ECONOMICS

Visit the *Economics, fourth edition* Companion Website at www.pearsoned.co.uk/ison to find valuable **student** learning material including:

- Answers to mini case studies throughout the chapters of the book
- Responses to the pause for thought boxes throughout the chapters of the book
- Answers to end of chapter progress and review questions
- Suggested outlines to essay questions

ECONOMICS
Fourth Edition

Stephen Ison
Loughborough University

Stuart Wall
Anglia Ruskin University

FT Prentice Hall
FINANCIAL TIMES

An imprint of **Pearson Education**
Harlow, England • London • New York • Boston • San Francisco • Toronto • Sydney • Singapore • Hong Kong
Tokyo • Seoul • Taipei • New Delhi • Cape Town • Madrid • Mexico City • Amsterdam • Munich • Paris • Milan

Pearson Education Limited

Edinburgh Gate
Harlow
Essex CM20 2JE
England

and Associated Companies throughout the world

Visit us on the World Wide Web at:
www.pearsoned.co.uk

Fourth edition published 2007

© Pearson Education Limited 2007

ISBN-13: 978-0-273-68107-6
ISBN-10: 0-273-68107-9

British Library Cataloguing-in-Publication Data
A catalogue record for this book is available from the British Library

Library of Congress Cataloging-in-Publication Data
Ison, Stephen.
    Economics / Stephen Ison, Stuart Wall. — 4th ed.
      p. cm.
    Includes bibliographical references and index.
    ISBN-13: 978-0-273-68107-6
    ISBN-10: 0-273-68107-9
    1. Economics—Textbooks. I. Wall, Stuart, 1946– II. Title.
  HB171.5.I84 2006
  330—dc22
                           2006047252

10 9 8 7 6 5 4 3 2 1
10 09 08 07 06

Typeset in 10/12pt Minion by 35
Printed and bound in Great Britain by Ashford Colour Press, Hampshire

The publisher's policy is to use paper manufactured from sustainable forests.

Contents

Part Two MACROECONOMICS

Chapter 13 Money, financial institutions and monetary policy

Chapter 17 Economic integration and the European Union

Preface

This fourth edition of *Economics* is somewhat of a departure from the previous editions in that it involves Stuart Wall as a co-author who has vast experience in terms of writing, editing and publishing in the area of economics and business management. His involvement in the revision of this book has substantially enhanced the final product.

As with the previous editions of this book, a key objective has been to introduce students to the main concepts, theories and applications of economics in a clear and concise manner. The fourth edition has been thoroughly updated with the addition of many new features. The new features include the following:

- *Learning objectives* at the beginning of each chapter, which carefully identify what the reader should learn from the particular chapter.
- *Pause for thought* boxes, to be found at strategic points throughout each chapter, to stimulate thinking about issues under discussion. Responses to these can be found on the website to accompany this book.
- *Examples* so that the reader can relate the concepts introduced to real world situations.
- *Mini Case Studies* and, on occasions, longer Case Studies based on up-to-date information and events, with questions asked and responses available at the back of the book, or on the student website, as indicated. As with the boxed *Examples*, the idea is to emphasise the relevance of economics to the real world.
- *Key points* at the end of each chapter, which serve as a check to help the reader focus on the main elements of the chapter.
- *Progress and review questions* at the end of each chapter, with answers and responses at the end of the book, or on the student website, as indicated, so that the reader can check on progress made.
- *Key terms* are to be found in the margins of each chapter, with the various economic terms defined the first time they appear in the text.

The eighteen chapters are divided into two parts, *microeconomic* related chapters (2–10) and *macroeconomic* related chapters (11–18), though it is readily acknowledged that this distinction is sometimes rather arbitrary. The book is aimed primarily at those students who are new to economics, taking the subject as part of a first year degree or degree equivalent programme or on professional courses. The book may also be useful to the more serious students engaged on A level economics and business studies courses.

There are certain topic areas which progress the subject beyond the level expected of the non-specialist or introductory economist. These topics are identified in the few chapters in which they occur and can be omitted without interfering with the flow of the book. Whilst these topics are more advanced than is usually required, if you feel that you can cope with them they are worth reading and will enhance your overall understanding of the subject.

Finally, every effort has been made to make the book as user-friendly as possible for students who are new to economics. This is quite a responsibility but I sincerely hope that you find the book both useful and interesting.

Stephen Ison
Nottingham
April 2006

Supporting resources

Visit **www.pearsoned.co.uk/ison** to find valuable online resources

Companion Website for students and instructors
- Answers to mini case studies throughout the chapters of the book
- Responses to the pause for thought boxes throughout the chapters of the book
- Answers to end of chapter progress and review questions
- Suggested outlines to essay questions

For instructors
- PowerPoint slides that can be downloaded and used for presentations

For more information please contact your local Pearson Education sales representative or visit **www.pearsoned.co.uk/ison**

Acknowledgements

Our combined thanks go to Eleanor for many long hours in helping us put the manuscript together. We would also like to thank our respective families for enduring long periods of our working in front of the computer screen. For Stephen, this especially involves Susanna, James, Naomi and Lydia, and for Stuart, Eleanor, Lizzy and Jonathan.

Our sincere thanks go to Alan Griffiths for much helpful support and content involving many chapters. Particular thanks also go to Carsten Zimmermann for contributing Chapter 17 on Economic integration and the European Union.

We would also like to thank Rachel Byrne and Paula Harris for much helpful advice and encouragement. Other thanks go to students undertaking economics as part of undergraduate courses in Air Transport Management and Transport and Business Management at Loughborough University who have used the book and made useful suggestions which have been incorporated in this new edition.

Finally, our thanks go to the four anonymous reviewers who made a number of insightful comments in terms of an early draft of the book. We found their contribution to be most useful and it certainly enhanced the final version. Of course, any errors and omissions are entirely our responsibility.

Stephen Ison and Stuart Wall

Publisher Acknowledgements

We are grateful to the following for permission to reproduce copyright material:

Financial Times for Mini Case Study 9.1; HMSO for an extract from *The Government's White Paper* on the Future of Air Transport (Cm 6046) published December 2003; Pearson Education for extracts adapted from *Economics for Business and Management 2005* by Griffiths and Wall.

In some cases we have been unable to trace the owners of copyright material and we would appreciate any information that would enable us to do so.

The nature of economics

By the end of this chapter you should be able to:

- Define what is meant by 'economics'.
- Outline the ways in which an economist thinks.
- Understand the importance of graphs, diagrams and charts to the economist.
- Understand the nature of the economic problem.
- Outline what is meant by the production possibility frontier and show how useful it is when analysing opportunity cost.
- Discuss the economic merits and weaknesses of the market economy.
- Outline the differences between a market economy and a planned economy.
- Define what is meant by 'public goods'.
- Distinguish between positive and normative economics.
- Distinguish between microeconomics and macroeconomics.

1 INTRODUCTION

What determines the demand for a good or service? What happens to the demand for a good if its price rises or falls? Why do firms supply goods? How can firms charge different prices for the same good or service to different groups of customers? What causes unemployment? What determines the wage level? What is the role of money in the economy? What causes inflation? Is there a need for government intervention in the economy? These are the types of questions economists are interested in and around which theories have been developed in order to aid our understanding.

This chapter seeks to introduce a number of the basic concepts which you will find useful as you progress through the book. The chapter introduces the way in which economists think and the use they make of economic models. In addition, economists make extensive use of graphs, diagrams, charts and tables, which are to be found throughout this book, and are therefore introduced in this chapter. The economic problem of scarcity and choice, which is central to economics, will also be covered in this chapter, together with an explanation of the free market, which is the main mechanism by which resources are allocated throughout the world. The use of a free market is an attempt by nations and the global economy to address this central economic problem of scarcity and choice.

2 DEFINING ECONOMICS

There is no one definition of economics, although a useful starting point is the well established definition provided by Lord Robbins as long ago as 1932. He defined *economics* as 'the science which studies human behaviour as a relationship between ends and scarce means which have alternative uses'. At first reading this may appear a difficult definition to understand; however, if it is studied in more detail it can be seen to offer a useful insight. We can dissect the definition as follows:

(a) Economics is a *'social science'* in that it uses scientific methods to study human behaviour.

(b) Human needs are unlimited whereas resources are in limited supply, hence the problem of *scarcity*.

(c) The resources can be put to *alternative uses* in order to meet certain *ends*, such as the building of a power station or a new hospital. Since resources are scarce, *choices* have to be made as to how resources are utilised.

2.1 The ways in which an economist thinks

Economics has its own 'language' which makes extensive use of selected words and which you will encounter throughout this book, such as production possibility frontier, demand, supply, elasticity, consumer surplus, the multiplier, comparative advantage and so on.

Economic models form an important part of the economists' thinking. They represent a simplification of the real world and often incorporate assumptions, making it easier to understand how the world operates. For example, when international trade is studied the economist may assume that there are only two countries, each of which produces only two products. This is in fact the assumption that is made when studying the benefits from trade in Chapter 16, and using such a 'two-by-two' model allows us to focus our thoughts. However, the principles or ideas that apply in the 'two-by-two' model can usually be generalised to many countries and many products, though mathematics may be required to capture this more general relationship. Simple economic models will be used all the way through this book and they often utilise diagrams in order to aid in our understanding.

2.2 The use of tables and diagrams

Raw data refers to numbers and facts in their original form and which have not, as yet, been treated in any way. One of the simplest ways to give meaning to raw data is to construct a *table* in which some order or shape is given to the raw data. Such tables can often be expressed in visual form as a diagram. Diagrams are used extensively in economics and you will encounter them throughout this book. In order to think like an economist it is important to understand and be able to interpret diagrams. For example, data giving the demand for chocolate bars is presented in Table 1.1 and this can be represented in the form of a diagram as in Figure 1.1.

Diagrams have a vertical and horizontal axis each representing a different variable. The price of chocolate bars is measured on the vertical axis and the quantity demanded is measured on the horizontal axis. Remember to express the *unit* for each variable, pence

Table 1.1 A demand schedule for chocolate bars

Price (pence per bar)	Quantity demanded (million bars per week)
0	12
10	10
20	8
30	6
40	4
50	2
60	0

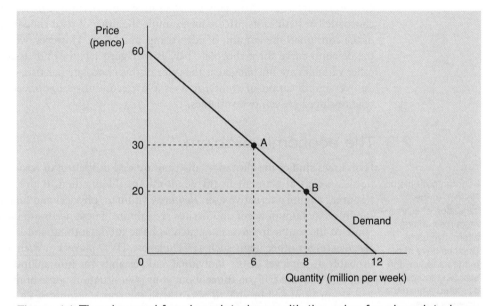

Figure 1.1 The demand for chocolate bars with the price for chocolate bars on the vertical axis and the quantity demanded (million bars demanded per week) on the horizontal axis.

for price and million bars for quantity. The quantity demanded also makes use of a time period, here 'per week'.

The dotted lines shown in the diagram are important, indicating specific parts of the diagram you wish to emphasise. For example, point A indicates two pieces of information, namely that at a price of 30 pence, 6 million chocolate bars will be demanded per week. Point B represents a different price and quantity situation, namely that at a price of 20 pence, 8 million bars will be demanded per week.

It is worth noting that the relationship between price and quantity shown in Figure 1.1 is a negative or inverse relationship. This means that the two variables move in the *opposite* direction, with a reduction in price leading to a rise in the quantity demanded, and vice versa. If the relationship had been positive, then the two variables would have moved in the *same* direction and the line would have sloped upwards from left to right.

The information presented in Table 1.1 and Figure 1.1 could have been presented mathematically, given by the equation of a straight line. This is beyond the scope of this book but you may like to consider what the equation for the demand curve would be given the above information.

Pause for thought 1

Can you find the equation for the straight line in Figure 1.1? Why do economists make use of diagrams?

By simplifying the situation and dealing with only two variables, economists are making use of the 'other things equal' (*ceteris paribus* in Latin) assumption. In practice, economists are aware that many variables may influence, say, the demand for a particular chocolate bar besides its price – for example the price of rival chocolate bars, the income of the consumer, the amount of advertising, and so on. However, when economists draw the demand curve for a chocolate bar, as in Figure 1.1, they are assuming that all these other variables are unchanged as the price of this chocolate bar rises or falls. Whilst this is an oversimplification of reality, it does allow economists to concentrate on important relationships between two variables.

2.3 The economic problem

Economic problem
Relates to the allocation of scarce resources among alternative uses. Choices have to be made as to how the scarce resources are allocated among the different ends, resulting in 'opportunity costs'.

Economics studies the allocation, distribution and utilisation of resources to meet human needs. A central element in the **economic problem**, then, is the allocation of scarce resources among alternative uses. *Resources* (human, physical and financial) are *limited* in supply while human needs and desires are infinite. These needs are usually called '*wants*'. Some of the wants are *necessities* such as basic food, clothing and housing but there are also desires for other items such as CD players, DVD players or even a night at the opera. Probably at the level of the individual and certainly for humankind as a whole, human wants are *unlimited*. If you think about your own situation, some of the goods and services you require you will be able to obtain with the scarce resources, i.e. income, available to you. There are likely, however, to be other items you would like to have but are unable to obtain because of limited resources. The same economic problem faces all individuals, organisations and societies – unlimited wants, limited resources.

Factors of production
The inputs used by an economy in the production of goods and services. They comprise land, labour, capital and entrepreneurial ability (in some definitions).

The resources an economy has at its disposal are used to satisfy the unlimited wants. These are often termed by economists *inputs* or *factors of production*. They are the means of producing the goods and services society requires to meet human needs and can normally be divided into three main categories:

a) *Land*, the natural resource
b) *Labour*, the human resource
c) *Capital*, the physical resource.

The factors of production will be dealt with in more detail in Chapter 5: Section 4.

Since the resources are limited in supply (i.e. scarce) and there is the existence of unlimited wants, *choices* have to be made – choices involving the allocation of scarce resources among alternative uses to achieve given ends. Economics is also concerned with the *distribution* of resources between different groups in society. So, in addition to the problem of what gets produced (allocation), there is the problem of who gets *what* is produced (*see* Chapter 8). Moreover, there is the problem of resource *utilisation*, ensuring that all the available resources are used effectively. This is the subject matter of macroeconomics and is dealt with in Part Two.

2.4 Opportunity cost

Macroeconomics
An area of economics that concentrates on the economic behaviour of the economy as a whole, dealing with issues such as inflation and unemployment.

Opportunity cost
The best alternative forgone.

Resources are limited in supply and have alternative uses. However, if they are used in the production of, say, iPods then they cannot be used in the production of DVD players. So if society chooses to produce more iPods it would have to forgo a certain quantity of DVD players which those same resources could have produced. In other words, the *opportunity cost* of producing more of the former is less of the latter. Opportunity cost can be defined as the *best alternative forgone*. This concept is central to the study of economics at a number of levels:

(**a**) *At the individual level*, if one decides to grow more potatoes in the garden then one has to reduce the production of, say, carrots. The limited space in the garden can be viewed as the scarce resource and one cannot produce more of one good, potatoes, and still produce the same amount of another, carrots.

(**b**) *At the level of the firm*, limited capital equipment (e.g. machinery) currently used to produce, say, milk chocolate cannot be used to manufacture plain chocolate.

(**c**) *At government level*, limited tax revenue may mean that a decision to build three new schools may be at the expense of the alternative option of building a new hospital.

When considering opportunity cost it is important to note that such choices are only required if all existing resources are being fully used. If this were not the case the idle resources, in our examples garden space, machinery and taxation revenue, could be used instead.

Society has to decide what goods and services it is going to produce. This will involve choices because producing more of one good or service will normally mean producing less of another if all existing resources are being fully utilised.

Example	Opportunity cost: extra spending on NHS

Production possibility frontier
This represents the boundary between those combinations of goods and services which can be produced and those which cannot.

The Wanless Commission into the NHS reported in 2002 that UK spending on health at 6.8% of National Income was well below the EU average of 8%. In the five-year plan for health spending from 2002–7, the Chancellor of the Exchequer (Gordon Brown) committed the UK to reaching the EU average by 2006, which implied government spending on the NHS rising by more than £100 billion a year. Of course, this extra government spending on the NHS means less tax revenue is available for spending on other public services such as transport and pensions, especially since the growth of public spending on education has also been protected up to 2007.

2.5 The production possibility frontier (PPF)

The central problem in economics of scarcity, choice, opportunity cost and resource allocation can be analysed by using a production possibility frontier or curve as shown in Figure 1.2.

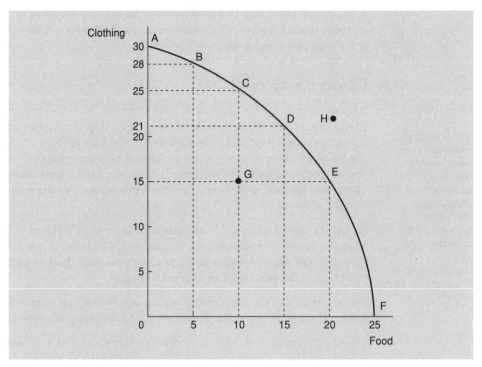

Figure 1.2 The production possibility frontier AF represents the boundary between the goods and services which can be produced, namely on or within the frontier, and those which cannot. The economy would prefer to be at a point such as C or D on the frontier than at a point such as G inside the frontier.

Figure 1.2 represents a hypothetical production possibility frontier AF for an economy producing two products: food and clothing. The PPF shows the alternative combinations of the two products that the country can produce if it fully utilises all of its resources. For example, if all the country's resources were used in the production of clothing then the total output would be 30 units of clothing and there would be no food production. This is represented by point A. If, however, all the resources were devoted to the production of food, the economy would be at point F with 25 units of food produced but zero clothing. Alternatively, the economy could be at any point on the PPF producing a certain amount of food and clothing. However, if the economy were at point G it would signify that the economy was under-utilising its resources. There would be unemployed resources and by bringing those resources into use the economy could move to a position on the curve such as point D, where more clothing and food could be produced.

It is clearly sensible for an economy to be on the PPF rather than inside it since at point G the economy is producing 15 units of clothing and 10 units of food, whereas at point D the economy is producing 21 units of clothing and 15 units of food. Once on the PPF it is not possible to increase the production of one of the two products without reducing the production of the other product. So, for example, if the economy were at point D a movement along the frontier to point E would involve a reallocation of resources. Hence an increase in food production of 5 units would require a reduction in clothing production of 6 units. Points outside the frontier such as H, representing other combinations of food and clothing output, are unattainable – given the existing resource availability and the state of technology. A shift outwards in the PPF, such as a shift to IJ in Figure 1.3, represents *economic growth*, which means the ability to produce more goods which in the example used means more food and clothing. This can be brought about either by technological change, i.e. new and better ways of producing the goods and services, or through an increase in the economy's productive capacity, achieved through an increase in the supply of the factors of production. This means that a point such as H which was previously unattainable is now attainable.

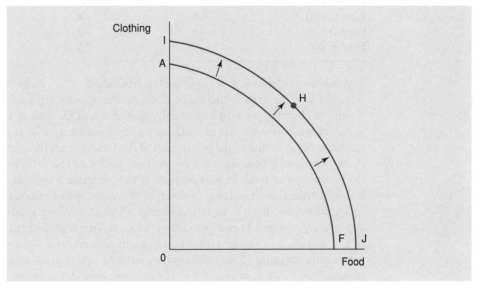

Figure 1.3 Technological change or an increase in the economy's productive capacity allows the production possibility frontier to shift to the right.

Example	Technological change in microchips

That technological change can shift the production possibility frontier outwards is well illustrated by developments in microchip production. The huge new global microchip fabrication plants ('fabs') use new technologies to produce microchips, enabling output per unit of input (i.e. productivity) to more than double. For example, more than 225 microchips can now be produced from a 'wafer' of silicon using these new technologies, compared to only 100 microchips in smaller, less technologically advanced plants. As a result, the average cost of microchips has fallen by 40% in recent years.

2.6 The PPF and opportunity cost

The frontier can be viewed in terms of opportunity cost since to produce more units of one product needs resources to be taken from the production of the other. In Figure 1.2 the frontier is concave to the origin and this means that the opportunity cost will change as we move along the frontier. If we start at point A and move down the curve we can see how the opportunity cost changes (*see* Table 1.2).

Table 1.2 The opportunity cost of food

Movement along the curve	Change in food	Change in clothing	Opportunity cost $\dfrac{\Delta \text{ in clothing}}{\Delta \text{ in food}} \times (-1)$
From A to B	+5	−2	0.4
From B to C	+5	−3	0.6
From C to D	+5	−4	0.8
From D to E	+5	−6	1.2
From E to F	+5	−15	3.0

A movement from A to B involving the production of 5 units of food requires a reduction of 2 units in the production of cloth. So the opportunity cost of 5 units of food is 2 units of clothing, with an opportunity cost of 0.4. (One unit of food has been gained at the expense of 0.4 units of clothing.) The opportunity cost is initially small as the resources better suited to the production of food move from the production of clothing.

As more food is produced, it is necessary to reallocate resources which are less suited to the production of food. In moving from B to C an extra 5 units of food production will involve a reduction in clothing production of 3 units, with a resulting opportunity cost of 0.6. A movement from C to D will require a loss in clothing production of 4 units (an opportunity cost of 0.8) and from D to E a loss of 6 units of clothing (an opportunity cost of 1.2). Finally, a movement from E to F, again with an extra 5 units of food production, will require forgoing 15 units of clothing with an opportunity cost of 3.0. This is more realistic than a PPF as in Figure 1.4. The figure illustrates a situation of constant opportunity cost, 0A/0B, where clothing can be exchanged for food at a constant rate.

Planned economy
An economic system in which decisions about the allocation of resources is undertaken by the state planning authority. These decisions concern what is produced, how and for whom.

Mixed economy
An economy where the decisions about what, how and for whom to produce are partly made via the market and partly by the government.

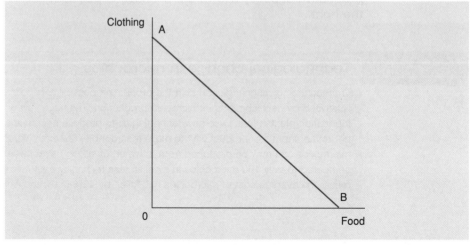

Figure 1.4 The production possibility frontier AB drawn as a straight line displays the characteristic of constant opportunity cost. This means that each additional unit of food produced requires that 0A/0B units of clothing be forgone. Every additional unit of clothing produced requires 0B/0A units of food to be forgone.

Pause for thought 2

Explain how the production possibility frontier provides an insight into the issues of scarcity and choice which an economy faces when deciding what goods and services to produce.

3 ECONOMIC SYSTEMS

Although all countries throughout the world have to face similar economic problems, the economic system they adopt as a means of dealing with them will differ. Essentially there are three approaches to tackling the economic problem of allocation, distribution and utilisation of resources:

Market economy
An economy where the allocation of resources is determined by the independent decisions and actions of individual consumers and producers in markets guided by price signals.

(a) A *market* economy allocates resources through the price mechanism, with market prices being determined by the forces of demand and supply.

(b) A *planned* economy allocates resources through administrative decisions. Although this type of economic system is no longer in evidence to any great extent worldwide, it may be useful to briefly outline how the planned economic system has operated in parts of the world.

(c) A *mixed* economy contains features of both the market and planned economic systems, with the government intervening in various ways to influence market prices. In practice most economies are, strictly speaking, mixed economies.

Example — Mixed economies are the rule

The following data shows the extent to which the governments of various countries in 2004 intervened in the economies of those countries. The figures show government spending as a percentage of total economic activity (i.e. gross domestic product: GDP) in those countries.

Country	Government spending as % of economic activity (GDP) in 2004
Australia	33.1%
France	48.5%
Japan	37.8%
Sweden	50.8%
UK	39.6%
USA	30.8%

Price mechanism
The way in which price acts as a 'signal' within a market economy to influence the demand for and supply of goods and services, thereby helping demand equal supply in a market economy.

Clearly governments intervene to a considerable extent in most economies, even though the extent of that intervention does vary.

Source: Adapted from *Economic Outlook*, OECD, 2005

4 THE MARKET ECONOMY

In a 'pure' free market economy there would be no government intervention and decisions as to the allocation of resources would be taken by individual producers and consumers through a system known as the *price mechanism* or market mechanism. The market or price mechanism is a central feature of a market economy. An outline of how the market mechanism works can be seen in Figure 1.5.

Throughout the economy millions of consumers are making decisions as to how to spend their income. By changing their preferences from good A to good B they are sending a signal to the producers of these goods. As the demand for good B increases and that of good A declines the prices of the two products will change and, *other things being equal,*

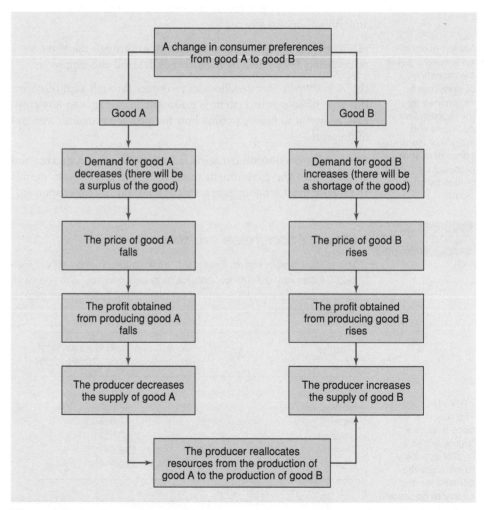

Figure 1.5 **The figure illustrates the market mechanism. Prices change in response to changes in demand and supply resulting in a reallocation of resources.**

the profit obtained from the two products will change. Profit is the key motivator in the market economy and the producers will reallocate their scarce resources to those goods and services which will yield the most profit.

One can see why this process is sometimes called the 'free' market because the allocation of resources occurs without government intervention – reallocation of resources is 'automatic'. The consumer has an important role to play in the market economy for it has been change in consumer tastes which have ultimately led to a change in what is produced. The scale of the influence depends on the level of income of the consumer. When consumers spend on a particular product, they are essentially voting for that product. The more income they have, the more *'money votes'* they can cast and, therefore, the greater their influence on what is produced.

4.1 Advantages of the market economy

(a) The market mechanism means that resources are allocated automatically without the need to resort to government intervention.

(b) By using 'money votes' the consumer dictates to the producers, through the market, what is produced.

(c) Producers are motivated by profit thus they have the incentive to respond quickly to changes in consumers' preferences.

4.2 Disadvantages of the market economy

(a) Those with higher income levels have more money votes and, therefore, a greater say in what is produced. The market mechanism is based on the 'ability to pay' and not on need, which means that certain members of society are unable to obtain the goods and services they require.

(b) The market mechanism generates competition between producers. But monopolies may develop, as larger companies take over or merge with smaller companies, or force them out of business. Monopolies may operate against the public interest, charging higher prices than in a competitive situation in the knowledge that the consumer has no alternative source from which to buy the product. Monopolies will be dealt with in more detail in Chapter 6: Section 4.

Externalities
Where economic decisions create costs or benefits for people other than the decision taker.

(c) In producing goods and services it is possible that **externalities** will occur. Externalities are costs (or benefits) which result from production or consumption but which fall on a third party. In terms of external costs such as pollution, and noise and traffic congestion, costs will be imposed on society which are not included in the decisions of consumers or suppliers. For example, as part of its productive process a chemical company may dump toxic waste into a river with the result that fish stocks are depleted. This can be viewed as an external cost on fishermen, a cost which is not taken into account by the chemical company. The chemical company is only likely to take account of their private costs, namely the rent, rates, raw material and labour costs incurred, and they are likely to ignore the costs they impose on others. To obtain the full *social cost* of production, the cost

Social cost
Private costs plus the external costs resulting from producing a good or providing a service.

(or benefit) of externalities should be added to the private cost. The external costs are likely to continue unchecked if left to the free market and are one of the reasons for government intervention. The whole area of externalities is dealt with in more detail in Chapter 10. Mini Case Study 1.1 below looks at externalities involved with air transport.

Public goods
Goods or services
which when
consumed by one
individual can still be
consumed by others
and from which no
one can be
excluded.

(**d**) Certain goods, namely public goods may be under-provided or not provided at all in a market economy. Public goods can be defined as those goods which when consumed by one individual can still be consumed by others and from which no one can be excluded. Examples include defence and flood control, and if they were paid for by one individual then others would be able to obtain a 'free ride'.

Whilst Mini Case Study 1.1 below has relevance here, you might also return to read it when you have read Chapter 10 relating to the environment.

Mini Case Study 1.1

Externalities and air transport

The Government recognises the benefits that the expansion in air travel has brought to people's lives and to the economy of this country. The increased affordability of air travel has opened up the possibilities of foreign travel for many people, and it provides the rapid access that is vital to many modern businesses. But we have to balance those benefits against the environmental impacts of air travel, in particular the growing contribution of aircraft emissions to climate change and the significant impact that airports can have on those living nearby.

Air travel has increased five-fold over the past 30 years, and demand is projected to be between two and three times current levels by 2030. Some of our major airports are already close to capacity, so failure to allow for increased capacity could have serious economic consequences, both at national and at regional level. That must be balanced by the need to have regard for the environmental consequences of air travel. The Government believes that simply building more and more capacity to meet demand is not a sustainable way forward. Instead, a balanced approach is required which:

● recognises the importance of air travel to our national and regional economic prosperity, and that not providing additional capacity where it is needed would significantly damage the economy and national prosperity;
● reflects people's desire to travel further and more often by air, and to take advantage of the affordability of air travel and the opportunities this brings;
● seeks to reduce and minimise the impacts of airports on those who live nearby, and on the natural environment;
● ensures that, over time, aviation pays the external costs its activities impose on society at large – in other words, that the price of air travel reflects its environmental and social impacts;
● minimises the need for airport development in new locations by making best use of existing capacity where possible;
● respects the rights and interests of those affected by airport development;
● provides greater certainty for all concerned in the planning of future airport capacity, but at the same time is sufficiently flexible to recognise and adapt to the uncertainties inherent in long-term planning.

As part of this approach, the Government believes more needs to be done to reduce and mitigate the impacts of air transport and airport development. At the global level, the government will play a major role in pressing for new solutions and stronger action by international bodies. And the White Paper sets out proposals to bring aviation within the European Union emissions trading scheme, to help limit greenhouse gas emissions.

Source: The government's White Paper on the Future of Air Transport (Cm 6046). Department for Transport, December 2003

Questions

1 *What is meant by 'externalities'?*

2 *Outline the advantages and disadvantages of an expansion in air travel.*

(Note that Chapter 10 covers the whole area of externalities in much more detail.)

Answers to questions can be found on the students' side of the Companion Website.

5 THE PLANNED ECONOMY

In a planned economy the government makes all the decisions about what is produced, how resources are allocated and at certain times, through rationing, how the finished products are distributed. A government planning office decides on the allocation of resources, estimating the types of products it considers individuals to want.

This kind of economy is rare today with even countries such as North Korea moving towards a market-based system. Prior to the late 1980s the countries of Eastern Europe allocated resources via a planned economy. Whilst this type of economic system no longer exists to any great extent, it is worthwhile briefly outlining its potential advantages and disadvantages.

5.1 Advantages of the planned economy

(a) The planning office decides what goods and services are produced, which, in theory at least, means that any wasteful competition is avoided.

(b) It has been argued that a planned economy can lead to a more equal distribution of income and wealth since the factors of production are controlled by the state.

(c) The planning office administers the prices of products and can, therefore, effectively control inflation. The result is that when shortages occur in the economy they manifest themselves in queues, rationing and the black market rather than in increased prices.

5.2 Disadvantages of the planned economy

(a) Since the allocation of resources is undertaken by the planning authority, they may misjudge the preferences of the consumers. This means there may be an overproduction of certain products and an underproduction of others. The shortages will result in long queues and rationing, whereas the overproduction of goods will lead to large stockpiles of unwanted products.

(b) As the state owns the assets of the economy it will mean that there is a reduced incentive to work harder. There can be a lack of motivation among management and workers since individuals do not own businesses or benefit directly from the profit those businesses earn.

(c) With business being organised as a state monopoly there is a lack of competition between companies, and a resulting lack of variety and quality of products. In fact, products tend to be rather standardised with the absence of product differentiation.

(d) In the market economy resources are allocated automatically via the market mechanism whereas in the planned economy a large bureaucracy has developed to administer the system. This bureaucracy can be viewed as a misuse of resources.

It is because of the failings of the planned economy that in recent years countries throughout Eastern Europe have moved towards a market economy system – in fact becoming more mixed economic systems.

Mini Case Study 1.2

Meeting the plan

The term 'communist bloc' was used in the West until the late 1980s to describe the operation of 25 economies under the Soviet sphere of influence. A characteristic of all these economies was an extensive central planning system, often termed a 'command economy'. The command economy dominated every aspect of life, telling factories where to buy their inputs, how much to pay their workers, how much to produce and where to sell their output. Individuals were trained in specialist schools and universities and directed to work at specific factories, which provided their wages, houses, health care – even holidays in enterprise-owned hotels and sanatoria. The national bank was told how much to lend to which factories and how much cash to print to pay wages.

As a theoretical concept, central planning was very elegant. Using 'input-output' analysis (a planning framework which calculated the inputs required for each factory in order for it to deliver its planned outputs to the next stage in the production process), the planning ministry could calculate precisely how much labour, capital and raw materials each enterprise required to achieve its production targets. The various production targets for raw materials and intermediate and final products all fitted together to ensure a perfectly balanced expansion of the economy. Input and output prices were carefully set to ensure that all firms could pay their wage bills and repay loans from the national bank, while at the same time pricing consumer goods to encourage consumption of socially desirable goods (e.g. books, ballet, theatre, public transport, etc.) and discourage consumption of politically unfavoured goods (e.g. international telephone calls, cars, luxury goods).

Questions

1 *Why do you think the command economy failed to deliver many of the benefits claimed for it in this Mini Case Study?*

2 *Can you find any clues in the Mini Case Study to explain why the transition from a command economy to a market economy has proved to be so painful for many of these states?*

3 *What would you consider to be the potential advantages and disadvantages for these states seeking to move from a command to a market economy?*

Answers to questions can be found at the back of the book (page 488).

6 THE MIXED ECONOMY

As the name suggests, this type of economic system aims to combine the merits of both the market and the planned economies. The main advantage of the market economy is the automatic working of the market mechanism. The mixed economy aims to allow the market to operate, with government intervening in the economy only where the market fails. This means providing those goods and services such as law and order, education and health services, which would have been under-provided if left to the market. The free market economy is also susceptible to:

(a) *booms and slumps* in the level of economic activity. In this area government intervention is geared towards creating a stable economic environment;

(b) *monopoly power*. There is, therefore, a role for government to monitor and control the activities or potential activities of monopolies – through the Monopolies and Mergers Commission in the UK;

(c) *inequalities*, for example in the distribution of income and wealth. This is something that government can attempt to correct through the taxation system (*see* Chapter 12) and through its expenditure.

(d) *externalities*. It is also possible for the government to make sure that companies take account of the externalities they create, e.g. by the Environmental Protection Act 1990.

In reality, most economies throughout the world are mixed economies.

Pause for thought 3

Why do you think it is that most economies are mixed economies?

7 POSITIVE AND NORMATIVE ECONOMICS

Positive economics Seeks to make statements that can be checked by reference to facts and avoids value judgements.

Normative economics Proposes action based on value judgements.

At this point it is useful to distinguish between *positive* and *normative* economics. Positive economics is concerned with issues such as how individuals behave in trying to maximise their satisfaction from a given income level or how firms behave in maximising their profits. Positive statements deal with *what is* or *what will be* – statements that can be empirically tested. For example, 'if the government increases income tax it will lead to a fall in the level of consumer expenditure' is a positive statement because it can be checked against the evidence and proved correct or incorrect. One of the main aims of economics has been to develop theories which could help explain economic behaviour and deal with positive statements.

Normative economics deals more with value judgements, statements which include the words *should* or *ought*. For example, 'income should be distributed more equally' is a normative statement. Unlike a positive statement, there is no way of proving it correct or incorrect.

8 MICRO- AND MACROECONOMICS

Microeconomics
An area of economics that concentrates on the economic behaviour of individual decision-making units, namely households and firms.

It is also important to distinguish between micro- and macroeconomics. Microeconomics deals with the decision making of individuals and firms, and how particular markets work. Macroeconomics studies the operation of the economy as a whole, covering areas such as unemployment, inflation and aggregate demand. Part One of *Economics* will deal with microeconomics and Part Two with macroeconomics.

KEY POINTS

- Economic models seek to represent certain aspects of the real world. They simplify reality by making certain assumptions which allow us to focus on key relationships, which can often be displayed in diagrams.

- The economic problem refers to the allocation of scarce resources among different uses. It is therefore necessary to make choices as to how those scarce resources are used amongst competing ends.

- Resources are often termed inputs or factors of production and they comprise land, labour and capital.

- Opportunity cost is defined as the best alternative forgone when resources are used in a particular way. Clearly when considering the concept of opportunity cost it is important to note that choices are only required if all existing resources are fully utilised.

- The production possibility frontier represents the boundary between the goods and services which can be produced and those which cannot within a particular economy. The frontier is concave to the origin since the opportunity cost of producing more of one particular product and less of another will change as movement occurs along the frontier. More specifically, the opportunity cost of an extra unit of a product will rise (i.e. more of the alternative product forgone) the greater the amount of that product already produced.

- 'Economic system' refers to the approach taken when dealing with the economic problem of allocating, distributing and utilising resources. These are three broad types of economic system, namely the market economy, where resources are allocated through the forces of demand and supply, the planned economy (no longer to be found to any great extent) where resources are allocated via the government or some centralised planning authority, and the mixed economy which contains features of both the market and planned economies.

- It is important to distinguish between micro- and macroeconomics. Microeconomics deals with the decision making at the level of the individual, firm or particular markets, such as the labour market. Macroeconomics on the other hand is the study of the operation of the economy as a whole, dealing with issues such as unemployment and inflation.

Further reading

Griffiths, A. and Wall, S. (2005) *Economics for Business and Management*, FT/Prentice Hall, Chapter 1.

Heather, K. (2004) *Economics Theory in Action*, 4th edition, FT/Prentice Hall, Chapter 1.

Parkin, M., Powell M. and Matthews, K. (2005) *Economics*, 6th edition, FT/Prentice Hall, Chapters 1 and 2.

Sloman, J. (2006) *Economics*, 6th edition, FT/Prentice Hall, Chapter 1.

Web references

The following website contains a wide range of data across micro- and macroeconomic issues, together with a discussion of techniques of data handling.

http://bized.ac.uk

A wide range of macroeconomic data can be found on the following website:

http://www.statistics.gov.uk/, the Official UK statistics site.

PROGRESS AND REVIEW QUESTIONS

Answers to most questions can be found at the back of the book (pages 489–90). Answers to asterisked questions can be found on the students' side of the Companion Website.

Multiple-choice questions

1 Which one of the following is *not* true with respect to the production possibility frontier (PPF)?

a) The PPF represents the boundary between the goods and services which can be produced and those which cannot within a particular economy.

b) The PPF is convex to the origin.

c) If an economy is operating on its PPF it is not possible to produce more of one product without producing less of another.

d) An outward shift in the PPF represents economic growth.

e) If the PPF is negatively sloped and linear it displays the characteristic of constant opportunity cost.

2 An economy can produce goods X and Y and their production possibility frontier is shown below. With the resources currently at their disposal, which bundles of goods can be produced?

a) Only A

b) Only A and B

c) Only B

d) Only A, B and C

e) Only D

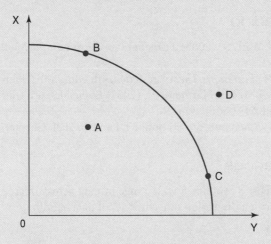

3 Which one of the following is *not* a feature of a market economy?

   a) Resources are allocated through the forces of demand and supply.
   b) Profit is a key motivator in a market economy.
   c) The consumer has an important role to play in the market economy.
   d) The government decides what should be produced.
   e) Firms decide how much labour to employ.

4 A mixed economy can be described as one in which:

   a) goods are produced for both the domestic and overseas market
   b) both agricultural and manufacturing goods are produced
   c) both capital and labour are employed in the production of goods
   d) both consumer goods and capital goods are produced
   e) production is decided partly by the market mechanism and partly by central government.

5 Which *two* of the following are features of a command economy?

   a) A dependence on price signals to allocate resources
   b) An extensive planning bureaucracy
   c) Little intervention by the state in the economy
   d) Government ownership of the means of production
   e) Extensive deregulation of economic activity

6 Which *two* of the following are normative statements?

   a) The reduction in the price of a product will lead to an increase in demand for the product.
   b) A reduction in income tax will lead to an increase in consumer spending.
   c) Reducing the rate of unemployment ought to be the main aim of any government.
   d) Income tax should be more progressive.
   e) The introduction of congestion charging in London has led to a reduction in the number of vehicles accessing the charging zone.

7 Which *two* of the following are microeconomic issues?

   a) British Petroleum seeking rights to explore a particular section of the North Sea
   b) A rise in the inflation rate
   c) An increase in the rate of economic growth
   d) The reaction of an individual consumer to an advertising campaign
   e) Higher unemployment

 ## Case study question

Work, work, work

In the nineteenth century the American Federation of Labour, campaigning to reduce long working hours, adopted the slogan: 'Eight hours for work, eight hours for rest, eight hours for what we will.' Though blessed with a pleasing symmetry, there is nothing sacred about this division of the day, as France set out to demonstrate by introducing the 35-hour week in 1999.

At the time, it might have seemed possible to see this as another small step on the road to Utopia, an idealised world in which machines did all the work and humankind lived a life of leisure. But just five years later, with the 35-hour week under attack not just in France, where it is a legal limit, but in Germany, where it is the industrial norm, we appear to be regressing to the nineteenth-century vision of how the day should be divided.

This is not what John Maynard Keynes, the distinguished British economist, foresaw. In a 1930 essay called *Economic Possibilities for our Grandchildren*, Keynes extrapolated economic growth and concluded that humankind was well on the way to solving the 'economic problem', the struggle for subsistence, that had hitherto been its most pressing concern. He looked ahead to an age of leisure and abundance in which the pursuit of wealth came to be regarded as detestable; in which the highest respect would go to 'the delightful people who are capable of taking direct enjoyment in things, the lilies of the field who toil not, neither do they spin'.

Today, that age seems as far off as ever. The word 'workaholic' has been invented to describe people who never leave the office. Britons moan about their long hours culture and lack of work/life balance. Laptop computers and mobile phones have helped work extend itself into people's private lives. And globalisation has thrown employees in developed countries into competition with those working longer hours for less money elsewhere.

In spite of it all, however, Keynes could still turn out to be right. Notwithstanding the reverses in France and Germany, study after study has shown that the long-term trend in working hours is still downwards. In the early 1800s, many people in the western world worked 70 hours a week. A century ago, the figure was more like 50. In Britain, government figures show that male, full-time employees worked an average of 39.1 hours a week in 2003 compared with 40.8 in 1995 – a fall of more than $1\frac{1}{2}$ hours a week in just eight years.

One reason why we think we are working harder, says the Chartered Institute of Personnel and Development, is because work is more stressful: people feel a need to succeed rather than merely earn a living. And with people now trying to cram so much into their lives it is little wonder some of them feel permanently exhausted. Whatever our perceptions to the contrary, it seems we are still working our way towards Utopia. It may simply be taking a little longer than we thought.

Questions

1 *With the use of a diagram explain how the introduction of a 35-hour week might affect the production possibility frontier.*

2 *What is meant by the term the 'economic problem' mentioned in the Case Study?*

True/false questions

1 The economic problem facing individuals, organisations and economies is one of limited wants and unlimited resources.

2 Opportunity cost can be defined as the best alternative forgone.

3 The production possibility frontier is convex to the origin.

4 In a pure 'planned economy' the market decides what should be produced.

5 A mixed economy combines elements of the market and planned economies.

6 A positive statement involves value judgements.

7 A macroeconomic issue tends to influence all the firms and households, rather than specific firms or households.

8 A firm polluting the environment without having to pay for that pollution is an example of an externality.

Essay questions

Answers to asterisked questions can be found on the students' side of the Companion Website. All other answers can be found at the back of the book (page 490).

1* Outline how the production possibility frontier can be used to explain the concept of opportunity cost. Why is the production possibility frontier concave to the origin?

2 Define opportunity cost and explain how useful the concept is.

3* What are the advantages and disadvantages of the market economy?

4 Over the last two decades the planned economies have introduced elements of the market mechanism into their economic systems. To what extent could it be argued that the market mechanism is better than the planned economy as a means of allocating resources?

Part One MICROECONOMICS

Demand, supply and market equilibrium

Learning objectives

By the end of this chapter you should be able to:

- Understand what is meant by the 'market'.
- Define demand and supply.
- Explain the factors that influence demand and supply.
- Understand the difference between a *movement along* and a *shift* in the demand and supply curve.
- Derive a market demand curve and a market supply curve.
- Explain what is meant by 'market equilibrium'.

1 INTRODUCTION

The previous chapter introduced the idea of the price or market mechanism. This chapter takes the idea of the market a little further and introduces the reader to the key concepts of demand and supply. The chapter aims to explain clearly what is meant by demand and supply and the factors which influence the demand for and supply of a particular good or service. What is the difference between a movement along and a shift in the demand and supply curve and how are the market demand and supply curves derived? This is followed by a discussion as to how the interaction of demand and supply determines the market 'equilibrium' price, i.e. that price which brings about a balance between the quantity demanded and quantity supplied. We also consider how the market will respond to various types of 'disequilibrium' situations and whether, and by what means, a new equilibrium price and quantity might be achieved.

2 THE MARKET

Market
Any situation that allows buyers and sellers to obtain information for the purpose of exchange.

The market for a product is not a particular place but rather any situation in which the buyer and seller of a product communicate with each other for the purpose of exchange. The collective actions of the buyers in the market determine the market demand for a particular product while the collective actions of the sellers determine the market supply. It is the interaction of these two forces (known as *market forces*) which determines the market price for the product.

The existence of a market does not mean that the buyer and seller have to meet although that may be the case. For example, buyers and sellers may be in contact with each other through a third party, such as an estate agent or a stockbroker.

Derived demand
Demand for a factor of production not for its own sake but the demand for the good or service which uses it.

The market may be *local*, as in the case of a fish and chip shop, *regional* as with a newspaper such as the *East Anglian Daily Times, national* such as the housing market which consists of many estate agents operating throughout the country, or *international* as is the market for oil. A market can take a number of different forms; it could be a *product market*, such as that for chocolate bars, or it could be a *labour market* where those individuals with particular skills supply their services to firms who demand those skills. In the latter case the demand is called *derived demand* because the labour demanded is determined by the demand for the product which that labour produces.

3 DEMAND

3.1 What is demand?

You may want a particular product but not have the money to pay for it or you may have the money to pay for a product but not desire it. Neither situation constitutes *effective demand*. Effective demand means there has to be the willingness and ability to buy a product.

In terms of demand it is not sufficient to say 'the demand for a good or service is 50 units' for it is also important to know at what price 50 units would be demanded and over what period of time. If the product is chocolate then in terms of the total market it might be 4 million bars demanded per week at 40 pence each. For newspapers it could be 1.5 million demanded per day at 50 pence each and for shoes it could be 2,000 pairs per month at £50 per pair.

Market demand
The total demand for a good or service by all consumers at a particular price over a particular period of time.

When you think of demand it is natural simply to consider an individual's demand but, although this is important, it is the *market demand* for the product which is of greater concern. We will deal with the relationship between individual and market demand later but for now we will simply consider the market demand for a product, which means the total amount that consumers demand at a particular price over a period of time.

The demand for a product, for example chocolate bars, depends upon a number of factors, namely:

a) the price of the product;
b) the price of all the other 'related' products in the economy;
c) the level of household income;
d) the tastes of the consumer;
e) advertising.

Ceteris paribus
All other things of relevance remaining the same or other things being equal.

It is not possible to study at the same time all of the factors which influence demand so the economist makes use of *ceteris paribus*, which means 'other things remaining unchanged'. It is, therefore, possible to study the relationship between demand and each of the variables in turn, assuming the other factors remain constant.

3.2 Factors influencing demand

This section outlines the factors which influence the demand for a product. The example of chocolate is used.

(**a**) *Changes in the price of the product.* A change in the quantity of chocolate bars demanded may result from a change in its price. The relationship between the quantity demanded and price can be shown in the form of a *demand schedule* such as in Table 2.1.

Table 2.1 The demand schedule for chocolate bars (showing the relationship between the quantity demanded and price)

Price (pence per bar)	Quantity demanded (million bars per week)
0	12
10	10
20	8
30	6
40	4
50	2
60	0
70	0

We might then present the information given in Table 2.1 in the form of a graph showing the *demand curve*, as in Figure 2.1.

This is a more convenient means of presenting the information and a number of important points can be noted:

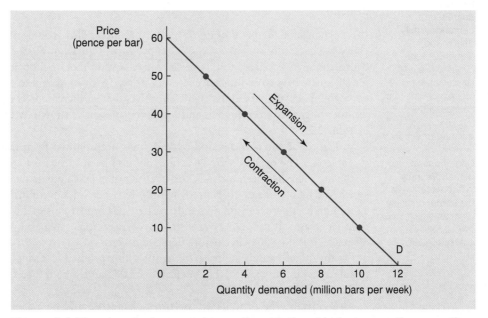

Figure 2.1 The demand curve shows the relationship between the quantity demanded of a good or service over a particular period of time and its price, assuming *ceteris paribus*. The quantity demanded is measured on the horizontal axis and the price on the vertical axis.

(*i*)   Price is on the vertical axis and the quantity demanded over a time period on the horizontal axis.

(*ii*) Demand is a *flow* concept which means that it is measured over a period of time.

(*iii*) The demand curve will normally slope down from left to right (a negative relationship). This is because the lower the price, the greater the quantity demanded and vice versa.

(*iv*) In Figure 2.1 the demand curve is a straight line although this does not necessarily have to be the case.

(*v*)   At a price of 60 pence the quantity demanded by the market is zero.

(*vi*) While considering the relationship between the quantity demanded and price we have assumed *ceteris paribus*, which you will remember means all other factors remaining unchanged.

(*vii*) A change in price will lead to a movement along the demand curve. For example, as the price rises from 20 to 30 pence the quantity demanded falls from 8 to 6 million bars per week. This is sometimes called a *contraction* of demand. If the movement had been in the opposite direction it would have been called an *expansion* of demand.

It is most important that the difference between a '*movement along*' a demand curve and a '*shift*' in a demand curve is fully understood. So far we have discussed the relationship between **quantity demanded** and the product's own price and have seen that this can be shown as a *movement along* the demand curve. We use the terms 'expansion' or 'contraction' for a movement along the demand curve. However, the other factors which influence demand will cause the whole demand curve to change its position. This is called a *shift* in the demand curve. We use the terms '**increase**' (shift to the right) or '**decrease**' (shift to the left).

These shift factors are discussed below and are sometimes called the '**conditions of demand**'.

(**b**) *A change in the price of other related products.* This would affect the demand for chocolate bars in one of two ways. If the product in question was a *substitute* product for chocolate, such as crisps, and its price rose relative to that of chocolate, then the demand for chocolate bars would increase at every price. This would lead to a shift in the demand curve for chocolate bars to the right. The effect that an increase in the price of a substitute product might have on the demand for chocolate bars is shown by the demand schedule in Table 2.2.

In Figure 2.2 the new demand curve D$_1$ has been plotted from the information given in Table 2.2. The original demand curve has also been included to allow comparisons to be made. There has been a rise in the quantity of chocolate bars demanded *at each price*, so whereas at a price of 20 pence 8 million bars per week were initially demanded now 12 million bars per week are demanded. There has been a *shift* in the demand curve to the right (increase). It can also be seen that, whereas initially demand was zero at a price of 60 pence, it is now 80 pence before demand is zero.

On the other hand, if the price of the substitute product was to fall then this could lead to a decrease in the quantity of chocolate bars demanded and, therefore, a shift to the left in the demand curve.

Alternatively, the product whose price changed could be a *complementary* product. Examples of complementary products include cars and petrol, and tennis balls and tennis racquets. In the above example it could be chocolate bars and cups of tea (which may be consumed together), although you may not see them as complements, for products which are complementary products are normally purchased together. If the price of the

Contraction or expansion of demand/supply Movement along a demand/supply curve due to a change in the product's own price.

Quantity demanded The amount of a good or service a consumer is willing and able to buy at a particular price over a particular period of time.

Increase or decrease of demand/supply Shift in the demand/supply curve to the right (increase) or left (decrease) due to a change in the 'conditions' of demand or supply.

Conditions of demand/supply Those variables in the demand/supply function which cause the respective curves to shift.

Table 2.2 The demand schedule for chocolate bars following an increase in the price of a substitute product

Price (pence per unit)	Quantity demanded following an increase in the price of a substitute product (million bars per week)
0	16
10	14
20	12
30	10
40	8
50	6
60	4
70	2
80	0

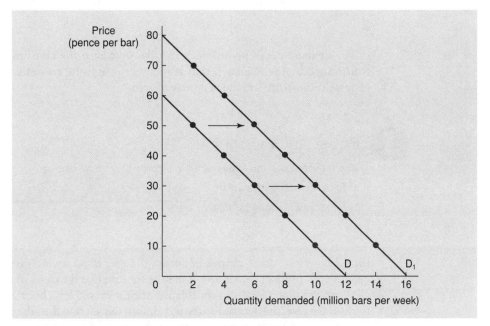

Figure 2.2 An increase in the price of a substitute product will result in a shift in the demand curve to the right from D to D₁.

complementary product tea fell, it would lead to an increase in the demand for chocolate bars and a shift in the demand curve to the right.

(c) *Change in the level of household income.* A change in the level of household income will normally lead to a pivoting of the demand curve around the intercept on the horizontal axis as in Figure 2.3. If the starting point is demand curve D_1 then, for a *normal good*, an increase in income will lead to the demand curve pivoting from D_1 to D_2. For an *inferior good*, however, an increase in income will result in the demand curve pivoting from D_1 to D_3.

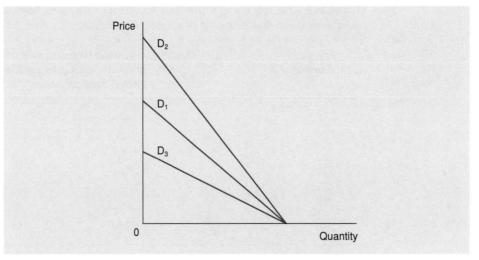

Figure 2.3 **The impact on demand caused by an increase in income.**

The demand curve pivots since if price were zero the consumption would not be constrained by income such that if income were to increase there would not be an increase/decrease in demand at a price of zero.

 Pause for thought 1

What effect would you expect a fall in income to have on demand

a) for a normal good/product

b) for an inferior good/product?

(**d**) *Changes in tastes.* A change in tastes will bring about an increase or a decrease in the quantity of a product demanded. It may be the case that the tastes of the chocolate-buying public will change away from chocolate in the future and less chocolate will be demanded. If this is the case, the demand curve will shift to the left. On the other hand there may be a change of tastes towards chocolate in which case the demand curve will shift to the right.

Example **Tastes change in favour of bread**

In 2005 it was reported by the UK Federation of Bakers that bread sales had increased by 10%, the first increase recorded in the past ten years. It believed this to be due to the collapse of confidence in the low-carb Atkins diet, with its emphasis on replacing carbohydrates such as flour, sugar, rice and potatoes with foods high in protein and fat. The UK Federation of Bakers noted that a whole range of Atkins-related products were now in decline and that there was now a shift of tastes away from 'faddy diets' and back towards a more balanced diet containing bread.

Example **Ageism increases demand for chocolate**

A rise in the average age of the UK population was reported in 2005 to be increasing the demand for chocolate. People over 55 years in the UK are eating their way through almost £700 million of chocolate every year. An ageing UK population is therefore helping the prospects for UK chocolate manufacturers.

(e) *Advertising*. Advertising is important in influencing the level of demand for a product. Successful advertising of a product will shift the demand curve to the right although successful advertising of a substitute product by a competitor will shift the demand curve for the product in question to the left. Advertising can also be linked to the previous factor in that a main function of advertising is to change tastes.

Mini Case Study 2.1

Budget flights grow

The popularity of low-fare flights has helped the air travel industry to recover after the 11 September 2001 terrorist attack in New York. Low-cost airlines now acount for 12% of the total scheduled flights, doubling their share since 2001. The director of corporate affairs at EasyJet claims that flights increased from 9 million passengers in 2001 to 26 million passengers in 2004. He puts this down to major seat promotions and reduced prices since 2001, whereas traditional airlines raised prices to cover their extra security costs.

Question

Use demand analysis to help explain this huge rise in passengers carried by EasyJet and other budget airlines since 2001.

Answer to question can be found on the students' side of the Companion Website.

3.3 'Movements along' and 'shifts in' the demand curve

It is important that you understand what brings about a movement along and a shift in the demand curve and Table 2.3 gives a summary of the factors.

Table 2.3 The factors leading to a movement along and a shift in the demand curve

A movement along the demand curve for chocolate bars	
The quantity of chocolate bars demanded	
Contracts if:	*Expands if:*
● the price rises	● the price falls

Table 2.3 (*cont'd*)

A shift of the demand curve

The quantity of chocolate bars demanded

Decreases (shifts to the left) if:	*Increases (shifts to the right) if:*
● there is a fall in the price of a related product (a substitute)	● there is a rise in the price of a related product (a substitute)
● there is a rise in the price of a complementary product	● there is a fall in the price of a complementary product
● there is a rise in household income and the product is an inferior good	● there is a rise in household income and the product is a normal good
● there is a change in tastes away from the product	● there is a change in tastes towards the product
● a competitor has a successful advertising campaign	● the company has a successful advertising campaign

3.4 The derivation of market demand

We stated earlier that the *market demand* curve is the total amount that consumers demand at a particular price over a given period of time. The market demand curve is derived from summing the individual demand curves horizontally. For example, if we assume just two individuals, A and B, then summing their demand curves horizontally would produce the market demand curve as shown in Figure 2.4 (*see* page 31). Thus at a price of 20 pence individual A demands 20 units per month of product X whereas individual B demands 15 units. The total market demand would therefore be 35 units. Obviously in the real world the market is made up of more than two individuals, but the way to calculate the market demand curve is just the same no matter how many individuals are involved.

Mini Case Study 2.2

Increase in demand for general air travel

Global air passenger traffic continued a steady recovery in 2004, rising 20% over 2003, according to the International Air Transport Association. The airline industry has been hit hard by a sluggish economy, rising fuel prices and travel fears related to the September 11, 2001 attacks on the United States and the conflict in Iraq.

However, in 2004 Middle Eastern air carriers posted a jump of 44.3% for passenger traffic, while the increase for passenger traffic in Asia was 35%, in North America 20% and in Europe the figure was 13%.

IATA noted that traffic figures were especially low in 2003 because the outbreak of severe acute respiratory syndrome, or SARS, frightened off many travelers. SARS had the greatest effect on Asian air travel. The disease struck hard in March 2003, infecting more than 8,000 people worldwide and killing 774, the vast majority in China, Hong Kong and Taiwan.

In recent years, airlines also have been hit by slumping passenger confidence after the September 11, 2001 attacks on the United States and the Iraq war, which caused a falloff in Middle East travel. The industry also has been hard hit by global economic sluggishness.

IATA also said the high price of jet fuel threatens the airline industry's recovery. At $50 a barrel in 2005, oil prices remain approximately US$14 per barrel above anticipated levels, which adds up to US$14 billion in costs to the industry, according to IATA. It believes that the prices charged for air travel will have to rise to meet these extra costs.

Source: AP Worldstream, 28 July 2004

Question

Outline the factors that influence the demand for world air travel.

Answer to question can be found at the back of the book (page 491).

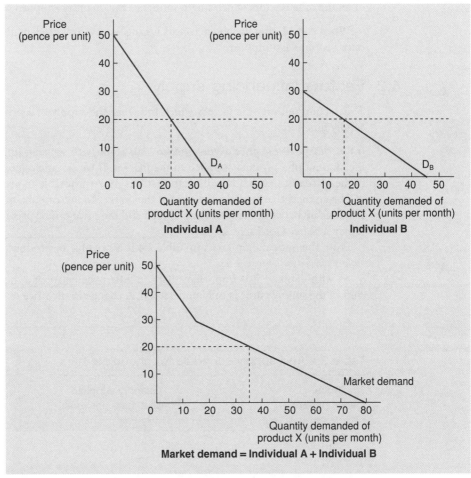

Figure 2.4 The market demand curve is obtained by summing the individual demand curves horizontally. The quantities demanded by each individual at each price are added together, so at a price of, say, 20 pence, individual A demands 20 units and individual B demands 15 units. The overall market demand is therefore 35 units at a price of 20 pence.

4	SUPPLY

4.1 What is supply?

The supply of a product is the quantity of the product that firms are willing and able to put onto the market at a particular price over a particular period of time. We will assume that the prime motive for supplying a product is to make a *profit* and that supply is the *market supply* rather than an individual firm's supply.

The factors which influence the quantity supplied are:

Quantity supplied
The amount of a good or service that producers plan to sell at a particular price over a particular period of time.

a) the price of product;
b) the price of all the other products in the economy;
c) the price of the factors of production;
d) the state of technology;
e) all the other factors which might influence the quantity supplied.

When considering the above factors it is necessary, as with demand, to make use of the *ceteris paribus* assumption.

4.2 Factors influencing supply

This section outlines the factors which influence the supply of a product, as given in the supply function.

(a) *A change in the price of the product.* This is likely to have an important influence on the amount of a product supplied to the market. If we assume *ceteris paribus*, an increase in the price of the product will mean that it is more profitable to produce and thus there will be an incentive for the producers in the market to increase the quantity supplied. The relationship between the quantity supplied and the price can be presented in the form of a *supply schedule* (*see* Table 2.4).

From the information given in Table 2.4 it is possible to produce a graph showing the *supply curve* (*see* Figure 2.5).

As with demand it is important that the difference between a movement along and a shift in the supply curve is fully understood. A change in the price of the product will lead

Table 2.4 **The supply schedule for chocolate bars**

Price (pence per bar)	Quantity supplied (million bars per week)
0	0
10	0
20	2
30	4
40	6
50	8
60	10
70	12

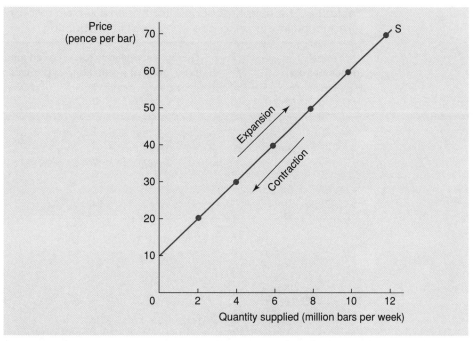

Figure 2.5 The supply curve normally slopes upwards since, as the price rises, the quantity supplied expands, assuming *ceteris paribus*. It can be noted that a change in price leads to a movement along the supply curve.

to a movement along the supply curve. We use the terms 'expansion' or 'contraction' for a movement along the supply curve. However, the other factors which influence supply will cause the whole supply curve to *shift* its position. We use the terms 'increase' (shift to right) or 'decrease' (shift to left).

These shift factors are discussed below and are sometimes called the 'conditions of supply'.

(b) *A change in the price of other products.* This is likely to influence the quantity of a product (in our case chocolate bars) supplied. *Substitutes in production* are other products which could be produced with similar resources to those used in producing chocolate bars. If the price of, say, boxed chocolates or candy bars fell, then assuming *ceteris paribus* these products would be less profitable to produce when compared to the chocolate bar. If this was the case then the quantity of chocolate bars supplied would increase at each and every price, as resources are reallocated from the production of the now less profitable boxed chocolates and candy bars to chocolate bars.

The information given in Table 2.5, which shows the new quantity supplied following a reduction in the price of another product such as boxed chocolates, can be plotted as in Figure 2.6. The initial supply curve has also been plotted so that a comparison can be made. It should now be possible to see how a *shift* in the supply curve has taken place from, say, 4 million bars supplied per week at a price of 30 pence to 6 million bars supplied per week at a price of 30 pence. In other words, the supply curve has shifted to the right (increased) from S to S_1.

Table 2.5 The supply schedule for chocolate bars following a reduction in the price of a substitute in production

Price (pence per bar)	Quantity supplied following a reduction in the price of a substitute in production
0	0
10	2
20	4
30	6
40	8
50	10
60	12
70	14

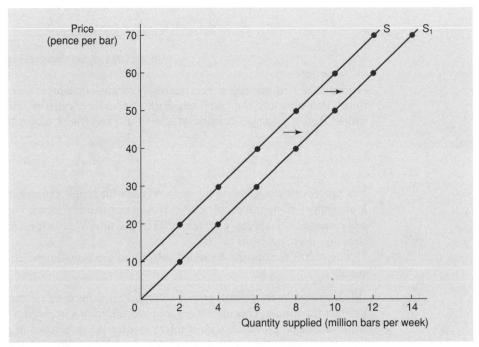

Figure 2.6 If the price of chocolate bars remains constant but there is a reduction in the price of a substitute in production this will lead to a shift in the supply curve for chocolate bars to the right from S to S₁.

Complements in production
This term refers to jointly-supplied products or by-products.

Of course, if, instead of a reduction in the price of boxed chocolates or candy bars, their price had risen then *ceteris paribus* the supply curve for chocolate bars would have shifted to the left (decreased).

There is no obvious **complement in production** for chocolate bars. However, other examples do exist – as more sheep are reared for meat (lamb or mutton), there will be more wool available. We say that mutton and wool are jointly-supplied products.

Pause for thought 2

How would you describe the change in supply of wool if there was a rise in price of its complement in production, mutton?

(c) *A rise in the price of the factors of production.* A rise, for example, in the price of labour used in the production of chocolate bars would make that product more costly and less profitable to produce and would lead to a shift in the supply curve to the left. If, however, there was a fall in the price of a factor of production used in the production of chocolate it would lead to a shift in the supply curve to the right (*see* Figure 2.6).

(d) *A change in the state of technology.* This would influence supply in that if there was an improvement in the technology used to produce chocolate, it would lead to an increase in the profitability of that product and, therefore, more would be supplied. This means that there would be a shift in the supply curve to the right.

(e) *All other factors which might influence the quantity supplied.* This refers to many possible factors, e.g. the weather conditions. Weather only affects particular products such as agricultural output. However, changes in government policy, such as the introduction of a tax on the product or a subsidy, will also influence supply because the level of profit made on that product will be affected.

4.3 The derivation of market supply

We stated earlier that the *market supply* is the total amount of the product that all the firms are willing and able to supply at a particular price over a given period of time. The market supply curve is derived from summing the individual firm supply curves horizontally. For example, if we assume just two firms, A and B, then summing their supply curves horizontally would give the market supply curve shown in Figure 2.7.

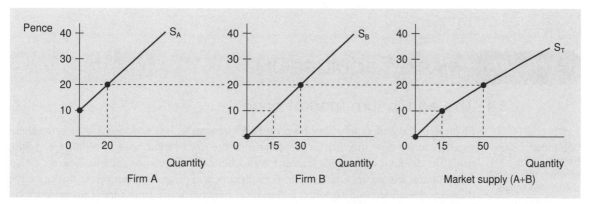

Figure 2.7 The market supply curve is obtained by summing the individual supply curves horizontally. The quantities supplied by each individual firm at each price are added together, so at a price of, say, 20 pence, firm A supplies 20 units and firm B supplies 30 units. The overall market supply is therefore 50 units at a price of 20 pence.

4.4 'Movements along' and 'shifts in' the supply curve

It is important that you understand the difference between a movement along and a shift in the supply curve and Table 2.6 gives a summary of the important points.

Table 2.6 The factors leading to a movement along and a shift in the supply curve

A movement along the supply curve for chocolate bars	
The quantity of chocolate bars supplied will	
Contract if:	*Expand if:*
● the price falls	● the price rises

A shift of the supply curve for chocolate bars	
The quantity of chocolate bars supplied will	
Decrease (shift to the left) if:	*Increase (shift to the right) if:*
● there is a rise in the price of a substitute in production	● there is a fall in the price of a substitute in production
● there is a fall in the price of a complement in production (jointly-supplied product)	● there is a rise in the price of a complement in production (jointly-supplied product)
● there is a rise in the price of a factor of production used in the production of chocolate bars	● there is a fall in the price of a factor of production used in the production of chocolate bars
● there is a deterioration in the technology used in the production of chocolate bars	● there is an improvement in the technology used to produce chocolate bars
● there is the introduction of a tax on the product	● there is the introduction of a subsidy on the product

5 | MARKET EQUILIBRIUM

5.1 The equilibrium market price

Equilibrium price Relates to the price at which the quantity demanded equals the quantity supplied.

So far demand and supply have been outlined separately. It is now possible to bring them together to see how they interact to determine the *equilibrium price and quantity*. Again, using the demand and supply curves for chocolate bars, it can be seen in Figure 2.8 that demand and supply are equal, i.e. in equilibrium, at a price of 35 pence. At this price the quantity demanded and supplied is 5 million bars per week and there is no pressure on the price to change.

However, if the price were 20 pence then the market would be out of equilibrium, in fact it would be in a *disequilibrium* situation. At this price the quantity demanded would be 8 million bars per week but producers would only be willing to supply 2 million bars to

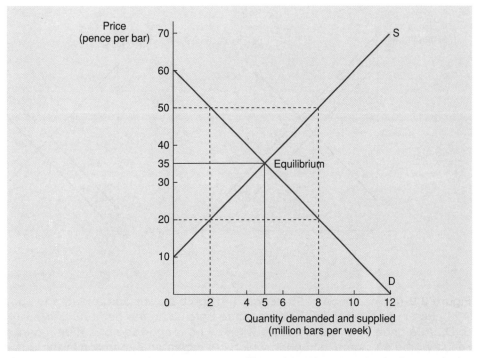

Figure 2.8 At a price of 35 pence, 5 million chocolate bars are demanded per week and 5 million supplied. There is neither excess demand nor excess supply and thus there is no incentive for the price to change. There is an equilibrium price and quantity. If, however, the price were 20 pence there would be excess demand of 6 million bars (a disequilibrium situation) and this would cause the price to rise. If the price were 50 pence there would be excess supply of 6 million bars (a disequilibrium) and this would cause the price to fall.

the market per week. There would, therefore, be a situation of *excess demand* of 6 million bars. In response to this, producers would raise their price. This would have the effect of increasing supply at the same time leading to a reduction in the quantity demanded. This would continue until the equilibrium price of 35 pence was reached. Conversely, the price could have been 50 pence per bar. Here the quantity demanded would have been 2 million and 8 million would have been supplied. In other words, there would have been *excess supply* of 6 million bars. Again, the market would be in a disequilibrium situation and the price would fall in response to the excess stocks held by the producers. This would have the effect of reducing the amount of the product the firms would be willing to supply to the market plus leading to an increase in the amount demanded. This would continue until the equilibrium price was reached.

5.2 Changes in the equilibrium market price

Once in equilibrium it is only possible for that equilibrium to change if there is a change in the demand or supply factors. For example, in Figure 2.9(a) the market is initially in an

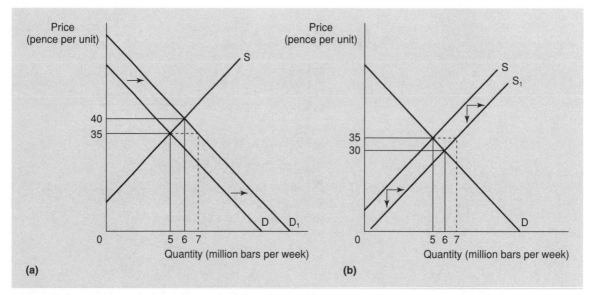

Figure 2.9 (a) At a price of 35 pence 5 million bars are demanded and supplied each week. A change in tastes in favour of chocolate bars shifts the demand curve to the right from D to D_1. At a price of 35 pence there will now be a shortage of 2 million bars per week. The result will be an increase in price which will cause an expansion in the quantity supplied and a contraction in the quantity demanded. The new equilibrium price will be 40 pence and the new equilibrium quantity will be 6 million bars per week.

(b) Given an initial price of the factor of production labour there would be an equilibrium price for chocolate bars of 35 pence and quantity of 5 million. Following a reduction in the price of labour required to produce chocolate bars the supply curve for chocolate bars will shift to the right (increase) from S to S_1. At the price of 35 pence there is now an excess supply of 2 million bars per week. The result will be a reduction in the price of chocolate bars which will cause an expansion in the quantity demanded and a contraction in the quantity supplied. The new equilibrium price will be 30 pence and the new equilibrium quantity will be 6 million bars per week.

equilibrium situation at a price of 35 pence and a quantity of 5 million bars. Suppose there is then a change in tastes and more of the product is demanded, the demand curve will shift to the right from D to D_1. Initially there will be a shortage of 2 million units (shown by the dotted line). This will lead to an increase in price which will stimulate producers to supply more and will also 'choke off' some of the demand, until the new equilibrium is reached at a price of 40 pence and a quantity of 6 million bars.

In Figure 2.9(b) the initial equilibrium is the same as in the previous example with a price of 35 pence and a quantity of 5 million bars. If there is then a reduction in the price of labour used in the production of the product, it is more profitable to produce (assuming *ceteris paribus*). The result would be a shift in the supply curve to the right and, although there would initially be an excess supply of 2 million units (shown by the dotted line), the price would fall until the new equilibrium is reached. This would be at a price of 30 pence and a quantity of 6 million bars.

Mini Case Study 2.3

Market for houses

Houses are valued as 12% more than the regional average if they are located in the same areas as the most successful secondary schools, according to research from the Halifax in 2005.

The study found a close correlation between school league tables and house prices. The 20 local education authorities with schools at the top of the league table have house prices 12% (or £25,000) higher than similar houses nearby but outside the education authority.

The Halifax study comes six months after a report from Nationwide in 2004 tried to put a figure on the premium to house prices generated by good performing local schools. It said that houses in areas where school performance was 10% above the national average would have 2.5% extra value. This was the case even when the houses were identical in characteristics and separated by only a few miles, and differed only in that some were in the catchment area of successful schools but others were outside the catchment areas (so that children had no right to attend the successful schools).

Questions

1 *From the study why do houses which are in similar locations with similar characteristics have different prices?*

2 *Can you use a demand/supply diagram to explain your answer?*

Answers to questions can be found on the students' side of the Companion Website.

KEY POINTS

- The market refers to any situation that allows buyers and sellers to obtain information for the purpose of exchange.

- The market demand for a product is the total amount which consumers demand at a particular price over a particular period of time.

- Effective demand means there is an ability and willingness to buy a particular product.

- *Ceteris paribus* is all important when studying demand and supply and it refers to all other things of relevance remaining the same or other things being equal.

- It is important to understand the difference between a *movement along* a demand and supply curve and a *shift* in a demand and supply curve.

- The market supply of a product refers to the total quantity that firms are willing and able to put onto a market at a particular price over a particular period of time.

- Equilibrium price relates to the price at which the quantity demanded equals the quantity supplied.

Further reading

Griffiths, A. and Wall, S. (2005) *Economics for Business and Management*, FT/Prentice Hall, Chapter 1.

Heather, K. (2004) *Economics Theory in Action*, 4th edition, FT/Prentice Hall, Chapter 2.
Parkin, M., Powell, M. and Matthews, K. (2005) *Economics*, 6th edition, FT/Prentice Hall, Chapters 3 and 6.
Sloman, J. (2006) *Economics*, 6th edition, FT/Prentice Hall, Chapters 2 and 3.

Web references

Useful data on demand and supply issues can be found at various websites, including:

http://thomasregister.com
http://www.foodanddrink.co.uk
www.cocacola.com
www.emigroup.com
www.virginrecords.com
www.bip.co.uk

Information on a range of market and demand related issues can be found at:

www.brandrepublic.com
www.keynote.co.uk
www.euromonitor.com
www.globalweb.co.uk

The market research society can be found at:

www.marketresearch.org.uk
www.bmra.org.uk

PROGRESS AND REVIEW QUESTIONS

Answers to most questions can be found at the back of the book (pages 491–3). Answers to asterisked questions can be found on the students' side of the Companion Website.

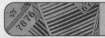 ## Multiple-choice questions

1 Which of the following could shift the demand curve for the VW Passat car to the right?

   a) An increase in income
   b) A reduction in the population
   c) A decrease in the price of the Vauxhall Vectra, a substitute
   d) An increase in the price of the VW Passat
   e) An increase in the price of fuel, a complement

2 The price of a product will increase if:

   a) demand for the product increases
   b) supply of the product increases
   c) the price of a complement increases
   d) if there is a surplus of the product
   e) none of the above.

3 A good can be seen as inferior if:

a) a reduction in the price of the good leads to an increase in the quantity of that good consumers wish to purchase

b) an increase in income leads to an increase in the demand for the good

c) the good is seen as being of low quality

d) an increase in income leads to a reduction in the demand for the good

e) an increase in the price of the good leads to a reduction in the quantity of the good consumers wish to purchase.

4

Price €	Quantity demanded	Quantity supplied
1	1,200	200
2	1,000	400
3	800	600
4	600	800
5	400	1,000
6	200	1,200

In terms of the above table, if a price of €2 is charged:

a) the market will be in equilibrium situation

b) there will be a surplus of 700 units

c) there will be a shortage of 700 units

d) the price of the good will tend to fall

e) none of the above.

5 In terms of the figure below, at a price of P_1:

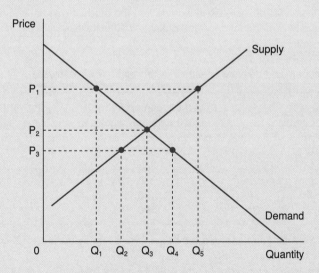

a) there will be a shortage of the amount Q_5-Q_1

b) the market will be in equilibrium

c) there will be a surplus of Q_5-Q_1

d) the price will rise

e) none of the above.

6 Recently there has been technological advance in terms of the manufacture of DVD players. As such, one would expect the price of DVD players to:

a) increase because of the technological advance
b) rise, leading to an increase in the demand for other forms of entertainment
c) fall, thus leading to a rise in the demand for DVD games purchased from retail outlets
d) fall, thus leading to a fall in the demand for DVD games purchased from retail outlets
e) none of the above.

 ## Data response questions

1 The demand and supply schedules for good X are given in the table below.

Px (£)	Quantity demanded	Quantity supplied
1	120	0
2	100	20
3	80	40
4	60	60
5	40	80
6	20	100

a) Define what is meant by the quantity demanded and the quantity supplied.
b) What is the equilibrium price and quantity?
c) What would be the excess demand or supply if the price were:
   (i) £2
   (ii) £6?
d) If there was an increase in income and the product was an inferior good what would be the new equilibrium price and quantity if 20 units less were demanded at each and every price?

2 The supply and demand situation for product X is as follows.

Price of X (£ per unit)	Quantity demanded of X (000 units per week)	Quantity supplied of X (000 units per week)
10	20	80
9	40	70
8	60	60
7	80	50
6	100	40

a) Draw a diagram showing the demand and supply curves for X and identify the equilibrium price and quantity.
b) Why is £9 not an equilibrium price? Use your diagram to explain how equilibrium will be restored in a market economy.
c) The government now introduces a maximum price of £6 per unit. Using your diagram explore the likely consequences of such a maximum price.
d) Suppose the government introduced a minimum price of £10 per unit. Using your diagram explore the likely consequences of such a minimum price.

Case study question

House prices slow down

In 2005 house prices in the UK are rising much more slowly than in previous years. In 2003 house prices rose on average by 20.3%, and in 2004 by 18.2%, but in 2005 house prices are rising at a slower rate. This fall in house price inflation has been linked to slower wage growth, interest rate rises (from 3% to 4.5% over the past two years) and lower expectations as to future house price rises by homeowners.

Question

1 *a) Why are house prices rising less rapidly than previously?*

   b) Can you use a demand/supply diagram to explain your reasoning?

Irish smoking ban

Ireland's ban on smoking in the workplace seems not to have triggered a feared collapse in its drinking industry in the six months following its introduction. Many publicans have complained that their takings have suffered since the Irish Republic became the first country to introduce a workplace smoking ban on 29 March 2004, but this is nothing like the meltdown that some had predicted. The Licensed Vintners' Association, which represents pub owners in Dublin, claims that about 2,000 jobs in the drinks industry have been lost and that, on average, Dublin pub sales are 16% lower. The Vintners' Federation of Ireland, which represents some 60,000 rural publicans, says that sales have fallen by an average of 15 to 25%. Without a doubt the publicans who have suffered most are those closest to Northern Ireland, where smokers can still puff away over a Guinness.

Question

2 *Use demand and supply diagrams to explain some of the impacts of the smoking ban on pubs in Ireland.*

True/false questions

1 A market is defined as a situation in which buyers and sellers communicate for the purpose of exchange.

2 The change in the price of a product will lead to a movement along the demand curve for that product.

3 If an increase in income results in a reduction in the quantity demanded then the good in question is said to be an inferior good.

4 The market demand curve for a product is derived from the vertical summation of individual consumers' demand curves.

5 Equilibrium quantity is the quantity bought and sold at the equilibrium price.

Essay questions

Answers to asterisked questions can be found on the students' side of the Companion Website. All other answers can be found at the back of the book (page 493).

1* Outline the factors that would bring about a movement along and a shift in the demand curve for an economics textbook.

2 With the aid of a demand and supply diagram show the effect on the market for DVD players if there is an increase in income (DVD players being a normal good) while at the same time the manufacturer of DVD players has introduced a new technique of production which significantly reduces the cost of production.

3* Using demand and supply diagrams outline the main factors which could affect the price of houses in the UK.

4 Why has the price of oil risen so sharply over the past few years?

Elasticity

Learning objectives

By the end of this chapter you will be able to:

- Understand the concept of elasticity of demand and supply.
- Identify the factors affecting price, income and cross elasticity of demand and price elasticity of supply.
- Explain the relationship between price elasticity of demand and total revenue.
- Understand the importance of elasticity.
- Apply the concept of elasticity to various situations.

1 INTRODUCTION

In Chapter 2 demand and supply curves were introduced. It was shown how, among other things, the demand for a product could be affected by a change in its price, a change in household income and a change in the price of other products and a change in tastes. It was also demonstrated how supply was, among other things, affected by a change in price, a change in the prices of factors of production, a change in technology and a change in taxes or subsidies.

Price elasticity of demand
The responsiveness of the quantity demanded of a good or service to a change in the price of that good or service, *ceteris paribus*.

The ways in which demand and supply respond to the above changes are important and can be measured by the use of a concept known as *elasticity*. In this chapter we deal with the four types of elasticity:

a) price elasticity of demand
b) income elasticity of demand
c) cross elasticity of demand
d) price elasticity of supply.

2 PRICE ELASTICITY OF DEMAND (PED)

2.1 What is price elasticity of demand?

It is possible to measure how the demand for a good responds to a change in its own price by using the concept of price elasticity of demand (PED). The relationship can be presented as a formula:

$$\text{PED} = \frac{\text{Percentage change in the quantity demanded}}{\text{Percentage change in the price}}$$

This can be rewritten as:

$$\text{PED} = \frac{\dfrac{\Delta q}{q} \times 100}{\dfrac{\Delta p}{p} \times 100} = \frac{\Delta q}{\Delta p} \times \frac{p}{q}$$

where:

q   = the original quantity
p   = the original price
Δq = the change in quantity
Δp = the change in price

For example, in Figure 3.1 a price increase from 10 pence to 20 pence causes the quantity demanded to fall from 10m to 8m per week.

This means that a 100% increase in price leads to a 20% fall in the quantity demanded, which will produce a price elasticity of demand (PED) equal to 0.2 or, to be absolutely correct, -0.2. This is obtained by:

$$\text{PED} = \frac{-2}{10} \times \frac{10}{10} = \frac{-2}{10} = -0.2$$

The reason for the negative sign is because of the negative slope of a normal demand curve (*see* Figures 3.1 and 3.2). If we ignore the negative sign and simply concentrate

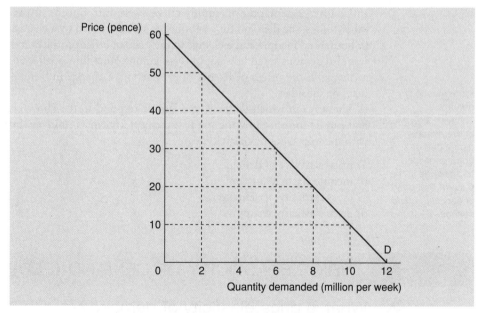

Figure 3.1 Using the equation given above it is possible to calculate the price elasticity of demand when price rises from 10 pence to 20 pence, from 20 pence to 30 pence, and so on. The demand curve is more elastic as we move up the demand curve from right to left.

on the value obtained then the price elasticity of demand is less than 1, i.e. demand is *inelastic*. This is because the percentage change in the quantity demanded is *less* than the percentage change in the price and demand is, therefore, not very responsive to a price change. The lower the elasticity of demand the less responsive is demand to a change in price. This has obvious implications for firms making their pricing decisions, as will be seen later in the chapter.

When the percentage change in the quantity demanded is greater than the percentage change in price then demand is said to be *elastic*. That means that demand is responsive to a price change. If the ratio is equal to 1, then the percentage change in the quantity demanded and the percentage change in price are equal. Here the elasticity is said to be *unity*. So the greater the elasticity value, the more responsive demand is to a price change.

Table 3.1 summarises the different numerical values for price elasticity of demand (ignoring the sign), together with the terminology used and what it actually means.

Table 3.1 **Price elasticity of demand: numerical value, terminology and description**

Numerical value	Terminology	Description
0	Perfectly inelastic demand	Whatever the % change in price no change in quantity demanded
0 < PED < 1	Relatively inelastic demand	A given % change in price leads to a smaller % change in quantity demanded
1	Unit elastic demand	A given % change in price leads to exactly the same % change in quantity demanded
1 < PED < ∞	Relatively elastic demand	A given % change in price leads to a larger % change in quantity demanded
∞ (infinity)	Perfectly elastic demand	An infinitely small % change in price leads to an infinitely large % change in quantity demanded

Normally the price elasticity of demand (PED) for a product will vary along the length of the demand curve. Again taking Figure 3.1, as the price rises from 20 pence to 30 pence demand falls from 8m to 6m per week and the PED is 0.5 (inelastic). A price increase from 30 pence to 40 pence causes demand to fall from 6m to 4m per week resulting in a PED of 1 (unity). A price increase from 40 pence to 50 pence results in a fall in demand from 4m to 2m per week and the PED is 2 (elastic). The demand curve is, therefore, more elastic as we move up the demand curve from right to left, from a price of 0 to a price of 60 pence.

Figure 3.2 is a graphical summary of price elasticity of demand and shows that the PED is unity halfway along the demand curve.

 Pause for thought 1

Why might a firm be interested in price elasticity of demand?

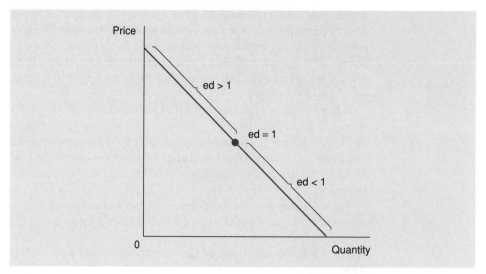

Figure 3.2 On a straight line demand curve the price elasticity of demand increases as the price rises and the quantity demanded falls. Above the mid point on the demand curve the price elasticity of demand is greater than 1 (elastic), below the mid point the price elasticity of demand is less than 1 (inelastic) and at the mid point the price elasticity of demand is equal to 1 (unity).

Although price elasticity of demand will usually vary along the length of the demand curve there are three exceptions (*see* Figure 3.3):

(a) A change in price in Figure 3.3(a) will have no effect on the quantity demanded. In this situation demand is perfectly inelastic along the length of the demand curve with a value of 0. No matter what price is charged for this good demand does not change.

(b) Demand is infinite at a price P_0 in Figure 3.3(b). If price were to increase to any level above P_0 then demand would fall to zero. In this situation demand is perfectly elastic with a value of infinity (∞).

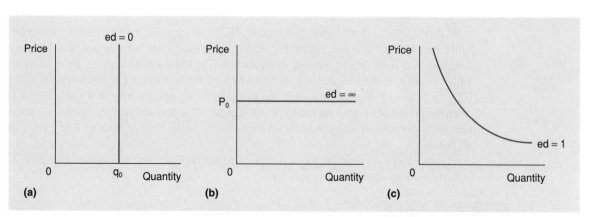

Figure 3.3 The three demand curves illustrated each have a constant elasticity. The vertical demand curve has a constant elasticity of zero, the horizontal demand curve has a constant elasticity of infinity and the rectangular hyperbola has a constant elasticity of 1.

(c) Any percentage increase or decrease in the price in Figure 3.3(c) leads to the same percentage decrease or increase in the quantity demanded and this will be the case along the length of the demand curve. The PED is, therefore, unity and a curve with this particular quality is called a *rectangular hyperbola*.

2.2 Price elasticity of demand and total revenue

Total revenue
A firm's total earnings obtained from the sale of a good or service. It is calculated by multiplying the price of the good or service by the quantity sold.

The price elasticity of demand for a product is important in relation to its effect on total revenue (TR). Total revenue will be covered in more detail in Chapter 6 but for the purposes of this section it can be defined as the total amount that is obtained from the sale of a product. Total revenue is, therefore, the price (P) of the product multiplied by the total quantity sold (q).

$$TR = P \times q$$

As can be seen in Figure 3.4(a), as the price falls from P_1 to P_2 the total revenue rises since the loss in revenue (−) from selling the original quantity at a now lower price is outweighed by the gain in revenue (+) from selling extra units at this lower price. This arises because demand is elastic. Note that the shaded area is 'common' to the revenue situation both before and after the price fall.

In Figure 3.4(b) a reduction in the price from P_3 to P_4 leaves total revenue unchanged as the revenue lost (−) is equal to the revenue gained (+). In this situation we have unit elasticity of demand.

In Figure 3.4(c) a reduction in the price from P_5 to P_6 leads to a fall in total revenue with the loss (−) being greater than the gain (+). In this situation we have inelastic demand.

The possible effects of a change in price on the total revenue and the resulting elasticity of demand are summarised in Table 3.2.

Mini Case Study 3.1

Price rises at the *Daily Mirror*

Sly Bailey, the Trinity Mirror chief executive, sought to boost revenues of the *Daily Mirror* in 2004 by increasing the price of the tabloid newspaper by 3p, from 32p to 35p. The move is a sharp U-turn of the policy of Philip Graf, her predecessor, who tried to boost *Daily Mirror* circulation by cutting the cover price, triggering a price war with its rivals *The Sun* and the *Daily Star*. Ms Bailey ended the price war as soon as she took over at Trinity Mirror in 2003. The *Daily Mirror* will now cost 5p more than *The Sun*, which is owned by News International, parent company of *The Times*. It appears that *The Sun* has no immediate plans to increase its price. The *Daily Mirror* last increased its price in September 1999 but the tabloid newspaper market in the UK is fiercely competitive and it is not clear what the effect on its circulation will be.

Question

What price elasticity of demand issues are raised in this case study?

Answer to question can be found on the students' side of the Companion Website.

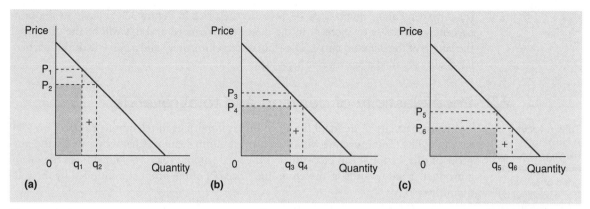

(a)   **(b)**   **(c)**

Figure 3.4 Elasticity can be considered by referring to total revenue. If, following a price reduction, there is a rise in total revenue as in (a), then demand is elastic. On the other hand, if, following a price reduction, there is a fall in total revenue as in (c), then demand is inelastic. If total revenue is constant after a price reduction then demand is unit-elastic as in (b).

Table 3.2 The relationship between price elasticity of demand and total revenue

Price elasticity of demand	Price	Effect on total revenue
Elastic > 1	Fall	Rise
	Rise	Fall
Unity = 1	Fall	No change
	Rise	No change
Inelastic < 1	Fall	Fall
	Rise	Rise

 Pause for thought 2

If the demand for a product is inelastic, what will be the effect on total revenue if the price of the product falls?

2.3 Factors determining price elasticity of demand

There are a number of factors which together determine the value of the price elasticity of demand for a given product including:

Substitute
A product seen by the consumer to be an alternative for another product.

(a) *Whether close substitutes are available.* If a product has a close substitute then it is likely that the demand for that product will fall if its price increases. The closer the substitute, the greater the contraction in demand for the product whose price has risen. If this is the case then demand will tend to be elastic. The reason for this is that consumers, faced with a price increase, will switch their expenditure to the close substitute. For example, a product such as petrol has a relatively inelastic demand since there are no close substitutes available, whereas *particular brands of petrol* have a much more elastic demand, as each brand can act as a close substitute for any other brand.

(b) *Time period.* The demand for most products is likely to be relatively more responsive to a price change in the long-run time period than in the short-run time period, since consumers often take time to adjust their purchasing habits.

Example

Elasticity and time

Figure 3.5 relates to the demand for petrol. Following a price rise from P_1 to P_2 the demand in the short run may contract from q_1 to q_2 along D_{SR} as consumers use their cars less. In the long run, however, the consumer may respond to the higher price for petrol by purchasing cars which have smaller engines, using less petrol. So, in the long run, demand is likely to fall further to q_3 along D_{LR}, with demand being relatively more elastic.

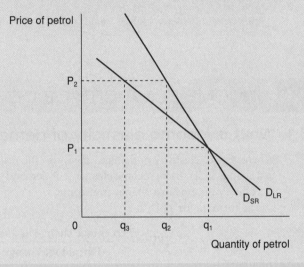

Figure 3.5 Demand is likely to be relatively more elastic in the long run than in the short run.

Mini Case Study 3.2

Elasticity of bus and rail travel

Table 3.3 Bus and rail fare price elasticities (UK values)

Length of forecast period	Elasticity (bus)	Elasticity (rail)
Short run	−0.42	−0.46
Medium run	−0.56	−
Long run	−1.01	−0.65

In the short run, price elasticities of demand for bus and rail fare average −0.42 and −0.46 respectively. Overall, short-run bus fare elasticity values have risen. This can be seen to reflect an increase in car ownership and less reliance over time on the bus. In the long run, bus fare elasticities average around −1.01. A number of reasons can be put forward for this. First, the longer the time period then the greater the range of options open to the bus user affected by the fare increase. In the short run the bus passenger can switch modes or stop making the journey. In the long run, however, more options are available such as moving homes, changing jobs or buying a car. In terms of rail elasticities the increase in value over time is not as great as for buses.

Source: Adapted from *The demand for public transport: a practical guide*, TRL Report TRL593, 2004

Questions

1 *Define price elasticity of demand and comment on the short-run values for bus and rail.*

2 *Why do you think the increase in the elasticity value of rail over time is not so great as that for bus?*

Answers to questions can be found at the back of the book (page 494).

3 INCOME ELASTICITY OF DEMAND (YED)

3.1 What is income elasticity of demand?

Income elasticity of demand
The responsiveness of the quantity demanded of a good or service to a change in income, *ceteris paribus*.

Whereas price elasticity of demand measures the responsiveness of demand for a product to a change in its price, income elasticity of demand (YED) measures how the demand for a product responds to a change in income.

The formula for YED is:

$$\text{YED} = \frac{\text{Percentage change in quantity demanded}}{\text{Percentage change in income}}$$

This can be rewritten as:

$$\text{YED} = \frac{\dfrac{\Delta q}{q} \times 100}{\dfrac{\Delta Y}{Y} \times 100} = \frac{\Delta q}{\Delta Y} \times \frac{Y}{q}$$

where:

q = the original quantity
Y = the original income
Δq = the change in quantity
ΔY = the change in income

Whereas price elasticity of demand measures a *movement along* a demand curve due to a change in the product's own price, income elasticity of demand measures a *shift* in the demand curve due to a change in income (one of the 'conditions of demand'). For most products a rise in income will lead to an increase in demand, with more of the product now bought at any given price, with the opposite being true for a fall in income. We call

Normal product
A good or service for which demand increases as income increases.

such products *normal products* or *normal goods*. The sign of income elasticity of demand (YED) will therefore be *positive* (+/+ or −/−) for normal products.

However, for some products as income rises beyond a certain level, the consumer may be able to replace a cheaper, but poorer quality product with a more expensive and better quality alternative. We call these cheaper, but poorer quality products *inferior products* or *inferior goods*. In other words, as income rises beyond a certain level demand for the inferior product decreases, with less of the product now bought at any given price. The sign of income elasticity of demand (YED) will therefore be *negative* (−/+ or +/−) over certain ranges of income for inferior products.

Inferior product
A good or service for which demand decreases as income increases.

Pause for thought 3

Can you explain why the inferior product might experience an increase in demand for a fall in income (+/− = −) over certain ranges of income?

3.2 Types of income elasticity of demand

Table 3.4 displays a number of examples of the response in demand to an increase in income.

The following situations can be noted:

(**a**) Here the product is normal with the percentage increase in the quantity demanded outweighing the percentage rise in income, so that a 10% rise in income results in a 15% increase in quantity demanded, giving a YED of +1.5. This would suggest that the product could be a consumer durable such as a CD player where the demand increases rapidly as income increases.

(**b**) Here the 10% rise in income leads to exactly the same 10% increase in quantity demanded, giving a YED of +1.

(**c**) Here the percentage increase in the quantity demanded is smaller than the percentage rise in income, so that a 10% rise in income results in a 5% increase in quantity demanded, giving a YED of +0.5. Basic foodstuffs is a type of product which could result in this response since we would not expect a substantial increase in the quantity of basic food purchased as income rises.

Table 3.4 Income elasticity of demand

	Change in income	Change in quantity demanded %	Ratio	Type of product	Income elasticity of demand
a	+10	+15	+1.5	Normal	Positive
b	+10	+10	+1.0	Normal	Unity
c	+10	+5	+0.5	Normal	Positive
d	+10	0	0		Zero
e	+10	−5	−0.5	Inferior	Negative

(d) Here the 10% rise in income has no effect on the quantity demanded, giving a zero income elasticity of demand.

(e) Here the 10% rise in income leads to a 5% *decrease* in the quantity demanded, giving a YED of −0.5. Clearly this is an *inferior product* or *inferior good*, with consumers switching away from this product to a better quality alternative which they can now afford.

The relationship between the quantity demanded of a product and income can be understood further by studying Figure 3.6.

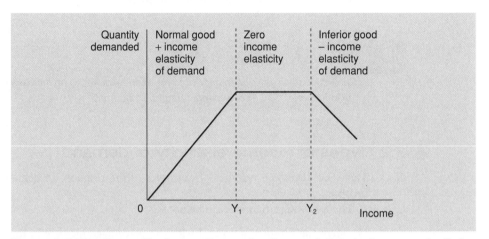

Figure 3.6 The figure illustrates three situations relating to income elasticity of demand. Up to an income level Y_1 the quantity demanded of the product increases as income rises, indicating a positive income elasticity of demand and thus a normal good. As income rises between Y_1 and Y_2 the quantity demanded of the product remains unchanged; the income elasticity of demand is thus zero. Finally, as income rises above Y_2 the quantity demanded decreases, thus illustrating negative income elasticity of demand and an inferior good.

With no income there is zero demand for the product; however, as income rises (up to Y_1) demand for the product increases. Up to an income level of Y_1, the product is normal with a positive income elasticity. As income rises from Y_1 to Y_2 there is no extra demand for the product because the household may have reached 'saturation' in terms of purchasing the product and the income elasticity of demand is zero. As income rises above Y_2 then the quantity demanded actually decreases, indicating that the product is now perceived by consumers as *inferior* and thus has a negative income elasticity of demand.

Although Figure 3.6 has given the three possible situations relating to income elasticity of demand, all products may not follow the pattern outlined and in fact the income elasticity of demand for most products may be positive at all income levels.

 ## Pause for thought 4

Use income elasticity of demand to explain the difference between a normal and an inferior product or good.

Mini Case Study 3.3

Spending on transport

Look carefully at Table 3.5 which shows household expenditure on transport according to which 10% of the gross income group the household happens to be in.

Table 3.5 Household expenditure on transport by gross income decile group

	Lowest 10%	Second decile group	Third decile group	Fourth decile group	Fifth decile group	Sixth decile group	Seventh decile group	Eighth decile group	Ninth decile group	Tenth decile group	All households
					Average weekly household expenditure						
Purchase of vehicles	3.00	6.20	11.00	13.40	15.90	26.20	31.90	37.10	49.80	62.10	25.70
New cars/vans	1.30	1.40	3.30	7.00	5.80	10.10	–	14.00	20.10	31.70	10.60
Second-hand cars/vans	1.70	4.60	7.60	6.30	9.50	15.10	19.50	21.80	28.60	29.10	14.40
Petrol, diesel and other motor oils	3.20	4.30	7.40	10.30	13.30	14.80	18.80	22.60	23.60	29.30	14.70
Repairs and servicing	1.10	1.80	2.90	4.30	5.00	5.00	6.60	6.30	7.20	10.60	5.10
Rail and tube fares	0.40	0.20	0.60	0.70	1.00	1.20	1.60	2.10	3.80	7.00	1.90
Bus and coach fares	0.90	1.10	1.20	1.40	1.40	1.90	1.80	1.70	2.00	1.20	1.50
Air travel	–	–	–	–	–	–	2.00		3.10	1.60	1.20

Source: Adapted from *Family Spending*, National Statistics, 2003

Questions

1 *Overall, what happens to travel expenditure as income increases?*
2 *Are there any items of expenditure which would suggest they are an inferior good?*

Answers to questions can be found on the students' side of the Companion Website.

---

4   CROSS ELASTICITY OF DEMAND (CED)

4.1 What is cross elasticity of demand?

Cross elasticity of demand (CED) refers to the response of demand for one product to the change in the price of another product. As with income elasticity of demand, CED measures a *shift* in the demand curve due to a change in the price of another product (one of the 'conditions of demand').

Cross elasticity of demand
The responsiveness of the quantity demanded of a good or service to a change in the price of another good or service, *ceteris paribus.*

The formula for cross elasticity of demand is:

$$CED = \frac{\text{Percentage change in the quantity demanded of product A}}{\text{Percentage change in the price of product B}}$$

This can be rewritten as:

$$\text{Cross elasticity of demand} = \frac{\dfrac{\Delta q_A}{q_A} \times 100}{\dfrac{\Delta p_B}{p_B} \times 100} = \frac{\Delta q_A}{\Delta p_B} \times \frac{p_B}{q_A}$$

where:

q_A = the original quantity of product A
p_B = the original price of product B
Δq_A = the change in the quantity of product A
Δp_B = the change in the price of product B

Three possible outcomes are shown in Figure 3.7, with the *sign* of CED telling us something about the relationship between the two products. The *size* (or magnitude) of CED tells us how close the two products are, whether as substitutes or complements in consumption.

Complement
Two products which are used/consumed together.

(a) *In situation (1)* as the price of B increases the quantity demanded of A increases. The cross elasticity of demand is therefore positive (+/+). For example, as the price of carrots rises the quantity of peas demanded may increase since they are often seen as substitutes for each other.

(b) *Situation (2)* relates to complementary products, in that as the price of product B rises (for example petrol), the quantity demanded of product A demanded (for example cars) decreases (−/+ = −).

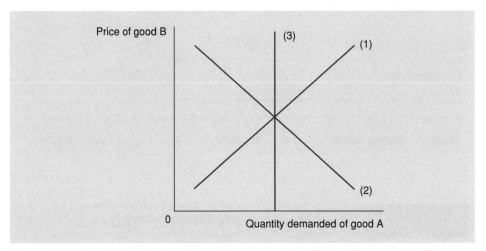

Figure 3.7 Line (1) illustrates a positive cross elasticity of demand with respect to a substitute in that as the price of product B rises the demand for product A increases. Line (2) illustrates a negative cross elasticity of demand with respect to a complement, in that as the price of product B rises the demand for product A decreases. Finally, line (3) illustrates a situation where the cross elasticity of demand is zero, in that as the price of product B rises there is no effect on the demand for product A.

(c) *Situation (3)* relates to two products which are totally unrelated. If, for example, the price of soap increased it is unlikely to result in a change in the quantity of ballpoint pens demanded.

Pause for thought 5

a) *Use the **sign** of CED to distinguish between a substitute product and a complement product.*

b) *Suppose CED is +3 for two products, but –3 for another two products. Explain what these results mean.*

---

5 PRICE ELASTICITY OF SUPPLY (PES)

5.1 What is price elasticity of supply?

Price elasticity of supply The responsiveness of the quantity supplied of a good or service to a change in the price of that good or service, *ceteris paribus*.

Just as price elasticity of demand refers to the responsiveness of demand for a product to a change in its own price, so *price elasticity of supply* (PES) refers to the responsiveness of supply of a product to a change in its own price. PES refers to *movement along* the supply curve, i.e. expansion/contraction of supply.

The relationship can be presented as a formula:

$$PES = \frac{\text{The percentage change in the quantity supplied}}{\text{The percentage change in price}}$$

This can be rewritten as:

$$PES = \frac{\frac{\Delta qs}{qs} \times 100}{\frac{\Delta p}{p} \times 100} = \frac{\Delta qs}{\Delta p} \times \frac{p}{qs}$$

where:
- qs = the original supply
- p = the original price
- Δqs = the change in supply
- Δp = the change in price

As noted in Chapter 2, supply curves generally have a positive slope so that the price elasticity of supply is usually positive (+/+ = +). Figure 3.8 illustrates three situations relating to price elasticity of supply.

(a) *In situation (a)* the supply curve S_1 is perfectly inelastic: as the price rises there is no change in the quantity supplied (the price elasticity of supply is zero).

(b) *In situation (b)* the supply curve S_2 is unit elastic (= 1). Any given percentage change in the price leads to exactly the same percentage change in the quantity supplied. Any straight line supply curve which passes through the origin has a price elasticity of supply equal to 1 at all points along its length.

(c) *In situation (c)* the supply curve S_3 is perfectly elastic with a numerical value equal to infinity. Suppliers in this situation would be willing to supply an infinite amount of the

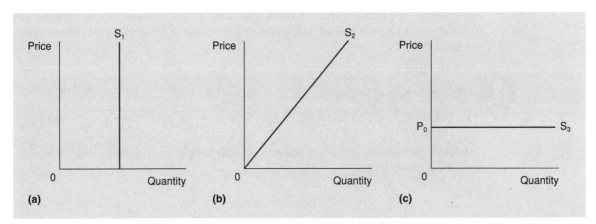

Figure 3.8 Each supply curve shown has a constant price elasticity of supply. The vertical supply curve in (a) has a constant elasticity of zero. The supply curve in (b) has a constant elasticity of 1, which is the case for any straight line supply curve which passes through the origin. In terms of the supply curve in (c) a horizontal supply curve has an elasticity equal to infinity.

product at a price of P_0. However, in this situation a small rise in the price would lead to the quantity supplied falling from infinity to zero.

5.2 Factors determining price elasticity of supply

The following factors determine the price elasticity of supply.

(a) *The existence of spare capacity.* Even if the price of the product rises a firm may not be able to expand supply if it does not have spare capacity. It may, in fact, be operating at full capacity so that, in the short run at least, supply may be perfectly inelastic. On the other hand, if the firm does have spare capacity with a plentiful supply of labour, capital equipment and raw materials it could respond to the price change by expanding output, in which case supply will be more elastic.

(b) *The availability of stocks.* The firm may have accumulated a large quantity of unsold stocks or inventories, which can be quickly supplied to the market. If this is the case then supply will tend to be more elastic.

(c) *Mobility of the factors of production.* If the firm can easily reallocate its resources (namely its land, labour, capital equipment and raw materials) from one type of production to another, then the supply for that product will tend to be more elastic. However, the labour force employed by a firm may be highly skilled in the production of a particular product and the capital equipment highly specialised. If this is the case then it may be difficult to shift resources from one use to another. In this situation the factors of production are said to be immobile and supply will tend to be relatively inelastic.

(d) *The time period.* It will take time for a firm to adjust supply to a change in a product's price, so that supply is likely to be more elastic in the long-run time period. In fact, the time period can be divided into three periods (*see* Figure 3.9).

The momentary period is where supply will be restricted to the amount currently on the market. Here the price elasticity of supply will be zero, shown by the supply curve S_0. In this case a price increase from P_0 to P_1 has no effect on the quantity supplied.

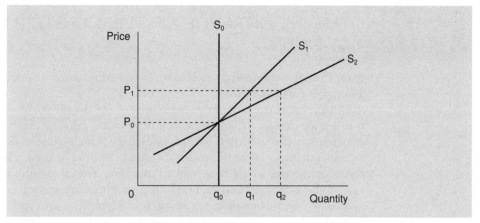

Figure 3.9 The figure illustrates momentary, short- and long-run supply curves. The long-run supply curve S_2 is more elastic than the short-run supply curve S_1, over the price range P_0 to P_1. The momentary supply curve S_0 is perfectly inelastic.

In the *short-run period* the firm may be able to transfer (reallocate) some of its resources and therefore expand from q_0 to q_1 (*see* Figure 3.9). For example, the workforce might be persuaded to work overtime and so the short-run curve could be represented by S_1.

In *the long run* it may be possible for the firm to expand all its resources, for example build a new factory and purchase more machinery, so that the firm's productive capacity rises. Supply will then expand to q_2 as price rises from P_0 to P_1, giving a supply curve of S_2, i.e. a more elastic supply curve.

Table 3.6 presents the numerical values, terminology and description for price elasticity of supply.

Table 3.6 Price elasticity of supply: numerical value, terminology and description

Numerical value of PES	Terminology	Description
0	Perfectly inelastic supply	Whatever the % change in price no change in quantity supplied
0 < PES < 1	Relatively inelastic supply	A given % change in price leads to a smaller % change in quantity supplied
1	Unit elastic supply	A given % change in price leads to exactly the same % change in quantity supplied
1 < PES < ∞	Relatively elastic supply	A given % change in price leads to a larger % change in quantity supplied
∞ (infinity)	Perfectly elastic supply	An infinitely small % change in price leads to an infinitely large % change in quantity supplied

6 THE IMPORTANCE OF THE ELASTICITY CONCEPT

Many firms find it important to obtain detailed estimates of the price elasticity of demand and supply for their products.

Reliable information on the *price elasticity of demand* (PED), i.e. how sensitive demand is to a price change, will allow the firm to be more confident about the effect on its revenue (and possibly its profit) when considering a price increase or decrease. If a firm considers its demand curve to be *elastic* around the price it is currently charging, then a reduction in price would raise total revenue. However, if the firm considers its demand curve to be *inelastic* around the price it is currently charging, then a rise in price would be needed to raise total revenue. For example, in Figure 3.1 a price increase from 10 pence to 20 pence (PED = 0.2) will raise total revenue from £1m to £1.6m.

In terms of income changes for households or for the whole economy, information on the *income elasticity of demand* (YED) will be vital for firms, for, if they are producing what can be classed as 'inferior goods', they are likely to find the demand for their product declining as incomes increase. If incomes are increasing then normal products with a high income elasticity of demand, such as luxury goods, would merit the firm's attention as possible items to produce.

Cross elasticity of demand (CED) will be of importance for firms when trying to assess the impact on demand for their products of changes in the prices of other products, whether substitutes or complements. For example, tyre producers need to be aware of CED between tyres and cars and between tyres and petrol, because a change in the price of cars or petrol will have implications for the tyre industry.

7 APPLICATIONS OF DEMAND AND SUPPLY

Having worked through Chapters 2 and 3, it is possible to introduce some applications of demand and supply analysis. There are numerous applications but this section will concentrate on just three, namely maximum price legislation, the minimum price legislation and the introduction of a tax on the sale of a commodity.

(a) *Maximum price legislation.* In Figure 3.10 the equilibrium price for, say, chocolate bars is 35 pence and the equilibrium quantity is 5 million. Attempts by governments to introduce a maximum price at anything lower than this equilibrium price will result in disequilibrium in the market. For example, if a maximum price of 25 pence were to be introduced by the government through legislation it would lead to an *excess demand* of 4 million bars. At a price of 25 pence, producers of chocolate bars would be willing to supply only 3 million bars to the market per week but consumers demand 7 million bars per week. There is therefore a danger of a *black market* developing since if it were possible for *black marketeers* to obtain that total supply, they could sell it illegally on the *black market* at a price of 45 pence per bar. This would mean that they would make a profit of £600,000 (the shaded area).

(b) *Minimum price legislation.* The introduction of a minimum price below which the product cannot be sold. Again using Figure 3.10, if the government were to introduce a minimum price of, say, 45 pence per bar the result would this time be an *excess supply* of 4 million bars and there would then be a glut of the product on the market. Given this

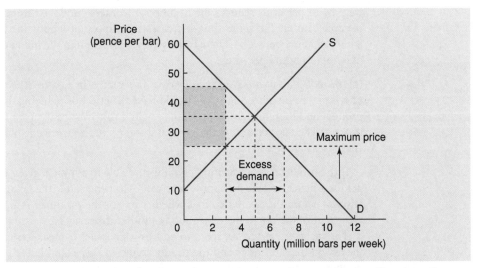

Figure 3.10 The introduction of a maximum price or price ceiling has the effect of artificially keeping the price below the equilibrium price. This creates an excess demand for the product concerned as illustrated.

situation the government would have to purchase the excess supply and *stockpile* it if it wanted to retain this maximum price.

The *minimum wage* is an example of a minimum price in the market for labour. Here it is illegal for employers to pay its workforce lower than a specified wage rate. This can be illustrated by reference to Figure 3.11. The demand curve for labour is D_L and the supply is S_L. If the market is unregulated then the wage rate will be £3 per hour and the quantity of labour employed will be 5 million hours per week. The introduction of a minimum

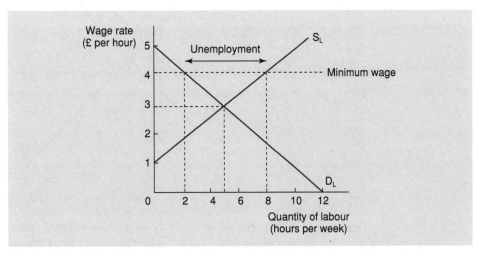

Figure 3.11 In the labour market illustrated, if a minimum wage of £4 per hour is set above the equilibrium wage of £3 per hour then it will create unemployment of 6 million hours per week.

wage of £4 per hour reduces the number of workers employed from 5 to 2 million hours per week but at the same time increases the supply of labour in the market from 5 to 8 million hours per week. There is thus a disequilibrium in the market with unemployment of 6 million hours per week.

(c) *Introduction of a tax on the sale of a commodity.* In Figure 3.12 a tax of 10 pence per unit is placed on a product. This would have the effect of reducing the profitability of that product and therefore the supply curve would shift vertically upwards and to the left, i.e. to S + t. The tax per unit is the vertical distance, *ac*, between the old and the new supply curve (*see* Figure 3.12).

If the producer was previously willing and able to supply a given quantity of the product for *x* pence, he/she must now receive *x* + 10 pence after the tax to be in the same situation as before the tax. Of course, whether or not the producer is actually able to pass on all or part of the tax to the consumer is another matter!

The *incidence of the tax* seeks to address this issue. It measures the relative burden of the tax on the consumer and the producer and in this example the incidence falls equally on them both, i.e. the consumer pays 5 pence per unit in tax (*ab*) and the producer pays 5 pence per unit in tax (*bc*). Overall, the taxation revenue to the government is £400,000, of which the consumer and producer both pay £200,000. After the tax has been paid, the producer is left with £1,200,000.

If, however, demand for the product were perfectly elastic or perfectly inelastic then the incidence of the tax would be different. This can be illustrated by use of Figures 3.13(a) and 3.13(b).

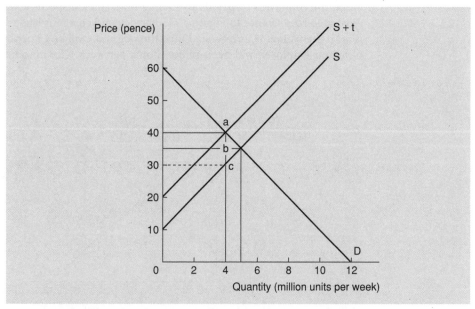

Figure 3.12 The initial equilibrium is at a price of 35 pence and quantity of 5 million units per week. The introduction of a tax of 10 pence per unit will result in a shift in the supply curve from S to S + t. The tax is represented by the vertical distance *ac* with the consumer paying *ab* per unit and the producer *bc* per unit.

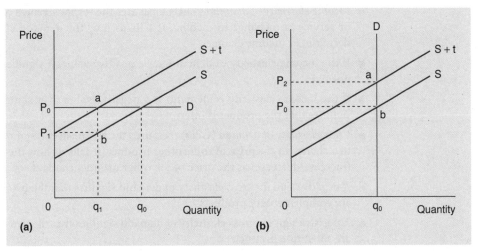

Figure 3.13 In (a) demand is perfectly elastic and if a tax is imposed on the product then the supplier has to bear the whole burden of the tax. In (b), however, demand is perfectly inelastic and as such the consumer of the product would bear the whole tax burden.

In Figure 3.13(a), demand is *perfectly elastic* and if, following the imposition of a tax *ab* on the sales of the commodity, the supplier were to raise the price, then demand would fall to zero. In this situation, therefore, the supplier has to bear the whole burden of the tax. There is no change in the price charged, i.e. P_0, but the supplier has to provide the government with tax revenue equal to P_0abP_1.

In Figure 3.13(b) demand is *perfectly inelastic* and the supplier can raise the price of the product by the full amount of the tax, *ab*. In this situation the consumer will bear the whole tax burden, with government tax revenue being P_2abP_0.

KEY POINTS

- *Price elasticity of demand* (PED) measures the responsiveness of the demand for a good or service to a change in its own price. It tells us about *movements along* a demand curve (expansion/contraction).
- If the percentage change in demand is less than the percentage change in price, then demand is said to be relatively inelastic.
- If the percentage change in demand is greater than the percentage change in price, then demand is said to be relatively elastic.
- If the percentage change in demand is exactly equal to the percentage change in price, then demand is said to be unit elastic.
- Factors which determine the price elasticity of demand (PED) include: whether there are close substitutes available, or the time period being considered.

- *Income elasticity of demand* (YED) measures the responsiveness of demand for a good or service to a change in income. It tells us how the demand curve *shifts* (increase/decrease) as income changes.

- If the income elasticity of demand has a positive value, it signifies that the product is normal.

- If the income elasticity of demand is a negative value over some range of income, it signifies that the product is inferior.

- *Cross elasticity of demand* (CED) measures the responsiveness of demand for a product to a change in the price of some other product. It tells us how the demand curve shifts (increase/decrease) as the price of the other product changes.

- A negative sign for cross elasticity of demand signifies that the two products in question are complementary products.

- A positive sign for cross elasticity of demand signifies that the two products in question are substitute products.

- *Price elasticity of supply* (PES) measures the responsiveness of supply for a good or service to a change in its own price.

- Factors which determine the price elasticity of supply include: whether spare capacity exists, whether stocks are available, the mobility of the factors of production and the time period taken for the firm to adjust to a change in the product's price.

Further reading

Griffiths, A. and Wall, S. (2005) *Economics for Business and Management*, FT/Prentice Hall, Chapter 2.

Heather, K. (2004) *Economics Theory in Action*, 4th edition, FT/Prentice Hall, Chapter 2.

Parkin, M., Powell, M. and Matthews, K. (2005) *Economics*, 6th edition, FT/Prentice Hall, Chapter 4.

Sloman, J. (2006) *Economics*, 6th edition, FT/Prentice Hall, Chapter 2.

Web references

The Business Owner's Toolkit has a section on pricing and elasticity:

www.toolkit.cch.com

Information on a range of market and demand related issues can be found at:

www.brandrepublic.com
www.keynote.co.uk
www.euromonitor.com
www.globalweb.co.uk

The market research society can be found at:

www.marketresearch.org.uk
www.bmra.org.uk

PROGRESS AND REVIEW QUESTIONS

Answers to most questions can be found at the end of the book (pages 494–5). Answers to asterisked questions can be found on the students' side of the Companion Website.

Multiple-choice questions

1 The concept used to reveal the responsiveness of demand for a product to a change in the price of that product is termed:

a) price elasticity of supply
b) price elasticity of demand
c) cross elasticity of demand
d) income elasticity of demand
e) none of the above.

2 If a small percentage drop in the price of a good leads to a large percentage increase in the quantity of that good demanded then:

a) demand is inelastic
b) demand is elastic
c) demand is unit elasticity
d) demand is perfectly inelastic
e) demand is perfectly elastic.

3 If a 10% increase in price leads to a 4% reduction in the quantity of a good demanded then the price elasticity of demand is:

a) −0.4
b) −0.6
c) −2.5
d) −4.0
e) −10.0

4 If a demand curve is horizontal it indicates that:

a) income elasticity of demand is zero
b) price elasticity of demand is infinity
c) price elasticity of demand is zero
d) price elasticity of demand is between zero and one
e) none of the above.

5 The revenue obtained from the sale of a good will fall if:

a) income increases and the good is a normal good
b) price increases and demand is inelastic
c) price increases and demand is elastic
d) price falls and demand is elastic
e) income falls and the good is an inferior good.

6 A rise in the price of product Y from €50 to €54 has resulted in the demand for product X increasing from 100 to 104 units per month. The cross elasticity of demand is:

a) 0.2

b) 0.5

c) 1.0

d) 2.0

e) 2.4

7 If the cross elasticity of demand between two goods X and Y is positive then:

a) the two goods are substitutes

b) the two goods are complements

c) the demand for the two goods is price inelastic

d) the demand for the two goods is price inelastic

e) none of the above.

8 A 5% increase in income leads to an increase in the quantity demanded from 24 units per week to 27 units per week. The income elasticity of demand is:

a) 1.0

b) 1.5

c) 2.0

d) 2.5

e) 3.0

9 If the demand curve for a product is perfectly inelastic then the incidence of a tax on that product falls:

a) totally on the supplier

b) equally on the buyer and seller

c) totally on the buyer

d) mostly on the supplier

e) none of the above.

10 A company supplies 20 units of a particular product per month at a price of €24. If the price elasticity of supply is 4 then how many units would the company supply at a price of €30?

a) 5

b) 10

c) 15

d) 20

e) 40

Data response questions

1

Price £	Quantity demanded per week	Quantity supplied per week
20	20	0
40	16	4
60	12	8
80	8	12
100	4	16

a) What is the price elasticity of demand when the price increases from £40 to £60?

b) What is the effect of a price increase from £40 to £60 on the total revenue?

c) Calculate the price elasticity of supply following a price increase from £60 to £80.

2 The figure below illustrates the demand and supply curves for a good before and after the introduction of a tax on the product.

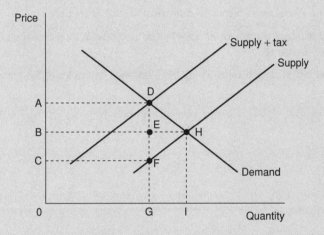

a) What is the tax on each unit?

b) What is the incidence of the tax on the consumer?

c) What is the incidence of the tax on the producer?

d) What is the government revenue from the tax?

True/false questions

1 If a product has price elasticity of demand greater than 1 then a rise in the price of the good will lead to a rise in total revenue received.

2 An inferior good is one for which demand increases as income increases.

3 Goods A and B are complementary if a rise in the price of good A leads to a fall in the demand for good B.

4 Price elasticity of supply refers to how supply for a good responds to a change in the good's price.

5 The incidence of a tax refers to the relative tax burden on the consumer and producer.

Essay questions

Answers to asterisked questions can be found on the students' side of the Companion Website. All other answers can be found at the back of the book (page 495).

1* Explain the meaning of these estimates of elasticities and how the values recorded might be of use to the agricultural industry.

	Beef and veal	Potatoes	All food
Price elasticity of demand	−1.25	−0.21	–
Income elasticity of demand	+0.08	−0.48	+0.01

2 Outline the factors which influence price elasticity of supply.

3* What is meant by 'the incidence of a tax' and how is the incidence affected by price elasticity of demand?

4 Under which circumstances might you advise a firm to lower the price of its product?

Consumer theory

Learning objectives

By the end of this chapter you should be able to:

- Understand what is meant by the 'utility'.
- Explain the law of diminishing marginal utility.
- Derive a demand curve from utility theory.
- Define an indifference curve and budget line.
- Understand the marginal rate of substitution.
- Explain the income and substitution effect.
- Use indifference curve analysis to distinguish between a normal and inferior good.

1 INTRODUCTION

This chapter looks more closely at what lies behind the demand curve. We are interested in why consumers behave the way they do and why it is that the consumer will normally buy more of a product when its price falls and less of a product when its price rises. This is sometimes referred to as the 'law of demand'. Consumer behaviour is often explained using two main approaches, namely *marginal utility theory* and *indifference curve analysis*. The theory of consumer behaviour will be used to determine the shape of a demand curve for a single product.

Note as stated in the Preface to this book there are certain topics, including utility theory and indifference curve analysis, detailed in this chapter, which may be more advanced for some courses. If these topics do *not* appear in your course, then you could omit this chapter.

2 MARGINAL UTILITY THEORY

2.1 What is marginal utility theory?

This theory is based on the premise that the amount of satisfaction or *utility* obtained from the consumption of a particular product can be *measured* in the same way that physical units can be measured. The theory was developed by Alfred Marshall who introduced an imaginary unit called the *util* as a means of measuring utility. Hence, if an individual consumed a bar of chocolate which resulted in them deriving 30 utils and a packet of crisps which resulted in 15 utils, then comparisons between the different levels of satisfaction could be made and a measure of the overall level of satisfaction could be obtained. This approach was termed *cardinal* since cardinal numbers could be used to measure utility.

2.2 Total utility

Total utility is the total satisfaction obtained from all the units of a particular product consumed over a period of time. If we take an example of a particular product, product x consumed over a period of time, say one week, then as the quantity consumed rises, the total utility will rise (*see* Table 4.1). There will, however, be a point at which total utility will begin to fall and in the example given this is after the fourth unit of the product is consumed.

2.3 Marginal utility

Marginal utility
The addition to total utility from consuming the last unit of a product.

Marginal utility is the addition to total utility derived from the consumption of one more unit of the product. As can be seen in Table 4.1, the marginal utility falls with each extra unit consumed, becoming negative for the fifth and sixth unit consumed.

2.4 The law of diminishing marginal utility

Law of diminishing marginal utility
Each extra unit consumed adds less to total utility than the previous unit consumed.

The declining marginal utility can be expressed as the *principle* or *law of diminishing marginal utility* with the first unit of the product yielding 30 utils of satisfaction, the second 16 utils of satisfaction, and so on until the fifth unit is consumed, which actually reduces total utility. The marginal utility derived from the fifth unit is negative, in other words the product yields *disutility*. In essence, therefore, the principle of diminishing marginal utility states that the more an individual has of a product, the less additional utility will be gained from each extra unit consumed. This can be seen in Figure 4.1 which has been produced from the data in Table 4.1.

 Pause for thought 1

Explain the law of diminishing marginal utility.

Table 4.1 Total and marginal utility illustrating the principle of diminishing marginal utility

Quantity of product x consumed per week	Total utility (TU) (Utils per week)	Marginal utility (MU)
0	0	
1	30	30
2	46	16
3	56	10
4	60	4
5	55	−5
6	45	−10

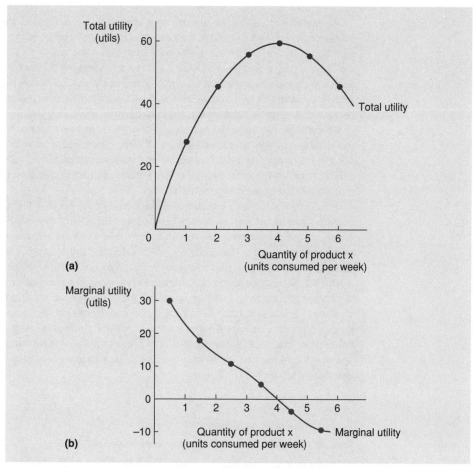

(a)

(b)

Figure 4.1 The figure illustrates total and marginal utility. As the consumption of product x rises, as seen in (a), then the total satisfaction (utility) obtained by the individual rises up to a certain point. Marginal utility (b) relates to the extra satisfaction obtained from consuming one extra unit of the product over a given period of time. The figure illustrates diminishing marginal utility.

Mini Case Study 4.1

Utility and happiness

Richard Layard, in his book *Happiness* (Allen Lane, 2005), argues that extra income does make us happier because we are able to satisfy certain basic wants. But once incomes are above $20,000 a year, the relationship breaks down. What is more, it is clear that while a boost to our spending power makes us feel good for a while, the effect soon wears off as we become used to our new income level. The impact of getting a rise is dulled if everyone else at work gets one too.

An experiment conducted at Harvard and cited by Layard makes the point. Students were asked to choose between two imaginary worlds: in the first they would earn $50,000 a year while the average for everybody else would be $25,000, while in the second they would earn $100,000 against an average of $250,000. Conventional economics would suggest that any rational individual would choose the latter option since they would be twice as well off. Actually, a majority chose the former; they were happier to be poorer if that meant they were higher in the pecking order.

Interestingly the same did not apply when the researchers looked at holidays. In one world, students would have two weeks off while others had one week's holiday; in the second they would have four weeks off and everybody else would have eight. This time only 20% of the students chose the first option, suggesting that they valued extra leisure more highly than they valued extra income.

The picture, according to Layard, is not a pretty one. He says that a study of 50 countries has found that six factors can account for 80% of the variations in happiness. These are the divorce rate, the unemployment rate, the level of trust, membership of non-religious organisations, the quality of government and the fraction of the population that believes in God. Divorce and unemployment are higher than they were 40 years ago, the levels of trust, memberships of societies and religious belief are down. We live in a rich but barren environment, insecure about our jobs and worried about crime. So what is to be done? Layard says happiness should become the overarching goal of government policy and comes up with a number of novel ideas for how this might be done, including compulsory classes in parenting in schools, lessons in emotional intelligence from the age of five, greater security from being fired, a more sceptical approach to the whole question of labour market flexibility.

Questions

1 *What influences happiness in this study?*

2 *What implications are there for government policy?*

Answers to questions can be found on the students' side of the Companion Website.

2.5 The consumer equilibrium

The 'consumer equilibrium' is the consumption bundle where total utility is a maximum. In considering the consumer equilibrium a number of assumptions are made, namely that the individual:

a) has a limited income;
b) acts in a rational manner;
c) aims to maximise his or her total utility subject to the income constraint.

The individual consumer is said to be in *equilibrium* when it is not possible to switch a single penny's worth of expenditure from product x to product y and obtain an increase in total utility, given the individual's income level and the prices that he or she faces. This occurs when the ratio of marginal utility to price is equal for all the products consumed. In other words when:

$$\frac{MU_x}{P_x} = \frac{MU_y}{P_y} = \frac{MU_n}{P_n}$$

where:

MU = marginal utility

P = the price

x, y and n = the individual products concerned.

The above equation states that the consumer equilibrium is where the marginal utility from the last penny spent on product x exactly equals the marginal utility from the last penny spent on product y equals the utility from the last penny spent on product n, thereby taking into account all of the products the individual consumes. When this situation is reached it is not possible for the individual to increase his or her total utility by reallocating expenditure. In other words, when the above condition is fulfilled, the consumer has allocated his or her income in such a way that maximum utility has been achieved.

The consumer equilibrium can be explained by referring to Table 4.2. We assume that there are only two products the individual can consume, product x costing £2.00 per unit and product y costing £4.00 per unit, and that the individual has an income per time period of £16.00. Given this situation, it can be seen that the consumer is in equilibrium when he or she consumes four of product x and two of product y. Here MU/P is the same, 8 for both products, and it is impossible for the consumer with an income of £16.00 to obtain a higher level of total utility. Note that in equilibrium the consumer obtains total utility of 268 utils. If the consumer were not in equilibrium it would be possible for him or her to reallocate income and obtain a greater level of satisfaction.

Table 4.2 **Consumer equilibrium**

Product x (price £2.00 each)			Quantity demanded of product x and y	Product y (price £4.00 each)		
Total utility	Marginal utility	$\frac{MU}{P}$		Total utility	Marginal utility	$\frac{MU}{P}$
80	80	40	1	68	68	17
132	52	26	2	100	32	8
152	20	10	3	128	28	7
168	16	8	4	152	24	6
176	8	4	5	172	20	5

 Pause for thought 2

Use Table 4.2 to show why consuming two units of product x *and three units of product* y *is not a consumer equilibrium.*

2.6 Derivation of the demand curve

It is possible to use marginal utility as a means of deriving a demand curve. If in Table 4.2 the price of product *y* were to fall to £2.00 then, assuming everything else remained constant, there would be a new column for MU/P and a new equilibrium would result. The consumer would reduce consumption of product *x* by 1 unit and raise consumption of product *y* by 3 units, hence consuming 3 of product *x* and 5 of product *y*. The fall in the price of product *y* by £2.00 has led to an expansion in demand by 3 units (*see* Figure 4.2). You may find it useful at this point to calculate the new MU/P for product *y* when its price has fallen and prove that the equilibrium is where the individual consumes 3 of product *x* and 5 of product *y* given an income of £16.00, with the consumer obtaining total utility of 324 utils.

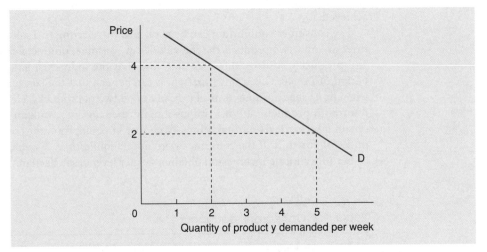

Figure 4.2 A fall in the price of product *y* from £4 to £2 results in an expansion in the quantity demanded from 2 to 5 units per week.

3   INDIFFERENCE CURVE ANALYSIS

3.1 What is indifference curve analysis?

The marginal utility theory approach to consumer behaviour has been criticised in that it is not possible to measure utility, which in any case can be viewed as a rather abstract and subjective idea. With this in mind, certain economists including John Hicks in the 1930s developed an *ordinalist approach* to consumer behaviour. The idea was that although the consumer could not measure utility, they could *order* or *rank* their preferences, say preferring bundle of products A to bundle of products B and so on. The ordering of preferences meant that the measuring of utility was not required, and the theory became known *as indifference curve analysis.*

3.2 Indifference curves

If again we assume two products, *x* and *y*, it is possible to produce an *indifference schedule* (*see* Table 4.3) which shows different combinations of the two products which yield the same level of satisfaction.

Table 4.3 An indifference schedule

Combination	Units of product *x*	Units of product *y*
A	10	30
B	20	16
C	30	9
D	40	5

Table 4.3 can be represented diagrammatically (*see* Figure 4.3) and the individual obtains the same level of satisfaction whether at point A, B, C or D or, in fact, at any points in between. It is possible to define an *indifference curve* as a line that joins all the combinations of two products which give the consumer the same level of satisfaction.

There are certain points to note with regard to indifference curves:

Indifference curves Lines representing different combinations of commodities that yield a constant level of utility or satisfaction to the consumer.

(a) They are *convex to the origin*, i.e. bent towards the origin (*see* Figure 4.3). The reason for this should be obvious from Table 4.3, for when the individual is at point *A* he or she has relatively large amounts of product *y* and is willing to give up 14 units of that product in return for 10 extra units of product *x*. This will leave the individual at the same level of utility or satisfaction. However, in a move from B to C the individual would be willing to give up only 7 units of product *y* in return for 10 units of product *x*, as product *y* is

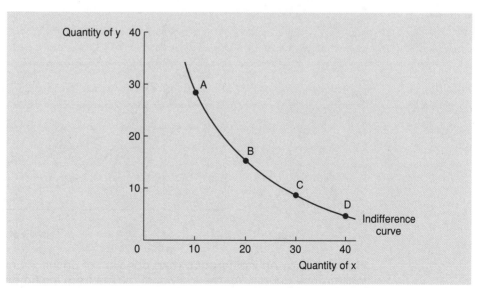

Figure 4.3 An indifference curve shows all the combinations of two products between which the consumer is indifferent. In other words, combinations of two products which yield the same level of satisfaction.

Diminishing marginal rate of substitution
In a two-product context, it suggests that consumers will be willing to sacrifice progressively less of one product (Y) for an extra unit of another product (X) the more of that product (X) they already consume (keeping utility unchanged).

becoming relatively scarce. To move from C to D he or she would be willing to give up only 4 units of product y in return for an additional 10 units of product x to remain at the same level of utility. The measure of the amount of one product an individual is prepared to give up in order to acquire additional amounts of the other product, and leave him or her at the same level of utility, is called the *marginal rate of substitution* and it can be seen to vary as we move along the indifference curve. In fact we can speak of a *diminishing marginal rate of substitution* between the two products, since the more of one product (here x) the consumer has, the progressively less of the other product (here y) the consumer is willing to give up for more of x. To be absolutely accurate, the marginal rate of substitution is given by the slope of a tangent to the indifference curve at a particular point.

(b) It is possible to produce an *indifference map* (*see* Figure 4.4(a)). There are an infinite number of indifference curves although only three are shown in the figure, and a move to

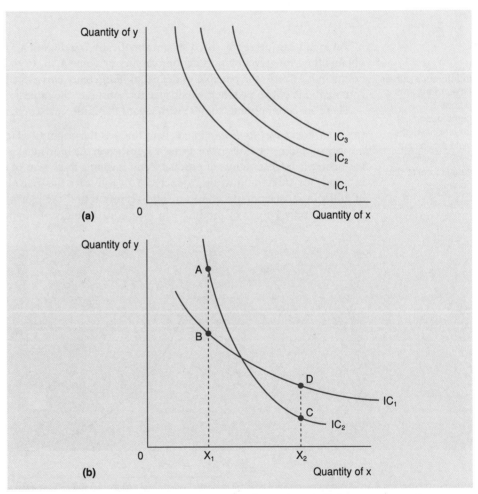

Figure 4.4 (a) An indifference map consists of an infinite number of indifference curves. As the individual moves from indifference curve IC_1 to IC_2 to IC_3 it represents a higher level of satisfaction. (b) The intersection of the two indifference curves results in consumer choices being inconsistent or irrational.

an indifference curve further from the origin, say from IC_1 to IC_2 represents an increase in the level of utility or satisfaction. This is because indifference curves further from the origin represent consumption bundles containing more of *both* products, which can be expected to mean higher utility or satisfaction. Unlike the cardinalist approach to consumer theory, no attempt is made to quantify the increase in satisfaction.

(c) *Indifference curves cannot cross* for this would suggest inconsistent or irrational consumer behaviour. For example, suppose we have the following consumer ranking of three bundles of products x and y, with the respective bundles shown as A, B and C in Figure 4.4(b).

$$A > B$$
$$B > C$$

Then, via consistent consumer behaviour, we can say:

$$A > C$$

If this assumption holds true, then indifference curves cannot intersect. However, if consumer preferences are not consistent, then indifference curves can intersect, as they do in Figure 4.4(b) (see opposite).

In Figure 4.4(b) A > B (more of y, same x)
A = C (on same indifference curve)
B = D (on same indifference curve)
But D > C (more of y, same x)

Clearly when indifference curves intersect, this indicates that consumers are not acting consistently in their rankings of different bundles of products.

Mini Case Study 4.2

Changing tastes over time

We have seen that an indifference curve captures the different bundles of products that give the consumer a constant level of utility. There is no doubt that the bundles of products that yield a certain amount of utility in the past are very different from the bundles that give a similar amount of utility today!

For example, each year the Office of National Statistics (ONS) monitors the most popular products in the nation's shopping baskets in the UK. The basket in 2003 contained 650 goods and services that a typical household bought over the last 12 months, and each year the basket is adjusted to reflect changing consumer behaviour. Table 4.4 presents the products that were included for the first time in 2003 and those products that were excluded.

The shopping basket was first introduced in 1947 as a basis for accurately calculating the rate of inflation. In the 1960s the products entering included sliced bread, fish fingers and crisps, jams and 'meals out' in restaurants. During the 1970s in came frozen foods, aluminium foil, wine, hardboard for home improvements and the cost of visiting stately homes. The 1980s saw the introduction of microwaves, video recorders, CDs and CD players and low alcohol lager, and the 1990s included for the first time the Internet,

Table 4.4 Changes in the UK 'shopping basket' in 2003

Products in	Products out
Coffee shop caffe latte	Tinned spaghetti
Takeaway burger	Frozen fish in sauce
Takeaway kebab	Brown ale
Draught premium lager	Vinyl floor covering
Dried potted snack	Fixed telephone
Diet aid drink power	Dog mixer
Single serve cat food	Dry cat food
Complete dry dog food	Women's shoe repair
Booster injection for dog	Men's belt
Designer spectacles	Battery powered clock
Dental insurance	Electronic keyboard
Hair gel	Leaded petrol
Shower gel	
Slimming club fees	
Aid fares	
Car CD player	
Golf fees	
Horseracing admissions	

satellite dishes, camcorders, computer games, CD-ROMs, Internet subscriptions and foreign holidays.

In 2003 it was caffe latte, takeaway burgers and kebabs and other convenience foods that made their first entry into this typical shopping basket. Indeed, expenditure on such foods has risen by 40% over the past five years, and they join the vegetarian and reduced-calorie ready meals which appeared for the first time in 2002. Spending on healthcare is also rising rapidly in the UK and even pre-prepared pet food is now in, replacing the effort previously made in preparing home-made foods for pets.

Questions

1 *Look again at Table 4.4. Can you explain any of the patterns and trends in the UK which might help explain why some products are 'in' and some 'out' of the typical shopping basket?*

2 *Does your answer to question 1 help explain the products in the shopping basket observed in the earlier decades of the 1960s, 1970s, 1980s and 1990s?*

3 *What products might you expect to appear in, and disappear from, the typical shopping basket over the next ten years? Explain your reasoning.*

Answers to questions can be found at the end of the book (page 496).

3.3 The budget line

Indifference curves reveal the consumer's preferences for product x and y but they do not tell us which combination of the two products will be chosen. The consumer is constrained by his or her income level and the price of the products. It is necessary, therefore,

Budget line
Describes the various combinations of two (or more) products that can be purchased if the whole household income is spent on these products.

to introduce what is known as the *budget line* or the *consumption possibility line* which reveals all combinations of the two products that are obtainable, given the individual's income and the prices of the two products.

For example, the individual may have £100 to spend on the two products per week. Table 4.5 shows the possible combinations of the two products assuming the individual spends all of the £100 with the price of product *x* being £20.00 and that of product *y* £10.00. This can be produced diagrammatically as in Figure 4.5. The individual can be at point A purchasing 10 of product *y* but unable to buy any of product *x*, or at point F purchasing 5 of product *x* but none of product *y*, or alternatively the consumer could be at a point between A and F on the budget line. Points above and to the right of the budget line are unobtainable and the slope of the budget line depends upon the relative prices of the two products.

Table 4.5 **The budget constraint with income equal to £100**

	Quantity of product *x* Price = £20.00	Quantity of product *y* Price = £10.00
A	0	10
B	1	8
C	2	6
D	3	4
E	4	2
F	5	0

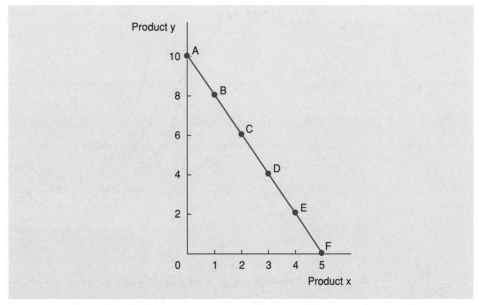

Figure 4.5 **The budget line AF represents all the possible combinations of products *x* and *y* which can be purchased given the individual's income and the price of the two products.**

4 THE CONSUMER EQUILIBRIUM UNDER INDIFFERENCE CURVE ANALYSIS

The consumer is in equilibrium, reaching the highest level of satisfaction that his or her income allows, where the budget line is tangential to the indifference curve furthest from the origin. At this tangency the slope of the budget line (as given by the relative prices of the two products) is equal to the slope of the indifference curve (the marginal rate of substitution). This can be seen in Figure 4.6 at point E which is the position of maximum utility (IC_2) for the consumer. As stated, any point on the budget line is feasible but movements to points such as C or D in Figure 4.6 would place the consumer on a lower indifference curve (IC_1) which represents a lower level of satisfaction. Given the consumer's income level and the price of the two products, indifference curve IC_3 is unattainable.

Having outlined the basics of indifference curve analysis it is now possible to analyse how the equilibrium position is affected by changes both in the income level of the consumer and in the price of the two products. These will be analysed in turn.

 Pause for thought 3

Using indifference curve analysis show, with the aid of a diagram, how a consumer maximises satisfaction from a given expenditure on two products.

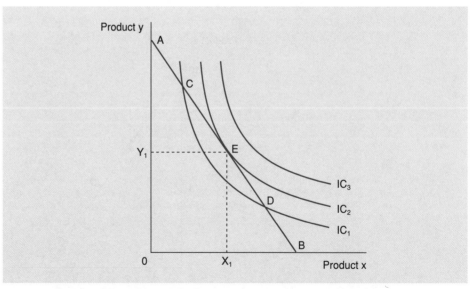

Figure 4.6 The individual is at the highest level of satisfaction possible, given income level and the price of the two products, where the indifference curve IC_2 is tangential to the budget line AB. This is represented by point E which is where the marginal rate of substitution is equal to the relative prices of the two products.

4.1 A change in income

Income–consumption curve
Shows how the quantity consumed of two products changes as the income changes, assuming no change in relative prices. A line which joins the set of tangency points between budget lines and highest attainable indifference curves.

An increase in income, assuming the price of the two products remains unchanged, will lead to a *parallel* shift in the budget line to the right, allowing the consumer to buy more of both products.

This can be seen in Figure 4.7 where the budget line shifts from AB to CD, thus allowing the consumer to move onto a higher indifference curve IC_2 with a new equilibrium of E_2. The line through the equilibrium positions is called the *income–consumption curve* and it shows how the consumption of the two products responds to an income change.

If there had been a fall in income the budget line would have shifted parallel and to the left.

4.2 A change in price

If there is a change in price of one of the goods, with income remaining unchanged, the budget line will *pivot*.

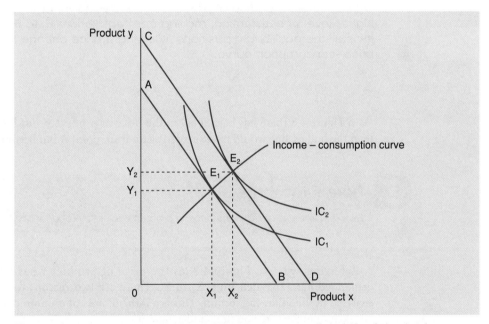

Figure 4.7 An increase in income leads to a parallel shift of the budget line to the right and this allows the individual to achieve a higher level of satisfaction. It can be seen that the individual consumes more of product *x* and product *y* following an increase in income, thus both are normal goods. The line which joins all the equilibrium positions following an income change is called the income–consumption curve.

In Figure 4.8 the initial budget line is AB and the consumer is in equilibrium at E_1, where the budget line is tangential to the indifference curve. Following a fall in the price of product *x* the budget line pivots to AC, thus allowing the consumer to move onto a higher indifference curve (IC_2) resulting in a new equilibrium of E_2. A line that joins all of the points of consumer equilibrium is called the *price–consumption curve*.

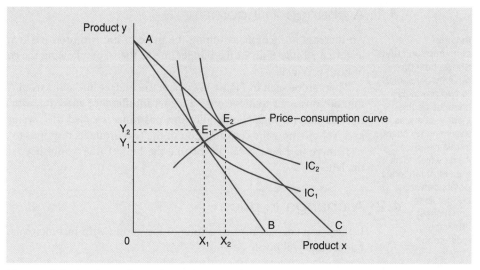

Figure 4.8 As the price of product x falls the individual is able to achieve a higher level of satisfaction, moving from equilibrium E₁ to E₂. The line which joins all the equilibrium positions following a price change is called the price–consumption curve.

In Figure 4.8 there has been a fall in the price of product *x*, but if the price had risen then the budget line would have pivoted again from point A but become steeper.

Pause for thought 4

How would a rise or fall in the price of product y affect the budget line?

Referring again to Figure 4.8, as the price of product *x* has fallen the quantity demanded has expanded from X_1 to X_2. There are two reasons for this which will be analysed in the following section. This is a difficult area of economic theory so care must be taken to make sure you fully understand it.

5 THE SUBSTITUTION AND INCOME EFFECT

Substitution effect
The additional amount of a product purchased as a result of its price being cheaper relative to other substitutes in consumption.

As the price of product *x* falls it becomes cheaper relative to product *y* and for this reason the consumer will substitute product *x* for product *y*. This is called the *substitution effect* of a price change. It will always be the case that the consumer will substitute towards the product which has become relatively cheaper.

As the price of product *x* falls it also means that the consumer has more money to spend on other products. It can be said that the consumer's real income has increased since it costs less to buy a given quantity of goods. This *may* mean that the consumer buys more of product *x* and this is called the *income effect* of a price change.

CHAPTER 4 · CONSUMER THEORY

Income effect
The additional purchasing power resulting from a fall in price of one or more products in the consumption bundle.

It is possible to distinguish between the substitution and income effect and this is shown graphically in Figure 4.9.

AB is the original budget line with the consumer in equilibrium at point a. If the price of product x falls this will lead to a pivot in the budget line to AC, allowing the consumer to reach a higher indifference curve (IC_2) and a new equilibrium of point c. The result of this is that the quantity of product x bought has risen from X_1 to X_3.

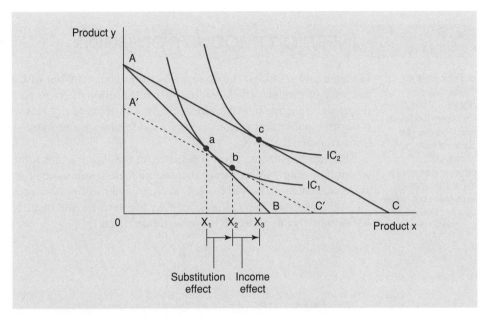

Figure 4.9 Given a budget line of AB and an indifference curve of IC_1 a consumer is in equilibrium at point a. The price of product x falls, hence the budget line pivots to AC. The substitution effect involves a move from point a to b, where the relative prices of products x and y have changed but real income has remained constant. The income effect involves a move from b to c, where real income increases while relative prices remain unchanged.

It is possible to distinguish between the income and substitution effect of the price change by first *eliminating* the income effect, which means hypothetically removing the increase in real income until the consumer is back on the original indifference curve. This is achieved by shifting a line back, parallel to the new budget line AC, until it is tangential to the original indifference curve with the consumer obtaining the same level of utility as that prior to the price change. In Figure 4.9 this is represented by the hypothetical budget line A′C′ which is tangential to the original indifference curve at b. We can now say that the movement from a to b is the *substitution effect* (having eliminated the income effect) and there is an expansion in the quantity consumed from X_1 to X_2.

Giffen good
Named after the nineteenth-century economist Sir Robert Giffen, who claimed to identify an upward-sloping demand curve for certain inferior goods. To be a Giffen good it is necessary, but not sufficient, that the good be inferior.

We can now restore the level of income by shifting the budget line in parallel fashion from A′C′ back to AC. The movement from point b to point c represents the *income effect*, allowing the consumer to reach a higher indifference curve IC_2 and consume more of product x, i.e. a move from X_2 to X_3. Figure 4.9 refers to a normal good (*see* section 3: 5) because the income effect is positive, meaning that an increase in income has led to a rise in the quantity demanded with the income effect reinforcing the substitution effect. The income effect can, however, be negative as in the case of inferior goods which includes **Giffen goods**.

Pause for thought 5

Distinguish between the income and the substitution effect of a price change.

6 INFERIOR PRODUCT OR GOOD

Inferior goods
Cheap but poor quality substitutes for other goods. As real incomes rise above a certain 'threshold', consumers tend to substitute more expensive but better quality alternatives for certain products.

In Figure 4.10 we follow the same process as in Figure 4.9 but with one difference. Again the price of product x falls leading to a substitution effect towards the product, i.e. a movement from a to b, with more being consumed (X_1 to X_2). However, the income effect is negative, unlike the previous example, and this means a movement from b to c with less being consumed, X_2 to X_3.

Although the income effect is negative, in this case it is not sufficient to outweigh the substitution effect, which means that overall there is still more of the product demanded as the consumer has moved from X_1 to X_3. In other words, the demand curve for product x is still downward sloping. It is possible, however, for the negative income effect to be sufficiently large to outweigh the substitution effect.

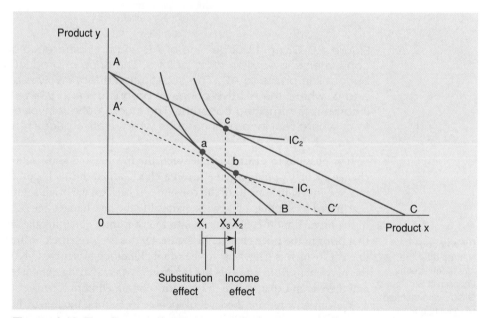

Figure 4.10 The figure relates to an inferior good with the income effect (represented by a move from b to c) working in the opposite direction to the substitution effect (represented by a move from a to b) following a fall in the price of product x. The substitution effect is greater than the income effect and so the demand curve for the product is still downward sloping.

7 GIFFEN GOOD

A *Giffen good* refers to a situation where the substitution effect is outweighed by the negative income effect. This can be seen in Figure 4.11 where the total effect of a price change reveals that the total quantity of the product demanded falls (X_1 to X_3) as the price of the product falls.

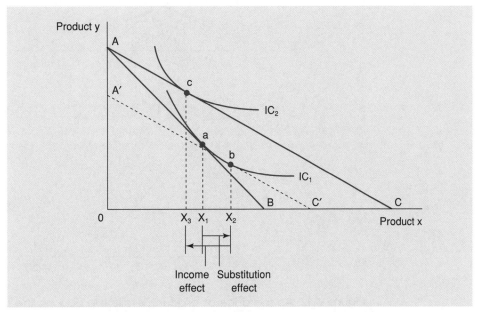

Figure 4.11 For a Giffen good the figure is similar to Figure 4.10, the only difference being that the income effect outweighs the substitution effect. The result is a positively sloped demand curve.

In this situation the demand curve is upward sloping from left to right (a positive slope) and this special type of demand curve relates to a type of product which is referred to as a *Giffen good*. The Giffen good (so named after a nineteenth-century economist) is one where demand falls as the price of the product falls and vice versa.

It is true to say that Giffen goods are very rare in practice.

 ## Pause for thought 6

In your own words, can you distinguish between an inferior good and a Giffen good?

8 DERIVATION OF THE DEMAND CURVE

It is possible to use the preceding analysis to derive a consumer's demand curve (*see* Figure 4.12, page 86). As the price of product *x* falls, represented by the budget line pivoting from AB to AC to AD, the quantity of product *x* demanded rises from X_1 to X_2 to X_3, thus giving a downward sloping demand curve.

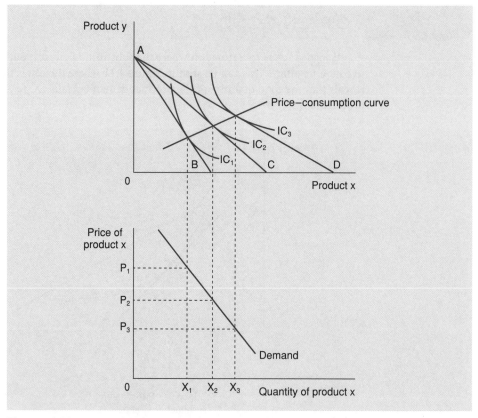

Figure 4.12 As the price of product x falls the budget line pivots from AB to AC to AD and this allows the consumer to reach higher indifference curves demanding more of product x. Thus a fall in the price of the product leads to an expansion in the quantity demanded and therefore a downward sloping demand curve.

KEY POINTS

- The budget line describes the various combinations of two (or more) products that can be purchased if the whole household income is spent on these products.
- Diminishing marginal rate of substitution in a two-product context, suggests that consumers will be willing to sacrifice progressively less of one product (Y) for an extra unit of another product (X) the more of that product (X) they already consume (keeping utility unchanged).
- In terms of the law of diminishing marginal utility, each extra unit consumed adds less to total utility than the previous unit consumed.
- The Giffen good is named after the nineteenth-century economist Sir Robert Giffen, who claimed to identify an upward-sloping demand curve for certain inferior goods. To be a Giffen good it is necessary, but not sufficient, that the good be inferior.

- The income-consumption line shows how the quantity consumed of two products changes as the income changes, assuming no change in relative prices. A line which joins the set of tangency points between budget lines and highest attainable indifference curves.
- The income effect reveals the additional purchasing power resulting from a fall in price of one or more products in the consumption bundle.
- Indifference curves represent lines of different combinations of commodities that yield a constant level of utility or satisfaction to the consumer.
- Inferior goods are cheap but poor quality substitutes for other goods. As real incomes rise above a certain 'threshold', consumers tend to substitute more expensive but better quality alternatives for certain products.
- Marginal utility represents the addition to total utility from consuming the last unit of a product.
- The substitution effect represents the additional amount of a product purchased as a result of its price being cheaper relative to other substitutes in consumption.

Further reading

Griffiths, A. and Wall, S. (2005) *Economics for Business and Management*, FT/Prentice Hall, Chapter 2 and Appendix 1.

Heather, K. (2004) *Economics Theory in Action*, 4th edition, FT/Prentice Hall, Chapters 3 and 4.

Parkin, M., Powell, M. and Matthews, K. (2005) *Economics*, 6th edition, FT/Prentice Hall, Chapters 7 and 8.

Sloman, J. (2006) *Economics*, 6th edition, FT/Prentice Hall, Chapter 4.

Web references

There are few, if any, websites involving indifference curves as such. However, useful websites on consumer behaviour include the following:

www.brandrepublic.com
www.keynote.co.uk
www.euromonitor.com
www.globalweb.co.uk

The market research society can be found at:

www.marketresearch.org.uk
www.bmra.org.uk

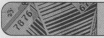

PROGRESS AND REVIEW QUESTIONS

Answers to most questions can be found at the back of the book (pages 496–8). Answers to asterisked questions can be found on the students' side of the Companion Website.

Multiple-choice questions

1 If marginal utility of a good is equal to zero then:

   a) total utility will also be zero
   b) the good gives no utility
   c) the good is worth nothing
   d) the consumer is in equilibrium
   e) total utility is at a maximum.

2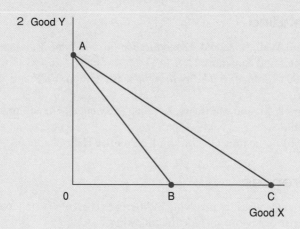

In terms of the figure above, a shift of the budget line from AB to AC is brought about by:

   a) a reduction in the price of good Y
   b) an increase in the price of good Y
   c) a reduction in the price of good X
   d) an increase in the price of good X
   e) none of the above.

3 In terms of indifference curve analysis, consumer equilibrium is the point at which:

   a) the indifference curve is tangential to the budget line
   b) it is outside and to the right of the budget line
   c) it is inside and to the left of the budget line
   d) the indifference curve cuts the budget line
   e) it is on the highest indifference curve given on the indifference map.

4 In terms of the figure below, consumer equilibrium is at point:

   a) A
   b) B

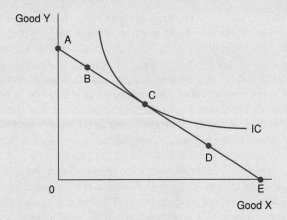

c) C

d) D

e) E

5 In terms of a Giffen good:

a) the income effect is negative but does not outweigh the substitution effect

b) the income effect is negative and outweighs the substitution effect

c) there is no income effect

d) the income effect is positive, reinforcing the substitution effect

e) none of the above.

Data response question

Complete the table using only the words 'positive' or 'negative'.

Type of product	Substitution effect	Income effect	Total effect
Normal			
Inferior (but not Giffen)			
Giffen			

Case study question

The Hoover free flight promotion

Companies such as Hoover, Hotpoint, Philips and Electrolux produce appliances such as washing machines, refrigerators, dishwashers, tumble dryers and vacuum cleaners. This market for 'white goods' is dominated by a few firms and is an example of an oligopolistic market structure. In recent years there has been growing interest by firms in the use of free *gifts* as a means of attracting new, or maintaining existing, customers. This has been particularly true of promotions involving free air miles or air tickets. One such promotion which has received a great deal of attention is the Hoover free flight promotion.

Households tend to purchase products such as vacuum cleaners only when their existing appliance has irrevocably broken down or perhaps when they are moving house. The market for such products is therefore by nature rather static, a situation not helped at times of economic slow down. Given these factors, Hoover launched a free flight promotion as a means of stimulating demand and gaining market share at the expense of its competitors' products. Customers who spent a minimum of £100 on the purchase of one of their products qualified for two free return flights to one of six European cities. This was subsequently extended to include US destinations. In reality, consumers had to spend at least £119, since that was the price of the cheapest Hoover product, namely a vacuum cleaner, which qualified for free air tickets.

The notion of free gifts, and in particular the Hoover free flight promotion, can be understood by the use of indifference curve analysis. In brief, available free flights produces a *notched* budget line shown in the figure below. The horizontal axis measures the quantity of Hoover products and free air flights and the vertical axis the quantity of all other goods. In the absence of free air flights the consumer would face a budget line of AF. Given the preference of the consumer there would be an equilibrium at point E where AF is tangential to the highest indifference curve I_1. In this case OQ_1 of Hoover products are consumed and OG of all other goods. With the launch of the Hoover offer the consumer who spent a minimum of £100 was eligible for the free flights. The amount of Hoover products purchased for £100 is represented by Q_1Q_a in the figure above, i.e. more Hoover appliances are bought and less of other goods. This entitles the consumer to free air flights represented by T, or Q_aQ_b in the figure. Given the situation illustrated in the figure, once the free air flights had been obtained, and provided the price of Hoover products relative to all other goods did not change, then the budget line would continue along a line CD. Overall, therefore, the budget line would be *notched*, represented by ABCD, as opposed to AF before the promotion. The offer represents an increase in the consumer's *real income* but it does not allow the consumer to increase expenditure on other goods. The air tickets cannot be exchanged for cash, thus it is not possible for the consumer to buy more of other goods, i.e. move along the dotted section marked HC.

If a consumer has indifference curves as illustrated in the figure below then they would be attracted by the offer and would purchase a Hoover product which qualifies them for the free flight. This will have the effect of moving the consumer onto a higher indifference curve, I_2,

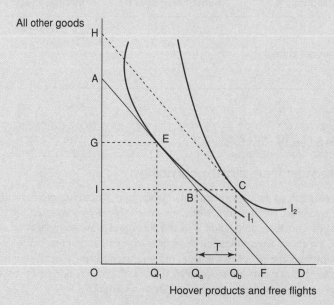

which results in an increase in the level of satisfaction at a new equilibrium of C. At this new equilibrium there will be less spent on other goods, OI as opposed to OG. It is likely to be the case that the reduced expenditure on other goods would include appliances produced by Hoover's main competitors.

However, consumers will be affected in different ways by the free flight promotion. For example, the consumer may have indifference curves as illustrated in the figure below.

In such a situation the consumer would choose not to take advantage of the Hoover offer. The indifference curves are relatively flat compared to the previous figure, such that the level of satisfaction is greater in the initial situation, point E on indifference curve I_1, than it would be if advantage was taken of the offer. Partaking of the offer would result in a lower level of satisfaction with the consumer being at point C on indifference curve I_2. It is important to *note* that the two figures are based on the fact that the consumer already purchases Hoover products, equal to OQ_1, prior to the free gift offer. However, the two figures could have been presented on the basis that the consumer did not initially purchase any Hoover product. This would have meant that the consumer indifference curve, I_1, would have touched the vertical axis at point A.

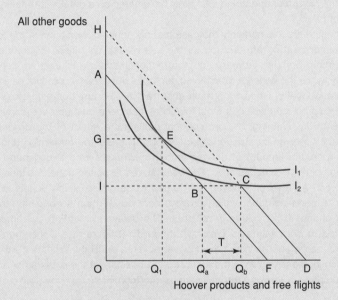

The aim of any promotion is to expand the sale of the product, thus increasing revenue and to strengthening *brand loyalty* by means of 'non-price' competition. In the situation illustrated in the first figure on page 90, the free flight offer has been successful in persuading the consumer to purchase the product. This could have been achieved by a reduction in the price of the product provided that the price elasticity of demand was favourable. This response has been extensively used in the past, particularly in times of recession, and although still practised it is now somewhat less popular. The problem with a policy of reducing the price is that it creates a degree of uncertainty in the market and the possibility of stimulating a *price war*. It may also cause the customer to question whether a lower price means lower quality and this could be potentially damaging for the product's image.

The Hoover promotion was successful in terms of the level of demand it generated, but it created a number of major difficulties. First, additional labour had to be employed and the factory had to be placed on seven-day working in order to meet the increased demand for appliances. Secondly, it soon became apparent that consumers were buying the product for the free flight offer rather than for the product itself. This is evident by advertisements which began to appear in the second-hand section of local newspapers and *Exchange and Mart* for Hoover appliances, mainly vacuum cleaners, which had been bought but never used. This was hardly a policy aimed at improving brand loyalty. Thirdly, and arguably the most problematic area, was the fact that the offer exceeded all expectations and thus proved to be a *costly* promotion. With all promotions it is forecast that a good percentage of those buying the product will not actually 'take up' the promotional offer for which they are eligible. For travel related promotions it is estimated that the level of take up is 10% or below. In terms of the Hoover promotion a higher than expected number of consumers had indifference curve schedules like those illustrated in the figure on page 90 as opposed to the figure on page 91. As a result Hoover found it difficult and expensive to cater for the demand for free airline tickets for which its customers were eligible. With hindsight Hoover could have possibly made the offer more restrictive. For example, they could have set the point of eligibility at £200 rather than £100 or offered only one free ticket rather than two. In many promotions the customer has to apply for the offer of a free gift and this often involves them having to make additional purchases such as hotel accommodation or restaurant meals. This would have proved to be an additional cost to the customer and could ultimately have acted as a deterrent to taking advantage of the free flight offer.

In recent years it is certainly the case that non-price competition in the form of promotional activity incorporating offers such as the use of free air miles, air tickets or holidays have become more popular. However, any promotional activity includes an element of risk for the company, while the benefits, if achieved, are ones of increased product sales and a strengthening of brand loyalty. One of the most important assets any company possesses is the *brand name* of its products, which in most instances has been built up over many years.

Therefore in planning any promotional activity the effect of the promotion on the brand name must be given careful consideration. In this case, the promotion undertaken by Hoover created a certain amount of unease among customers who experienced difficulty in taking advantage of the free flights offer. The offer proved to be too generous thus stimulating enormous interest. As a result Hoover was forced to purchase airline tickets on the open market in order to meet demand, which proved more costly than its original strategy of obtaining cheaper charter flight tickets in advance. The delays in meeting customers' demand for air tickets led to complaints to Trading Standards Officers, the Consumers' Association and numerous newspapers which gave Hoover adverse publicity. What is clear is that any promotion which increases sales in the *short run* but possibly at the expense of a loss of confidence in the company in the *long run* has serious shortcomings.

Questions

1 *With the use of indifference curve analysis, illustrate a situation in which a consumer is indifferent between taking advantage of, and not taking advantage of, the Hoover 'free flights' offer.*

2 *What lessons can a company learn from the 'free flights' offer, when considering a promotional campaign?*

True/false questions

1 Marginal utility is the overall satisfaction derived from the consumption of a particular product over a particular period of time.

2 Total utility is the total satisfaction obtained from all the units of a particular product consumed over a period of time.

3 The law of diminishing returns states that the more an individual has of a product the greater the marginal utility will be from each additional unit consumed.

4 An indifference curve reveals all combinations of two products which yield the same level of satisfaction.

5 As an individual moves onto a higher indifference curve it represents the same level of satisfaction.

6 Indifference cannot cross since this would suggest irrational consumer behaviour.

7 A parallel shift of the budget line to the right represents an increase in consumer income.

 ## Essay questions

Answers to asterisked questions can be found on the students' side of the Companion Website. All other answers can be found at the back of the book (page 498).

1* Briefly outline what is meant by total and marginal utility and explain the law of diminishing marginal utility. Using marginal utility theory, when is a consumer in equilibrium?

2 Outline what is meant by an indifference curve. Using indifference curve analysis show, with the aid of a diagram, how a consumer maximises satisfaction from a given expenditure on two goods.

3* What is the effect on the consumer equilibrium of:

a) an increase in income
b) an increase in price?

Distinguish between the income and the substitution effect of a price change.

4 With the use of indifference curve analysis, outline the effect a change in the price of a product would have on the demand for that product if:

a) the income elasticity of demand is positive
b) the income elasticity of demand is negative.

Production and costs

```
0101
1010
1010
1110
1101
1010
```

Learning objectives

By the end of this chapter you should be able to:

- Understand the different types of business enterprise.
- Explain why and how firms grow.
- Examine the linkages between production and factor inputs in both the short and long run.
- Explain the different types of cost in both the short and long run.
- Discuss the sources and importance of economies and diseconomies of scale.

1   INTRODUCTION

Production can be defined as the transformation of inputs, namely land, labour and capital, into goods and services in order to satisfy human wants. Some would add 'enterprise' or 'entrepreneurship' to this list of inputs or, as they are often known, factors of production. This chapter deals with the different types of business organisation, how they grow in size and the factors of production they use in the creation of goods and services.

The costs of production in the short-run and the long-run time periods are also covered in this chapter. Obviously the length of time which corresponds to these time periods will depend very much on the product under consideration. For example, a new electricity generating plant may require five years to plan, build and get operational. In this case we would say the short run is five years and the long run five plus years. It is essential that you understand the relationship between the total, average and marginal cost as these concepts will be used again in Chapters 6 and 7 and in many other chapters of the book.

Note: There are certain topics in this chapter which do not appear in some courses, such as topics in Sections 5.4 to 9 which cover production in the long run, isoquants, isocosts and the long-run expansion path. If these topics do not appear on your syllabus, you could go straight from the end of Section 5.3 to Section 10.10.

2 TYPES OF BUSINESS ENTERPRISE

2.1 Sole trader

Sole traders
Businesses that
are owned by one
person who has
unlimited liability.

This type of business is also called a *sole proprietor* business and, as the name implies, it is owned by one person. On the whole they tend to be small businesses and are common in retailing and in the provision of personal services such as hairdressing. Since the owner of this type of business is in sole charge, decisions can be taken quickly because no one else has to be consulted. There is also the advantage that they only require a small amount of capital to start up. Also, since the owner is working for him or herself there is an incentive to operate the business as efficiently as possible.

There are, however, a number of disadvantages in this type of business, for example the owner may not be able to specialise in certain functions within the business. Additionally, the owner stands to lose all of his or her personal belongings if the business goes bankrupt – the owner is said to have *unlimited liability*.

2.2 Partnership

Partnership
Comprises two
or more owners,
generally with a
maximum of 20.

As the name implies, a **partnership** comprises two or more owners. Partnerships are generally allowed to have between two and twenty members. All the partners have equal responsibility for the debts of the business, if they occur, since all the partners have unlimited liability. It is, however, possible to have what are known as *sleeping* or *dormant partners* who simply provide capital for the partnership on which they receive a return, but who take no active part in the day-to-day running of the company. These partners have *limited liability*.

Partnerships have the advantage in that the various partners may bring different ideas and extra capital into the business. They may also be able to specialise in a particular area of the partnership's work in which they have expertise. The main disadvantages are that, like a sole trader, the partners have unlimited liability for all the debts of the business, and the actions of one of the partners are legally binding on the other partners.

2.3 Joint stock company

Unlike sole traders and partnerships, joint stock companies have *limited liability*. This means that if the company goes bankrupt, the owners'/shareholders' responsibility ends with the money they have invested in the company – they will not be liable to lose all of their personal possessions. The individual will not, therefore, be put off from investing in a limited company by, for instance, fear of losing their home.

There are two types of joint stock company:

**Private limited
companies (Ltd)**
Tend to be small
family businesses.

(a) *Private limited company.* These can be identified by 'Ltd' after the name of the company. With this type of enterprise its shares cannot be advertised and offered for sale to members of the general public. They are not, therefore, available for sale on the Stock Exchange. The number of shareholders can start at two, with no upper limit. Private limited companies are a common form of business and tend to be small family concerns. The advantage of such businesses is that the owners are protected from losing their personal possessions, with the company having limited liability. The company has its own legal identity, unlike a sole trader business or a partnership.

A possible disadvantage for a sole trader or a partnership which has become a private limited company is that they will lose some of their control over how the business is run, for they will be accountable to the shareholders.

Public limited companies (plc)
Issue shares which can be advertised and sold to members of the general public. Once issued the shares can be traded on the Stock Exchange.

(b) *Public limited company*. These can be identified by the letters PLC (or plc) after the name of the company. As with the private limited company, the number of shareholders can range between two and no upper limit. However, unlike a private limited company, the shares can be advertised and sold to members of the general public and, once issued, the shares can be traded on the Stock Exchange. The shareholders have certain rights, namely to attend and vote at the annual general meeting (AGM), receive the company annual report and elect the board of directors. PLCs are normally much larger than private limited companies.

The potential advantages of a PLC are that, like the private limited company, the shareholders have limited liability and, since they are able to sell shares on the open market, PLCs are able to grow and take advantage of internal economies of scale (*see* Section 10.5).

2.4 Public sector companies

Public sector companies
Are owned by the state on behalf of the general public.

These are enterprises owned by the state on behalf of the general public. There are two types, namely public corporations and nationalised industries. Public corporations are established by a Royal Charter (such as the BBC, set up in 1927). Nationalised industries were established by an Act of Parliament. Nationalised industries have a separate identity from the government, although the government appoints the chairman who, along with the board of directors, is responsible for the day-to-day running of the industry. Unlike PLCs, there are no shareholders in public sector companies as they are owned by the state.

Over the last 20 years the majority of nationalised industries have been privatised, i.e. state owned assets have been returned to the private sector, and the status of many state-owned companies has changed from being a nationalised industry to being a PLC. The whole issue of privatisation will be dealt with in Chapter 9, Section 3.

Pause for thought 1

Can you provide examples of all these different types of company?

3 THE GROWTH OF FIRMS

3.1 Why do firms wish to grow?

There are a number of reasons why a firm may wish to grow:

(a) In order to reduce their average costs and hence take advantage of economies of scale (*see* Section 10.4).

(b) To diversify, producing a wider range of products in order to ensure their long-term survival. By spreading their risks it can be argued that companies are in a better position to withstand a recession in the economy or a failure of one of their products.

(c) In order to increase their profit and market share and possibly, therefore, its monopoly power.

Mini Case Study 5.1

Alternative Investment Market (AIM)

In June 1995 the Alternative Investment Market (AIM) was opened to meet the demand for a low cost and accessible investment market for small and growing companies. Its trading rules are less demanding than those for a full listing on the London Stock Exchange as indicated in the table below.

Table 5.1 The differences between the main market and AIM

Listing criteria	Main market	AIM
% of free-floating shares	Minimum 25% in public hands	No minimum
Trading history	Three years' trading record normally required	No prior trading record required
Listing fees	Companies required to pay a listing fee of between £5,125 and £256,250, depending on market capitalisation	Flat fee of £4,000 per company
Shareholder participation	Prior shareholder approval needed for certain transactions	No prior shareholder approval required
Reporting requirements	Required to report profits twice a year	Required to report profits twice a year

By the end of 2003, there were 693 companies trading on the AIM with a total of £5 billion having been raised since 1995. Companies on the AIM include Centre Parcs, Peel Hotels, Majestic Wine and Ask Central (restaurants), Hardy Amies (fashion house), Pixology (photographic software) and Aberdeen Football Club. In 2003 almost as much money was raised by small and medium-sized enterprises (SMEs) on AIM (£1.6 billion) as on the London Stock Exchange.

Question

How might you justify government support for the Alternative Investment Market?

Answer to question can be found on the students' side of the Companion Website.

The next question to ask is, *how* do firms grow?

Pause for thought 2

How does growing larger increase a firm's 'market power'?

3.2 Internal growth

There are essentially two methods of growth, the first being internal growth which is also called 'organic growth'. This is where the firm ploughs back its profits into the company and by so doing increases its productive capacity. This is obviously easier if the demand for the company's product(s) is increasing. Advantages of internal growth are that there is less risk to the firm, since having no creditors means the firm cannot be put into receivership or administration. Of course, using one's own profits for investment implies the 'opportunity cost' of not using these profits for something else.

3.3 External growth

External growth has become a common method of growth and involves a *takeover* or a *merger*.

A *takeover* is where one firm purchases another firm from its shareholders, normally with the agreement of the shareholders of the acquired company. It may, however, involve what is known as the 'predatory' company buying up shares in the company it wishes to acquire over a period of time. By making attractive offers to the shareholders it hopes to persuade them to sell their shares, with the aim of obtaining 51% of the shares in the 'targeted' company.

A merger, on the other hand, is where both companies agree to combine their resources into a single company. A merger is normally a voluntary agreement.

The amalgamation of two or more companies in the form of a merger can also be called *integration* and this can be classified in the following way:

Vertical integration
Occurs when firms amalgamate at different stages of the productive process.

(a) *Vertical integration*. This occurs when firms amalgamate at different stages of the productive process. Vertical integration can be divided into backward and forward integration:

(*i*) *Backward vertical integration* refers to a situation where one firm amalgamates with another firm at an *earlier* stage of the productive process. An example of this is a tea producer such as Brooke Bond acquiring a tea plantation. There are certain benefits in that the acquiring firm can directly control the quality and the supply of their raw material requirements. It is also possible to make sure that delivery of the raw material is on time and that other producers (possibly competitors) are denied the raw material supply. It is also the case that the profits which would have been earned by the supplier of the raw material now accrue to the firm at the next stage of production.

(*ii*) *Forward vertical integration* occurs when a firm acquires another firm at the *next* stage of the productive process. Examples of this include a brewery acquiring a public house or an oil producer acquiring a chain of petrol stations. The reason for this type of integration is that the producer is able to control the quality of the outlet. If a firm, such as a brewing company, has spent substantial amounts of money on advertising its product it will want to make sure that the outlet or the 'point of sale' for its product is satisfactory. Additionally, with a brewing company, the acquisition of a number of public houses also ensures that those outlets are tied to the manufacturer's product.

Horizontal integration
Occurs when firms merge at the same stage of the production process.

(b) *Horizontal integration*. This occurs when a firm amalgamates with another firm at the same stage of the productive process. An example of this was the acquisition of Rowntree by Nestlé in the 1980s. There are obvious advantages gained by horizontal integration. Economies of scale can be obtained (*see* Section 10.4) and it also allows for rationalisation, with the closure of plant if there is excess capacity. Horizontal integration can also lead to a reduction of competition in the industry and can, therefore, benefit the firm from increased monopoly power.

Conglomerate integration Occurs when firms merge with no discernable links between the goods and services they produce.

(c) *Conglomerate integration.* This occurs when firms merge with no obvious link between the goods and services they produce. One of the main advantages of this is the 'spreading of risk' as production is diversified. It is also possible that economies of scale, namely managerial and financial, can be achieved through conglomerate mergers.

! Pause for thought 3

Can you provide more examples of each of these types of integration?

Mini Case Study 5.2

Morrisons acquires Safeway

In December 2003 Wm Morrison took over its larger supermarket rival, Safeway, in a £3 billion agreed deal. More than 1,200 jobs will go – mainly at Safeway's head office in Hayes, Middlesex. The enlarged group will have combined sales of more than £13 billion giving it a 15.6% market share, behind J. Sainsbury with 16%, Asda with 16.7% and market leader Tesco, which holds a 26.8% share of the market. 'Putting Morrisons and Safeway together will create a powerful national retailer able to challenge the other three majors,' said Sir Ken Morrison, chairman of the group and architect of its recent successes. Analysts expect further pressure on prices as Morrisons introduces its low-price formula to Safeway, but Sir Ken dismissed speculation about a new industry price war. The company – formed by Sir Ken's father through a series of market stores in West Yorkshire – has been growing fast, gradually moving out of the north and Midlands into the south. It now has 109 stores and will acquire a further 479 mainly southern-based outlets from Safeway, although it will be forced by the competition ruling to dispose of 52. That forced sale has dented the potential synergies to be achieved in the tie-up, with Morrisons now targeting savings of £215 million by the end of January 2008 rather than the £250 million by January 2007 it had earlier predicted. Morrisons expects to boost sales by 21% at Safeway's larger stores and 10% at its medium-sized ones, which will be converted to the Wm Morrison brand. The Safeway label will be retained for the 138 smaller stores, although Sir Ken indicated that these could be sold. Expressions of interest have already been received for them.

	Number of employees	Number of stores	Turnover	Pre-tax profit	Forecast 2004 profits
Tesco	225,000	835	£28.6bn	£1.4bn	£1.6bn
Sainsbury's	145,000	505	£18.5bn	£695m	£675m
Asda	125,815	259	£12.1bn	£546m	(unavailable)
Safeway	89,745	479	£8.6bn	£329.7m	£310m
Morrisons	50,000	109	£4.3bn	£275.4m	£320m

Question

What factors would seem to lie behind the takeover deal?

Answer to question can be found at the back of the book (page 499).

4   THE FACTORS OF PRODUCTION

4.1 What are the factors of production?

There are certain inputs or resources called the factors of production which are the means by which goods and services are produced. These resources can be divided into the three categories of land, labour and capital.

Land
Can be viewed as a natural resource. It not only comprises the earth's surface but also includes agricultural production, mining, fishing and forestry. Land comprises both renewable and non-renewable resources.

4.2 Land

This can be classed as a natural resource. It is not simply the surface of the earth on which houses and factories can be built but is also the natural resources which can be found on or below the surface. Land, therefore, includes agricultural production, mining such as coal and oil, and the resources obtained from the sea and forests (e.g. timber, medicine). Land can be separated into *renewable* and *non-renewable resources*. For example, renewable energy (such as wind, wave and solar power) can be used over and over again, whereas non-renewable energy (e.g. coal, oil, gas) cannot be used more than once.

4.3 Labour

Labour
The human resource providing time, effort and expertise which individuals allocate to producing goods and services.

If land can be classified as the natural resource, labour can be seen as the human resource. Labour is not simply the physical or manual work undertaken by individuals but also the intellectual and mental skills used in the production of goods and services. The supply of labour is all important and it is determined by the size of the population which in turn depends upon the birth rate, the death rate and the level of migration. Obviously not all of the population will be of working age, i.e. between the ages of 16 and 65, and not all those of working age will be available for work, for example those in full-time higher education. Chapter 8 looks in more detail at labour as a factor of production.

4.4 Capital

Capital
Includes items such as plant, machinery, tools and factory buildings used in the production of goods or services.

Unlike land and labour, capital is a human-made resource which can be used in the production of goods and services. It includes plant, machinery and factory buildings. Capital can be divided into *fixed* and *circulating capital*. Fixed capital includes such items as machinery and factories and can be used over a period of time. Circulating capital, which is sometimes called working capital, includes the stock of raw materials, partly finished products and all the finished products in the factory waiting to be sold. An important point to remember when considering capital is that it does not refer to money, for capital consists of real assets.

5   PRODUCTION

5.1 Production function

The production of goods and services requires inputs of the factors of production. The relationship between the two can be summarised in the *production function*, generally given as:

$$Qx = f(F_1, F_2, \ldots F_n)$$

where:

Qx = the output of product x over a period of time

f = the functional relationship

$F_1, F_2 \ldots F_n$ = the factor inputs

So the output of product x is a function of (depends on) the inputs of land, labour and capital. The above equation can be simplified to give the following:

$$Qx = f(L, K)$$

where:

L = the quantity of labour

K = the quantity of capital

Short run
That period of time for which at least one of the factors of production is fixed,

Long run
That period of time for which all of the factors of production can be varied.

It is important to distinguish between production in the short run and in the long run. In the short run, at least one of the factors of production is fixed. This is normally taken to be capital because it is not possible to construct a new factory or purchase new machinery overnight. It is, however, possible to employ extra units of labour and to purchase extra raw materials in the short run, hence they are called the *variable factors*. In the long run, all of the factors of production can be varied.

5.2 Production in the short run: law of diminishing returns

In the short run, as a firm employs more of the variable factor, it will eventually experience *diminishing returns to the variable factor*. This is known as the *law of diminishing returns* and is illustrated for labour as the variable factor in Table 5.2.

We assume that the quantity of capital and the state of technology are fixed, with the only variable factor being labour. Labour is also assumed to be homogeneous (each worker is identical). Table 5.2 shows what happens to production as there is an increase in the number of workers employed. The terms used in the table are defined below.

Table 5.2 Total, average and marginal product illustrating the law of diminishing returns

Number of workers	Total product (TP)	Average product (AP)	Marginal product (MP)
1	5	5	5
2	24	12	19
3	57	19	33
4	100	25	43
5	150	30	50
6	180	30	30
7	189	27	9
8	176	22	−13
9	153	17	−23
10	100	10	−53

Total product
The total amount produced by a firm over a particular period of time.

(a) *Total product* (TP). This is the total output that the firm produces over a given period of time as the number of workers employed is varied. The total product will increase up to a maximum of 189 units of output, when seven workers are employed.

Average product
Output per worker.

(b) *Average product* (AP). The average product of labour represents the output per worker. It is measured by dividing total product by the number of workers, thus if five workers are employed and total output is 150 units then AP is 30:

$$AP = TP/L$$

Marginal product
The addition to total output obtained by employing one extra worker.

(c) *Marginal product*. The marginal product is the extra output obtained from the employment of one extra worker. In other words, it is the change in total product as a result of employing an additional worker:

$$MP = \Delta TP/\Delta L$$

where ΔTP is the change in the total product and ΔL is the change in the quantity of labour employed.

The law of diminishing returns, which is sometimes called the *law of variable proportions*, states that as successive units of the variable factor are combined with the fixed factors (land and capital) both the average and the marginal product of the variable factor will eventually decline. Thus in Table 5.2 diminishing marginal returns to labour occur after the fifth worker is employed and diminishing average returns occur after the sixth worker is employed.

The information from Table 5.2 can be reproduced in a diagram (*see* Figure 5.1). Note that the MP is plotted at the mid points between 0 and 1, 1 and 2, etc., and that at some point MP becomes negative, when employing additional units of the variable factor actually reduces the total product of the firm. This occurs after the seventh worker is employed.

Pause for thought 4

Distinguish between total, average and marginal product.

5.3 The average and marginal concept

These are important concepts which you will come across throughout this book. Note from Figure 5.1 that the MP of labour cuts the AP of labour at its maximum point. This can be explained by use of the batting average of a cricketer. His latest innings is his marginal score and his average score is the total number of runs he has made so far divided by the number of innings he has batted (the assumption is made that he is out each time). If he has only batted in 4 innings so far and has made scores of 20, 30, 50 and 60, his average is 40. If in the next innings (his 5th) he makes 50, although his marginal score has declined from the previous one of 60, his average, which is now 42, is still increasing because his marginal score was above his average. If in his 6th innings he only scores 42, which is exactly equal to his average score, then his average score does not change. At this point the marginal and the average score are the same. If, however, in the 7th innings the cricketer scores only 28, his average will start to fall, now being only 40. This is because his marginal score is now below his average score.

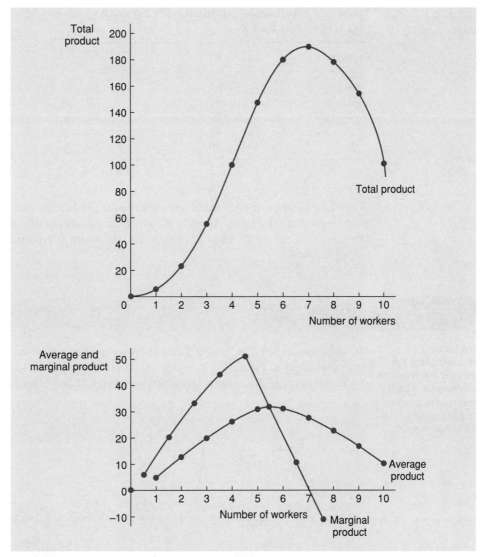

Figure 5.1 The figure illustrates the relationship between total, average and marginal product. The average and marginal product curves will eventually decline as diminishing returns occur. Note that when marginal product is above average product then average product is increasing. When marginal product is below average product then average product is decreasing. When marginal product and average product are equal then average product is at its maximum.

5.4 Production in the long run

In the *long run* it is possible to vary all of the factors of production. This can be illustrated by involving two factors of production, namely capital and labour. Given the two factors it is possible for the firm to choose different combinations of capital and labour to produce a particular level of output. In Table 5.3 the firm might be able to produce one unit

Table 5.3 Alternative processes for producing one unit of product x

Process	K	L
A	140	30
B	90	50
C	60	80
D	50	110
E	40	160

of product x using one of five different processes of production. For example, one unit of x can be produced by using 140 units of capital and 30 units of labour, process A, a capital intensive process, or 40 units of capital and 160 units of labour, process E, a labour intensive process.

6 ISOQUANTS

Isoquant
A curve giving the various combinations of capital and labour required to produce a given quantity of a particular product.

The information given in Table 5.3 can be reproduced in a diagram (*see* Figure 5.2). The curve illustrated in Figure 5.2 is referred to as an *isoquant*. An isoquant can be defined as a curve showing the various combinations of capital and labour required to produce

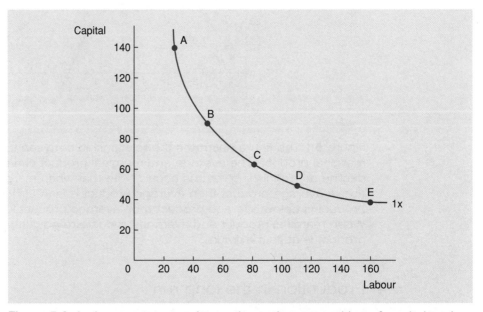

Figure 5.2 An isoquant curve shows the various quantities of capital and labour required to produce a particular quantity of a particular product in the most efficient way. The figure shows just five of a whole range of combinations of capital and labour in producing one unit of product x.

a given *quantity* of a particular product, in the most efficient way. The slope of the isoquant reveals the *marginal rate of technical substitution* of labour for capital. This shows how much capital can be replaced by *one* extra unit of labour, with output remaining constant.

Given the current state of technology, if extra units of x are to be produced then it will require at least one more of the inputs. For example, in terms of Figure 5.3, 2x can be produced by employing 70 more units of capital, a move from point B to F, or 60 more units of labour, a move from B to G. Equally, the firm could employ more of both capital and labour which would be along the FG segment of the 2x isoquant.

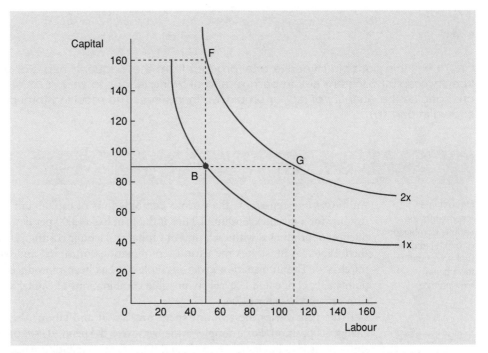

Figure 5.3 In producing extra units of product x, then more of at least one of the inputs will be required. Starting at point B, if 70 more units of capital are used (a move to point F) then one extra unit of x will be produced. Alternatively, this can be achieved by employing 60 more units of labour (a move to point G). It is also possible to produce one more unit of x by employing more capital and labour (a move to a point on the 2x isoquant between F and G).

There is an isoquant for each level of output, and a series of isoquants is called an *isoquant map*. Thus, isoquant curves above and to the right of lower isoquants represent higher levels of output.

In Section 5.2 production in the short run was introduced. Figure 5.4 illustrates how, if capital is held constant, such as $\bar{k}$, and the amount of labour is varied, then the horizontal section through the isoquant map reveals the total product curve as given in Figure 5.1.

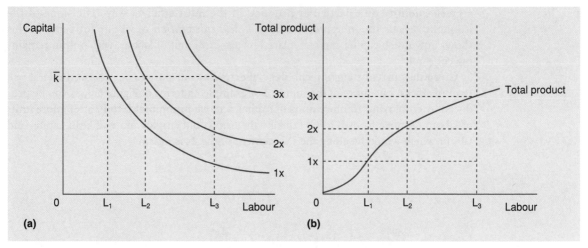

Figure 5.4 It is possible to derive total product from the isoquant map. For example, by keeping capital constant at k̄ in part (a) and allowing labour to vary, it reveals how output changes as the quantity of labour employed increases. The resulting total product curve is shown in part (b).

7   ISOCOST

Isocost line
Represents the various combinations of capital and labour that a firm can buy for a given expenditure.

An *isocost line* represents the various combinations of capital and labour that the firm can buy for a given expenditure. Thus if the firm has £1,000 per day to spend on the production of product x, with each unit of capital and labour costing £10 and £5 respectively, then Table 5.4 illustrates the various combinations of capital and labour which can be purchased. The information given in Table 5.4 has been reproduced in Figure 5.5. The points a, b, c, d, e and f reveal six possible combinations of capital and labour which the firm can purchase for £1,000.

If the firm varies the amount spent on capital and labour then the isocost would change its position. For example, if the firm were to spend £1,500 then the isocost would shift upwards as in Figure 5.6 to C_3, and if the firm's expenditure was reduced to £500 the isocost would shift inwards to C_1.

It is important to note that the *slope* of the isocost is given by the relative price of the factor inputs, capital and labour. From Figure 5.5, we can see that the slope of the isocost line is 100:200, i.e. the same as the price of labour:price of capital.

Table 5.4 Isocost schedule

Combinations	K (£10 per unit)	L (£5 per unit)
a	100	0
b	80	40
c	60	80
d	40	120
e	20	160
f	0	200

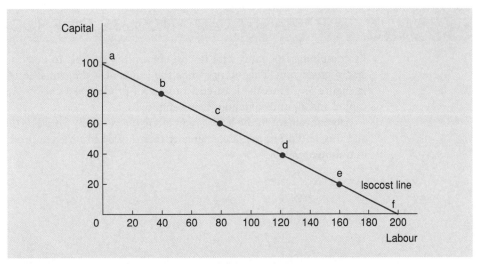

Figure 5.5 An isocost line represents the various combinations of capital and labour a firm can buy for a given expenditure. Thus, as illustrated in the figure, if the firm has £1,000 to spend per day, and capital and labour cost £10 and £5 per unit respectively, then the firm can purchase 100 units of capital (point a) or 200 units of labour (point f). Alternatively, the firm could purchase a combination of the two, such as points b, c, d or e.

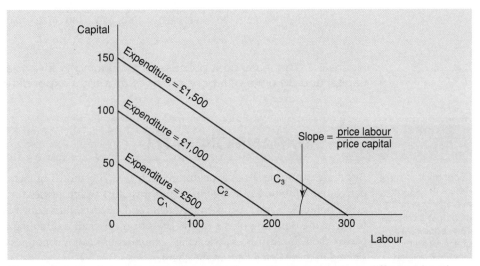

Figure 5.6 Each isocost such as C_1, C_2 or C_3 represents a different level of expenditure. The slope of the isocost line is determined by the relative price of capital and labour. The slope of C_3 is 150:300, i.e. the ratio of the price of labour:price of capital (ie £5:£10). All the isocost lines have the same slope.

8   THE LEAST-COST PROCESS OF PRODUCTION

By combining isoquants with isocost curves it is possible to determine the *least-cost process of production*. This occurs when the isoquant is tangential to the isocost, at point c, in Figure 5.7. Thus the least-cost process of producing 1x costs £1,000 with 60 units of capital and 80 units of labour being employed.

Any movement to the left or right along the isoquant would be outside the isocost line and this would indicate a cost greater than £1,000 in order to produce the same level of output, that is 1x.

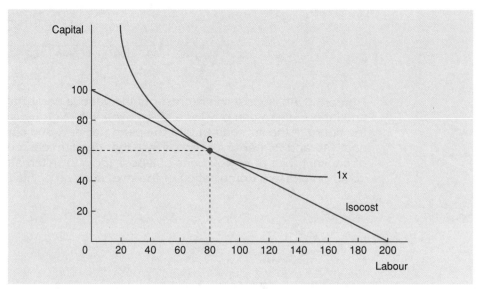

Figure 5.7 The least-cost process of producing 1x involves 60 units of capital and 80 units of labour (point c) at a total expenditure of £1,000.

9   THE EXPANSION PATH

Economies of scale
Refers to long-run average cost falling as output increases. The economies of scale can be technical (related to production) and non-technical (related to marketing, distribution, finance and so on).

By taking various levels of expenditure such as C_1, C_2 and C_3 in Figure 5.8 it is possible to derive the *minimum cost expansion path* (MCEP) which passes through successive tangency points a, b and c between isoquants and isocosts. *Increasing returns to scale* are said to occur if a doubling of the inputs leads to more than a doubling in the output. If this occurs then the firm is experiencing *economies of scale*. Economies of scale will be considered in more detail later in the chapter.

If a doubling of the inputs leads to a doubling of the output then this is referred to as *constant returns to scale*. There could, however, be *decreasing returns to scale*, where a doubling of inputs leads to less than a doubling in output. This is called *diseconomies of scale* (*see* 10.7).

 Pause for thought 5

Differentiate between the terms constant, increasing and decreasing returns to scale.

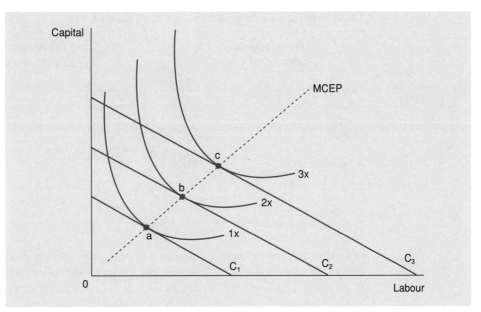

Figure 5.8 **The tangency points between isoquants and isocosts such as a, b and c in the figure reveal the firm's minimum cost expansion path.**

10 COSTS

10.1 What are costs?

Costs can be viewed as the total amount paid by a firm for the factors of production it uses, such as labour, in the productive process. It is important when considering costs to distinguish between the accountant's and the economist's method of measurement. The accountant measures historical cost which is the price originally paid for the factors of production whereas the economist measures the opportunity cost. Opportunity cost (*see* Chapter 1, Section 2.4) is a measure of the best alternative forgone. In certain situations the historical cost and the opportunity cost measurements are the same. For example, when a firm buys raw materials and uses them soon after they are purchased then the historical cost and the opportunity cost are the same because the money spent on the raw materials could have been used to purchase something else. However, the historical cost of the accountant and the opportunity cost of the economist may differ.

Take for example a firm owned by one person (a sole trader) who may obtain a revenue of £140,000 for the sale of his or her product over the year. According to the accountant, subtracting the explicit costs on such things as the purchase of raw materials and the wages of hired labour totalling £100,000 would leave the firm with a profit of £40,000 as shown in Table 5.5.

The economist, however, would view this as an overestimate of the profit earned by the firm. In calculating costs, the economist would also take into account the implicit costs, which refer to the inputs owned and used by the firm when producing goods and services. These costs can be viewed as imputed (or estimated) costs because no actual expenditure has taken place. The imputed costs are based on what the inputs could have earned in their best alternative use and include what the owner of the firm could have earned if he

Diseconomies of scale
Refers to long-run average cost rising as output increases beyond a certain level.

Table 5.5 Accounting cost and opportunity cost

The accountant (accounting cost)		The economist (opportunity cost)	
	£		£
Sales revenue:	140,000	Sales revenue:	140,000
Less:		Less:	
Explicit costs	100,000	Explicit costs	100,000
		Imputed cost of owner's time	15,000
Accounting profit	40,000	Opportunity cost of finance	5,000
		Opportunity cost of factory	10,000
		And machinery	
		Economic profit	10,000

or she had worked for another company. For example, the owner could earn say £15,000 if he or she was employed by someone else and this is the opportunity cost of the owner's time, which is included in the economist's calculation of costs but not the accountant's.

The economist's *opportunity cost* is also concerned with the funds the owner has tied up in the business. The opportunity cost is the amount these funds could have earned elsewhere. For example, if the owner has £50,000 in the business this could have been placed in a bank and earned a rate of interest of, say, 10%. The sum of £5,000 interest is the opportunity cost of finance and is also included in the economist's cost calculation.

The sole trader may also own the factory and machinery used in production and it is possible that both could be rented out. The imputed cost is the rent it could have received by letting it out to another business and this could be estimated at £10,000.

As seen in Table 5.5, using the economist's method of calculating cost reduces the profit figure from £40,000 to £10,000. After taking the costs into account as calculated by the economist, the firm is still making a profit. This is called economic profit, pure profit or supernormal profit, and is a true indicator of how the firm is doing. If the figure had been negative it would have been better for the sole trader to close down the business, place his or her money in the bank, rent out the factory and work for someone else. The concept of supernormal profit will be considered in more detail in Chapter 6.

Pause for thought 6

Distinguish between accounting cost and economic cost.

10.2 Short-run and long-run costs

When considering costs it is important to distinguish between the short run and the long run. In the short run certain factors are fixed while others are variable. This means that some costs, namely *fixed costs*, will have to be paid even if there is no output being produced. The fixed costs, which are also called overhead or unavoidable costs, include rent paid on the premises, rates, interest payments on loans and hire purchase repayments. *Variable costs* include raw materials, wages of the operative staff and the cost of fuel. When no output is produced, no variable costs are incurred. As output increases, the firm will incur increasing variable costs and because of this they are also called direct or avoidable costs. In the long run, all the factors of production are variable costs.

Pause for thought 7

Can you give some examples of fixed costs and variable costs for a firm known to you?

10.3 Total, average and marginal cost

Table 5.6 gives the figures for total, average and marginal cost for a hypothetical firm producing a particular good.

Total cost
The cost of producing a particular level of output.

(a) *Total cost (TC)*. Total cost is just that, it is the total cost of producing a particular level of output. Total cost can be divided into total fixed cost (TFC) and total variable cost (TVC), so that:

$$TC = TFC + TVC$$

It can be seen from Table 5.6 and Figure 5.9 (which is based on the data in the table) that total fixed costs do not vary with output and are constant at £30. The total variable costs are zero if no output is produced and then increase as output increases. As illustrated in Figure 5.9 (page 112), both total variable cost and total cost increase with output, with the vertical distance between the two being equal to the total fixed cost.

Table 5.6 Total, average and marginal cost

Units of output (Q)	TFC (£)	TVC (£)	TC (£)	AFC (£)	AVC (£)	ATC (£)	MC (£)
0	30	0	30				
							30
1	30	30	60	30.0	30.0	60.0	
							11
2	30	41	71	15.0	20.5	35.5	
							8
3	30	49	79	10.0	16.3	26.3	
							9
4	30	58	88	7.5	14.5	22.0	
							12
5	30	70	100	6.0	14.0	20.0	
							15
6	30	85	115	5.0	14.1	19.1	
							20
7	30	105	135	4.2	15.0	19.2	
							25
8	30	130	160	3.75	16.25	20.0	
							30
9	30	160	190	3.33	17.7	21.0	
							41
10	30	201	231	3.0	20.1	23.1	

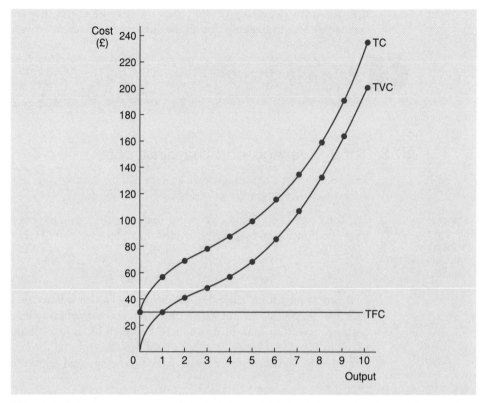

Figure 5.9 The figure illustrates total cost (TC). A firm's total cost is made up of total fixed cost (TFC), which does not vary with output, and total variable cost (TVC), which increases as output increases. The vertical distance between the TC and TVC curves is equal to the TFC.

Average total cost
The cost per unit.
Average total cost is average fixed cost plus average variable cost.

(b) *Average cost (AC).* Average cost is the cost per unit and is obtained by dividing total cost by the number of units produced. *Average total cost* (ATC) comprises *average fixed cost* and *average variable cost* so that:

$$ATC = AFC + AVC$$

Average fixed cost is given by

$$AFC = TFC/Q$$

and is shown in Figure 5.10 (using the data from Table 5.6). AFC declines continuously as output increases. This is because the fixed cost is spread over more units of production and is therefore sometimes called 'spreading the overheads'. Average variable cost is given by

$$AVC = TVC/Q$$

and is shown in Figure 5.10, again obtained by using the data from Table 5.6.

Marginal cost
The addition to total cost of producing one extra unit.

(c) *Marginal cost (MC).* Marginal cost is the change in the total cost as a result of a change in output of one unit. It can be written as:

$$MC = \frac{\Delta TC}{\Delta Q}$$

The marginal cost cuts the average cost at its minimum point (*see* Figure 5.10).

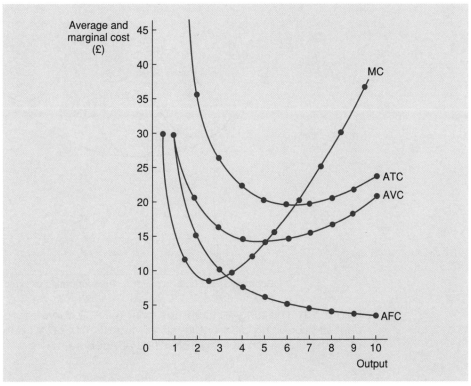

Figure 5.10 These are short-run cost curves. The average fixed cost declines continuously as output increases. The average variable cost and average total cost curves are U-shaped with the vertical distance between the two representing the average fixed cost. The marginal cost (MC) curve is also U-shaped and cuts the AVC and ATC curves at their minimum points.

> ! **Pause for thought 8**
>
> *Define total, average and marginal cost.*

10.4 Long-run average cost (LRAC) and economies of scale

Long-run average cost curve
The envelope of all the short-run average cost curves, representing the lowest cost of producing different levels of output when all factors of production can be varied.

In the long run all the factors of production are variable and this means that output can be varied using different capacity.

The long-run average cost (LRAC) curve is the envelope of all the short-run average cost (SRAC) curves and it represents the lowest cost of producing different levels of output (*see* Figure 5.11). All points above the LRAC curve are attainable levels of cost, whereas the points below the curve are unattainable levels of cost.

Up to an output level of q* the LRAC curve is declining, which signifies that the firm is benefiting from economies of scale, there being increasing returns to scale. The minimum point q* is the minimum efficient scale of production and after q* the LRAC curve increases, which signifies diseconomies of scale, with the firm experiencing decreasing returns to scale.

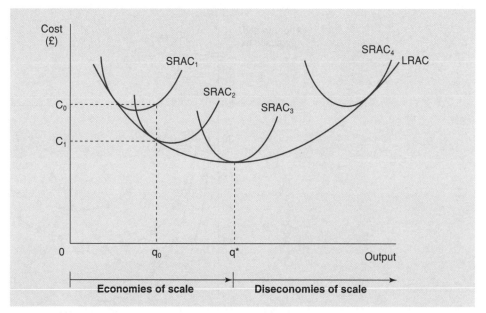

Figure 5.11 The long-run average cost (LRAC) curve represents the lowest cost of producing different levels of output. The LRAC curve is an envelope of all the short-run average cost (SRAC) curves.

An output of q_0 could be produced by using the capacity implicit within the short-run average cost curve ($SRAC_1$) at a cost of C_0, but by expanding its capacity to $SRAC_2$, the firm's cost of producing q_0 could be reduced to C_1.

10.5 Sources of economies of scale

As a firm grows in size it is possible for them to reduce their cost of production. The reduction in costs as a result of increasing production are called economies of scale and in Figure 5.11 they are obtained by the firm up to a level of output q^*, the lowest point on the firm's long-run average cost curve.

The sources of economies of scale can be outlined as:

(a) *Technical economies.* As a firm grows in size it may be able to take advantage of increased *specialisation*. If the firm produces only a small output it may not be possible to employ a worker solely on one process but as the level of production increases workers may be able to specialise, leading to a lowering of the firm's costs.

As the firm grows it can also reduce its costs through what is known as *increased dimensions*. For example, if the size of a container is doubled its surface area is increased four-fold and its volume is increased eight-fold. It is possible, therefore, to obtain cost savings by making use of larger containers, say, for the storage or distribution of finished products since the cost per unit will fall.

A large firm may also devote proportionately more resources to *research and development* which could lead to an improvement in the quality of the goods and services produced, and possibly to a lowering of the cost per unit.

(b) *Marketing economies*. When a firm buys its raw materials in *bulk* it may obtain preferential terms in the form of a discount, thus reducing the cost of each unit. A large firm may employ specialist buyers whose sole responsibility it is to purchase raw materials at the cheapest price. Administration, advertising, and packaging costs may also be lower for larger companies since they can spread the cost over larger orders. For example, the packaging costs per item for 1 million units is likely to be substantially lower than if 100 items were packaged.

(c) *Financial economies*. Larger firms may be able to obtain finance on favourable terms, obtaining loans from financial institutions at lower rates of interest. Banks will be more willing to loan on preferential terms to a large, well-known company, which can offer more collateral as security for the loan, than it will to a smaller company.

Mini Case Study 5.3

Scale economies in the skies

In late 2005 we can expect the huge Airbus A380 super-jumbo jet to take off on its maiden test flight, before entering service in spring 2006. Although the absolute costs of building the 555–650 seater A380 super-jumbos are dramatically higher than for today's 350–400 seater jumbos, the *cost per passenger seat* is estimated to be some 15% to 20% lower than for the widely used Boeing 747-400.

How can this be? Certainly the hugely expensive $10.7 billion (£6.7 billion) programme will require 6,000 engineers at factories in Germany, France, Spain and Britain, with an assembly hall in Toulouse more than twice the size of a football pitch! To bring all the component parts of the A380 to Toulouse from the 15 different manufacturing plants in the four countries will also be hugely expensive. For example, purpose-built roll-on roll-off ferries, barges and road trailers have had to be designed and built to transport to Toulouse in Southern France the huge wings (from Broughton, Wales), the rear and forward fuselage (from Hamburg, Northern Germany), the tail piece (from Cadiz, Southern Spain) and the centre fuselage and cockpit (from St Nazaire, Western France). Roads are having to be widened and secure overnight parking facilities provided (e.g. three nights stops needed for transporting the slow moving road convoys in France).

Nevertheless, a 'value chain' for production which involves specialising in these individual parts using firms in the different countries is thought to be cost and quality efficient and to more than compensate for the huge costs and logistical problems in transporting them for final assembly in Toulouse.

The design of the A380 has taken into account the views of numerous focus groups of potential users from many airlines. It has been designed with 20% of the airframe made from the most modern, tough, lightweight plastic materials to keep within the maximum take-off weight of 560 tonnes. The basic version with 550 passengers will be able to travel some 8,000 miles without refuelling, and an extended version will carry 650 passengers an extra 1,000 miles (i.e. 9,000 miles in total).

Airbus will need to sell around 250 of these A380 jets to break even, and stated that it was over halfway to that total by late 2003, with orders from ten different airlines. Airbus estimate the total market for aircraft in the 400 plus seat category to be around 1,100 over the next 20 years. It also predicts an air-freight version will be in demand, with some 300 extra customers attracted.

The annual traffic growth for air passengers has been predicted at around 4.7% per annum over the next 20 years. However, much of this growth will involve the Asia-Pacific region, and Airbus has yet to receive orders from Japan Air Lines or All Nippon Airways – both major carriers to that region. Other companies also challenge the Airbus strategy, with its main rival, Boeing, believing the market will be better met by flying smaller aircraft into a wider range of smaller airports, rather than huge aircraft into a few hub-to-hub centres.

Vital statistics of A380

Assembly	Toulouse
Price	$260m
Capacity	556–650 seats
Range	8,000–9,000 miles
Take-off weight	560 tonnes
Entry into service	Spring 2006
Programme cost	$10.7 billion

Source: Economics for Business and Management, Griffiths and Wall (FT/Prentice Hall, 2005)

Questions

1 *What sources of economies of scale are helping the A380 achieve the projected 15% to 20% lower seat cost?*

2 *Can you identify some of the benefits and costs (e.g. risks) to Airbus in following this scale economy strategy?*

Answers to questions can be found on the students' side of the Companion Website.

10.6 Economies of scope

Economies of scope Refers to the situation in which a firm can reduce its average cost by changing the mix of products.

Firms will normally produce more than one product and are, therefore, in a position to take advantage of *economies of scope*. Economies of scope refer to the reduction in average total cost (ATC) made possible by a firm increasing the number of different goods it produces. For example, Cadbury Schweppes could produce a range of confectionery products at a lower ATC than if separate firms were to produce each particular product. The reason for this is that Cadbury Schweppes is able to take advantage of skilled staff and technology which can be shared by the different confectionery goods produced. Economies of scope therefore exist when costs are spread over a range of products, with the result that there are lower costs of production for each good.

10.7 Diseconomies of scale

As seen in Figure 5.11, at a certain level of output the firm's average costs may increase in the long run with the firm experiencing diseconomies of scale.

The sources of diseconomies are:

(a) As a company grows in size it will possibly have a larger management team and, unlike a sole trader, it will find it difficult to make decisions quickly. This can often be the case where companies have merged and there are two sets of management with different ideas. It may be difficult to coordinate planning, marketing, production and so on, with a resulting increase in the company's cost per unit.

(b) The workforce may feel remote and alienated from the management. They may find their jobs boring and repetitive, particularly if mass production methods are used, and this may result in low morale and poor motivation. There may be a feeling on the part of the workforce that they are not part of the firm and this may lead to a deterioration in the quality of work undertaken. A 'them and us' situation may also develop between the management and the workforce, possibly resulting in an increase in the number of industrial disputes.

Pause for thought 9

What is meant by economies and diseconomies of scale? Can you use an industry known to you to provide possible examples of economies of scale?

KEY POINTS

- Sole traders are owned by one person whereas partnerships comprise two or more owners, generally with a maximum of 20. Both have unlimited liability. Private limited companies (Ltd) tend to be small family businesses whereas public limited companies (plc) issue shares which can be advertised and sold to members of the general public. Once issued the shares can be traded on the Stock Exchange. Public sector companies, however, are owned by the state on behalf of the general public.

- Vertical integration occurs when firms amalgamate at different stages of the productive process whereas horizontal integration occurs when firms merge at the same stage of the production process. Conglomerate integration occurs when firms merge with no discernable links between the goods and services they produce.

- Land can be viewed as a natural resource. It not only comprises the earth's surface but also includes agricultural production, mining, fishing and forestry. Land comprises both renewable and non-renewable resources. Labour is the human resource providing time, effort and expertise which individuals allocate to producing goods and services. Capital includes items such as plant, machinery, tools and factory buildings used in the production of goods or services.

- Total product is the total amount produced by a firm over a particular period of time. Average product is output per worker and marginal product is the additional to total output obtained by employing one extra worker.

- The short run is that period of time for which at least one of the factors of production is fixed whereas the long run is that period of time for which all of the factors of production can be varied.

- An isoquant represents a curve giving the various combinations of capital and labour required to produce a given quantity of a particular product whereas an isocost line represents the various combinations of capital and labour that a firm can buy for a given expenditure.

- The total cost is the cost of producing a particular level of output; average total cost is the cost per unit comprising average fixed cost plus average variable cost, and marginal cost is the addition to total cost of producing one extra unit.

- The long-run average cost curve is the envelope of all the short-run average cost curves, representing the lowest cost of producing different levels of output when all factors of production can be varied.

- Economies of scale refer to long-run average cost falling as output increases. The economies of scale can be technical (related to production) and non-technical (related to marketing, distribution, finance and so on). Diseconomies of scale refer to long-run average cost rising as output increases beyond a certain level. Economies of scope refer to the situation in which a firm can reduce its average cost by changing the mix of products.

Further reading

Griffiths, A. and Wall, S. (2005) *Economics for Business and Management*, FT/Prentice Hall, Chapter 3 and Appendix 2.

Heather, K. (2004) *Economics Theory in Action*, 4th edition, FT/Prentice Hall, Chapter 5.

Parkin, M., Powell, M. and Matthews, K. (2005) *Economics*, 6th edition, FT/Prentice Hall, Chapters 9 and 10.

Sloman, J. (2006) *Economics*, 6th edition, FT/Prentice Hall, Chapter 5.

Web references

The following website contains a wide range of company data, including production and cost related data:

http://bized.ac.uk

www.dti.gov.uk

www.eubusiness.com

Companies House: **http://www.companieshouse.gov.uk/** The place for getting information on all English and Welsh companies.

Chinese business activity: **www.cbbc.org**

Japanese business activity: **www.jetro.org**

EU business activity: **www.euromonitor.com**

PROGRESS AND REVIEW QUESTIONS

Answers to most questions can be found at the back of the book (pages 499–501). Answers to asterisked questions can be found on the students' side of the Companion Website.

Multiple-choice questions

1   Which *one* of the following is a characteristic of a sole trader?

   a) Limited liability

   b) Unlimited liability

   c) Economies of scale

   d) Ease of access to capital

   e) None of the above.

2 Which *one* of the following is a characteristic of a public limited company (plc)?

   a) Unlimited liability
   b) Potential lack of continuity of business
   c) Risk of takeover by other firms buying shares on the Stock Exchange
   d) Cannot sell shares to the general public
   e) None of the above.

3 Which *one* of the following situations is most favourable to the small firm's survival?

   a) Serves 'niche' markets, often too small for large firms to service profitably
   b) Extensive 'outsourcing' possible, reducing costs within larger firms
   c) Substantial economies of scale exist
   d) Large 'bulk purchase' economies are available
   e) None of the above.

4 Limited liability describes a situation where:

   a) all shareholders are equally responsible for all the debts of the company
   b) the responsibility of shareholders for the debts of a company is limited to the amount they agreed to pay for the shares when they brought them
   c) the responsibility of shareholders for the debts of a company is limited to the number of debentures they hold in the company
   d) the responsibility of shareholders for the debts of a company is limited to the value of their personal wealth.
   e) none of the above.

5 If the marginal product of labour is less than the average product of labour then:

   a) the average product of labour is increasing
   b) the average product of labour is decreasing
   c) the marginal product of labour is increasing
   d) the average product of labour is at its maximum
   e) the total product curve is negatively sloped.

6 An isoquant curve reveals:

   a) the various amounts of capital and output, with a fixed amount of labour
   b) the various amounts of labour and capital required in order to produce the same level of output
   c) the various amounts of labour and capital required in order to produce an increased level of output
   d) the various amounts of labour and capital required in order to produce a reduced level of output
   e) none of the above.

7 If a firm remains on the same isoquant it means that:

   a) output must decrease
   b) output must stay the same
   c) output must increase
   d) the quantity of labour and capital employed must stay the same
   e) none of the above.

8 In terms of producing a certain output a firm's average total cost is €4 and its average variable cost is €3.50. Overall, the firm's total fixed cost is €1,000. As such, the firm's total output is:

   a) 100 units
   b) 250 units

c) 750 units
d) 1,000 units
e) 2,000 units

9 The figure below represents the short-run average and marginal cost curves. The average fixed cost curve is represented by:

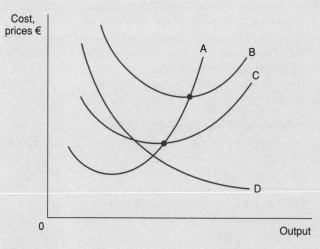

a) A
b) B
c) C
d) D
e) none of the above.

10 If the average variable cost is decreasing then:

a) marginal cost is below average variable cost
b) marginal cost is above average variable cost
c) marginal cost is equal to average variable cost
d) average fixed cost is increasing
e) none of the above.

Case study question

Hidden costs

A study in July 2004 claims that Britain's booming compensation culture is driving jobs offshore and posing a severe threat to the competitiveness of UK plc. More than 70% of businesses feel that the 'have-a-go' culture is placing an unsustainable burden on industry. Most – 96% – blame the government for failing to take action to tackle the issue.

The study, of more than 500 private and public sector organisations, was conducted by Aon, the insurance broking and risk management group. It provides the first hard evidence of the wider effects of the blame culture on the UK economy. The report also undermines a recent study by the government's Better Regulation Taskforce, which claimed that the compensation culture was a myth. But 60% of employers questioned said that, far from being a myth, the growing trend by individuals and employees to litigate was hampering their business. More than 60% had seen an increase in the cost of claims they faced over the past five years and 50% had seen an increase in the number of claims. Many said that the time and money they now spend managing and fending off claims is a deterrent to employing people in the UK and is strengthening the trend for sending work offshore. The study calls for swift action by the government and demands a crackdown on advertisements by so-called 'no-win-no-fee' firms – named in the study as the driving force behind the growth in claims – and more rigorous screening by the courts to root out spurious claims.

It also calls for greater promotion by ministers of mediation and other dispute resolution procedures to ensure that the courts become the remedy of last resort. The study illustrates how other countries have dealt effectively with the problem, highlighting the example of New South Wales in Australia. Reforms instituted there are deemed by experts to have been highly successful in curbing claims. A Civil Liability Act (2002) prevents a lawyer from taking up a frivolous claim by imposing a bar on the provision of legal services unless he believes the case has a better than even chance of success. Bob Carr, the state premier, said that the number of lawsuits in the state had dropped by 25%. The CBI (Confederation of British Industry), meanwhile, has suggested creating a working fund to pay for treatment of injured employees as one alternative way to ease the burden.

Question

How does the so-called 'compensation culture' influence business costs? What remedies might be available?

Data response questions

1

Output	TC	TFC	TVC	ATC	AFC	AVC	MC
0	15	15	0			0	
1	30						
2	35						
3	39						
4	45						
5	60						

a) Complete the above table.
b) Plot the AC and the MC on graph paper. (Remember to plot the MC at the mid point, i.e. between 1 and 2, etc.)
c) Outline the relationship between total, average and marginal cost.

2 Look carefully at the data on economies of scale in car production shown in the tables below.

Car output per plant per year	Index of unit average production costs (car)
100,000	100
250,000	83
500,000	74
1,000,000	70
2,000,000	66

Optimum output per year (cars)	
Advertising	1,000,000
Sales	2,000,000
Risks	1,800,000
Finance	2,500,000
Research and Development	5,000,000

What does the data suggest about the benefits of size in the car industry?

 True/false questions

1 The shares of a private limited company can be sold on the Stock Exchange.

2 Horizontal integration is where firms amalgamate at different stages of the productive process.

3 In terms of short-run production then at least one of the factors of production is fixed.

4 An isocost line measures the various combinations of capital and labour that a firm can buy with a given expenditure.

5 When a firm's marginal costs are at a minimum, then marginal cost equals average cost.

6 Average fixed cost plus average variable cost equals average total cost.

7 Average fixed cost declines continuously as output increases.

8 Marginal cost is the increase in total cost which results from an increase in output by one unit.

9 Increasing returns to scale means that the percentage change in the firm's output is less than the percentage change in the firm's input.

10 In the long run, the resulting reduction in costs per unit as production increases in called economies of scale.

 Essay questions

Answers to asterisked questions can be found on the students' side of the Companion Website. All other answers can be found at the back of the book (pages 500–1).

1* Outline the main differences between a sole trader, partnership and a public limited company. What are the main reasons for a firm growing in size?

2 Define the terms 'isoquant' and 'isocost'. What is meant by the least-cost process of production?

3* Outline what is meant by economies and diseconomies of scale and how they affect the shape of the long-run average cost curve.

4 Using a particular industry or sector, explain what is meant by economies of scale and economies of scope. How have these affected the sector you have identified?

Theory of the firm: perfect competition and monopoly

By the end of this chapter you should be able to:

- Understand the concepts of revenue, cost and profit.
- Explain what is meant by perfect competition.
- Examine the equilibrium situations for perfect competition in the short-run and long-run time periods.
- Discuss the relevance of 'contestable market theory'.
- Explain what is meant by monopoly.
- Assess the price and output policies under monopoly, including price discrimination.
- Understand the concept of consumer surplus.

1   INTRODUCTION

An industry can be defined as a group of firms which produce close substitutes. For example, there are product similarities for a group of firms in the confectionery industry, the car manufacturing industry and the textile industry respectively. An industry is made up of a number of firms and it is possible, by summing the output of those individual firms, to obtain the output of the industry as a whole. Industries have different numbers of firms operating within them and this chapter analyses how this may affect the behaviour of firms in their price and output decisions.

The benchmark cases which form the extremes of what is called the *market structure* are *perfect competition* and *monopoly*. In perfect competition there are a large number of firms producing an identical product and there are no barriers to entry into the industry. At the opposite extreme is a 'pure' monopoly in which the firm is the industry. This situation is maintained through the imposition of barriers to entry of new firms. Monopoly is more generally defined as a situation where more than 25% of the output of an industry.

The chapter concludes by reviewing the important idea of consumer surplus and its links to price discrimination. Sometimes an industry may look more like a monopoly than perfect competition, but the firms within it may act as though it was competitive. Contestable market theory deals with this situation, where the absence of barriers to entry may result in even large firms responding in ways similar to that of the small, competitive firm.

Perfect competition and monopoly will be dealt with in this chapter, while the other types of market structure (*see* Figure 6.1) which lie between these two extremes, namely

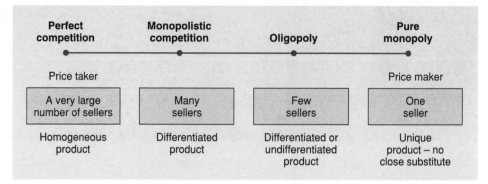

Figure 6.1 **The different types of market structure with perfect competition (a price taker) at one extreme and 'pure' monopoly (a price maker) at the other. Between these two extremes lie monopolistic competition and oligopoly.**

monopolistic competition and *oligopoly* will be discussed in Chapter 7. However, a short explanation may be useful here. *Monopolistic competition* occurs where there are a large number of firms in competition with each other, each producing a similar but not identical product. *Oligopoly*, on the other hand, is a market form in which there are a small number of large firms, each of which recognises that the actions and reactions of the other large firms can have serious implications.

2 REVENUE, COSTS AND PROFIT

Central to the theory of the firm is the concept of profit maximisation and in order to analyse the various market structures using profit maximisation a clear understanding of revenue and cost is required. The concept of *cost* was dealt with in Chapter 5 and although *total revenue* was introduced in Chapter 3, a little more detail on revenue is required.

2.1 Revenue

Table 6.1 presents a revenue schedule revealing how the demand for a product changes as the price falls.

Table 6.1 **Total, average and marginal revenue**

Quantity demanded	Price/average revenue (£)	Total revenue (£)	Marginal revenue (£)
1	30	30	30
2	25	50	20
3	20	60	10
4	15	60	0
5	10	50	−10
6	5	30	−20

Total revenue
The amount earned from the sale of a firm's product. It is calculated by multiplying the price by the quantity sold.

Average revenue
This is the revenue per unit of output sold. It is calculated by dividing total revenue by the quantity sold and it is also equal to the price of the product (when this is sold at a uniform price).

(a) *Total revenue* is the price of the product multiplied by the quantity:

$$\text{Total Revenue (TR)} = \text{Price (P)} \times \text{Quantity (q)}$$

As seen in Table 6.1, as the price of the product falls total revenue will initially increase and then decrease. This can be presented graphically (*see* Figure 6.2).

(b) *Average revenue* is total revenue divided by quantity:

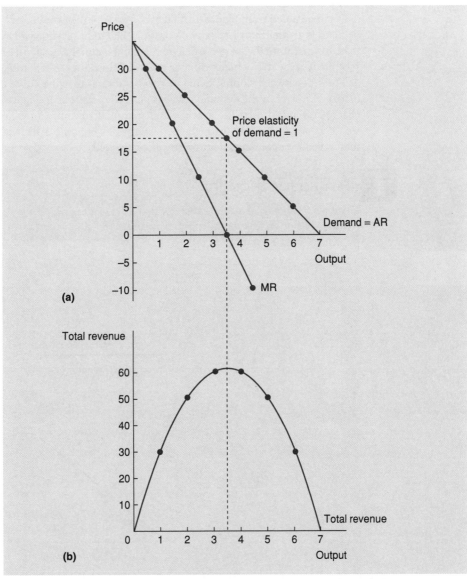

(a)

(b)

Figure 6.2 Given the demand curve it is possible to plot the total revenue (TR) curve. The marginal revenue (MR) curve shows how the TR changes when output is changed by one unit. It can be seen to lie below the demand curve. When MR is zero then TR is at a maximum.

$$\text{Average revenue (AR)} = \frac{\text{Total revenue}}{\text{Quantity}}$$

Since average revenue is also $\frac{P \times q}{q}$, average revenue is also equivalent to the price.

Marginal revenue
The change in total revenue resulting from the sale of one extra unit.

(c) *Marginal revenue* is the change in total revenue resulting from a change of one unit in the total number of units sold. For example (*see* Table 6.1), when the price falls from £25 to £20 the quantity demanded expands from 2 to 3 units, with total revenue rising by £10, which is the marginal revenue.

It can be noted from Figure 6.2 that as the price of the product falls and price elasticity of demand is greater than 1 (relatively elastic), then total revenue will rise. This will continue to be the case until the price elasticity of demand is equal to unity (*see* 3: 2) and the marginal revenue is zero, after which point, as the price continues to fall, total revenue will fall.

For a downward sloping demand curve the total revenue curve is as shown in Figure 6.2(b). However, if the demand curve is perfectly elastic as in Figure 6.3(a), then the price charged would also be the average and marginal revenue, and the total revenue curve would be a straight line through the origin as in Figure 6.3(b), with the gradient of the total revenue curve dependent on the price charged.

 ## Pause for thought 1

Using a revenue schedule like that in Table 6.1, work out why, if the price is constant, it will also be equal to both the marginal and the average revenue.

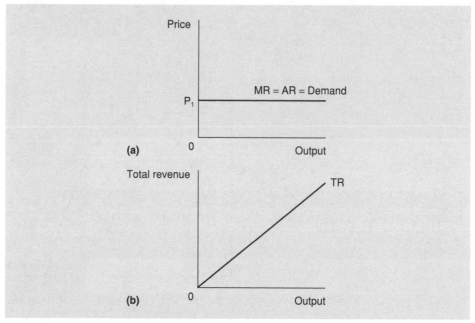

Figure 6.3 If demand is perfectly elastic, with a value of infinity, then the price charged will also be the average and marginal revenue. This will give a total revenue curve which is a straight line through the origin, the gradient of which depends on the price charged.

2.2 Profit maximisation

Profit maximisation
Refers to a situation in which the difference between total revenue and total cost is the greatest. This is also where marginal revenue equals marginal cost.

Before dealing with the concept of **profit maximisation** it is important to note a number of points from Figure 6.4.

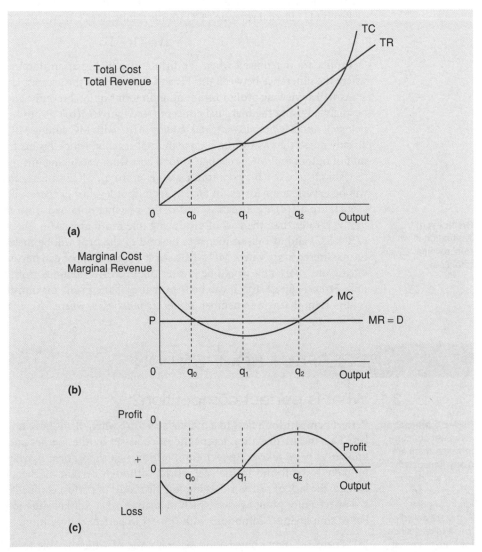

(a)

(b)

(c)

Figure 6.4 (a) Illustrates the total revenue and total cost curves. The area between the curves represents total profit or total loss, with the maximum profit being at an output of q_2 where the vertical distance between the total revenue curve and the total cost curve is at its greatest. The maximum loss is at an output of q_0. At an output of q_1 there is zero profit and this is the break even point. In (b) profit maximisation can be seen to occur where marginal cost equals marginal revenue, with marginal cost cutting marginal revenue from below. In (c) we have the profit curve. As in (a) it reveals that profits are maximised when output q_2 is produced.

(a) Figure 6.4 refers to a perfectly competitive firm. This can be seen by the fact that the demand curve in Figure 6.4(b) is perfectly elastic and the resulting total revenue curve in Figure 6.4(a) is a straight line through the origin. The demand curve will be referred to later in the chapter.

(b) Figure 6.4 relates to the short run since in Figure 6.4(a) the total cost curve intersects the vertical axis, which means that there is an element of fixed cost.

Profit (Π) is total revenue (TR) minus total cost (TC):

$$\Pi = TR - TC$$

Profits are maximised when the firm is producing at an output, q_2 in Figure 6.4(a), where the difference between the TR and TC curves is the greatest and is positive.

As well as viewing profit maximisation in terms of total revenue and total cost it can also be analysed using the marginal concept (*see* Figure 6.4(b)). Profit maximisation is where *marginal cost (MC) equals marginal revenue (MR)*, with MC cutting MR from below. We have already noted that MR is the change in total revenue which results from selling one more unit of output and MC is change in total cost from producing one more unit of output.

Using Figure 6.4(b), as output expands up to q_0, MC is greater than MR and the firm will be experiencing losses. In fact, at an output level of q_0 there will be maximum losses (*see* Figure 6.4(c)). Between q_0 and q_2 the revenue obtained from the sale of one more unit is greater than the cost of producing one more unit. At q_1 the firm is *breaking even* (TR = TC) and as output increases beyond q_1 the firm will be making profit. Profit will be maximised at q_2, where MC = MR, for if output is expanded beyond q_2, the MC of producing one more unit would be greater than the MR obtained from the sale of one extra unit. From Figure 6.4(c) it can be seen that q_2 is the profit-maximising level of output. It is important that you remember *profits are maximised where MC = MR*.

Break even
A situation in which total revenue equals total cost.

---

3 PERFECT COMPETITION

3.1 What is perfect competition?

Perfect competition
A market structure in which there are many firms, each selling an identical product at an identical price. Firms are called 'price takers' since they are too small by themselves to influence the market price. There are many buyers and no barriers to new firms entering the market. Both buyer and sellers possess perfect knowledge.

Perfect competition refers to a market structure where firms have no power over the market. This means that they accept the price as set by the market and, therefore, they are known as *price takers*. Perfect competition is a theoretical market structure which is unlikely to be found in the real world, although certain markets do tend towards it. Despite the lack of real world examples, the model of perfect competition provides a standard or reference point against which to analyse other market situations. There are a number of simplifying assumptions with respect to perfect competition.

(a) There are many buyers and sellers, none of which is able to influence the market. Each firm is very small in relation to the whole market and is, therefore, unable to affect the price charged. As stated, they are price takers which means that they face a perfectly elastic demand curve at the price set by the market (*see* Figure 6.5).

The industry's demand curve is the normal shape (Figure 6.5(a)) and the demand curve for the firm is such that if they raise their price above P_0 then the demand for their product would fall to zero.

(b) Both the producers and consumers have *perfect knowledge*; they are aware of the ruling market price, P_0. If the producer charges above P_0, consumers, given that in perfect competition there are many small firms, will purchase their products elsewhere.

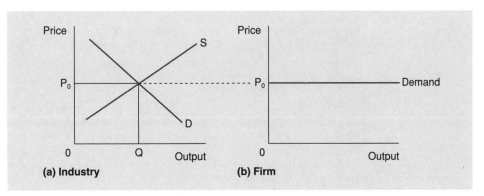

Figure 6.5 In perfect competition the price is determined by the intersection of demand and supply in the industry. In (a) this is illustrated by a price of P_0. The firm faces a price of P_0 irrespective of how much it produces. The firm's demand curve in (b) is perfectly elastic at the market price.

(c) The product is *homogeneous*, which means that each unit of the product is identical. Thus, following on from the previous assumption, buyers have no preference as to where they purchase the product – they are indifferent – hence the demand curve in Figure 6.5(b).

(d) In a perfectly competitive market there is freedom for firms to enter into and leave the industry. Existing firms cannot prevent the entry of new firms into the market.

 ## Pause for thought 2

What are the assumptions on which perfect competition is based?

3.2 Short-run equilibrium in perfect competition

Figure 6.6 gives three alternative situations for the firm in perfect competition, in the short run.

(a) *In situation (a)* the firm is profit maximising, producing an output q_1 where MC = MR. The cost curves incorporate an element of profit called *normal profit*. Normal profit is the return necessary to keep the firm in its present business. The total revenue is OP_1Aq_1 and total cost is $OCBq_1$, hence the firm is making supernormal profit of P_1ABC, represented by the shaded area.

(b) *In situation (b)* the firm is profit maximising, producing an output q_2 and covering its total cost. The firm is breaking even, making normal profit.

(c) *In situation (c)* the firm is profit maximising, producing an output of q_3. However, in this situation, the firm is actually *loss minimising*, making a loss equal to P_3DEF.

In the long run the firm in this situation will close down, although it may continue to operate in the short run if it can cover its average variable cost (AVC). The reason for this is that in the short run the firm will have to pay its fixed costs even if it produces nothing, so by producing an output of q (*see* Figure 6.7), the firm can cover its AVC, such as raw materials, wages and fuel costs, and part of its fixed costs.

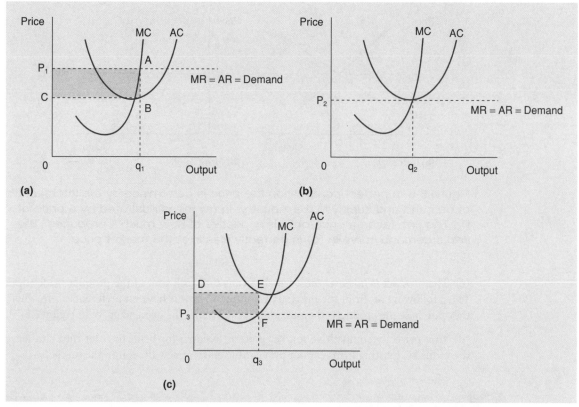

Figure 6.6 In the short run the firm's profit in perfect competition can be positive as in (a), zero (break even) as in (b), or negative as in (c). To determine whether a firm is making a profit or a loss it depends on whether the price is above or below the average cost (AC) curve.

In Figure 6.7 the firm's total revenue is represented by the area OP_0Cq and therefore the firm can cover all of its total variable costs, represented by area $OEDq$, and some of its fixed costs, represented by areas EP_0CD. The firm is not, however, able to cover P_0ABC of its fixed costs and this represents a loss to the firm. It is, therefore, worth this firm operating in the short run for its total revenue is greater than its total variable cost. If the price line were below point F, then the firm would close down in the short run for it would not even be covering the purchase of such things as raw materials and labour, i.e. the variable costs. At prices above the AVC curve the firm will equate price (marginal revenue) with marginal cost and, in fact, the marginal cost curve above the AVC curve (i.e. point F) represents the firm's supply curve. The industry supply curve (*see* Figure 6.5(a)) is derived from the horizontal summation of the individual firms' marginal cost (supply) curves.

> **!** **Pause for thought 3**
>
> *Can you explain why it is that the firm's marginal cost curve above the AVC curve (i.e. point F) in Figure 6.7 represents the supply curve of the firm in perfect competition?*

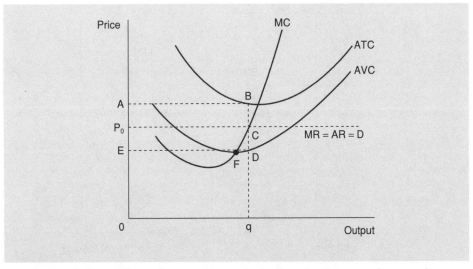

Figure 6.7 A firm will continue to operate in the short run so long as it can cover its average variable cost (AVC). This is the case for the firm illustrated. Its total revenue is represented by the area OP_0Cq, and its total cost by the area OABq. By operating, however, it is covering its total variable costs, given by area OEDq and part of its total fixed costs, given by area EP_0CD. The firm is still making a loss of area P_0ABC, but this is less than the loss would be if the firm did not operate at all. If the firm ceased operating the loss would be EABD.

3.3 Long-run equilibrium in perfect competition

In the long run a firm such as that in Figure 6.6(c) would close down, whereas a firm such as that in Figure 6.6(b) would continue to operate since it is breaking even. The existence of supernormal profit, as in Figure 6.6(a), would attract new firms into the industry since profits act as a 'signal' in a competitive market for other firms to enter the industry. The entry of new firms into the industry would result in a shift in the industry's supply curve to the right and the price would be forced down until all the firms in the industry were earning normal profit.

In the long-run equilibrium each firm will be operating at the minimum point on both their short-run and long-run average cost curves, obtaining the full economies of scale (*see* Chapter 5, Section 10.4). Figure 6.8 can be used to see how this occurs. The firm in Figure 6.8(a) is of a size such that its short-run average and marginal cost curves are $SATC_1$ and SMC_1 respectively. With a market price of P_1 and an output of q_1 the firm is making super-normal profit equal to the shaded area. This encourages the firm to increase its capacity, allowing it to move on to a lower average and marginal cost curve such as $SATC_2$ and SMC_2 in order to obtain economies of scale. In addition, the existence of this supernormal profit will encourage new firms to enter the industry. This will lead to an increase in the industry supply, indicated by a shift in the supply curve to the right from S_1 to S_2 in Figure 6.8(b). Hence the market price will fall, until the long-run equilibrium price of P_2 and output Q_2 is reached.

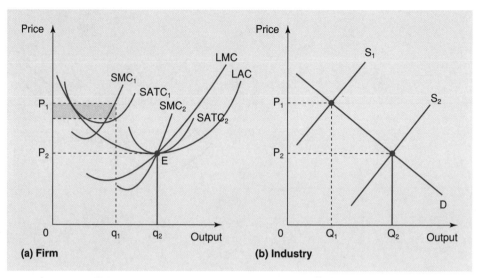

Figure 6.8 In the long run as the firms expand their output, supply will increase and the price will fall. The long-run equilibrium occurs where the price is P_2 and each firm is operating at point E. This is at the lowest point on the firm's long-run average cost curve.

In terms of the individual firm illustrated in Figure 6.8(a), its capacity has increased such that the $SATC_2$ and SMC_2 curves are the new short-run average and marginal cost curves. The firm is now operating at the lowest point on both its short-run and long-run average cost curves after obtaining the full economies of scale. The firm will be in *long-run equilibrium*, producing an output of q_2 with average costs at their minimum level of E. Any increase or decrease in output from q_2 would result in the firm making a loss.

3.4 Allocative and productive efficiency

If long-run equilibrium could be achieved in a perfectly competitive market, that would have important implications for the economy. For example, in economics a fundamental issue for each firm is the optimal use of its scarce resources and that is achieved in a perfectly competitive market. We saw in Figure 6.8(a) that in the long run a perfectly competitive firm will operate where marginal cost equals the price charged, which is point E, the lowest point on the long-run average cost curve. In perfect competition consumers are charged a price which is exactly equal to what it costs the firm to produce the extra or marginal unit of output, and as such *allocative efficiency* is said to occur. In other words, because price is equal to marginal cost the market is said to have achieved allocative efficiency.

Equally, since the firm is operating at the lowest point on the long-run average cost curve, so obtaining all the available economies of scale, the firm is said to be *productively efficient*. This is the case since the cost per unit of production in the long run is as low as is technically possible. Overall, therefore, a perfectly competitive market structure produces a situation in which both allocative and productive efficiency are achieved.

Chapter 17 takes these issues of allocative and productive efficiency further in the context of the EU competition authorities.

Pause for thought 4

Using examples of specific industries, distinguish between the short- and long-run time periods.

3.5 Contestable market theory

Contestable market theory
Where few barriers to entry exist and firms act and react as though they were in a competitive industry.

Barriers to entry
Impediments, either legal or natural, protecting firms from competition from potential entrants into a market.

The idea of *contestable markets* broadens the application of competitive behaviour beyond the strict conditions needed for perfect competition. In other words, instead of regarding competitive behaviour as existing only in the perfectly competitive market structure, it could be exhibited in any market structure that was contestable. Generally speaking, the fewer the barriers to entry into a market, the more contestable that market. In this sense some monopoly and oligopoly markets could be regarded as contestable.

The absence of entry barriers increases the *threat* of new firms entering the market. It is this threat which is assumed to check any tendency by incumbent (existing) firms to raise prices substantially above average costs and thereby earn supernormal profit.

(For further discussion on contestable markets *see* Chapter 7, Section 6.)

Mini Case Study 6.1

Perfect competition and the Internet

It has been argued in recent years that the explosive growth of retailing on the Internet has made this form of retailing resemble an almost perfectly competitive market. Consumers appear to have perfect information about both prices and products at their fingertips by merely logging onto the Net in search of the best deals. In a perfectly competitive market products are identical; there are a large number of buyers and sellers; there are no search costs; customers are perfectly informed; there is free entry into and exit out of the industry, and profit margins would be 'normal' in the long run.

The Internet does seem to have some of these attributes of a perfect market. For example, studies have shown that online retailers tend to be cheaper than conventional retailers and that they adjust prices more finely and more often. The Internet has also led to the growth of people who use 'shopbots', i.e. computer programmes that search rapidly over many websites for the best deal. These provide customers with a more complete knowledge of the market, hence minimising search costs. In addition, entry and exit from Internet sites is relatively easy for sellers so there are no obvious barriers to entry. Under these conditions one would expect prices for the same or similar products to be virtually identical on the Internet, as under perfect competition.

However, a closer study of the Internet retail market shows that there may still be important elements of imperfection in the market. Studies in the US by the Sloan School of Management have shown that there is still an element of price dispersion (i.e. difference between the highest and lowest prices for a given product or service) in the Internet retail market. This would tend to indicate that the market is inefficient, with some retailers still being able to charge more than others. For example, price dispersion for identical books, CDs and software amongst different online retailers can differ by as much as 33% and 25% respectively. Researchers at the Wharton School in Pennsylvania found that airline tickets from online travel agents differed by an average of 28%!

Source: *Economics for Business and Management*, Griffiths and Wall (FT/Prentice Hall, 2005)

Questions

1 *Why does a degree of price dispersion suggest that we do not have a perfect market?*

2 *Which factors might explain why various retailers can still charge different prices for the same product over the Internet, despite the claim that it resembles a perfect market?*

Answers to questions can be found on the students' side of the Companion Website.

4 MONOPOLY

4.1 What is monopoly?

Monopoly
An industry where more than 25% of the output is in the hands of a single firm or group of linked firms – see also 'pure' monopoly.

Pure monopoly
An industry in which there is one supplier of the product. Barriers to entry protect the supplier from new firms entering the market and obtaining market share.

Whereas in perfect competition there are many sellers of an identical product, with a 'pure' monopoly there is a single seller of a product for which there is no close substitute. The firm is the industry and, unlike a perfectly competitive firm which is a price taker, a monopolist is a *price maker*. This means that the demand curve is downward sloping from left to right as in Figure 6.9.

Since the demand curve (average revenue curve) is downward sloping, marginal revenue must be less than the average revenue. This was explained earlier in Section 2. The monopoly diagram is given in Figure 6.9, with marginal revenue such that it cuts the horizontal axis halfway between the origin and where the average revenue curve cuts the

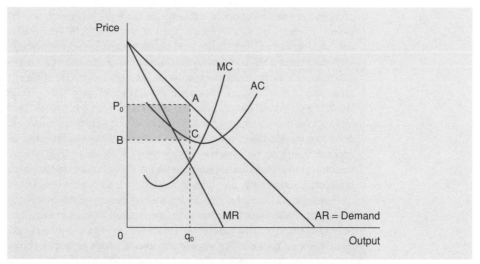

Figure 6.9 A profit maximising monopolist will operate where marginal cost equals marginal revenue. This occurs at a price of P_0 and an output of q_0. The monopoly profit is represented by the shaded area BP_0AC.

horizontal axis. The monopolist profit maximises where marginal cost equals marginal revenue. The price charged is P_0 and an output of q_0 is produced, and this results in the supernormal profit of the shaded area. Total revenue is equal to OP_0Aq_0 and the total cost $OBCq_0$, giving supernormal profit as stated of BP_0AC. As with a perfectly competitive firm, the monopolist must make sure that it is covering its average variable cost in the short run.

In the long run the monopolist can continue to earn supernormal profit and the excess of price over marginal cost is an indication of the firm's monopoly power. For supernormal profit to be earned in the long run it is necessary for there to be *barriers to entry* into the industry.

Pause for thought 5

Using actual industries as examples, suggest some barriers to entry in those industries.

4.2 Barriers to entry

There are a number of reasons why monopolists are able to earn supernormal profit in the long run:

(a) The monopolist may have sole ownership of a natural resource. Control over, for example, the supply of a raw material will create an effective barrier to entry.

(b) The monopoly may have been created by the state, making it a legal monopoly.

(c) With either a patent or copyright the firm will have the sole right to produce a particular good or service.

(d) The productive process may be such that a high level of output is required to obtain the full economies of scale. With this being the case, new firms considering entry into the market will face high production costs and will, therefore, find it difficult to compete.

Mini Case Study 6.2

Car barriers

Competition Commission reports in the past few years have pointed to barriers in the car market which have raised prices higher. In fact, car buyers have been paying on average £1,100 too much for new models as a result of a complex monopoly operating in Britain's new car market.

British car buyers have, over recent years, had to pay 10% to 12% more than those in France, Germany and Italy for the same models.

The Competition Commission has blamed the high prices squarely on the monopolies operated in favour of 17 suppliers, which together accounted for 94% of new car sales in Britain last year. The Commission has focused on the system of car distribution to main dealerships, known as 'selective and exclusive distribution'. Dealers have been specifically deterred from obtaining cheaper models from other European states and

→

were not allowed to sell cars from more than one company on the same premises. So BMW dealers could not, for example, also offer new Mercedes models for sale.

The Commission found conclusively that the system of franchises and the restrictions placed on the dealerships have operated 'against the public interest' and that the overall effect of the suppliers' practices has been to raise the UK price of new cars sold to private customers. This system has been prevented from operating in the UK since 2002. The Commission has also stated that car companies operate a cartel system on price – suppliers appear to set their list prices at about the same level of their competitors – and compete instead on marketing, temporary offers, product quality or specifications.

Questions

1 *What practices suggest that the new car market acts as a monopoly?*

2 *What are the consequences of being a monopoly market?*

Answers to questions can be found at the back of the book (page 501).

4.3 Advantages of a monopoly

There are a number of advantages with a monopoly:

(a) Being a large producer of a particular product may mean that the monopolist can benefit from *economies of scale* (*see* Chapter 5, Section 10.4) which are not possible under perfect competition. In this case the monopolist's marginal cost curve could be lower than the supply curve obtained under perfect competition. This is shown in Figure 6.10 where the monopoly equates MC with MR and produces q_m at a price of P_m.

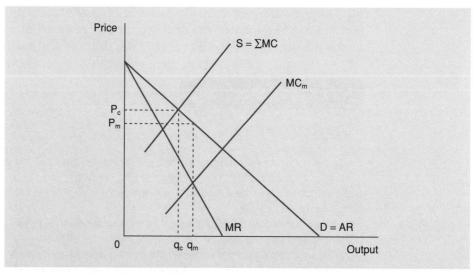

Figure 6.10 It may be the case that the monopolist's marginal cost curve is lower than that of a competitive industry. As such, the monopolist's price P_m is lower than that obtained under perfect competition, P_c, whereas the quantity produced is higher, q_m as opposed to q_c.

Under perfect competition the supply curve is the summation of the individual firms' MC curves and the industry will equate supply and demand, producing an output of q_c at a price of P_c. It is, therefore, the case that economies of scale could be so large that the output is higher and the price lower under monopoly than under a perfectly competitive industry.

(b) The fact that monopolies earn supernormal profit in the long run means that they can allocate resources to research and development in order to improve the quality of the product, and therefore benefit society.

(c) The existence of long-term supernormal profit under a monopoly situation may mean that they can innovate, not only improving existing products but also introducing new products.

4.4 Disadvantages of a monopoly

There are a number of reasons why a monopoly could be seen as operating against the *public interest*:

(a) There could be an imaginary situation in which a perfectly competitive industry comprising many small firms is taken over by a profit maximising monopolist. This can be analysed by referring to Figure 6.11 in which D is the demand curve for the industry and S_c is the supply curve in perfect competition obtained by the summation of individual firms' marginal cost (MC) curves.

In the perfectly competitive situation the quantity produced is q_c and the price charged by each firm is P_c. If the perfectly competitive industry was then taken over by a single firm, i.e. a monopolist with identical cost and demand conditions, then the monopolist would equate MC and MR in order to profit maximise. The perfectly competitive industry's supply curve would then become the monopolist's MC curve (MC_m) and the monopolist would thus reduce its output level to q_m and increase its price to P_m.

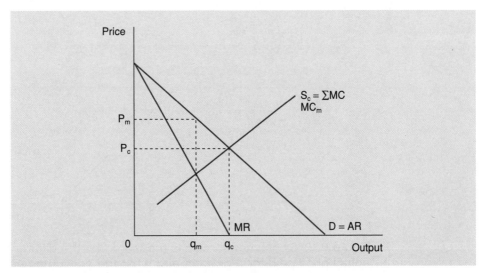

Figure 6.11 When a perfectly competitive industry is taken over by a monopolist, with costs unchanged, then the price increases from P_c to P_m and the quantity produced reduces from q_c to q_m.

(b) Monopolies are able to earn above normal profit in the long run because of the barriers to entry. This represents a redistribution of income from the consumer to the producer which can be criticised on equity grounds.

(c) Since there are barriers to entry, monopolies face no pressure from competition and because of this the quality of the product may decline. This is not the case with perfectly competitive markets where competition forces firms to be efficient, operating at the lowest point on the average cost curve in the long run.

5 PRICE DISCRIMINATION

Price discrimination
A practice used of charging certain consumers a higher price than others for an identical good or service.

So far we have assumed that the monopolist charges only one price; however, it is possible for a monopolist to charge different prices in separate markets and to obtain some of the consumer surplus which would otherwise go to the buyer of the product. The markets can be separated *geographically*, as with an exporter charging different prices for the home and overseas market, or on the basis of *time*, as with car parking space. Car parking spaces can be charged differently depending on short stay or long stay.

5.1 Consumer surplus

Consumer surplus
The difference between the value the consumer places on a product and the price actually paid.

In terms of Figure 6.12 the market price of the product is P_0 at which q_0 units would be sold. However, certain individuals would have been willing to pay a price for the product in excess of P_0. Some, in fact, would have been willing to pay a price as high as P_1, and the shaded area under the demand curve and above the price is the **consumer surplus** (area ABC).

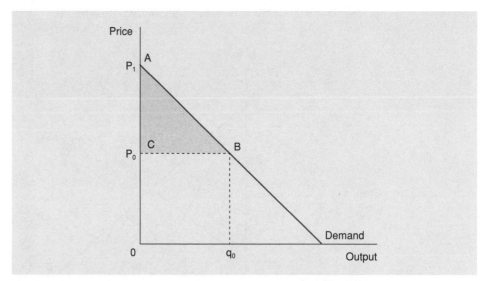

Figure 6.12 Consumer surplus is measured by the difference between the actual price paid for a product and what the consumer would have been willing to pay. In the figure certain consumers would be willing to pay a price as high as P_1 whereas the price actually paid is P_0, thus consumer surplus is represented by the area ABC.

Pause for thought 6

Use your own experiences and preferences to explain the idea of consumer surplus.

5.2 First degree price discrimination

First degree price discrimination
Sometimes called perfect price discrimination, where the firm sells each unit of a product separately, charging the highest price each consumer is willing to pay.

First degree price discrimination is sometimes called *perfect price discrimination* and involves the monopolist in selling each unit of the product separately, charging the highest price each consumer is willing to pay.

In Figure 6.13, assuming constant marginal cost (MC), the profit maximising monopolist (before perfect price discrimination) would charge a price of P_m and produce an output q_m. By perfect price discrimination the consumer willing to pay the highest price for the product could be charged P_1. Having sold this unit the second unit could be sold for a slightly lower price and so on. The producer would thus price down the demand curve, which in fact becomes the marginal revenue curve. The marginal revenue of the last unit is the price that unit is sold for. As such, the monopolist will continue to produce up to point E with a quantity of q_1 being sold. The result is that through perfect price discrimination the monopolist is able to extract the entire consumer surplus. Perfect price discrimination is not common in the real world, not least because the monopolist requires precise information about the shape of the consumers' demand curve in order to establish just how much they are prepared to pay.

 Pause for thought 7

What is meant by first degree price discrimination?

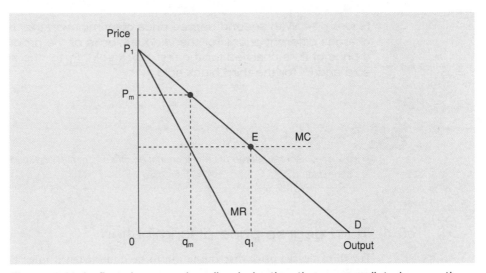

Figure 6.13 In first degree price discrimination the monopolist charges the consumer the highest price they are prepared to pay for each unit sold. The result is that the entire consumer surplus is obtained by the monopolist.

5.3 Second degree price discrimination

Second degree price discrimination
A situation in which a firm charges the consumer a certain amount for the first number of units purchased, but a smaller amount for the next number of units purchased and so on.

Third degree price discrimination
A situation in which the firm divides consumers into specific groups and charges each group a different price for the same product.

Second degree price discrimination involves charging a *uniform* price per unit for a specific quantity of the product consumed, a lower price per unit for the next *block* consumed and so on.

Second degree price discrimination is illustrated in Figure 6.14, with the first block up to a quantity q_1 being sold for a price P_1, the second block from q_1 to q_2 being sold for a price of P_2 and the third block q_2 to q_3 being sold for a price of P_3. For this reason it is sometimes called *block pricing*. By this form of price discrimination the monopolist is able to extract some but not all of the consumer's surplus.

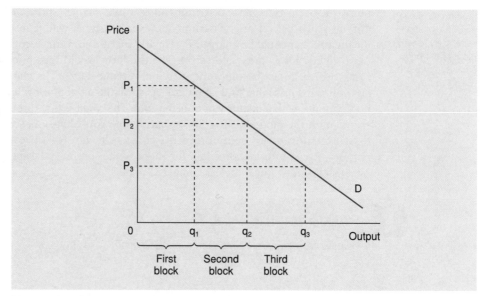

Figure 6.14 With second degree price discrimination the monopolist charges different prices for the various blocks of the product sold. Thus a price of P_1 is charged for the first block sold, P_2 for the second block sold and P_3 for the third block sold.

 ### Pause for thought 8

How does second degree price discrimination differ from first and third degree price discrimination?

5.4 Third degree price discrimination

For third degree price discrimination to be undertaken it must be both possible and profitable to segment the market into two or more groups of consumers, with a different price charged to each group.

To be possible, the firm must be able to prevent consumers moving from the higher priced market segment to the lower priced market segment. In other words, there must be 'barriers' separating the respective market segments. Such barriers could include geo-graphical distance (domestic/overseas markets), time (peak/off-peak), personal iden-tification (young/old), etc.

To be profitable, the price elasticity of demand must be different in each separate market segment.

Figure 6.15 outlines the situation of third degree price discrimination.

In Figure 6.15 we assume that the large oligopoly firm produces in one location and sells its output to two separate markets, A and B, with different price elasticities of demand in each market. Market B has a much higher price elasticity of demand than Market A. The corresponding *total market* marginal and average revenue curves are obtained by summing horizontally the *individual market* marginal and average revenue curves.

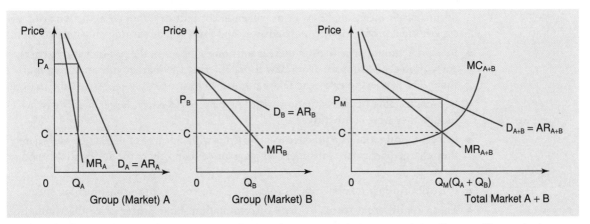

Figure 6.15 **When price elasticity is different in two market segments, the profit maximiser will charge a higher price in that market when demand is less elastic.**

With production in a single location there is one MC curve, giving the overall profit maximising output of Q_M, which might be sold at a single price P_M. However, total profit can, in this situation, be raised by selling this output at a different price to each group (market).

The profit maximising condition is that MC for whole output must equal MR in each separate market:

$$\text{i.e. } MC_{A+B} = MR_A = MR_B$$

In Figure 6.15 total output Q_M will be allocated so that Q_A goes to group (market) A and Q_B to group (market) B, resulting in the respective prices P_A and P_B.

Any other allocation of total output Q_M must reduce total revenue and therefore, with unchanged costs, reduce total profit.

We can illustrate this by considering a single unit reallocation from market A to market B. The addition to total revenue (MR_B) of this unit when sold in market B is less than C, whereas the loss to total revenue (MR_A) of not selling this unit in market A is C. The overall change in total revenue from this unit reallocation is clearly negative, which, with total costs unchanged, must reduce total profit.

As we can see from Figure 6.15 the implications of third degree price discrimination is a higher price in the market with lowest price elasticity of demand ($P_A > P_B$).

KEY POINTS

- Total revenue is the amount earned from the sale of a firm's product (calculated by multiplying the price by the quantity sold). Average revenue is the revenue per unit of output sold (calculated by dividing total revenue by the quantity sold). Marginal revenue is the additional revenue obtained from the sale of one extra unit.

- Profit maximisation occurs at the output for which marginal revenue equals marginal cost. It also occurs at the output for which the difference between total revenue and total cost is the greatest.

- A perfectly competitive market structure is one in which there are many firms selling an identical product with many buyers and no barriers to entry. Each firm is a 'price taker', assuming it can sell all it produces at the going market price. The existence of super-normal profit means that new firms will enter the industry, though in the long run any supernormal profit will be competed away and firms will be earning only normal profit.

- In a 'pure' monopoly situation there is only one supplier of the product and barriers to entry protect the supplier from new firms entering the market and obtaining market share. The barriers to entry can take a number of forms most notably legal and natural.

- In a contestable market situation with few barriers to entry, larger firms may act as though they were competitive.

- Price discrimination is a practice used by firms with a degree of market power whereby they charge particular consumers a higher price than others for an identical good or service.

- Price discrimination allows firms to capture some or all of the consumer surplus.

- There are different forms of price discrimination. First degree price discrimination occurs where a firm sells each unit of a product separately, charging the highest price each consumer is willing to pay. Second degree price discrimination occurs where a firm charges the consumer a certain amount for the first number of units purchased, a lower amount for the next number of units purchased and so on. Third degree price discrimination occurs where the firm divides consumers into specific groups and charges each group a different price for the same product.

Further reading

Griffiths, A. and Wall, S. (2005) *Economics for Business and Management*, FT/Prentice Hall, Chapter 6.

Heather, K. (2004) *Economics Theory in Action*, 4th edition, FT/Prentice Hall, Chapters 6 and 7.

Parkin, M., Powell, M. and Matthews, K. (2005) *Economics*, 6th edition, FT/Prentice Hall, Chapters 11 and 12.

Sloman, J. (2006) *Economics*, 6th edition, FT/Prentice Hall, Chapter 6.

Web references

The following website contains a wide range of company data:

http://bized.ac.uk
www.dti.gov.uk
www.eubusiness.com

Companies House: **http://www.companieshouse.gov.uk/** The place for getting information on all English and Welsh companies.

Chinese business activity: **www.cbbc.org**
Japanese business activity: **www.jetro.org**
EU business activity: **www.euromonitor.com**

PROGRESS AND REVIEW QUESTIONS

Answers to most questions can be found at the back of the book (pages 501–2). Answers to asterisked questions can be found on the students' side of the Companion Website.

Multiple-choice questions

1 If marginal revenue is zero, total revenue is:

a) at its maximum
b) at its minimum
c) rising
d) falling
e) also zero.

2 Profit maximisation is where:

a) average revenue equals average cost
b) marginal revenue equals marginal cost
c) total revenue equals total cost
d) marginal cost equals average cost
e) none of the above.

3

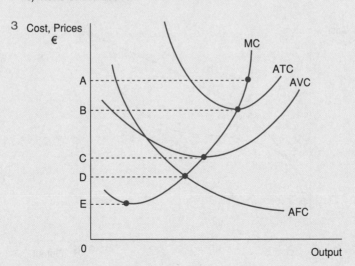

The diagram above shows the cost curves for a firm operating under perfect competition with A to E referring to the prices charged. The price below which the firm would close down in the short run is:

a) A
b) B
c) C
d) D
e) E

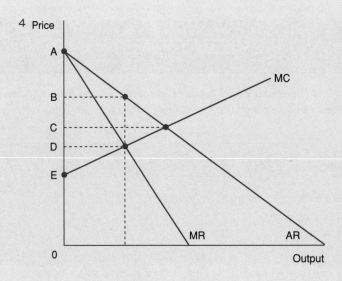

In the diagram above the price charged by a profit maximising monopolist is:

a) A
b) B
c) C
d) D
e) E

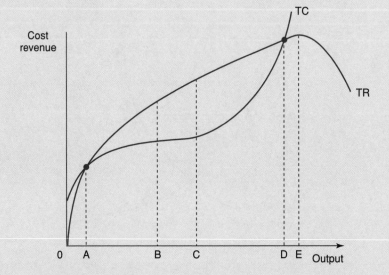

5 In terms of the diagram above, total revenue is at a maximum at:

   a) A
   b) B
   c) C
   d) D
   e) E

6 In terms of the diagram above, profit maximisation is at:

   a) A
   b) B
   c) C
   d) D
   e) E

7 In terms of the diagram above, the firm breaks even at:

   a) A and B
   b) C only
   c) A and D
   d) E only
   e) none of the above.

8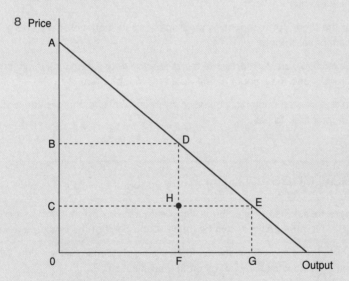

   In the above diagram an increase in consumer surplus brought about by a reduction in the price of the product from 0B to 0C is:

   a) ABD
   b) BCED
   c) DHE
   d) CBDH
   e) ACE

9 If a firm undertakes perfect price discrimination it means that it will:

   a) minimise total costs
   b) produce where marginal cost equals the lowest price charged

c) be making normal profit

d) charge only one price for the product

e) none of the above.

True/false questions

1 Total revenue is the price of a product multiplied by the quantity sold.

2 Marginal revenue is calculated by dividing total revenue by quantity sold.

3 A firm's profits are maximised where marginal revenue equals marginal cost, with marginal cost cutting marginal revenue from below.

4 In perfect competition each firm faces a perfectly elastic demand curve.

5 In perfect competition a firm will continue to operate in the short run so long as it is covering its fixed costs.

6 In perfect competition in the long run each firm will be making normal profit.

7 Monopoly operators are able to make supernormal profit in the long run because of barriers to entry.

8 In the theory of monopoly a profit maximising monopolist will charge the lowest price it can for its product.

9 Consumer surplus represents the difference between the value an individual places on a product and the amount actually paid for that product.

10 In first degree price discrimination each individual is charged the maximum amount they are prepared to pay.

Essay questions

Answers to asterisked questions can be found on the students' side of the Companion Website. All other answers can be found at the back of the book (page 502).

1* Outline the relationship between total, average and marginal revenue. With the use of a diagram, outline what is meant by profit maximisation.

2 Why is a firm in a perfectly competitive market said to be a 'price taker'? Distinguish between the short-run and long-run equilibrium in perfect competition.

3* Why is it possible for a monopolist to earn supernormal profit in the long run?

4 Outline the assumptions necessary for price discrimination to take place. Distinguish between first, second and third degree price discrimination.

Theory of the firm: monopolistic competition and oligopoly

By the end of this chapter you will be able to:

- Understand what is meant by monopolistic competition.
- Explain the equilibrium situation for monopolistic competition in the short run and long run.
- Understand what is meant by oligopoly.
- Explain how the kinked demand curve is derived.
- Assess price and non-price competition under oligopoly where no collusion exists.
- Outline the methods of collusion and assess their implications.
- Explain what is meant by game theory and the use of payoff matrices.

1 INTRODUCTION

Monopolistic competition
Refers to market structure in which there are a large number of small firms all competing with each other producing goods and services which are slightly differentiated from their competitors.

Chapter 6 dealt with the theories of perfect competition and monopoly, with the perfectly competitive firm seen as a 'price taker' and the monopolist a 'price maker'. This chapter deals with the theories of monopolistic competition and oligopoly, where firms are able to exercise a degree of control over the prices they charge.

In *monopolistic competition* there are many firms producing slightly different products and, although they are in competition with each other, their product is unique in some way, thereby giving them a certain degree of monopoly power. *Oligopolistic* markets are dominated by few large firms which are *interdependent*, closely monitoring their competitors' actions and responding accordingly.

2 MONOPOLISTIC COMPETITION

2.1 What is monopolistic competition?

The theory of **monopolistic competition** incorporates features of both perfect competition and monopoly. As with perfect competition there are a large number of firms in the market and there is freedom of entry into the industry. However, unlike perfect competition each firm produces goods and services which are slightly different from those of their

Product differentiation
The way in which a firm makes its goods or services slightly different from that of the firms it competes with.

competitors. The existence of such *product differentiation* means that firms have a certain degree of monopoly power, so that if they raise their price they do not lose all of their customers, even though they produce products which are close substitutes. This is because some consumers prefer their (differentiated) product, even at a higher price. If they lower their price, they do not gain all those who currently buy the (now more expensive) rival products because some consumers prefer these (differentiated) rival products. The result is a downward sloping demand curve, albeit a relatively elastic demand curve. Thus a monopolistically competitive firm is *not* a price taker facing a perfectly elastic demand curve at the going market price. Product differentiation can be reinforced through advertising which produces an element of *brand loyalty*.

 Pause for thought 1

Can you give examples of industries which might be described as monopolistic competition?

2.2 Short-run equilibrium in monopolistic competition

Assuming the monopolistically competitive firm is a profit maximiser, the *short-run equilibrium* is similar to that of a monopoly. The only difference here is that the demand curve is relatively more elastic and each firm is producing only a small proportion of the overall market output. As previously explained (*see* 6: **2.2**), profit maximisation occurs where marginal cost equals marginal revenue, and in Figure 7.1 the firm is in a profit maximising equilibrium where it is producing an output of q_0 which it sells at a price of P_0. Supernormal profit is then given by the shaded area P_0ABC.

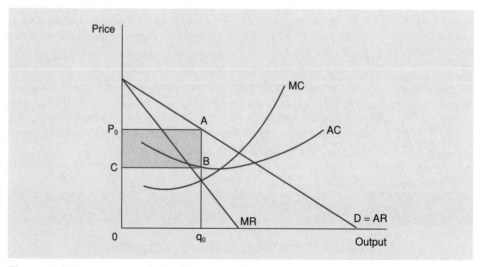

Figure 7.1 The monopolistically competitive firm faces a downward sloping demand curve. It maximises its profits by producing an output of q_0 and charging a price of P_0. The figure illustrates the short-run profit maximising situation, with supernormal profit represented by the shaded area.

2.3 Long-run equilibrium in monopolistic competition

Given the assumption of freedom of entry into the industry, the existence of supernormal profit will act as an incentive for new firms to enter the industry. We do *not* treat this as an increase in supply, where more of an identical product is supplied at any given price. This is because the product is not identical from the different producers. Rather we treat the entry of new firms as capturing some consumers who previously bought the (differentiated) product of existing firms. This will result in a shift in the firm's demand (average revenue) curve to the left, which will also lead to a shift in the associated marginal revenue curve to the left.

The supernormal profit will be competed away until, in the long run, the firm will be earning normal profit and producing where price (average revenue) equals average cost, with the firm breaking even (*see* Figure 7.2). At this point there will be no further entry into the industry.

Note that in equilibrium the average cost curve is tangential to the demand curve at point E which is above the minimum point on the average cost curve. Although in the long run firms are making normal profit, this does not mean that the consumer obtains the same benefit from monopolistically competitive firms as they do from perfectly competitive firms. For example, here, unlike long-run perfect competition, the firm is producing above the minimum point on the average cost curve so the consumer is having to pay a higher price than that paid in perfect competition in the long run. Under monopolistic competition, however, the consumer enjoys a greater variety of products and therefore the higher price may, to some extent, reflect the consumer's desire for a wider choice.

In Figure 7.2 the firm is operating on the downward sloping section of its average cost curve at an output of q_0. Average cost is at a minimum denoted by point F, at an output

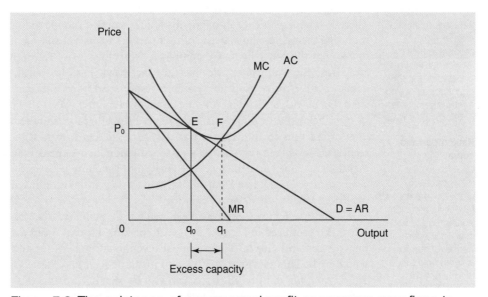

Figure 7.2 The existence of supernormal profit encourages new firms to enter the industry. The result is a shift of the firm's demand and marginal revenue curves to the left, which leads to an erosion of their supernormal profit. In the long run the firm will produce an output of q_0 and charge a price of P_0, making normal profit. At this point there is no further entry of firms into the industry.

of q_1. In monopolistic competition, firms are not, therefore, operating at the point of *full productive efficiency*, in fact they are operating with spare or excess capacity. In Figure 7.2 the difference between q_0 and q_1 is this *excess capacity*.

3 OLIGOPOLY: NON-COLLUSIVE

Here we consider price and non-price competition by firms in **oligopoly** markets which do not collude with one another, i.e. do not get together to 'fix' the market.

3.1 What is oligopoly?

Oligopoly refers to a situation where a few firms dominate the market, often producing a large number of branded products. Each firm is of a sufficiently large size that the decision taken by one firm will affect the decisions taken by the other firms in the market. The firms are, therefore, *mutually dependent* and any theory of oligopoly needs to take this into account.

3.2 The kinked demand curve and price rigidity

Oligopoly
Refers to a market structure in which there are a small number of firms which dominate the industry. In such a market, firms recognise their interdependence and are aware that their actions are likely to encourage counter-action by their rivals.

Kinked demand curve
Used to explain how, in oligopolistic markets where a few firms dominate, prices tend to be stable for substantial periods, i.e. the price is often rigid (price rigidity or price stability).

Figure 7.3 relates to a single firm operating in an oligopolistic market where there are several producers of similar products. The aim of the **kinked demand curve**, developed by Paul Sweezy in 1939, was to explain price stability and the absence of price warfare in oligopolistic markets.

Using Figure 7.3(a), suppose the oligopolist is producing an output q_0 at a price of P_0. There is interdependence in oligopolistic markets and the individual firm believes that if they *raise* their price above P_0 the other firms in the market will not follow. The reason for this is that the other firms are content to keep their price fixed and attract consumers away from the firm whose price has now increased. The oligopolist, therefore, expects its demand curve to be relatively elastic in response to a price increase, hence the demand curve D_1D_1, with a marginal revenue curve of MR_1. If, however, the individual firm *lowers* its price below P_0 the oligopolist believes that the other firms in the market will also lower their prices, thus creating a price war. The firm, therefore, expects the demand curve to be relatively inelastic in response to a price reduction, hence the demand curve D_2D_2, with a marginal revenue curve of MR_2. The oligopolist therefore believes that it is facing a *kinked demand curve* D_1AD_2 (*see* Figure 7.3(a) and there is little or no incentive to raise or lower the price, which is *stable* or *sticky* at P_0.

We can use Figure 7.3(b) to explain this price stability. The demand curve of Figure 7.3(a) is reproduced in Figure 7.3(b) with the kink at point A representing the junction of the two demand curves. The marginal revenue curve faced by the oligopolist is represented by BCDE (*see* Figure 7.3(b)) and it can be seen that there is a *discontinuity* of CD. The *discontinuity* in the MR curve can also be seen as a reason why the price tends to be stable at P_0. Given that the oligopolist is a profit maximiser, producing where marginal cost (MC) equals marginal revenue (MR) at point D, it follows that MC can increase (shift upwards) up to MC_1 without there being any effect on the price charged. It is only when marginal cost increases above MC_1 that there is a need for the profit maximising firm to raise the price of the product.

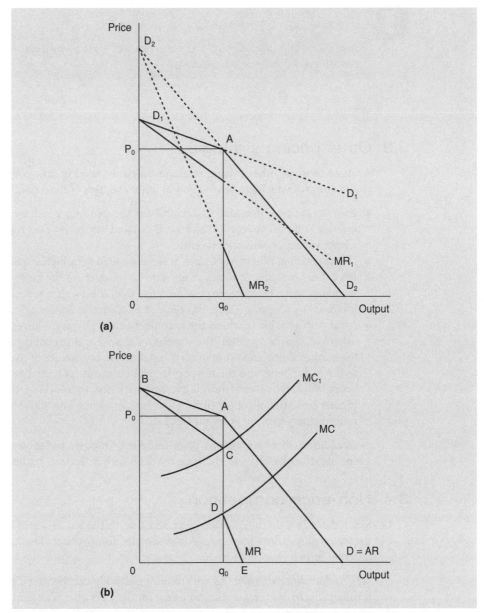

Figure 7.3 The oligopolist believes it has a kinked demand curve illustrated by BAD in (b). This is derived from two demand curves D_1 and D_2 illustrated in (a). If the firm raises its price above P_0 it perceives its demand curve as being relatively elastic with the other firms unwilling to match the price increase. If, however, the firm lowers its price below P_0, then demand is perceived as being less elastic since the oligopolist believes that the other firms in the market will also lower their price. Since the demand curve is kinked it means that the marginal revenue curve has a discontinuity illustrated by CD in (b). It follows that the marginal cost can rise from MC to MC_1 without there being any change in the profit maximising price and output of the firm.

Pause for thought 2

Draw your own kinked demand curve and use it to explain why it is that oligopolistic markets may experience price stability.

3.3 Other pricing strategies

A whole range of other pricing strategies might be used in non-collusive oligopoly situations, some of which are touched on in other chapters of this book.

- *Price elasticity of demand.* If demand for the product is relatively inelastic, a price increase will raise revenue. However, if demand for the product is relatively elastic then a price reduction will raise revenue.
- *Prestige pricing.* Where higher prices are associated with higher quality ('Veblen effect').
- *Price discrimination.* If demand for a given product can be broken down into market segments, some being more price sensitive than others, then revenue and profits can be increased by charging a different price in each market segment.
- *Limit pricing.* This is where the incumbent firm charges a lower price than it might otherwise charge to 'limit' the chances of a new, and probably smaller firm, to enter the market. Being smaller it will not benefit from economies of scale to the same extent as the incumbent, and the lower price will reduce its potential average profit (average profit = average revenue minus average cost). Strictly speaking, the 'limit price' is the highest price the oligopoly firm believes it can charge and still avoid encouraging new (and smaller) firms to enter the market.

In addition, there are various 'price-leadership' models, but these are often regarded as a type of tacit collusion and are therefore dealt with in Section 4.3 below.

3.4 Non-price competition

Since there is a threat of price wars and due to the existence of effective alternative strategies, oligopolists may engage in non-price competition. This can take a number of different forms:

(a) *Product differentiation.* As with monopolistically competitive firms oligopolists can, through advertising, create a brand image for their product. The firm may offer a particular after-sales service or package the product in a particular way.

(b) *Promotional offers.* These can take a number of different forms such as 'buy two and get one free', '20% extra free', or free gifts such as drinking glasses – commonly used by petrol companies.

Pause for thought 3

Can you think of any other types of non-price competition?

4 OLIGOPOLY: COLLUSION

Collusion
In terms of oligopoly, collusion exists when firms agree to restrict their competition between each other, either formally or informally. This can be done in a number of ways such as setting quotas or fixing prices.

Given the level of uncertainty which exists in oligopolistic markets, there is much to be gained from *collusion*, i.e. from firms coming together and trying to influence the market outcome in their favour. Collusion is a way of dealing with interdependence since coming to an agreement as to what price should be charged or what level of output should be produced makes it possible for oligopolists to act as a monopoly, thereby achieving maximum profits for their industry. Mini Case Study 7.1 looks at possible collusion in the cigarette industry.

Mini Case Study 7.1

Price fixing in cigarettes

In 2004 the Office of Fair Trading began an investigation into what it believes may be evidence of a price-fixing cartel operating in Britain's cigarette markets. The sale of 56 billion cigarettes a year in the UK is dominated by London-listed firms Gallaher and Imperial Tobacco, which together control almost 90% of the market. Latest accounts show both firms generate operating profit margins, after duty, of about 50% – making Britain one of the most profitable markets in the world, despite relatively high duty levels. British American Tobacco, which controls a further 6% of the market, is also being targeted by the competition watchdog's investigation. A spokeswoman for Gallaher, which owns brands including Benson & Hedges and Mayfair, confirmed the company had recently provided the OFT with requested information relating to agreements with its British retail partners.

Shares in all the companies involved fell by around 5% following the news of the investigation. A spokesman for Imperial Tobacco, whose brands include Richmond and market leader Lambert & Butler, confirmed it had complied with a similar request.

OFT scrutiny of the cigarette grade comes less than a year after the OFT began its ongoing inquiry into possible fixing of prices on rolling tobacco papers, a sector dominated by Imperial through its Rizla brand. It is understood that as the cigarette paper inquiry progressed, evidence of possible price fixing in the wider tobacco sector came to light prompting the OFT to write to Britain's three largest cigarette makers.

The price for a packet of 20 cigarettes ranges from £3.60 to £4.60, which manufacturers are expected to argue offers customers a spread of budget and premium brands. Manufacturers are expected to hotly dispute suggestions that cigarettes should be traded as a commodity, stating that costly marketing and publicity campaigns justify higher prices for more fashionable and more profitable brands.

Question
What issues are raised by these allegations for both producers and consumers?

Answer to question can be found on the students' side of the Companion Website.

4.1 Methods of collusion

Collusion can take the following forms:

(**a**) *Formal collusion*. This can be called *overt* collusion, with agreement being reached between the firms as to what price to charge or what output to produce. This type of formal agreement is known as a *cartel* and is illegal in the UK, although some international cartels such as OPEC (Oil Producing and Exporting Countries) are legal.

(**b**) *Tacit collusion*. This is where firms behave in a cooperative way but do not have a formal agreement. Firms in an oligopolistic market may view covert collusion as being in their mutual interest. The most common form of tacit collusion is *price leadership* where one firm sets the price and the other firms follow.

4.2 Cartels

Formal collusion involves establishing and maintaining some kind of organisation which seeks to direct the policy of its members to reach some agreed end. For example, OPEC (Oil Producing and Exporting Countries) seeks to control the output of its member countries in order to keep the oil price above a target level previously agreed.

The operation of a cartel can be illustrated in terms of Figure 7.4.

If no agreement is reached among suppliers, the suggestion in Figure 7.4 is that an equilibrium price P_e and quantity Q_e will result from the market. However, suppose the producers establish an organisation which seeks to prevent prices falling below P^*. In effect, the cartel must prevent output rising above Q^*. It can do this by capping output at Q^*, causing the original supply curve SS to take the shape SVS' in Figure 7.4.

An obvious problem is that at price P^* the producers would (in the absence of the cartel) have supplied quantity Q_1, giving *excess supply* $Q^*–Q_1$. In order to limit the output of members to Q^* big cartels often allocate quotas, i.e. a maximum production level for each member such that, when aggregated, no more than Q^* is produced in total. Of

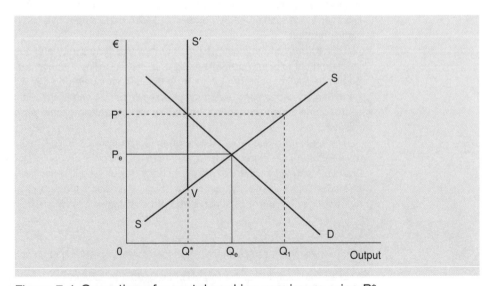

Figure 7.4 Operation of a cartel seeking maximum price P*.

course, if members cheat and produce more than their quota, overall supply will rise above Q* and price will fall below P*.

Mini Case Study 7.2 reviews a number of cartels found to have operated in the UK and EU in recent years.

Mini Case Study 7.2

Cartels and collusion

Companies in oligopolistic markets such as Coke and Pepsi or Exxon Mobil and Shell can generally set prices at levels that match mutual profit requirements, without either price wars or secret meetings. However, cartels still happen and the following examples will help show the degree of formal collusion which often occurs.

In 2000 the three largest UK producers of ordinary Portland cement (OPC), namely Blue Circle plc, Castle Cement Ltd and the Rugby Group, refused to supply OPC in bulk to concrete producers such as Readymix when they heard that the concrete producers intended to resell the cement themselves in bag form to builder's merchants. This was because they, themselves, sold OPC in bag form to other customers. However, the three producers were forced to supply cement after the Office of Fair Trading (OFT) found that refusing to supply OPC in bulk for ultimate resale in bags was anti-competitive.

In December 1999 the OFT had discovered that Vitafoam Ltd of Rochdale, Carpenter plc of Glossop, Derbyshire and Reticel Ltd of Alfreton, Derbyshire, had met to agree on the price rises of 8% for foam rubber and 4% for reconstituted foam which they supplied to the upholstery business. Cartel members agreed that the price rises announced by Vitafoam, the market leader, would be matched by similar announcements from Carpenter and Reticel.

On a much larger scale, the European Commission identified a 'vitamin cartel' in 2001, when eight pharmaceutical companies led by the Swiss firm, Hoffman La Roche, were found to have been operating secret market sharing and price fixing cartels in the supply of vitamins throughout the 1990s. These vitamins were used in a multitude of products from cereals and biscuits to cosmetics. The Commission found that the companies led by Hoffman La Roche allocated sales quotas, agreed on and implemented price increases, and engaged in regular meetings between the senior executives of the companies. The Commission imposed a record fine of £534 million on the companies for operating an illegal cartel.

Questions

1 *In what ways do the examples above show that cartel activity can take various forms?*

2 *Why are cartels widely believed to be against the public interest?*

3 *Draw a simple supply and demand diagram to illustrate a supply based cartel and indicate what conditions are necessary for the cartel to be successful.*

Answers to questions can be found at the back of the book (page 503).

4.3 Price-leadership models

Tacit collusion may involve various types of price-leadership understandings, rather than the more formal collusion of a cartel.

(a) *Dominant firm price leadership*. Often the price leader in an oligopolistic market is the dominant firm. In this situation the largest or the most efficient firm takes the lead in setting the price which the other firms follow, possibly because they fear that not doing so would lead to a price war.

A formal model of the dominant firm price leadership can be explained by the use of Figure 7.5.

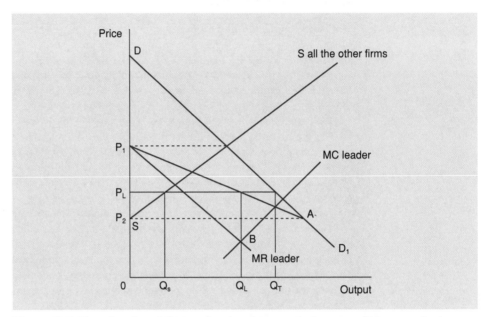

Figure 7.5 The dominant firm price leader maximises profit by producing Q_L and charging P_L. The small firms in the market, who act as perfect competitors, accept the price set by the price leader and therefore produce Q_S and also set their price at P_L.

The assumption is made that the oligopolistic market consists of one profit maximising dominant firm and many small firms whose behaviour is typical of perfect competition. In Figure 7.5 the total market demand curve is shown as DD_1 and the supply curve of all the small firms in the industry is SS. This is derived from the individual firms' marginal cost curves. Given the market demand curve it is possible for the dominant firm to derive its own demand curve. At a price of P_1 the whole market could be supplied by the small firms, therefore the demand for the dominant firm's product is zero. At a price of P_2, however, the small firms would supply nothing and the dominant firm would have the market to itself. The demand curve faced by the dominant firm is, therefore, P_1AD_1. Having obtained the dominant firm's demand curve it is possible to construct its MR curve (which is labelled MR leader). If the dominant firm has a MC curve of MC leader then it will profit maximise by producing Q_L at a price of P_L given that MC equals MR at point B. The leader sets the price at P_L and the other small firms in the oligopolistic market follow this price and in doing so supply Q_S. The total market demand is Q_T of which the dominant firm supplies Q_L and the small firms supply Q_S. The total market output Q_T equals Q_S plus Q_L.

(b) *Barometric firm price leadership*. The price leader may be a small firm but one which has a close knowledge of the market and the prevailing economic conditions. In this situation the *barometric* firm may institute a price change which the other firms in the oligopolistic market follow.

Pause for thought 4

How does the dominant firm price-leadership model work?

5 GAME THEORY

Game theory
A study of the strategic behaviour of firms in oligopolistic markets. Their behaviour depending on the assumptions they make about their rivals' behaviour.

As stated in Section 7: 1 a key feature of oligopolistic markets is interdependence. Oligopolists attempt to second guess their rivals' reactions to their own moves or actions. One way to analyse the behaviour of firms in oligopolistic markets is through the use of *game theory*. Firms in such markets can undertake various *strategies* which may range from price changes to promotional campaigns. Game theory illustrates the strategic inter-action between rational decision-making firms operating in a situation of uncertainty. Game theory can be illustrated using either a *zero* or *non-zero sum game* situation.

5.1 Zero sum games

This situation can be illustrated by use of Table 7.1 and it refers to a situation in which two firms A and B (a duopolistic market) are in competition with each other. The two firms have various strategies open to them, in this case three strategies, namely changing the price of their product, advertising and promotional activity. The table is called a *pay-off matrix* with the figures in the matrix referring to profit in € million based on the pos-

Zero sum game
Where any gain to one 'player' is exactly offset by losses to another player (or players).

sible combinations of strategies adopted by the two firms. It is called a *zero sum game* in that one firm's loss in terms of profit is exactly matched by the other firm's gain in terms of profit. In other words, whatever firm A wins firm B loses, with the total gains plus total losses summing to zero.

The payoff matrix is produced from firm A's perspective such that if firm A were to *change its price* then firm B would either change its price, advertise or promote such that firm A would either increase its profit by €4 million, have no increase in profits or obtain an increase of €12 million respectively. This would mean that firm B would find either its profits reduced by €4 million, have no change in profits or find that they are reduced by €12 million. On the other hand, if firm A was to *advertise* and firm B were to change its

Table 7.1 Payoff matrix for firm A (profit € million)

	STRATEGIES	Firm B			COLUMN MINIMUM
		Price change	Advertising	Promotion	
Firm A	Price change	4	0	12	0
	Advertising	8	−4	−16	−16
	Promotion	−12	−8	16	−12
	ROW MAXIMUM	8	0	16	

price in response then firm A would increase its profit by €8 million at the expense of firm B. If the response by firm B was to advertise then firm A would find its profits reduced by €4 million with firm B's profits increasing by €4 million and so on. The matrix has been produced in terms of profit but it could equally refer to market share or some other measure.

Firm A has to decide which is the best strategy to pursue. Suppose firm A assumes that firm B will seek to respond with a strategy which minimises firm A's gain and thus minimises firm B's losses. The right-hand column, labelled *COLUMN MINIMUM*, refers to the minimum payoff to firm A in each of the rows. For example, if firm A seeks to change its price then it believes that firm B will advertise, since this minimises firm A's gains and therefore minimises firm B's losses, so zero is entered in the right-hand column. If firm A were to advertise then it believes firm B will promote, leaving firm A with a €16 million loss of profit. Similarly, if firm A promotes then it believes firm B will change its price, leaving firm A with a €12 million loss of profit.

Maxi-min decision rule
Select the strategy which yields the best (maxi) of the worst possible (min) outcomes.

One possible approach or 'decision rule' for firm A is that of **maxi-min**, where firm A selects the best of these minimum (worst possible) outcomes for each of its three strategies. This is often regarded as a 'conservative' or pessimistic decision rule, since firm A is always assuming that, for any strategy it follows, firm B reacts in the worst (for A) possible way. Given the *maxi-min* approach to the game, firm A will change its price and firm B will choose to advertise, leaving firm A's profits unchanged. A change in price will be the best of the three possible strategies for firm A and it is called the *dominant strategy*.

 ## Pause for thought 5

Based on the illustrated payoff matrix, why will firm B change its price if firm A promotes its product?

If the payoff matrix is viewed from firm B's perspective then it is important to analyse the *ROW MAXIMUM*, which represents the maximum losses that firm B will incur as a result of each strategy it pursues. Of course, the impact on firm B's profits of each of its strategies depends on what firm A itself does. If firm B adopts a price change, then the maximum loss for firm B occurs if firm A has advertised, i.e. a loss of €8 million. The maximum losses firm B will incur for each of its strategies are shown in ROW MAXIMUM as €8 million, no loss at all or a loss of €16 million. If firm B also follows the *maxi-min* decision rule it will choose the best of the worst possible outcomes. It will therefore choose the strategy which results in the minimum of the maximum losses, which is an advertising strategy which leads to no change in its profits.

In terms of the example used in the payoff matrix, the maximum of firm A's minimum payoffs equals the minimum of firm B's maximum losses. This is a *stable equilibrium* and could mean that the price change undertaken by firm A is responded to by the advertising strategy of firm B. There is no tendency to change since each firm is selecting what it regards as its optimum strategy under the *maxi-min* decision rule, and the other firm is responding in a way consistent with that optimum strategy. In this equilibrium neither firm gains or loses profit.

Mini-max decision rule
Select the strategy which yields the worst (mini) of the best possible (max) outcomes.

A more 'optimistic' decision rule is **mini-max**. Here each firm works out the best possible outcome for each strategy, i.e. it assumes the other firm reacts to each of its strategies in a way that is best for it. So firm A in Table 7.1 would assume that if it changes prices firm B will respond by changing price, giving a €4 million profit to firm A.

COLUMN MINIMUM becomes COLUMN MAXIMUM and then firm A selects the worst (minimum) of these maximum outcomes.

Can you see that if firm B adopts this same *mini-max* decision rule then the ROW MAXIMUM of Table 7.1 will become the ROW MINIMUM?

Pause for thought 6

*What will the **mini-max** decision rule suggest is the strategy chosen by firm A and firm B respectively in Table 7.1? Is this an equilibrium?*

5.2 Non-zero sum games

Non-zero sum game
Where any gain to one 'player' is *not* offset by equivalent losses elsewhere.

Prisoners' dilemma
Refers to a specific situation in which two prisoners/firms are independently trying to decide on the best strategy, but who result in a worse position than if they had colluded.

The **non-zero sum game** is a situation in which one firm's losses do not exactly equal the other firm's gain. As such, the total gains plus total losses do not sum to zero hence the term 'non-zero sum games'. This situation can be analysed by what is called the **prisoners' dilemma** which is illustrated in Table 7.2.

The prisoners' dilemma refers to a situation in which two individuals, Stuart and Steve, have been arrested by the authorities on suspicion of a crime and are put into *separate* cells. They are then told that if they confess to the crime, thereby implicating their partner, then they will be allowed to go free but that their partner will be given 10 years in prison. If they both confess they are told they will each be given a prison sentence of 5 years. Alternatively, if neither confesses, the authority has enough evidence to convict them of a minor offence and they will each be given a 2-year prison sentence. There is hence a prisoners' dilemma. The left-hand side of each box refers to the number of years Steve will spend in prison whereas the right-hand side refers to the number of years Stuart will spend in prison.

Pause for thought 7

What would you do in this situation: confess or not confess?

Each prisoner has two strategies, either to confess or not confess, and the prison term given depends on the strategy each chooses. The best strategy for both Stuart and Steve is to confess, since by so doing each would either be given a 5-year prison sentence or set free. On the other hand, by not confessing each would either be given a 10- or 2-year prison term. By confessing each of the two prisoners is following a *maxi-min* decision rule with confession as the dominant strategy, as a result of which each receives a 5-year prison sentence. They are both expecting the worst from their partner.

Table 7.2 The prisoners' dilemma

		Stuart			
		Confess		Don't confess	
Steve	Confess	5	5	0	10
	Don't confess	10	0	2	2

The payoff matrix clearly illustrates that the prisoners could have done better if they had *colluded* (or, in terms of an oligopolistic market, formed a cartel), so that both refused to confess. By so doing they would each have received a 2-year prison sentence. Neither Stuart nor Steve, however, would have undertaken this strategy independently of each other for fear of the other confessing, resulting in a 10-year prison sentence for their partner.

Pause for thought 8

What benefits are there for the two criminals if they were both to collude?

This analysis clearly has relevance for firms operating in oligopolistic markets. It reveals the benefits to be gained from colluding in order to either reduce the prison term or, in oligopoly terms, possibly increase joint profits by operating a cartel (were the payoff matrix in Table 7.2 to refer to an oligopolistic market). Once a collusive agreement has been reached, however, it is not always certain that the cartel will be stable, for there is often a temptation to cheat on any agreement reached. Referring to Table 7.2, with both individuals/firms colluding and undertaking a 'don't confess' strategy, there are gains to be made by reneging on (breaking) the agreement. In such a situation the cartel would break down.

Pause for thought 9

Can you use Table 7.2 to show how breaking an agreement might benefit Stuart or Steve?

6   CONTESTABLE MARKETS

Contestable markets
A market structure in which entry into an industry is free and exit is costless. Even the threat of a new firm entry causes incumbent firms to act as though such potential entry actually exists. Instead of regarding competitive behaviour as existing only in a perfectly or monopolistically competitive market, it could exist in markets which are contestable.

Contestable markets is a recent theory of market structure and is based on the effect potential new entrants have on price and output decisions. Like perfect competition, and to a certain extent monopoly, contestable markets are not so much a description of the real world but rather a benchmark against which other theories can be assessed.

A contestable market can be defined as one in which entry is free and exit is costless. Free entry means that potential entrants to a market are not at a disadvantage in terms of possessing higher costs or from consumers preferring the products of other firms. Costless exit means that firms can leave the industry without financial penalty. In other words, there are no *sunk costs*, since the capital they invested in when they entered the industry can be resold. This is an important aspect of the theory of contestable markets since if exit were not costless then by definition it would be a cost of entry. This all means that potential entrants are not put off entering a market by the possibility of existing firms cutting their prices, since they can always leave the industry without financial penalty. As a result, contestable markets experience '*hit and run entry*' as the existence of supernormal profit leads to new firms entering a market, obtaining a share of the profits and leaving the industry when the profits have been '*creamed off*'. It is also the case that the threat of potential entry encourages existing firms to be efficient by minimising their costs of production.

A contestable market would appear to be similar to a perfectly competitive market and it is true that perfectly competitive markets are also perfectly contestable. The reverse is not true, however, since a contestable market could be one in which only a few firms exist. In a contestable market the size and number of firms will be determined by the market.

The interest in the model stems from the fact that it has less restrictive assumptions than the perfectly competitive model, which is seen as the ideal market structure. Even so, it is true to say that the theory of contestable markets should not be viewed as a realistic model of market structure but rather a benchmark case against which other market structures can be analysed. The theory indicates that the structure of a market and how firms behave within that market cannot be determined just by counting the number of firms in the industry.

 Pause for thought 10

What is meant by a contestable market? Can you think of any examples?

KEY POINTS

- A *monopolistically competitive* market structure refers to a situation in which there are a large number of small firms each producing a slightly different product from their competitor. They have a degree of market power and as such have some influence over the price charged, but equally there are close substitutes to the goods or services they produce.

- An *oligopolistic* market structure refers to a situation in which there are a few firms which dominate the industry often producing a large number of brands. Each firm in the market is of a sufficient size that any decision they take will have an effect on the other firms in the market. As such there is an interdependency and rivalry.

- The *kinked demand curve* illustrates why it may be that prices are stable in oligopolistic markets. The demand curve is seen to be kinked, with the price stable around the kink. If a firm increases its price then other firms in the market are unlikely to follow, whereas if a firm lowers its price then other firms do follow and lower their prices also.

- *Non-price competition* refers to competition which takes the form of product promotion, such as advertising and packaging, and/or innovative approaches to the design and the development of the product.

- *Collusion* is one way in which oligopolistic firms deal with the issue of interdependence. Through collusion firms can reach agreement as to what price they charge or what output they produce and as such they can increase their joint profits.

- *Price leadership* is a common form of informal (tacit) collusion whereby one firm will set the price and the other firms in the market will follow that price. Price leadership can take a number of different forms, most notably dominant firm price leadership and barometric firm price leadership.

- *Game theory* is one way of analysing the behaviour of firms in oligopolistic markets. In game theory firms will undertake various strategies, trying to identify the possible reaction of its rival in response to each of these strategies.

- *Contestable markets* refer to a market situation in which entry barriers are absent and the *threat* of new firms entering the market checks the tendency of incumbent firms to raise their prices and earn supernormal profit.

Further reading

Griffiths, A. and Wall, S. (2006) *Applied Economics*, 11th edition, FT/Prentice Hall, Chapter 6.

Griffiths, A. and Wall, S. (2005) *Economics for Business and Management*, FT/Prentice Hall, Chapter 6.

Heather, K. (2004) *Economics Theory in Action*, 4th edition, FT/Prentice Hall, Chapters 7 and 8.

Parkin, M., Powell, M. and Matthews, K. (2005) *Economics*, 6th edition, FT/Prentice Hall, Chapter 13.

Sloman, J. (2006) *Economics*, 6th edition, FT/Prentice Hall, Chapter 7.

Web references

The following website contains a wide range of company data:

http://bized.ac.uk

Mergers and acquisitions involving UK: **www.competition-commission.org.uk**

Mergers involving EU: **http://europa.eu.int/comm/competition/index_en.html**

Mergers involving US: **http://www.ftc.gov/ftc/antitrust.htm**

www.dti.gov.uk

www.eubusiness.com

Companies House: **http://www.companieshouse.gov.uk/** The place for getting information on all English and Welsh companies.

Chinese business activity: **www.cbbc.org**

Japanese business activity: **www.jetro.org**

EU business activity: **www.euromonitor.com**

PROGRESS AND REVIEW QUESTIONS

Answers to most questions can be found at the back of the book (pages 503–4). Answers to asterisked questions can be found on the students' side of the Companion Website.

 ## Multiple-choice questions

1 The reason for product differentiation is to:

   a) make the demand curve more elastic

   b) make the demand curve less inelastic

   c) make the demand curve less elastic

   d) lower the firms costs of production

   e) none of the above.

2 One difference between a firm operating under perfect competition and one operating under monopolistic competition is that under monopolistic competition:

 a) profit maximisation is where marginal revenue equals marginal cost
 b) marginal revenue is not equal to price
 c) average revenue equals price
 d) marginal cost cuts average cost at its minimum point
 e) none of the above.

3 In terms of the kinked demand curve, the basis of the approach is that:

 a) a rival firm will leave their price unchanged if a competitor lowers their price
 b) oligopolists sell their product to consumers who are less sensitive to a price increase than a price decrease
 c) an oligopolist will expect a rival to react to any fall in price by reducing the price of their own product
 d) an oligopolist will increase the price of their product if the price charged by a competitor is increased
 e) none of the above.

4 If a firm operating in an oligopolistic market increases its price then a rival firm:

 a) can have no effect on that firm's market share by reacting to the price increase
 b) will always increase its price
 c) will increase their market share if they keep their price constant
 d) will always decrease their price
 e) none of the above.

5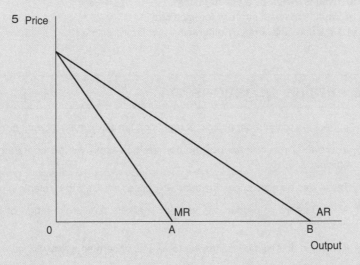

The diagram above refers to a monopolistically competitive profit maximising firm with zero costs. The equilibrium level of output is:

 a) 0A
 b) zero
 c) 0B
 d) between 0 and A
 e) between A and B.

6 For the successful operation of a cartel:

a) there must be free entry into the industry

b) there must be close substitute products available to the consumer

c) the majority of firms in the industry must cooperate

d) the demand curve for the product sold by the cartel must be elastic

e) none of the above.

Data response question

1 The following table illustrates a payoff matrix for firms X and Y, with two alternative strategies (advertising and price cutting).

Firm Y

		Advertising		Price cutting	
Firm X	Advertising	4	4	0	5
	Price cutting	5	0	3	3

Note: The matrix is given in terms of profit. The left side of each box refers to firm X and the right to firm Y.

a) What is meant by a payoff matrix?

b) What is the best strategy for each firm?

c) How does this strategy differ if the two firms collude?

True/false questions

1 In the long run in monopolistic competition firms will make normal profit.

2 In the long run in monopolistic competition firms will be operating at full productive efficiency.

3 The kinked demand curve illustrates why prices are likely to be stable in oligopolistic markets.

4 A key feature of certain oligopolistic markets is a proliferation of different brands of products.

5 If a firm in an oligopolistic market lowers its price then a rival will increase their price.

6 Formal collusion is where firms in an oligopolistic market fix what price to charge or what output to produce.

7 In the dominant firm price-leadership model the dominant firm will set the price and the other firms in the market will follow.

8 In game theory the reaction of a rival to the decisions a firm takes are unimportant.

9 In a contestable market entry is free and exit is costless.

10 In a contestable market new firms can enter, 'cream off' the profits and leave without any financial penalty.

 ## Essay questions

Answers to asterisked questions can be found on the students' side of the Companion Website. All other answers can be found at the back of the book (page 504).

1* In what way is monopolistic competition (a) similar to, and (b) different from, monopoly?

2 Why is there likely to be price stability in oligopolistic markets?

3* What forms can non-price competition take in monopolistic competition and oligopoly?

4 What are the reasons for collusion in oligopolistic markets and what form does the collusion take?

Wages, rent and profit

By the end of this chapter you should be able to:

- Understand what is meant by the 'marginal productivity theory' of labour.
- Explain how wages are determined for occupations using demand and supply curves for labour.
- Examine the levels of wages and employment in imperfect product and labour markets, such as monopsony and monopoly labour markets.
- Understand what is meant by a monopsonistic buyer of labour.
- Understand what is meant by 'economic rent' and 'transfer earnings'.
- Review the role of profit in allocating factors of production.

1 INTRODUCTION

The aim of this chapter is to analyse the reward to the factor of production labour. The demand for labour can be viewed as a *derived demand*, which means that labour is not simply demanded for its own sake but for what it can contribute to the productive process. In a market economy the price of the factor of production is determined by the market demand and supply conditions. Throughout this chapter the *marginal productivity theory* will be used to analyse the demand for labour under competitive labour market conditions.

Of course, in reality, 'market failure' occurs in labour markets as well as in product markets (*see* Chapter 9). In labour markets such imperfections can involve trade unions (monopoly in the supply of labour) or large employers or groups of employers (monopoly in the demand for labour). This latter situation is sometimes called 'monopsony' in the labour market.

2 MARGINAL PRODUCTIVITY THEORY OF WAGES

The **marginal productivity theory** is based on the principle of profit maximisation which was introduced in Chapter 6. Profit maximising firms will employ additional workers up to the point where the extra cost of the additional unit of labour employed is equal to the extra revenue obtained from that employment.

In outlining the theory we will initially assume a perfectly competitive product and labour market.

2.1 Perfectly competitive product and labour market

Marginal productivity theory
This suggests that firms will continue to employ factors of production up to the point where the marginal unit of each factor adds as much to revenue as it does to costs.

Marginal revenue product
Refers to the additional total revenue received from the employment of one more unit of the factor of production with the quantity of all other factors of production remaining constant.

Marginal physical product of labour
Refers to the total, physical output obtained from employing one more unit of labour.

Average revenue product of labour
Refers to output per unit of labour. It is calculated by multiplying the average physical product by the price of the product.

Assuming a perfectly competitive product market means that a firm can sell each unit of output at the same price, assumed to be £10 in the hypothetical data given in Table 8.1. In other words, the firm is a 'price taker' and thus faces a perfectly elastic demand curve for its product at the going market price (£10).

Perfect competition in the labour market means that the firm can employ extra workers at the same wage rate, assumed to be £200 per worker per week in Table 8.1. We also make the assumption that labour is the only variable factor.

The data given in Table 8.1 can be plotted as in Figure 8.1.

The **marginal revenue product** (MRP) of labour is the extra revenue obtained by employing one extra unit of labour. It is the extra output from employing the last worker, i.e. the **marginal physical product** (MPP) **of labour** multiplied by the price of the product. Hence:

$$MRP = MPP \times price$$

The **average revenue product of labour** (ARP) is derived by multiplying the average physical product by the price of the product. Both the ARP and the MRP rise and then decline since labour is subject to the law of diminishing returns (*see* Chapter 5, Section 5.2), although in Figure 8.1 it can be seen that diminishing marginal returns to labour set in *before* diminishing average returns to labour. The supply curve of labour is shown as perfectly elastic at a wage (W) of £200 and this represents both the marginal cost (MC_L) and the average cost (AC_L) of labour.

The profit maximising position for the firm is where:

$$MRP = MC_L$$

In Figure 8.1 this is where 6 workers are employed. The firm would not employ the 7th worker since he or she would only add £90 to revenue but would cost the firm £200 – hence a reduction in profit of £110 (*see* Table 8.1).

Table 8.1 The marginal revenue product (£)

Number of workers	Marginal physical product (MPP)	Price of the product (P = MR = AR) (£)	Marginal revenue product (MRP) (£)	Wage rate (W) (£)	Additional profit (MRP – W) (£)
1	5	10	50	200	−150
2	19	10	190	200	−10
3	33	10	330	200	+130
4	43	10	430	200	+230
5	50	10	500	200	+300
6	30	10	300	200	+100
7	9	10	90	200	−110

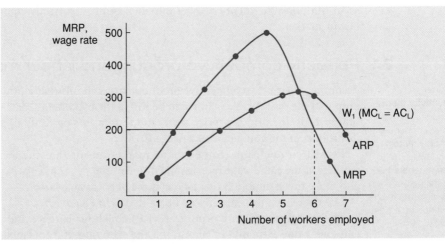

Figure 8.1 The figure illustrates the average and marginal revenue product (MRP) curves for labour. MRP eventually decline as the quantity of labour employed rises due to the 'law of diminishing returns' which causes marginal physical product (MPP) of the variable factor, labour, to fall. The portion of marginal revenue product curve below the average revenue product curve represents the firm's demand curve for labour. The firm will employ labour up to the point at which the wage rate (the marginal cost of labour MC_L) equals the marginal revenue product of labour.

 Pause for thought 1

Explain why the marginal cost of labour equals the average cost of labour equals £200 in Figure 8.1.

2.2 The firm's demand curve for labour

The profit maximising firm in Figure 8.2 faces a perfectly elastic supply curve for labour (MC_{L1}) which means that all additional labour can be hired at the same wage rate W_1 (*see* Section 3), and thus the quantity of labour employed is qL_1.

If the wage rate was to increase to W_2 then the labour supply curve would shift to MC_{L2} and the profit maximising firm would reduce the number of workers employed to qL_2. The MRP curve thus represents the firm's demand curve for labour, with an increase in the wage rate leading to a movement along the curve from A to B. It is important to note that the demand curve is only the downward sloping section of the MRP curve below the ARP curve. This is because if the wage rate rose above W_3 (in Figure 8.2) then the firm would be unable to earn sufficient revenue to cover all its variable costs and would close down.

 Pause for thought 2

Can you explain why the firm would be unable to cover all its variable costs if the wage rate rose above W_3 in Figure 8.2?

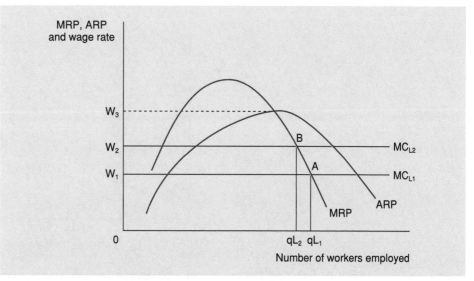

Figure 8.2 If the wage rate is W₁, then the profit maximising firm will equate the wage rate to the MRP (point A) and will employ qL₁ units of labour. If the wage rate were to increase to W₂ the quantity of labour employed would fall to qL₂.

3 THE SUPPLY OF LABOUR

The total supply of labour to a market depends on the price of labour (i.e. the wage rate), the size of the population, the age composition of the population, the labour force participation rate, the occupational and geographical distribution of the labour force and the tastes of the labour force in terms of their trade-off between work and leisure. The wage rate is all important in determining the supply of labour and this section begins by deriving the supply curve of labour for an individual. The market supply curve is simply the summation of the individual supply curves.

(a) *The individual's supply curve of labour.* The supply curve of labour may be backward bending (*see* Figure 8.3). This means that after a certain wage rate, higher wages will result in fewer hours being worked per day, with individuals demanding more leisure time. In Figure 8.3, as the wage rate increases from W_1 to W_2 the individual is prepared to increase the number of hours worked from H_1 to H_2. At a wage rate above W_2, however, the supply curve is backward bending or negatively sloped, with the individual supplying less hours of labour and preferring to use his or her income on leisure activities. So as the wage rate increases from W_2 to W_3, the number of hours worked is reduced from H_2 to H_3.

The backward bending supply curve can be analysed using indifference curve analysis and, in particular, the income and substitution effect (*see* 4: 5). As the wage rate increases, assuming leisure is a normal good, individuals will substitute extra hours of work for leisure, hence the *substitution effect*. An increase in the wage rate will increase the individual's income and as this takes place there will be an increase in the demand for normal goods, including leisure time. The *income effect* operates in such a way that fewer hours of

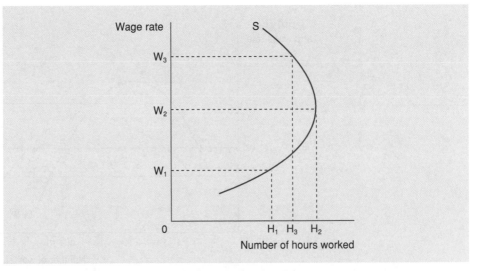

Figure 8.3 The individual's supply curve for labour may be backward bending. As the wage rate increases from W_1 to W_2 the individual is prepared to work H_2 to H_1 hours more. Above the wage rate W_2 a further increase will result in a decrease in the number of hours the individual is prepared to work. Thus an increase in the wage rate from W_2 to W_3 results in a reduction in the number of hours worked from H_2 to H_3.

work are supplied as income increases. When the income effect outweighs the substitution effect, higher wages can lead to less hours worked and a backward bending supply curve.

(b) *The industry's supply curve of labour.* This is obtained by the horizontal summation of the supply curves of individuals and it will normally be positively sloped. As the wage rate rises in a particular industry, workers will be encouraged to transfer into that industry from other industries.

 Pause for thought 3

What is meant by a backward bending supply curve for labour?

4 THE LABOUR MARKET EQUILIBRIUM

Having derived the market demand and supply curves for labour in a particular industry, it is possible to determine the labour market equilibrium.

Figure 8.4 gives the market demand (D_{L1}) and the market supply (S_L) for labour in a particular industry, with an equilibrium wage of W_1 and employment of L_1.

If we take the example of the construction industry, an increase in the demand for buildings will, assuming *ceteris paribus*, lead to an increase in the demand for labour, labour being a derived demand. The demand curve for construction workers will, therefore,

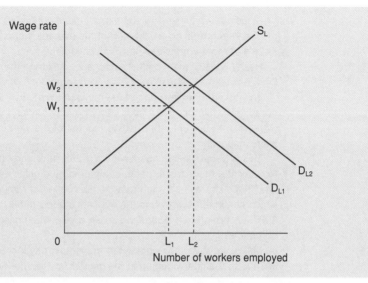

Figure 8.4 In a particular labour market with the demand for labour (D_{L1}) and the supply (S_L) then there will be an equilibrium wage of W_1 and employment L_1. If the demand for labour were to increase (D_{L1} to D_{L2}) then there would be a new equilibrium wage rate of W_2 and employment L_2.

shift to the right (D_{L2} in Figure 8.4) and there will be a new equilibrium wage and level of employment (W_2 and L_2 respectively).

 ## Pause for thought 4

If the government imposed a minimum wage above the equilibrium wage in Figure 8.4, what might happen?

The Mini Case Study below presents some information on wages and earnings in the UK labour market, suggesting that labour market 'equilibrium' solutions have little to do with ethical issues such as promoting greater equality!

Mini Case Study 8.1

Increasing wage inequality

Two-thirds of the workforce in 2004 were earning less than the average wage as a result of soaraway pay deals for executives and directors.

Pay researchers at Incomes Data Services (IDS) say that wage inequality is rising, despite Labour's introduction of the minimum wage, because top pay is increasing faster than for the rest of the workforce. The widening divide is wrecking the government's drive to engineer a fairer society.

Since 1990 pay rises for top earners have continued to outstrip those for the rest of the workforce to such an extent that the average wage has been pulled upwards, leaving more and more employees earning beneath it.

Nearly 65% of the workforce now earn less than the full-time average weekly wage of £488 a week before tax. Ten years ago, some 60% of workers earned less than average.

The government introduced the minimum wage in April 1999, but the IDS researchers noted that while this put a floor under poverty pay and stopped the lowest 10% of workers from falling further behind the rest of the workforce, it has had little impact on wage inequality.

This is because earnings for the top 25% and particularly the top 10% have continued to grow at a much faster pace, outstripping the gains made by those at the bottom. The late 1990s shares boom led to an explosion in the remuneration packages of executives, which continued even when the markets started to fall. Executive pay rose by 18% in 2003, according to a *Guardian* survey, a year when billions was wiped off the value of companies.

Male executives have pocketed the largest pay increases, a factor which contributed in 2002 to the first widening in the gender pay gap for five years.

Questions

1 *Can you explain how two-thirds of UK workers can be on less than average pay?*

2 *What factors have contributed to these findings?*

3 *What policy implications are suggested for reducing such income inequality?*

Answers to questions can be found on the students' side of the Companion Website.

The previous sections have assumed that all markets are perfectly competitive; however, labour markets are likely to contain imperfections. These can be on the *demand side*, in terms of the employer, who may be a producer monopoly or a monopsonist (i.e. a monopoly buyer of labour), or on the *supply side*, in terms of the employee, who may belong to a trade union.

However, before turning to these imperfections in the labour market, we first consider what happens when there are imperfections in the *product market*.

Monopsonist
A significant buyer of labour who can influence the price of labour by its hiring decisions.

4.1 Labour demand and imperfect product markets

The firm's demand curve for labour has so far assumed that any extra output by the firm and indeed by all firms in the industry can be sold at a constant product price. When we relax this assumption of a perfectly competitive product market then the MRP curve for the firm and the industry may need to be adjusted if it is to still be regarded as the demand curve for labour. As we shall see, strictly speaking we should describe the curve we have been using for both the firm and industry demand curve as the value marginal product (VMP) curve, as indicated below.

In reality, the constant product price assumption may not even hold true for an individual firm. For example, a firm in a monopoly or oligopoly product market will face a downward sloping demand curve for its product. This means that the firm must lower the price charged for the product if it wishes to sell more. We can, therefore, distinguish between the *value of the marginal product* (VMP) which is the marginal physical product (MPP) multiplied by the price of the product (P):

$$VMP = MPP \times P$$

and the *marginal revenue product* (MRP) which is strictly speaking the marginal physical product (MPP) multiplied by the marginal revenue (MR):

$$MRP = MPP \times MR$$

This can be seen in Figure 8.5, with the MRP curve below the VMP curve, since the marginal physical product (MPP) is now multiplied by a falling price. This in turn means that MR is less than price (AR).

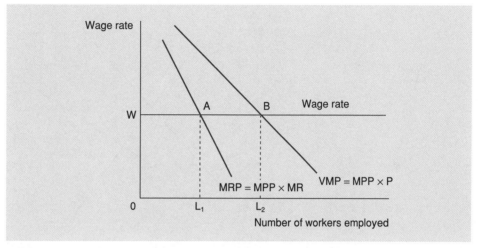

Figure 8.5 A product monopolist or oligopolist will face a downward sloping demand curve for its product and thus the marginal revenue product (MRP) curve will lie below the value of the marginal product (VMP) curve. As a result the wage rate will be W and L_1 units of labour will be employed. If the product market were perfectly competitive then L_2 units of labour would be employed.

The assumption is made in Figure 8.5 that the wage rate remains constant at W. The profit maximising monopolist or oligopolist will employ L_1 workers at the wage rate W, the equilibrium being illustrated by point A. If the product market had been perfectly competitive then the price and the marginal revenue would have been the same, with the MRP equal to the VMP and L_2 rather than L_1 units of labour would have been employed, illustrated by point B in Figure 8.5. A monopolist would, therefore, employ less labour than a firm in perfect competition.

5   A MONOPSONY MARKET FOR LABOUR

When buyers of labour are large and can influence the wage rate by the amount of labour they demand, we call this a *monopsony* labour market. The individual firm may be a large hirer of labour, nationally or regionally, or firms may group together to hire labour, e.g. an employers' association. If this is the case then we can no longer assume that hiring extra workers will not influence the wage rate (i.e. that there is a perfectly elastic supply of labour to the firm at the going wage rate. Rather for the firm or association to recruit additional workers, a higher wage rate must be offered. This is illustrated in Figure 8.6 with the marginal cost curve for labour (MC_L) being above the average cost curve for labour (AC_L). The reason for this can be explained by the use of a simple example. At a wage rate of £100, 50 workers may be employed. If, however, the monopsonist wishes to employ one more worker he or she may be forced to offer £101, the increase being paid to all workers. The average cost is now £101 but the marginal cost is £151, comprising £101 paid to the 51st worker plus £1 paid to each of the 50 original workers.

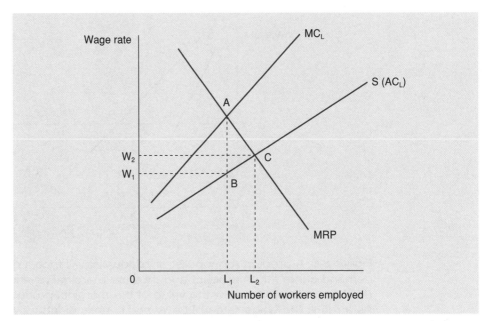

Figure 8.6 If there is a single buyer of labour, a monopsonist, then the marginal cost of labour (MC_L) will be above the average cost curve of labour (AC_L). The monopsonist will equate the marginal cost of labour with marginal revenue product in order to maximise profit, thus L_1 units of labour will be employed. The wage rate is given by the average cost curve of labour (AC_L) and will be W_1. If the market were perfectly competitive then the wage would be W_2 and L_2 units of labour would be employed.

The monopsonist, being a profit maximiser, will employ where the MC_L is equal to the MRP, i.e. point A in Figure 8.6, hence L_1 units of labour will be employed. The wage rate, however, is given by the average cost curve $S(AC_L)$ and this will be W_1. The overall wage bill to the monopsonist will, therefore, be OW_1BL_1. In a perfectly competitive non-labour market the wage and numbers being employed would have been W_2 and L_2 respectively.

 ## Pause for thought 5

What then is the impact of a monopsony labour market on wage rate and level of employment as compared to a competitive labour market?

6 TRADE UNIONS AND THE MARKET FOR LABOUR

Trade union
An organisation
representing a
group of workers
essentially for
the purpose of
improving pay and
conditions.

Trade unions are made up of groups of workers who have a common interest. This could be a common skill, a similar job or working in the same industry.

6.1 Impacts of trade unions

The aims of a trade union can range from improving the working environment to taking up the case of those members the union see as being unfairly dismissed. An important function is to increase the wage rate of its members and this section will concentrate on the way in which trade unions seek to achieve that objective.

(**a**) *Restrict the supply of labour.* Restricting the supply of labour could be achieved through the use of a closed shop or by lengthening the time it takes to complete an apprenticeship.

Over a period of time the trade union could reduce the supply of labour to an industry, shifting the supply curve from SL_1 to SL_2 (*see* Figure 8.7). The result would be an increase in the wage rate from W_1 to W_2, but with a reduced number employed, i.e. L_2 instead of L_1.

(**b**) *Collective bargaining.* Collective bargaining involves the direct negotiation between a trade union, bargaining collectively on behalf of its members, and the employer(s). Successful collective bargaining could raise the wage rate from W_1 to W_2, as illustrated in Figure 8.8.

The trade union may be unwilling to supply labour below the wage rate of W_2; therefore, the supply curve becomes W_2AS_L, being perfectly elastic over the section W_2A. At the

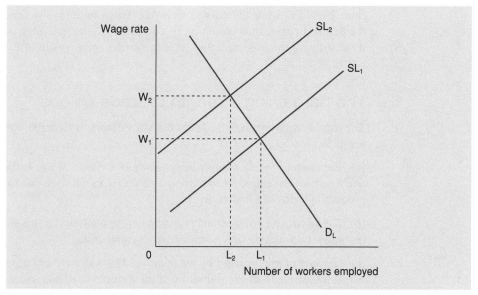

Figure 8.7 If the trade union restricts the supply of labour to an industry, reducing the supply from SL_1 to SL_2, then the wage rate will increase from W_1 to W_2. There will, however, be a reduction in the units of labour employed from L_1 to L_2.

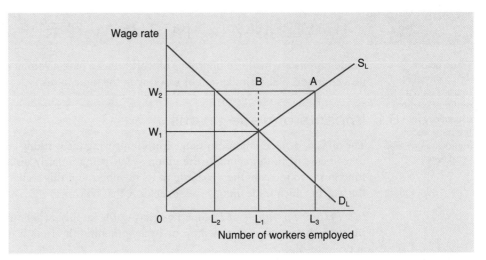

Figure 8.8 Collective bargaining between the trade union and the employer could raise the wage rate above the market equilibrium, from W_1 to W_2. The result will be L_2 units of labour employed and $L_3 - L_2$ unemployed.

equilibrium wage of W_1, with no trade union involvement, L_1 workers would be employed. However, with a wage of W_2, only L_2 are demanded and therefore $L_3 - L_2$ are unable to find employment. There may be individuals who are willing to work for a wage below W_2 but they would be prevented from doing so by the union agreement.

Through collective bargaining a wage rate of W_2 has been agreed, with L_2 being employed. The union, however, could attempt to maintain employment at the equilibrium level of L_1 while obtaining a wage W_2. This would involve forcing the employer off the demand curve, thus obtaining position B in Figure 8.8. This will only be successful if the firm is profitable and, thus, able to sustain employment at L_1 while paying a wage rate of W_2.

6.2 The bargaining strength of trade unions

The bargaining strength of trade unions when dealing with employers depends on a number of factors:

(a) *The demand for the product being relatively inelastic.* If this is the case then it is relatively easy for the employer to pass on an increase in the wage rate to the consumer of the product in terms of a higher price.

(b) *The labour cost being a small proportion of the total cost.* In this situation an increase in the wage rate will have only a small effect on total cost.

(c) *The level of profit earned by the industry.* This will have an important bearing on the bargaining strength of the union, for if the industry is earning substantial profit there is more chance of the trade union obtaining a wage increase for its members.

(d) *The ease of substituting the factors of production.* It may be easy for an industry to substitute capital for labour. If this is the case, it will weaken the bargaining strength of the trade union.

(e) *The strength of the trade union itself.* If the majority of the workers in a particular industry belong to the union or the union has sufficient funds to withstand a prolonged period of industrial action, it will have added strength when bargaining with the employer.

(f) *The economic and political climate.* In a period of high unemployment, with a government determined to resist wage increases, the power of a trade union will be severely restricted.

Pause for thought 6

What factors will increase the bargaining strength of the trade union?

Mini Case Study 8.2

Trade unions and labour markets

Look carefully at the data in Table 8.2.

Table 8.2 **Trade union membership in Great Britain: 1991–2003**

Year	Number of members (thousands)	Union density Employees (%)
1991	8,602	37.5
1992	7,956	35.8
1993	7,767	35.1
1994	7,530	33.6
1995	7,309	32.1
1996	7,244	31.2
1997	7,154	30.2
1998	7,155	29.6
1999	7,277	29.5
2000	7,351	29.4
2001	7,370	29.0
2002	7,390	29.0
2003	7,420	29.1

Source: Adapted from *Labour Market Trends*, July 2002 and March 2004

Questions

1 *What does the data suggest?*

2 *What implications might it have for union bargaining?*

Answers to questions can be found at the back of the book (pages 504–5).

7   ECONOMIC RENT AND TRANSFER EARNINGS

7.1 Economic rent

Economic rent can be defined as the amount paid to a factor of production over and above that necessary to keep it in its present occupation. It relates to any factor of production, not just land.

Example

A footballer may earn £100,000 per week given the particular skills he possesses. His next best occupation may be a salesman for which he could earn only £400 per week; the £99,600 difference between the two is called *economic rent* or *rent of ability*.

 Pause for thought 7

How much of David Beckham's earnings would you regard as economic rent?

7.2 Transfer earnings

If the earnings of a factor of production decline, there will come a point when the factor will transfer to another use. The minimum payment necessary to keep the factor of production in its present occupation is called its *transfer earnings*. The excess of earnings above the transfer earnings is called the *economic rent*.

7.3 Economic rent versus transfer earnings

Economic rent
A return over and above that which is necessary for the factor of production to be supplied. A type of 'surplus' payment.

Transfer earnings
A necessary return for the factor of production to be supplied.

These two concepts can be illustrated by reference to Figure 8.9. Although the figure relates to the labour market it could equally be the market for any other factor of production. The equilibrium wage rate in this particular labour market is P and the numbers employed q. Thus total earnings are OPEq. The shaded area SPE represents economic rent and is the amount above the minimum payment necessary to keep labour in the particular industry concerned. The last worker employed may only be willing to work for P, thus he or she obtains zero economic rent. All previous workers would receive economic rent and their transfer earnings are represented by the area OSEq. SE in Figure 8.9 is the 'necessary supply price', i.e. the minimum payment necessary to keep the factor in its present occupation.

Two extreme situations are represented in Figures 8.10(a) and (b). In Figure 8.10(a) the supply curve for labour is perfectly inelastic (S_1). If this is the case then with a demand curve (D_1) the earnings are OW_1Eq_1 and this is all economic rent since q_1 units of labour would have been willing to work for nothing. The situation in Figure 8.10(b) is somewhat different in that the supply curve (S_2) is perfectly elastic at a wage rate W_2, and total earnings are represented by area OW_2Eq_2 and this represents all transfer earnings. The reason for this is quite simple in that if the employer reduced the wage rate below W_2, labour

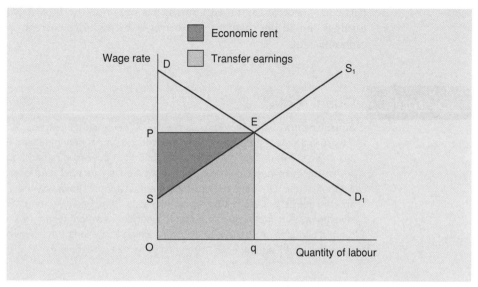

Figure 8.9 The figure illustrates economic rent and transfer earnings.
The transfer earnings, given by area OSEq, are the minimum payments
necessary to keep the factor of production in its present use. The excess
of earnings above the transfer earnings SPE is called the economic rent.

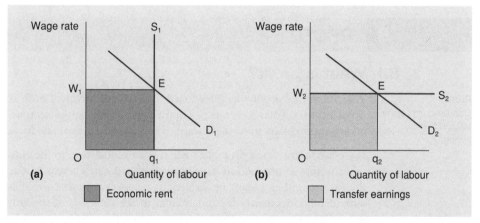

Figure 8.10 If the supply curve is perfectly inelastic as in (a) then economic
rent is represented by the area OW₁Eq₁. Alternatively, if the supply curve
is perfectly elastic as in (b) then transfer of earnings are represented by
area OW₂Eq₂.

would be unwilling to supply its services. It should be clear from Figures 8.10(a) and (b),
therefore, that the more inelastic the supply curve, the greater the economic rent.

We have analysed economic rent and transfer earnings in terms of labour and the
wage rate but it would have been equally valid to have used capital. For example, if a

particular piece of capital equipment has only one use then it will have zero transfer earnings and all the payments it receives in excess of its current operating costs will be economic rent.

Example	Quasi rent

A machine may be expected to earn €10,000 per annum in excess of its operating costs. If there is a recession, however, the capital equipment may only earn €1,000 but it will still make sense to keep the capital equipment in operation rather than scrap it. This will be the case in the short run so long as it covers its operating cost since it has no alternative use. Once the capital equipment wears out, however, the situation is different and the equipment will not be replaced unless it has been deemed to be an unwise investment. Any factor payment that is a surplus payment (economic rent) in the short run but contains an element of transfer earning in the long run, is called 'quasi rent'. The return to capital equipment is often placed in this category.

Pause for thought 8

What is meant by transfer earnings?

8 PROFIT

8.1 What is profit?

Profit
Can be seen as the reward for risk taking.

The concept of profit was introduced in 5: **10** and involves both revenue and cost (e.g. Total Profit = Total Revenue – Total Cost). Profit can be seen as the reward for risk-taking and it differs from the reward to the other factors of production in several ways:

(a) *Uncertainty surrounds profit* since it is a residual paid to the entrepreneur after all the other factors of production have been rewarded. So, whereas labour receives a reward in the form of either a wage or a salary, it is not certain that the shareholders will receive a dividend. Uncertainty is fundamental to the activities of the entrepreneur and it will generally be the case that the greater the uncertainty, the greater the risk and the potential rewards.

(b) *Profit can be negative* in which case the firm is making a loss. This is unlike the returns to the other factors of production which are positive since they are contracted prior to the commencement of production. For example, labour is paid an agreed contractual amount.

(c) *Profit can fluctuate much more than the other factor rewards*. With regard to wages, for example, the rates are normally fixed by the employer for a particular period of time, so too is rent, but profit depends on the cost of production and the demand for the product – which may change dramatically.

8.2 Profit as a cost of production

If the profit of a particular company falls below a particular level the entrepreneur will switch into another form of economic activity. It is, therefore, the case that the entrepreneur must earn 'normal profit' to prevent him or her transferring to another type of economic activity in the long run. *Normal profit* is the minimum return necessary to keep the entrepreneur in a particular line of business and it can, therefore, be seen as a cost of production. Profit above normal profit is often referred to as *supernormal profit*.

8.3 The function of profit

In the free market economy (*see* 1: 4) the profit motive is all important as a key motivator in allocating resources in line with consumer demand. Consumers indicate their preferences by being willing to pay a higher price for a certain quantity of a particular good or service. If this is the case, it will encourage the entrepreneur to increase the supply of that good or service since the higher price, assuming other things remain constant, will increase the sales revenue and, therefore, the total profit received. Demand for other products may have fallen, leading to a reduction in price, and thus a fall in sales revenue and total profit. The result of this will be a reduction in the supply of these products since there is less profit to be earned and resources will reallocate to more profitable areas of production.

Profit acts as an incentive to reallocate resources, for it is the prospect of profit that encourages firms to enter a market and add to the productive capacity of that particular industry. There are, however, certain sectors of the economy where it is not feasible to operate on the basis of the profit motive as a means of allocating resources. This is frequently the case with public services which are state controlled and run as public corporations.

8.4 Determination of profit

The total profits earned by a particular company depend upon the relationship between total revenue and total cost. The gap between revenue and cost (i.e. profit) may depend on how successful the entrepreneur is in:

(a) Raising revenue or in anticipating changes in the market demand for particular products.

(b) Reducing costs, such as by installing new and more productive techniques, lowering the firm's costs and to leading to an increase in the company's profit.

(c) Taking advantage not only of internal but also of external economies of scale (*see* 5: 10.4–10.5).

(d) Restricting the entry of new firms into the market.

 Pause for thought 9

Why is Manchester United such a profitable football club?

KEY POINTS

- Marginal productivity theory of labour suggests that firms will continue to employ labour up to the point at which the marginal person employed adds as much to revenue as he/she does to costs.

- The marginal revenue product (MRP) curve for labour is the firm's demand curve for labour in a competitive labour market.

- If the *product market* is monopsonistic, less labour will be employed and at a lower wage rate than if it is competitive.

- If the *labour market* is unionised, then the union might be able to raise wages and retain employment if it has considerable bargaining strength.

- A monopsony is a market in which there are significant buyers or employers of labour who can influence the wage rate by their hiring policy.

- Economic rent is the income obtained by the owner of a factor of production over and above what is necessary to induce the owner to supply the factor of production.

- Transfer earnings refer to the income that the owner of a factor of production requires in order to induce them to supply that factor.

- Trade unions are organisations which represent a group of workers essentially for the purpose of improving pay and conditions.

- Profit can be seen as the reward for risk taking with total profit defined as total revenue minus total cost.

Further reading

Griffiths, A. and Wall, S (2006) *Applied Economics*, 11th edition, FT/Prentice Hall, Chapter 15.

Griffiths, A. and Wall, S. (2005) *Economics for Business and Management*, FT/Prentice Hall, Chapter 7.

Heather, K. (2004) *Economics Theory in Action*, 4th edition, FT/Prentice Hall, Chapter 11.

Parkin, M., Powell, M. and Matthews, K. (2005) *Economics*, 6th edition, FT/Prentice Hall, Chapter 14.

Sloman, J. (2006) *Economics*, 6th edition, FT/Prentice Hall, Chapter 9.

Web references

National Statistics: **http://www.statistics.gov.uk/** The official UK statistics site.

Trade Union Congress: **http://www.tuc.org.uk/** The main UK labour coordinating organisation.

Confederation of British Industry: **http://www.cbi.org.uk/** The main employers federation in the UK.

ACAS: **http://acas.org.uk/** The main UK advisory, conciliation and arbitration service.

Department of Trade and Industry: **http://www.dti.gov.uk/er/nmw/** Information regarding the national minimum wage.

Eurostat: **http://europa.eu.int/comm/eurostat/** EU data.

Trade unions: **http://www.psr.keele.ac.uk/area/** Information about trade unions and labour organisations.

Unison: **http://www.unison.org.uk/** The website of the UK's largest union.
International Labour Office: **http://www.ilo.org/** The international labour organisation with comparative statistic on labour, social conditions, etc.
Global trade unions: **http://www.vicnet.net.au/vicnet/labour/global.htm** information on trade unions from a global perspective.

PROGRESS AND REVIEW QUESTIONS

Answers to most questions can be found at the back of the book (pages 505–7). Answers to asterisked questions can be found on the students' side of the Companion Website.

Multiple-choice questions

The figure below illustrates a profit maximising monoponistic buyer of labour and refers to questions 1 and 2.

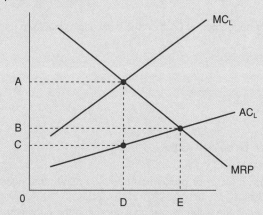

1 The amount of labour employed is:

a) A
b) B
c) C
d) D
e) E

2 The wage rate is:

a) A
b) B
c) C
d) D
e) E

The figure below illustrates a situation of collective bargaining and refers to questions 3 and 4.

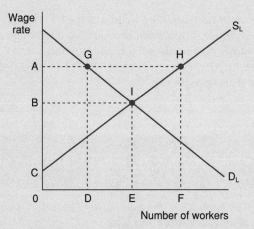

3 If, through collective bargaining, the wage rate is negotiated above the market equilibrium, the supply curve for labour is:

a) CEHS$_L$
b) BEH
c) AGHS$_L$
d) DGH
e) FHG

4 If the wage rate is negotiated at 0A then the individuals unable to find employment is measured by:

a) AB
b) DE
c) EF
d) DF
e) AC

5 Economic rent can be defined as the:

a) reward for risk taking
b) amount paid for a factor of production over and above that necessary to keep it in its present occupation
c) difference between the value placed on a good and the price actually paid
d) minimum payment necessary to keep the factor of production in its present occupation
e) none of the above.

6 In a competitive labour market, the *demand curve for labour* is given by which *one* of the following?

a) Total physical product
b) Total revenue product
c) Marginal physical product
d) Marginal revenue product
e) Marginal cost

7 A *monopsony* type of market failure is said to occur for which *one* of the following?

a) Suppliers of labour have market power
b) Suppliers of products have market power
c) Buyers of labour have market power
d) Buyers of products have market power
e) There is a natural monopoly

8 Which *two* conditions are most likely to lead to a rise in union bargaining power?

a) Rise in the percentage of the workforce in the union

b) Increased competition in the product market

c) A sustained rise in GDP

d) Relatively high elasticity of demand for labour

e) Monopsony in the labour market

9 Which of the following refers to a situation where the return to the factor is greater than is needed for it to supply itself?

a) Quasi rent

b) Transfer earnings

c) Interest

d) National Minimum Wage

e) Economic rent

Data response questions

1

Number of workers employed	1	2	3	4	5	6
Total product (output per week)	10	22	36	44	50	50

a) If the price of the product is €20 per unit, given the information in the table, calculate the marginal physical product of labour and the marginal revenue product of labour.

b) Assuming the producer is a profit maximiser, how many workers would be employed if the wage rate was €160 per week?

c) How many would be employed if the wage rate fell to €80?

2 Look carefully at the data in Table 8.3.

Table 8.3 Earnings of occupational groups: average (gross weekly) earnings of full-time male employees in selected occupations, as a percentage of average (gross weekly) earnings of all full-time male employees (April, 2002)

Non-manual	
Managers and administrators	152
Professional occupations	132
Associate professional and technical	113
Sales	76
Personal and protection services	76
Clerical and secretarial	63
Manual	
Craft and related occupations	78
Plant and machine operators	71
Other occupations	60

Source: Adapted from *New Earnings Survey*, ONS, 2002

Can you explain the earnings differentials given in the table?

True/false questions

1 The marginal revenue product of labour is the marginal physical product (MPP) multiplied by the marginal revenue.

2 Average revenue product is derived by multiplying marginal physical product by average revenue.

3 The industry's supply curve for labour is derived by the horizontal summation of the supply curves of individual supply curves.

4 A single buyer of labour can be called a monopsonist.

5 Trade unions comprise groups of workers who have a common interest, most notably to improve the working environment of its members.

6 The minimum payment necessary to keep the factor of production in its present occupation is called economic rent.

7 If the supply curve for labour is perfectly elastic there is no economic rent.

8 Profit can be seen as a reward for risk taking.

Essay questions

Answers to asterisked questions can be found on the students' side of the Companion Website. All other answers can be found at the back of the book (pages 506–7).

1* How will the firm's demand for labour be affected by a fall in the wage rate, assuming:

a) all other firms hold their output constant?
b) all other firms expand their output?

2 Distinguish between economic rent and transfer earnings. How does the elasticity of supply affect economic rent?

3* How does profit differ from the other factor rewards? What role does profit play in the allocation of resources?

Regulation, deregulation and competition

0101
1010
1010
1110
1101
1010

Learning objectives

By the end of this chapter you should be able to:

- Define regulation, deregulation and privatisation.
- Understand the reasons for deregulation.
- Explain public interest theory.
- Understand the reasons for and against privatisation.
- Explain the meaning of natural monopoly.
- Discuss the key elements in UK and EU competition policy.

1 INTRODUCTION

Regulation
Involves rules laid down by government in order to restrict or control economic activity by price setting, output setting, controlling entry into a market, markets served and services supplied within a particular industry.

This chapter studies the government regulation of markets for goods and services and seeks to explore why, since the late 1970s, there has been a tendency to deregulate markets. Deregulation is the process of removing regulations or other restrictions to economic activity. Privatisation of previously state owned assets is sometimes regarded as a type of deregulation.

This chapter draws on the ideas of economic welfare considered earlier in the book: for example, the ideas of consumer surplus (Chapter 4) and producer surplus (Chapter 5). 'Public interest theory' examines the impacts of regulation or deregulation in terms of the *net* effect of any proposed change on economic welfare, defined as the sum of consumer and producer surplus.

The theoretical underpinnings of competition policy in the European Union (and indeed in the UK) are considered in more detail in Chapter 17.

2 REGULATION

Regulation involves the imposition of controls on prices, output, entry and exit, markets served and services supplied within a particular industry.

2.1 Types of regulation

It is somewhat difficult to categorise all the different types of regulation that can be imposed on firms by the UK government or the EU. Two general types can be identified:

1 Regulations aimed at protecting the consumer from the consequences of market failure.

2 Regulations aimed at preventing the market failure from happening at all.

These two types of regulation can be illustrated by considering regulations imposed by the EU on business.

1 In the Financial Sector, the EU *Deposit Guarantee Directive* protects customers of accredited EU banks by restoring at least 90% of any losses up to a maximum of £12,000 following the failure of a particular bank. Protecting customers is partly a response to 'asymmetric information', since customers do not have the information in order to evaluate the credit worthiness of a particular bank, and might not be able to interpret that information correctly even if it were available.

Asymmetric information
Where one person or firm knows more than another person or firm.

2 The EU *Capital Adequacy Directive* is aimed at preventing market failure from taking place at all. This seeks to prevent market failure (such as a bank collapse) by directly relating the value of the capital a bank must hold to the riskiness of its business. The idea is that the greater the value of capital available to a bank, the larger the 'buffer stock' it has in place should it need to absorb any losses. Various elements of the Capital Adequacy Directive force the banks to increase their capital base if the riskiness of their portfolio (indicated by various statistical measures) is deemed to have increased.

Deregulation
Involves the removal of restrictions on economic activity in terms of price and output setting, controlling entry into a market, markets served and services supplied within a particular industry.

The regulatory system for EU financial markets is seeking to provide a framework within which greater competition between banks can occur, while at the same time addressing the fact that greater competition can increase the risk of bank failure. It is seeking both to protect the consumer, should anything untoward occur, and at the same time to prevent anything untoward actually occurring.

As well as regulating a sector a government can also intervene by *removing* such regulation, i.e. by using policies of *deregulation*.

2.2 Reasons for deregulation

Public interest theory
A theory of regulation stating that regulation is introduced in order to satisfy the demands of consumers and producers. As such, it usually involves the ideas of consumer and producer surplus.

The following can be seen as reasons for deregulating markets, namely:

- *Opening markets up to competition* If removing regulation stimulates market competition then consumers can benefit from the extra choice and lower prices that usually follow.
- *Removing unnecessary obstacles to business efficiency* Firms, small, medium and large regularly complain about the time and money 'wasted' having to comply (e.g. form-filling) with what they regard as unnecessary bureaucratic regulation.
- *Raising economic welfare* If regulation has become so complex, time consuming and expensive for businesses and employees to comply with, then there may be a case for removing elements of that regulation. 'Public interest theory' would propose removing regulations where it can be shown that 'economic welfare', defined as consumer surplus plus producer surplus, is increased by removing the regulations.

 ## Pause for thought 1

Suggest some reasons for deregulating the airline industries, which used to be dominated by large state-run airlines.

2.3 Deregulation and public interest theory

Economic welfare can be defined as consumer surplus plus producer surplus.

Consumer surplus
The difference between the value placed on a good and the price actually paid.

Producer surplus
The price a producer obtains for a product minus the opportunity cost of producing it.

- The *consumer surplus* is the amount consumers are willing to pay over and above the amount they need to pay.
- The *producer surplus* is the amount producers receive over and above the amount they need for them to supply the product.

Public interest can be analysed by reference to Figure 9.1. In the figure the initial demand curve DD and supply curve SS give a market equilibrium price P_1 and quantity Q_1.

The market may have been *regulated* in order to prevent the price falling below P_2, with the government setting a *quota* restricting output of the product to $0Q_2$. In terms of Figure 9.1, if the quota is set at Q_2, then the effective supply curve becomes SaS′, since no more than Q_2 can be supplied whatever the price.

The result is to raise the 'equilibrium' price from P_1 to P_2 and reduce the 'equilibrium' quantity to Q_2. In this case, the quota regulation has resulted in a loss of economic welfare equivalent to the area B plus C. The reduction in output from Q_1 to Q_2 means a loss of consumer surplus of area B and a loss of producer surplus of area C. The higher price does, however, result in a gain of area A to the producer. This involves a transfer of income from the consumer to the producer and also represents a loss of consumer surplus. This means that the *net* welfare change is negative, i.e. there is a 'deadweight loss' of areas B plus C.

'Public interest theory' suggests that deregulation should occur whenever the net welfare change of removing regulations is seen to be positive. In terms of Figure 9.1 it could be argued that removing the regulation by which the government has restricted output to keep price artificially high at P_2 will give a net welfare change which is *positive*, namely a

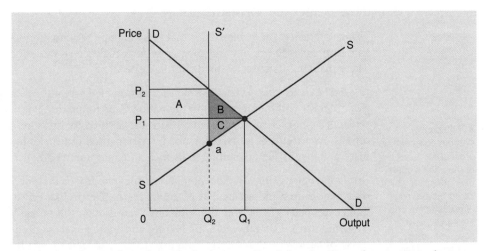

Figure 9.1 A regulated market such as the introduction of a quota scheme set at $0Q_2$ will lead to an increase in price to P_2, above the market level of P_1. This will result in a loss of economic welfare equal to the area B plus C. Using public interest theory there is a need for the market to be deregulated since economic welfare will then be increased.

net gain of area B plus C. By allowing the free market equilibrium price P_1 and quantity Q_1 to prevail, this restores the previous loss of economic welfare which was the result of regulation.

Deregulation is designed to improve competitiveness and this process can be frustrated by the absence of privatisation. As such, deregulation and privatisation are seen to be more desirable.

Pause for thought 2

What do you understand is meant by public interest theory?

3 PRIVATISATION

Privatisation
The process of selling public sector companies or assets to the private sector or shareholders.

Privatisation is usually used to refer to a situation in which a good or service previously provided by the public sector is now provided by the private sector. In the UK some important nationalised industries such as coal, telecommunications, gas, water and railways were until recently run by public corporations, not private firms. In 1979 the nationalised industries were a significant part of the economy, producing 9% of GDP, being responsible for 11.5% of UK investment and employing 7.3% of all UK employees. Since 1979, however, privatisation in the UK has reduced the number of nationalised industries to less than 2% of UK GDP, around 3% of UK investment and under 1.5% of UK employment.

The scale of the transfer of public sector businesses since 1979 to private ownership is indicated in Table 9.1 which lists the businesses privatised by their sector of operations.

The arguments for and against privatisation are now considered.

3.1 The case for privatisation

Greater efficiency The suggestion is that breaking up the state monopoly and allowing private companies to provide the good or service, makes resource allocation more efficient. Three main points are often made in this respect.

X-inefficiency
Without competitive pressure a monopolist's costs may increase, which could be the result of overstaffing or a failure to invest in new technology. The effect of this X-inefficiency is to make the MC and AC curves higher than they would be otherwise.

(a) *Public choice theory* This sees politicians and civil servants seeking to maximise their own interests (utility functions) in the nationalised industries. Politicians seek votes, civil servants support their departments which are lobbied by pressure groups, such as trade unions. As a result objectives pursued by nationalised industries have tended to be confused and inconsistent, resulting in inefficient management and operation of the industry.

(b) *Property rights theory* This emphasises the inability of the public to exercise control over nationalised industries. For example, the public (unlike private shareholders) have limited property rights over the company even though the public 'owns' them. In contrast, the private shareholders, by buying and selling shares, attending AGMs, and the threat of takeovers, all resulting from private share ownership, are thought to increase the 'efficiency' of corporate activity.

(c) *X-inefficiency* is the term often given to the result of these shortcomings; i.e. management failing to minimise cost in producing a given output – or failing to maximise output from a given set of resources.

Table 9.1 Major privatisations in the UK: a sectoral breakdown

Mining, oil, agriculture and forestry
British Coal
British Petroleum
Enterprise Oil
Land Settlement
Forestry Commission
Plant Breeding Institute

Distribution, hotels, catering
British Rail Hotels

Transport and communication
British Railways
National Freight, National and Local Bus
Companies
Motorway Service Area Leases
Associated British Ports, Trust Ports, Sealink
British Airways, British Airways Authority
(and other airports)
British Telecommunication, Cable and Wireless

Banking and finance
Girobank

Manufacturing, science and engineering
AEA Technology
British Aerospace, Short Bros, Rolls-Royce
British Shipbuilders, Harland and Wolff
British Rail Engineering
British Steel
British Sugar Corporation
Royal Ordnance
Jaguar, Rover Group
Amersham International
British Technology Group Holdings
(ICL, Fairey, Ferranti, Inmos)

Electricity, Gas and Water
British Gas
National Power, PowerGen
Nuclear Electric
Northern Ireland Electric
Northern Ireland Generation (4 companies)
Scottish Hydro-Electric
Scottish Power
National Grid
Regional Electricity Distribution
(12 companies)
Regional Water Holding Companies
(10 companies)

This can be illustrated by reference to Figure 9.2. The figure refers to a monopoly situation (*see* Chapter 6, Section 4.1) such as a nationalised industry. It is assumed that costs are constant, hence marginal cost equals average cost, and the monopolist seeks to profit maximise. If the marginal and average cost is $MC_1 = AC_1$ the profit maximising output will be Q_1 and the price P_1. Suppose the arguments above using 'public choice' theory and 'property rights' theory apply, so that the nationalised industry fails to control costs. As a result the nationalised industry will become increasingly inefficient, and it may be expected that the marginal and average cost curves drift upwards to $MC_2 = AC_2$. The tendency for productive efficiency to decline is termed X-inefficiency and in order to maximise profits the monopolist will reduce its output to Q_2 and raise its prices to P_2.

Greater managerial freedom The nationalised industries, being dependent on the Treasury for finance, had long complained of insufficient funds for investment. When the industry is privatised these constraints no longer apply, and management can now seek to raise finance for investment from the capital market (e.g. share issues).

Wider share ownership In 1979, before the move to privatisation took place, only 7% of UK adults owned shares. Today around 20% own shares, many having bought shares for the first time in privatised companies. As such, privatisation has helped create a 'property

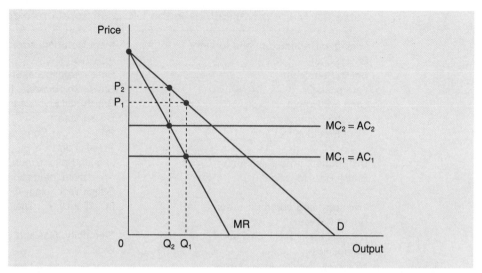

Figure 9.2 Firms operating in the public sector without the competitive pressure may find that they become inefficient with an increase in their costs from MC_1/AC_1 to MC_2/AC_2. This is termed X-inefficiency and leads to an increase in the price the consumer pays.

owning democracy' resulting in shareholders sympathetic to a capitalist/market based economy and a more committed and efficient workforce as a result of owning shares in the company.

More government revenue The privatisation programme since 1979 has raised in the region of £50 billion for the Treasury.

3.2 The case against privatisation

It simply converts a state monopoly to a private monopoly The argument here is that economies of scale are so large for many of the industries and sectors privatised (*see* Table 9.1) that it will only ever be efficient to have one, or at most a few, large firms in those sectors. This criticism of privatisation suggests that it simply changes a 'state monopoly' for a 'private monopoly', with few, if any, benefits of lower price and extra consumer choice.

Need for industry regulation and extra bureaucracy Related to the previous point, governments have appointed industry regulators to protect the public from the market power of large private companies that have replaced the nationalised industries. For example, OFGAS, OFWAT and OFTEL attempt to limit price increases and impose conditions on the operations of the now large private companies in gas, water and telecommunications. Firms in these industries often complain as to their lack of freedom to manage with excessive 'red tape' and bureaucracy because of industry regulators.

Concentration of share ownership Whilst more individuals own shares, the larger shareholding institutions such as pension funds, insurance companies and unit trusts have increased their share holdings and together own almost 60% of all shares in the UK. Only these shareholders who have a significant stake in the company can, in practice, influence company policy and as such having each owning a few shares each does little to bring about a true 'property owning democracy'.

Loss of government revenue At the time of privatisation the new shares were offered to the public at largely 'knock-down' prices to create public interest in the privatisation. This undervaluation of shares lost the Treasury considerable potential revenue at the time of these privatisations and was seen as simply selling off the family silver.

Pause for thought 3

Suggest some reasons for and against the privatisation of the UK telecommunication industry.

3.3 'Natural monopoly' argument

Natural monopoly Refers to a situation in which one firm can supply the whole market at a lower price than a number of firms.

The *natural monopoly* argument is often advanced in favour of public ownership of certain industries and therefore against privatisation. Economies of scale in railways, water, electricity and gas industries are perhaps so great that the tendency towards monopoly can be termed 'natural'. In terms of our earlier analysis (*see* Chapter 5, Section 10.4) the *minimum efficient size* (MES) is so large that the economy can only sustain one efficient firm in that particular industry. It then follows that creating competition in providing such goods and services, with duplication of investment would, in this view, be wasteful of resources.

Figure 9.3 illustrates the natural monopoly argument. The falling long-run average total cost curve (LRAC) indicates that significant economies of scale occur as output rises.

The demand (AR) curve for the product is such that it is not possible for this industry to even have one firm producing at the minimum efficient size (MES). Output Q_1 is the highest output the nationalised industry could produce and still break even (Price = AR = AC). However, even at this output the LRAC curve is still falling. To create private sector

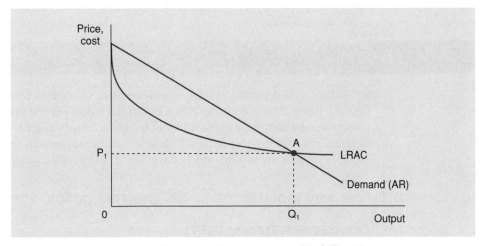

Figure 9.3 In the case of a natural monopoly with falling long-run average cost, it is not possible for one firm to achieve the minimum efficient size. At the break even point A the LRAC curve is still falling.

competition in such a 'natural monopoly' situation would mean smaller outputs than $0Q_1$ at higher average costs and higher prices than is needed to break even.

 Pause for thought 4

Can you suggest any possible examples of a natural monopoly?

4 REGULATION OF PRIVATISED COMPANIES

The privatisation of public utility companies with 'natural' monopolies creates the possibility that the companies might abuse their monopoly power. As such UK privatisation have incorporated reassurance to the public in the form of regulatory offices for each privatised utility, for example OFTEL for telecommunications and OFWAT for the water industry.

4.1 Objectives of regulators

Regulators have two fundamental objectives.

(a) They attempt to create the environment which companies would experience in a competitive market environment. For example, companies in competitive markets must take account of what their competitors are doing when setting their prices and are under competitive pressure to improve their service to consumers in order to gain market share. Regulation can stimulate the effects of a competitive market by setting price caps and performance standards.

(b) Regulators have the longer-term objective of encouraging actual competition by promoting the entry of new producers into the market and by preventing privatised monopoly power maintaining barriers to entry.

5 UK COMPETITION POLICY

In Chapter 5 the potential benefits of increased size via various economies of scale were detailed, whereas the monopoly section of Chapter 6 detailed that the extra market power from increased size can lead to higher prices, lower output and reduced choice for consumers. Competition policy in the UK seeks to balance the potential benefits of mergers and acquisitions with the need to protect the public from possible excesses of market power.

5.1 The key institutions in UK merger policy

Office of Fair Trading (OFT)

This is an independent statutory body which has been given the task of keeping markets under review and promoting competition. In the *Enterprise Act 2002* it was given the key role in deciding which mergers should be permitted and which should be investigated further. For those mergers to be investigated further it advises the *Secretary of State for Trade and Industry* on whether, and under what conditions, the proposed merger should be allowed.

Sometimes the OFT bases that advice on in-depth investigations conducted by the *Competition Commission* (CC) to which it can refer proposed mergers. For a proposed merger to be referred to the Competition Commission, two key conditions must apply, and if they do it becomes a '*relevant merger*'.

1 *Either* that the enterprise being taken over has a UK turnover exceeding £70 million (the 'turnover test') *or* that the merged enterprises together supply at least 25% of the UK market (the 'share of supply' test). It is implicit in this criterion that at least one enterprise must trade within the UK.

2 If the above condition is satisfied, the OFT will still only refer the proposed merger to the Competition Commission (CC) for further scrutiny if it is expected to result in a substantial 'lessening of competition' within the UK. 'Lessening of competition' would generally mean a situation where it is expected that product choice or quality would be reduced, prices raised, or innovation restricted as a result of the merger activity.

Sometimes the OFT might decide *not* to make a reference to the CC if the OFT itself believes that the 'public benefits' (e.g. higher choice, lower prices, higher quality or innovation) resulting from the merger outweigh the substantial 'lessening of competition'.

● *Competition Commission* (CC)
  It is an independent statutory body which conducts in-depth investigations of any potential merger situations referred to it by the OFT or the Secretary of State for Trade and Industry. The CC, when considering a merger in more depth, will weigh the 'lessening of competition' effect against the 'public benefits' effect before making its final decision.

● *Competition Appeals Tribunal* (CAT)
  There is a new appeals mechanism giving a right to those parties involved in the merger to apply to the Competition Appeals Tribunal (CAT) for a statutory judicial review of a decision of the OFT, CC or the Secretary of State for Trade and Industry, a Cabinet Minister in the UK government.

Mini Case Study 9.1

OFT loses power in merger decisions

Mergers stand to cost more and take longer after a ground-breaking decision in December 2003 by the *Competition Appeals Tribunal*, which urged the Office of Fair Trading to refer more takeovers to the *Competition Commission*. In comments about the first merger decision to be challenged before the three person tribunal, Sir Christopher Bellamy, its president, said that 'only exceptionally' should the OFT try to resolve mergers where there was a 'real question as to whether there is a substantial lessening of competition'.

Competition lawyers said the decision was likely to encourage competitors to take more merger challenges to the tribunal and would probably lead to more references to the *Competition Commission*. 'We're going to see a much higher level of contention,' predicted Chris Bright, lawyer at Shearman & Sterling. The decision came after the OFT cleared a planned £800 million merger in November 2003 between Torex and iSoft, which supply software to hospitals and healthcare companies. Under rules brought in by the *Enterprise Act 2003* ministers have been taken out of the merger decision process and a new appeals procedure against OFT decisions has been introduced.

Both Torex and iSoft are bidding to participate in the modernisation of the National Health Service's computer system, the world's biggest IT project. The OFT itself decides, without reference to a more thorough investigation by the Competition Commissions, that the merger was not likely substantially to reduce competition. That view was challenged by IBA Health, an Australian-listed healthcare software provider. It claimed the OFT's decision was unlawful because of the anti-competitive implications. It pointed out that, for example, the combined group would have a market share of 46% in the electronic patient record sector and 100% of the installed base in Scotland.

The Competition Appeals Tribunal also took issue with the OFT's approach. 'We are not satisfied the OFT applied the right test or . . . reached a conclusion that was reasonably open to them,' it said.

'In a merger case where it is clear that there are material and complex issues relating to what is potentially a substantial lessening of competition between horizontal competitors in a sector [of] national importance, we do not think it likely that parliament intended that those issues were to be resolved at the stage of the OFT,' Sir Christopher added in his remarks.

The tribunal quashed the OFT's decision and referred the matter back. This could either involve a fresh decision from the OFT or see it handed to the Competition Commission.

Source: FT 4 December 2003

Questions

1 *Why did the Competition Appeals Tribunal overrule the OFT in this particular case?*

2 *What implications does this have for merger policy in the UK?*

Answers to questions can be found on the students' side of the Companion Website.

So far our concern has been with mergers policy in the UK. However, UK competition policy also includes dealing with various 'restrictive practices'.

5.2 Restrictive practices legislation

The *Restrictive Trades Practices Act 1956* specified that restrictive practice operated by groups of firms had now to be registered with a *Registrar of Restrictive Practices*. It was the Registrar's responsibility to bring cases to the *Restrictive Practices Court*, consisting of five judges and ten lay members with the status of a High Court.

Such restrictive practices were deemed against the public interest unless they could satisfy at least one of seven 'pathways'.

1 That it protects the public against injury.
2 That it confers special benefits on consumers.
3 That it prevents local unemployment.
4 That it counters existing restrictions on competition.
5 That it maintains exports.
6 That it supports other acceptable restrictions.
7 That it assists the negotiations of fair trading terms for suppliers and buyers.

In 1968 an eighth 'gateway' was added, namely 'that the agreement neither restricts nor deters competition'.

Even having satisfied one or more of the 'gateway' conditions, the firms had still to show that the overall benefits from the restrictive practice were clearly greater than the costs incurred. This was largely responsible for the prohibition of many restrictive practices.

The *Fair Trading Act 1973* gave permission for restrictive practices legislation to be extended to cover services as well as the production of goods. The *Restrictive Practices Act 1976* consolidated previous legislation.

Despite these changes, the adequacy of restrictive practices legislation has been questioned. For example, under the Restrictive Practices Act there were no financial penalties for failing to register a restrictive agreement and many such practices were able to continue. Of particular concern was the legislation dealing with *cartels*, which has been considerably strengthened in recent years.

5.3 Cartels in the UK

The UK approach to cartels has been considerably strengthened in recent years.

(a) Under the *Competition Act 1998* the OFT was given civil powers to fine companies for anti-competitive behaviour involving formal or informal cartels.

(b) Under the *Enterprise Act 2002* the OFT was given additional *criminal powers* when investigating such cartels. The OFT now has the power to investigate people suspected of price fixing, bid rigging or limiting production or supply of goods dishonestly. Regulators from the OFT can now use force to enter offices or homes under a search warranty and can bring in the Serious Fraud Office to prosecute any criminal offence suspected. In effect, the OFT can do much more than impose fines, it can now take actions which result in the possible imprisonment of directors and others involved in cartel related activity.

6 EU COMPETITION POLICY

European competition policy has been criticised for its lack of comprehensiveness and in December 1989 the Council of Ministers agreed for the first time on specific cross-border merger regulations. The criteria for judging whether a merger should be referred to the European Commission covered three aspects.

1 The companies concerned must have a combined world turnover of more than €5 billion (though for insurance companies the figure was based on total assets rather than turnover).
2 At least two of the companies concerned in the merger must have an EU-wide turnover of at least €250 million each.
3 If both parties to the merger have two-thirds of their business in one and the same member state, the merger was to be subject to national and not EU controls.

The European Commission must be notified of merger proposals which meet the criteria within one week of the announcement of the bid and it then vets each proposed merger against a concept of '*a dominant position*'. Any creation or strengthening of a dominant position will be seen as incompatible with the aims of the EU if it significantly impedes '*effective competition*'.

The European Commission has one month after notification to decide whether to start proceedings and then four months to make a final decision. If a case is being investigated by the European Commission it will *not* also be investigated by national bodies such as the UK Competition Commission, for example.

Member states may prevent a merger which has already been permitted by the EU only if it involves public security, some aspect of the media or if competition in a local market is threatened.

Mini Case Study 9.2

Ryanair and Charleroi

The wide-ranging problems resulting from EU rulings on the legitimacy of state and subsidies is usefully illustrated by the recent experience of Ryanair, the Irish carrier. In February 2004 the European Commission ruled that Ryanair had received around £11 million (€15 million) in state aid from the Belgium authorities to fly to and from Charleroi airport in Southern Belgium and ordered the no-frills airline to return up to £3 million (€4 million) of the money. According to the judgement, Ryanair's controversial benefits from the Walloon regional government which owns Charleroi included €1.92 million in subsidies to launch new routes, €768,000 for pilot training, €250,000 towards hotel costs and a landing charge of only €1 per passenger, compared to the standard rate of €8 to €13.

Loyola de Palacio, the EU transport commissioner, said she thought the ruling would force Ryanair to put up its prices by an average of up to €8 (£6) per return ticket but Mr O'Leary, Ryanair's owner, said it was likely to be double that.

The ruling is also expected to affect Ryanair's cut-price fares to other destinations since it has similar subsidy arrangements with 19 state-owned airports in France which include popular second-home destinations for British travellers such as Montpellier, Biarritz, Carcassonne and Pau.

Ms de Palacio made it clear that some forms of aid were acceptable, including one-off help from airports to provide marketing support for new routes. She also indicated that introductory discounts for new airlines could be acceptable for up to five years, rather than the 15 years agreed at Charleroi.

The ruling is only applicable to state-owned airports, which means that destinations in countries such as Britain and Germany, where airports are privatised, will be unaffected.

The European Low Fares Airline Association, which represents nine low-cost carriers, also criticised the European Commission ruling. The Association of European Airline's secretary general, Ulrich Schulte-Strathaus, said, 'Are we expected to believe that there is a natural market at Charleroi that can support three Boeing 737 services a day to London and two a day to Venice? The Charleroi routes only make economic sense if, first, they are represented as serving Brussels and, secondly, they are supported by subsidies.'

Source: Economics for Business and Management, Griffiths and Wall (FT/Prentice Hall, 2005)

Questions

1 *Why have the regional governments owning these airports been willing to offer such aid and subsidies to Ryanair?*

2 *What is the European Commission's attitude to such aid and subsidies?*

3 *Consider some of the implications that might follow from this ruling against Ryanair.*

Answers to questions can be found at the back of the book (page 507).

7 EU RESTRICTIVE PRACTICES AND EU LEGISLATION

As in the UK, the EU competition policy seeks to deal with much more than merger activity. The reasoning behind European competition policy is exactly that which created the original European Economic Community (EEC) over 40 years ago. Competition is viewed as bringing consumers greater choice, lower prices and higher quality goods and services.

Promoting 'fair and free' competition The European Commission has a set of *directives* in this area which are designed to underpin 'fair and free' competition. They cover cartels (price fixing, market sharing, etc.), government subsidies (direct or indirect subsidies for inefficient enterprises – state and private), the abuse of dominant market position (differential pricing in different markets, exclusive contracts, predatory pricing, etc.), selective distribution (preventing consumers in one market from buying in another in order to maintain high margins in the first market), and mergers and takeovers.

Avoiding excessive use of state aid One of the most active areas of competition policy has involved *state aid*. The Commission has attempted to restrict the aid paid by member states to their own nationals through Articles 87 and 88 which cover various aspects of the distorting effect that subsidies can have on competition between member states. However, it is likely that the progressive implementation of single market arrangements will result in domestic firms increasing their attempts to obtain state aid from their own governments as a means of helping them meet greater European-wide competition. Overall, the amount of aid given by member states to their domestic industry has been running at around 2% of their respective GNPs during the 1990s and early years of the millennium.

Pause for thought 5

Make sure you understand what constitutes UK and EU competition policy.

Mini Case Study 9.3

EU Directive and the NHS

The UK managed to delay the full implementation of the EU Working Time Directive and to impose a higher limit for working hours to 58 hours per week for hospital doctors (rather than the standard 48 hours per week). Nevertheless, most NHS hospitals in England have found it difficult to operate legally since 1 August 2004 when this European Directive came into force limiting junior doctors' hours to 58 hours per week, falling to 48 hours per week in 2009. Written replies from 75 of the 173 NHS acute and specialist trusts to *The Guardian* showed 53% expect difficulties in cutting the juniors' hours to a maximum of 58 a week, as required by the new law.

Although most hospitals have tried to organise shift systems to comply with the Directive, many cannot find enough qualified house officers and registrars to staff them. The survey identified particular shortages in paediatrics, anaesthetics and maternity services. It found 13 hospitals – 17% – admitting openly that they could not comply fully by the deadline. But many more gave answers raising suspicion that they will also be operating outside the law. If the NHS trusts do not comply they could be prosecuted by the Health and Safety Executive and fined or – in extreme circumstances – forced to close down overworked departments.

But the Health and Safety Executive said it would wait for evidence of malpractice over several months before initiating proceedings and the first legal action is likely to be launched by the British Medical Association in local employment tribunals. It said it will name and shame hospitals which allow the new limits to reduce the quality of training. The Working Time Directive was passed in 2000 and applied to hospitals in an attempt to stop the long-standing practice in many member states of overworking doctors during their period of training to become consultants. For many years the medical establishment argued that long hours were necessary to give the juniors enough experience. More recently the Royal Colleges accepted that juniors working 80 or 90 hours a week were too exhausted to work safely and the shifts have been getting shorter. But the 37,000 juniors in England – including house officers, senior house officers and registrars – have not been entitled to the rest breaks required under European law. The Directive requires 11 hours' rest in every 24 hours, breaks during shifts and a maximum of eight hours' work in every 24 for night workers. Other groups of employees have a maximum working week of 48 hours and this will apply to junior doctors from 2009.

The Royal College of Nurses believes that nurses could take over work previously allotted to junior doctors.

Question

Discuss the issues raised in the Mini Case Study from the point of view of both employers and employees.

Answer to question can be found on the students' side of the Companion Website.

KEY POINTS

- Regulations are widely used in all economic sectors in order to protect consumers from 'market failure' and to prevent such failures actually occurring.
- There is considerable momentum behind removing regulations (i.e. deregulation) where this can be shown to be in the 'public interest'.
- Privatisation is the transfer of assets or economic activity from the public sector to the private sector.
- The term 'privatisation' is often used to cover many situations: the outright sale of state-owned assets, part-sale, joint public/private ventures, market testing and the contracting out of central/local government services.
- The case for privatisation is based on greater productive efficiency (lower costs) via the introduction of market pressures. These are seen as creating more flexibility in labour markets, higher productivity and reduced unit labour costs.
- The case against privatisation includes suggestions that state monopolies have often merely been replaced by private monopolies, with little benefit to consumers, especially in the case of the public utilities.

- Regulators have been appointed for a number of public utilities in an attempt to simulate the effects of competition (e.g. limits to price increases and to profits) when there is little competition in reality.

Further reading

Griffiths, A. and Wall, S. (2006) *Applied Economics*, 11th edition, FT/Prentice Hall, Chapter 8.

Griffiths, A. and Wall, S. (2005) *Economics for Business and Management*, FT/Prentice Hall, Chapter 8.

Heather, K. (2004) *Economics Theory in Action*, 4th edition, FT/Prentice Hall, Chapters 10 and 17.

Parkin, M., Powell, M. and Matthews, K. (2005) *Economics*, 6th edition, FT/Prentice Hall, Chapters 16 and 17.

Sloman, J. (2006) *Economics*, 6th edition, FT/Prentice Hall, Chapters 11 and 12.

Web references

The data sources below offer a range of useful data and information on companies, including regulations involving merger and acquisition activities.

Mergers and acquisitions involving UK: **www.competition-commission.org.uk**
Mergers involving EU: **http://europa.eu.int/comm/competition/index_en.html**
Mergers involving US: **http://www.ftc.gov/ftc/antitrust.htm**
http://bized.ac.uk
Companies House: **http://www.companieshouse.gov.uk/** The place for getting information on all English and Welsh companies.
EU Common Agricultural Policy:
http://europa.eu.int/comm/agriculture/capreform/index_en.htm
UK intellectual property rights: **www.patent.gov.uk**
US intellectual property rights: **www.uspto.gov**
World intellectual property rights: **www.wipo.int**
TRIPS: **http://www.wto.org/english/tratop_e/trips_e/trips_e.htm**

PROGRESS AND REVIEW QUESTIONS

Answers to most questions can be found at the back of the book (pages 507–9). Answers to asterisked questions can be found on the students' side of the Companion Website.

Multiple-choice questions

1 Which *two* of the following reasons are often used to support a policy to nationalise certain industries?

a) More difficult to take into account any divergence between private cost and social cost.

b) Easier to take into account any divergence between private cost and social cost.

   c) Few economies of scale exist in the industry.

   d) Economies of scale are so large that the industry is a 'natural monopoly'.

   e) It is expensive and inefficient to establish a bureaucracy of civil servants to run the industry.

2 Which *two* of the following reasons are often used to support a policy to privatise certain industries?

   a) Firms exposed to market forces are likely to be more efficient.

   b) Firms insulated from market forces are likely to be more efficient.

   c) Firms can more easily take into account any negative externalities in their decision making.

   d) The stock market can exert a useful discipline on the firm, with less successful firms being more likely to be taken over by more successful ones.

   e) The public finances are likely to deteriorate.

3 Which *two* of the following are problems that often confront regulators of particular industries?

   a) Setting the price floor

   b) Setting the price cap

   c) Establishing the share price

   d) Restricting competition

   e) Encouraging competition

4 Which *one* of the following refers to a situation in which the minimum efficient size for firm output is greater than the current output of the industry?

   a) Natural monopoly

   b) Public good

   c) Positive externality

   d) Negative externality

   e) Asymmetric information

5 Which *one* of these is an independent statutory body which conducts in-depth investigations of potential merger situations referred to it?

   a) Office of Fair Trading

   b) Secretary of State for Trade and Industry

   c) Competition Appeals Tribunal

   d) Competition Commission

   e) Court of Appeal

6 Which *one* of these has the initial task of deciding whether the potential merger should be classified as a 'relevant merger' and investigated further?

   a) Office of Fair Trading

   b) Secretary of State for Trade and Industry

   c) Competition Appeals Tribunal

   d) Competition Commission

   e) Court of Appeal

7 Which *two* of the following might lead the government to increase tax on an activity?

   a) Marginal private cost exceeds marginal social cost

   b) Marginal social cost exceeds marginal private cost

   c) Marginal private benefit exceeds marginal social benefit

    d) Marginal social benefit exceeds marginal private benefit

    e) Marginal private benefit equals marginal social benefit

8 Which *two* of the following might lead the government to subsidise an activity?

    a) Marginal private cost exceeds marginal social cost

    b) Marginal social cost exceeds marginal private cost

    c) Marginal private benefit exceeds marginal social benefit

    d) Marginal social benefit exceeds marginal private benefit

    e) Marginal private benefit equals marginal social benefit

 ## Case study question

Read the text then answer the questions.

State aid

One of the most active areas of competition policy has involved state aid. The Commission has attempted to restrict the aid paid by member states to their own nationals through Articles 87 and 88 (formerly Articles 92 and 93 of the original Treaty of Rome). These Articles cover various aspects of the distorting effect that subsidies can have on competition between member states. However, it is likely that the progressive implementation of single market arrangements will result in domestic firms increasing their attempts to obtain state aid from their own governments as a means of helping them meet greater Europe-wide competition. Overall, the amount of aid given by member states to their domestic industry has been running at around 2% of their respective GNPs during the 1990s.

    Currently, some 45 billion ECU per year is spent on state aid to EU manufacturing. Germany tops the league of aid recipients as it tries to help its new *Länder* in the former East Germany to restructure their industry. The main problem with state aid is that the big, industrially powerful countries – Germany, France, UK and Italy – account for some 85% of the total state aid given by EU countries to their domestic industry. This arguably gives such economies considerable advantages over the four 'cohesion' countries – Greece, Portugal, Spain and Ireland.

    To counter some of these trends, the EU Commission has begun to scrutinise state aid much more closely – especially where the aid seems to be more than is needed to ensure the ultimate viability of the recipient organisations. For example, in April 1998 the Commission decided that aid paid to the German porcelain firm, Triptis Porzellan GmbH, should be recovered because it believed the aid to be more than was needed to restore the firm's viability, thereby distorting competition in the market.

    Article 87 determines all state aid to be illegal unless it conforms to one or more of a number of exceptions:

- Aid to promote improvements of a social character
- Aid to promote economic development in areas with high unemployment or low living standards
- Aid to promote a project of common EU interest
- Aid to the former German Democratic Republic
- Aid to disaster areas
- Sectoral aid to assist in the restructuring of an individual sector in structural decline, e.g. shipbuilding.

Source: *Economics for Business and Management*, Griffiths and Wall (FT/Prentice Hall, 2005)

Questions

1 *Consider the case in favour of 'state aid' as a policy to correct market failure.*

2 *Now consider the problems with such a policy.*

True/false questions

1 A 'natural monopoly' refers to monopoly power in the provision of natural resources.

2 A benefit of nationalisation is that it encourages wider share ownership.

3 If regulation can be shown to result in a net welfare loss then this may be used as an argument in favour of deregulation.

4 Information asymmetry is where both parties have the same knowledge.

5 Public choice theory helps strengthen the case for privatisation.

6 Public interest theory helps strengthen the case for state ownership.

7 Privatisation helps widen share ownership in the short run and long run.

8 State involvement can help decision makers reflect social costs and benefits more readily than privatisation.

Essay questions

Answers to asterisked questions can be found on the students' side of the Companion Website. All other answers can be found at the back of the book (page 508).

1* Outline the reasons for deregulating a market.

2 Assess the arguments for and against privatisation.

3* Examine the role of the competition policy in the UK using examples to illustrate your arguments.

4 Why do governments often intervene in markets?

The environment

By the end of this chapter you should be able to:

- Understand the relationship between the economy and the environment.
- Develop a model of pollution and understand the concept of an optimum level of pollution.
- Examine different approaches to solving environmental problems such as bargaining and negotiations, environmental taxes, tradable permits and the setting of standards.
- Analyse the various options aimed at dealing with the problem of transport related pollution and congestion.

1 INTRODUCTION

In recent years there has been increasing interest in the impact that economic activity has on the environment. The disposal of household and industrial waste, traffic related pollution in urban areas, deforestation, acid rain and global warming are but a few of the issues causing concern. There is a growing awareness that the frequency and severity of events such as hurricanes in the Gulf of Mexico (Katrina and its impacts on New Orleans), the melting of the polar ice caps and the expansion of drought and desert conditions, can all be linked in some way to the impacts of humankind on the environment.

The aim of this chapter is to describe the link between the economy and the environment and to outline an economic model of pollution. In addition, the chapter will outline the various policy options available when dealing with environmental problems, namely bargaining, environmental taxes, tradable permits and the setting of environmental standards. Finally, a major polluter is transport and in particular the private car and as such the link between transport and the environment is examined.

2 THE ECONOMY AND THE ENVIRONMENT

In Chapter 11 the concept of the circular flow of income is introduced which examines the flow of income and expenditure between households and firms. Households receive income in return for their factor services and households use some of this income to purchase goods and services from firms. However, this conventional circular flow analysis fails to take account of constraints imposed on the economy by environmental factors. Figure 10.1 addresses this issue by providing a link between the economy (the circular flow of income) and the environment.

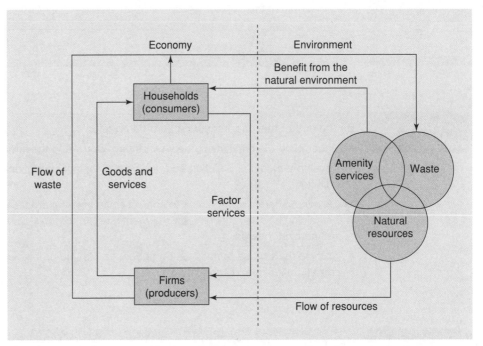

Figure 10.1 Relationship between the economy and the environment. The environment is linked to the economy in terms of providing natural resources and amenities as well as acting as a dumping ground for waste products.

The environment is linked to the economy in three ways:

(a) *Natural resources*, such as forests and coal deposits are to be found in the natural environment and are used in the production process. They can be classified as renewable and non-renewable resources.

(b) *Amenity services*, in that the natural environment provides households with benefits such as recreational space and areas of natural beauty such as National Parks.

(c) *Waste products*, generated by both households and firms such as carbon monoxide associated with road vehicles and discharged into the atmosphere. Likewise, sewage and litter are the by-products of consumer activity. The natural environment is ultimately the dumping place for all the waste products.

Figure 10.1 illustrates that all three are interlinked and in certain respects competitive. For example, the Alaska coastline is an area of natural beauty which provides an amenity service in terms of tourism and the residents who benefit from the beautiful scenery. At the same time the coastline provides resources such as commercial fishing activity. A discharge of waste or an oil spillage such as that from the oil tanker the *Exxon Valdez* in 1989 has major consequences in terms of using this natural resource. If the coastline cannot assimilate the discharge of oil then the resulting pollution will mean the amenity and resource functions, such as herring fishing, of the coastline are destroyed.

 ## Pause for thought 1

Give examples of natural resources, amenity services and waste products.

---

3   A MODEL OF POLLUTION

The effect that pollution, such as an oil spill or the discharge from a factory, has on the use of an amenity can be studied through the use of a model of pollution. In Figure 10.2 the horizontal axis measures the scale of economic activity (which means the output from a particular firm) and also the level of pollution, which is assumed to be directly related to the level of economic activity. The vertical axis relates to the costs and benefits, both to the firm and society, measured in monetary terms.

Marginal net private benefit (MNPB) measures the extra net benefit, i.e. of profit, received by the firm in producing one more unit while *marginal external cost* (MEC) measures the extra damage to society as a result of producing one more unit. If the firm is not constrained in terms of its scale of activity and aims to maximise its profits, then it

Marginal external cost (MEC)
The extra cost imposed on others when one more unit is produced.

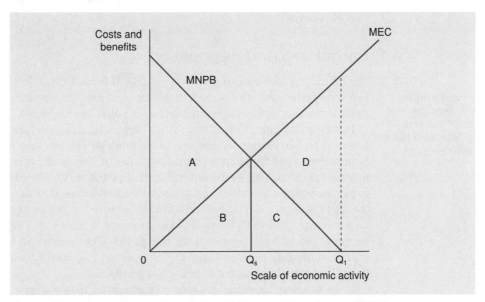

Figure 10.2 An optimum level of pollution exists where MNPB equals MEC with the firm producing Q_s. If a firm produces an amount below Q_s the benefits the firm derives in terms of profit is greater than the cost on society in terms of MEC, thus output should be expanded. If the firm is producing an output above Q_s then the cost on society is greater than the benefits the firm is deriving and so output should be reduced. As such a scale of activity Q_s is termed the social optimum.

will produce an amount Q_1. At this output the total net private benefit (total profit) is maximised, i.e. the area under the MNPB curve, A + B + C is maximised. At a level of output Q_1, however, there are total external costs of B + C + D. The optimum level of pollution, the *social optimum*, is achieved at a scale of activity Q_s, where MNPB = MEC. If the firm operated at a level of activity *above* Q_s then the MEC would be greater than the MNPB, with each extra unit of output causing more external damage than internal profit. At a level of activity below Q_s the converse would be true, less external damage than the internal profit it contributes. It is important to note that the optimum level of output Q_s involves an amount of pollution equal to area B in Figure 10.2. It follows that prohibiting an economic activity just because it generates external costs is rarely in society's interest. This does however raise the problem of identifying the *optimum* level of pollution since there are difficulties in measuring the costs and benefits.

Pause for thought 2

What area represents the net benefit to society when output is at Q_s?

4   POLICY OPTIONS

There are a number of options which can be used to achieve a more socially optimum level of pollution.

4.1 Bargaining and negotiation

Property rights
The legal rules that determine what firms or individuals can do with their property.

The bargaining solution is based on the insight of Ronald Coase in 1960. The argument is that if *property rights* are assigned, that is the legal rights to a resource, then *bargains* may be undertaken such that the optimum level of pollution is achieved.

In terms of Figure 10.2, if there is no bargaining then the firm will produce Q_1. If, however, property rights are assigned to the *firm that pollutes*, then those who suffer may be prepared to pay the polluter to reduce its scale of activity and therefore the level of pollution. In order to achieve the optimal level of pollution, Q_s, the sufferers may be willing to pay the polluter an amount up to a maximum of C plus D. This is an amount equal to the total loss incurred. The polluter would be prepared to reduce its output from Q_1 to Q_s for a sum not less than C, the profit earned through that activity. There is clearly scope for bargaining to take place between the two parties. The amount paid by the sufferers will thus be somewhere between C and C plus D with the amount actually paid depending on the relative bargaining strengths of the two parties.

If the property rights are assigned to the *sufferers* then a similar outcome will result. Here the polluter will find it advantageous to produce the social optimum Q_s and compensate the sufferers of pollution with an amount equal to B, thus retaining an amount of profit A. If the polluter produced an amount greater than Q_s the gains obtained in terms of profit would be less than the losses incurred in terms of compensation paid to the sufferers. As with the previous example there is scope for bargaining to take place. Whether the polluter compensates the sufferers or the sufferers pay the polluter the outcome is the same. In terms of equity, however, the two outcomes are very different.

Pause for thought 3

Can you use the letters in Figure 10.2 to indicate how the income distribution will differ depending on who has the property rights?

The success of the bargaining solution depends in part on the numbers involved. If there are a large number of sufferers and polluters then organising the two sides could be costly. In this case, the government may resort to alternative methods of dealing with pollution, most notably environmental taxes, tradable permits and emission standards. Game theory was introduced in Chapter 7, Section 5. It was used to analyse how firms might react in oligopolistic circumstances but it can also be used to study the notion of bargaining and the fact that one of the difficulties with such an option is the possibility of the 'free-rider' effect.

4.2 Bargaining, game theory and the free-rider problem

Assume there are two sufferers from the pollution emitted from a factory. The two sufferers, individuals A and B each have a level of utility equal to 50 utils. Individuals A and B are thinking about involving themselves in negotiation with the factory polluter. In reaching their decision there are *four* scenarios:

1 *Both individuals A and B decide not to negotiate with the polluter.* The outcome is that both continue to suffer and obtain a utility of 50 utils.
2 *Both individuals A and B decide to negotiate with the polluter.* There is a cost in negotiating which is equal to 70 utils each. If they negotiate together, however, they are likely to obtain major concessions, which could be equal to 100 utils for each individual. In this situation both individuals A and B benefit by a further 30 utils, resulting in each having utility of 80 utils.
3 *Individual A decides to negotiate while B free-rides.* In this situation the bargaining strength of the sufferers will be somewhat less and as such the gains from negotiation could be only 40 utils. In this situation the expected utility from negotiation for A would now be 10 utils (the original 50 utils plus the gain of 30 utils minus the cost of 70 utils). For individual B, however, the expected gain is 40 utils with no negotiation costs involved because of free-riding. Thus B's expected utility is 90 utils.
4 *Individual B decides to negotiate while A free-rides.* In this situation A's expected utility is 90 utils and B's 10 utils.

The information above can be presented in terms of a game theory payoff matrix, as in the table below.

		Individual B			
		Negotiate		Free-ride	
Individual A	Negotiate	*80*	80	*10*	90
	Free-ride	*90*	10	*50*	50

Each individual has one of two options, either to negotiate or free-ride. The left-side of each box (in italics) refers to individual A's outcomes (payoffs) and the right-side to individual B's outcomes (payoffs). Taking free-ride might seem an attractive option for each individual, yielding the highest payoff (90) in the belief that the other individual will indeed negotiate. However, if both decide to free-ride this essentially means both decide not to negotiate and the outcome is a less attractive payoff (50). The situation is the same as in the prisoner's dilemma, which is also part of game theory (*see* Chapter 7, Section 5.2).

If each selects the best outcome for itself independent of the reaction of the other, then each will choose to free-ride, believing it can achieve a payoff of 90 utils. This is the so-called 'dominant strategy' for the game, but in fact the outcome from following this strategy is only 50 utils each. Had each individual sought to negotiate rather than free-ride, then each would have been better off with 80 utils apiece. If sufferers are more likely to attempt to free-ride in this way, then giving them the property rights by making the polluter pay may be the best way of ensuring that the socially optimum bargaining outcome is achieved.

4.3 Environmental taxes

Pigouvian tax
A tax on the producer of an externality which is exactly equal to the marginal external cost imposed.

In terms of Figure 10.3, if a tax of t (a **Pigouvian tax**) is imposed on the polluter it has the effect of shifting the MNPB curve to the left, thus giving MNPB – t. The tax would be paid on each unit of pollution and the polluter would now maximise net private benefits at a level of activity equal to Q_s. If the firm produced an amount greater than Q_s then it would pay more in tax on the extra units sold than it would receive in revenue. The tax would be equal to MEC at the optimum level of pollution.

Using an environmental tax is a way of *internalising* the external cost. In other words, the firm now has the incentive to take the external cost into account when making its decisions. There are problems with using an environmental tax, not least in determining

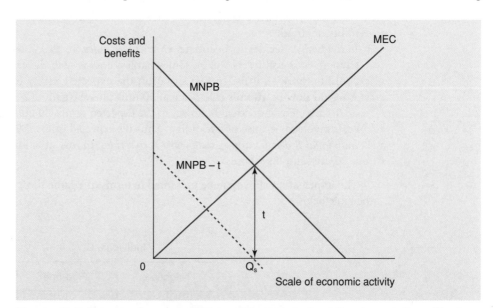

Figure 10.3 If an environmental tax of t were to be introduced, the effect would be to shift the MNPB curve to the left. If the tax is set correctly it will achieve an optimal level of economic activity, Q_s.

Market failure
Imperfections in the market which prevent it achieving an efficient allocation of resources.

the tax rate which will equate MNPB with the MEC. An environmental tax is consistent with the idea of the 'polluter-pays principle' in that the polluter should incur the cost of environmental degradation caused. The polluter-pays principle thus seeks to rectify *market failure*.

Pause for thought 4

What is meant by a Pigouvian tax?

4.4 Tradable permits

Tradable permits
Gives the holders the right to emit a specific level of pollution. These permits can be traded on markets.

As with an environmental tax, **tradable permits** are a market-based solution to the problem of pollution. With this policy option the polluter is issued with a number of permits to emit a specified amount of pollution. The total number of permits in existence places a limit on the total amount of emissions allowed. Polluters can buy and sell the permits to each other, at a price agreed between the two polluters. In other words, the permits are *transferable*.

The underlying principle of tradable permits is that those firms which can achieve a lower level of pollution can benefit by selling permits to those firms which at present find it either too difficult or expensive to meet the standard set.

The market for permits can be illustrated by use of Figure 10.4. In order to achieve an optimum level of pollution, the agency responsible for permits may issue Q_s permits. With demand for permits at D_1 the price will be set at P_1. If new polluters enter the market the demand for permits will increase, as with D_2 in the figure. As such, the permit price will increase to P_2.

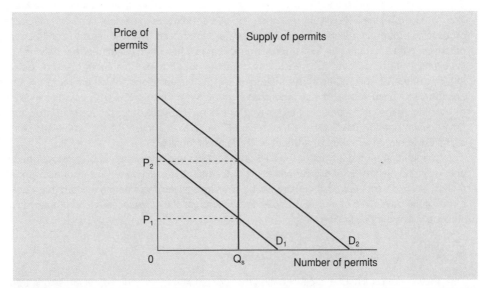

Figure 10.4 The market price for permits will be determined by the demand for and the supply of permits. With the supply of permits fixed at Q_s and the demand for permits being D_1, the price of permits will be P_1. If demand increases to D_2, the price of permits will rise to P_2.

If for any reason the agency wishes to relax the standard set then more permits will be issued and the supply curve for permits will shift to the right. Alternatively, the standard could be tightened, by the agency purchasing permits on the open market from polluters, which would have the effect of shifting the supply curve to the left.

The EU Emissions Trading Scheme uses the idea of tradable permits in seeking to reduce greenhouse gas emissions.

Mini Case Study 10.1

The EU Emissions Trading Scheme

In the EU an Emissions Trading Scheme (ETS) is being seen as a key economic instrument in a move to reduce greenhouse gas emissions. The ETS is to aid the EU in meeting its commitments as part of the Kyoto Protocol. The EU took upon itself as part of the Protocol to reduce greenhouse gas emissions by 8% (from 1990 levels) by 2008–2012. The idea behind the ETS is to ensure that those companies within certain sectors responsible for greenhouse gas emissions keep within specific limits by either reducing their emissions or by buying *allowances* from other organisations with lower emissions. The ETS is essentially aimed at placing a cap on emissions.

Background

The emission of greenhouse gases is seen as a major cause of climate change, which has environmental and economic implications, not least in terms of floods and drought. In October 2001 the European Commission proposed that an ETS should be established in the EU in order to deal with the greenhouse gas emissions. The result is that an ETS, in the first instance covering only CO_2 (carbon dioxide) emissions commenced on 1 January 2005, representing the world's largest market in emissions allowances. In the first phase, which runs from 2005–2007, the ETS will cover companies of a certain size in sectors such as energy, production and processing of ferrous metals, the mineral industrial sectors and factories making cement, glass, lime, brick, ceramics, pulp and paper. In the larger Member States it has been estimated that between 1,000 and 2,500 installations will be covered, whereas in the other Member States the number could be between 50 and 400. In terms of the UK this represents in the region of 1,500 installations, which emit approximately 50% of the economy's CO_2 emissions. The second phase, that will run from 2008–2012, could include other sectors such as aviation. In the UK a number of organisations will be responsible for the issue of allowances, namely the Environment Agency, the Scottish Environment Protection Agency, the Northern Ireland Department of the Environment and the Department of Trade and Industry.

In preparation for the advent of the ETS an electronic registry system is being developed such that when a change in the ownership of allowances takes place then there will be a transfer of allowances in terms of the registry system accounts. This registry will be similar to a banking clearing system that tracks accounts in terms of the ownership of money. In order to buy and sell the allowances each company involved in the scheme will require an account.

How will emissions trading work?

This section details a hypothetical situation that will aid in understanding how emissions trading will operate. In the following analysis we assume there are two companies, A and B, each emitting 60 million and 40 million tonnes of CO_2 per annum respectively. Each company is illustrated in Figure 10.5. The marginal abatement cost (MAC) curves refer to the extra cost to the firm of avoiding emitting the last unit of pollution. The MAC for

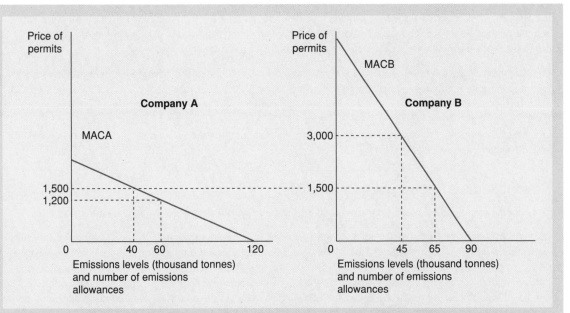

Figure 10.5 Marginal abatement cost (MAC) and the trading in emissions allowances.

company A increases more slowly than for company B indicating that the cost of abatement is more costly for company B when compared with A.

With no controls on the level of emissions then the total level of CO_2 emissions will be 210 million tonnes (120 million tonnes from company A and 90 million from company B). If we now assume that the authorities want to reduce CO_2 emissions by 50% (so that 105 million tonnes is the maximum) then this can be achieved by issuing 105 emission allowances. If they are issued on the basis of previous emission levels then company A would receive 60 million emission allowances (or tradable permits) and company B 45 million, based on one allowance representing the right to emit one tonne of CO_2. If this were the case then company A would have to reduce its emissions to 60 million tonnes and company B to 45 million tonnes. Based on this company A would have a MAC of £1,200 and company B £3,000. Given this situation company B would buy permits if it could pay less than £3,000 and company A would sell them for a price greater than £1,200. Company A would sell them since the revenue earned from the sale would be greater than the additional abatement cost incurred by reducing emissions. There is thus a basis for trade in emissions allowances and this will continue until the MAC's are identical. In Figure 10.5 this can be seen as £1,500 with 40 million tonnes of CO_2 emitted by company A and 65 million by company B, with company A selling 20 million emissions allowances to company B. Overall, the price of the allowances will be determined by supply and demand.

Potential advantages of the ETS

A number of potential advantages have been put forward in terms of the use of an ETS when dealing with issues such as the control of emissions affecting climate change, most notably:

(a) Unlike pollution taxes, which begin by making companies pay for something they were once getting for free, emissions allowances begin by creating and distributing a new type of *property right*.

(b) It is politically easier to get companies to agree on a pollution control policy that begins by distributing a valuable new property right than by telling them that they will have to pay a new tax. The reason for this is that the emission allowance will have a market value as long as the number of allowances created is limited. In other words, it is a more acceptable policy instrument to those directly involved in the ETS.

(c) They are cost effective since they provide incentives for polluters with low abatement costs to abate and sell the permits no longer required while providing incentives for polluters with higher abatement costs to purchase these permits rather than abate. As such a ready made market exists.

(d) According to the White Paper on the Future of Aviation (2003) one of the advantages of emissions trading is that it guarantees the desired outcome in a way not achieved by the other market – and non-market-based instruments, such as the introduction of a charge. Companies have flexibility in that they can achieve their emission reduction levels based on their own strategy. That is by reducing emissions or by purchasing emissions allowances. Either way the desired environmental outcome is achieved since the cap on overall emissions has been established.

Potential disadvantages of the ETS

The scheme came into force on 1 January 2005 and there are a number of potential disadvantages:

(a) An appropriate system of initially allocating the emissions allowances is all-important. In terms of the hypothetical situation outlined above, the allowances were allocated on the basis of current emissions with companies A and B each receiving allowances representing half their emission levels. There are, however, difficulties with this in that companies may have successfully reduced their level of emissions and been penalised for doing so by receiving less of the allowances. An alternative to this *grandfathering* approach could be to allocate allowances equally to those companies that are part of the ETS. This method also has inherent difficulties in that companies may differ in terms of the amount of pollution they currently emit. In terms of the EU ETS a final decision on individual allocations will be taken by the end of September 2004.

(b) A related issue is whether the allowances will be allocated freely or auctioned. The EU ETS will allow for a proportion of the allowances to be sold but at least 95% of the allowances must be allocated free in the first period of the scheme. The UK view is that there should be 100% free allocation in the first phase, which as stated runs from 2005–2007. If they are freely allocated then the price of allowances will be determined by the market that develops for trading EU ETS allowances.

(c) In terms of the philosophy underpinning the use of an emissions allowance scheme it can be argued that it gives the owner of an allowance the right to pollute. In other words, a permit to emit pollutants.

(d) It is possible that a few polluters may purchase all the available permits making it difficult for new companies to enter a particular sector. As such allowances could act as a *barrier to entry* and thus be seen as anti-competitive. It has been stated however that the idea behind the ETS is to limit emissions not output. There is a need to be aware of the potential difficulties new entrants to a sector may face.

(e) Any scheme of this nature will have an administration cost not least in terms of maintaining the electronic registry system. There is also a need to monitor the allowance transactions so that companies are only emitting what they are entitled to. There is also the cost of monitoring the scheme. It has been stated that as part of the EU ETS if companies do not surrender allowances necessary to cover their annual emissions then they will be liable to a penalty. In the first phase of the scheme this will be €40 per tonne of CO_2 emitted for which now allowances have been forthcoming.

Conclusions

The EU ETS represents a relatively new market-based approach to dealing with the issue of CO_2 emissions and their related impact on climate change. The scheme was introduced in the EU in January 2005 and is administered by a number of Environmental Bodies throughout the UK. The scheme has a number of potential advantages notably the fact that it is establishing a new form of property right, its acceptance relative to pollution taxes, its cost effectiveness and its flexibility. There are, however, potential difficulties not least in terms of allocating the emissions allowances, the ethical aspect of creating a right to pollute, the possibility of companies cornering the market in emissions allowances and the administrative costs.

Overall, time will tell as to the success of such a relatively new market-based solution to the problem of greenhouse gas emissions.

Questions

1 *With the use of diagrams briefly discuss how the price of allowances within an Emissions Trading Scheme is likely to be determined.*

2 *Outline the relative arguments for and against the implementation of an ETS.*

Answers to questions can be found on the students' side of the Companion Website.

4.5 Environmental standards

Environmental standards
The setting of standards, e.g. upper limits of acceptable air and water pollution, and then allowing the polluter to decide how best to meet these standards.

Setting standards is a common option in terms of controlling pollution. For example, minimum standards are set in terms of air and water quality and the polluter is then free to decide how best to meet the standard. A regulator then monitors the situation and action is taken against any polluter who fails to maintain the standard set.

A standard St_1 could be set as illustrated in Figure 10.6. This would achieve the optimum scale of economic activity Q_s and the optimum level of pollution. As with an environmental tax, standards require accurate information on MNPB and MEC. For example, the standard could be set at St_2 which would require a scale of economic activity equal to Q_A. This is not an optimum position since the benefits derived by the polluter $Q_A X$ are greater than the external costs $Q_A Y$. In other words, the standard is too severe. In addition, in terms of Figure 10.6, the penalty Pen_1 imposed on polluters who violate the standard set is not adequate. In fact, the polluter will be tempted to pollute up to Q_B since

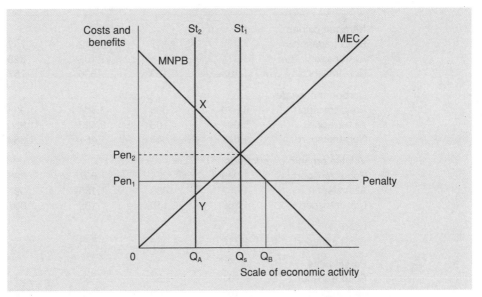

Figure 10.6 The setting of a standard such as St_1 will achieve the optimum level of economic activity and therefore pollution, provided that the penalty is set at Pen_2.

the penalty will be less than the profits received by the polluter, as measured by the MNPB curve. The polluter will not produce in excess of Q_B since the penalty incurred would be greater than the profit obtained from that production. Of course, it is always possible that the pollution will go undetected and therefore no penalty will be imposed. With an optimal standard of St_1 the penalty should be Pen_2 and consistently enforced.

5 | TRANSPORT AND THE ENVIRONMENT

In 1950 there were 3,970,000 motor vehicles licensed in Great Britain, whereas by 2003 the number had risen to 31,207,000, an increase of approximately 686%. Over the same period there was a increase in passenger kilometres travelled from 218 to 794 billion, made up predominantly by the private car. This growth in traffic has major environmental implications, be it congestion, noise or air pollution. Road traffic congestion is readily identifiable, traffic pollution, however, is more insidious and the costs on society not too easy to quantify. There is a range of pollutants associated with road vehicles as shown in Table 10.1.

The table illustrates that road transport is a major polluter in terms of nitrogen oxide and carbon monoxide. The decline in lead emissions is the result of the growth in the sale of unleaded petrol in the UK since 1986.

Table 10.1 Pollutant emissions from transport and other sources in the UK, 1992–2002

	Thousand tonnes				
	1992	1995	1998	2002	Per cent of total in 2002
Nitrogen oxides					
Road transport	1,260	1,117	1,012	762	48
All transport	1,371	1,215	1,102	825	52
Non-transport	1,195	2,189	836	757	48
Carbon monoxide					
Road transport	4,979	4,086	3,404	1,935	60
All transport	5,001	4,106	3,423	1,950	60
Non-transport	1,871	1,545	1,451	1,288	40
Volatile organic compounds					
Road transport	1,045	864	637	385	28
All transport	1,062	880	1,185	397	29
Non-transport	1,368	2,136	1,185	967	71
Lead					
Road transport	1,716	1,053	575	1	1
Particulates					
Road transport	61	57	50	41	26
All transport	65	60	52	43	27
Non-transport	234	180	158	118	73

Source: Adapted from *Transport Statistics Great Britain 2004*, October 2004

Mini Case Study 10.2

Alternatives to oil

Volkswagen and Archer Daniels Midland (ADM) agreed a joint research project in 2004 into biodiesel fuels for the automotive industry. They said it was the first time one of the world's largest carmakers had joined forces with a global agricultural group to develop clean, renewable fuels. Biodiesel fuels combine diesel petroleum with natural substances such as rapeseed or soybean oil and can be used in conventional diesel engines. They reduce harmful emissions substantially.

Biodiesel is available at some fuel stations in Europe, but has not been available in the US because of lower penetration of diesel vehicles and because the quality of diesel fuel in the US is inferior to that in Europe. 'The significance of the agreement is that we will work with the major agricultural company to help develop a higher quality fuel that could be used in our diesel engines in the US,' VW said. VW, which already sells some diesel cars in the US, in 2004 unveiled for the US market a version of its Touareg sports utility vehicle that can be run on standard diesel or biodiesel fuel. The agreement with ADM comes as carmakers continue to look for ways to reduce vehicle emissions and produce vehicles that will appeal to an increasingly environmentally conscious motoring public. That is partly being driven by a desire, strongly expressed in the US, to reduce dependence on fossil fuels and therefore on Middle East supplies (e.g. Saudi Arabia). Bernd Pischetsrider, VW chief executive, said the agreement would help persuade regulators to adopt diesel in the US: 'Biodiesel has no sulphur at all,' he said.

Question

How might these developments affect the market for oil?

Answer to question can be found at the back of the book (page 509).

5.1 The economic background

In 10: 3 an economic model of pollution was developed relating primarily to emissions as a result of a firm's economic activity. In terms of transport and its environmental implications it is necessary to introduce a slightly different model as in Figure 10.7 (*see* page 218).

In Figure 10.7 it is assumed that there is a single road and the flow of traffic is measured along the horizontal axis. In undertaking a journey the motorist is likely to consider only his or her own marginal private cost (MPC). The MPC, which is assumed to increase with an increase in traffic flow, comprises the generalised cost of making a trip and includes the price of petrol, the wear and tear on the vehicle and travel time, which involves an opportunity cost. There will, however, be costs incurred on other road users which the individual motorist does not take into account. These will consist of such costs as congestion, air pollution and noise. If congestion is considered to be the only externality then this can be shown as MPC + *congestion cost* in Figure 10.7. As the flow of traffic increases then so does the *divergence* between the MPC and the MPC + *congestion cost*. The reason for this is that as additional drivers enter the road it imposes extra delays on every other road user.

Road users will equate their MPC with the marginal benefit (MB) obtained from making a trip, as measured by the demand curve. They will take no account of the congestion

---

Marginal private cost (MPC)
The extra cost incurred by those in producing one more unit of the product.

Generalised costs
Refers to vehicle operating cost (namely the fuel cost plus the wear and tear of a vehicle) plus the time cost involved in making a journey.

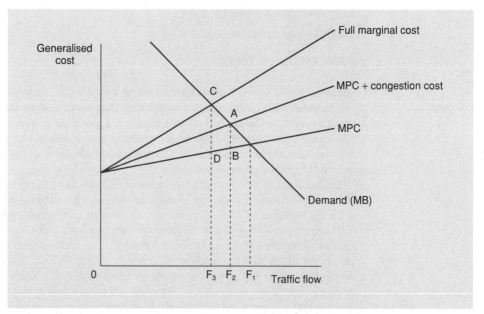

Figure 10.7 As the flow of traffic increases, the cost of undertaking journeys increases primarily because of the extra time taken. As such the MPC curve will increase. If the cost of congestion is included (the cost on other road users), then the MPC + congestion cost curve can be derived. Also taking account of the further environmental implications of road transport would give the full marginal cost curve. An optimum flow of traffic F_3 could be achieved if a road price of CD were introduced.

or environment cost they cause on the rest of society. There will thus be a flow of traffic equal to F_1. If congestion costs are added to the private costs (MPC) then costs would be MPC + congestion cost, and the flow of traffic would fall to F_2. Thus at a flow of F_2, the private cost of making trips would be F_2B and the congestion cost would be AB. In other words, a tax or congestion charge of AB could be introduced to cover the real cost of congestion. If, however, the environmental implications of road transport are also considered, as illustrated in Figure 10.7, the full marginal cost would be much greater. The optimal traffic flow, if the environmental costs as well as congestion are taken into account, would be F_3, where the full marginal cost equals the marginal benefit. Here the MPC would be F_3D and the overall congestion and environmental costs of CD could be covered by a road user charge (a road price) on the motorist of CD. Road pricing as a possible policy measure is discussed in more detail in the following section.

5.2 Possible policy options

The types of policy option aimed at dealing with vehicle emissions and congestion can be divided into two categories, namely those aimed at making vehicle engines cleaner (*see* (a)–(c) below) and those aimed at reducing the overall volume of road traffic (*see* (d)–(f) below).

(a) *Catalytic converters.* Catalytic converters have been fitted since 1992 to all new cars with petrol engines in order to meet EU regulations. This should result in reduced emissions of nitrogen oxides, volatile organic compounds and carbon monoxide, 60% of which was attributed to road transport in 2002. The converters, however, will only act as a temporary check on emissions, since the benefits of the converter will eventually be outweighed by the growth in traffic. A catalytic converter is fitted inside the exhaust and comprises a honeycomb of either ceramic or metal coated with platinum, palladium and rhodium which convert the pollutants into less harmful forms. A limitation of the catalytic converter is that they only become effective after they have reached a certain temperature. Thus on shorter journeys it may be of little use. In addition, the converter can only be used in cars that run on unleaded petrol.

(**b**) *Tighter government controls.* The introduction of emission tests for carbon monoxide as part of the MOT test and an increase in the roadside enforcement programme in order to weed out the worst offenders in terms of emission levels are both examples of tighter government controls.

(**c**) *Enforcing the speed limit.* Immediate benefits result from motorists adhering to the 60 mph and 70 mph speed limit. In this respect one option would be fitting cars with speed-limiting devices. Speed governors on cars would restrict the speed and with it reduce the carbon emissions by up to 1 million tonnes.

(**d**) *Increasing fuel duties.* An increase in the price of petrol in real terms is one method of tackling the environmental costs of pollutants. An increase in the price of fuel is likely to result in a reduction in fuel consumption and the volume of traffic on UK roads.

(**e**) *Limiting car use.* Traffic calming measures such as limiting access of vehicles to city centres and increased pedestrianisation are possible ways of reducing the environmental cost of vehicle exhaust emissions. It could be argued however that such physical control measures restrict vehicle access and result in longer journeys and therefore even more pollution. Other measures such as those used in Athens, where cars with odd and even registration number plates are allowed into the city on alternate days, might prove more difficult to implement in the UK.

Congestion charging
The direct charging of motorists for the use of road space.

(**f**) *Congestion charging* is gaining in popularity as a means of dealing with transport congestion and its associated environmental effects. Congestion charging involves charging the motorist for road use and it could be implemented by using meters attached to cars which are activated as the vehicle enters a designated area, with monetary units deducted from a smartcard. In terms of Figure 10.7, a road price of CD would be the optimum charge.

Mini Case Study 10.3

London congestion charging

On 17 February 2003 in London the Mayor, Ken Livingstone launched the first major congestion charging scheme in Britain, a scheme to charge motorists for the use of the road network within a specified area of Central London between certain times. The aim of the scheme is to reduce congestion and it forms one of only a small number of charging schemes worldwide, the Singapore Electronic Road Pricing scheme being the other main example. Whilst the main aim was one of reducing congestion it also had environmental benefits. Other cities throughout Europe have tended to use regulation rather than the

→

price mechanism in order to reduce congestion. For example, German cities have adopted extensive pedestrianised shopping areas and Athens only allows certain cars into the city on alternate days.

London congestion

Britain is one of the most congested countries in Europe and London one of the most congested cities. As revealed in Table 10.2 average vehicle speeds in London have declined in successive periods since 1974. The reduction in average speeds has been experienced both in the morning and evening peak periods and in fact the daytime off-peak period in Central London is equally congested. Clearly this is something the London authorities, namely the Transport for London, have been keen to address.

Building new roads as a way of dealing with congestion is not an option in London, and equally it can be argued that as a measure it simply leads to more traffic being generated and therefore ultimately the same level of congestion, but with additional environmental fallout. The system is aimed at reducing total traffic levels, measured in terms of vehicle miles, by 10–15% within the zone itself, leading to an increase in traffic speeds of between 10–15%.

Table 10.2 **Average speeds in London (miles per hour)**

Morning peak period	Central area	Inner area
1974–6	14.2	15.9
1980–2	12.1	14.2
1986–90	11.5	11.8
1994–7	10.9	13.4
2000–03	9.9	11.6
Daytime off-peak		
1974–6	12.9	18.6
1980–2	11.6	17.2
1986–90	11.0	14.6
1994–7	10.9	15.0
2000–03	9.0	13.7
Evening peak period		
1974–6	13.2	15.5
1980–2	12.2	14.1
1986–90	11.0	11.6
1994–7	10.8	12.8
2000–03	9.6	11.3

Source: Adapted from *Transport Statistics Great Britain 2004*, October 2004

The congestion charging scheme

Congestion charging covers a 21sq km of Central London. Motorists entering the zone between the hours of 7a.m. and 6.30p.m. Monday – Friday (excluding public holidays) are charged £8 (originally £5).

Enforcement of the scheme is via 700 video cameras, which are able to scan the rear numberplate of the 250,000 vehicles that on average enter the area during a working week. It is predicted that every vehicle in the charging zone will pass an average of five cameras over the 11½ hours that the charge is in operation each day. Each evening the information obtained is matched against a database of motorists who have paid the charge. Payment can be made by phone, the Internet, at shops or petrol stations. In fact there are 150 paypoints at retail locations, 100 machines in car parks, 112 BT Internet kiosks within the zone and more than 1,500 retail locations. If the motorist has failed to pay the charge before midnight a fine of £80 is imposed. If the offender pays within 14 days then the fine falls to £40.

A number of exemptions have been built into the scheme. Certain listed vehicles receive a 100% discount – this includes all alternative fuel vehicles namely gas, electric and fuel cell vehicles, exempt on environmental grounds. Blue and orange badge holders are also exempt, that is vehicles driven by disabled people. In addition, certain NHS staff, patients and emergency vehicles (fire engines, police vehicles and ambulances) are in this category. Certain vehicles such as those with more than nine seats and military vehicles used by the armed forces are also exempt.

Residents within the charging zone are eligible for a 90% discount.

Exempt vehicles include motorbikes and mopeds, black cabs and London-licensed mini-cabs.

The advantages and disadvantages of the scheme

Advantages: Congestion in urban areas can be viewed as *market failure* with the actions of road users in Central London affecting other road users. Congestion has a cost associated with it not least in terms of the increased time taken to undertake a journey and the opportunity cost that involves. The intention of the charge is to reduce congestion, expected to be in the region of 15%, thus freeing up the road network and so reduce the time taken to complete a journey.

Economics is concerned with the optimum use of scarce resources and since road space in Central London can be viewed as a scarce resource then charging for its use will mean that it can be used more efficiently.

The revenue raised from congestion charging, is used to improve public transport.

Individuals tend not to like being charged and as such the use of regulation has tended to be more acceptable. The use of regulation, however, tends to be a 'blunt instrument', something which cannot be fine tuned to tackle varying demand conditions and unlike congestion pricing it produces no revenue.

Disadvantages: Clearly one issue with congestion charging is the invasion of privacy given that the system relies on taking a photograph of the vehicle numberplates.

The issue of equity and fairness can be raised in terms of congestion charging. The charge can be viewed like a regressive tax in that those who pay the charge and are on lower incomes pay a larger proportion of their income than higher income earners in order to drive in Central London. In order to negate this claim the use of the revenue is all important. If the revenue is used to subsidise public transport as an alternative to the car, most notably the bus, then the charge can be seen as less unfair.

The cost has been seen as a disadvantage of congestion charging. It has been estimated that the cost of setting up the scheme has been £200 million and it will cost an additional £80–90 million in operating costs per annum.

Safety has been raised as an issue since there is the temptation for van drivers to run to finish their delivery inside the zone before the 7a.m. start time for charging. Such drivers may be tempted to break the speed limit raising safety implications. In addition, it is envisaged that one result of introducing the charge is an increase in the use of motorbikes, scooters and bikes in order to avoid paying the charge. This coupled with the fact that vehicles inside the zone are likely to be travelling faster increases the potential for accidents.

The scheme utilises a rather simplistic technology. Namely cameras on all the roads into the central area and a fixed price of £8, the charge not changing in line with the level of congestion experienced. This may change over time and as the scheme evolves it could see the use of global positioning satellites (GPS) and cars fitted with satellite receivers in order to allow a charge to be made based on distance, time and location, getting somewhat closer to a charge of CD illustrated in Figure 10.7.

Questions

1 *Outline the trends illustrated in Table 10.2.*

2 *What are the arguments for and against the introduction of a congestion charging scheme?*

Answers to questions can be found on the students' side of the Companion Website.

KEY POINTS

- Market failure refers to the various market imperfections which prevent it achieving an efficient allocation of resources. The existence of externalities is one aspect of market failure.

- The notion of property rights is central to the study of the environment as these define the legal rules that determine rights and responsibilities over assets.

- The 'optimum' level of pollution occurs where the returns to society is maximised. In our analysis this occurred at the level of output for which marginal net private benefit exactly equalled the marginal external cost.

- Marginal external cost occurs when economic decisions result in costs for individuals other than the decision takers, such as air and water pollution.

- Marginal private costs refer to the wages, raw materials, capital and other costs incurred by the production of an extra unit.

- The Pigouvian tax has been advocated as a means of dealing with the problem of environmental pollution whereby the producer of an externality is taxed by an amount exactly equal to the marginal external cost imposed.

- Tradable permits are a relatively new concept whereby the holders of such permits are given the right to emit a specific level of pollution. These permits can be traded on markets.

- Environmental standards involve the setting of upper limits, for example, in terms of air and water pollution, and then allowing the polluter to decide how best to meet the standard. Setting standards also involves the need for monitoring compliance and imposing penalties for firms not adhering to the standards set.

- Transport is a major source of environmental pollution, especially when congestion occurs.

Further reading

Griffiths, A. and Wall, S. (2006) *Applied Economics*, 11th edition, FT/Prentice Hall, Chapter 10.

Griffiths, A. and Wall, S. (2005) *Economics for Business and Management*, FT/Prentice Hall, Chapter 12.

Heather, K. (2004) *Economics Theory in Action*, 4th edition, FT/Prentice Hall, Chapter 12.

Parkin, M., Powell, M. and Matthews, K. (2005) *Economics*, 6th edition, FT/Prentice Hall, Chapter 18.

Sloman, J. (2006) *Economics*, 6th edition, FT/Prentice Hall, Chapter 12.

Web references

Pressure group websites include:

www.foe.co.uk
www.tiwf.co.uk
www.greenpeace.org.uk

The issue of sustainability can be considered at:

www.sustainability.co.uk

Visit the Body Shop website for material on human rights and environmental issues:

www.body.shop.co.uk

KPMG has a section devoted to business ethics:

www.kpmg.com/ethics
www.panda.org

The National Environmental Trust is at www.environet.policy.net/
Visit the Co-op Bank at www.co-opbank.co.uk

The issue of congestion charging in London, visit:

www.london.gov.uk

PROGRESS AND REVIEW QUESTIONS

Answers to most questions can be found at the back of the book (pages 509–12). Answers to asterisked questions can be found on the students' side of the Companion Website.

Multiple-choice questions

1 The optimum level of pollution is achieved where:
   a) marginal net private benefit is greater than marginal external cost;
   b) marginal external cost is greater than marginal net private benefit;
   c) marginal net private benefit is equal to marginal external cost;
   d) marginal net private benefit is zero;
   e) marginal external cost is zero.

Questions 2 and 3 are based on the figure below.

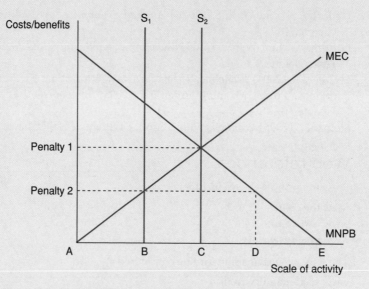

2 If no standard is set by the authority the scale of activity will be:

a) A
b) B
c) C
d) D
e) E

3 If a standard is set at S_1 and the penalty for non-compliance is set at Penalty 2, then the scale of activity is likely to be:

a) A
b) B
c) C
d) D
e) E

4 Congestion charging is a concept that involves:

a) the fitting of catalytic converters to all vehicles using the road network;
b) tighter controls set on the use of road space;
c) a charge to motorists for using the road space;
d) an increase in the price of fuel;
e) none of the above.

Data response questions

Look carefully at the date in Table 10.3.

1 What does the table indicate?

2 Examine policy options for dealing with transport issues implied by the table.

Table 10.3 Average vehicle speeds in London for selected time periods, dates and locations

Morning peak period	Central area	Inner area
1974–6	14.2	15.9
1980–2	12.1	14.2
1986–90	11.5	11.8
1994–7	10.9	13.4
2000–03	9.9	11.6
Daytime off-peak		
1974–6	12.9	18.6
1980–2	11.6	17.2
1986–90	11.0	14.6
1994–7	10.9	15.0
2000–03	9.0	13.7
Evening peak period		
1974–6	13.2	15.5
1980–2	12.2	14.1
1986–90	11.0	11.6
1994–7	10.8	12.8
2000–03	9.6	11.3

True/false questions

1 Natural resources comprise renewable and non-renewable resources.

2 The optimum level of pollution is where there is zero economic activity.

3 The bargaining solution to achieving a more socially optimum level of pollution involves the allocation of property rights.

4 A Pigouvian tax is a tax which is equal to the marginal external cost at the optimum level of pollution.

5 The introduction of an environmental tax shifts the MNPB curve to the right.

6 Tradable permits can be transferred from one polluter to another for a price.

7 Generalised cost comprises vehicle operating cost and the time cost of a journey.

8 Congestion charging is a charge made for the use of road space.

9 The optimal flow of traffic is where the full marginal cost curve equals the marginal benefit from journeys undertaken.

10 Increasing the price of fuel is a market based approach to the problem of traffic related pollution.

 **Essay questions**

1 Discuss the notion that the 'bargaining solution' to environmental problems results in the same outcome whether the polluter compensates the sufferers or the sufferers pay the polluter to reduce their levels of emissions. Discuss the relative merits of bargaining as a solution to environmental problems.

2 The EU Emissions Trading Scheme (ETS) will commence on 1 January 2005 but the first phase, which will run from 2005–2007, does not include aviation. Outline the potential issues, which need to be resolved if ETS is to be extended, for example, to include aviation.

3 'Road user charging is a more effective and acceptable way of dealing with the effects of traffic-related pollution in urban areas when compared with the use of public transport subsidies.' Examine this statement.

4 Outline the trends illustrated in Table 10.1. Critically assess the possible policy options available for dealing with vehicle emissions and congestion.

Part Two MACROECONOMICS

CHAPTER 11

National income and its determination

Learning objectives

By the end of this chapter you should be able to:

● Understand how national income is measured and what is meant by the various definitions of national income.

● Outline the relevance of national income data to both national and international comparisons of standards of living.

● Explain the meaning of 'equilibrium' national income and show how such an equilibrium is brought about.

● Use both the withdrawal/injection diagram and the 45° aggregate expenditure diagram to assess changes in the equilibrium levels of national income.

1   INTRODUCTION

In the preceding chapters we have concerned ourselves with microeconomics, dealing with specific aspects of the economy, including how individual consumers and firms behave, how the price of a product is determined and how certain markets, such as the labour market, operate.

The following chapters in Part 2 of this book concentrate on macroeconomics, which deals with the economy as a whole. The chapters will cover topics such as national income, unemployment, inflation, exchange rates, fiscal and monetary policy, all of which affect the whole economy. Part 2 will also examine aspects of the global economy which influence the prospects of any national economy, paying particular attention to international trading relationships, regional trading blocks such as the European Union and the increasing tendency to 'offshore' and outsource elements of the value chain. The implications of these global patterns and trends for the developing economies is also considered.

Central to the study of macroeconomics is the notion of *national income*, which is the subject matter of Chapter 11. We begin this chapter by dealing with how national income is measured, the possible problems encountered in its measurement and what purpose the national income statistics serve.

2   THE CIRCULAR FLOW OF INCOME

National income
Total value of income (output or expenditure) generated within the economy in a particular year.

National income is a measure of the value of the *output* of the goods and services produced by an economy over a period of time, usually one year. It is also a measure of the *incomes* which flow from that output and the *expenditure* involved in purchasing that output. It follows that all three methods can be used to measure national income and we briefly review each in turn. However, before doing so it will help to introduce the so-called 'circular flow of income' and define some terms widely used when discussing national income.

2.1   Circular flow of income: simplified

Circular flow of income
A model to show how the 'equilibrium' level of national income is determined in an economy.

Figure 11.1 presents a simplified approach to the **circular flow of income** within a domestic economy characterised by firms (producers) and households (consumers). It is 'simplified' in that we initially assume no savings, no investment, no government expenditure or taxation and no international trade (so no exports or imports). Nevertheless, this approach is useful in indicating that output, income and expenditure are all involved in the circular flow of income.

Note: We use the term 'domestic' throughout to refer to firms and households *located within* the domestic economy (e.g. within the UK).

Consumption expenditure
Where domestic households purchase the output of domestic firms.

Domestic households provide factor services (labour, loan capital, entrepreneurship, land) to domestic firms which use their services to produce an *output* of goods and services. These factor services from households are rewarded by *income* in the form of wages, rent, interest and profit. With no savings in our simplified economy, no tax and no spending on imports, all the income received by domestic households goes in *consumption expenditure* (C) on the output of domestic firms.

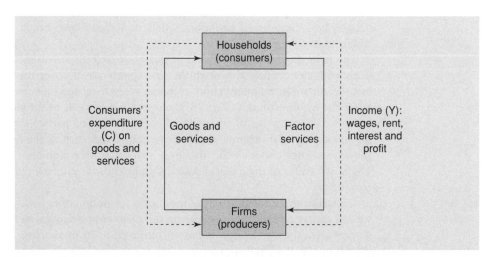

Figure 11.1 The circular flow of income and expenditure between domestic households and domestic firms when there are no withdrawals and no injections. Households receive income in return for their factor services and households use that income to purchase goods and services from firms.

In this simplified circular flow, any initial money value of income can be sustained indefinitely, since there are no withdrawals and no injections. In Figure 11.1 the dashed line refers to 'monetary' flows, involving income and expenditure, whereas the solid lines refer to 'real' flows of factor services and the resulting output of goods and services.

It will be useful to consider a more realistic model of the circular flow of income before exploring the *three* alternative methods of measuring national income.

2.2 Circular flow of income: withdrawals and injections

Withdrawals
Leakages from the circular flow of income (e.g. S, T and M).

Injections
Additions to the circular flow of income (e.g. I, G and X).

We now relax our assumptions of no saving or investment, no government involvement and no international trade. As we can see from Figure 11.2 we now have certain *withdrawals* (W) from the circular flow of income, shown by a minus (−) sign, and certain *injections* (J), shown by a plus (+) sign.

Withdrawals (W)

Although it may seem over fussy it is very important to carefully define the terms we use in the circular flow.

We define a *withdrawal* (W) from the circular flow as either:

● any income received by a domestic household (H) not passed on to a domestic firm (F); or
● any income received by a domestic firm (F) not passed on to a domestic household (H).

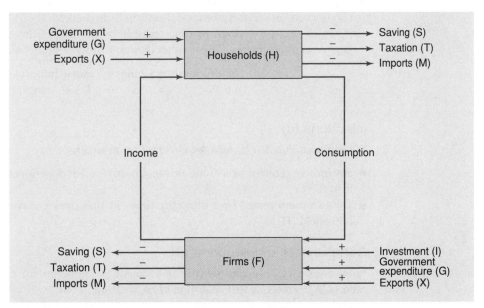

Figure 11.2 The circular flow of income and expenditure between domestic households and domestic firms with withdrawals (W) and injections (J) identified. Withdrawals (W) include savings (S), taxes (T) and imports (M). Injections (J) include government expenditure (G), investment expenditure (I) and export expenditure (X).

Components of withdrawals (W)

As we see in Figure 11.2, some income received by domestic households (H) or domestic firms (F) is *not passed on* in the circular flow. In other words, it is saved (S), taxed (T) or spent on imports (M).

- *Savings* (S) These can be either personal savings by domestic households (H) or business savings (e.g. undistributed profits) by domestic firms (F).
- *Taxes* (T) These can be either taxes paid by domestic households (H), such as income tax and council tax, or taxes paid by domestic firms (F), such as corporation tax, business rates and VAT. Although we, as individuals and households, see ourselves as paying VAT on our purchases, strictly speaking it is firms who have the legal liability to pay VAT.

Example	Taxation in various economies

It is often said that the UK is overtaxed. Currently, around 38% of all UK national income is taken in various forms of taxation, which actually places the UK as only a middle-ranked country in terms of tax burden. Of the twenty largest world economies, ten have a higher tax burden than the UK. For example, over 53% of national income is taken in tax in Sweden, 49% in Denmark, 46% in Austria, 45% in Belgium, Norway and Finland, though only around 30% in the USA.

- *Imports* (M) These can be imports either by domestic firms (F) or domestic households (H) of goods or services from *overseas* firms or households.

   In all the above cases, income received by domestic firms or households *is not passed on* in the circular flow to other domestic firms or households.

$$\text{Withdrawals} = \text{Savings} + \text{Taxes} + \text{Imports}$$
$$\text{i.e. W} \quad = \quad \text{S} \quad + \quad \text{T} \quad + \quad \text{M}$$

Injections (J)

We define an *injection* (J) into the circular flow as either:

- any income received by a domestic household (H) that does not come from a domestic firm (F); or
- any income received by a domestic firm (F) that does not come from a domestic household (H).

Components of injections (J)

From Figure 11.2 we can identify investment (I), government expenditure (G) and exports (X) as meeting this definition of an injection.

- *Investment* (I) Here income is received by domestic firms (F) which does not come from domestic households (H) but from *other domestic firms* who purchase capital equipment, buildings etc., for investment purposes. (Of course, here we are using 'investment' in its strict, national income accounting definition which involves expenditures seen as pushing outwards the production possibility frontier.)

- *Government expenditure* (G) Here income is received by domestic firms (F) which does not come from domestic households (H) but from *the government* (e.g. government contracts). Alternatively, income is received by domestic households (H) which does not come from employment by domestic firms (F) but from employment by *the government* (e.g. public sector workers).

Example	**Government spending in various economies**

Although the UK government is sometimes criticised for excessive spending, at 41% of national income, government spending is less than the 44% average across the EU countries, but more than the 31% of national income recorded for government spending in the USA. In fact, in 2004, out of 14 major countries, the UK was only tenth highest in terms of the share of national income given to government expenditure.

- *Exports* (X) Here income is received by domestic firms (F) which does not come from domestic households (H) or domestic firms (F) but from *overseas households and firms*. Alternatively, income is received by domestic households (H) from *overseas firms and households* (e.g. interest and dividend payments from overseas, consultancy payments from overseas etc.).

$$\text{Injections} = \text{Investment} + \text{Government expenditure} + \text{Exports}$$
$$\text{i.e. J} \quad = \quad \text{I} \quad + \quad \text{G} \quad + \text{X}$$

Figure 11.2 above brought these components of withdrawals (W) and injections (J) together on one diagram.

3 NATIONAL INCOME: DEFINITIONS AND MEASUREMENT

Having introduced the various withdrawals from and injections into the circular flow, we are now in a better position to consider the different definitions of national income and the three methods for measuring national income.

Gross domestic product (GDP) Value of output produced (and incomes received) by factors of production located within that country.

3.1 National income definitions

Various definitions are widely used.

Gross domestic product (GDP)

This is the value of output produced (and incomes received) by domestic residents, in other words, by firms and households located within the domestic economy (e.g. within the UK).

Gross national product (GNP) Value of output produced (and incomes received) by residents of that country wherever they are located. GNP = GDP + *net* property income from abroad.

Gross national product (GNP)

This is the value of output produced (and incomes received) by domestic residents from their *ownership of resources*, wherever these resources happen to be located, whether inside or outside the domestic economy. For example, GNP takes account of the fact that some UK residents (firms and households) earn incomes such as profits, interest and rent from owning resources located abroad whilst overseas residents (firms and households) earn

Net property income from abroad
Inward payments received by residents from their ownership of overseas property minus outward payments made by residents from their ownership of domestic property.

such incomes from owning resources located in the UK. The *net* value to UK residents of these receipts from abroad and their equivalent payments abroad is called 'net property income from abroad' in the national accounts.

$$GNP = GDP + \text{net property income from abroad}$$

Net national product (NNP)

Net national product (NNP)
Since capital equipment will have depreciated over the year via wear and tear or because technological change has made it obsolescent, NNP = GNP − depreciation.

Gross national product is the total value of output produced and incomes received by UK residents in the course of a year. It therefore includes the full value of *new* plant and equipment produced during the course of the year (i.e. gross domestic fixed capital formation). However, over this period *existing* plant and equipment will have depreciated (i.e. declined in value due to wear and tear and obsolescence). In order to obtain a true measure of national income an appropriate deduction for capital depreciation must be made.

$$NNP = GNP - \text{depreciation}$$

'Market prices' and 'factor cost'

Market prices
The various measures of national output/income *include* indirect taxes and subsidies.

All these measures of national income can be expressed either at 'market prices' or at 'factor cost'.

- *Market prices* Here the value placed on any output uses the prices observed in the marketplace (where these are available). Such prices may, however, be distorted by taxes and subsidies. For example, the market prices of some products may be higher than they otherwise would be due to the taxes levied on them. Alternatively, the market prices may be lower than they otherwise would be due to subsidies received on them. 'Market prices' is a valuation approach which includes these impacts on price of both taxes and subsidies.

Factor cost
The various measures of national output/income *exclude* indirect taxes and subsidies.

- *Factor cost* Here the value placed on any output seeks to *exclude* the 'distorting' impacts on the prices of products of any taxes or subsidies.
  a) Taxes are subtracted from the valuation at market prices.
  b) Subsidies are added to the valuation at market prices.

3.2 National income measurement

We now briefly consider the output, income and expenditure methods for measuring national income. Strictly speaking, the national income accounts are defined in such a way that the three methods of measurement should give exactly the same result.

The output method

Output method
Where national income is measured by taking the value added at each stage of production.

A country's national income can be calculated from the *output* figures of all firms in the economy. However, this does not mean that we simply add together the value of each firm's output. To do so would give us an aggregate many times greater than the national income because of *double counting*.

- *Avoiding double counting* The outputs of some firms are the inputs of other firms. For example, the output of the steel industry is used in part as an input for the automobile industry and so on. To avoid including the total value of the steel used in automobile production twice (double counting) we adopt one of two possible approaches. Either sum only the *value added* at each stage of production or alternatively we sum only the *value of final output* produced for the various goods and services.

Example

In producing a packet of crisps costing 50 pence to the consumer the manufacturer will need to purchase potatoes from a farmer. The value of this input, as seen in Table 11.1, is 25 pence and this is included, along with the value added by the manufacturer, in the price the wholesaler pays the manufacturer for the packet of crisps. In other words, the manufacturer has turned the potatoes into crisps adding value to the product of 10 pence. The wholesaler will sell the crisps to the retailer for 40 pence after adding further value added of 5 pence to the price, possibly through marketing and the delivery of the crisps to the retailer. Finally, the retailer will sell the crisps to the consumer for 50 pence, which includes value added of 10 pence in the form of the retailer's factor costs and profit. If we include the total value of all transactions, i.e. £1.50, in the calculation of national income we would be guilty of double counting.

Table 11.1 Value added in the production of a packet of crisps

	Total paid/received (£)	Value added (£)	Sector
Potato farmer	–	0.25	Primary
Crisp manufacturer	0.25	0.10	Secondary
Wholesaler	0.35	0.05	Tertiary
Retailer	0.40	0.10	Tertiary
Retailer sells to the consumer	0.50		
Total	1.50	0.50	

This problem can be overcome by either totalling the *value added* at each stage of production, giving us 50 pence in the example above, or taking the *final value*, namely the price of the packet of crisps when bought by the consumer, which again is 50 pence. All the other transactions involve the sale or purchase of intermediate goods or services.

- *Inventories* We must also ensure that any additions to 'stock and work in progress' (inventories) are included in the output figures for each industry since any build-up in stock during a year must represent extra output produced during that year.
- *Public goods and merit goods* We have already seen in Chapter 8 that the government provides many goods and services through the non-market sector, such as education, healthcare, defence, police and so on. Such goods and services are clearly part of the nation's output, but since many of these are not sold through the market sector, strictly they do not have a market price. In such cases, the value of the output is measured at resource cost or factor cost. In other words, the value of the service is assumed to be equivalent to the cost of the resources used to provide it.
- *Self-provided commodities* A similar problem arises in the case of self-provided commodities, such as vegetables grown in the domestic garden, car repairs and home improvements of a do-it-yourself type. Again, these represent output produced, but there is no market value of such output. The vast majority of self-provided commodities are omitted from the national income statistics because it is impractical to monitor their production.
- *Exports and imports* Not all of the nation's output is consumed domestically. Part is sold abroad as exports. Nevertheless, GDP is the value of *domestically produced* output and so the value of exports must be included in this figure. On the other hand, a great deal of domestically produced output incorporates imported raw materials and

components. Hence the value of the import content of the final output must be deducted from the output figures if GDP is to be accurately measured.

- *Net property income from abroad* This source of income to domestic residents will not be included in the output figures from firms. We have already noted that the net inflow (+) or outflow (−) of funds must be added to GDP when calculating the value of *domestically owned* output, i.e. GNP.

The income method

Income method
Where national income is measured by adding incomes which correspond to productive activities.

When calculating national product as a flow of *incomes* it is important to ensure that only the rewards for factor services which have contributed to output in that year are included. In other words, only those incomes paid in return for some productive activity during that year and for which there is a corresponding output are included. Of course, it is the *gross value* of these factor rewards which must be aggregated, since this represents the value of the output produced. Levying taxes on factor incomes reduces the amount the factors actually received, but it does not reduce the value of the output they produced!

Transfer payments
Payments received out of tax revenue without production taking place (e.g. pensions).

- *Transfer payments* These are simply transfers of income within the community, and they are not made in respect of any productive activity. Indeed, the bulk of all transfer payments within the UK are made by the government for social reasons. Examples include social security payments, pensions, child allowances and so on. Since no output is produced in respect of these payments they must be excluded from the aggregate of factor incomes.
- *Undistributed surpluses* Another problem in aggregating factor incomes arises because not all factor incomes are distributed to the factors of production. For example, firms might retain part or all of their profits to finance future investment. Similarly, the profits of public bodies may accrue to the government rather than to private individuals. Care must be taken to include these undistributed surpluses as factor incomes.
- *Stock appreciation* Care must be taken to exclude changes in the money value of inventory or stock caused by inflation. These are windfall gains and do not represent a real increase in the value of output during the year.
- *Net property income from abroad* When moving from GDP to either GNP or NNP we have seen that it is necessary to *add* net property income from abroad to the aggregate of domestic incomes.

The expenditure method

Expenditure method
Where national income is measured by expenditures on the final output of goods and services.

The final method of calculating national income is as a flow of *expenditure* on domestic output.

- *Final output* It is only expenditure on final output which must be aggregated otherwise there is, again, a danger of double counting, with intermediate expenditure on raw materials and components being counted twice.
- *Current output* It is only expenditure on current output which is relevant. Second-hand goods are not part of the current flow of output and factors of production have already received payment for these goods at the time they were produced. We should note, however, that any income earned by a salesman employed in the second-hand trade, or the profits of second-hand dealers, *are* included in the national income statistics. The services these occupations render during that year are part of current production!

Using the symbols of Figure 11.2 (page 231) we can say that, using the expenditure method:

$$GDP = C + I + G + X - M$$

where

    C = Consumer expenditure
    I = Investment
    G = Government expenditure
    X = Exports expenditure
    M = Imports expenditure

As with the output and income methods, the value of expenditure in the economy must be adjusted if it is to measure national income accurately.

- *Consumers' expenditure* (C) This is the major element in expenditure and in 2004 accounted for over 50% of total domestic expenditure in the UK.
- *Investment expenditure* (I) Expenditure on fixed capital, such as plant and machinery, must obviously be included in calculations of total expenditure. Gross domestic fixed capital formation (GDFCF) incorporates this item and in 2004 this was around 12% of total domestic expenditure. What is not so obvious is that additions to stock and work in progress also represent investment. The factors of production which have produced this, as yet unsold, output will still have received factor payments. To ignore additions to stock and work in progress would therefore create an imbalance between the three aggregates of output, income and expenditure. Additions to stock and work in progress are therefore treated as though they have been purchased by firms. Care must be taken to include them in the aggregate of total domestic expenditure.
- *Government expenditure* (G) Since only domestic expenditure on the current output of goods and services is relevant, care must be taken to deduct any expenditure on transfer payments by the government or other public authorities. Transfer payments do not contribute directly to the current flow of output and, therefore, we must only include that part of government current expenditure which is spent directly on goods and services. In 2004 government (central and local) expenditure on goods and services was just over 20% of total domestic expenditure.
- *Exports* (X) *and Imports* (M) We have already seen that it is important to include exports and exclude imports from our calculation of national income. Care must be taken to ensure this when aggregating total expenditures.
- *Net property income from abroad* As before, when moving from GDP to GNP or NNP, it is important to include net property income from abroad when aggregating total expenditures.
- *Taxes and subsidies* In measuring the value of expenditure, we are attempting to measure the value of payments made to the factors of production which have produced that output. Indirect taxes raise total expenditure on goods and services relative to the amount received by the factors of production. Subsidies have the opposite effect. In order to avoid a discrepancy between the income and expenditure totals, it is necessary to remove the effects of taxes and subsidies from the latter. The expenditure total is adjusted to *factor cost* by deducting indirect taxes and adding subsidies.

Note: The 'black economy'

One way in which the so-called 'black economy' can be estimated is through the difference between national income when measured by the *income* method and when measured by the *expenditure* method. Apart from errors and omissions these are defined in the national accounts in such a way that they come to the same value. If, however, people receive income and do not declare it in tax returns, it will not appear on the income side, though expenditure will increase as the unrecorded income is spent on goods and services. In recent years the 'income' valuation – based on tax returns – has fallen short of the 'expenditure' valuation by progressively larger amounts. Some estimates have the 'black economy' as high as 10–12% of GDP in the UK. The 'black economy' is a term often used to refer to those activities and associated incomes which are 'unofficial' in the sense that the tax authorities are unaware of their existence.

3.3 National income accounts

Each year the Office for National Statistics (ONS) publishes the *United Kingdom National Accounts* (called the Blue Book) which gives detailed figures of the three approaches. In September 1998, the ONS introduced the most extensive changes in the format of the UK national accounts since the first publication of the 'Blue Book' in 1952. Previously, different accounting standards were used in different countries which made inter-country comparisons difficult. The changes have adopted an internationally agreed system of national accounts which makes international comparisons more straightforward. The figures for 2003 are to be found in Table 11.2.

In the national income accounts before 1998 the key indicator of the state of the economy was gross domestic product (GDP) at factor cost. However, *headline* GDP is now GDP at market prices and so this is widely used as the key indicator, in common with

Table 11.2 UK gross domestic product and national income accounts in 2003 (£ million)

The income approach £million		The output approach £million		The expenditure approach £million	
Total operating surplus of corporations, gross	242,473	Gross value added, at basic prices: output of goods and services	2,038,326	Household final consumption expenditure	693,551
Other income	101,866	*Less* intermediate consumption	1,062,178	Final consumption expenditure of non-profit bodies	27,532
Compensation of employees	614,917	*Total gross value added*	*976,148*	General government expenditure	229,892
Gross value added at factor cost	*959,256*	Value added taxes (VAT) on products	*77,864*	Total gross capital formation	181,380
Taxes on production *less* subsidies	140,147	Other taxes on products	53,599	*Total domestic expenditure on goods and services at market prices*	*1,132,355*
Statistical discrepancy	493	Less subsidies on products	−7,313	Exports of goods and services	277,539
Gross domestic product at market prices	**1,099,896**	Statistical discrepancy	−402	*Gross final expenditure*	*1,409,894*
		Gross domestic product at market prices	**1,099,896**	*Less* imports of goods and services	309,998
				Statistical discrepancy	−214
				Gross domestic product at market prices	**1,099,896**

Source: United Kingdom National Accounts (Various)

other EU member countries. GDP at market prices in the UK was £1,099,896 million in 2003, as seen in Table 11.2. All three methods give the same value for this indicator, as indeed they must since they are defined in such a way (i.e. they are 'accounting' identities).

 Pause for thought 1

What is the entry, in terms of the actual data in Table 11.2, that makes sure the different methods give the same result?

4 USING NATIONAL INCOME STATISTICS

Two of the main reasons for calculating national income are:

(a) as a means of expressing changes in the nation's standard of living over time;

(b) as a means of comparing the standard of living in different countries.

4.1 Comparing national living standards over time

Great care has to be taken when using national income figures as an indication of living standards. In the UK in 1980 gross national income at market prices was £226,801 million but by 2003 it had risen to £1,099,896. However, this does not mean that we were four times better off in 2003. The reasons for this are:

(a) There has been *inflation* over the 23-year period which needs to be taken into account. We are not interested in *money* gross national income, as given by the above figures, but *real* national income so that the effect of price changes can be eliminated and comparisons between 1980 and 2003 can be made. 2003 prices need to be expressed as 1980 prices, which is achieved by using index numbers. A simple example can clearly explain this point.

Example

If the national income figures in Table 11.3 are taken at face value they would seem to suggest an increase in national income between Year 1 and Year 2 of over 33% (£18 million to £24 million). Over that period, however, inflation has been at 10% so part of the 33% increase in national income has been due to an increase in prices rather than an increase in output. By dividing the Year 2 national income by the price index for Year 2 (110) and multiplying by 100, the real national income in Year 2 at Year 1 prices can be obtained. The result is that instead of an increase in national income of some 33% the increase is only from £18 million to £21.8 million, i.e. an increase of only around 21%.

Table 11.3 **Money and real values of national income**

	Year 1	Year 2
National income	£18m	£24m
Price index	100	110
Real national income [Year 2 national income expressed at Year 1 prices]		£21.8m $\left[24 \times \dfrac{100}{110}\right]$

(b) Although real national income may have increased, there may have been an increase in *population* over the period in question. If this is the case the real national income would have to be shared out among more people. It is important, therefore, that changes in the population are taken into account. It is possible to obtain *real per capita income* (or real income per head) by dividing real national income by the population. This will give an average figure for how much national income there is for each member of the economy.

(c) Obtaining a figure for real income per head may still not give a true picture of the nation's living standards. Real income per head could have increased as a result of a *longer working week*. With less leisure time there may, in fact, be a reduction in the well-being of society, not an increase. Furthermore, real income per head is as stated 'an average'; it does not, therefore, indicate how the real national income is distributed in the economy. There may be a skewed distribution with a small percentage of very rich people, and a large percentage of the population who are very poor and not sharing in any increase in living standards.

(d) The figure for per capita income cannot take account of changes in *quality*. A car purchased in 2004 will give a better performance and be more reliable – and, therefore, arguably confer a larger increase in welfare – than a car purchased in 1959.

(e) A major limitation of per capita income is its failure to take account of *environmental* issues. An increase in pollution and transport congestion will influence living standards negatively but this effect is not yet measured in the national income statistics.

The Mini Case Study 11.1 looks at various problems with using time series of GDP data to measure changes in the standard of living especially data involving public sector output.

Mini Case Study 11.1

New national income data

Controversial economic growth figures based on better measures of public sector output could be published soon. Sir Tony Atkinson, the Oxford University academic charged with reviewing the way public services are measured, is expected to show the economic value of services such as hospitals, schools and social services have been under-recorded, allowing the government to say the economy is growing faster than first thought. The government has repeatedly said the figures fail to capture the true value to society of public services, which in turn reduces the reported productivity of the UK economy.

Sir Tony published his interim report in July 2004 which laid out the foundations for his review. He said: 'Public services output should be measured by the incremental contribution to individual or collective welfare. That implies measuring and including the quality of services.' The first results found NHS output had risen 29% between 1995 and 2003, rather than the 19% previously calculated, adding as much as 0.1% to annual GDP. The Atkinson review will cover about 60% of total government spending, of which health makes up half. The next largest sector is education, which takes up 17% of state resources. Until 1998, statisticians assumed the output of state services was equal to the amount of money going in. Since then the Office for National Statistics (ONS) has made attempts, such as including an assumption of a 0.25% annual quality improvement when measuring numbers of state school pupils. Now it has until 2006 to meet new EU rules that will outlaw any use of the 'output equals input' rule. Sir Tony's task is to establish a rulebook to allow statisticians to measure outputs of a range of services such as schools, hospitals, prisons, police, social services, fire brigades and the legal system. Sir Tony outlined five 'principles', such as ensuring output measures the 'value added' to the individual from the service. He said he was confident the transparency of the process would ensure it would not be 'dominated by the UK domestic agenda'.

Question

Consider the implications of this Mini Case Study for measuring national income and productivity in the UK.

Answer to question can be found on the students' side of the Companion Website.

4.2 Comparing living standards of different nations

National income statistics are used to compare the living standards of different countries. Apart from the problem of exchange rate fluctuations over time between the countries being compared, there are a number of other difficulties when making international comparisons.

(a) There may be differences not only in the way national income is calculated but also in the *reliability* of the collected data. Although the changes introduced in 1998 with the adoption of a new internationally agreed system of national accounts should go some way to dealing with the problem.

(b) The two countries in question may have different *climates*. So, for example, when comparing Sweden and Greece, Sweden may need to spend a higher proportion of its national income on heating and clothing in order to achieve the same 'quality of life' as Greece. Countries will, therefore, have different needs and tastes which cannot be readily taken into account when making international comparisons.

(c) The two countries may provide other differences in *quality of life* which are even more difficult to reflect in terms of a monetary value, e.g. feelings of safety from attack, freedom to express one's viewpoint without fear of retribution, access to the countryside.

(d) Other factors that make international comparisons difficult might include variations between countries in any or all of the following:

- *The level of unrecorded activity*, such as activity in the informal ('black') economy.
- *Numbers of hours* that people work.
- The level of *public provision* of goods and services.
- The *distribution* of national income (i.e. levels of inequality).
- The levels of *negative externalities* such as road congestion/pollution.

We return to this issue, namely the use of national income statistics for international comparison, in more detail in Chapter 18.

5 NATIONAL INCOME DETERMINATION

After introducing the idea of the circular flow of income, the emphasis so far has been on how national income is measured, the problems encountered in its measurement and the use to which national income statistics can be put. This section is concerned with what determines the size of the national income since, as we have seen, the size is an important influence on our living standards.

The circular flow of income was introduced in Section 2 of this chapter and a simple model of the whole economy was shown in Figure 11.2 (page 231) which identified certain *injections* into and *withdrawals* from the circular flow of income between domestic households (H) and domestic firms (F).

5.1 Equilibrium in the circular flow: W/J approach

Equilibrium national income: W/J diagram
Where withdrawals (W) equal injections (J), so that national income/output is then in balance or sustainable over time.

Exogenous variable
One which influences the system or model but which is determined *outside* that system or model.

'Equilibrium' or balance in the circular flow will occur, using this approach, when the value of withdrawals (W) from the circular flow exactly matches the value of injections (J) into the circular flow.

i.e. W = J is the equilibrium condition

All the relationships in Figure 11.3 are assumed to be linear, so that the 'curves' can be drawn as straight lines.

In terms of the circular flow, we treat the various injections (I, G and X) as *exogenous variables*, i.e. we assume that these are determined outside the model and are independent of national income (Y) so that I, G and X remain constant when national income (Y) changes. As a result we show the injections schedule (J) as a horizontal line at some particular value in Figure 11.3, being unchanged as national income (Y) varies in value.

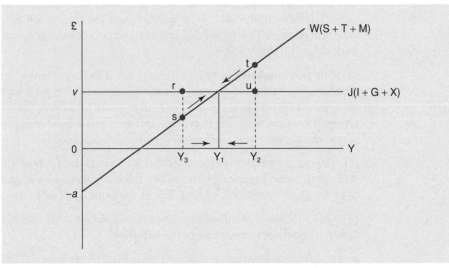

Figure 11.3 Equilibrium in the circular flow of income occurs only at Y_1, where total withdrawals (W) exactly match total injections (J) at value *v*.

 ## Pause for thought 2

Although, for simplicity, we assume that I, G and X remain constant as national income (Y) varies, can you think of any reasons why reality might be different from our assumption?

Endogenous variable
One which is determined inside the model or system.

However, we treat the various withdrawals (S, T and M) as *endogenous variables*, i.e. we assume that these are determined inside the model and are dependent on national income (Y). In this case the various withdrawals are all assumed to rise as national income (Y) rises and fall as national income (Y) falls.

As a result we show the withdrawals schedule (W) as sloping upwards from left to right in Figure 11.3, varying directly with the level of national income (Y).

Before examining the individual components in Figure 11.3 more carefully, we can use the diagram to indicate why the *equilibrium* value for national income is Y_1. To do this we might look at values for national income that are *not* equilibrium values.

- *National income level Y_2* Here withdrawals exceed injections (by $t - u$) so the value of the circular flow of income (Y_2) will fall. It will continue to fall until withdrawals have fallen sufficiently to exactly equal the unchanged value of injections at national income level Y_1.
- *National income level Y_3* Here injections exceed withdrawals (by $r - s$) so the value of the circular flow of income (Y_3) will rise. It will continue to rise until withdrawals have risen sufficiently to exactly equal the unchanged value of injections at national income level Y_1.

Only at national income level Y_1, where W = J, is there no further tendency for national income to change. We then say we have an *equilibrium* (balanced) level of national income at Y_1.

We now look rather more carefully at the withdrawals and injections schedules. We will come across the important ideas of *marginal propensities* and *average propensities* in this part of our analysis.

Withdrawals schedule (W) and national income (Y)

Here we examine in more detail the suggestion of Figure 11.4 below that each component of W (i.e. S, T and M) varies directly with the level of national income (Y), i.e. rising as Y rises, falling as Y falls.

The savings (S), taxes (T) and imports (M) schedules are all drawn as straight lines, which assumes a *linear* relationship between each component and national income (Y). One difference is immediately apparent, namely that the savings schedule (S) does *not* go through the origin (zero). Rather Figure 11.4(a) shows S as having a negative value ($-a$) when national income (Y) is zero. The suggestion here is that at zero income, households will still have to spend some money on consuming various goods and services, and this can only come from running down past savings (i.e. *dissaving* or negative savings).

Also it is often assumed, as in Figure 11.4(b), that at zero income the government receives no tax revenue and, as in Figure 11.4(c), that at zero income there is no spending on imports. It follows that the T and M schedules go through the origin (zero).

In Figure 11.4(d) the withdrawals schedule (W) is shown as the aggregate of the three previous schedules (S + T + M).

For example, suppose we have the following relationships for S, T and M with respect to national income (Y).

$$S = -4 + 0.1Y$$
$$T = 0.2Y$$
$$M = 0.3Y$$

Then
$$W = -4 + 0.6Y$$

We can use this last relationship to explore the ideas of *marginal propensity to withdraw* and *average propensity to withdraw*. This important but rather technical material is considered in Box 11.1.

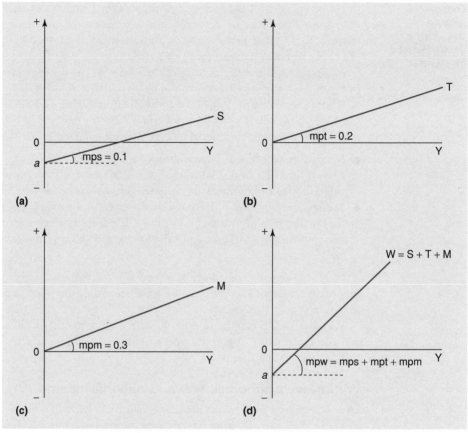

Figure 11.4 How savings (S), taxes (T), imports (M) and total withdrawals (W) vary with national income (Y).

Box 11.1	Marginal and average propensity to withdraw

Marginal propensity to withdraw (mpw)

This is a ratio of the change in total withdrawals (ΔW) to the change in national income (ΔY). For example, if the household withdraws 60 pence out of an extra £1 of income, then mpw = 0.6. For any straight line (linear) withdrawals schedule this is given by the slope of the line and is a constant over its entire length.

$$\text{Marginal propensity to withdraw } (mpw) = \frac{\text{Change in withdrawals}}{\text{Change in national income}}$$

$$= \frac{\Delta W}{\Delta Y}$$

where Δ = 'change in'

The *mpw* is shown in Figure 11.4(d) as the slope of the straight line withdrawals schedule (W). We have found this to be 0.6, suggesting that for every £1 rise in national income, 60 pence is withdrawn.

You should be able to see that:

$$\text{Marginal propensity to save } (mps) = \frac{\text{Change in savings}}{\text{Change in national income}} = \frac{\Delta S}{\Delta Y} = 0.1$$

$$\text{Marginal propensity to tax } (mpt) = \frac{\text{Change in taxation}}{\text{Change in national income}} = \frac{\Delta T}{\Delta Y} = 0.2$$

$$\text{Marginal propensity to import } (mpm) = \frac{\text{Change in imports}}{\text{Change in national income}} = \frac{\Delta M}{\Delta Y} = 0.3$$

$$mpw = mps + mpt + mpm = 0.6$$

Average propensity to withdraw (apw)

However, we are often interested in the *average* as well as marginal propensities. The difference between *apw* and *mpw* is shown in Figure 11.5.

$$\text{Average propensity to withdraw } (apw) = \frac{\text{Total withdrawals}}{\text{Total national income}} = \frac{W}{Y}$$

Using the withdrawals (W) schedule in Figure 11.5:

$$W = -4 + 0.6Y$$

At, say, $Y_1 = 20$

$$W_1 = -4 + 0.6 (20)$$

i.e. $\quad W_1 = 8$

We can therefore say that at a level of national income (Y_1) of 20:

$$apw = \frac{8}{20} = 0.4$$

We should be able to see from Figure 11.5 that *apw* is the slope of the straight line drawn from the origin to the relevant point on the withdrawals schedule (W). We should also be able to see that apw (unlike mpw) will rise continuously as the level of national income rises.

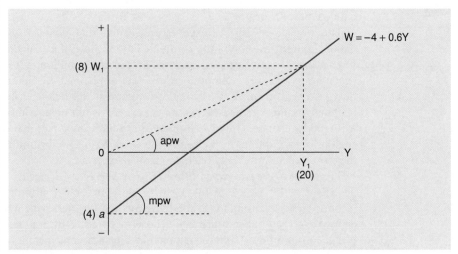

Figure 11.5 Average propensity to withdraw (*apw*) and marginal propensity to withdraw (*mpw*).

Injections schedule (J)

As already mentioned, we assume that each component of J (i.e. I, G and X) does *not* vary with national income, even though this may be something of an oversimplification. The injection schedule (J) is therefore drawn as a horizontal straight line at some given value *v* in Figure 11.3 above (page 242).

Put another way, we are treating each component of injections (i.e. I, G and X) as an *exogenous variable*, i.e. one which affects the equilibrium value of the circular flow but whose value is determined outside the circular flow.

5.2 Equilibrium in the circular flow: 45° diagram approach

Equilibrium national income: 45°
Where 'planned' expenditure equals national income/ output which is then in balance or sustainable over time.

An alternative approach to the W/J diagram in finding the equilibrium level of national income involves the 45° diagram. This approach makes use of the expenditure method (page 236) of calculating national income.

Note: Planned and unplanned expenditure

In terms of *measuring* national income, we noted earlier (page 230) that we can use either the expenditure, output or income methods. In other words, expenditure is defined in the national income accounts in such a way that it yields the same value for national income as the output or income methods of measurement. Using our earlier terminology (page 239) the expenditure, output and income methods are 'accounting identities' with any differences in their recorded values due to measurement problems, such as the existence of a 'black economy' (page 237). We should note that when we use this national income definition of 'expenditure' we are referring to *actual* expenditure, both planned and unplanned.

However, when we use the term 'expenditure' in determining the *equilibrium* level of national income, i.e. in establishing whether any level of national income can be sustained, we only refer to *planned* expenditure. 'Planned' expenditure is that expenditure which households, firms and governments *intend* to spend on the output of domestic firms. Only when **national output** reaches a level where there is an intention to purchase it in its entirely (i.e. planned expenditure = national output) do we speak of *equilibrium* in national output/income.

National output
(*See* national income)

The 'unplanned' level of expenditure ensures that 'actual' expenditure always equals national output/income in the accounts. For example, if in any one year *actual* expenditure (planned + unplanned) = national output at £10 billion, but £1 billion is unplanned expenditure, then the attempt to reduce that 'unplanned' £1 billion of expenditure in the next year will mean that national output must fall below £10 billion in the future. National output/income is not sustainable, i.e. it is not in 'equilibrium' or in balance, but will tend to change. Only when *planned* expenditure = national output do we have an equilibrium condition. In the rest of this section on equilibrium national output/income the term 'expenditure' only refers to planned expenditure.

The term *aggregate expenditure* (E) (or *aggregate demand*) is sometimes used to describe C + I + G + X in the 45° diagram approach to finding equilibrium national income. However, using the expenditure method for measuring national income we have defined aggregate expenditure as C + I + G + X − M. Why are they different? The answer is that consumption (C) in the national income accounts includes consumer expenditure on *all* goods and services (wherever they are produced) whereas in the 45° diagram consumption (C) only includes expenditure on the output of *domestic firms*. It follows that expenditure on imports (M) from overseas firms has already been subtracted from consumption (C) when we use the 45° diagram approach.

Under the 45° diagram approach, the equilibrium level of national income occurs where the value of planned aggregate expenditure (E) exactly equals the value of aggregate output (Y).

$$E = Y$$
i.e. $C + I + G + X = Y$ in equilibrium

Figure 11.6 represents this situation, with equilibrium national income at Y_1 (where $E_1 = Y_1$). Notice that the 45° line represents all the values in the diagram for which $E = Y$.

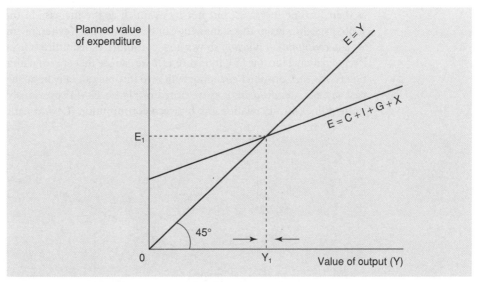

Figure 11.6 Equilibrium in the circular flow of income occurs where the value of planned aggregate expenditure (E_1) exactly equals the value of aggregate output (Y_1).

 Pause for thought 3

Can you use the idea of a right-angled triangle to prove why E = Y at all points along the 45° diagram?

It follows that only where the planned aggregate expenditure schedule E *intersects* the 45° diagram do we fulfil the equilibrium condition $E = Y$.

- At levels of national income *above* Y_1, the value of planned expenditure *is less than* the value of output (i.e. $E < Y$), so the value of output falls.
- At levels of national income *below* Y_1, the value of planned expenditure *is greater than* the value of output (i.e. $E > Y$), so the value of output rises.
- Only at Y_1 where the planned aggregate expenditure schedule intersects the 45° line do we have the value of planned expenditure *exactly equal* to the value of output, i.e. an equilibrium ($E_1 = Y_1$) at which the value of output does not change.

The *planned aggregate expenditure* schedule (E) in Figure 11.6 includes the *consumption schedule* (C) sometimes called the *consumption function*. We now consider this consumption function in rather more detail, together with the important ideas of the marginal propensity to consume (*mpc*) and the average propensity to consume (*apc*).

The consumption function

Consumption is the most important single element in aggregate expenditure in the UK, accounting for around half its total value. John Maynard Keynes related consumption to current disposable income and his ideas are embodied in the so-called consumption function. In the book *General Theory*, Keynes argued that 'the fundamental psychological law . . . is that men are disposed, as a rule and on the average, to increase their consumption as their income increases, but not by as much as the increase in their income' (Keynes, 1936, page 96). From this statement can be derived the Keynesian consumption function.

The *consumption function* shows how consumer expenditure (C) varies directly with the level of national income (Y). In Figure 11.7 we can see that at zero national income consumption (C) is +*a*. Consumer spending with zero income can only be achieved by running down past savings (i.e. *dissaving*), as we noted in Figure 11.4(a) previously. Again we assume a straight line (linear) relationship between consumption (C) and national income (Y).

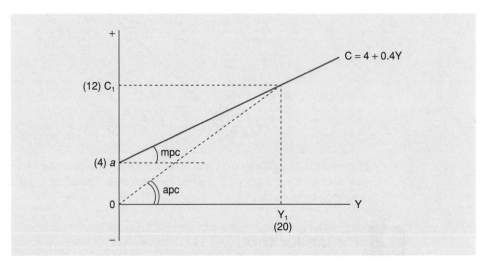

Figure 11.7 The consumption function (C), the average propensity to consume (apc) and the marginal propensity to consume (mpc).

It may be useful at this point to explore the ideas of *marginal propensity to consume* and *marginal propensity to withdraw*. This important but rather technical material is considered in Box 11.2.

| Box 11.2 | Marginal propensities to consume and withdraw |

Marginal propensity to consume (mpc)

The marginal propensity to consume (*mpc*) is a ratio of the change in total consumption (ΔC) to the change in national income (ΔY). For example, if the consumer spends 40 pence out of an extra £1 of income, then *mpc* = 0.4. For any straight line (linear) relationship this is given by the slope of the line and is a constant over its entire length.

$$\text{Marginal propensity to consume } (mpc) = \frac{\text{Change in consumption}}{\text{Change in national income}} = \frac{\Delta C}{\Delta Y}$$

where Δ = 'change in'

The mpc is shown in Figure 11.7 as the slope of the straight line consumption function (C) and has the value 0.4. This suggests that for every £1 rise in national income, 40 pence is consumed.

mpc and mpw

It is worth noting an important relationship between mpc and mpw

$$mpc + mpw = 1$$

This must follow from our earlier Figure 11.2 (page 231) which showed that any income received by domestic households (H) is either consumed (passed on in the circular flow) or withdrawn from the circular flow.

$$Y = C + W$$

It follows that for any change in Y $\Delta Y = \Delta C + \Delta W$

and dividing throughout by ΔY $\dfrac{\Delta Y}{\Delta Y} = \dfrac{\Delta C}{\Delta Y} + \dfrac{\Delta W}{\Delta Y}$

$$1 = mpc + mpw$$

We can therefore also say that: $1 - mpc = mpw$

Other influences on consumer spending

- *Interest rates* If interest rates rise then individuals are assumed to feel more secure as to the future returns from their asset holdings (i.e. positive 'wealth effect'). If individuals do perceive a rise in the real value of their wealth then they may be inclined to spend more at any given level of national income (Y). In terms of Figure 11.7, the consumption function (C) will shift vertically upwards. Of course, the higher interest rates may mean that individuals now have less income to spend from any given value of their total ('gross') income, since more of their total income is now required to pay the higher mortgage and loan commitments. In terms of Figure 11.7, the reduction in 'disposable' national income at any given level of total or 'gross' national income (Y), will mean that the consumption function (C) will shift vertically downwards. The *net* impact of higher interest rates on consumption (C) will depend on the relative strength of these opposing effects.
- *Price level* If there is a rise in the general level of prices (inflation) then the value of people's money balances will fall. They may, therefore, spend less of their current income in order to increase their money balances in an attempt to restore their initial real value. In terms of Figure 11.7, the consumption function (C) will shift vertically downwards as a result of this so-called 'real balance' effect.

Note: Too little consumption

Worried that the government may not be able to afford to pay for their future pensions, Japan's ageing population prefers to save rather than spend. Even with interest rates effectively zero per cent, this concern for the future has meant that Japanes banks are awash with savings. Unfortunately, over the past decade, so few firms have wanted to borrow these savings for investment that with so much saving and so little consumer spending the Japanese economy has barely grown.

Mini Case Study 11.2

National income and consumer behaviour

The consumer has been widely seen as sustaining the level of national income in the UK economy by continuing to purchase goods and services, creating extra output and employment. However, there is major concern that the growing 'debt overhang' may reduce consumer spending sharply in the near future. Figures from the Bank of England in 2004 showed that the average indebted household in Britain owed £3,516 in unsecured debt (hire purchase, credit cards, personal loans, overdrafts).

A major concern for analysts is that any sustained rise in interest rates will make it extremely difficult for UK households to keep up their repayments on all types of debt, secured and unsecured. For example, in 2004 almost £11 billion was borrowed in one month alone, some £9 billion of this being borrowed against property in the form of mortgages. This extra borrowing in just one month amounted to the equivalent of 1% of the country's entire annual wealth!

Mortgage debt is secured debt but will create major problems for consumers should interest rates rise. In October 2003, London and Country Mortgage brokers estimated the following impact of rises in mortgage rates above the then 3.5% per annum. The following table indicates the inreases in monthly payments on different values of mortgages if interest rates rose by specified amounts.

Table 11.4 How mortgage payments could rise

Mortgage	Current monthly payments	Increase if base rate rises to		
		4.0%	4.5%	5.0%
£100,000	£292	£42	£83	£125
£250,000	£729	£103	£208	£313
£500,000	£1,458	£208	£417	£625
£750,000	£2,198	£313	£625	£938

Interest rates reached 4.5% in 2005. Many people are projecting the UK interest rates will indeed rise to 5.0% or more during 2007 and beyond.
Source: M. O'Quigley in Griffiths and Wall, *Economics for Business and Management* (FT/Prentice Hall, 2005)

Questions

1 *What impact would higher interest rates have on the consumption function in Figure 11.7 (page 248)?*

2 *How would this influence the equilibrium level of national income?*

3 *Are there any policy measures which government might take to help reduce this potential problem?*

Answers to questions can be found at the back of the book (page 512).

5.3 Equivalence of the two approaches

Suppose we are faced with the situation shown in Table 11.5.

Table 11.5 National income equilibrium

National income (Y) (£bn)	Planned consumption (C) (£bn)	Planned withdrawals (W) (£bn)	Planned injections (J) (£bn)	Planned expenditure (E = C + J) (£bn)	Change in national income
0	12	−12	4	16	Increase
10	18	−8	4	22	Increase
20	24	−4	4	28	Increase
30	30	0	4	34	Increase
40	36	4	4	40	No change
50	42	8	4	46	Decrease
60	48	12	4	52	Decrease
70	54	16	4	58	Decrease
80	60	20	4	64	Decrease

Figure 11.8 presents the data in Table 11.5 using both the W/J and 45° diagram approach.

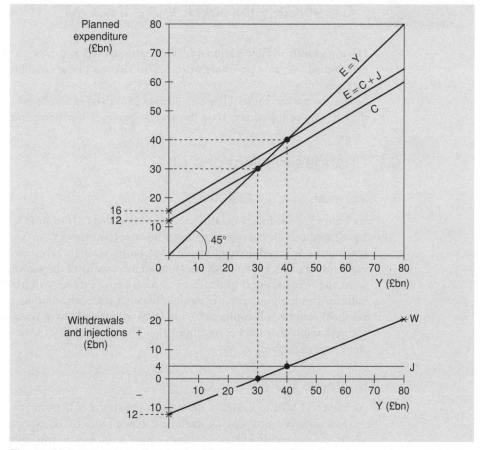

Figure 11.8 This shows that the W/J and 45° diagram approaches will both give the same value for equilibrium national income.

W/J approach

At all levels of national income below £40 billion, planned injections exceed planned withdrawals (J > W). More is being added to the circular flow than is being withdrawn from it, so the value of that flow (national income) must rise.

At all levels of national income above £40 billion, the opposite is true (J < W) and national income must fall.

At £40 billion national income planned injections of £4 billion exactly equal planned withdrawals of £4 billion (J = W) and the level of national income is stable, i.e. in equilibrium.

45° diagram (aggregate expenditure) approach

At all levels of national income below £40 billion, planned aggregate expenditure (E = C + J) exceeds the value of national output/national income (i.e. E > Y). The value of Y must rise: either the quantity of output rises or prices rise or both.

At all levels of national income above £40 billion, the opposite is true (i.e. E < Y) and the value of national output/national income (Y) must fall.

6 CHANGES IN NATIONAL INCOME

Having examined how national income is measured and how an equilibrium value is determined, we now pay more attention to *changes* in the equilibrium level of national income.

We can use our earlier Figure 11.3 (page 242) to consider the effect of changes in withdrawals (W) or injections (J) on the *equilibrium* level of national income.

6.1 Changes in injections (J)

Increase in J (I + G + X)

As Figure 11.9(a) indicates, an *increase* in injections (ΔJ) from J_1 to J_2, will (other things equal) result in an *increase* in national income (ΔY) from Y_1 to Y_2. This upward shift in the injections schedule may result from an increase in investment (ΔI), government expenditure (ΔG), exports (ΔX) or from an increase in all three components.

At the original equilibrium Y_1, injections now exceed withdrawals, so the value of national income must rise. As national income rises, withdrawals rise (move along W). National income will continue to rise until withdrawals have risen sufficiently to match the new and higher level of injections (J_2). This occurs at Y_2, the new and higher equilibrium level of national income.

Decrease in J (I + G + X)

As Figure 11.9(b) indicates, a *decrease* in injections (ΔJ) from J_1 to J_2, whether from a decrease in investment (ΔI), government expenditure (ΔG), exports (ΔX) or decrease in all three components will (other things equal) result in a *decrease* in national income (ΔY) from Y_1 to Y_2.

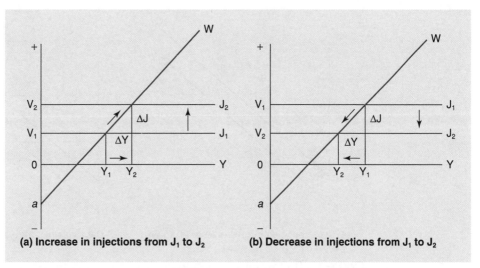

(a) Increase in injections from J_1 to J_2 (b) Decrease in injections from J_1 to J_2

Figure 11.9 Changes in equilibrium national income (ΔY) following a change in injections ($\Delta J = \Delta I + \Delta G + \Delta X$).

 ## Pause for thought 4

Can you explain the mechanism involved in moving from the original equilibrium Y_1 to the new equilibrium Y_2 following a decrease in J from J_1 to J_2? How would a change in injections be captured on the 45° diagram? For example, how would an increase in injections affect the aggregate expenditure schedule (E) and why? What impact would this have on equilibrium national income?

6.2 Changes in withdrawals (W)

Increase in W (S + T + M)

As Figure 11.10(a) indicates, an upward shift in the withdrawals schedule from W_1 to W_2 will result in a decrease in national income (ΔY) from Y_1 to Y_2. With the new withdrawals schedule W_2 there is now a higher level of withdrawals from any given level of national income (i.e. higher *apw*). This may be due to an upward shift in any or all of the savings (S), taxation (T) or imports (M) schedules shown in Figure 11.4 (page 244).

At the original equilibrium Y_1, withdrawals now exceed injections so the value of national income must fall. As national income falls, withdrawals fall (move along W_2). National income will continue to fall until withdrawals have fallen sufficiently to match the original level of injections (J). This occurs at Y_2, the new and lower equilibrium level of national income.

Decrease in W (S + T + M)

As Figure 11.10 indicates, a *downward shift* in the withdrawals schedule from W_1 to W_2 will result in an *increase* in national income (ΔY) from Y_1 to Y_2.

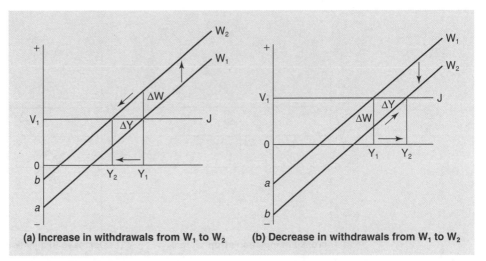

Figure 11.10 Changes in national income (ΔY) following a change in withdrawals ($\Delta W = \Delta S + \Delta T + \Delta M$).

Pause for thought 5

Can you explain the mechanism involved in moving from the original equilibrium Y_1 to the new equilibrium Y_2 following a decrease in W from W_1 to W_2? How would a change in withdrawals be captured on the 45° diagram? For example, how would an increase in withdrawals affect the aggregate expenditure schedule (E) and why? What impact would this have on equilibrium national income?

7 NATIONAL INCOME AND EMPLOYMENT MULTIPLIERS

7.1 National income multiplier

Multiplier
The change in national income (or employment) resulting from an initial change in injections or withdrawals.

The *national income* **multiplier** seeks to explain why any given change in injections (or withdrawals) may result in a change in national income which is often larger than (some multiple of) that initial change. In Figure 11.11 we see that an increase in injections of £10 million results in an increase in national income of £40 million, suggesting a national income multiplier (K) of 4.

We define the national income multiplier (K) as:

$$K = \frac{\Delta Y}{\Delta J} = \frac{40}{10} = 4$$

It may be useful to first consider the idea behind the multiplier. Suppose a firm invests, say, £1 million in building an extension to its factory or office in a town. This £1 million will in the first stage yield income to the various people involved in planning and building the extension. Suppose these people spend 60% of any extra income received ($mpc = 0.6$)

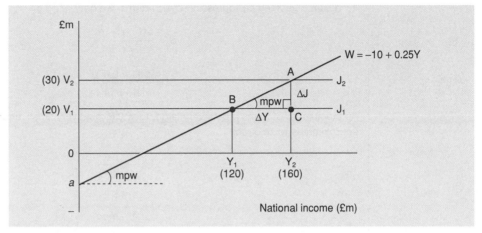

Figure 11.11 Finding the national income multiplier. A given change in injections (ΔJ) results in a larger change in national income (ΔY).

and withdraw (via savings, tax and spending on imports) 40% of any extra income received ($mpw = 0.4$). Some £600,000 is therefore spent in this second stage on goods and services of various types in (and outside) the town. Suppose those receiving this £600,000 as income (e.g. various shops, restaurants, entertainment centres, landlords etc.) in turn spend 60% of this £600,000 of new income, i.e. £360,000 in the third stage. Clearly at each stage extra income (and spending) is being created. We then have the following (geometric) progression of new income received at each stage if mpc is always 0.6.

£1m + £600,000 + £360,000 + £216,000 + £129,600 which eventually will sum to £2.5 million (*see* Box 11.3 below).

We can now say that the national income multiplier (K) is

$$K = \frac{1}{1 - mpc} \quad \text{or} \quad \frac{1}{mpw}$$

$$\text{i.e. } K = \frac{1}{1 - 0.6} = \frac{1}{0.4} = 2.5$$

In other words, the extra income created at each stage from an initial injection of £1 million is £2.5 million. Box 11.3 provides a more technical proof of our formula for the multiplier.

Box 11.3 **Deriving the multiplier**

A geometric progression is of the form a, ar, ar^2, ar^{n-1} where:

a = initial value
r = common ratio
n = number of terms
In our earlier example:
a = the change in injections (ΔJ) of the £1m
$r = mpc = 0.6$

→

If we *sum* a geometric progression over *n* terms, we get

$$S_n = \frac{a(1 - r^n)}{1 - r}$$

$$S_n = \frac{\Delta J(1 - 0.6^n)}{(1 - 0.6)}$$

As the number of terms *n* gets very large, then 0.6^n gets very small, and eventually approximates to zero, so:

$$S_n = \Delta J \times \frac{1}{(1 - 0.6)}$$

$$S_n = \Delta J \times \frac{1}{1 - mpc}$$

$$\text{where } K = \Delta J \times \frac{1}{1 - mpc} = \frac{1}{mpw}$$

Pause for thought 6

Can you draw the 45° diagram and use it to demonstrate the multiplier? For example, start with an equilibrium level of national income, then assume an increase in injections (ΔJ). Show the multiplier effect on your diagram.

Of course, the national income multiplier can work both ways:

- *raising* national income by some multiple of a given increase in injections or decrease in withdrawals (i.e. '*expansionary multiplier*')
- *reducing* national income by some multiple of a given decrease in injections or increase in withdrawals (i.e. '*deflationary multiplier*').

Multiplier and the marginal propensities to save, tax and import

Remember that the marginal propensity to withdraw is the sum of the marginal propensity to save, tax and import (*see* page 245).

$$\text{i.e. } mpw = mps + mpt + mpm$$

$$\text{so, } K = \frac{1}{mpw} = \frac{1}{mps + mpt + mpm}$$

For example, if $mps = 0.1$, $mpt = 0.2$ and $mpm = 0.3$

$$K = \frac{1}{0.1 + 0.2 + 0.3} = \frac{1}{0.6} = 1\tfrac{2}{3}$$

In other words, we can now find the value of the national income multiplier (K) by dividing 1 by the marginal propensity to withdraw (*mpw*).

7.2 Employment multiplier

As well as the national income multiplier there is also the *employment multiplier*. This compares the *total* (direct and indirect) increase in employment to the *initial* increase in employment (direct) which begins the multiplier process. Suppose a building project initially employs 100 extra people but, when all the 'ripple' effects of their extra spending works through the economy, a total of 400 extra people are employed, then the 'employment multiplier' is 4.

The Mini Case Study below looks at a practical application of national income and employment multipliers.

Mini Case Study 11.3

Levi jeans and the multiplier

The good life has come to an end for workers at Levi Strauss's last two factories in America. In October 2003 members of the 2,000 strong workforce of the plant in San Antonio, Texas, queued up to collect their last pay cheques. Over their last few weeks, as well as sewing labels, zippers and rivets, they had been attending workshops and a job fair to help them prepare for life after Levi Strauss.

The closure ends a momentous chapter in the history of the jeans company, established 150 years ago by a 24-year old Bavarian immigrant to clothe miners in the goldrush. The jeans with signature red tag, considered as American as Coca-Cola, Ronald Reagan and mom's apple pie, will from now on be made in Mexico and China. Levi Strauss, which in the 1980s had more than 60 factories in the US, has outsourced all its manufacturing to Latin America, Asia and the Caribbean in the face of fierce competition and price pressures from companies such as Wal Mart.

Around half of these workers are expected to remain unemployed and those who do get a job are likely to find their earnings are much lower. Data from the Bureau of Labor Statistics in the US shows that while around 70% of all displaced US workers find a job eventually, for manufacturing the figure is only around 35%.

It is estimated that the 'ripple effects' of these job losses and earnings reductions on the whole economy of the towns affected will bring about many more job losses and threaten a downward spiral in the fortunes of these communities.

Question

Explain the likely multiplier impacts resulting from this Mini Case Study.

Answer to question can be found on the students' side of the Companion Website.

KEY POINTS

● National income can be measured using income, output, expenditure approaches.

● In terms of the national income accounts, expenditure includes both 'planned' and 'unplanned' expenditure.

● In the 'circular flow of income', *injections* (J) consist of investment (I), government expenditure (G) and exports (X) whilst *withdrawals* (W) consist of savings (S), imports (M) and taxes (T).

- 'Equilibrium' or balance in the circular flow occurs where injections into the flow (J) are exactly matched by withdrawals from the flow (W).

- 'Equilibrium' national income can be shown using *either* the withdrawals/injections diagram or the aggregate expenditure (45°) diagram.

- In terms of 'equilibrium' national income, expenditure (E) refers only to 'planned' expenditure.

- We define planned aggregate expenditure (E) as consumer expenditure (C) *plus* injection expenditure (J).

- The national income multiplier tells us the change in national income resulting from either a change in injections or a change in withdrawals.

Further reading

Griffiths, A. and Wall, S. (2005) *Economics for Business and Management*, FT/Prentice Hall, Chapter 9.

Heather, K. (2004) *Economics Theory in Action*, 4th edition, FT/Prentice Hall, Chapters 12 and 13.

Parkin, M., Powell, M. and Matthews, K. (2005) *Economics*, 6th edition, FT/Prentice Hall, Chapters 19, 20, 22 and 23.

Sloman, J. (2006) *Economics*, 6th edition, FT/Prentice Hall, Chapters 13 and 17.

Web references

The data sources below offer a range of useful data and information on aspects of consumption and saving.

National Statistics: **http://www.statistics.gov.uk/** The Official UK statistics site.

HM Treasury: **http://www.hm-treasury.gov.uk/** UK macroeconomic data, forecasts and government tax and spending plans.

Institute of Fiscal Studies: **http://www1.ifs.org.uk/** An independent research organisation providing economic analysis of public policy. Data on UK tax system.

Webecon: **http://netec.mcc.ac.uk/WebEc/** Web resources and data sets for economics.

Eurostat: **http://europa.eu.int/comm/eurostat/** EU data.

Resource centre for access to data on Europe: **http://www-rcade.dur.ac.uk/academic/academic.htm**

World Bank: **http://www.worldbank.org/** World economic data.

IMF: **http://www.imf.org/** Economic and financial data for most countries.

InfoNation: **http://www.un.org/Pubs/CyberSchoolBus/infonation/e_infonation.htm** A United Nations statistical database that enables comparisons to be made of UN member countries.

OECD: **http://www.oecd.org/** Statistics for most developed economies and some transition and emerging economies.

Economic models and simulation

Economic modelling is an important aspect of economic analysis. There are a number of sites that offer access to a model for you to use, which can be a useful way of finding out how economic theory works within an environment that claims to reflect reality. In this case variations in levels of injections and withdrawals can be seen to affect the economy.

Virtual Economy: **http://bized.ac.uk/virtual/economy**
WinEcon: **http://www.webecon.bris.ac.uk/winecon/**
About.com Economics: **http://economics.about.com**
Estima (statistical analysis): **http://www.estima.com/**
SPSS (statistical analysis): **http://www.spss.com/**
National Institute of Economic and Social Research: **http://www.niesr.ac.uk/**

PROGRESS AND REVIEW QUESTIONS

Answers to most questions can be found at the back of the book (pages 513–15). Answers to asterisked questions can be found on the students' side of the Companion Website.

 ## Multiple-choice questions

1 The value of national output produced by residents located within the country, before depreciation and including the influence of taxes and subsidies, is known as:

a) GDP at market prices
b) GDP at factor cost
c) GNP at market prices
d) GNP at factor cost
e) NNP at factor cost.

2 The value of national output produced by residents of a country, whether located at home or overseas, after depreciation and excluding the influence of taxes and subsidies, is known as:

a) GDP at market prices
b) GDP at factor cost
c) GNP at market prices
d) GNP at factor cost
e) NNP at factor cost.

3 Of the following items, which *one* would be considered an investment in the UK national income accounts?

a) The purchase of a new lorry by a road haulier.
b) The purchase of 100 shares of UK stock on the London Stock Exchange.
c) The purchase of a 100-year old house that was just put on the protected historic sites list in the year in question.
d) The purchase of a British government bond.
e) All of the above.

4 Which *one* of the following items would be included in UK GDP?

a) Payments made to unemployed workers during the year as part of their unemployment compensation.

b) The cost of the tools used by a car mechanic.

c) The cost of the pollution caused during the processing of steel during the year.

d) The purchase of stocks on the New York Exchange by a resident located in the US.

e) The purchase of stocks on the London Exchange by a UK resident located in the US.

5 Which *one* of the following is a component of the factor incomes approach to GDP?

a) Government purchases

b) Transfer payments

c) Corporate profits

d) Net exports

e) Value added

6 Other things equal, which *one* of the following will lead to an increase in aggregate demand?

a) An increase in taxes

b) An increase in imports

c) A decrease in the rate of government spending

d) A decrease in the interest rate

e) A decrease in the money supply

7 The marginal propensity to consume

a) equals 1

b) is between 0 and 1

c) is negative

d) exceeds 1

e) can be any one of the above depending upon circumstances.

8 Which *one* of the following represents the difference between GNP at market prices and GDP at market prices?

a) The value of depreciation

b) The value of taxes and subsidies

c) Exports

d) Imports

e) Net property income from abroad

9 Which of the following is a widely used measure of the standard of living?

a) Nominal output (income) per employed person

b) Nominal output (income) per head of population

c) Real output (income) per head of population

d) Real output (income) per employed person

e) Real output (income) per unit of capital

10

Disposable income (£)	Consumption expenditure (£)
100	225
200	300
300	375
400	450
500	525
600	600

Using the table above, if income is either consumed or saved and if disposable income is £400, then saving is:

a) £100
b) −£75
c) −£50
d) £0
e) £50

11 If there are no taxes or imports and MPC = 0.67, the multiplier is:

a) 1.5
b) 0.33
c) 6
d) 0.05
e) 3

12 If the multiplier is 4.0 and, owing to a decrease in expected future profit, investment decreases by £2.5 billion, the equilibrium national income:

a) rises by less than £10 billion
b) falls by £10 billion
c) does not change
d) falls by more than £30 billion
e) rises by £10 billion.

Matching pairs

1 In this question you have a description of a particular type of transaction in the circular flow of income. Try to match the *lettered* description with the correct *numbered* term.

Descriptions

a) The publisher Pearson UK sells 50,000 books to South Africa.
b) A successful advertising campaign by Ford results in greater car sales in its domestic (UK) market.
c) A rise in the pound:euro exchange rate causes Ford UK to switch from UK based component suppliers to those located in the Eurozone.
d) The main GlaxoSmithKline production plant in the UK purchases new machinery from another UK firm to produce its pharmaceuticals.
e) A rise in UK interest rates raises the amount of money placed by domestic residents in various types of interest-bearing deposit accounts.
f) A government contract to build a major trunk road is withdrawn because of environmental protests.

Terms

i)   Consumption expenditure (C)
ii) Investment expenditure (I)
iii) Government expenditure (G)
iv) Exports (X)
v)   Savings (S)

vi) Taxes (T)
vii) Imports (M)

2 In this question you will see a description of a particular type of measurement used for national output/income and a list of terms. Try to match the *lettered* description with its correct *numbered* term.

Descriptions

a) GNP minus the depreciation of physical assets.
b) Pensions paid by the government to residents of that country.
c) The gross income received by residents minus the direct taxes they pay.
d) The value of incomes received by residents of a country from their ownership of resources, wherever these are located (but excluding direct taxes and subsidies).
e) Inward payments received by residents from their ownership of overseas property minus outward payments made by residents from their ownership of domestic property.
f) The value of incomes received by residents located within a country (including indirect taxes and subsidies).

Terms

i)   Disposable income
ii)   Net property income from Abroad
iii)   GDP at market prices
iv)   GDP at factor cost
v)   GNP at market prices
vi)   GNP at factor cost
vii)   Net national product (NNP)
viii) Transfer payment

3 The value of national income (output) can be expressed in a number of different ways. Try to match the *lettered* description with its correct *numbered* term.

Descriptions

a) This measure takes into account the fact that some capital equipment will have depreciated over the year via wear and tear or because technological change has made it obsolescent.
b) Value of output produced (and incomes received) by residents of that country wherever they are located.
c) Measures of national output/income which *include* indirect taxes and subsidies.
d) Measures of national output/income which *exclude* indirect taxes and subsidies.
e) Value of output produced (and incomes received) by factors of production located within that country.

Terms

i) Gross domestic product (GDP)
ii) Gross national product (GNP)
iii) Net national product (NNP)
iv) Market prices
v) Factor cost

Data response and stimulus questions

1 Look carefully at Tables (i) and (ii) below which show national income in Country A, using the *income* and *expenditure* approaches respectively.

(i) Income method (£bn)

National account	
Income from employment	1,042.8
Income from profit and rent	426.4
Other	157.2
GDP factor cost	1,626.4
Indirect cost less subsidies	260.4
GDP at market prices	1,886.8
Net property income from abroad	6.0
GNP at market prices	1,892.8

(ii) Expenditure method (£bn)

National account	
Expenditure by households	1,189.6
Expenditure by government and non-profit organisations	395.4
Investment spending	334.2
Exports–Imports	(−32.4)
GDP at market prices	1,886.8
Net property income from abroad	6.0
GNP at market prices	1,892.8

a) What do you notice?

b) From Table (i), explain why GDP at market prices is higher than GDP at factor cost.

c) From Table (i), explain why GNP at market prices differs from GDP at market prices.

d) What types of income have not been included in Table (i) when measuring GDP or GNP?

e) From Table (ii), identify 'aggregate expenditure'.

f) From Table (ii), explain what contribution 'Exports–Imports' is making to calculating GDP at market prices.

g) What types of expenditure have *not* been included in Table (ii) when measuring GDP or GNP?

2 Look carefully at the table below

National income (Y)	Planned savings (S)	Planned taxation (T)	Planned expenditure on imports (M)	Planned investment (I)	Planned government expenditure (G)	Planned export sales (X)	Tendency to change in national income
0	−2,000	0	0	1,200	1,800	1,000	
2,000	−1,600	400	200	1,200	1,800	1,000	
4,000	−1,200	800	400	1,200	1,800	1,000	
6,000	−800	1,200	600	1,200	1,800	1,000	
8,000	−400	1,600	800	1,200	1,800	1,000	
10,000	0	2,000	1,000	1,200	1,800	1,000	
12,000	400	2,400	1,200	1,200	1,800	1,000	
14,000	800	2,800	1,400	1,200	1,800	1,000	
16,000	1,200	3,200	1,600	1,200	1,800	1,000	

a) Fill in the last column using *one* of the three words 'increase', 'decrease', 'no change'.

b) Use the information in the table to complete the following.

National income (Y)	Withdrawals (W)	Injections (J)
0		
2,000		
4,000		
6,000		
8,000		
10,000		
12,000		
14,000		
16,000		

c) Draw the W/J diagram.

d) Can you express each of the following as a schedule? The first has been done for you. (Check back to Figure 11.3, page 242.)

Savings (S) $= -2{,}000 + 0.2Y$

Taxes (T) $=$

Imports (M) $=$

Withdrawals (W) $=$

e) Now use the information given above to complete the following table.

National income (Y)	Consumption (C)	Injections (J)	Aggregate expenditure (E)
0			
2,000			
4,000			
6,000			
8,000			
10,000			
12,000			
14,000			
16,000			

Hint: Any income received by domestic households is either passed on in the circular flow (consumed) or withdrawn.

i.e. $Y = C + W$

so $Y - W = C$

f) Draw the 45° diagram.

g) What is equilibrium national income using this 'aggregate expenditure' approach? What do you notice?

3 Read the following text and try to answer the question.

Saving can be counterproductive!

Sometimes we talk about the 'paradox of thrift'. A paradox is a contradiction, something that is against logic or expectation. A very commonly discussed paradox revolves around time travel: if I went back in time and killed my mother when she was a child, then I would never have been born. If I was never born I would never have been alive to go back in time! The paradox of thrift does not give rise to quite so many interesting novels and films but it is rather more useful. It was put forward by the economist John Maynard Keynes and goes something like this:

A thrifty person is a careful person who wishes to spend within their means and always be able to pay their way. Being thrifty is considered to be a good thing, a virtue. However, Keynes pointed out two very important points about being thrifty.

1 What may be a virtue in one person is not necessarily virtuous if *everyone* does it. What is good for one is not necessarily good for all.
2 The more savings that people intend to make, the less savings that may actually occur.

Thriftiness would therefore seem indeed to be a paradox, leading to possibly unexpected outcomes.

a) Can you use the W/J schedule to explain why the above might occur?

4 Read the text then answer the questions which follow.

The multiplier and the London Olympic bid

London successfully bid for the 2012 Olympics, narrowly defeating Paris and Madrid. Here it may be useful to consider an important aspect of that bid, i.e. the regeneration of parts of London and other benefits to the rest of the UK.

It is important to remember that people and businesses are at the centre of the workings of the so-called national income multiplier. Take, for example, London's bid for the 2012 Olympic Games, which is predicted to give a huge boost to London and surrounding areas in terms of extra income (and jobs) well beyond the initial £2.4 billion of extra government spending promised for the project. The organisers have stated their intentions to stage the most compact games in the history of the Olympics, with 17 of the 28 sports to be held in venues within a 15 mile radius of the Olympic Village to be constructed in Stratford, East London. Some 70,000 extra people will be hired to work in and around London before and during the games to provide support services at the various venues, all receiving an income and spending part of it on food, drink, leisure activities, accommodation, transport and so on. Those selling these goods and services to those extra workers will in turn expand output, hire new employees and generate still further employment and income.

Of course, many more firms and individuals will benefit. Barbara Cassani, the first Chairman of the London bid, had said, '2012 will be a powerful catalyst for regeneration. It will lead to massive development with new sports facilities, new jobs and new housing. There will be massive benefits for the construction industry.'

One of the biggest beneficiaries of the games will be the east London borough of Newham, one of the most deprived areas in the country, where the main Olympic venues will be built, leading to major regeneration with new parks and community facilities. Once the games are over, the athletes' village will be used for affordable housing for the local community.

Around £17 billion will be spent on improving road, train and underground links now that London has secured the 2012 games; the government has already given guarantees that the work will be carried out.

A new rail link from King's Cross to Stratford will be constructed for the Olympics, with the journey taking six and a half minutes. Major refurbishment work will be carried out on tube lines to Stratford while a £115 million extension will be built to City airport in east London. The government and the Mayor of London have agreed a package that allows for nearly £2.4 billion of public funding. This will comprise £1.5 billion from the National Lottery and up to £625 million from an increase in the London council tax. The London Development Agency has agreed to give £250 million if it is needed.

a) Suggest why incomes are expected to rise by much more than the £2.4 billion to be injected by the government into the games.

b) Will all the benefits of this multiplier effect occur in London?

c) What might help the final multiplier effect from the proposed £2.4 billion of government expenditure to be larger or smaller?

 ## Essay questions

Answers to asterisked questions can be found on the students' side of the Companion Website. All other answers can be found at the back of the book (page 515).

1* Explain how GDP at factor cost can be found using the *expenditure* method.

2 Why are national income measures inadequate when comparing the standard of living between developed and developing countries?

3* Using any model you wish, explain what might be the consequences for the circular flow of income of:

a) an increase in government spending

b) an increase in tax revenue.

4* What is the 'national income multiplier'? How useful is it for policy purposes?

Public expenditure, taxation and fiscal policy

Learning objectives

By the end of this chapter you should be able to:

- Outline the case for public sector involvement in an economy.

- Discuss the size and nature of public expenditure in the UK economy and the reasons for its growth.

- Review the different types of tax, their relative importance in the UK and their impacts on the economy.

- Understand the role of fiscal policy in managing the economy.

- Assess the contribution of both built-in stabilisers and discretionary fiscal policies.

1   INTRODUCTION

The next three chapters examine various government policies which might influence the equilibrium level of national income in the economy. We saw in Chapter 11 that any changes in consumption or injection expenditure will influence aggregate expenditure (E = C + I + G + X) in the 45° diagram and therefore equilibrium national income. Similarly, any changes in withdrawals (S + T + M) or injections (I + G + X) in the W/J diagram will influence equilibrium national income. Government fiscal policy (expenditure/taxation), monetary policy (money supply/interest rates) and exchange rate policy will affect many of these variables.

In this chapter we first review the case for public sector involvement in the economy before considering the size and nature of public expenditure in the UK and the difficulties surrounding its control. Major increases in public expenditure over the period 2003–06 were announced in the Comprehensive Spending Review of November 2002, raising the projected ratio of public expenditure to GDP to around 42% by 2006. We then turn our attention to the existing pattern of taxation and the implications of such taxes for incentives to work, save and take risks. The chapter concludes by bringing public expenditure and taxation together in the context of government fiscal policy.

2 RATIONALE FOR A PUBLIC SECTOR

It is possible to identify a number of reasons for the involvement of the public sector in the economy.

(a) *Provision of goods and services.* There are certain goods and services which would be under-provided if left to the market mechanism. Examples include *public goods* such as defence, law and order and flood control schemes, and *merit goods* such as education and health.

Public goods have two main characteristics:

(*i*) If they are provided to one individual then they are provided to all, which means there is *non-excludability* (it would be difficult, if not impossible, to restrict the benefits of a defence force to specific sections of the population). If individuals cannot be excluded from consuming a product, whether they pay for that product or not, then clearly private markets will not exist, since revenue cannot be collected.

(*ii*) Consumption by one individual does not impede its consumption by others, which means there is *non-rivalry*. (The fact the I benefit from the UK police force does not restrict your ability to benefit from the same police force.)

Public goods are consumed *collectively* rather than on an individually charged basis and so it is difficult to finance their supply through the market. Thus there is the need for them to be provided by the state, financed by general tax revenue out of the public purse.

Merit goods such as education and health are viewed as being desirable by the government so that their consumption should be encouraged. Since it is possible to exclude non-payers from consuming merit goods, these can be provided through the market mechanism, but they are unlikely to be provided in the quantity deemed necessary by the government. As a result the government will often intervene in the marketplace to provide these merit goods itself or to heavily subsidise their supply. When the social benefits of providing goods or services exceed the private benefits of those supplying them, as in the case of merit goods, we speak of *positive externalities* (*see* Chapter 1, page 11).

(b) *The control of negative externalities.* In producing goods and services the private sector tends to take account only of their private costs, i.e. the costs of raw materials, labour and energy. They often fail to take account of the costs incurred on *society*, such as pollution, noise and congestion. These costs are called 'negative externalities' (*see* Chapter 10, page 207). State involvement can make sure that the private sector accounts for these negative externalities, either through the imposition of taxes or by the use of legislation to impose minimum standards.

(c) *The redistribution of income and wealth.* The aim of the public sector may be to obtain a more equitable distribution of income and wealth. This can be achieved through a progressive tax structure (*see* page 278) and the use of transfer payments, such as the retirement pension, sickness benefit, child benefit and unemployment benefit. Transfer payments (*see* Chapter 11, page 236) are an important part of public expenditure as indicated by the amount devoted to social security in Table 12.2 below.

(d) *To encourage competition.* The allocation of resources through the market mechanism requires competition both in the factor and product markets. Over time, an unrestrained free market could lead to the creation of monopolies which operate against the public interest. There is a need, therefore, for public sector involvement in the economy in order to ensure competition, using regulatory bodies such as the *Competition Commission*, which investigates mergers and acquisitions which might produce monopolies. A company can be referred to the *Competition Commission* if it supplies 25% or more of the market, and the investigation examines whether or not such market power is acting 'contrary to the public interest'. We considered government intervention to help prevent a range of 'market failures' in Chapter 9.

It could, however, be argued that throughout the twentieth century the state has restricted competition via a policy of nationalisation. In response to this the 1980s and 1990s have seen large-scale privatisations.

(e) *To regulate the level of economic activity.* Later in the chapter we outline how the public sector can influence the level of economic activity through changes in government expenditure and taxation. Such *fiscal policy* has been used extensively to achieve the objective of full employment, price stability, economic growth and a balance-of-payments equilibrium.

Mini Case Study 12.1

Preventing unfair competition

The Office of Fair Trading (OFT) is a government body regulating competition (*see* Chapter 9, page 194) and it uncovered the following data in its investigation of allegedly 'unfair' ticket pricing for major events.

Table 12.1 What you pay: total price of tickets purchased on the Internet and delivered by post (evening show, 3 July 2004, West End, London, reserved seating)

	Face value	Total booking fee	Total price of ticket	Fee as a % of face value
Chicago				
Abbey Box Office	£42.50	£11.00	£53.50	26%
Keith Prowse	£42.50	£7.90	£50.40	19%
See Tickets	£42.50	£5.70	£48.20	13%
Ticketmaster	£42.50	£2.75	£45.25	6%
Hamlet				
Abbey Box Office	£37.50	£9.70	£47.20	26%
Keith Prowse	£37.50	£6.90	£44.40	18%
See Tickets	£37.50	£5.25	£42.75	14%
Ticketmaster	£37.50	£2.25	£39.75	6%

Source: Adapted from Office of Fair Trading, 'Random purchasing exercise'

Question

Use the data to explain why the OFT intervened in the market to order all ticket prices from May 2005 to be displayed on posters and adverts for concerts, musicals, plays or sports events, with details of commission fees to be published.

Answer to question can be found on the students' side of the Companion Website.

3   GOVERNMENT EXPENDITURE

3.1 What is government expenditure?

Table 12.2 gives a broad breakdown of the share of various departments and programmes in UK total government spending in 2004/05.

Clearly social security, health and education are the key spending areas, taking around 56% of all government expenditure. The impact on business of extra government spending will depend on the sectors in which the money is spent. Obviously, defence contractors will benefit directly from extra spending on the armed services. However, as we noted in Chapter 11 the 'multiplier effect' from the extra government spending will increase output, employment, income and spending indirectly in many sectors of economic activity.

Table 12.2 Components of total UK government spending, 2004/5

Department/Programme	%
Social security	28
Health	17
Education	11
Debt interest	7
Defence	6
Law and order	6
Industry and employment	4
Housing/environment	3
Transport	2
Contributions to EU	1
Overseas aid	0.5
Other	5

Source: Adapted from *Pre-Budget Report*, ONS

3.2 Growth of public expenditure

Attempts to control public expenditure are nothing new; they began long before Gladstone. Although the last Conservative government was pledged to cut back public expenditure, the evidence suggest that it failed with real public spending between 1979 and 1997, showing an average growth rate of 1.4% per annum. Nevertheless, public expenditure did fall *as a proportion of GDP* from around 48% in 1980 to as low as 38% in 2000. However, major increases in public expenditure over the period 2003–06 were announced by the Comprehensive Spending Review of November 2002, raising the projected ratio of public expenditure to GDP to around 42% by 2005/06.

Public sector net cash requirement (PSNCR)
Previously called the 'public sector borrowing requirement' (PSBR).

Although 'general government expenditure (GGE)' has been a widely used measure of public spending, as we note below *total managed expenditure* (TME) has now been widely adopted. Similarly, any excess of public expenditure over revenue is no longer to be called the public sector borrowing requirement (PSBR) but rather the *public sector net cash requirement* (PSNCR).

Pause for thought 1

Using the 45° diagram or W/J diagram of Chapter 11, show how an increase in government expenditure will affect equilibrium national income.

3.3 Total managed expenditure (TME)

The *Economic and Fiscal Strategy Report* in June 1998 reformed the planning of the control regime for public spending.

- Overall plans were to use a new distinction between current and capital spending
- Three-year plans for each spending department (*Departmental Expenditure Limit*, DEL) were to provide certainty and flexibility for long-term planning and management.
- Spending outside DELs, which could not reasonably be subjected to three-year spending commitments, was to be reviewed annually as part of the budget process. This *annual managed expenditure* (AME) is also subject to constraints.
- *Total managed expenditure* (TME) was defined as consisting of DEL plus AME and was to be widely used as the overall measure of government expenditure (replacing general government expenditure (GGE)).

3.4 Fiscal 'rules'

In 1998 the Labour government committed itself to the following two important 'fiscal rules'.

Golden rule
Over the economic cycle the government will only borrow to invest and not to fund current expenditure.

(a) *The 'golden rule'*: over the economic cycle the government will only borrow to invest and will not borrow to fund current expenditure. In effect the 'golden rule' implies that current expenditure will be covered by current revenue over the economic cycle. Put another way, any PSBR (now public sector net cash requirement) must be used only for investment purposes, with 'investment' defined as in the national accounts.

(b) *The 'public debt rule'*: the ratio of public debt to national income will be held over the economic cycle at a 'stable and prudent' level. The 'public debt rule' is rather less clear in that the phrase 'stable and prudent' is somewhat ambiguous. However, taken together with the 'golden rule' it essentially means that, as an average over the economic cycle, the ratio of PSBR (PSNCR) to national income cannot exceed the ratio of investment to national income. Given that, historically, government investment has been no more than 2–3% of national income, then clearly the PSBR (PSNCR) as a percentage of national income must be kept within similar strict limits.

The need to abide by these 'rules' inevitably brings into focus the procedures for the planning, monitoring and control of public expenditure.

3.5 Explanations of the growth in public expenditure

Microeconomic analysis

Explanations based on microeconomic analysis suggest that additional public spending can be seen as the result of governments continually intervening to correct market failure. This would include the provision of 'public goods' such as collective defence and the police. An extra unit of the public good can be enjoyed by one person, without anyone else's enjoyment being affected. In other words, the marginal cost of one more person using the good is zero, and it is often argued in welfare economics that the 'efficiency' price should, therefore, be zero. Private markets are unable to cope with providing goods at zero price, so that public provision is the only alternative should this welfare argument be accepted. Microeconomic analysis would also cover extra public spending due to a change in the composition of the 'market', such as demographic change raising the number of pensioners in the next few decades. It has been estimated that the UK 'dependency ratio' – the non-working population divided by the working population – will have risen from the current 0.52 to 0.62 by 2030. By 2030, therefore, each worker will be required to contribute almost 20% more real income to sustain the current level of welfare provision. It is scenarios such as this which have led to renewed scrutiny of the practicability of a welfare state along present lines.

Example Ageing population

It is expected that somewhere around the year 2014 the number of people over 65 years in the UK will actually exceed the number of children under 16. The situation is similar for the EU as a whole, where the percentage of over 65s has increased by almost 50% since 1970.

Indeed, ageing populations are occurring in countries across the world. For example, between 1950 and 2003 the median age (at which 50% of the population is below and 50% above) of the world's population rose by only 3 years, from 23.6 years in 1950 to 26.4 years in 2003. However, over the next 50 years or so the UN projects that the median age will rise dramatically to 37 years by 2050, with 17 advanced industrialised economies having a median age of 50 years or above. This has major implications for international business in terms of productive location (e.g. adequate supply of labour of working age) as well as the range of products likely to be in global demand.

Pause for thought 2

Why is an ageing population of concern to governments?

Macroeconomic analysis

There are also explanations of the growth of public spending based on long-run macro-economic theories and models. The starting point in this field is the work of Wagner, who used empirical evidence to support his argument that government expenditure would inevitably increase at a rate faster than the rise in national production (*see* Bird, R., 1971). Wagner suggested that 'the pressures of social progress' would create tensions which could only be resolved by increased state activity in law and order, economic and social services, and participation in material production. Using the economists' terms, Wagner was in effect suggesting that public sector services and products are 'normal', with high income elasticities of demand. Early studies in the UK by Williamson during the 1960s tended to support Wagner, indicating overall income elasticities for public sector services of 1.7, and for public sector goods of 1.3, with similar results in other advanced industrialised countries.

Further evidence in favour of Wagner's ideas came during the 1980s when studies by the OECD concluded that the proportion of GNP absorbed by public expenditure between 1954 and the early 1980s on 'merit goods' (education, health and housing) and 'income maintenance' (pensions, sickness, family and unemployment benefits) had doubled from 14% to 28%, as an average across all the advanced industrialised countries, with high income elasticities playing a major part in this observed growth.

Peacock and Wiseman's 'displacement theory', covering the period 1890–1953, suggested that public spending was not rising with the smooth, small changes predicted by Wagner, but that it was displaced (permanently) upwards by social upheavals associated, for instance, with depression or wars leading to demands for new social expenditure. Displacement theory has, however, been criticised for giving insufficient weight to political influences on the level of public expenditure.

The conclusion that must be drawn from reviewing such work is that there is no definite micro- or macro- explanation of the growth path for public expenditure. It then follows that there is no inevitable 'law' ensuring that public expenditure becomes a progressively rising proportion of national income. However, in a recessionary period such as that of the early 1990s, increased spending on unemployment and social services may indeed cause a sharp increase in the share of public expenditure in national income. The same result can be expected from explicit attempts by the UK government to raise the quality of public services and spending per head on those services to levels already reached within the EU economies. The continued growth of public expenditure as a proportion of national income is also supported by 'behavioural theories' which point out that the growth in public expenditure creates special interest and pressure groups (e.g. public sector unions and employer associations) which will benefit from yet more growth.

4 PLANNING, MONITORING AND CONTROL

Governments must seek to plan levels of public expenditure several years into the future, especially since any rise in public expenditure must be financed either by additional taxation or by increased borrowing. Governments must also develop and apply procedures to monitor and control public expenditure. All three elements are involved to some extent in the Public Expenditure Survey 'rounds', to which all the spending departments must submit on a regular and ongoing basis.

4.1 Public Expenditure Survey (PES)

Planning public expenditure for the next three years begins with the Public Expenditure Survey (PES). As part of this process the spending departments discuss their spending proposals with the Public Expenditure Division of the Treasury, with all proposals expressed in cash terms. This PES 'round' usually takes place between April and September of each year, with the results of the PES announced at the end of November when the Chancellor presents his budget statement to Parliament. To avoid any planning 'surprises' the major spending departments, such as the Department of Social Security, actually undergo two PES rounds each year, the second lasting from October to April.

4.2 Control total (CT)

We have already noted the importance attached to the 'golden rule', which has resulted in the government paying less attention to monitoring and controlling cyclical components of expenditure such as unemployment benefit and various types of income support. This has led to the government establishing a new *control total* (CT) for public expenditure which covers around 85% of the value of spending.

Of course, the more effective control of the growth of public expenditure is not without its 'costs'.

Example | **Impacts of public expenditure control**

In the 2004/05 spending review, Gordon Brown announced that he was planning to cut projected annual government spending by £21.5 billion by 2008. He intends to do this by cutting 70,000 public sector jobs following a government review of the civil service by Sir Peter Gershon. A further 15,000 civil servants will be switched from 'back office' jobs to frontline services in benefit offices and elsewhere, and around 20,000 civil servant jobs will be relocated out of London and the South East to the Midlands and northern regions.

 Pause for thought 3

Consider some of the likely impacts of these changes in the civil service on the UK economy, using your analysis of national income (e.g. 45° and W/J diagrams) in Chapter 11.

---

5 | REASONS FOR THE CONTROL OF PUBLIC EXPENDITURE

A main aim of government has been to reduce public expenditure, taxation and government borrowing. Both taxation and government borrowing will be discussed later in this chapter but, in terms of public expenditure, a number of possible reasons can be outlined as to why the control of public expenditure is seen as so important.

5.1 More freedom and choice

The suggestion here is that excessive government expenditure will result in the following:

- First, it is feared that it spoonfeeds individuals, taking away the incentive for personal provision, as with private insurance for sickness or old age.
- Secondly, that by impeding the market mechanism it may restrict consumer choice. For instance, the state may provide goods and services that are in little demand, whilst discouraging others (via taxation) that might otherwise have been bought.
- Thirdly, it has been suggested that government provision may encourage an unhelpful separation between payment and cost in the minds of consumers. With government provision, the good or service may be free or subsidised, so that the amount paid by

the consumer will understate the true cost (higher taxes, etc.) of providing him or her with that good or service, thereby encouraging excessive consumption of that item.

5.2 To control the money supply

Growth in public expenditure and a resulting increase in the public sector net cash requirement (PSNCR), formerly known as the public sector borrowing requirement (PSBR), can, depending on how it is funded, lead to an increase in the money supply and hence inflation. For example, we note in Chapter 13 that government attempts to fund the extra spending by issuing Treasury Bills and Bonds might result in an increase in the money supply (Chapter 13, page 315). This has led many to believe that it is necessary to restrict public expenditure in order to control the growth in the money supply and, therefore, inflation.

5.3 Crowding out

It is possible that an excessive growth in public expenditure can lead to what has become known as the *crowding out effect* on the private sector. The growth in public expenditure might result in an increase in the PSNCR which is then financed through the sale of government securities (e.g. bills and bonds). An increase in the number and value of government securities on the market requires the interest rate to rise in order to encourage individuals, companies and governments to acquire them. Higher interest rates increase the cost of private sector investment, thereby reducing (crowding out) private sector investment. In other words, the increase in public expenditure is seen here as absorbing productive resources which could have been more effectively used in the private sector. If the notion of 'crowding out' is accepted, then the control of public expenditure will allow the private sector greater access to scarce resources (such as investment funds), which many believe they would then use in a more efficient way than the public sector.

5.4 Incentives to work, save and take risks

The control of public expenditure should make it possible for there to be a reduction in taxation, in particular in income tax, which could act as an incentive to work, since more *net* income is available from work, and also to save, since less of the return on savings will then be subject to tax. If there is a reduction in tax on businesses (e.g. corporation tax), then there may also be greater incentives to invest (take risks), since profits on the returns from such investments will then pay less tax. The evidence as to the effects of reductions in taxes on these incentives to work, save and take risks is, however, inconclusive.

Mini Case Study 12.2

International comparisons of public expenditure

Clearly public expenditure has grown over time in the UK, but how do we compare with other countries? Conclusions based on OECD surveys indicate that UK public expenditure patterns are similar to those in most other advanced industrialised countries, although inferences drawn from international surveys must be treated with caution. The OECD definitions are frequently different from national ones, public sector boundaries vary between countries, and fluctuating exchange rates compromise any attempt at a standard unit of value.

Look carefully at the data in the following table.

Table 12.3 Public spending as % of GDP, rankings and growth rates

Tax as a % of GNP	1981		2001		GDP growth (yearly average) 1981–2001	
	Percentage	Rank	Percentage	Rank		
Australia	33.5	14	31.5	15	3.4	3
Austria	49.6	4	45.7	3	2.4	=9
Belgium	49.6	4	45.3	5	2.0	=11
Canada	40.0	12	35.2	=13	2.8	=5
Denmark	55.6	3	49.0	2	2.1	10
Finland	39.6	13	45.4	4	2.7	6
France	47.6	7	36.4	=12	2.0	=11
Germany	42.3	9	36.4	=12	2.0	=11
Greece	31.6	16	40.8	9	1.9	=12
Ireland	41.6	10	29.2	17	5.5	1
Italy	33.4	15	41.8	8	1.9	=12
Japan	28.3	19	27.1	18	2.6	7
Luxembourg	40.0	11	42.4	7	5.2	2
Netherlands	49.4	6	39.9	10	2.4	=9
Norway	48.7	2	44.9	6	2.8	=5
Spain	27.2	20	35.2	=13	2.8	=5
Sweden	56.9	1	53.2	1	1.9	=12
Switzerland	30.8	18	34.5	14	1.4	13
United Kingdom	42.4	8	37.4	11	2.5	8
United States	31.3	17	29.6	16	3.1	4

Source: Adapted from Revenue Statistics, OECD (2002); Economic Outlook, No. 71, June, OECD (2002)

Questions

1 What do you notice from this data?

2 How might this data influence government policy?

Answers to questions can be found at the back of the book (page 516).

6 TAXATION

As long ago as the eighteenth century, Adam Smith laid down the rules for a 'good tax' in his so-called 'canons of taxation'. A tax should be:

1 *equitable* (fair): those who can afford to pay more should do so;
2 *economic*: more should be collected in tax than is needed to cover the costs of administration;
3 *transparent*: individuals should know how much tax they are paying;
4 *convenient*: the taxpayer should not find it difficult to pay the tax.

6.1 Direct and indirect taxes

Taxes are often grouped under these headings depending on the administrative arrangements for their collection, as can be seen in Figure 12.1.

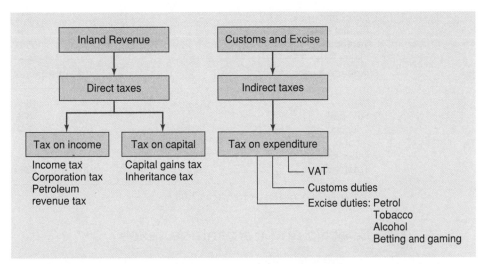

Figure 12.1 Illustrates the direct and indirect taxes levied by central government. Direct taxes are paid directly out of income to the Inland Revenue (now part of 'Customs and Excise'). Indirect taxes are paid indirectly to central government out of expenditure.

(a) *Direct taxes* These taxes are paid directly to the Exchequer by the taxpayer, whether by individuals (e.g. income tax, employees' national insurance, capital gains tax) or by companies (e.g. corporation tax, employers' national insurance). Most of the revenue from direct taxes comes from taxing the *income* of the individuals and companies. Table 12.4 shows that *direct taxes* contribute some 55% of total tax revenue, when we include employers' and employees' national insurance contributions, corporation taxes on company profits and capital gains and inheritance taxes.

(b) *Indirect taxes* These taxes are paid indirectly to the Exchequer by the taxpayer, e.g. via retailers. Other indirect taxes include a range of excise duties (on oil, tobacco and cars) and import duties. Most of the revenue from indirect taxes comes from taxing the *expenditure* of individuals and companies. Table 12.4 shows that *indirect taxes* contribute some 28% of total tax revenues, and with VAT the most important. Other taxes (e.g. council tax, business rates, etc.) make up the other 17%.

Later we look in more detail at the advantages and disadvantages of both direct and indirect taxation.

 Pause for thought 4

Using the 45° diagram or W/J diagram of Chapter 11, show how an increase in total taxation (direct + indirect) will affect equilibrium national income.

Table 12.4 Types of tax: % of tax revenue in 2004

Direct taxes	% of total tax revenue
Income tax	29%
National insurance (Employees + Employers)	16%
Corporation tax	7%
Capital gains, Inheritance	3%
Total direct	**55%**

Indirect taxes	% of total tax revenue
VAT	16%
Fuel duties	6%
Tobacco	2%
Alcohol	2%
Other indirect	2%
Total indirect	**28%**

Source: Adapted from *Pre-Budget Report*, ONS

6.2 Specific and percentage taxes

(a) *Specific tax*: this is expressed as an absolute sum of money per unit of the product. Excise duties are often of this kind, being so many pence per packet of cigarettes or per proof of spirit or per litre of petrol.

(b) *Percentage tax*: this is levied not on volume but on value, e.g. in the UK in 2004/05 VAT was 17.5% of sales price, and corporation tax was 30% of assessable profits for larger companies and 19% of assessable profits for smaller companies. These percentage taxes are sometimes called *ad valorem* (to vary) since the absolute sum of money paid per unit of the product varies with the price.

6.3 Progressive and regressive taxes

Progressive taxes
Where the proportion of total income paid in tax rises as income rises.

(a) *Progressive taxes*: these occur when, as incomes rise, *the proportion of total income paid in tax rises*. Income tax is progressive, partly because of allowances for low paid workers before any tax is paid, and partly because tax rates rise for higher income groups.

Regressive taxes
Where the proportion of total income paid in tax falls as income rises.

(b) *Regressive taxes*: these occur when, as incomes rise, *the proportion of total income paid in tax falls*. VAT is regressive since the spending on products subject to VAT does not rise proportionately with income, which means that for those on higher incomes a lower proportion of such higher incomes is paid in VAT and most other indirect taxes. Those who suggest that more tax revenue should come from indirect taxes on expenditure are, according to this analysis, supporting a more regressive tax regime.

Proportional taxes
Where the proportion of total income paid in tax is unchanged as income rises.

(c) *Proportional taxes*: these occur when, as incomes rise, *the proportion of total income paid in tax remains unchanged*.

It is important to remember when differentiating between the three types of taxation that it is not sufficient to discuss them in terms of the *amount* of tax paid, for in all three examples in Table 12.5 the amount paid actually increases as income increases. It is the *percentage* of income paid in tax which is the distinguishing feature.

Table 12.5 Progressive, regressive and proportional taxes

Income £	Progressive tax		Regressive tax		Proportional tax	
	Income tax (£)	% of income paid in tax	Income tax (£)	% of income paid in tax	Income tax (£)	% of income paid in tax
100	10	10	10	10	10	10
1,000	200	20	80	8	100	10
10,000	3,000	30	600	6	1,000	10
100,000	40,000	40	4,000	4	10,000	10

7   INDIVIDUAL TAXES

Here we consider some of the different taxes in a little more detail.

7.1 Income tax in the UK

Not all income is taxed; everyone is allowed to earn a certain amount before paying tax, which is shown in the tax code. For example, in 2004/05 each single person in the UK under 65 years had an allowance of £4,615 before tax.

Most workers have their tax paid for them by their employer using PAYE (Pay As You Earn). This conforms to the third and fourth 'canons of taxation', namely that taxes should be *transparent* and *convenient*. Employers have to give the worker a salary advice form showing the amount of tax deducted for the current time period (a week or a month) and the amount of accumulated tax deducted in the current tax year.

Table 12.6 shows how UK income tax rates have been simplified and lowered in the 17 years from 1987/8 to 2004/05.

Table 12.6 UK income tax schedules 1987/8 and 2004/05

Rate of tax (%)	1987/8 taxable income (£)	Rate of tax	2004/05 taxable income (£)
	–	10	0–1,920
	–	22	1,921–29,900
27	0–17,900		
40	17,901–20,400	40	over 29,900
45	20,401–25,400		–
50	25,401–33,300		–
55	33,301–41,200		–
60	over 41,200		–

Source: Adapted from *Pre-Budget Report*, ONS

7.2 Other direct taxes in the UK

- *National insurance* A tax on employment, paid by both employees and employers.
- *Capital gains tax* A tax on the increased value of an asset when it is sold.
- *Inheritance tax* A tax on inheritance or gifts.
- *Corporation tax* A tax on company profits.

Mini Case Study 12.3

Corporation tax

Gordon Brown's pre-budget report in January 2005 gave the predictions shown in Table 12.7 for the total amount of revenue to be raised by various taxes in 2004/05.

Table 12.7 Predicted tax receipts in 2004/05

Type of tax	Receipts
1. Income tax	£128bn
2. National insurance	£78bn
3. VAT	£73bn
4. Corporation tax	£35bn
5. Fuel	£24bn
6. Council and business tax	£39bn
7. Stamp duty	£9bn
8. Tobacco	£8bn
9. Alcohol	£8bn

Source: Adapted from *Pre-Budget Report*, ONS

In 2004/05 corporation tax is expected to yield £35 billion of tax revenue. The Treasury is forecasting that this will rise to as much as £54 billion in 2009. The Institute of Fiscal Studies and others have criticised the Treasury as being much too optimistic in its forecasts for future corporation tax. It noted that Treasury forecasts of corporation tax receipts have been 1% higher than the actual out-turn when looking one year ahead and 13% too high when looking two years ahead.

Questions

1 *Why might the Treasury forecasts for corporation tax receipts be too high?*

2 *Does the Treasury being too optimistic matter?*

Answers to questions can be found on the students' side of the Companion Website.

7.3 Indirect taxes in the UK

- *Value added tax* (VAT) A tax on expenditure on most goods and services (currently 17.5% in the UK). Some items (e.g. children's clothes) are VAT exempt. VAT is a tax on expenditure levied by all EU countries, though at different rates.
- *Excise duties* A specific tax of an absolute amount levied on goods such as tobacco, petrol, alcohol.

Example	VAT, Blackpool Pleasure Beach and United Biscuits

VAT was invented in 1965 by Maurice Laure, a French civil servant, for use in the then European Common Market. The UK adopted the system in 1973. Because VAT is not supposed to be levied on 'essential' products but only on 'luxuries', various businesses have sought to be VAT exempt, sometimes with controversial results (e.g. cakes are VAT exempt, biscuits are not).

In 1974 Blackpool Pleasure Beach brought one of the first claims against Britain's new tax. They said their Big Dipper rollercoaster was a form of transport (VAT exempt) and argued that passengers should therefore be exempt from VAT. Custom and Excise did not agree. United Biscuits got into a wrangle with the authorities when it claimed its Jaffa Cakes snacks were cakes and not biscuits, thereby making them exempt from VAT. After taking the case to a tribunal the company won.

Total revenues since the introduction of VAT in 1973 add up to £826 billion. The annual revenue for this tax in 2004 was around £645 billion, up from £2.5 billion in 1973. At 25% Denmark and Sweden have the highest VAT rates in Europe.

7.4 Other taxes in the UK

Some UK taxes are difficult to define or put into neat categories, such as the BBC licence, road fund licence, council tax, stamp duty, airport tax, fees paid by local residents to the council for parking and prescription charges.

8   TAXES AND ECONOMIC INCENTIVES

There is an ongoing debate as to whether or not taxes are 'excessive' in the UK and whether current tax rates act as a disincentive to UK households and businesses.

8.1 Taxes and incentives to work

Many empirical studies have been conducted on tax rates and incentives, with no clear results. However, one widely accepted approach does warn governments against imposing too higher an *overall tax rate*.

Laffer curve
A curve relating tax revenue to tax rate.

Laffer curve

Professor Art Laffer derived a relationship between tax revenue and tax rates of the form shown in Figure 12.2. The curve was the result of econometric techniques, through which a 'least squares line' was fitted to past US observations of tax revenue and tax rate. The dotted line indicates the extension of the fitted relationship (continuous) line, as there will tend to be zero tax revenue at both 0% and 100% tax rates. Tax revenue = tax rate × output (income), so that a 0% tax rate yields zero tax revenue, whatever the level of output. A 100% tax rate is assumed to discourage all output, except that for subsistence, again yielding zero tax revenue. Tax revenue must reach a maximum at some intermediate tax rate between these extremes.

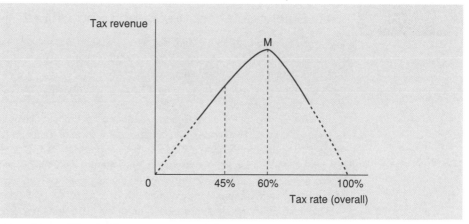

Figure 12.2 The Laffer curve suggests that if the composite rate of tax rises above 60% then there is a net disincentive effect which will reduce the value of tax revenue.

The London Business School has estimated a Laffer curve for the UK using past data. Tax revenue was found to reach a peak at around a 60% 'composite tax rate', i.e. one which includes both direct and indirect taxes, as well as various social security payments, all expressed as a percentage of GDP. If the composite tax rate rises above 60% then the disincentive effect on output is so strong (i.e. output falls so much) that tax revenue (tax rate × output) actually falls, despite the higher tax rate.

The Laffer curve in fact begins to flatten out at around a 45% composite tax rate. In other words, as tax rate rises to about 45%, the disincentive effect on output is strong enough to mean that little extra tax revenue results. Econometric studies of this type have given support to those in favour of limiting overall rates of tax. In fact, the reduction in the top income tax rate to 40% in the UK in 1988/9 was inspired by the Laffer curve.

Mini Case Study 12.4

The flat tax

Flat tax
A system using a single tax rate on all earned income and therefore a much simplified tax structure.

The idea of a single, low income tax rate to be paid by all, i.e. a 'flat tax', has been much discussed in recent times. For example, the Adam Smith Institute (ASI) has proposed a 'flat tax rate' of 22% with a personal allowance of £15,000 (three times higher than the current allowance). The cost of setting such a high level of personal allowances – to lift the poorest out of tax – would be £63 billion, but the ASI believed this could be recouped in three years as lower taxes create incentives for us all to work harder and to stop avoiding tax. The suggestions of supporters of the flat tax is that the British tax system has become so complex that few can understand it, unintended disincentives to work frequently occur and failure to follow simpler, lower tax regimes present in the rest of the world is undermining UK international competitiveness.

However, critics of the 'flat tax' approach point out that it is a myth that the poor will benefit from lower tax rates. For example, Brian Reading, of Lombard Street Research, noted in 2005 that 50% of the total income tax revenue is actually paid by the top 10%

of income earners, so this 10% (3 million people) would gain the most and the other 90% (27 million people) would lose the most from a move to a 'flat tax' regime which collected the same amount of income tax revenue as is currently collected and kept the same personal allowances. This would require a flat tax rate of 23% and would potentially result in 24 million losers 'net'.

Table 12.8 provides some useful data in this respect. The average tax rate is currently 18%, but the flat tax rate would have to be set higher than this because of personal allowances which remove taxes from initial slices of income.

Table 12.8 Impacts of various 'flat tax' options

Average tax rate on taxpayers' total income	Flat tax rate on taxed income	Allowances and deductions	Losers – millions (net number)	Tax revenue lost
18	23	Unchanged	27	nil
15	20	Personal allowances raised by £2,500	8	£10bn
13	18	Unchanged	zero	£20bn

Source: Adapted from *Lombard Street Research*, B. Reading (2005)

Questions

1 *How do the ideas behind the 'Laffer curve' relate to the 'flat tax' debate?*

2 *What arguments might the government use in responding to an opposition party which proposes a 'flat tax' regime at the next general election?*

Answers to questions can be found at the back of the book (page 516).

8.2 Comparative tax rates

Table 12.9 provides some useful data on comparative tax rates between the UK and some other advanced industrialised economies.

Despite the rise in UK tax burden over the last few years, and contrary to popular public opinion, the UK is only a middle-ranked country in terms of tax burden. From Table 12.9 we see that in 1981 the UK was the eighth ranked country out of 20 in terms of tax burden, below the Scandinavian countries and close to France. OECD data in 2001 gave the UK a lower ranking of eleventh. Despite the high level of tax revenue as a proportion of GDP over this 20-year period, the UK tax burden in 2001 continued to lie well below that in the Scandinavian countries, where between 45% and 53% of GDP was taken in tax and social security contributions in that year, and was very similar to other major competitors such as France and Germany.

 ## Pause for thought 5

What does Table 12.9 suggest as to the linkage between tax burden and economic growth?

Table 12.9 Comparative tax burdens and economic growth

Tax* as % of GNP	1981		2001		GDP growth (yearly average) 1981–2001	
	%	Rank	%	Rank	Percentage	Rank
Australia	33.5	14	31.5	15	3.4	3
Austria	49.6	4	45.7	3	2.4	−9
Belgium	49.6	4	45.3	5	2.0	−11
Canada	40.0	12	35.2	−13	2.8	−5
Denmark	55.6	3	49.0	2	2.1	10
Finland	39.6	13	45.4	4	2.7	6
France	47.6	7	36.4	−12	2.0	−11
Germany	42.3	9	36.4	−12	2.0	−11
Greece	31.6	16	40.8	9	1.9	−12
Ireland	41.6	10	29.2	17	5.5	1
Italy	33.4	15	41.8	8	1.9	−12
Japan	28.3	19	27.1	18	2.6	7
Luxembourg	40.0	11	42.4	7	5.2	2
Netherlands	49.4	6	39.9	10	2.4	−9
Norway	48.7	2	44.9	6	2.8	−5
Spain	27.2	20	35.2	−13	2.8	−5
Sweden	56.9	1	53.2	1	1.9	−12
Switzerland	30.8	18	34.5	14	1.4	13
United Kingdom	42.4	8	37.4	11	2.5	8
United States	31.1	17	29.6	16	3.1	4

* Including social security contributions.
Source: Revenue Statistics, 1965–2001, OECD (2002); *Economic Outlook,* No. 71, June, OECD (2002)

9 DIRECT VERSUS INDIRECT TAXES

It might be useful to consider in more detail the advantages and disadvantages of direct and indirect systems of taxation. For convenience we shall compare the systems under four main headings, with indirect taxes considered first in each case.

9.1 Macroeconomic management

Indirect taxes can be varied more quickly and easily, taking more immediate effect, than can direct taxes. Since the Finance Act 1961, the Chancellor of the Exchequer has had the power (via 'the regulator') to vary the rates of indirect taxation at any time between budgets. Excise and import duties can be varied by up to 10% and VAT by up to 25% (i.e. between 13.13% and 21.87% for a 17.5% rate of VAT). In contrast, direct taxes can only be changed at budget time. In the case of income tax, any change involves time-consuming revisions to PAYE codings. For these reasons, indirect taxes are usually regarded as a more flexible instrument of macroeconomic policy.

9.2 Economic incentives

We have already seen how, in both theory and practice, direct taxes on income affect incentives to work. We found that neither in theory nor in practice need the net effect be one of disincentive. Nevertheless, it is often argued that if the same sum were derived from indirect taxation then any net disincentive effect that did occur would be that much smaller. In particular, it is often said that indirect taxes are less visible (than direct), being to some extent hidden in the quoted price of the product. However, others suggest that consumers are well aware of the impact of indirect taxes on the price level. Certainly for products with relatively inelastic demands any higher indirect taxes will be passed on to consumers as higher prices and will therefore not be less visible than extra direct taxation.

9.3 Economic welfare

It is sometimes argued that indirect taxes are, in welfare terms, preferable to direct taxes, as they leave the taxpayer free to make a choice. The individual can, for instance, avoid the tax by choosing not to consume the taxed commodity. Although this 'voluntary' aspect of indirect taxes may apply to a particular individual and a particular tax, it cannot apply to all individuals and all taxes. In other words, indirect taxes cannot be 'voluntary' for the community as a whole. If a chancellor is to raise a given sum through a system of indirect taxes, individual choices not to consume taxed items must, if widespread, be countered either by raising rates of tax or by extending the range of goods and services taxed.

Another argument used to support indirect taxes on welfare grounds is that they can be used to correct 'externalities'. Earlier (Chapter 1) we noted that an externality occurs where private and social costs diverge. Where private costs of production are below social costs, an indirect tax could be imposed, or increased, so that price is raised to reflect the true social costs of production. Taxes on alcohol and tobacco could be justified on these grounds. By discriminating between different goods and services, indirect taxes can help reallocate resources in a way that raises economic welfare for society as a whole.

On the other hand, indirect taxes have also been criticised on welfare grounds for being regressive since the element of indirect tax embodied in product prices takes a higher proportion of the income from lower paid groups. Nor is it easy to correct this. It would be impossible administratively to place a higher tax on a given item for those with higher incomes although one could impose indirect taxes mainly on the goods and services consumed by higher-income groups, and perhaps at higher rates.

9.4 Administrative costs

Indirect taxes are often easy and cheap to administer. They are paid by manufacturers and traders, which are obviously fewer in number than the total of individuals paying income tax. This makes indirect taxes, such as excise and import duties, much cheaper to collect than direct taxes, though the difference is less marked for VAT which requires the authorities to deal with a large number of mainly small traders.

Even if indirect taxes do impose smaller administrative costs than direct taxes for a given revenue yield, not too much should be made of this. It is, for instance, always possible to reform the system of PAYE and reduce administrative costs. The Inland Revenue is, in fact, considering a change from PAYE to an American system of income tax, with the obligation on taxpayers themselves to estimate and forward tax, subject to random checks. Also, the computerisation of Inland Revenue operations may, in the long run, significantly reduce the administrative costs associated with the collection of direct taxes.

In summary, there is no clear case for one type of tax system compared to another. The macroeconomic management and administrative cost grounds may appear to favour indirect taxes, though the comparison is only with the current system of direct taxation. That system can, of course, be changed to accommodate criticisms along these lines. On perhaps the more important grounds of economic incentives and economic welfare the case is very mixed, with arguments for and against each type of tax finely balanced. To be more specific we must compare the particular and detailed systems proposed for each type of tax.

Mini Case Study 12.5

Indirect taxes

Look carefully at Table 12.10 which shows the impact of indirect taxes on the various quintile (20%) income groups in the UK.

Table 12.10 Impacts of indirect taxes (2002/03)

Quintile groups of households	Indirect taxes as % of disposable income per household		
	VAT	Other indirect taxes	Total indirect taxes
Bottom fifth	12.9	21.8	34.7
Next fifth	9.0	14.5	23.5
Middle fifth	8.5	12.9	21.4
Next fifth	7.5	10.7	18.2
Top fifth	5.9	7.2	13.1

Source: Adapted from *The Effects of Taxes and Benefits on Household Income 2002/03*, April, ONS (2004)

Question

What conclusions might you draw from the data shown in the table?

Answer to question can be found on the students' side of the Companion Website.

---

10   POVERTY AND UNEMPLOYMENT 'TRAPS'

One area where the facts do strongly suggest that the current level and type of taxation may have eroded incentives, concerns the 'poverty' and 'unemployment' traps. The families in these traps are enmeshed in a web of overlapping tax schedules and benefit thresholds, developed and administered by two separate departments (Department of Social Security and the Treasury) with differing objectives in mind.

Poverty trap
Where a person on low income gains very little, or even loses, from an increase in gross earnings.

10.1 Poverty trap

The 'poverty trap' describes a situation where a person on low income may gain very little, or even lose, from an increase in gross earnings. This is because as gross earnings rise, the amount of benefits paid out decreases while income tax deductions increase. In extreme circumstances, net income may actually fall when a person's gross earnings rise, i.e. an implicit marginal tax rate (or marginal net income deduction rate) of over 100%. After 1988 the government tried to resolve the gross disincentive effects of such high rates of deduction by relating benefits to net income after tax. However, the problems of the poverty trap dilemma still occur (if not to the same extent as before).

Table 12.11 shows the net income situation of a married man with two children in June 2002 when his gross income rises from £125 to £250 per week. We can see that net income rises little over this range. For example, an increase in income from £150 to £200, i.e. £50 per week, gives only an extra £15.81 in income after deductions, i.e. £34.19 is lost. This results in an implicit marginal tax rate (or marginal deduction rate) of about 68% (£34.19/50). In 1992, using a similar family situation and gross income change, the rate was as high as 124%. The improvements in the family credit arrangements since 1992 have eased such extreme situations but the rates are still high and often provide little encouragement for those in the area of the poverty trap to work harder. On a general level, the number of families where the head of the household faced a relatively high implicit marginal tax rate of 70% and over nearly doubled after 1988 to 645,000 by 1999–2000, but has fallen substantially since then. A high implicit tax rate (marginal deduction rate) can therefore act as a major disincentive to low income earners.

Table 12.11 Married couple (one earner working more than 30 hours per week) with two children under 11 (rent £52.27, council tax £16.40 per week)

| | June 2002 | | | |
	(£pw)	(£pw)	(£pw)	(£pw)
Gross earnings*	125.00	150.00	200.00	250.00
Plus child benefit	26.30	26.30	26.30	26.30
Working family tax credit	112.26	99.88	80.56	61.86
Housing benefit	5.53	0.00	0.00	0.00
Council Tax benefit	2.02	0.00	0.00	0.00
Less Income tax	0.00	0.00	9.87	20.87
National insurance	3.60	6.10	11.10	16.10
Net income	267.51	270.08	285.89	301.19

Notes: Calculations are for a married man with two children under 11, Local Authority rent of £52.27 a week and council tax of £16.40 a week.
* 30 hours per week at the minimum wage (June 2002) was £123.00.
Source: Adapted from DSS, Tax/Benefit Model Tables (June 2002)

10.2 Unemployment trap

Unemployment trap
Where employment results in little or no extra income as compared to unemployment.

As we noted, the 'poverty trap' relates to people who are in work but find little incentive to improve their situation by extra work effort. On the other hand, some workers never even enter the labour market because of another problem, often called the '**unemployment trap**'.

The 'unemployment trap' occurs when people find that their income when employed is not better than if they were unemployed. Taking figures for June 2002, Table 12.12 shows that when the gross wage of the married man in our example is £150 per week, the net income after various allowances and deductions is £270.08. If he was unemployed, his net income would be £253.82, i.e. the replacement rate is 94%. The replacement rate measures the proportion of a person's net income that will be 'replaced' by the benefit system if that person loses his or her job. The introduction of family credit in 1988 has helped to decrease the number of people with replacement rates of over 100%. The replacement rate for a person in the same situation as our present example in 1992 was 104%, so things have got marginally better. However, the fact that the income of a person when out of work is still 94% of his income when in work provides little incentive to work. There were still 590,000 people in the UK with replacement rates of 70% and over in 1999/2000, although this number has fallen substantially since then.

From these examples, we can see that both poverty and unemployment traps provide a disincentive to work because people caught in these problematic situations find it difficult, if not impossible, to improve their position through their own efforts.

Replacement rate
The proportion of a person's net income that will be 'replaced' by the benefit system if that person loses his or her job.

Table 12.12 Unemployed married couple (one earner previously working more than 30 hours per week) with two children under 11 (rent £52.27, council tax £16.40 per week), June 2002

In work	£pw	Out of work	£pw
Gross earning	150.00	Jobseeker's allowance	151.75
Child benefit	26.30	Child benefit	26.30
Working family tax credit	99.88	Meals & welfare	7.10
Housing benefit	..00.00	Housing benefit	52.27
Council tax benefit	00.00	Council tax benefit	16.40
Less income tax	0.00		
Less national insurance	6.10		
Net income	270.08	*Net income*	253.82
Replacement ratio	$\frac{253.82}{270.08} = 94\%$		

Notes: Calculations are for a married man with two children under 11, Local Authority rent of £52.27 a week and council tax of £16.40 per week.
Source: Adapted from DSS, Tax/Benefit Model Tables (June 2002)

10.3 The black economy

Tax avoidance is legal; tax evasion is illegal, involving concealment in one form or another, and therefore fraud. The Inland Revenue has estimated that tax evasion was equal to between 6% and 8% of GDP in the UK – often called the 'black economy'. However, other estimates have suggested that the black economy may even be as high as 10–12% of GDP. This would mean that the UK's black economy is the same size as Portugal's entire economy or is as much as the Treasury earns from income tax every year. One way in which the black economy can be estimated is through the difference between national income when measured by the income method and when measured by the expenditure method. Apart form errors and omissions, these are defined in the national accounts in such a way that they come to the same value. If, however, people receive income and do not declare it in tax returns, it will not appear on the income side, though expenditure will increase as the unrecorded income is spent on goods and services. In recent years the 'income' valuation – based on tax returns – has fallen short of the 'expenditure' valuation by progressively larger amounts.

11 FISCAL POLICY

'Fiscal policy' is the name given to government policies which seek to influence government revenue (taxation) and/or government expenditure. We have already seen how changes in either can influence the equilibrium level of national income, with implications for output, employment and inflation.

Major changes in fiscal policy in the UK are normally announced at the time of the budget, which in the UK traditionally takes place just before the end of the tax year on 5 April. Both revenue raising and expenditure plans are presented together at the Budget.

11.1 The Budget

The Budget occurs annually when the Chancellor of the Exchequer makes a financial statement both to Parliament and the nation. In the Budget the Chancellor reviews economic policy and proposes taxation changes for the coming year. This is published in the *Economic and Fiscal Strategy Report and Financial Statement and Budget Report* (known as the Red Book). On certain occasions the government has viewed it necessary to have an extra budget, known as a mini budget.

Changes in government expenditure are also announced by the Chancellor and since November 1993 both the Budget and Chancellor's announcements on expenditure have been held together.

11.2 Budget terminology

A number of terms are often used to describe a budget.

Budget deficit
When tax revenue falls short of public expenditure.

Budget surplus
When tax revenue is greater than public expenditure.

Balanced budget
When tax revenue equals public expenditure.

- *Budget deficit* When tax revenues fall short of public expenditure (T < G).
- *Budget surplus* When tax revenue exceeds public expenditure (T > G).
- *Balanced budget* When tax revenue equals public expenditure (T = G).

Similarly, a number of terms are often used to describe the *consequences* of these budget situations.

(a) *Public sector borrowing requirements (PSBR)* Until recently this term has been widely used to describe the outcome of a budget deficit since the government will have to borrow to cover the excess of government spending over tax revenue (G > T), at least in the short run. This borrowing may involve issuing government bills and bonds to the financial markets.

(b) *Public sector net cash requirement (PSNCR)* In recent years this has been the term more usually used in the UK to refer to situations previously described by the PSBR.

As we noted earlier, the Labour government has committed itself to two key 'fiscal rules' (*see* page 271), namely the 'golden rule' and the 'public debt rule'.

12 FISCAL POLICY AND STABILISATION

Fiscal policy can help to 'stabilise' an economy, avoiding excessive 'boom' or 'bust' scenarios. It can do this by making use of **'built-in' stabilisers** or by using 'discretionary' fiscal policy.

12.1 Business cycle

Built-in stablisers
Result in a
net increase in
withdrawals in
'boom' conditions
and a *net* increase
in injections during
recession.

Business cycle
The tendency for
economies to move
from economic
boom into economic
recession and vice
versa.

The terms **business cycle** or trade cycle are often used to refer to the tendency for economies to move from economic boom into economic recession, or vice versa. Economic historians have claimed to observe a five- to eight-year cycle of economic activity between successive peaks (A,C) or successive troughs (B,D) around a general upward trend (T) of the type shown in Figure 12.3.

From a business perspective it is clearly important to be aware of such a business cycle since investment in extra capacity in boom year A might be problematic if demand had fallen relative to trend by the time the capacity came on stream in the recession year B.

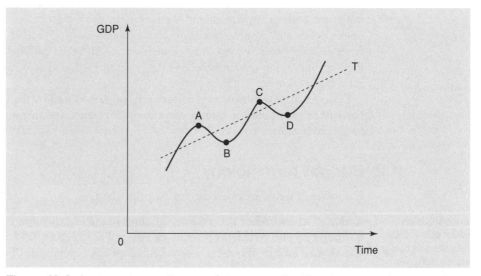

Figure 12.3 A stereotype picture of the so-called business cycle around a trend growth (T) in national income.

Example	Microchip manufacture

In the boom dot.com years of the late 1990s many of the major chip-making firms such as Intel, Samsung, Fujitsu and Siemens invested in extra chip-making plants. Unfortunately, by the time many of these were ready for operation, the dot.com boom had turned to bust and many of these state-of-the-art plants had to be closed when excess chip supply resulted in plunging prices.

From a government perspective, investment might be better timed to take place at or around points B or D in Figure 12.3, depending on the time lags involved. Even better would be a situation in which government fiscal policies had 'smoothed' or stabilised the business cycle around the trend value (T) by making use of 'built-in' stabilisers or by using 'discretionary' fiscal policy. It is to this policy objective that we now turn.

12.2 Built-in stabilisation

Some of the tax and spending programmes we have discussed will act as built-in (or automatic) stabilisers. They do this in at least two ways.

(a) Bringing about an *automatic* rise in withdrawals and/or fall in injections in times of 'boom'. For example, when the economy is growing rapidly, individual incomes, business incomes and spending on goods and services will all be rising in value, thereby increasing the government's revenue from both direct and indirect taxes. At the same time, unemployment is likely to be falling, reducing the government's spending on social security, unemployment and other benefits. This 'automatic' rise in withdrawals and reduction in injections will help to dampen any excessive growth in national income which might otherwise result in rapid inflation and unsustainable 'boom' conditions.

(b) Bringing about an *automatic* fall in withdrawals and/or rise in injections in times of recession. For example, when the economy is contracting, individual incomes, business incomes and spending on goods and services will all be falling in value, thereby reducing the government's tax revenue from both direct and indirect taxes. At the same time, unemployment is likely to be rising, increasing the government's spending on social security, unemployment and other benefits. This 'automatic' fall in withdrawals and rise in injections will help to stimulate the economy and prevent national income from falling as far as it otherwise might have done.

 Pause for thought 6

How can the government use fiscal policy to increase the extent of built-in (automatic) stability in the economy?

12.3 Discretionary fiscal stabilisation

On occasions governments will intervene in the economy for specific purposes, such as reinforcing the built-in stabilisers already described.

- If the economy is tending to expand too rapidly, so that inflationary pressures are building up, then the government may seek to reduce G or raise T.
- If the economy is tending to slow down, so that unemployment is rising and output falling, then the government may seek to raise G or reduce T to stimulate the economy.

These are examples of *discretionary* fiscal policy, where the government makes a conscious decision to change its spending or taxation policy. As compared to built-in stabilisers, discretionary fiscal stabilisation policy faces a number of difficulties involving time lags. At least two time lags can be identified.

1 *Recognition lag* It takes time for the government to collect and analyse data, recognise any problems that may exist, and then decide what government spending and taxation decisions to take.

2 *Execution lag* Having made its fiscal policy decisions it takes time to implement these changes and it also takes time for these changes to have an effect on the economy.

In terms of discretionary fiscal policy these time lags can result in the government *reinforcing* the economic cycle, rather than stabilising it, as indicated in Figure 12.4.

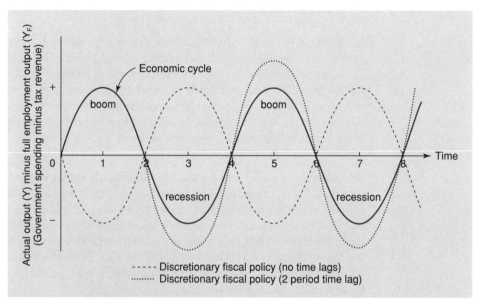

Figure 12.4 The business (economic) cycle and discretionary fiscal policy seeking to stabilise the business cycle. This discretionary fiscal policy is shown with no time lags and with a two period time lag.

The business trade cycle is shown as a continuous line in the diagram, with a complete cycle (peak to peak) lasting four time periods. For the economic cycle the relevant variable on the vertical axis is actual output (Y) minus full employment output (Y_F).

● Where this is *positive*, as in time periods 1 and 2, we have our familiar 'inflationary gap' (since $Y > Y_F$).

● Where this is *negative*, as in time periods 3 and 4, we have our familiar 'deflationary gap' (since $Y < Y_F$).

Discretionary fiscal policy is shown as both a dashed line (no time lag) and a dotted line (two period time lag) in the diagram. For discretionary fiscal policy the relevant variable on the vertical axis is government spending minus tax revenue.

● Where the economic cycle is experiencing an 'inflationary gap' (time periods 1 and 2), the appropriate discretionary fiscal policy is a *budget surplus* (G < T). This is the case with the dashed line.

● Where the economic cycle is experiencing a 'deflationary gap' (time periods 3 and 4), the appropriate discretionary fiscal policy is a *budget deficit* (G > T). This is again the case with the dashed line.

If the timing of the discretionary fiscal policy is correct, as with the dashed line (no time lag), then intervention by the government will help to 'stabilise' the economic cycle, with discretionary fiscal policy resulting in a net withdrawal in times of 'boom' and a net injection at times of recession.

However, when the recognition and execution time lags are present, discretionary fiscal policy can actually turn out to be 'destabilising'. This is the case in Figure 12.3 if these time lags cause a *two time-period-delay* in discretionary fiscal policy to come into effect. The dotted line of Figure 12.4 shows the previous government intervention now resulting in a budget surplus at times of recession (time periods 3 and 4) and a budget deficit at times of boom (time periods 5 and 6). This is exactly the opposite of what is needed for a discretionary fiscal policy to help stabilise the economic cycle.

Pause for thought 7

Why might an inaccurate estimate of the national income multiplier by government also pose a problem for the use of discretionary fiscal policy?

13 FISCAL POLICY AND GLOBALISATION

So far we have assumed that fiscal policy is mainly governed by the needs of the domestic economy being used to stimulate economic activity in periods of recession and to dampen it in periods of boom. However, the suggestion has been made that in an increasingly globalised world (*see* Chapter 16) where international finance and capital is highly geographically mobile, there will be an *external* discipline on a government's ability to run budget deficits. The argument here is that such international capital flows will respond adversely to imprudent macroeconomic policies (Stiglitz, 2000; OECD, 2005). The suggestion that such financial globalisation will act as an external constraint on overexpansive fiscal policy receives some empirical support in that average budget deficits across the developed and developing countries have fallen from an average of some 5% of GDP during the late 1990s to around 2% in 2005. Tytell and Wei (2004) found some evidence that a rise in financial globalisation (measured by the ratio of gross foreign assets and liabilities to GDP) has indeed curbed the frequency and intensity of budget deficits.

Financial globalisation The increased geographical mobility of international financial capital.

KEY POINTS

- Successive government spending reviews since 2000 have resulted in substantial real-term increases in government spending, which is projected to take around 42% of national income by 2005/06.

- Total managed expenditure (TME) has now been widely adopted as a replacement for general government expenditure (GGE).

- International comparisons do not suggest that UK public expenditure is exceptionally high as a percentage of GDP. In 2004 it was only tenth highest out of 14 countries investigated, and some five percentage points below the EU average.

- Many of the reasons put forward for controlling public expenditure involve the desire to cut the PSBR (now the public sector net cash requirement – PSNCR). The government concern is that too high a PSBR (PSNCR) will force higher taxes and interest rates, with adverse effects on incentives and investment in the public sector.

- Taxes on income in the UK account for around 48% of all tax receipts, with taxes on expenditure around 37%.

- UK direct taxes are progressive while indirect taxes are regressive. Overall, the UK has a broadly proportional tax system.

- The UK is a middle-ranked country in terms of tax revenue as a percentage of GDP, i.e. in terms of 'tax burden'. The UK tax burden as a percentage of GDP has averaged over 35% over the past decade.

- The 'Laffer curve' suggests that extremely high tax rates may reduce tax revenue by acting as a disincentive to work and take risks. However, the composite tax rate has to be over 60% for these disincentive effects to occur.

- The 'flat tax' has been proposed as a means of simplifying the tax system and creating greater incentives. There is considerable debate over the number of potential 'winners' and 'losers' from such a system, depending on the particular approach adopted.

- The 'poverty trap' has improved since 1992 with implicit marginal tax rates for some households falling from 124% in 1992 to much lower percentages today. Low hourly wages tend to worsen the poverty trap situation, though the minimum wage may help in this respect.

- The 'unemployment trap' has eased slightly with replacement rates for an unemployed married couple with two children falling from 104% in 1992 to nearer 90% today.

- 'Built-in' stabilisers such as a progressive income tax system and the benefit system can help automatically relieve economic recessions and dampen economic boom without explicit fiscal policy decisions by government.

- Discretionary fiscal policy may still be needed at times to reinforce such built-in stabilisers. Such discretionary fiscal policy may be restrained by the increasing 'financial globalisation' of international capital markets. For example, budget deficits regarded as 'excessive' by the financial markets may lead to a substantial and rapid loss of international financial capital.

Further reading

Griffiths, A. and Wall, S. (2006) *Applied Economics*, 11th edition, FT/Prentice Hall, Chapters 18 and 19.

Griffiths, A. and Wall, S. (2005) *Economics for Business and Management*, FT/Prentice Hall, Chapter 10.

Heather, K. (2004) *Economics Theory in Action*, 4th edition, FT/Prentice Hall, Chapter 16.

Parkin, M., Powell, M. and Matthews, K. (2005) *Economics*, 6th edition, FT/Prentice Hall, Chapters 15 and 24.

Sloman, J. (2006) *Economics*, 6th edition, FT/Prentice Hall, Chapter 20.

Web references

You can find current data and information on many aspects of taxation and public expenditure from the following websites.

National Statistics: **http://www.statistics.gov.uk/** The official UK statistics site.

HM Treasury: **http://www.hm-treasury.gov.uk/** UK macroeconomic data, forecasts and government tax and spending plans.

Eurostat: **http://europa.eu.int/comm/eurostat/** The sources for EU data.

Institute for Fiscal Studies: **http://www.ifs.org.uk** The IFS is a useful source of information on various aspects of taxation and expenditure.

Department of Social Security: **http://www.dss.gov.uk** *The DSS is a useful source on areas of taxation, spending and social security data.*

OECD: **http://www.oecd.org/** This provides statistics and articles on comparative taxation.

Inland revenue: **http://www.inlandrevenue.gov.uk** The main site for statistics and comments on taxation matters.

Webecon: **http://netec.mcc.ac.uk/WebEc/** Web resources and data sets for economics.

Resource centre for access to data on Europe: **http://www-rcade.dur.ac.uk/academic/academic.htm**

World Bank: **http://www.worldbank.org/** World economic data.

IMF: **http://www.imf.org/** Economic and financial data for most countries.

InfoNation: **http://www.un.org/Pubs/CyberSchoolBus/infonation/e_infonation.htm** A United Nations statistical database that enables comparisons to be made of UN member countries.

OECD: **http://www.oecd.org/** Statistics for most developed economies and some transition and emerging economies.

Economic models and simulation

Economic modelling is an important aspect of economic analysis. There are a number of sites that offer access to a model for you to use, which can be a useful way of finding out how economic theory works within an environment that claims to reflect reality. In this case variations in levels of taxation and public expenditure can be seen to affect the economy.

Virtual economy: **http://bized.ac.uk/virtual/economy**

WinEcon: **http://www.webecon.bris.ac.uk/winecon/**

National Institute of Economic and Social Research: **http://www.niesr.ac.uk/**

References

Bird, R. M. (1971) 'Wager's Law of Expanding State Activity', *Public Finance*, 26, 1.

OECD (2005) *World Economic Outlook*, IMF, Washington DC, April.

Stiglitz, J. (2000) 'Capital Account Liberalisation, Economic Growth and Instability', *World Development Report*, Vol. 28, No. 5.

Tytell, I. and Wei, S. (2004) 'Does Financial Globalisation Induce Better Macroeconomic Policies?', paper presented to the Fifth Annual IMF Conference, Washington DC, 4 November.

PROGRESS AND REVIEW QUESTIONS

Answers to most questions can be found at the back of the book (pages 516–18). Answers to asterisked questions can be found on the students' side of the Companion Website.

Multiple-choice questions

1 Which *two* of the following are consistent with the idea of automatic fiscal stabilisers?

   a) The fact that the tax of unleaded petrol is lower than that on leaded petrol.
   b) The fact that as people's incomes increase the amount that they pay in taxes also increases.
   c) The fact that people sent to prison do not receive benefits.
   d) The fact that government spending falls during 'boom' times as unemployment falls.

2 Which *two* of the following represent explanations of the rise in government spending which are based on 'microeconomic analysis'?

   a) 'Displacement theory' which suggests that public spending is ratcheted upwards over time by social upheavals – as in the case of economic depressions or wars.
   b) The state providing 'public goods' and 'merit goods' free at the point of use, which private markets are unable to do.
   c) Rise in a country's real national income, when public services are 'normal' products with high income elasticities of demand.
   d) Change in the composition of the various public sector 'markets' leading to greater public spending (e.g. ageing population incurring greater expenditure on healthcare).
   e) Increased privatisation reducing the role of the public sector.

3 Which *two* of the following represent explanations of the rise in government spending which are based on 'macroeconomic analysis'?

   a) 'Displacement theory' which suggests that public spending is ratcheted upwards over time by social upheavals – as in the case of economic depressions or wars.
   b) The state providing 'public goods' and 'merit goods' free at the point of use, which private markets are unable to do.
   c) Rise in a country's real national income, when public services are 'normal' products with high income elasticities of demand.
   d) Change in the composition of the various public sector 'markets' leading to greater public spending (e.g. ageing population incurring greater expenditure on healthcare).
   e) Increased privatisation reducing the role of the public sector.

4 Which *two* of the following are often used as arguments for *restricting* the size of the public sector?

   a) Public sector 'crowding out' the private sector
   b) Lower taxes reducing incentives to work, save and take risks
   c) Higher taxes reducing incentives to work, save and take risks
   d) Greater public provision is needed to offset poverty and inequalities
   e) 'Market failures' of various kinds can only be corrected by government intervention

5 Which *two* of the following are often used as arguments for *expanding* the size of the public sector?

   a) Public sector 'crowding out' the private sector
   b) Lower taxes increasing incentives to work, save and take risks
   c) Higher taxes reducing incentives to work, save and take risks
   d) Greater public provision is needed to offset poverty and inequalities
   e) 'Market failures' of various kinds can only be corrected by government intervention

6 Which *two* of the following are defined as sources of government revenue from indirect taxes?

   a) Petroleum revenue tax
   b) VAT
   c) Inheritance tax
   d) Capital gains tax
   e) Fuel duties

7 Which *two* of the following are the most accurate indicators of the government's budgetary situation (fiscal stance) in any given year?

   a) Public sector net cash requirement
   b) Public sector receipts
   c) Income tax schedules
   d) Public sector borrowing requirement
   e) Surplus on current account.

8 Which *two* of the following are often claimed to be the advantages of an indirect system of taxation?

   a) It helps households to avoid the 'unemployment trap'
   b) It can be varied more quickly and easily
   c) It imposes smaller administrative costs
   d) It decreases the tax burden as a percentage of GDP
   e) It stimulates government revenue when demand is elastic

9 Which *one* of the following terms represents a tax system where the marginal rate of taxation is higher than the average rate of taxation

   a) Regressive tax system
   b) Proportional tax system
   c) Welfare minimising tax system
   d) Progressive tax system
   e) Welfare maximising tax system

10 Which *two* of the following are consistent with the idea of discretionary fiscal policy?

   a) The fact that the tax of unleaded petrol is lower than that on leaded petrol.
   b) The fact that as people's incomes increase the amount that they pay in taxes also increases.
   c) The fact that the government increases spending during a recession.
   d) The fact that congestion charges reduce traffic in city centres.
   e) The fact that government raises tax rates during a 'boom' period.

 Data response questions

1 Look carefully at the data in the table below showing what happens to tax taken from this family as gross earnings rise.

Table 12.13 Married couple (one earner working more than 30 hours per week) with two children under 11 (rent £52.27, council tax £16.40 per week)

	June 2002			
	(£pw)	(£pw)	(£pw)	(£pw)
Gross earnings	125.00	150.00	200.00	250.00
Plus child benefit	26.30	16.30	26.30	26.30
Working family tax credit	112.26	99.88	80.56	61.86
Housing benefit	5.53	0.00	00.00	00.00
Council tax benefit	2.02	0.00	00.00	00.00
Less: Income tax	0.00	0.00	9.87	20.87
National insurance	3.60	6.10	11.10	16.10
Net income	*267.51*	*270.08*	*285.89*	*301.19*

Source: Adapted from DSS, Tax/Benefit Model Tables (June, 2002)

a) What does this table suggest?
b) What implications are there for government policy?

2 Look carefully at Figure 12.5 which shows the percentage reduction in net income from a 1% rise in VAT.

What does the data in Figure 12.5 suggest?

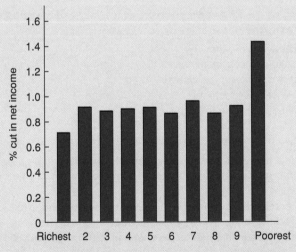

Figure 12.5 Percentage cut in net income from a 1% VAT rise.

Source: Adapted from *Institute of Fiscal Studies* data, 2004/05

Case study question

Higher rate tax payers

The number of people paying higher rate income tax (40%) has increased by more than 50% since Labour came to power in 1997. Is this an assault on the middle classes or of concern only to the wealthy few?

Many people near the top of the income range seem to believe they are more 'average' than they are. In 2004 the higher rate of tax was paid on incomes before tax in excess of £35,115. Imagine lining everyone in the country up from the lowest income to the highest. The income of the person in the middle – the median – would be £11,800 before taxes. If you lined up households rather than individuals the median would be £21,700 – still well below the higher rate of tax threshold.

In fact, despite the increase in number since 1997, there are still only 3.3 million higher rate taxpayers in Britain – only 7% of adults and only 11% of those with incomes high enough to be paying any income tax. So it looks hard to argue that the increase has really hit the middle classes – if by that we mean households around median income.

But the story is a little more complicated that that. A household's position in the income distribution depends not only on the cash coming in but also on how many people share it. To achieve the same standard of living as a childless couple, government statisticians typically assume that a single person requires only 61% as much income while a couple with two children (aged four and thirteen) needs 145%. However, even after taking household size and composition into account (i.e. adjusting gross incomes to give 'income equivalent' values for different types of household), 66% of higher rate taxpayers are still found in the richest tenth of the population and 94% in the richest three-tenths.

(You can see how your income compares with the rest of the population at **www.ifs.org.uk/wheredoyoufitin**. Type in your take-home income, your council tax bill and your family details, and you can see your position on a chart of the income distribution.)

Questions

1 *Discuss the suggestion that too many individuals earning middle-income are now having to pay higher rate income tax.*

2 *Does the analysis change if we use households rather than individuals?*

Essay questions

Answers to asterisked questions can be found on the students' side of the Companion Website. All other answers can be found at the back of the book (pages 517–18).

1* Consider the reasons for government intervention in the economy.

2 Government expenditure has tended to grow rapidly in most advanced industrialised economies. Explain why some believe that it is important to restrict the growth in public expenditure. Suggest how public expenditure might be controlled.

3* Examine the case for moving the tax system away from indirect taxes and towards direct taxes.

4 Explain why governments try to make use of 'built-in' stabilisers. Suggest some possible problems for this policy.

5* Review the case for and against a 'flat tax' regime.

Money, financial institutions and monetary policy

By the end of this chapter you should be able to:

- Outline the key functions of money.
- Understand the difference between money and near money commodities.
- Explain the different measures of money in the UK and the means by which money can be 'created'.
- Examine the role of the various financial intermediaries in the UK and of the Bank of England.
- Assess the factors determining the rate of interest.
- Understand the contribution of monetary policy (controlling money supply and interest rates) to economic management.
- Evaluate the impacts of increased 'financial globalisation' on the conduct of domestic monetary policy.

1   INTRODUCTION

Money
Anything which is generally acceptable as a means of payment and which fulfil the four key 'functions of money', namely acting as a medium of exchange, unit of account, store of value and standard of deferred payment.

The chapter begins by considering what is meant by the term 'money'. To this end the functions of money are outlined, including the money commodity acting as a medium of exchange, a unit of account, a store of value and a standard of deferred payment. The official measures of the money supply, as used by the Bank of England, are defined and reviewed. The chapter examines the role of the various financial institutions in the UK and also deals with the main determinants of the demand for and the supply of money. Particular attention is paid to the importance of and the factors determining the rate of interest. The role of the Bank of England and its operation of monetary policy are reviewed. The chapter concludes by assessing the possible constraints of 'financial globalisation', i.e. the enhanced geographical mobility of international financial and capital flows on the conduct of domestic monetary policy.

2   THE FUNCTIONS OF MONEY

When considering money it is useful to consider the four widely recognised functions of money, namely to act as a medium of exchange, a unit of account, a store of value and a standard of deferred payment.

2.1 A medium of exchange

The medium of exchange function can be viewed as the main function of money. Money allows us to specialise in the production of certain goods and services. Without money the economy would revert to a system of *barter*, where goods and services would be exchanged directly for each other. This is an inefficient system of exchange not least because of the need for ***double-coincidence of wants.*** This means that if I want a particular good, not only must I find someone who has that good but that person must also want what I have. There is also the problem of what exchange value to attach to the goods concerned. Barter is a time-consuming process and leads individuals to produce for themselves the majority of products they require. It is inappropriate for a modern economy, producing a wide range of goods and services.

Double coincidence of want
Where I must have what you want and you must have what I want for exchange to take place.

For money to perform the function of a medium of exchange it does not necessarily have to have any *intrinsic value* (i.e. it need not, in itself, be valuable) but it must be generally acceptable as a medium of exchange, i.e. have a claim on the goods and services with intrinsic value.

Pause for thought 1

How might the production possibility frontier (see Chapter 1) of a barter economy differ from that of a money based economy?

2.2 A unit of account

Where money is used as a unit of account every good and service is valued against a common standard, namely money, rather than against each other. Money as a unit of account allows a quick comparison to be made between the value of different goods and services. In this function money is acting as a common denominator against which value in exchange can be expressed.

2.3 A store of value

Money is not perishable and so it has yet another advantage over barter in that it allows us to delay the purchase of a good or service. In other words, money makes *saving* possible, i.e. assets can be built up. However, it is important to note that if the economy is experiencing inflation this will reduce the value of money and affect people's preparedness to hold it as a store of value. In this function money is permitting a time lag to exist between the sale of one thing and the purchase of something else.

2.4 A standard of deferred payment

Money allows for payments to be delayed (deferred), as for example by making it possible for contracts to be agreed involving payment in the future. But, as with a store of value, inflation will affect the willingness of people to accept a given sum of money in future settlement of a debt.

Mini Case Study 13.1

Plastic replaces cash

An economic era came to an end in January 2005 when plastic officially replaced cash as Britain's most popular method of payment. Figures released for 2004 suggested that, for the first time ever, British shoppers had spent more in stores on their credit card payments than in cash payments, namely £269 billion in payments by plastic cards in 2004 compared to £268 billion in payments by cash. The first plastic cards appeared in June 1966, and in only 40 years have supplanted cash. The introduction of debit cards have played a key role in this outcome in recent years, with almost two-thirds of all plastic spending using debit cards compared to one-third using credit cards.

British consumers have 123 million multifunction plastic cards plus another 23 million cash-only cards and 22 million store cards. More than 90% of adults have at least one plastic card.

Question

Consider some of the possible implications of the use of plastic cards to replace cash payments.

Answer to question can be found on the students' side of the Companion Website.

3   MONEY SUPPLY

3.1 What is money?

Sight deposits
Current account deposits – bearing little or no interest.

Money can be defined as any item which is generally acceptable as a means of payment in settling a debt and which is capable of fulfilling the functions already identified. The item must obviously enjoy the confidence of those using it, but there still remains the question of what exactly constitutes money in a modern economy. Banknotes and coins are generally acceptable as a means of payment, as are current accounts (also known as *sight deposits*) on which cheques are drawn. In terms of the functions of money, notes and coins and sight deposits act as a medium of exchange and also fulfil the unit of account, store of value and standard of deferred payment functions of a money commodity.

Near money
Commodities which fulfil only *some* of the functions of money.

3.2 Near money

Time deposits
Deposit accounts often requiring notice of withdrawal and bearing interest.

Commodities which fulfil only some of the functions of money cannot be classed as money. Credit cards and luncheon vouchers, for instance, can sometimes be used as a medium of exchange for transactions, but they are not money because they cannot always be used, nor do they fulfil the other functions of money. Paper assets, such as government securities, serve as a store of value, but they cannot be used as a medium of exchange. However, liquid assets, i.e. those which can easily be converted into money without loss of value, form a potential addition to the money stock and are often referred to as '**near money**'. Assets normally classed as 'liquid' include **time deposits**, treasury and commercial bills, and certificates of deposit (Figure 13.1). Other assets become more liquid the nearer is their maturity date. Many of the assets shown in Figure 13.1 are considered in more detail later in this chapter.

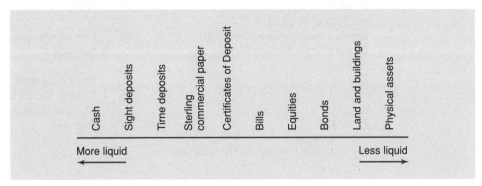

Figure 13.1 A liquidity spectrum ranging from cash as the most liquid asset to physical assets of various kinds as the least liquid assets.

3.3 Measuring the money supply

Official estimates of the money supply have been published in the UK since 1966. Some of these measures have been described as *narrow* as they include only the most liquid assets in their definition. Others have been described as *broad* as they include a variety of less liquid assets. At present there are two official measures of the money supply used by the Bank of England, namely M0 and M4, and these measures differ in terms of their levels of liquidity.

M0
The narrowest definition of the money supply consisting of notes and coins and operational deposits of the Bank of England, often referred to as the 'Monetary base'.

M4
A broader definition of the money supply including notes and coins in circulation, sight and time deposits and various other deposits held by a range of financial intermediaries.

(a) M0 is the narrowest definition of the money supply. It consists of all the notes and coins in circulation outside the Bank of England, that is notes and coins in the hands of the general public and the till money of banks and building societies, plus operational deposits (*see* page 313) held by the banks at the Bank of England. M0 is often referred to as the *monetary base*, the central stock of cash on which all money supply expansion is based. As we can see from Table 13.1 the total for M0 was £43,395 million in 2005.

(b) M4 is a broader definition of the money supply (though not as regards the notes and coins component). It includes only the notes and coins in circulation with the private sector plus non-interest bearing sight (current account) bank deposits, private sector interest bearing *sight* (current account) and *time* (deposit account) bank deposits, as well as sterling certificates of deposit. It also includes the private sector holdings of building society shares and deposits, certificates of deposit and building society holdings of bank deposits and bank certificates of deposit and notes and coins. M4 was introduced in 1987 as a measure of the money supply in order to account for the increased importance of building societies. As we can see from Table 13.1 the total for M4 was much larger than for M0, reaching £862,478 million in 2005.

At the present time M0 and M4 are the only aggregates which are monitored by the government. The main reason for defining and monitoring the rate of growth of the money supply is the belief that the money supply influences levels of prices and the output in the economy. We return to this issue below.

Table 13.1 **Components of M0 and M4 (£ million) in March 2005**

M0		M4	
Notes and coins in circulation outside the Bank of England	42,299	Notes and coins	34,918
Bankers operational deposits with Bankers Department of Bank of England	96	Non-interest bearing bank deposits	53,631
		Other bank retail deposits	616,930
		Building society and retail shares and deposits	157,999
Total M0	42,395	*Total M4*	863,478

Source: Adapted from *Financial Statistics* (2005) May

3.4 Credit creation

In the previous section it was noted that bank and building society deposits form part of the money supply. Banks and building societies are able to create new deposits through a process known as *credit creation*. A simplified model of credit creation is illustrated in Figure 13.2.

Credit creation
The process by which financial intermediaries are able to create new deposits (which can then be spent).

Credit creation in a single bank system

It will help to make a number of simplifying assumptions when considering the concept of credit creation.

(a) The economy has a single commercial bank, a monopoly bank, which has a number of branches.
(b) The bank has found from experience that it needs to hold 10% of its assets in the form of cash to meet the normal demand for cash withdrawals from its customers.
(c) All the loans made by the bank are re-deposited with it. In practice this is unlikely to be the case.
(d) There are sufficient borrowers willing to take up the loans issued by the bank.

Suppose a customer deposits an extra £1,000 cash in the bank, illustrated by stage 1 in Figure 13.2. The new deposit is classed as a liability since the bank owes that money to its account holder and must pay it back whenever the holder demands it. The deposit is in fact a claim against the bank. Having obtained the initial deposit of £1,000 the bank, given assumption (b), needs to maintain a 10% cash ratio. Thus, on the asset side, £100 cash is held to meet customer requirements for cash withdrawals. The remaining 90% or £900 can be loaned out. Given the assumption that assets loaned out will be spent and find their way back into the bank, then in stage 2 re-deposits of £900 will occur. Of this re-deposited amount £90 (10%) will be held in the form of cash in order to meet claims on the bank and the remaining £810 (90%) will be loaned out. This process will continue with the amount available for lending continually declining, as with stages 3 and 4 in Figure 13.2, until eventually total liabilities and assets will equal £10,000. Thus, from an original deposit of £1,000 cash, £10,000 of new deposits and £9,000 of new loans have been made. There has thus been a multiple expansion of credit.

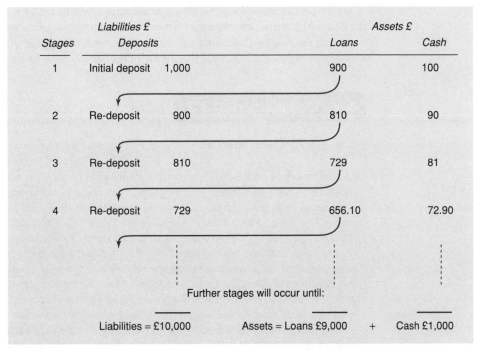

| | Liabilities £ | | Assets £ | |
Stages	Deposits		Loans	Cash
1	Initial deposit	1,000	900	100
2	Re-deposit	900	810	90
3	Re-deposit	810	729	81
4	Re-deposit	729	656.10	72.90

Further stages will occur until:

Liabilities = £10,000   Assets = Loans £9,000   +   Cash £1,000

Figure 13.2 The figure illustrates how, say, a single bank can create money. In stage 1 a new deposit of £1,000 is made with the bank. Given the assumption that the bank needs to maintain a 10% cash ration then £100 will be retained to meet customer withdrawals. The remaining 90% (£900) can be loaned out. Since the assumption was made that there is only one bank and that all loans are re-deposited then the £900 will ultimately be re-deposited. The whole process will now be repeated, stages 2, 3, 4, etc., with the amount available for lending continually declining until total deposits, which are part of the money supply, equal £10,000. *Note*: Only deposits resulting from lending are newly created money.

The credit multiplier

Credit creation can be analysed by use of the *credit* or *bank multiplier*. The extent of the creation of new deposits depends upon the size of the cash ratio banks maintain. Thus if the cash ratio is 10% then the credit multiplier is 10 since:

$$\text{The credit multiplier} = \frac{1}{\text{Cash ratio}}$$

Credit creation in a multi-bank or multi-building society system

The concept of credit creation is more complicated in a multi-bank (or multi-building society) system. The reason is that when a bank makes a loan to a customer, say to buy a new car, then the garage from which the car is purchased will not necessarily deposit the money in the same bank which initially gave the loan. Even though this is the case, the end result in terms of credit creation is exactly the same provided all the banks in the economy create deposits to the limit of the cash ratio.

Of course the money supply, however measured, will be influenced by the activities of the financial institutions, especially where broader measures of money are involved. After reviewing the role of these financial institutions we return (page 314) to a discussion of how governments can influence the supply of money available in an economy.

Mini Case Study 13.2

Clearing payments

The time taken to clear both electronic payments and cheques has actually increased in recent years, despite technological progress. The operation of the electronic payment system and cheque clearance have both become high profile topics in recent years as bank profits have soared whilst the time taken to 'clear' electronic payments and cheques has risen from 3 days to 6 days. The Office of Fair Trade reported in May 2005 on these practices and has requested that the electronic payments system (more widely used than cheques nowadays) be speeded up within a two-year period. The banks argue that they need time to adjust their technologies to make them compatible between banks and other financial intermediaries. They also argue that the increased time for clearing such payments has been an attempt to reduce fraud rather than raise profits. The OFT is likely to press for a speed-up in clearing times for cheques in a separate report in the near future.

Question

Consider some of the benefits and costs to the various parties of the changes being proposed.

Answer to question can be found at the back of the book (page 518).

4 | FINANCIAL INSTITUTIONS

Financial system
Consists of lenders and borrowers, financial intermediaries and financial markets.

It will be useful to begin by reviewing the role of the **financial system** and the financial intermediaries as a whole before turning to the different types of financial institutions. The discussion in this section follows closely that of Webb (2006).

4.1 The role of the financial system

Financial intermediaries
Come between savers and lenders to provide brokerage, maturity transformation, risk transformation and size transformation services.

The basic rationale of a financial system is to bring together those who have accumulated an excess of money and who wish to save with those who have a requirement to borrow in order to finance investment. The process arguably helps to better utilise society's scarce resources, increase productive efficiency and ultimately raise the standard of living.

Figure 13.3 provides an overview of the structure of the financial system in the UK. Essentially there are three kinds of operator in the UK financial system.

1 *Lenders and borrowers* – these include persons, companies and government.
2 *Financial intermediaries* – consisting of financial institutions which act as intermediaries between lenders and borrowers. **Financial intermediaries** take one of two general

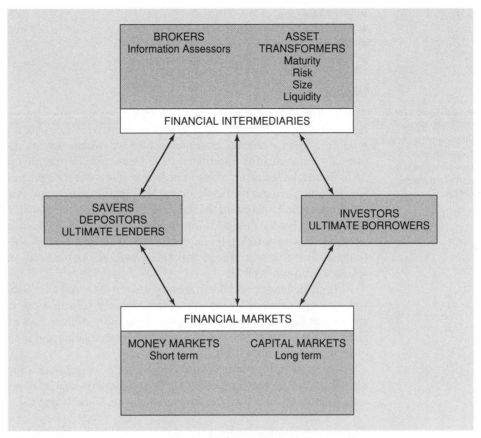

Figure 13.3 A useful overview of the linkages between lenders and borrowers, financial intermediaries and the financial markets, which together comprise the UK financial system.

forms: brokers (bringing together lenders and borrowers by evaluating market information) and asset transformers (transforming the financial assets of lenders by varying the maturity, risk, size and **liquidity** of the liabilities of borrowers).

3 *Financial markets* – where money is lent and borrowed through the sale and purchase of financial instruments. They play an essential role in reducing the cost of placing, pricing and trading such instruments. In the UK, the financial markets can be defined as short-term money markets and long-term capital markets.

Liquidity
Commodities which can easily be converted into cash, with little or no risk, are referred to as 'more liquid'.

4.2 The role of financial intermediaries

Financial intermediaries come between those wishing to save (lend) and those wishing to invest (borrow). They provide a service that yields them a profit via the difference which exists between the (lower) interest they pay to those who lend and the (higher) interest they receive from those who borrow. That they can earn such profits reflects the fact that they are offering a useful service to both lenders and borrowers which can be disaggregated into at least four separate functions:

- brokerage
- maturity transformation
- risk transformation
- collect and parceling – size transformation.

Brokerage

Brokerage function
Where financial
intermediaries bring
together lenders and
borrowers who have
complementary
needs.

The **brokerage function** is rather different from the other three, which might all be regarded as including elements of 'asset transformation'. A broker is an intermediary who brings together lenders and borrowers who have complementary needs and does this by assessing and evaluating information. The lender may have neither the time nor the ability to undertake search activities in order to assess whether a potential borrower is trustworthy, is likely to use the funds for a project that is credible and profitable, and is able to pay the promised interest on the due date. By depositing funds with a financial intermediary the household avoids such information gathering, monitoring and evaluation costs, which are now undertaken by the specialised financial intermediary. The borrower needs to know that a promised loan will be received at the time and under the conditions specified in any agreement.

By bringing lenders and borrowers together in these ways, the various information and transactions costs are reduced so that this brokerage function can command a 'fee'. The size of that fee will, of course, be greater the more difficult and expensive it is for the financial intermediary to develop procedures for evaluating and monitoring borrowers in order to minimise 'default risks'.

The next three functions involve elements of asset transformation in which the liabilities (deposits) are transformed by the financial intermediaries into various types of asset with differing characteristics in terms of maturity, liquidity and risk.

Maturity transformation

Here the financial intermediaries bridge the gap between the desire of lenders to be able to get their money back quickly if needed and the desire of borrowers to borrow for a long period. In fulfilling this function the financial intermediaries hold liabilities (e.g. deposits) that have a shorter term to maturity than their assets (e.g. loans), i.e. they borrow short and lend long. For example, a building society will typically hold around 70% of its liabilities in the form of deposits repayable 'on demand', i.e. which can be withdrawn at any time without penalty. In contrast, around 75% of its assets are repayable only after five years or more.

**Maturity
transformation**
Where financial
intermediaries bridge
the gap between the
desire of lenders for
liquidity and of
borrowers for
illiquidity.

Financial intermediaries are able to perform this **maturity transformation** function in part because of the 'law of large numbers', which implies that while some depositors will be withdrawing funds others will be making new deposits. This means that, overall, withdrawals minus new deposits are likely to be small in relation to the value of total deposits (liabilities). As a result the 'funding risk', namely that depositors might wish to withdraw more funds than the banks have available in liquid form, is greatly reduced. This enables the financial intermediaries to hold a sizeable proportion of less liquid assets (e.g. long-term loans) in their portfolio.

Risk transformation
Where financial
intermediaries shift
the burden of risk
from lenders to
themselves.

Risk transformation

This involves the financial intermediaries in shifting the burden of risk from the lender to themselves. Their ability to do so depends largely on economies of scale in risk management. The large amounts of deposits (liabilities) the financial intermediaries collect allow them to diversify their assets across a wide variety of types and sectors. 'Pooling' risk and reward in this way means that no individual is exposed to a situation in which the default of one or more borrowers is likely to have a significant effect.

Collection and parcelling
Where financial intermediaries collect a large number of small amounts from savers and parcel these into larger amounts for borrowers.

Collection and parcelling

Financial intermediaries also transform the nature of their assets through the collection of a large number of small amounts of funds from depositors and their parcelling into larger amounts required by borrowers. Often the financial intermediaries have relied on obtaining many small deposits from conveniently located branches of their operations. This process is known as 'size intermediation' and benefits borrowers because they obtain one large loan from one source, thus reducing transaction costs. Of course this loan is an asset to the financial intermediary and a liability to the borrower.

The common characteristics of all financial intermediaries are therefore as follows. First, they take money from those who seek to save, whether it be in exchange for a deposit account bearing interest or in exchange for a paper financial claim. Secondly, they lend the money provided by those savers to borrowers, who may issue a paper asset in return. Thirdly, in exchange for such lending they acquire a portfolio of paper assets (claims on borrowers) which will pay an income to the intermediary and which it may 'manage' by buying and selling the assets on financial markets in order to yield further profits for itself.

Pause for thought 2

In Chapter 11 (page 264) we spoke of the so-called 'paradox of thrift', whereby attempting to save more, while virtuous for an individual can be damaging for a nation. What contribution might the financial institutions make that might help avoid that paradox?

5 UK FINANCIAL INTERMEDIARIES

The UK financial system incorporates different types of financial intermediary, offering lenders and borrowers a variety of instruments which have different maturities, liquidities and risk profiles. A popular method of classification is to distinguish between the bank and non-bank financial intermediaries.

- *Bank sector* All the UK financial institutions that have been issued with a banking licence, including the high street commercial banks, the corporate wholesale banks and the foreign banks, are regarded as being part of the bank sector.
- *Non-bank sector* The other financial intermediaries, including the building societies, insurance companies, pension funds, unit trust and investment trust companies, are classified as part of the non-bank sector.

Although the distinction between banking and non-banking institutions has become increasingly blurred, it may be helpful to consider the UK financial intermediaries under the following three headings: banking financial intermediaries, non-bank financial intermediaries, and the Bank of England.

5.1 The UK banking financial intermediaries

The retail banks

These include banks which either participate in the UK clearing system or have extensive branch networks. Retail banks, through their extensive branch networks, have historically been primarily engaged in gathering deposits and creating loans, usually at high margins given that they could obtain deposits at low interest rates and could offer loans to individuals and firms at high interest rates. The retail banks offer a wide array of services to personal customers including savings accounts, unsecured and secured loans, mortgages, overdrafts, automated cash machines, home banking, foreign currency transactions and general financial advice. They also offer a range of services to corporate customers including leasing and hire purchase, export and import facilities, payroll services and international financial transfers.

Note: Islamic banks

In 2004 the Financial Services Authority gave the go-ahead for Britain's first totally Islamic bank in a move that for the first time will allow Britain's 1.8 million Muslims to obey their religious beliefs on charging interest.

The Islamic Bank of Britain operates in line with Islamic Sharia principles, which include a stipulation that money must be invested ethically and that the giving or receiving of interest is forbidden.

Whereas a traditional bank would charge interest on a loan granted to a customer, the Islamic Bank of Britain said it would deal in real items rather than lend money. If a customer wished to buy a computer, the Bank would buy it and then sell it to the customer at a fixed price, or lease it and charge a rental until the item was fully paid for.

To ensure that the Bank is operating in a wholly Sharia compliant way, its services, activities and investments will be overseen by a supervisory committee made up of Islamic scholars. The bank will not invest in businesses deemed to be unethical – such as tobacco, alcohol and pornography – and is opposed to the idea that money can be simply traded for money.

The wholesale banks

These include around 500 banks which typically engage only in large-scale lending and borrowing transactions, namely transactions in excess of £50,000. The wholesale banks include the following.

- *merchant banks*, of which there are about 40 including the Accepting Houses;
- *other British banks*, a general category covering banks with UK majority ownership;
- *overseas banks*, which include American banks, Japanese banks and a variety of other overseas banks and consortium banks.

The majority of transactions by the wholesale banks involve corporate clients, with individual transactions being 'wholesale', that is of a high value (greater than £50,000) but, more typically, in excess of £1 million so that sizeable absolute levels of a profit can still be made. Wholesale banking takes place mainly in foreign currencies, which reflects the substantial presence of Japanese and American banks in this sector. However, the sector also includes the British merchant banks, whose major business includes the acceptance of bills, underwriting, consultancy, fund management and trading in the financial markets.

Mini Case Study 13.3

Banks and ethics

Banks and ethics are not widely seen as being synonymous with one another, but the Co-op bank is trying to change that perception. It turned down £87 million in business in 2004 because of ethical and ecological concerns.

The amount of business lost to the bank because of its ethical stance rose from £6.9 million the previous year. The Manchester-based society also reaped rewards from its holier than thou stance as it attributed 34% of its £132 million profits in 2004 to its ethical policies. That compares with 29% in 2003. More loan and savings account customers joined up and stayed with the bank for ethical reasons, it said.

Simon Williams, a spokesperson for the Co-op Bank, said, 'When we launched our ethical stance back in 1992, its initial appeal was very much to individual customers who wanted to know what happened to their money while it was in the bank. Now, 13 years on, 36% of personal customers and a quarter of the bank's corporate customers join us precisely because we are prepared to turn away certain sorts of business.'

Refusing to provide banking services to companies on ecological grounds cost the bank £3.8 million last year, while the cost of turning away business for animal welfare reasons was £1.29 million.

Declining to do business with companies associated with poor human rights and labour practices lost it £847,000 and rebuffing organisations that are involved in the production of controversial chemicals cost it £688,000.

The number of companies turned down increased because the Co-op widened the scope of background checks made on business customers applying for an account. For instance, in property finance it routinely assesses the ethical record of not only the developers but also any tenants that may underpin the development or acquisition.

Question

What implications might follow from this Mini Case Study for the UK banks and financial intermediaries?

Answer to question can be found on the students' side of the Companion Website.

5.2 UK non-bank financial intermediaries

The institutions in this sector fulfil a number of specialist functions such as providing mortgage finance, insurance and pension cover. They typically specialise in matching the needs of borrowers for long-term finance with the needs of lenders for paper assets denominated in small units which are readily saleable. The UK non-bank financial intermediaries include the building societies, insurance companies, pension funds, unit trusts and investment trusts.

The building societies

These are mutually owned financial institutions which have traditionally offered loans in the form of mortgages to facilitate house purchase. Mutuality means that they are owned by their 'members', namely those who have purchased shares in the form of deposits and those who have borrowed from them. Until the early 1980s, building societies were the only institutions offering mortgages and competition was restricted by various agreements and regulations between the various building societies.

Competition in this sector has, however, intensified since the early 1980s when deregulation of the retail banking sector allowed banks to offer mortgage finance and thereby to threaten the position of the building societies. This led to demands for deregulation to be extended to the building society sector in order to allow the building societies to respond by competing with banks in financial and other markets where previously they had been restricted. The Building Societies Act 1986, the subsequent Orders in Council of 1988 and the Building Societies Act 1997 have permitted building societies to offer a whole range of new banking, investment and property related housing services, in addition to their traditional savings and home loan business.

Nevertheless, building societies have remained true to their basic principles and remain predominantly mortgage finance providers, with the building society sector providing around nine times more mortgage lending by value in 2005 than consumer credit lending.

Insurance companies and pension funds

About half of all personal savings are channelled into these institutions via regular and single-premium life assurance and pension payments. These savings from the personal sector are used to acquire a portfolio of assets. The institutions then manage these assets with the objective that they yield a sufficient return to pay the eventual insurance and pension claims as well as providing a working rate of return for the financial institutions themselves. The insurance companies and pension funds are major investors in the financial markets and exert considerable influence in these markets. They hold large amounts of long-term debt and help absorb ('make markets in') large volumes and values of new issues of various equities, bills and bonds.

Although these insurance companies and pension funds compete strongly against each other in the personal savings market, their portfolio choices differ because the structures of their liabilities differ. For example, the life assurance companies hold a larger proportion of assets as fixed-interest securities because many of their liabilities are expressed in nominal terms (e.g. money value of payments in the future on policies is known). Pension funds, however, hold a larger proportion of assets in the form of equities which historically have yielded higher real rates of return because many of their liabilities are expressed in real terms (e.g. pensions paid in the future are often index linked).

 ## Pause for thought 3

How have the types of asset held by pension funds played a part in the so-called 'pensions crisis'? What other factors have helped cause this 'pensions crisis'?

Unit and investment trusts

Both unit and investment trusts offer lenders a chance to buy into a diversified portfolio of assets and thereby reduce risk while at the same time receiving attractive returns. These institutions can achieve this by pooling the funds received from a large number of small investors and then implementing various portfolio management techniques not available to such small investors.

5.3 The Bank of England

The Bank of England is the Central Bank of the UK and can be referred to as 'the Bank'. Most countries have a central bank, for example the Deutsche Bundesbank in Germany and the Federal Reserve System in the USA. As seen in Table 13.2, it is divided into two departments, namely the *Issue Department* and the *Banking Department*.

(a) *The Issue Department* is responsible for the note issue. Since notes are promises by the Bank to pay the holders then the *liabilities* of the Issue Department consist of notes in circulation and notes held in the Banking Department ready for issue to the banking sector. The *assets* of the Issue Department consist of securities since these represent monies owed to the Bank.

(b) *The Banking Department* is concerned with the business of the Bank. The *liabilities* of the Banking Department include the following.

(*i*) *Public deposits* which are deposits of the central government.

Bankers' deposits Operational deposits of the clearing banks held at the Bank of England for clearing purposes.

(*ii*) *Bankers' deposits* which are deposits of the commercial clearing banks held by the Banking Department for operational (e.g. clearing) purposes.

(*iii*) *Reserves and other accounts* which are deposits of overseas central banks and of local authorities and public corporations. There are also a number of private sector accounts.

Table 13.2 Bank of England balance sheet (£ million), March 2005

Issue Department

Liabilities		*Assets*	
Notes in circulation	37,212	Government securities	14,870
Notes in Banking Department	8	Other securities	22,350
	37,220		37,220

Banking Department

Liabilities		*Assets*	
Public deposits	525	Government securities	1,810
Bankers' deposits	2,162	Advances and other accounts	12,093
Reserves and other accounts	17,767	Premises, equipment, etc.	6,550
		Notes and coins	1
	20,454		20,454

Source: Adapted from *Financial Statistics* (2005) May

The *asset side* of the Banking Department consists of government securities, advances and other accounts, premises, equipment and notes and coins ready for issue to the clearing banks, which they can obtain through their operational balances.

Functions of the Bank of England

The Bank has a range of functions, as detailed below, and they are related to achieving three objectives:

(a) maintaining the integrity and value of the nation's currency;

(b) ensuring the stability of the financial system;

(c) promoting the efficiency and competitiveness of the financial system.

The functions of the Bank can be seen as:

(a) *Banker to the banking sector.* The Bank of England holds accounts of other banks. These operational balances are used for inter-bank settlements at the end of each banking day.

(b) *Banker to the government.* The Bank acts as the government's bank, responsible for their finances. Taxation revenue is paid into, and government expenditure is taken out of, the Exchequer Account at the Bank of England.

(c) *Banker to other customers.* The Bank holds accounts for a number of overseas central banks as well as for a few private individuals.

(d) *Manager of the Exchange Equalisation Account.* This is an account managed by the Bank which is composed of sterling and foreign currency and is used to intervene in foreign exchange markets in order to influence the value of sterling.

Monetary policy
The use of various techniques to change the money supply and/or the rate of interest.

(e) *Note issue.* The Bank is the sole issuer of notes in England and Wales. This function includes the printing, issue and withdrawal of banknotes.

(f) *Supervision of the financial system.* In order to maintain the international reputation of the UK financial sector.

Monetary Policy Committee
Nine members, some from the Bank of England, others independent, who meet monthly at the Bank of England to set interest rates.

(g) *Implementation of **monetary policy**.* The Bank is responsible for the implementation of the government's monetary policy. This includes control of the money supply and the rate of interest and will be covered in more detail in Section **6**. The target for monetary policy is a rate of inflation of $2\frac{1}{2}\%$. The decision with respect to the interest rate is made by the Bank's **Monetary Policy Committee** (MPC) which has a remit set by the government. If inflation deviates by more than 1% either side of this figure then the MPC is required to write to the Chancellor of the Exchequer explaining the situation.

6 MONEY SUPPLY AND THE BANK OF ENGLAND

As noted above, the Bank of England through the MPC has the responsibility for monetary policy and in particular for setting the *short-term interest rate* in order to achieve the inflation target as determined by the government. However, in the UK, as in most developed countries, monetary policy cannot focus exclusively on determining the 'price' of money (i.e. the rate of interest) alone. It must take into account the overall supply of, and demand for, money which together provide the market context in which the 'price' of money can be determined.

We first examine various policy instruments used by the Bank of England to influence the *supply* of money.

6.1 Supply of money

(a) *Open market operations* (OMO) involve the Bank of England in buying and selling government securities such as Treasury Bills on the open market. The Bank of England holds accounts of the banks ('operational balances') which are used for the settlement of debt between the banks at the end of each day (*see* page 313). The banks are expected to hold positive balances in their accounts at the Bank daily.

If the Bank wishes to *increase* the money supply it will purchase government securities such as Treasury Bills, with the individuals or institutions who sell these bills receiving cheques drawn on the Bank of England. The individuals or institutions will present the cheques for payment to their own banks and the result will be a transfer of money from the Bank to the bank's operational balances at the Bank. The effect of this will be an increase in the bank's cash reserves at the Bank of England. The credit multiplier (*see* page 305) will begin to operate, helping increase the money supply.

Pause for thought 4

What might the Bank of England do in terms of OMOs if it wishes to decrease the money supply?

In terms of OMOs the bank has usually dealt in Treasury Bills, but of more importance currently are gilt repos. 'Gilt repos', which is short for *sale and repurchase agreement*, is a transaction where one party sells a financial asset to another party and agrees to repurchase equivalent financial assets at a specified time in the future. They are in effect a cash loan with gilts (government bonds) as the security. The gilt repo market was introduced in January 1996 and is a major tool by which the Bank of England provides refinancing to the banking sector.

The following are policy instruments not currently used by the Bank but which have been used over the years.

(b) *Special deposits*. Special deposits are not currently being used as a method of controlling bank liquidity. The Bank can, however, if it so wishes, call for special deposits from the institutions in the banking sector. These deposits would be placed in an account at the Bank and, although they would receive a rate of interest, they would be frozen until the Bank viewed it as the correct time to return them to the banks.

If the Bank called for special deposits it would have the effect of reducing bank liquidity. This would lead the banks to reduce their lending and, therefore, result in a contraction of the money supply. A release of special deposits on the other hand would have the effect of leading to an expansion of the money supply. A call for special deposits has not been made since 1979, the reason being that the Bank can create a shortage of liquidity through open market operations without the use of special deposits.

(c) *Funding*. Funding involves altering the composition of government borrowing. By the issue of more long-term debt, such as gilts, and less short-term debt, such as Treasury Bills, the maturity of the government debt is effectively lengthened. Longer-term debt is likely to be bought by the non-banking sector, unlike short-term debt. The effect of this is to reduce the liquidity of the banks' assets, which restricts the banks' ability to engage in the multiple expansion of credit.

(d) *Ceilings*. From time to time ceilings have been placed on the growth of deposits, allowing banks to increase them by, say, no more than 6%. This type of *quantitative control* could be supplemented with *qualitative controls*, whereby the Bank instructed or offered guidance as to the composition of bank lending – such as discouraging personal lending and the borrowing for property deals. Ceilings were used in the 1950s and 1960s but were abolished in 1971. The reason they were abolished was because they introduced rigidities into the financial system and reduced competition. International financial markets are sophisticated and it is certainly the case that borrowers and lenders would be successful in circumventing such controls.

(e) *Changing the reserve ratio.* The banks could be required to keep a certain proportion of their assets in a particular form, the proportion being some percentage of their liabilities. The effect of this would be a reduction in the banks' ability to create credit. It will be useful at this point to review the factors influencing the *demand for money*. Various theories have been suggested and we shall consider these in the next section which also deals with interest rates, which are often linked to the demand for and supply of money or savings.

7   MONEY DEMAND AND INTEREST RATES

As well as initiating changes in the money supply, the Monetary Policy Committee of the Bank of England can change the interest rate at its monthly meetings.

7.1 What is interest?

The rate of interest has two roles. *To a borrower* the rate of interest is the payment which has to be made in order to obtain liquid assets, namely cash. *To the lender* it is the reward received for parting with liquid assets. When the term 'the rate of interest' is used it appears to imply a single rate of interest. There are, however, many rates of interest on such things as mortgages, bank loans and government securities, with the rate depending on such factors as how credit-worthy the borrower is and the length of time the loan is required for. The level of inflation present in the economy will also affect the rate of interest. If inflation is increasing then one would expect lenders to seek a higher rate of interest to compensate for the expected future loss in the real value of their capital.

It is important to distinguish between nominal and real rates of interest. The *nominal* or *money rate of interest* is the annual amount paid on funds which are borrowed, whereas the *real rate of interest* takes account of inflation, therefore:

Real rate of interest = Nominal rate of interest − Inflation rate

7.2 Theories of money demand and interest rate determination

Various theories have been proposed as to the factors influencing the interest rate, most involving the supply of money and the demand for money in its liquid forms (*see* Figure 13.1 above). The interest rate is then seen in many of these theories as the equilibrium 'price' at which the quantity of money supplied will be held by those demanding the money asset. Whilst the 'Keynesian' and the 'Loanable funds' and other theories of interest seek to emphasise rather different factors involved in the demand for money, a common thread running through all the theories is the suggestion that the demand for money to hold is sensitive to both the level of household income and the rate of interest. Although the terms 'transactions' and 'precautionary' motives for holding money are most often associated with Keynes, similar motives feature in other theories of interest.

The transactions demand for money

Individuals need to hold money in order to meet daily transactions such as buying petrol, paying for groceries or purchasing a newspaper. Everyone will hold a certain amount of money since they are normally paid weekly or monthly whereas their expenditure is spread over the whole period. The average amount held for *transactions purposes* depends upon the level of money income, the price level and the frequency of pay days. In terms of *money income*, the higher the money income, the greater the average expenditure on goods and services over the time period, and therefore the higher the level of transactions balances required. If the *price level* increases, then it is also likely that the demand for money for transactions purposes will be higher, since more money will need to be held to purchase the now more expensive goods and services over the time period. In the case of the *frequency of pay days*, the less frequent the pay days over any given time period, the higher the transactions demand for money. A person receiving £700 in a weekly wage who spends all the money at an even rate over seven days, will hold an average of £400 per day (700 + 600 + 500 + 400 + 300 + 200 + 100 divided by 7). However, £2,800 received monthly in a four week month will, under the same assumption, result in holding an average of £1,600 per day.

More sophisticated treatments of the transactions demand for money suggest interest rates may also be influential. Higher interest rates mean that the opportunity cost of holding idle transactions balances rises (i.e. more interest payments forgone). This would suggest that the transactions demand for money will contract as interest rates rise and expand as interest rates fall.

The precautionary demand for money

The demand for money is also based on the desire to provide for the unexpected. The *precautionary demand* for money allows the individual to cover unforeseen events, such as the car breaking down, a lengthy period off work through illness, or an unexpected redundancy. The higher the income received per time period, the more costly any unforeseen event (e.g. loss of employment) is likely to be, and therefore the greater the precautionary demand for money to hold. Of course it is also likely to be the case that as the rate of interest rises, the precautionary demand for money will contract since the opportunity cost of 'holding' idle money has risen in terms of income forgone.

Figure 13.4 shows that a fall in interest rates will cause the transactions and precautionary demand (T + P) for money to expand, and vice versa. We have already noted that the *level of income* is directly related to the transaction and precautionary demands for money. A rise in income from Y_1 to Y_2 can be expected to *shift* the T + P curve to the right, with more money demanded for transactions and precautionary purposes at any given level of income.

Pause for thought 5

*What would you expect to happen to the T + P curve if: a) the price level falls,
b) payments to employees change from monthly to weekly?*

Box 13.1 presents a further motive for holding money which is particularly associated with the theory of Keynes. You can omit this if your course does not involve this particular approach to holding money.

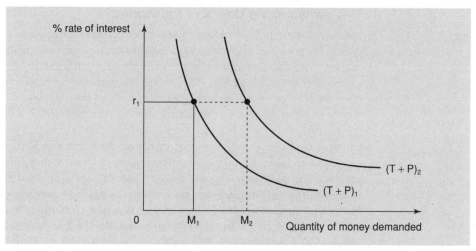

Figure 13.4 Transactions (T) and precautionary (P) demands for money are shown here as inversely related to the rate of interest, with T + P rising as the interest rate falls, and vice versa. At any given rate of interest (e.g. r_1) a rise in the level of income will shift the T + P curve to the right, raising the quantity of money demanded from M_1 to M_2.

Box 13.1

The speculative demand for money

The motive for holding money differs from the other two. The transactions and precautionary motives relate to the function of money as a medium of exchange, whereas the *speculative demand for money* is based on the expectation of making a speculative gain or avoiding a speculative loss. Keynes outlined the speculative demand for money in terms of the desire to hold either money or fixed income bonds, and in order to explain the speculative demand for money it is necessary to outline the relationship between the price of bonds and the rate of interest.

It is important to note that the *price of bonds* and the *rate of interest* are inversely related. For example, consider a bond with a nominal face value (i.e. stamped on the certificate) of £100 which yields £10 per year forever (a perpetual bond). If the price of the bond is £100 on the market then the effective rate of interest from holding the bond for one year is 10%. If the rate of interest were to rise to 20% then the market price of this nominal £100 bond would fall to £50, since £50 invested in an income earning asset at 20% would yield £10. We can say that if the interest rate rises then the price of such fixed return (perpetual) bonds falls, making bonds a less attractive proposition to investors than money. If, on the other hand, the rate of interest were to fall to 5%, then the market price of this nominal £100 bond would rise to £200, since £200 invested in an income-earning asset at 5% would yield £10. We can say that the price of such fixed return (perpetual) bonds rises, making them a more attractive proposition for an investor than money. It can thus be seen that there is an *inverse* relationship between the price of a fixed income bond and the rate of interest.

The speculative demand for money is influenced by what individuals *expect* to happen to the rate of interest, bearing in mind that investors will have different expectations of how the rate of interest, and hence bond prices, will move. Some investors will expect the rate of interest to rise, while others will expect it to fall. When the rate of interest is perceived to be unduly high by individuals, most will assume that the next move is in a downward direction. As already noted, when the rate of interest falls the price of bonds increases and so there are capital gains to be made. This being so, when the rate of interest is high there will be a substantial demand for bonds and hence a low speculative demand to hold money. If, however, the rate of interest is perceived to be unduly low then most individuals will assume that the next move is upwards, resulting in a fall in bond prices and, therefore, a capital loss for those who own bonds. If this is the case the demand for bonds is likely to be low and those owning bonds will be looking to sell them *before* the price falls. In this situation the speculative demand for money to hold will be high.

The speculative demand for money can be observed by studying Figure 13.5. At a rate of interest r_1 the speculative demand for money is SD_1, whereas at a rate of interest r_2 the speculative demand is SD_2. At a rate of interest r_3 the rate of interest can be viewed as being so low that everyone believes that it must rise. In other words, the price of bonds is perceived to be so high that it is expected that the only way they can move is in a downward direction, hence no one wants to hold bonds and everyone wants to hold cash, so the speculative demand for money is perfectly elastic. In other words, any extra money supplied will readily be absorbed (demanded) at this rate of interest. On the other hand, the rate of interest can be viewed as being so high, such as r_4, that everyone expects the rate of interest to fall, thus leading to an increase in the price of bonds and, therefore, to a capital gain. As a result no one wants to hold money and everyone wants to hold bonds, hence the speculative demand for money is zero.

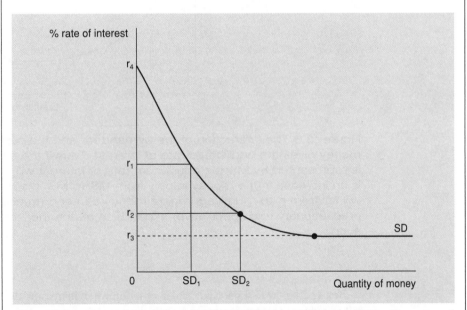

Figure 13.5 The speculative demand (SD) for money. A fall in the rate of interest from r_1 to r_2 leads to an expansion in the speculative demand for money. At a low rate of interest, r_3, the speculative demand for money is perfectly elastic. At a high rate of interest, r_4, the speculative demand for money is zero.

The determination of the rate of interest

It is assumed that the money supply is determined by the monetary authorities and is taken to be fixed for the purposes of analysing the determination of the rate of interest. This being so, the interaction of the demand for money and the supply of money will give the equilibrium rate of interest. This can be seen in Figure 13.6, where the money demand curve MD_1 and the money supply curve MS_1 intersect to give the equilibrium rate of interest r_1. If the money supply were to increase to MS_2 then the equilibrium rate of interest would fall to r_2. The reason for this is that if the money supply were to increase at the initial equilibrium rate of interest r_1 from MS_1 to MS_2, there would be an excess supply of money. Individuals would respond (at least some would) by demanding more bonds, which would bid up their price. As stated earlier, a rise in the price of bonds has the effect of bringing down the rate of interest and as this occurs the transaction, precautionary, and speculative demands for money would expand until the new equilibrium rate of interest r_2 is reached.

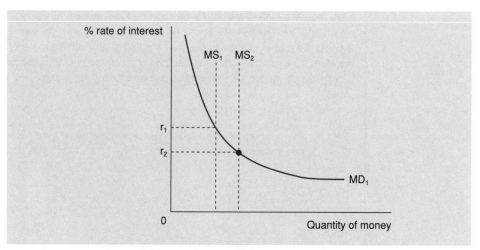

Figure 13.6 The interaction of the demand for and the supply of money gives the equilibrium rate of interest. Thus if the money supply is represented by MS_1 the equilibrium rate of interest will be r_1. If there is an increase in the money supply from MS_1 to MS_2 the rate of interest will fall from r_1 to r_2 until aggregate money demand (transactions and precautionary and speculative) expands to match the increased money supply.

Box 13.2 below looks at a particular situation when increasing the money supply might fail to reduce the rate of interest. This analysis is closely associated with Keynes' theory of interest and relates closely to Box 13.1 above. If you omitted Box 13.1, then omit Box 13.2 as well.

Box 13.2	The liquidity trap

Liquidity trap
The suggestion that interest rates are so low that everyone expects them to rise (and therefore the market price of bonds to fall), so that no one wants to hold bonds and everyone wants to hold money.

The **liquidity trap** occurs when an increase in the money supply – such as that shown in Figure 13.7 by a movement from MS_1 to MS_2 – has no effect on the rate of interest. The reason for this is that at a very low rate of interest, such as r*, everyone expects the rate to rise and, therefore, the bond price to fall causing a capital loss. In this situation no one wants to hold bonds (seen here as the alternative to money) so that an increase in the money supply is simply absorbed into speculative demand for money (into what are called *idle balances*) and the rate of interest is unchanged. This rate of interest r* at which the demand for money is perfectly *elastic*, is known as the *liquidity trap.*

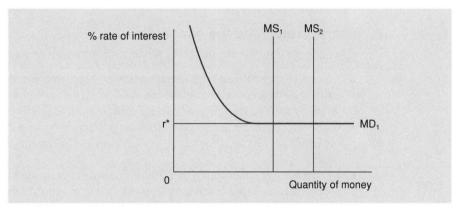

Figure 13.7 An increase in the money supply from MS_1 to MS_2 has no effect on the rate of interest which remains constant at r*. This is referred to as the liquidity trap.

8 MONETARY POLICY

8.1 Controlling the money supply

The ways in which the Bank of England, operating on behalf of the government, can influence the money supply have been considered earlier (page 314). When the government wishes to stimulate the economy, it is likely to seek to *increase* the money supply and when it wishes to dampen down the economy, it is likely to seek to *reduce* the money supply.

● Deciding on the value of notes and coins to be issued through the Bank of England and by the Royal Mint.
● Making available more liquid assets in the financial system (e.g. Treasury Bills). For example, the Bank of England might be instructed to buy securities in the 'open market' with cheques drawn on the government. This will increase cash and liquidity for the financial institutions and individuals selling their bonds and bills.

Today, less emphasis is placed on controlling the money supply than was the case in the past. Instead, rather more attention is now given to controlling the demand for money using interest rates.

8.2 Rate of interest

Since 1997 the Bank of England has been given independence by the government and is now responsible for setting the interest rate each month. This is done at a monthly meeting of the nine members of the *Monetary Policy Committee* (MPC) at the Bank of England. The MPC takes into account the 'inflation target' the government has set and projections for future inflation when deciding upon the rate of interest.

There are, in fact, many rates of interest charged by different lenders. For example, a loan for a longer period of time will tend to carry a higher rate of interest, as might a loan to smaller companies or to individuals considered to be 'higher risk' by the lender. However, all these rates of interest tend to move upwards or downwards in line with the monthly rate of interest set by the Bank of England.

Interest rates and the economy

Changing the interest rate affects the economy in a number of ways.

- *Savings* Higher interest rates encourage saving, since the reward for saving and thereby postponing current consumption has now increased. Lower interest rates discourage saving by making spending for current consumption relatively more attractive.
- *Borrowing* Higher interest rates discourage borrowing as it has now become more expensive, whilst lower interest rates encourage borrowing as it has now become cheaper.
- *Discretionary expenditure* Higher interest rates discourage such expenditure. For many people their mortgage is the most important item of expenditure. To avoid losing their home, people must keep up with the mortgage repayments. Most people are on variable rate mortgages, so that if interest rates rise they must pay back more per month, leaving less income to spend on other things. Similarly, if interest rates fall, there will be increased income left in the family budget to spend on other things.
- *Exchange rate* Higher interest rates in the UK tend to make holding sterling deposits in the UK more attractive and an increased demand for sterling is likely to raise the exchange rate for sterling (*see* Chapter 14). Raising the exchange rate will make exports more expensive abroad and imports cheaper in the UK. Lowering interest rates will have the opposite effect, reducing the exchange rate for sterling, thereby making exports cheaper abroad and imports dearer in the UK.

---

9 MONETARY POLICY AND FINANCIAL GLOBALISATION

Financial globalisation
The increased geographical mobility of international financial capital.

The dramatic increase in cross-border financial transactions over the past 20 years has placed increasing strain on the conduct of monetary policy by national governments (OECD, 2005). If the international financial markets regard a domestic government as conducting an 'imprudent' monetary policy, such as excessive growth in the money supply or unduly low interest rates, then this increasing tendency towards **financial globalisation** can result in substantial movements of funds out of the financial centres of that country. This outward flow of financial capital may well reduce the domestic money supply and force higher domestic interest rates to help retain the confidence of foreign investors.

Tytell and Wei (2004) in their survey of 62 developed and developing countries found that such increased financial globalisation did indeed exert a disciplinary effect on the conduct of domestic monetary policy. They found a significant correlation between their measure of financial globalisation (the ratio of gross foreign assets and liabilities to GDP) and the conduct of monetary policy, with a rise in financial globalisation correlated with more restrictive domestic monetary policies. Rogoff (2003) found that a rise in financial globalisation was indeed correlated with more restrictive monetary policies, as evidenced by progressively lower levels of inflation worldwide.

There is also evidence (OECD, 2005) to suggest that changes in domestic interest rates now have a greater impact on a country's exchange rate (*see* Chapter 14) than previously. Global financial flows appear to be more sensitive to *interest rate differentials* than in the past, with a rise in domestic interest rates now likely to cause a more substantial increase in demand for that currency and sharper rise in the exchange rate than previously. Conversely, a fall in domestic interest rates is now likely to cause a more substantial decrease in demand for that currency and sharper fall in the exchange rate than previously. In other words, under the influence of globalisation, changes in interest rates now have a more substantial impact on exchange rates, increasing the importance of the interest rates as the 'transmission mechanism' by which monetary policy influences the domestic economy.

KEY POINTS

- Money functions as a unit of account, a medium of exchange, a store of value and a standard of deferred payments.

- Money avoids the inefficiency of a barter system, permitting greater specialisation and associated scale economies.

- As well as cash, there are a range of 'near money' assets of varying degrees of liquidity.

- M0 is the official definition of money which most closely corresponds to the idea of a 'cash base'.

- Deposits at financial institutions are the most important component of broad money.

- Definitions of money are constantly evolving because of financial deregulations and innovation.

- Monetary policy involves influencing the money supply and/or the rate of interest.

- Since 1992 the Bank of England has adopted an inflation target as the nominal anchor for monetary policy.

- The Bank of England was granted operational independence on 6 May 1997 and its Monetary Policy Committee now sets interest rates each month.

- Interest rate theories see interest rates as the 'equilibrium price' which results from both the demand for holding money and the supply of money.

- In most theories of interest rate, the demand for money to hold is seen as sensitive to changes in the interest rate, rising as interest rates fall, and vice versa.

- Financial globalisation has given the interest rate greater impact in economic policy terms since the exchange rate is now more sensitive to changes in interest rate differentials.

Further reading

Griffiths, A. and Wall, S. (2006) *Applied Economics*, 11th edition, FT/Prentice Hall, Chapters 20 and 21.

Griffiths, A. and Wall, S. (2005) *Economics for Business and Management*, FT/Prentice Hall, Chapter 10.

Heather, K. (2004) *Economics Theory in Action*, 4th edition, FT/Prentice Hall, Chapters 14 and 18.

Parkin, M., Powell, M. and Matthews, K. (2005) *Economics*, 6th edition, FT/Prentice Hall, Chapters 25–7.

Sloman, J. (2006) *Economics*, 6th edition, FT/Prentice Hall, Chapters 18 and 20.

Web references

National Statistics: **http://www.statistics.gov.uk/** The official UK statistics site.
HM Treasury: **http://www.hm-treasury.gov.uk/** A main source for UK financial data.
Institute for Fiscal Studies: **http://www.ifs.org.uk** The IFS is a useful source of information on various aspects of money and EMU.

You can find current data and information on many aspects of financial institutions and markets from the following websites.

Bank of England: **http://www.bankofengland.co.uk/**
Bank of England Monetary and Financial Statistics: **http://www.bankofengland.co.uk/mfsd/**
Banque de France: **http://www.banque-france.fr/home.htm**
Bundesbank (German central bank): **http://www.bundesbank.de/index.en.php?print=no&**
Central Bank of Ireland: **http://www.centralbank.ie/**
European Central Bank: **http://www.ecb.int/home/html/index.en.html**
Eurostat: **http://www.europa.eu.int/index_en.htm**
US Federal Reserve Bank: **http://www.federalreserve.gov/**
Netherlands Central Bank: **http://www.dnb.nl/dnb/homepage.jsp**
Bank of Japan: **http://www.boj.or.jp/en/index.htm**
Reserve Bank of Australia: **http://www.rba.gov.au**
Bank Negara Malaysia (English): **http://www.bnm.gov.my/**
Monetary Authority of Singapore: **http://www.mas.gov.sg/masmcm/bin/pt1Home.htm**
National Bank of Canada: **http://www.bankofcanada.ca/en/**
National Bank of Denmark (English): **http://www.nationalbanken.dk/dnuk/specialdocuments.nsf**
Reserve Bank of India: **http://www.rbi.org.in/home.aspx**
About.com link to central banks: **http://economics.about.com/?once=true&**

Economic models and simulation

Economic modelling is an important aspect of economic analysis. There are a number of sites that offer access to a model for you to use, which can be a useful way of finding out how economic theory works within an environment that claims to reflect reality. In this case variations in variables such as the money supply and rate of interest can be assessed as to how they influence the economy.

Virtual economy: **http://bized.ac.uk/virtual.economy**
WinEcon: **http://www.webecon.bris.ac.uk/winecon/**
National Institute of Economic and Social Research: **http://www.niesr.ac.uk/**

References

Rogoff, K. (2003) 'Globalisation and global disinflation', paper presented to the Federal Reserve Bank of Kanses City, Wyonming, August.
Tytell, I. and Wei, S. (2004) 'Does Financial Globalisation Induce Better Macroeconomic Policies?', paper presented to the fifth Annual IMF Conference, Washington DC, 4 November.
Webb, R. (2006) 'Financial Institutions and Markets' in A. Griffiths and S. Wall, *Applied Economics*, FT/Prentice Hall.

PROGRESS AND REVIEW QUESTIONS

Answers to most questions can be found at the back of the book (pages 518–19). Answers to asterisked questions can be found on the students' side of the Companion Website.

Multiple-choice questions

1   Which *one* of the following is NOT a function of money?

   a) Unit of account
   b) Medium of exchange
   c) Store of value
   d) Means of barter
   e) Standard of deferred payment

2   Which one of the following is an example of using money as a store of value?

   a) Betting £10 that you will pass an exam
   b) Paying cash for a new car
   c) Paying your rent with a cheque
   d) Keeping £200 on hand for an emergency
   e) Paying for a new dress with a credit card

3   A customer deposits £500 in a bank. According to the 'credit multiplier' theory, if all banks have a reserve ratio of 20% then the amount of new deposits eventually created is:

   a) £250
   b) £1,600
   c) £2,500
   d) £1,500
   e) £400

4 If the Central Bank carries out an open market operation and sells government securities, it is likely that the interest rate:

 a) falls and the quantity of money decreases
 b) may rise or fall depending upon the state of the economy
 c) rises and the quantity of money increases
 d) falls and the quantity of money increases
 e) rises and the quantity of money decreases.

5 Which *two* of the following are still published in the UK as measures of the stock of money?

 a) M0
 b) M1
 c) M2
 d) M3
 e) M4

6 Which *one* of the following most accurately represents the function where money is generally acceptable in ways that help us avoid a barter economy?

 a) Unit of account
 b) Medium of exchange
 c) Store of value
 d) Standard of deferred payment
 e) Double-coincidence of wants

7 Which *one* of the following represents the function where money allows a comparison to be made between the value of different goods and services

 a) Unit of account
 b) Medium of exchange
 c) Store of value
 d) Standard of deferred payment
 e) Double-coincidence of wants

8 The suggestion that holdings of money depend in part on the value of expenditures undertaken by households in any given time period is called:

 a) precautionary demand for money
 b) quantity theory of money
 c) transactions demand for money
 d) money supply multiplier
 e) open market operations

9 The suggestion that holdings of money depends on providing for possible unexpected events is called:

 a) precautionary demand for money
 b) quantity theory of money
 c) transactions demand for money
 d) money supply multiplier
 e) open market operations

10 Which of the following terms is used to refer to purchases or sales of government bills and bonds?

a) Precautionary demand for money
b) Quantity theory of money
c) Transactions demand for money
d) Money supply multiplier
e) Open market operations

True/false questions

1 The number of exchange possibilities that exist in a money economy exceeds the number in a barter economy.

2 An increase in the length of time for which money is held will reduce the velocity at which money circulates in the economy.

3 The Keynesian 'speculative demand for money' suggests that a fall in the rate of interest will cause investors to switch from holding assets such as bonds to holding cash, thereby increasing the demand for money.

4 M0 is the most widely used measure of 'broad' money.

5 Monetary policy can involve changes in the money supply and/or the rate of interest.

6 The demand for money is directly related to changes in the interest rate.

7 Financial globalisation refers to the increased geographical mobility of financial and capital flows.

8 The interest rate is now a less important element in monetary policy as a result of financial globalisation.

Case study question: High risk credit cards!

Britain's credit card companies will come under pressure to target customers on lower incomes as the traditional card market reaches saturation, according to a 2005 survey by PricewaterhouseCoopers (PwC).

The accountancy firm predicts that card companies will begin to aim their products at consumers on low incomes or social benefits and those with poor credit histories in an attempt to maintain the high level of growth in card issuance. The prediction comes as consumer groups are becoming increasingly concerned at the spiralling level of indebtedness in the UK.

A 2004 survey conducted by MORI found that 1 million credit card holders are in 'a potentially dangerous credit situation'. In 2004 borrowers racked up £50 million of arrears on their cards. PwC estimates that the average balance owed by borrowers on credit cards in 2004 ranged from £575 for HSBC customers to nearly £1,500 for Capital One customers.

Encouraging people on low incomes to borrow more on credit cards could also exacerbate already serious levels of indebtedness. The PwC report says, 'The issuing of credit cards to higher risk customers is not well developed in the UK markets and it is likely that there is a relatively low penetration rate of the non-prime adult population.' The report adds, 'PwC expects the non-prime market to be one of the future sources of growth available to lenders.' According to PwC, 8 million consumers in the UK can be considered in this category.

Already banks such as HSBC are considering expanding in the non-prime market. HSBC, Britain's biggest bank by market capitalisation, in 2004 completed the purchase of Household International, the American consumer loan company that aims credit products at the non-prime market in the US.

Question

Examine the possible implications of extending credit card usage to the 'non-prime' market.

Essay questions

Answers to asterisked questions can be found on the students' side of the Companion Website. All other answers can be found at the back of the book (pages 518–19).

1* What do you regard as the main functions of money? Assess the relative importance of these functions.

2 Briefly review the main features of the UK financial system. Explain the importance of this system to the efficient working of the UK economy.

3* How might the Bank of England seek to reduce the liquidity within the UK economy?

4 Consider the factors that might result in a higher interest rate for the economy.

Exchange rates and the balance of payments

Learning objectives

By the end of this chapter you should be able to:

- Understand how exchange rates are determined on the foreign exchange market.

- Examine the different types of exchange rate.

- Define the terms of trade, identify patterns and trends in the terms of trade for the UK economy and discuss various policy implications.

- Examine the role of exchange rates and elasticity conditions in influencing the value of international trade flows.

- Review the impact of changes in the exchange rate on different price indices over time.

- Explain why the short-run impacts of a fall in the exchange rate might be adverse ('J-curve effect') and why expenditure reducing policy instruments may also be required.

- Assess the case for and against adopting a single currency, such as the euro.

- Outline the key components of the balance of payments and evaluate the impacts of high oil prices on both the balance of payments and the economy as a whole.

1 INTRODUCTION

The previous two chapters have examined fiscal and monetary policy respectively, noting their impacts on the level of economic activity. This chapter gives more detailed attention to the impacts of exchange rate policy on the domestic economy. Chapter 11 touched on many of these issues, as for example the contribution of exports and imports in determining the level of national income. Here we go further by reviewing the impacts of changes in the exchange rate on the price of exports in the overseas markets and the price of imports in the domestic market.

We notice the importance of price elasticity of demand and other elasticities (*see* Chapter 3) in determining how consumers respond to such price changes in both overseas and domestic markets. The case for and against sterling becoming a member of the eurozone, with the euro as the single currency, is then reviewed. We also note the diffusion path which different price indices follow after a change in the exchange rate. This delayed impact of exchange rate changes on various prices, together with the 'adjustment lag' of households and businesses in responding to such price changes, may help explain the so-called 'J-curve effect'. This is the observation that the initial impact of a fall (depreciation) in the exchange rate may be to worsen, rather than improve, any balance of payments deficit. Attention is also drawn to the fact that the exchange rate is an 'expenditure switching' policy instrument, changing the relative prices of exports and imports and inducing households and businesses to change their patterns of consumption. However, for a fall in the exchange rate to improve the balance of payments it may need to be accompanied by 'expenditure reducing' policy instruments, such as reducing the budget deficits of governments. This may be needed in order to create spare productive capacity for increased volumes of exports and import substitutes to take advantage of the lower price of exports overseas and higher price of imports at home.

The different types of exchange rate system are reviewed including fixed (gold standard), adjustable peg (IMF) and floating exchange rate systems. This provides a useful background for discussing the advantages and disadvantages of joining the single currency, here the euro. The measurement of the *values* of exports, imports and other international trade flows is also considered in some detail, using the UK balance of payments accounts by way of illustration and paying particular attention to the oil market.

2   EXCHANGE RATE

This can be quoted as the number of units of the *foreign currency* that is needed to purchase one unit of the domestic currency: e.g. £1 = €1.50. Alternatively, it can be quoted as the number of units of the *domestic currency* needed to purchase one unit of the foreign currency: e.g. €1 = £0.666.

The exchange rate is a key 'price' affecting the competitiveness of UK exporters and UK producers of import substitutes.

Depreciation
A fall in the exchange rate of one currency against another. Often used in the context of floating exchange rates.

- *A fall (**depreciation**) in the sterling exchange rate* makes UK exports cheaper abroad (in the foreign currency) and imports into the UK dearer at home (in £ sterling).
- *A rise (**appreciation**) in the sterling exchange rate* makes UK exports dearer abroad (in the foreign currency) and imports into the UK cheaper at home (in £ sterling).

We can illustrate the latter using the £:$ exchange rate. In recent times sterling has risen (appreciated) significantly in value against the US dollar.

Appreciation
A rise in the exchange rate of one currency against another. Often used in the context of floating exchange rates.

Example: £1 = $1.50 (2002)
£1 = $1.85 (March, 2005)

As a result a £100 export from the UK costing $150 in the US in 2002 costs $185 in 2005. Similarly, an import from the US costing $150 would sell for £100 in the UK in 2002 but £81.08 in 2005.

The change in value of UK exports and UK imports after a change in the exchange rate will depend crucially on the *price elasticity of demand* (PED) for both exports and for imports (*see* Chapter 3). The more elastic the demand for exports and for imports, the greater the impact on the balance of payments of any change in the exchange rate, and vice versa. We return to this issue of elasticity of demand for exports and imports in Section 4 below.

2.1 Determination of exchange rates

Floating exchange rate system
Where demand for and supply of a currency determines its exchange rates against other currencies.

Most exchange rates are determined by the demand for and the supply of that currency on world foreign exchange markets. This system is often called a *floating exchange rate system* since changes in world demand/supply for the currency cause the exchange rate to 'float' upwards or downwards, second by second.

Figure 14.1 shows how the *demand* for the pound sterling and the *supply* of the pound sterling will determine its equilibrium exchange rate, in this case against the US dollar.

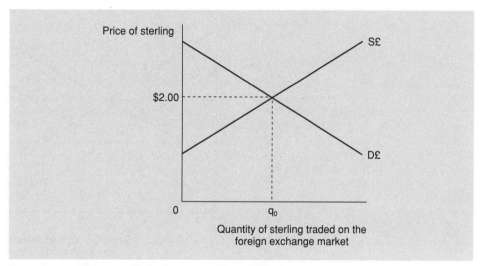

Figure 14.1 The equilibrium exchange rate.

We can see from Figure 14.1 that only at an exchange rate of £1 = $2.00 is there balance or equilibrium.

- At an exchange rate *above* the equilibrium, there will be *excess supply* of £s, so its 'price' will fall.
- At an exchange rate *below* the equilibrium, there will be an *excess demand* of £s, so its 'price' will rise.

We should note that exports of goods or services from the UK, or capital inflows into the UK, will cause a *demand* for sterling. In other words, flows of goods, services or financial capital which have a *positive* sign in the balance of payments correspond to a demand for sterling.

 Pause for thought 1

Can you explain why exports of goods and services from the UK and capital inflows into the UK cause (at least potentially) a demand for sterling?

Similarly, imports of goods or services into the UK, or capital outflows from the UK, will cause a *supply* of sterling. In other words, flows of goods, services or financial capital which have a *negative* sign in the balance of payments correspond to a supply of sterling.

Pause for thought 2

Can you explain why imports of goods and services from the UK and capital inflows into the UK cause (at least potentially) a supply of sterling?

Figure 14.2 shows possible shifts in the demand curve for sterling or supply curves of sterling and their impacts on the equilibrium exchange rate for sterling.

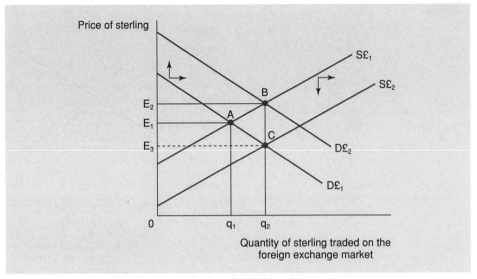

Figure 14.2 If the original equilibrium is point A then, other things equal, an increase in a demand for sterling will raise the exchange rate from E_1 to E_2. However, if, starting at point A, there was an increase in supply of sterling then the exchange rate would fall to E_3.

For example, suppose we start at an initial equilibrium at point A. If UK exports and capital inflows (+ signs) now rise in value then, other things equal, the demand for £ sterling increases, shifting from $D£_1$ to $D£_2$, raising the sterling exchange rate from E_1 to E_2.

Returning back to our initial equilibrium point A, suppose that UK imports and capital outflows (− signs) now rise in value, other things equal. This time the supply of sterling increases, shifting from $S£_1$ to $S£_2$, lowering the sterling exchange rate from E_1 to E_3.

● Rise in exports and/or capital inflows increases the demand for sterling and, other things equal, raises the sterling exchange rate.
● Rise in imports and/or capital outflows increases the supply of sterling and, other things equal, lowers the sterling exchange rate.

2.2 Types of exchange rate

● *Nominal exchange rate* This is the rate at which one currency is quoted against any other currency. The nominal exchange rate is therefore a *bilateral* (two country) exchange rate.
● *Effective exchange rate* (EER) This is a measure which takes into account the fact that sterling varies in value by different amounts against other currencies. It is calculated as

a *weighted average* of the bilateral rates against all other currencies and is expressed as an index number relative to the base year. The EER is therefore a *multilateral* (many country) exchange rate, expressed as an index number.

- *Real exchange rate* (RER) is designed to measure the rate at which home products exchange for products from other countries, rather than the rate at which the currencies themselves are traded. It is thus a measure of competitiveness. When we consider *multilateral* UK trade, it is defined as:

$$RER = EER \times P(UK)/P(F)$$

In other words, the real exchange rate for the UK (RER) is equal to the effective exchange rate (EER) multiplied by the ratio of home price, P(UK), to foreign price, P(F), of products.

- If UK prices rise relative to foreign prices, the real exchange rate (RER) will rise unless the sterling effective exchange rate (EER) falls sufficiently to offset this impact.
- Similarly, if the sterling effective exchange rate (EER) rises, the real exchange rate will rise unless UK prices fall sufficiently relative to foreign prices.

Table 14.1 outlines the nominal rate of exchange for sterling against other currencies and the overall sterling effective exchange rate (EER) against a 'basket' of other currencies.

Notice the rapid *appreciation* in the nominal exchange rate of sterling against the US dollar since 2002 (i.e. the US dollar has *depreciated* significantly against sterling). However, sterling has *depreciated* in value against the euro in the last few years.

Pause for thought 3

How are the changes in the sterling exchange rate over the last few years shown in Table 14.1 likely to affect the UK balance of payments?

Table 14.1 Sterling nominal exchange rates: 1990–2004

	US dollar	French franc	Japanese yen	German mark	Sterling effective exchange rate (1990=100)	Euro
1990	1.79	9.69	257	2.88	100.0	
1991	1.77	9.95	238	2.93	100.7	
1992	1.76	9.33	224	2.76	96.9	
1993	1.50	8.50	167	2.48	88.9	
1994	1.53	8.48	156	2.48	89.2	
1995	1.58	7.87	148	2.26	84.8	
1996	1.56	7.98	170	2.35	86.3	1.21
1997	1.64	9.56	198	2.84	100.6	1.45
1998	1.66	9.77	217	2.97	105.3	1.49
1999	1.62	–	240	–	103.8	1.52
2000	1.50	–	264	–	105.6	1.60
2001	1.44	–	175	–	105.8	1.61
2002	1.50	–	188	–	106.0	1.59
2003	1.69	–	189	–	102.4	1.40
2004	1.85		190		103.2	1.44

The impact of exchange rate changes are considered in many chapters of this book since they clearly have an important impact on the competitiveness of exports in foreign markets and of imports in domestic markets.

Mini Case Study 14.1

China revalues the yuan

For many years China has locked its currency, the yuan, to the US dollar. As a result, as the dollar has fallen in recent years, so too has the yuan, giving China an even greater competitive advantage in its international trading relationships. In the US, many politicians blame China for the large and growing US deficit in trade with China, rising from $40 billion in 1995 to almost $200 billion in 2005.

In July 2005 China made a small concession to this pressure, allowing the yuan to rise in value from its pegged value of 8.28 yuan to the US dollar, a revaluation of 2.1%. The People's Bank of China said that this was to 'bring imports and exports into balance'. However, few believe that such a small change in the exchange rate will have much effect, though it is regarded as a step in the right direction.

To maintain any pegged value the economic authorities in China must intervene on the foreign exchange markets. For China, to keep the yuan down to even the new rate of 8.11 yuan to the US dollar, this means China must buy large amounts of US dollars with its own currency otherwise the yuan would rise against the US dollar on the foreign exchange market.

Questions

1 *Why might a revaluation of the yuan be in the interests of the US?*

2 *Explain why the yuan would rise against the US dollar if China did not intervene on the foreign exchange market.*

Answers to questions can be found on the students' side of the Companion Website.

3 | THE TERMS OF TRADE

The terms of trade are calculated by taking a weighted average of export prices and dividing by a weighted average of import prices, both expressed as an index number:

Terms of trade index
Ratio of export prices to import prices, with some specific year as the base (100).

$$\text{Terms of trade index} = \frac{\text{Index of export prices}}{\text{Index of import prices}} \times \frac{100}{1}$$

The concept of index numbers is outlined in Chapter 15. In relation to the terms of trade, the index number incorporates weights which are attached to each good and service based on their relative importance in total exports and total imports respectively. The terms of trade for the period 1998–2003 can be seen in Table 14.2.

The base year is 2001 where the indexed price of exports and imports are made equal to 100, thus giving a terms of trade of 100. In 2003 the UK terms of trade was 105.6 which was obtained by dividing 101.1 by 95.7 multiplied by 100.

Table 14.2 The UK terms of trade (2001=100)

Year	Index of export prices	Index of import prices	Terms of trade
1998	106.9	100.3	106.6
1999	103.0	98.9	104.1
2000	101.0	100.5	100.5
2001	100.0	100.0	100.0
2002	99.9	96.9	103.1
2003	101.1	95.7	105.6

Source: Adapted from *UK Balance of Payments: The Pink Book*, ONS (2004)

Between 2001 and 2003 there was thus a *rise* in the terms of trade index of 5.6 points, with the indexed price of exports rising relative to the indexed price of imports. Between 1998 and 2001 the indexed price of exports fell relative to the indexed price of imports, thus the terms of trade index *fell*. (Notice that between 2001 and 2003 *both* export and import price indices fell, but that for imports fell faster.) A rise in the terms of trade is called a *favourable movement* whereas a fall is called an *unfavourable* movement.

Pause for thought 4

Can you think of situations where a rise in the terms of trade might not in fact be 'favourable' to a country?

Care must be taken when interpreting the terms of trade. A 'favourable' movement does not necessarily imply a value of over 100, but simply an improvement on the previous year's value. Again, although a rise in the relative price of exports in relation to imports means that more imports can be obtained per unit of exports, this may still have a detrimental effect on the trade in goods and services. For example, the rise in export prices may be due to higher costs of domestic production, implying a loss in global competitiveness, rather than an increase in demand for the exported products. Such a cost-based rise in the relative price of exports may then, if export demand is relatively elastic, lead to a reduction in the total value of export sales. Similarly, a fall in import prices might, if import demand is relatively elastic, lead to a rise in the total value of imports. A rise in the indexed price of exports relative to the indexed price of imports might not, in these circumstances, be of benefit to the country.

4   THE MARSHALL–LERNER ELASTICITY CONDITION

As we note in more detail in Section 8, the balance of payments involves exports of goods and services and various inward flows of capital and finance, all of which are given a positive sign in the balance of payments accounts. On the other hand, imports of goods and services and various outward flows of capital and finance are given a negative sign in the balance of payments accounts. We have seen that a depreciation in the exchange rate will tend to make a country's exports cheaper abroad and imports dearer at home. However, whether or not the balance of payments is likely to improve from this fall in the exchange rate depends to a significant extent on the price elasticity of demand for exports and for imports.

Marshall–Lerner elasticity condition
Elasticity condition which must be satisfied if a depreciation (fall) in the exchange rate is to improve the balance of payments. Namely that the price elasticity of demand for exports + the price elasticity of demand for imports > 1.

The *Marshall–Lerner* **elasticity condition** relating to the depreciation of a particular currency states that an improvement in an economy's balance of payments following a fall in the exchange rate will only occur if the *sum* of the price elasticity of demand for its exports and the price elasticity of demand for its imports is greater than unity. This can be outlined by reference to Figure 14.3 where, following a depreciation of the pound, the price of imports increases and the price of exports decreases.

In Figure 14.3(a) a depreciation of the pound has resulted in a rise in the sterling price of imports from P_1 to P_2 and reduced their demand from M_1 to M_2. This leads to an increase in sterling expenditure on imports of area A but a reduction in sterling expenditure on imports of area B. There will be an overall reduction in expenditure on imports of B − A if the demand for imports is elastic. In Figure 14.3(b) the depreciation of the pound has resulted in a reduction in the foreign price of exports from P_3 to P_4 and an expansion in the demand for exports from X_1 to X_2. This will lead to a reduction in expenditure by foreigners on UK exports by area C, but at the same time there will be a rise in expenditure by foreigners on UK exports of area D. There will be an overall increase in expenditure by foreigners on UK exports of D − C if the demand for exports is elastic.

In terms of the balance of payments, the effect will have been an improvement of (B − A) + (D − C), which will be greater the higher the respective elasticities of demand for imports and exports. However, it can be shown that the cut-off value for these respective elasticities is where the *sum of their values equals 1*. In this situation a fall (depreciation) in the exchange rate will leave the balance of payments unchanged. However, if the sum of these respective elasticities is *less than 1*, then a fall (depreciation) in the exchange rate will cause the balance of payments to worsen. Only if the sum of these elasticities is greater than 1 and the Marshall–Lerner condition is fulfilled, will a depreciation (eventually) improve the balance of payments.

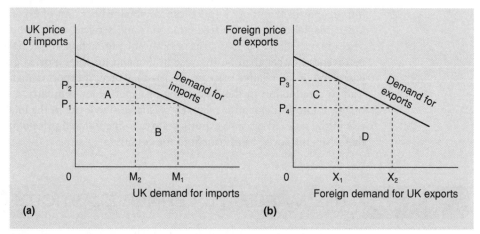

Figure 14.3 The figures relate to the depreciation of the £ sterling and the effect it has on the demand for imports and exports. It illustrates that there will be a more substantial improvement in the balance of payments following depreciation of the £ sterling the greater the sum of the price elasticity of demand for imports and the price elasticity of demand for exports.

5   THE J-CURVE

J-curve
Since short-run
elasticities of
demand for exports
and imports are
lower than longer-
run elasticities, often
takes 18 months or
more before a fall in
the exchange rate
improves the
balance of
payments.

This refers to the fact that even if the Marshall–Lerner elasticity condition is fulfilled, it may take some time for the change in exchange rate to influence the balance of payments. In particular it may take time for a fall (depreciation) in the exchange rate to improve the balance of payments. This time lag has been estimated at around two years in the UK.

In Figure 14.4 the economy is initially assumed to be at point A, experiencing a current account deficit (*see* page 347).

In response to the current account deficit, the economy's currency may depreciate. Initially this will cause the deficit to worsen, noted by a movement to point B in Figure 14.4. The reason for this is that it takes time for the economy to adjust to the change in the external value of its currency. At least two reasons may be involved in such a time lag: the fact that various prices take time to respond to the fall in the exchange rate and that households and businesses take time to adjust their expenditure patterns to these (eventual) changes in price.

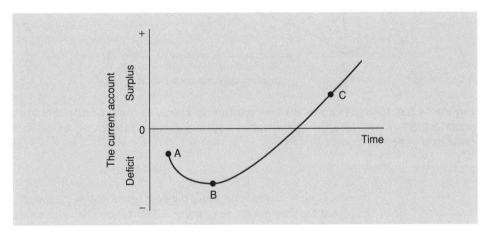

Figure 14.4 A depreciation of the currency occurs at a time when the economy is at point A. Initially the trade deficit will worsen, illustrated by a movement to point B. After a period of time, however, the trade deficit will reduce and a situation such as point C could be obtained. Hence the J-curve.

5.1   Diffusion path for price changes following a currency depreciation

Sterling depreciation will raise the cost, expressed in sterling, of imported items. However, both the magnitude and the speed of price rise will vary with the type of import. This can be illustrated by reference to a short-term forecasting model that has been used by the Bank of England. As we can see from Figure 14.5 the full effect of the sterling depreciation on import prices for consumers (curve A) will only be felt after more than two years. Imported fuel and industrial material prices (curves F and G) will, with less elastic demands, respond most substantially and most rapidly to the depreciation. This is in part

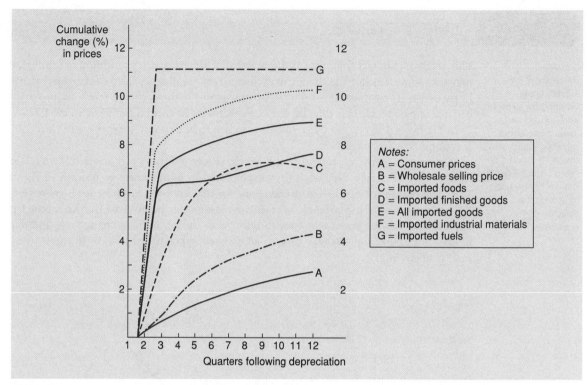

Figure 14.5 A 10% fall in the sterling exchange rate will raise overall consumer prices (A) by around 2.5%, i.e. a quarter of the fall in exchange rate. However, this overall effect may take over two years to occur.

because the less elastic is demand, the easier it is to pass on cost increases to consumers. Imported finished goods' prices (curve D) rise by a smaller amount, and less quickly, because some of these goods face extensive competition on home markets, i.e. face more elastic demand curves. Imported food prices will tend to be less affected, at least initially, because of the operation of the Common Agricultural Policy (*see* Chapter 17).

The final effect on consumer prices following a hypothetical 10% depreciation in Figure 14.5 can be seen to be about 2.5% for overall consumer prices (curve A), i.e. about one-quarter of the sterling depreciation, and then only after more than two years.

For any depreciation, the final effect on consumer prices will depend on a number of factors:

1 The import content of production
2 The extent to which cost increases can be passed on to consumers, i.e. price elasticity of demand
3 The import content of consumption
4 The sensitivity of wage demands to cost-of-living increases.

Figure 14.5 is drawn on the assumption of no wage response, i.e. that (4) above is zero. Any such response would increase wholesale and consumer prices still further.

Whereas a fall in the sterling exchange rate (depreciation) will increase inflation, a rise in the exchange rate (appreciation) will reduce it. There is, of course, another side to the picture. A high sterling exchange rate, although helping the fight against inflation, may adversely affect output and employment. UK producers may now find it more difficult to sell their goods and services: first, because competition from cheaper imports drives them out of home markets and, secondly, because UK exports become expensive on foreign markets.

5.2 Time lag in adjustment of consumer behaviour to price changes

It will also take time for domestic households and businesses to adjust their consumption patterns and switch to cheaper domestically produced substitutes for the now more expensive imported products. Similarly, overseas households and businesses may take time to adjust their consumption patterns to the now cheaper exported products sold in the overseas markets. After a period of time, however, the current account will begin to improve, eventually moving into a situation of surplus such as point C in Figure 14.4.

Pause for thought 5

If the fall in the exchange rate does improve the balance of payments, can you use a) the 45° diagram, and b) the W/J diagram of Chapter 11 to consider the likely impacts on national income?

6 EXPENDITURE SWITCHING V EXPENDITURE REDUCING POLICY INSTRUMENTS

A further possible explanation of the J-curve effect may be found in the need for domestic businesses to expand their *output* to produce substitutes for the now more expensive imported products and to produce more of the now cheaper exported products. To explain this it may be useful to make a distinction between 'expenditure switching' and 'expenditure reducing' policy instruments for correcting a balance of payments deficit.

Expenditure switching policy instruments Involve a change in the relative prices of exports and imports (e.g. depreciation of exchange rates).

- *Expenditure switching policy instruments:* these policy instruments seek to improve the balance of payments by raising the relative attractiveness of domestic products as compared to foreign products so that domestic consumers switch from the now relatively more expensive foreign imports to domestically produced goods and overseas consumers switch away from their home produced products to the now relatively less expensive exports from the domestic country. Changes in the exchange rate have this effect. For example, a fall in the exchange rate makes imported foreign products more expensive in the domestic market and domestic products cheaper in foreign markets, encouraging just such a 'switching' of expenditures.

Expenditure reducing policy instruments Involve a reduction in aggregate demand to create the spare capacity to produce more exports and import substitutes.

- *Expenditure reducing policy instruments:* these policy instruments seek to dampen domestic aggregate expenditure, especially consumption expenditure (C) and government expenditure (G) within aggregate expenditure (E = C + I + G + X).

Sometimes correcting the balance of payments may need a combination of both expenditure switching and expenditure reducing policy instruments. For example, if the economy is at or near 'fall capacity' output, there may need to be a reduction in aggregate expenditure in the domestic economy. This will help to create the 'spare capacity' needed if domestic industry is to produce more substitute products to replace imports and to shift output from the (easier) domestic market to overseas markets to raise exports.

Box 14.1	The 'absorption approach'

The so-called 'absorption approach' can help illustrate the need for policies which reduce aggregate expenditure in the domestic economy if the 'expenditure switching' opportunities from a depreciation in the exchange rate are to be fully exploited. This is especially so where the domestic economy is operating at or near full capacity.

We noted in Chapter 11, using the 45° diagrams, that equilibrium in the national income occurs where the value of planned expenditure on domestic output (E) equals the value of that output (Y):

$$E = Y \quad\text{.. (1)}$$
$$\text{i.e.} \quad C + I + G + X - M = Y \quad\text{.. (2)}$$

where:

C = domestic consumption expenditure
I = investment expenditure
G = government expenditure
X = exports
M = imports
Y = national income

We can re-write (2) as:

$$A + (X - M) = Y \text{... (3)}$$

where A is the domestic absorbtion of resources used for consumption, investment or government expenditure purposes and $(X - M)$ is the balance of payments surplus (if positive) or deficit (if negative).

Suppose Y is at or near the full capacity level Y* then

$$(X - M) = Y^* - A \text{... (4)}$$

In other words, any improvement in the balance of payments (higher surplus or reduced deficit) can only take place if the domestic absorbtion of resources (A) is reduced, given that Y* is already at or near full capacity and, at least in the short run, is fixed in real terms.

7	EXCHANGE RATE POLICY AND FINANCIAL GLOBALISATION

The previous two chapters have noted the impact of the greater volumes and frequency of financial and capital flows across geographical boundaries on fiscal and monetary policy

Financial globalisation
The increased geographical mobility of international financial capital.

respectively. Here we consider some of the impacts of such **financial globalisation** on the exchange rate.

The more open borders which characterise globalisation (*see* Chapter 16) have resulted in a substantial growth in volumes and values of world exports and imports. As a result, any movement in the exchange rate has a greater impact on X (exports) and M (imports) in the aggregate demand function than ever before. Further, financial globalisation is creating new opportunities for governments to influence the exchange rate. For example, *interest rate differentials* across countries are now having a more substantial impact on international financial flows. If interest rates in your country rise relative to those in other countries, you can expect a more substantial inflow of financial capital, raising demand for your currency on foreign exchange markets and, other things equal, raising the exchange rate. Alternatively, a reduction in interest rates relative to those in other countries is likely to lead to a substantial exodus of financial capital, increasing the supply of your currency on foreign exchange markets and thereby reducing the exchange rate.

Pause for thought 6

Use a demand and supply diagram for £ sterling to illustrate the likely impacts of a) a rise in UK interest rate differentials, and b) a fall in UK interest rate differentials.

This analysis would suggest that exchange rate changes are, as a result of financial globalisation, more sensitive to interest rate policies of national governments than was previously the case. Of course, for the UK, the opportunities for the government to use this development to influence the exchange rate are limited since interest rates are now determined independently of the government by the *Monetary Policy Committee*.

Of course, the financial markets pay attention to more than interest rate differentials. For example, even if a government raises its interest rates so that the differential rises, if the markets perceive that the interest rate rise is a sign of economic 'weakness' (e.g. higher interest rates to dampen rapidly accelerating inflationary pressures), then net flows of financial capital may still be outwards rather than inwards.

8   EXCHANGE RATE SYSTEMS

It will be useful to review the various types of exchange rate systems which have operated over time before considering the case for a single currency.

8.1   Fixed exchange rates (gold standard)

Gold standard
A fixed system of exchange rates.

As the nineteenth century progressed, and as world trade expanded, the use of gold as a means of international payment broadened to take in almost all the major trading countries. The 'price' of each major currency was fixed in terms of a specific weight of gold, which meant that the price of each currency was fixed in terms of every other currency, at a rate that could not be altered. The **gold standard** was therefore a system of *fixed exchange rates*. Any difficulties for the balance of payments had to be resolved by expanding or contracting the domestic economy. A rather stylised account of the adjustment mechanism will highlight the main features of the gold standard system.

Suppose a country moved into balance of payments *surplus*. Payment would be received in gold which, because domestic money supply was directly related to the gold stock, would increase the money supply. This would expand the economy, raising domestic incomes, spending and prices. Higher incomes and prices would encourage imports and discourage exports, thereby helping to eliminate the initial payments surplus. In addition, the extra money supply would lead to a fall in the 'price' of money (the rate of interest), encouraging capital outflows (a minus sign in the accounts) to other countries which had higher rates of interest. A payments surplus would in these ways tend to be eliminated.

For countries with payments *deficits*, gold outflows would reduce the gold stock and with it the domestic money supply. This would cause the domestic economy to contract, reducing incomes, spending and prices. Lower incomes and prices would discourage imports and encourage exports. The reduction in money supply would also raise the 'price' of money (interest rate) – encouraging capital inflows – a plus sign in the accounts. Payments deficits would, therefore, also tend to be eliminated.

This whole system came to be regarded as extremely sophisticated and self-regulating. Individual countries need only ensure (a) that gold could flow freely between countries, (b) that gold backed the domestic money supply, and (c) that the market was free to set interest rates. Of course, this meant that countries with payment surpluses would experience expanding domestic economies, and those with payments deficits contracting economies.

The breakdown of the gold standard system during the inter-war period found no ready replacement. The result was a rather chaotic period of unstable exchange rates, inadequate world liquidity and protectionism during much of the 1920s and 1930s. It was to seek a more ordered system of world trade and payments that the Allies met in Bretton Woods in the US, even before the Second World War had ended. What emerged from that meeting was an entirely new system under the auspices of the IMF.

8.2 Adjustable peg system (IMF)

Revaluation
A rise in the par value of a currency under the IMF adjustable peg exchange rate system.

Devaluation
Reduction in the par value of a currency under the IMF adjustable peg exchange rate system.

Adjustable peg exchange rate system
IMF system from 1947–71 under which currencies had par values, with limited scope for change.

Under the IMF system, which lasted from 1947 to around 1971, the dollar was the common unit of all exchange rates. A country had a 'right' to change its initial exchange rate (par value) by up to 10%. For changes in par value which, when cumulated, came to more than 10%, the permission of the IMF was required. The IMF would only give such permission if the member could demonstrate that its balance of payments was in 'fundamental disequilibrium'. Since this term was never clearly defined in the Articles of the IMF, any substantial payments imbalance would usually qualify. A rise in par became known as a *revaluation*; a fall in par, a *devaluation*. As well as changing par value, a member could permit its exchange rate to move in any one year ± 1% of par, but no more. Because the IMF system sought stable, but not totally fixed, exchange rates, it became known as the *adjustable peg exchange rate system*.

Changes in exchange rate were a means by which deficits or surpluses could be adjusted. For instance, a devaluation would lower the foreign price of exports and raise the domestic price of imports. The IMF system was, however, criticised for in practice permitting too little flexibility in exchange rates. Between 1947 and 1971 only six adjustments took place: devaluation of the French franc (1958 and 1969) and of sterling (1949 and 1967) and revaluations of the Deutschmark (1961 and 1969). It is true, of course, that adjustments of exchange rates are subject to an extremely fine balance: too many adjustments and the system loses stability and confidence; too few and the system generates internal tensions of unemployment and/or lower real incomes which may eventually destroy it.

Between 1971 and 1976 various problems beset this adjustable peg exchange rate system of the IMF, not least problems with the very currency on which the whole system of exchange rates was based, namely the US dollar. By 1976 almost all IMF members had adopted some type of floating exchange rate system. The IMF meeting of that year in Jamaica officially recognised this new system of floating exchange rates.

8.3 The floating exchange rate system

According to basic economic theory, a system of freely floating exchange rates should be self-regulating. If the cause of a UK deficit were, say, extra imports from the US, then the pound should fall (depreciate) against the dollar. This would result from UK importers selling extra pounds sterling on the foreign exchange markets to buy US dollars to pay for those imports. In simple demand/supply analysis (*see* Figure 14.2, page 332) the extra supply of pounds sterling will lower its 'price', i.e. the sterling exchange rate. As we have already seen, provided the Marshall–Lerner elasticity conditions are fulfilled (price elasticity of demand for UK exports and imports together greater than 1), then the lower-priced exports and higher-priced imports will contribute to an improvement in the balance of payments, perhaps after a short time lag.

As it has developed since 1973, however, the system has not been one of 'freely floating' rates. Instead, governments have tended to intervene from time to time to support the values of their currencies. The setting by governments of particular 'targets' for the exchange rate has resulted in a system of 'managed' exchange rates, sometimes described as a 'dirty floating system'.

In the last 60 years we have moved, as we have noted, from a fixed to a floating exchange rate regime. However, the countries of the emerging European Union had a particular problem after the Treaty of Rome in 1958 in that it was clearly not possible to create the intended unified single market without fixed parities: for example, ever changing exchange rates would make realistic price comparisons impossible across a future single market, removing one of the reasons (transparency) for creating such a market! The European economies have moved progressively towards linking their exchange rates ever more closely. This move began in 1979 by operating an Exchange Rate Mechanism (ERM) which pegged currencies to a central unit then known as the European Currency Unit (ECU), with a restricted band for divergence. The value of the 'ECU' was based on a weighted average of the exchange rates of the participating currencies.

The Exchange Rate Mechanism (ERM) was seen as an intermediate step towards a **European Monetary Union** with a single currency.

European Monetary Union (EMU)
The system since 1999 of a single currency (euro), with a European Central Bank and other institutional arrangements.

9 SINGLE CURRENCY (EURO)

Single currency
Where the currencies of member countries are replaced by a single currency, e.g. the euro.

Eventually the Exchange Rate Mechanism was transformed from currencies closely linked to one another, with only minor adjustments in exchange rate permitted, to a **single currency** in which, effectively, exchange rates are fixed for all time against other member currencies. This took place when eleven countries formally replaced their national currencies with the euro on 1 January 1999, with Greece becoming the twelfth member of this eurozone in 2001. Harrison (2006) has outlined some of the advantages and disadvantages of membership of the single currency.

9.1 Advantages of single currency

- *Lower costs of exchange.* When goods are imported the trader receiving the goods must obtain foreign currency to pay the exporter. Banks will happily supply foreign currency, but they will levy a service charge for the transaction. For the economy as a whole these charges are sizeable and, in general, they will be passed on to consumers through higher prices. For the EU as a whole the transaction costs associated with intra-community trade are estimated at 0.4% of the EU's GDP. These figures give an idea of the resource savings to those countries which adopted the euro and provide an encouraging argument about why these resource savings might be reflected in lower prices within the euro area.

- *Reduced exchange rate uncertainty.* Inside the euro area, exchange rates are irrevocably fixed and there is no uncertainty over future rates of exchange. This is important because traders often negotiate contracts for delivery and payment stretching six months and longer into the future. Outside the euro area, exchange rate risk exists for traders involved in international transactions. It is, of course, possible for traders to hedge the foreign exchange risk in the forward market where rates of exchange can be agreed today for delivery of currency at some future point in time. However, such arrangements are costly and so raise the cost of a transaction. A different alternative might be for traders to find a domestic producer instead of trading internationally. The implication is that exchange rate risk might raise the cost of trading internationally or discourage international trade altogether. To the extent that this is the case, a single currency will reduce the cost of transacting business across frontiers (because of the costless elimination of exchange rate risk) and will increase international trade with all the associated benefits of comparative advantage. These advantages include the increased variety of products that become available, lower prices due to competition (because price differences between markets will no longer be masked by being quoted in different currencies) and greater economies of scale because of the larger market.

- *Eliminating competitive devaluations.* Between the two world wars, several European countries engaged in what became known as 'competitive devaluations' when a devaluation in one country was matched by a devaluation in other countries. While such competitive devaluations have been avoided in the latter half of the century, the possibility that they might recur still exists; in fact, all devaluations adversely affect inflationary expectations in the devaluing country. Given the increasing scale of intra-European trade, any return to competitive devaluations (or any other form of protectionism) would have devastating effects on Europe's economies. The possibility of these disruptions disappears when a common currency exists.

- *Preventing speculative attacks.* Where different currencies exist, there is also the possibility of a speculative attack on one or more currencies. The problem is exacerbated when a fixed exchange rate exists because speculators have a one-way bet. If the currency they have bet against is not devalued all they have lost is their transactions costs on the deal, whereas betting correctly can result in speculator gains. Governments can defend currencies against such attacks but this often involves raising interest rates, which reduces business investment and hampers economic growth. To the extent that exchange rate disruption is avoided, trade, investment and economic growth will be encouraged and there will be resource savings (e.g. no longer necessary for the authorities to hold reserves of foreign currency to defend the exchange rate). The latter will again have a positive impact on investment and growth.

9.2 Disadvantages of single currency

The advantages of adopting the euro seem encouraging, but these advantages do not come without costs. It is to a consideration of these that we now turn.

● *Loss of independent monetary policy.* Countries participating in the euro relinquish the right to implement an independent domestic monetary policy. Instead they accept the monetary policy implemented by the European Central Bank (ECB). However, this 'one size fits all' monetary policy might not suit all countries equally, for example when there is a recession in one country but not in others. If that country is outside the euro area, the country's central bank could reduce interest rates and stimulate economic activity. However, the ECB is unlikely to respond in this way if the recession is only country-specific because this will raise inflation throughout the Union. Monetary policy actions for the ECB, as with the Bank of England, will involve changes in the rate of interest. However, a 'one size fits all' monetary policy might be less effective than the policy an independent country could pursue.

  The ECB has announced that monetary policy will target the rate of inflation. In other words, changes in monetary policy will be initiated whenever the forecast rate of inflation for the euro area as a whole rises above the ECB's target rate of 2%.

● *Loss of an independent exchange rate policy.* Similarly, when a common currency exists, countries lose the ability to devalue the exchange rate to offset a loss of competitiveness. The exchange rate, like the rate of interest, is a powerful weapon for bringing about changes in demand and economic adjustment. In the event of a balance of payments deficit inside a common currency area, the burden of adjustment is thrown on to the domestic economy. For example, cutting aggregate demand to reduce imports and curb any price inflation will be reflected in lower domestic output and employment. This will continue until rising unemployment depresses real wages far enough to restore competitiveness. Adjustment is less painfully achieved when the rate of exchange can be devalued to restore competitiveness.

● *Loss of an independent fiscal policy.* It might be argued that fiscal policy could fill the vacuum left by the loss of monetary policy sovereignty and exchange rate policy sovereignty. However, since the maximum allowable budget deficit for any country in the eurozone is 3% of that country's GDP, scope for an active fiscal policy is clearly limited. It will be limited even further if current thinking on harmonising taxation within the eurozone is adopted!

● *Loss of convergence.* Loss of policy sovereignty might not be so important if economies are reasonably convergent, in which case country-specific shocks are less likely to occur. Unfortunately not all economies have the same levels of unemployment, inflation or growth so that a monetary policy that fits one may not fit another.

Note: The treasury's five tests

● Is the UK economy becoming sufficiently compatible – similar growth, inflation, etc., with the other economies in the eurozone to adopt the 'one size fits all' interest rate determined by the European Central Bank in Frankfurt?

● Is there sufficient flexibility within the eurozone's economic structures – for example, the stability and growth pact which determines government deficits – to cope with economic change?

● Would joining the European Monetary Union create better conditions for firms making long-term decisions to invest in Britain?

- What impact would entry into the EMU have on the competitive position of the UK's financial services industry, particular the City's share, bond and foreign exchange markets?
- In summary, will joining the EMU promote higher UK growth, stability and a lasting increase in jobs?

9.3 Developments in the eurozone

For the potential benefit of the European Monetary Union (EMU), with its single currency and a European Central Bank, to be fully realised in the long run, three factors will be desirable.

- *Sustainable economic convergence* For the smooth working of the euro, the economies of the participating countries must be in the same stage of the economic cycle and be relatively homogeneous.
- *Strong political commitments to EMU discipline.* The European Council of Economic and Financial Ministers (ECOFIN), consisting of the finance ministers of the EU, are able to impose severe fines on member states whose budget deficits exceed the ratio of 3% of GDP. The fines could reach as much as 0.5% of GDP.
- *Credible European Central Bank* (ECB) The ECB's independence is enshrined in the Maastricht treaty of 1992, as is its commitment to price stability. Short-term interest rates are set with a view to achieving such price stability. However, political pressure for more expansionary monetary policies might arise if the EU experiences slow growth and high unemployment.

9.4 The 'Growth and Stability Pact'

To maintain stability in the eurozone, a 'Growth and Stability Pact' has been operating since January 1999 which is designed to ensure that the euro maintains its value over time by committing the participating countries to form 'convergence contracts'. These contracts are necessary to make sure that members of the eurozone continue to maintain their economies under the same economic criteria as when they entered. In particular, the Pact was designed to ensure that the medium term budgetary discipline criteria were met. At least every two years the European Commission and the European Central Bank (ECB) reports to ECOFIN on the fulfilment of the convergent criteria. If member states exceed the criteria for government budget deficit (set at 3% of GDP) or government debt (set at 60% of GDP) they would be penalised. Penalties for excessive government deficits can involve members having to lodge with the European Commission a non-interest bearing deposit of up to 2% of a country's GDP, a large amount of money on which no interest return is forthcoming.

However, the Growth and Stability Pact has fallen into disrepute in recent years when the constant infringement of the budget deficit provision by France, Germany and Italy (who have had budget deficits consistently higher than 3% of GDP) led to no penalties being imposed. The Pact has also been heavily criticised for concentrating more on stability than on growth.

 Pause for thought 7

Can you explain the basis for the criticism that too much emphasis in the Pact has been placed on stability?

10 BALANCE OF PAYMENTS

The UK balance of payments is often broken down into the *current account, capital account* and *financial account*.

10.1 Current account

Balance on goods
Net value of trade in tangible goods (exports +, imports –). Previously known as the 'visible trade balance'.

This consists of two main sub-accounts, the '**balance on goods**' (formerly 'visible trade balance') and the '**balance on services**' (formerly 'invisible trade balance'). Exports are given a positive sign, imports a negative sign: when exports exceed imports, we speak of a 'surplus' and when imports exceed exports, a 'deficit'.

- Balance on goods is split into oil goods and non-oil goods.
- Balance on services includes shipping, insurance, finance etc.

Balance on services
Net value of trade in intangible services (exports +, imports –). Previously known as the 'invisible trade balance'.

The current account is completed by adding two further items: the 'investment income balance' (i.e. net income from interest, profits and dividends) and the 'transfer balance' (i.e. net value of government transfers to institutions such as the EU, World Bank etc.). Table 14.3 presents the components of the UK current account over the past twelve years.

Note: Oil prices and UK balance of payments

We can see from Table 14.3 that the positive UK balance on oil is diminishing as oil reserves are progressively exploited. By 2020 UK oil reserves from the North Sea are predicted to be largely exhausted. However, the high oil prices of recent years (well over $50 a barrel) are making it more attractive to seek for new North Sea oil fields. These are more expensive to operate than oil fields in deserts, but provided high oil prices are expected to continue over the long term, they will become more commercially viable, encouraging more exploration of the North Sea.

Table 14.3 Components of UK current account, 1992–2003 (£ million)

	Trade in goods and services					Investment Income[1] balance	Transfer balance	Current balance
	Balance on goods			Balance on services	Balance on goods & services			
Year	Total	Oil	Non-oil					
1992	−13,050	+1,610	−14,660	+5,482	−7,568	+128	−5,534	−12,974
1993	−13,066	+2,612	−15,678	+6,581	−6,485	−191	−5,243	−11,919
1994	−11,126	+3,937	−15,063	+6,379	−4,747	+3,348	−5,369	−6,768
1995	−12,023	+4,323	−16,346	+8,481	−3,542	+2,101	−7,574	−9,015
1996	−13,722	+4,810	−18,532	+9,597	−4,125	+1,204	−5,788	−8,709
1997	−12,342	+4,560	−16,902	+12,528	+186	+3,906	−5,812	−1,720
1998	−21,813	+3,042	−24,855	+12,666	−9,147	+12,558	−8,225	−4,814
1999	−27,372	+4,449	−31,182	+11,794	−15,578	+2,536	−6,687	−19,729
2000	−30,326	+6,536	−36,862	+11,838	−18,488	+9,312	−10,032	−19,208
2001	−40,620	+5,577	−46,197	+13,000	−27,620	+16,188	−6,188	−18,038
2002	−46,455	+5,487	−51,942	+15,166	−31,289	+21,119	−8,795	−18,817
2003	−47,290	+4,806	−52,096	+14,617	−32,673	+22,097	−9,854	−20,430

[1] = This total includes both 'compensation to employees' and 'investment income' but in statistical terms it is nearly all investment income.
Source: Adapted from ONS (2004) *UK Balance of Payments*; ONS (2004) *Data Releases* (various)

10.2 Capital account

The **capital account** records the flow of money into the country (positive sign) and out of the country (negative sign) resulting from the purchase or sale of fixed assets (e.g. land) and selected capital transfers.

10.3 Financial account

Capital account
Records the flows of money into the country (positive sign) and out of the country (negative sign) resulting from the purchase or sale of fixed assets (e.g. land) and selected capital transfers.

This records the flows of money into the country (positive sign) and out of the country (negative sign) resulting from investment related or other financial activity.

- *Direct investment* usually involves physical assets of a company (e.g. plant, equipment).
- *Portfolio investment* involves paper assets (e.g. shares, bonds).
- *'Other financial flows'* may involve the movement of deposits between countries.

If the net value of the items mentioned in the three accounts so far are negative, we speak of a *balance of payments deficit*; if positive, of a *balance of payments surplus*.

10.4 Balancing item

The overall accounts are constructed so that they *must* balance (accounting identity), with this balance achieved by either drawing on reserves (if deficit) or adding to reserves (if surplus). The 'balancing item' (or 'net errors and omissions') represents these values, which are required to maintain the accounting identity.

11 OIL PRICES AND THE GLOBAL ECONOMY

Financial account
Records the flows of money into the country (+) and out of the country (–) from investment related (direct and portfolio) or other financial activity (e.g. movement of deposits between countries).

Portfolio investment
Involves paper assets (e.g. shares, bonds).

Other financial flows
Records the movement of deposits between countries. Part of the 'financial account' of the balance of payments.

We noted above that higher oil prices have raised revenues from North Sea oil production, helped by both the relatively inelastic demand for oil and the continuous increases in global demand for oil. However, the IMF declared in late 2005 that high and volatile oil prices pose a significant risk to the global economy, with a one in five chance that the cost of crude oil could stay above $60 a barrel during 2006, given the disruptions to oil supplies of events such as Iraq and hurricanes in the Gulf of Mexico. Mini Case Study 14.2 looks in more detail at the oil price.

Mini Case Study 14.2

Oiling the wheels

In August 2005 the widely used measure for the price of crude oil, the West Texas Spot-rate, had reached $82 per barrel, some 250% higher than in August 2002. Indeed the crude oil price was as low as $11 a barrel as recently as summer 2001. Why has there been such volatility in price? Close examination of demand and supply conditions for oil may give us some clues!

Crude oil is refined into a vast number of products via the chemical process of 'cracking'. However, just three, namely petrol, diesel and fuel oil account for around

75% of oil derivative products and are mainly used in transport and electricity generating activities. Of course, the demand for transport and electricity is closely linked to economic growth; for example, every 1% rise in US national income has been estimated as raising US demand for crude oil by nine-tenths of 1%.

Few immediate substitutes exist for crude oil derivatives in transport and energy. Natural gas is perhaps the closest substitute and provides around 25% of total global energy. Estimates suggest that a 1% fall in price of natural gas leads to a three-quarters of 1% fall in demand for crude oil. However, other less obvious substitutes for oil are becoming more important. For example, all types of renewable energy sources (wind, water, sun etc.) are increasingly seen as more environmentally desirable (if more expensive) substitutes for oil in energy production in that they do not emit the carbon dioxide (CO_2) and other greenhouse gases which result from using oil-based products. The scientific linkage of these emissions with global warming led to 93 countries (but not the US) having ratified the Kyoto Protocol by 2003, with the developed countries committing themselves to an overall 5% reduction in the recorded 1990 emissions of greenhouse gases by 2012.

Climate itself can also influence the demand for oil. The OECD noted that in 2002 the Northern Hemisphere recorded the warmest ever first quarter of the year, and linked this to demand for crude oil from countries in the Northern Hemisphere falling by 1.1 million barrels per year.

Whilst the demand for oil is capable of significant shifts, so too is the supply. Around one-third of total supply of crude oil is in the hands of a small group of well-organised oil producing and exporting countries (OPEC). Members of OPEC include Saudi Arabia, Iraq, Iran, Qatar, Libya, Kuwait, United Arab Emirates, Nigeria, Indonesia and Venezuela. These countries meet regularly to decide on the total supply they should collectively produce, seeking to limit the total supply in order to keep the world price of crude oil at a 'reasonable' level (said to be around $25 a barrel as recently as 2004 but recent statements suggest a price nearer $40 is in view). Having fixed the total supply, OPEC then allocates a quota to each member state which specifies their maximum oil production in that year.

Questions

1 a) *Discuss some of the factors suggested in the Mini Case Study that might cause an increase in the world demand for oil.*

   b) *Now discuss possible reasons for a decrease in the world demand for oil.*

2 *We have seen that OPEC has tried to restrict the total supply of crude oil from its member countries to keep the world price at a 'reasonable' level of around $25 a barrel. Suppose it now aims for a higher world price of around $45 a barrel.*

   a) *How might it achieve this new target? (You could use a diagram here)*

   b) *What problems might OPEC encounter in trying to achieve this higher oil price?*

Answers to questions can be found at the back of the book (pages 519–20).

There were signs, the IMF said, that consumer confidence was being adversely affected and inflationary pressures were being stoked up by high oil prices. Whilst the IMF accepts that the impact of higher oil prices on global growth has so far been surprisingly moderate, it noted that further oil price increases could have a less benign impact. The point is that an oil price increase acts like an indirect tax on the world, reducing the aggregate demand available for spending on non-oil goods and services. The IMF said it had revised its forecasts for oil prices from $43.75 to $61.75 in 2006. Since crude oil prices started to rise in 2003, the IMF estimates that global GDP has been reduced by a cumulative 1 – 1.5% with every 10% increase in oil prices, ie. higher oil prices since 2003 are associated with a 0.1–0.15% reduction in annual global growth (Rajan, R., 2005).

Other analysts are less convinced that future oil prices will be as high as those forecast by the IMF. Cable (2005) notes that theory and experience teach us that the current high prices will affect both supply and demand. On the supply side, additional exploration and investment is already taking place, attracted by the high returns on oil, in existing oil areas and in new areas such as the Caspian Sea and the African continental shelf. Oil firms have developed new technologies for maximising yields and exploring inhospitable offshore reserves which are now profitable. Also, substitutes for oil are also being developed such as non-conventional oils like the 'tarsands' of Canada and Venezuela which are vast and believed to be profitable at around $30 a barrel, in effect setting a cap on the long-term price of oil itself.

Whilst the supply side looks encouraging, on the demand side, the scope for easy economies in oil use has been limited by advances already made, for example the oil intensity of western economies (and China) is much less than before as industry, already under pressure on energy costs, is having to economise on oil, as are households faced with higher oil bills.

 Pause for thought 8

What have been the reasons for a rapidly increasing global demand for oil? What other factors are responsible for the progressive rise in the oil price in recent years?

KEY POINTS

- The exchange rate is usually quoted as the number of units of the domestic currency that are needed to purchase a unit of foreign currency.

- The exchange rate is a key 'price' affecting the competitiveness of UK exporters and UK producers of import substitutes.

- A fall (depreciation) in sterling will, other things equal, make UK exports cheaper abroad and UK imports dearer at home.

- The terms of trade are usually expressed as an index involving the ratio of export prices to import prices, with some base year having the index of 100 for this ratio.

- A rise in the terms of trade index indicate a rise in export prices relative to import prices and is usually regarded as a 'favourable' movement, though this may not always be the case.

- The Marshall–Lerner elasticity conditions must be fulfilled if a fall in the exchange rate is to improve the balance of payments. Namely the sum of the price elasticities of demand for exports and imports must be greater than one.

- Because short-term elasticities are lower than long-term elasticities, the initial one to two years after a depreciation may not lead to an improvement in the balance of payments (the so-called 'J-curve' effect).

- A change in the exchange rate influences the relative prices of exports and imports and is sometimes referred to as an 'expenditure switching' policy instrument.

- If national output is at or near 'full capacity' it may be necessary to accompany an exchange rate change with a reduction in aggregate expenditure, i.e. by also using 'expenditure reducing' policy instruments.

- Financial globalisation is tending to make exchange rates more sensitive to changes in interest rate.

- The eurozone currently contains 12 members with a single currency and a European Central Bank. Problems with the implementation of the 'Growth and Stability Pact' have not as yet been resolved.

- The current account balance involves the balance on goods (oil and non-oil) and the balance on services.

- The overall balance of payments involves the balances on current account, capital account and financial account respectively. The 'balancing item' ensures that overall balance is achieved in the accounts.

- High oil prices may help the UK balance of payments in the short run but may contribute to a reduction in global economic growth which may reduce demand for UK non-oil exports in the longer run.

Further reading

Griffiths, A. and Wall, S. (2006) *Applied Economics*, 11th edition, FT/Prentice Hall, Chapters 26–8.

Griffiths, A. and Wall, S. (2005) *Economics for Business and Management*, FT/Prentice Hall, Chapter 10.

Harrison B. (2006) 'Money and EMU' in A. Griffiths and S. Wall *Applied Economics*, 11th edition, FT/Prentice Hall.

Heather, K. (2004) *Economics Theory in Action*, 4th edition, FT/Prentice Hall, Chapters 19 and 20.

Parkin, M., Powell, M. and Matthews, K. (2005) *Economics*, 6th edition, FT/Prentice Hall, Chapters 33 and 34.

Sloman, J. (2006) *Economics*, 6th edition, FT/Prentice Hall, Chapters 15, 23–5.

Web references

You can find current data and information on many aspects of exchange rates and trade performance from the following websites.

National Statistics: **http://www.statistics.gov.uk/** The official UK statistics site.

Eurostat: **http://europa.eu.int/comm/eurostat** The main site for EU statistics.

United Nations: **http://www.un.org** A main source of information and statistics.

Overseas investment into the UK: **www.invest.uk.com**

US exports and overseas business: **www.mac.doc.gov**

ASEAN: **www.aseansec.org**

Chinese business: **www.cbbc.org**

Japanese business: **www.jetro.org**

References

Cable, V. (2005) 'The price of oil will fall', *Guardian*, 8 September.

Harrison, B. (2004) 'Money and EMU' in A. Griffiths and S. Wall *Applied Economics*, 10th edition, FT/Prentice Hall.

Rajan, R. (2005) 'High oil prices a risk to global economy', *Guardian*, 22 September.

PROGRESS AND REVIEW QUESTIONS

Answers to most questions can be found at the back of the book (pages 520–1). Answers to asterisked questions can be found on the students' side of the Companion Website.

Multiple-choice questions

1 Which *two* of the following would have a positive sign in the UK balance of payments?

   a) Import of wheat into the UK
   b) Export of machinery from the UK
   c) A UK based firm investing in France
   d) A German based firm investing in the UK
   e) A French consumer purchasing Italian pasta

2 Which *two* of the following are (other things equal) likely to cause the UK's 'financial account balance' to improve?

   a) A rise in purchase of shares in US companies by UK residents.
   b) A rise in purchase of shares in UK companies by French residents.
   c) A rise in direct investment by UK firms in plant and machinery in the US.
   d) A rise in direct investment by US firms in plant and machinery in the UK.
   e) A transfer of sterling deposits by financial intermediaries in London to dollar deposits in New York.

3 Which *two* of the following would correspond to a deficit for the UK in the 'balance on goods' (formerly the 'visible trade balance')?

   a) Exports of oil and non-oil goods from the UK falling short of the value of imports of oil and non-oil goods into the UK.
   b) Exports of oil and non-oil goods from the UK exceeding the volume of imports of oil and non-oil goods into the UK.
   c) The surplus on the oil goods account exceeding the deficit on the non-oil goods account.
   d) The surplus on the oil goods account falling short of the deficit on the non-oil goods account.
   e) The surplus on the oil goods account exactly matching the deficit on the non-oil goods account.

4 Which *two* of the following would correspond to a surplus for the UK in the 'balance on goods' (formerly the 'visible trade balance')?

a) Exports of oil and non-oil goods from the UK falling short of the value of imports of oil and non-oil goods into the UK.

b) Exports of oil and non-oil goods from the UK exceeding the volume of imports of oil and non-oil goods into the UK.

c) The surplus on the oil goods account exceeding the deficit on the non-oil goods account.

d) The surplus on the oil goods account falling short of the deficit on the non-oil goods account.

e) The surplus on the oil goods account exactly matching the deficit on the non-oil goods account.

5 Which *two* of the following are (other things equal) likely to improve the UK's 'balance on goods'?

a) Rise in sterling value of oil exports

b) Rise in sterling value of oil imports

c) Fall in sterling value of exports for non-oil goods

d) Fall in sterling value of imports for non-oil goods

e) Rise in sterling value of imports for non-oil goods

6 Which *two* of the following are (other things equal) likely to cause the UK's balance on current account to deteriorate?

a) Rise in the sterling value of exports of financial services

b) Fall in the sterling value of the deficit previously experienced for trade in non-oil goods

c) Fall in the sterling value of the surplus previously experienced for trade in oil

d) Fall in the sterling value of imports of financial services

e) Rise in the sterling value of the deficit previously experienced for trade in non-oil goods

7 Which *three* of the following are (other things equal) likely to cause the UK's 'financial account balance' to deteriorate?

a) A rise in purchase of shares in US companies by UK residents.

b) A rise in purchase of shares in UK companies by French residents.

c) A fall in direct investment by UK firms in plant and machinery in the US.

d) A fall in direct investment by US firms in plant and machinery in the UK.

e) A transfer of sterling deposits by financial intermediaries in London to dollar deposits in New York.

8 Which *two* of the following would tend to increase the demand for sterling on the foreign exchange market?

a) Increased demand for imports into the UK

b) Increased demand for exports from the UK

c) Increased inflows of foreign currencies into sterling deposit accounts in the UK

d) Increased outflows of sterling into foreign currency accounts overseas

e) Increased aid by the UK government to developing economies

9 Which *two* of the following would tend to increase the supply of sterling on the foreign exchange market?

a) Increased demand for imports into the UK

b) Increased demand for exports from the UK

c) Increased inflows of foreign currencies into sterling deposit accounts in the UK

d) Increased outflows of sterling into foreign currency accounts overseas

e) Reduction in aid by the UK government to developing economies

10 A fall in the sterling exchange rate against the US dollar would have which *two* of the following impacts?

a) UK exports to US become cheaper (in dollars)

b) UK exports to US become dearer (in dollars)

c) UK imports from US become cheaper (in sterling)

d) UK imports from US become dearer (in sterling)

e) No change in export or import prices, whether in dollars or sterling

11 A rise in the sterling exchange rate against the euro would have which *two* of the following impacts?

a) UK exports to France become cheaper (in euros)

b) UK exports to France become dearer (in euros)

c) UK imports from France become cheaper (in sterling)

d) UK imports from France become dearer (in sterling)

e) No change in export or import prices, whether in euros or sterling

12 Under which *two* of the following circumstances would the sterling value of imports from the US be more likely to increase (other things equal)?

a) A fall in the sterling exchange rate against the dollar, with price elasticity of demand for imports from the US relatively inelastic.

b) A fall in the sterling exchange rate against the dollar, with price elasticity of demand for imports from the US relatively elastic.

c) A rise in the sterling exchange rate with price elasticity of demand for imports from the US relatively elastic.

d) A rise in the sterling exchange rate with price elasticity of demand for imports from the US relatively inelastic.

e) A rise in the sterling exchange rate with price elasticity of demand for imports from the US unit elastic.

13 Which *one* of the following was lost as a result of the arrival of the European Central Bank for members of the eurozone?

a) Ability to control interest rates

b) Ability to control maximum VAT rates

c) Ability to control common external tariff rate

d) Ability to control optimum social benefit rates

e) Ability to control GNP based income levy

Matching terms/concepts

Match each description involving exchange rates to the most appropriate term.

1 A bilateral (two country) exchange rate:

a) Depreciation in exchange rate

b) Appreciation in exchange rate

c) Nominal exchange rate

d) Effective exchange rate (EER)

e) Real exchange rate (RER)

2 As a result of this the prices of exports rise overseas and the prices of imports fall at home:

a) Depreciation in exchange rate

b) Appreciation in exchange rate

c) Fall in nominal exchange rate

d) Fall in effective exchange rate (EER)

e) Fall in real exchange rate (RER)

3 A weighted average exchange rate involving more than two countries:

a) Depreciation in exchange rate

b) Appreciation in exchange rate

c) Nominal exchange rate

d) Effective exchange rate (EER)

e) Real exchange rate (RER)

4 As a result of this the prices of exports fall overseas and the prices of imports rise at home:

a) Depreciation in exchange rate

b) Appreciation in exchange rate

c) Rise in nominal exchange rate

d) Rise in effective exchange rate (EER)

e) Rise in real exchange rate (RER)

5 An exchange rate which also takes into account the relative prices of products in the countries being compared:

a) Depreciation in exchange rate

b) Appreciation in exchange rate

c) Nominal exchange rate

d) Effective exchange rate (EER)

e) Real exchange rate (RER)

 ## True/false questions

1 A deterioration in the 'balance on non-oil goods' must lead to a deterioration in the 'balance on goods'.

2 A fall in the sterling exchange rate against the euro would help UK manufacturers importing components from eurozone countries.

3 A fall in the sterling exchange rate will reduce the sterling value of imports by more the greater the price elasticity of demand for those imports.

4 A fall in the sterling exchange rate will raise the foreign value of exports by more the greater the price elasticity of demand for those exports.

5 A rise in the sterling exchange rate will make UK exports cheaper abroad and imports dearer at home.

6 If a fall in the effective exchange rate between sterling and six other currencies is exactly offset by the rise in prices of UK products relative to the countries concerned, then the real exchange rate will be unchanged.

7 Members of the eurozone have a common currency but can adopt individual policies as regards the money supply and interest rates.

8 A fall in the exchange rate will improve the balance of payments of a country provided the Marshall–Lerner elasticity conditions are fulfilled.

 # Data response and stimulus questions

1 **Sony puzzles over future**

Sony is extremely concerned that the appreciation of sterling against the euro has made it increasingly difficult for Sony to export CD players from its UK plants to eurozone countries. By making exports from the UK more expensive in major overseas markets like Germany it has lost out, as it has in the important UK market since imports from rivals producing in eurozone countries have been cheaper in sterling. Only a significant depreciation of sterling against the euro can help remedy this problem, especially since the price elasticity of demand for CD players is relatively high.

What factors might cause sterling to depreciate against the euro? Why is price elasticity of demand for CD players relevant to Sony's prospects?

2 Given the data in the table, calculate the terms of trade for each of the months.

2005	Index price of exports	Index price of imports
July	89.8	88.0
August	89.5	88.0
September	89.1	87.6
October	89.1	86.4
November	89.3	86.3

3 Given the data in the table, calculate:

a) balance on goods and services
b) current account balance
c) capital and finance account balance
d) net errors and omissions.

	£bn
Trade in goods	−90
Trade in services	100
Investment income balance	130
Transfer balance	−90
Capital account balance	70
Financial account	−50

Essay questions

Answers to asterisked questions can be found on the students' side of the Companion Website. All other answers can be found at the back of the book (page 521).

1* How might a fall in the exchange rate (depreciation) improve the balance of payments?

2 Under what circumstances might a rise in a country's terms of trade really be regarded as an 'improvement'?

3* Examine the case for and against a single currency.

4 Consider the impacts on an economy of a rise in oil prices.

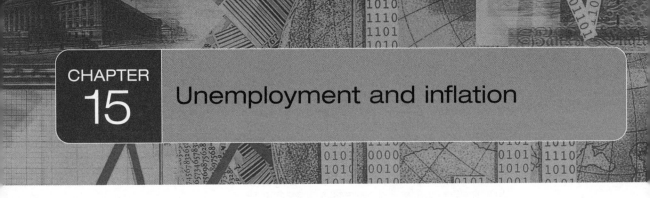

<table>
<tr><td>Learning objectives</td><td>By the end of this chapter you should be able to:</td></tr>
</table>

Learning objectives

By the end of this chapter you should be able to:

- Understand how aggregate demand and aggregate supply curves can be used to analyse the key issues of unemployment and inflation.
- Outline the different types of unemployment and the policy responses needed to tackle each type of unemployment.
- Explain the different approaches used in the measurement of inflation in the UK.
- Examine the different possible causes of inflation, their impacts and the policy responses available for tackling them.

1   INTRODUCTION

High unemployment has, from time to time, been a feature of the UK economy, as for example in the early 1990s when it rose to over 3 million. In October 2005, however, the unemployed total had fallen to only 1.8 million, some 5.1% of the economically active population. This chapter will seek to outline the nature of the unemployment problem and to analyse the possible causes of, and cures for, unemployment. However, any policy responses to unemployment must be taken by governments who at the same time must seek to control the rate of change of prices, i.e. inflationary pressures. This chapter will therefore combine the separate but interrelated topics of unemployment and inflation.

The chapter also introduces the important ideas of aggregate demand and aggregate supply in explaining changes in national income, building on the withdrawals/injections and 45° analyses discussed in Chapter 11. Aggregate demand and aggregate supply curves bring the levels of both prices and national output into consideration and are therefore well suited to dealing with both inflation and unemployment. The aggregate demand and supply curves are then used to further explore the causal factors of unemployment and inflation.

2   AGGREGATE DEMAND AND AGGREGATE SUPPLY ANALYSIS

It will be useful at this stage to introduce an approach which develops further our earlier work on finding the equilibrium value of national income. This approach makes use of

Aggregate demand
The total demand in
the economy, usually
expressed as C + I +
G + (X – M).

aggregate demand and aggregate supply curves rather than the W/J or 45° diagrams used so far. This aggregate demand/supply approach will be used in later chapters to consider a wide range of policy issues.

In using these aggregate demand and aggregate supply schedules we are seeking to establish linkages between the level of national output (income) and the general level of prices in a more realistic way than was possible using the W/J and 45° diagrams.

2.1 Aggregate demand schedule

Aggregate supply
The total output in
the economy, in
the short run a
rise in the average
price level is usually
assumed to exceed
rises in input costs.

We have already considered *aggregate expenditure* as consisting of consumption plus injection expenditure, i.e. C + I + G + X (page 247). However, the aggregate demand schedule uses a *broader measure of consumption* (C) which includes *all* consumer expenditure, whether on the output of domestic firms or overseas firms. We reconcile these two different measures of consumption by taking only the *net* contributions to aggregate demand from overseas trade, i.e. exports (injection) *minus* imports (withdrawal). This gives us our expression for *aggregate demand* (AD).

$$AD = C + I + G + X - M$$

where

C = consumer expenditure
I = investment expenditure
G = government expenditure
X = exports
M = imports

Aggregate demand and the price level

Another difference from our previous analysis is that we plot the general *price level* on the vertical axis and *national output* on the horizontal axis, as in Figure 15.1. Just as the *firm*

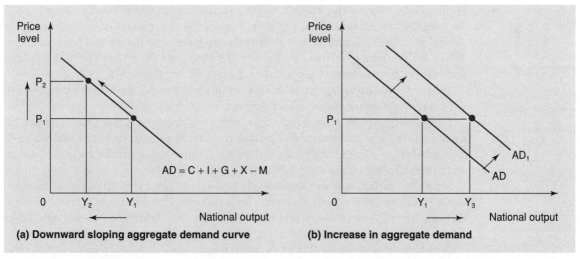

(a) Downward sloping aggregate demand curve **(b) Increase in aggregate demand**

Figure 15.1 The downward sloping aggregate demand (AD) curve is shown in Figure 15.1(a), with a rise in price level from P_1 to P_2 causing aggregate demand to contract from Y_1 to Y_2. This is a *movement along* an existing AD curve. However, the AD curve can also *shift* its position. Figure 15.1(b) shows an increase (shift to the right) in aggregate demand from AD to AD_1.

demand curve shows an inverse (negative) relationship between price and demand for its output, the suggestion here is that the *aggregate* demand curve shows a similar inverse relationship between the average level of prices and aggregate demand in the economy.

In Figure 15.1(a) we can see that a rise in the average price level from P_1 to P_2 reduces AD from Y_1 to Y_2. For example, a higher price level reduces the real value of money holdings which (via the 'real balance' effect, page 249) is likely to cut consumer spending (C), whilst a higher price level is also likely to result in interest rates being raised to curb inflationary pressures, with higher interest rates then discouraging both consumption (C) and investment (I) expenditures. As a result, as the average price level rises from P_1 to P_2, aggregate demand falls from Y_1 to Y_2.

In Figure 15.1(b) a rise in any one or more of the components of aggregate demand C, I, G or (X – M) will shift the AD curve rightwards and upwards to AD_1. Aggregate demand is now higher (Y_3) at any given price level (P_1).

The impact of changes in aggregate demand on equilibrium national output is considered further after we have introduced the aggregate supply curve (AS).

2.2 Aggregate supply schedule

We have previously noted a direct (positive) relationship between price and *firm* supply (e.g. Chapter 2). The suggestion here is that the aggregate supply (AS) curve shows a similar direct relationship between the average level of prices and *aggregate* supply in the economy.

However, for aggregate supply we often make a distinction between the *short-run* and *long-run* time periods. In the short run at least one factor of production is fixed, whereas in the long run all factors can be varied.

Short-run aggregate supply

Figure 15.2(a) shows the upward sloping short-run aggregate supply curve (AS). It assumes that some input costs, particularly money wages, remain relatively fixed as the general price level changes. It then follows that an increase in the general price level from P_1 to P_2 whilst input costs remain relatively fixed, increases the profitability of production and induces firms to expand output, raising aggregate supply from Y_1 to Y_2.

There are two explanations as to why an important input cost, namely wages, may remain constant even though prices have risen.

First, many employees are hired under fixed-wage contracts. Once these contracts are agreed it is the firm that determines (within reason) the number of labour hours actually worked. If prices rise, the negotiated *real wage* (i.e. money wage divided by prices) will fall and firms will want to hire more labour time and raise output.

Secondly, workers may not immediately be aware of price level changes, i.e. they may suffer from 'money illusion'. If workers' expectations lag behind actual price level rises then workers will not be aware that their real wages have fallen and will not adjust their money demands appropriately.

Both these reasons imply that as the general price level rises, real wages will fall, reducing costs of production and raising profitability thereby encouraging firms to raise output.

In Figure 15.2(b) a rise in the productivity of any factor input or fall in its cost will shift the AS curve rightwards and downwards to AS_1. Aggregate supply is now higher (Y_3) at any given price level (P_1). Put another way, any given output (Y_1) can now be supplied at a lower price level (P_2).

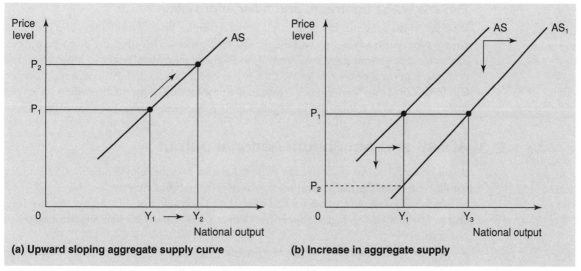

(a) Upward sloping aggregate supply curve   **(b) Increase in aggregate supply**

Figure 15.2 The upward sloping aggregate supply curve (AS) is shown in Figure 15.2(a) with a rise in price causing aggregate supply to expand from Y_1 to Y_2. This is a *movement along* an existing AS curve. However the AS curve can also *shift* its position. Figure 15.2(b) shows an increase (shift to the right) in aggregate supply from AS to AS_1.

Long-run aggregate supply

In the long run it is often assumed that factor markets are more flexible and better informed so that input prices (e.g. money wages) fully adjust to changes in the general price level and vice versa. If this is the case then we have the *vertical* long-run aggregate supply (AS) curve in Figure 15.3.

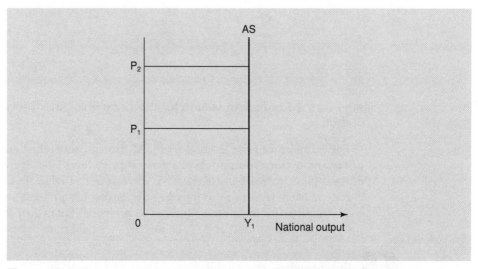

Figure 15.3 This shows the aggregate supply (AS) schedule in the long-run time period (or in the short-run time period if input costs do fully reflect any changes in prices).

Flexible wage contracts and fuller information

Workers in the long run can gather full information on price level changes and can rene-gotiate wage contracts in line with higher or lower prices. This time any given percentage increase in the general price level from P_1 to P_2 is matched by increases in input costs. For example, if general prices rise by 5% then wages rise by 5% so that the 'real wage' does not fall. In this situation there is no increase in the profitability of production when prices rise from P_1 to P_2, so that long-run aggregate supply remains unchanged at Y_1 in Figure 15.3.

2.3 AD/AS and equilibrium national output

It will be useful at this stage to look at how AD and AS schedules can be used to find the equilibrium levels for the general price level and for national output.

We initially assume that wages and other input costs do not fully adjust to price level changes to that the aggregate supply (AS) curve slopes upwards from left to right and is not vertical.

Only where AD and AS *intersect* at a general price level of P_1 and national output Y_1 in Figure 15.4, do we have an equilibrium outcome for the economy. Any other combina-tion of price level and national output is unsustainable, with an excess of either aggregate demand or aggregate supply.

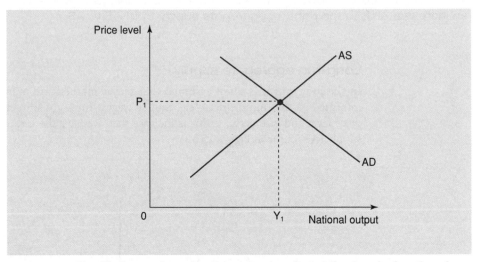

Figure 15.4 Equilibrium values for the price level and the level of national output.

For example, for price levels *above* P_1, AS exceeds AD putting downward pressure on prices and national output. As the general price level falls, aggregate demand (AD) expands (positive 'real balance effect' via increase in real value of wealth holdings, raising C and via likely reductions in interest rates raising C and I, etc.) and aggregate supply (AS) contracts (profitability is squeezed as prices fall faster than the less flexible input costs for producers). Only at P_1/Y_1 do we have an equilibrium outcome.

Pause for thought 1

Can you explain why price levels below P_1 are not sustainable in Figure 15.4?

As we consider unemployment and inflation in the remainder of this chapter, we shall use aggregate demand and aggregate supply analysis wherever appropriate.

3   UNEMPLOYMENT AND ITS CHARACTERISTICS

Here we review the definition, measurement and characteristics of unemployment in the UK.

3.1 Definition of unemployment

Unemployment
The number of people actively looking for work who are currently out of a job.

There are two methods of defining and measuring unemployment in the UK: the survey method and the claimant count.

(a) *Survey method* This involves undertaking *surveys* designed to provide information about the labour force. The UK government's Labour Force Survey (LFS) is undertaken quarterly using the *International Labour Office* (ILO) definition of unemployment. The ILO define unemployment as people who are out of work, who want a job, have actively looked for a job over the previous four weeks and who are available to start work within the next two weeks. One benefit of the ILO definition is that since surveys are conducted throughout the EU and OECD countries it is useful when making international comparisons.

(b) *Claimant count method* The second measure of unemployment uses *administrative records* in order to determine the number of people who claim unemployment-related benefits, such as the Jobseeker's Allowance (JSA). In order to claim the JSA people must declare that they are out of work but capable and available for work and be actively seeking work in the week in which they make the claim. This measure of unemployment is known as the *claimant count* and since the figures are a by-product of the administrative process they are available each month, at little extra cost, for all geographical areas. Since the claimant count is based on administrative records however, it is susceptible to changes in the way the statistics are calculated.

3.2 Measuring unemployment

Unemployment can be expressed as a number such as 1.8 million or a percentage, such as 5.1% of the workforce. The workforce (sometimes called the 'economically active' population) can be defined as those who are employed and unemployed. The unemployment rate (U) is the percentage of the workforce who are unemployed. Thus:

$$U = \frac{\text{Number of people unemployed}}{\text{Workforce}} \times 100$$

Over the period March–May 2005 unemployment as calculated by the ILO was 1,265,000 which represented an unemployment rate of 5.1%.

Unemployment is a *stock concept*, which means that it is measured at a point in time and there are inflows and outflows from the stock (*see* Figure 15.5).

For example, individuals may be sacked or made redundant and, though they are still part of the workforce, they represent an inflow into the unemployment total. An outflow can take the form of unemployed individuals emigrating.

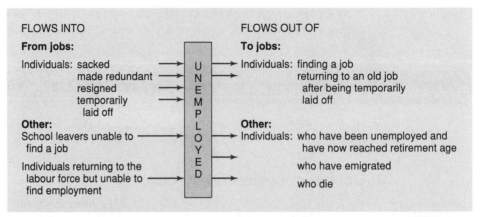

Figure 15.5 Unemployment can essentially be viewed as a *stock concept*. In other words, it can only be measured at a point in time. From the stock of unemployed there are inflows and outflows. As illustrated in the figure, individuals, for example, may be sacked, made redundant, or in fact resign. If they have no immediate job to go to then they will represent an inflow into the unemployed total. As regards the outflow from the stock individuals may, for example, find employment or emigrate.

3.3 The costs of unemployment

The 'costs' of unemployment take various forms. For example, there is the lost output which could have been produced had the unemployed been in employment. The unemployed labour represents a loss of resources and with it a resulting lower standard of living. Unemployment in the UK as a whole has fallen from some 9.7% in 1992 to around 5.1% in 2005. However, it is often useful to look at patterns and trends within this headline figure. Table 15.1 reveals that in Spring 2004 18,000 in the 18–24 age group, 272,000 in the 25–49 age group and 44,000 in the 50 years and over age group had been unemployed for more than two years.

Individuals who are unemployed for long periods of time become less attractive to prospective employers and less optimistic about their employment prospects. The result can be family unrest, depression and, possibly, an increase in the crime rate. Unemployment can also lead to the repossession of the unemployed person's house due to a failure to pay the mortgage. Encouragingly these figures are much lower than for the same groups in 2000 and 1996, indicating a reduced social cost in terms of the long-term unemployed.

An increase in unemployment can result in two main costs to the exchequer:

(*i*) Benefits such as unemployment benefit, social security and housing benefit are paid to those who are unemployed.

(*ii*) Those who become unemployed no longer pay income tax and, because they have a reduced amount of money to spend, it also means less indirect taxes (VAT and excise duty) to the exchequer. Both, therefore, represent a reduction in tax revenue to the government.

3.4 The characteristics of unemployment

Unemployment in the UK possesses the following characteristics:

Table 15.1 UK ILO unemployment by age and duration – male and female (in thousands), Spring quarters (March–May)

Age	Duration	1996	2000	2004
18–24	Up to 6 months	303	284	280
	Over 6 and up to 12 months	95	53	60
	All over 12 months	159	66	52
	All over 24 months	75	28	18
	All	557	403	392
25–49	Up to 6 months	492	418	393
	Over 6 and up to 12 months	217	120	107
	All over 12 months	535	246	157
	All over 24 months	348	141	72
	All	1,244	784	658
50 and over	Up to 6 months	120	116	108
	Over 6 and up to 12 months	55	43	35
	All over 12 months	203	116	72
	All over 24 months	148	75	44
	All	378	275	215

Source: Adapted from *Labour Market Trends* (2005), April, Vol. 113, No. 4

Regional unemployment
The geographical location of particular industries and changes in long-term demand play a key role here.

(a) *Regional unemployment.* Table 15.2 gives the UK regional unemployment figures over the period 1992–2004.

The figures reveal regional differences in the rates of unemployment with the North East, Yorkshire and Humberside and West Midlands usually having regional unemployment rates above the UK average at any point in time. The traditional explanation for such regional disparities in unemployment has been the decline of basic industries such as textiles, shipbuilding, steel and coal which have tended to be located in these specific regions.

It is more difficult to raise aggregate demand as a means of dealing with *regional unemployment* since the result is likely to be inflationary pressures elsewhere in the economy.

Table 15.2 Regional ILO rates of unemployment (%)

Spring quarter of each year	1992	1996	2000	2004
United Kingdom	9.7	8.2	5.8	5.1
North East	11.8	10.8	9.1	6.6
North West	9.1	8.4	5.7	5.1
Yorkshire and Humberside	10.1	8.1	6.2	5.5
East Midlands	8.8	7.4	5.3	4.3
West Midlands	10.7	9.2	6.4	5.4
Eastern	7.7	6.2	3.8	4.2
London			7.3	7.1
South East	7.8	6.0	3.5	3.9
South West	9.1	6.3	4.3	3.9
England	9.7	8.1	5.5	5.1
Wales	8.9	8.3	6.5	4.6
Scotland	9.5	8.7	7.7	5.7
Northern Ireland	12.3	9.7	7.2	5.4

Source: Adapted from *Regional Trends*, 2005

Regional policy has therefore been used as a remedy for regional disparities in unemployment (*see* page 370).

(b) *Female unemployment.* Table 15.3 reveals that female unemployment as a percentage of the labour force was lower than that of males over the period 1992–2004.

Table 15.3 Male and female ILO unemployment rates (%)

UK unemployment	Male	Female
1992	11.7	7.5
1996	9.8	6.5
2000	6.2	5.0
2004	5.4	4.2

Source: Adapted from *Labour Market Trends*, April 2005

(c) *Age-related unemployment.* In terms of the long-term unemployed, Table 15.1 reveals that in Spring 2004, 34.2% of the 50 years and over age group had been out of work for over 12 months, whereas for the 18–24 age group the figure was 12.6%. This would seem to suggest that those individuals who are over 50 years of age and out of work are more likely to remain unemployed for longer periods than those in the younger age group. Table 15.1 also reveals that 27% of the total unemployed are in the 18–24 age group. One of the possible reasons for this is that if a firm runs into difficulty employers are likely to cut back first on those who have not accumulated skills and experience.

4 THE CAUSES AND REMEDIES OF UNEMPLOYMENT

We briefly review various types of unemployment with some possible causes and remedies. A more detailed analysis of policy prescriptions for unemployment is undertaken later in this chapter.

4.1 Frictional unemployment

Frictional unemployment
Due to the time it takes workers to change jobs.

(a) *Causes.* This type of unemployment includes those individuals who are between jobs. Workers who leave one job in order to look for another need time to search because of the lack of information on all the possible jobs available. There are 'search' costs involved, in terms of lost earnings and travel expenses for such things as interviews, but they can be viewed as an investment.

(b) *Remedies.* There will always be individuals between jobs but measures to cut the search time involved will invariably reduce frictional unemployment. Improving the flow of information with regards to the availability of particular employment is one such measure. Some argue for a real reduction in unemployment related benefits as helping encourage the unemployed to seek work, although this is a controversial method. It could be argued that by reducing unemployment benefit individuals will spend less time searching for another job and therefore may end up in less appropriate (and less efficient) jobs, with a mismatch between their skills and those required in their job.

4.2 Structural unemployment

Structural unemployment
Arises from longer-term changes in the demand for, and supply of, labour in specific industries.

(a) *Causes.* The pattern of demand and methods of production are continually changing. There could be a change in the comparative costs of an industry, technological change may mean that an industry's labour requirements are somewhat less or demand for a particular product may simply decline. Any of these changes could lead to structural unemployment. Examples in the UK include unemployment resulting from a decline in the production of textiles, shipbuilding, coal and steel. Those workers who become structurally unemployed are available for work but they have either the wrong skills for the jobs available or they are in the wrong location. There is a mismatch between the skills and the location of labour and the unfilled vacancies.

(b) *Remedies.* The remedy for structural unemployment involves retraining those made redundant so that they can acquire the skills now required by the growing sectors of the economy. It may also involve the possible relocation of labour to other areas of the UK. Such schemes could include the Travel to Interview scheme, which offers help to those who are unemployed and who have to travel beyond daily travelling distance for a job interview, including paying travelling expenses and the cost of overnight stays where necessary. Regional policy (*see* page 370) can also be used to attract industry into those geographical areas suffering from structural unemployment.

4.3 Demand deficient unemployment

(a) *Causes.* This is often referred to as *Keynesian unemployment* or *cyclical unemployment.* It occurs when aggregate demand is too small in relation to aggregate output so that there is a deficiency of demand for goods and services. Since the demand for labour is a derived demand, the lack of demand for goods and services will also lead to a deficiency of demand for labour. This is the type of unemployment Keynes was concerned with in his *General Theory* (1936).

Demand deficient unemployment can be outlined by reference to Figure 15.6. The assumption is made that the economy is initially at full employment when aggregate demand – consisting of consumer expenditure, investment, government expenditure and exports minus imports – is AD_1, aggregate supply is AS and equilibrium national income is Y_1. Suppose there is now a reduction in investment, perhaps because of a fall in business confidence so that aggregate demand falls to AD_2 resulting in a reduction in equilibrium national income to Y_2. This being the case, the fall in national income/output from Y_1 to Y_2 will result in an increase in the numbers unemployed, i.e. demand deficient unemployment.

(b) *Remedies.* It is possible to use *fiscal policy* and *monetary policy* in order to reduce demand deficient unemployment. Their use is referred to as *demand management* and the aim is to influence the total demand for goods and services in the economy. *Fiscal policy* can increase aggregate demand, either through an increase in total government expenditure or by a reduction of taxes, or both. Referring again to Figure 15.6, assuming the economy is in equilibrium at a level of income Y_2, but that the full employment level of income is Y_1, then an increase in government expenditure would help shift aggregate demand from AD_2 to AD_1 and alleviate the demand deficient unemployment. *Monetary policy* can also influence the level of money or aggregate demand by means of the interest rate and the level of credit available. By influencing the amount and the terms on which households and firms can borrow to finance expenditure and investment, it is possible to influence the level of total demand in the economy. For example, a reduction in the interest

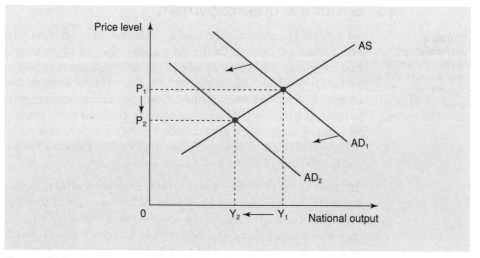

Figure 15.6 A fall in aggregate demand from AD_1 to AD_2 results in a reduction of national income from Y_1 to Y_2 and an increase in the numbers unemployed.

rate makes it cheaper to borrow for consumption and investment, and this will stimulate demand in the economy. For the way in which the Bank of England can influence the interest rate, *see* Chapter 13, page 314.

4.4 Real wage unemployment

Real wage unemployment
Rigidities in the labour market are seen as preventing the ratio of money wage to prices falling to a level that would 'clear' the market.

(a) *Causes.* This is often referred to as *classical unemployment* after the economists in the 1930s who believed that unemployment was the result of real wages being too high. This can be illustrated in Figure 15.7 where a real wage of $(W/P)_2$ is set above the equilibrium real wage $(W/P)_1$. The result will be an excess supply of labour equal to $q_{L3} - q_{L2}$. This *real*

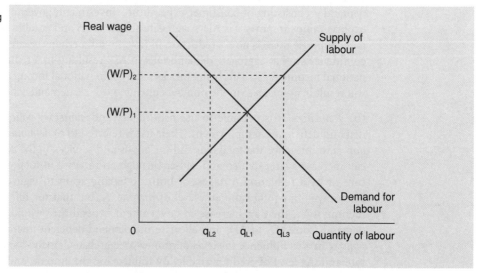

Figure 15.7 If a real wage $(W/P)_2$ is maintained above the equilibrium real wage $(W/P)_1$ then the result is an excess supply of labour equal to $q_{L3} - q_{L2}$, i.e. real wage unemployment.

wage unemployment is seen as resulting from workers being unwilling to accept a real wage of less than $(W/P)_2$. Classical unemployment is, therefore, the result of real wages being maintained above an equilibrium real wage $(W/P)_1$.

(b) *Remedies*. It is not easy to cure this type of unemployment for it involves the reduction of real wages which could require agreement between the government, trade unions and employers. An added problem is that a cut in real wages would reduce aggregate demand since real wages influence consumers' expenditure. A reduction in aggregate demand might then lead to a reduction in the equilibrium level of national income and, therefore, create demand deficient unemployment.

Real wage unemployment in a modern, globalised economy (*see* also Chapter 16) is an increasing problem when overseas countries can offer labour at highly competitive wage rates to those in the domestic country. In this event 'offshoring' may occur, as is indicated in Mini Case Study 15.1 below.

Mini Case Study 15.1

Losing jobs overseas

The falling price of consumer electronics has buoyed demand for items from microwave ovens to flat-screen televisions, filling our living rooms with games consoles and DVD players. But lower price tags and margins also make it uneconomic to manufacture these goods in high-cost countries such as Britain.

Prices fall as volume production ramps up, enabling big manufacturers to take advantage of economies of scale. The cost of silicon chips, for example, has reduced steadily even though the power of such chips has risen greatly.

David Alker, senior industry analyst at SRI Consulting Business Intelligence, said: 'The retail cost does not reflect the actual cost of consumer electronics. A digital camera that sold for £300 a few years ago retails for £100 now, but the actual cost of production is identical. It's just that prices were higher at first in order to recoup the research and development costs.'

The electronics industry has always relied on a small proportion of early adopters, the people who must have new gadgets as they arrive, in order to defray the high initial costs until demand ramps up. At this point other manufacturers pile in with similar products, bringing down prices. This pattern is far from unique to the electronics industry: it can be seen in every piece of new technology, from light bulbs to cars.

New technology also causes disruption for suppliers of the old products. The Samsung plant which closed in Teesdale in the late 1990s was planning to make fax machines at a time when few were predicting the rapid rise of e-mail. Saturation in certain key markets also plays a part in lowering margins, as PC makers and mobile manufacturers have found to their cost. But the most significant factor bringing down costs is the entry of manufacturers based in eastern Europe and China, where labour is much cheaper.

Source: *Economics for Business and Management*, Griffiths and Wall (FT/Prentice Hall, 2005)

Questions

1 *Why are electronic businesses in general coming under increased pressure to reduce costs?*

2 *What particular problems are facing electronics businesses located in Britain?*

Answers to questions can be found on the students' side of the Companion Website.

Offshoring

This issue of lower overseas costs is considered in further detail in Chapter 16. However, we might note here that countries which already have lower labour costs than the UK and other advanced industrialised economies are creating *even stronger* incentives for overseas businesses to locate production in their territories. For example, India is planning an aggressive drive to create *special economic zones* (SEZs) that would enable the country to compete better with China for foreign investment. Senior officials say New Delhi is planning to forgo India's restrictive labour laws within the country's planned 17 special economic zones. This would be designed to allay foreign investor concerns about India's low labour productivity. In addition, New Delhi would remove remaining bureaucratic obstacles to creation of the zones. India, which has roughly half the per capita income of neighbouring China, aims to increase its share of world trade to 1% by 2007, up from 0.7% in 2003. In 2002 India attracted roughly one-tenth the foreign investment that went to China. A senior government figure reported that they needed to create success stories in trade so that they can move forward in India. He also said that they need to increase foreign direct investment. The SEZs are key to this.

4.5 Regional unemployment

(a) *Causes.* Table 15.2 (page 365) has already noted the considerable variation in unemployment rates between different regions of the UK. For example, the unemployment rate in the North East of England is consistently higher than the average for the UK (6.6% in 2004 compared to 5.1% average). The geographical concentration of industries in decline (e.g. shipbuilding in the North East, textiles in the North West), in other words *structural unemployment*, clearly plays a role here. So too might factors such as lack of infrastructure and greater geographical distance to key markets.

(b) *Remedies.* Government support to less advantaged regions is a key policy measure for tackling regional unemployment. *Regional Selective Assistance (RSA)* is the main instrument of the UK in seeking to influence locational decisions for production activities in various regions. It is a discretionary grant towards projects of any size in both the manufacturing and service sectors, is open to both domestic and international firms and is available to help with the investment costs of projects with capital expenditures above £500,000. It has three overlapping objectives:

1 to create and safeguard jobs
2 to attract and retain internationally mobile investments
3 to contribute to improving the competitiveness of disadvantaged regions.

The RSA is usually administered either as capital related or job related.

- *Capital-related project grants* are normally used to help cover the costs of land purchase and site preparation or the acquisition of plant and machinery.
- *Job-related project grants* are normally used to help cover the costs of hiring and training staff.

The Department of Trade and Industry (DTI) administers the scheme and has spent over £750 million over the past decade on the RSA, safeguarding or creating some 180,000 UK jobs. However, the cost per job has been estimated at around £4,000 during this period.

Example	State aid sometimes fails

Samsung, the Korean electronics firm, located a major manufacturing plant for electronic equipment in Teeside, UK in 1994. To encourage Samsung to locate in Teeside it received £86 million of public money from the UK government, £58 million in the form of RSA to support the development of infrastructure needed by the new plant, training and other project costs. It was expected that 3,000 new jobs would be created and £600 million of new investment in a state-of-the-art electronic factory. In the event Samsung decided to close the manufacturing site in January 2004, claiming falling global prices for flat-panel screens and microwaves, two of its key projects. Samsung announced that it would disperse production to China and Slovakia, where labour costs were only 50 pence and £1 per hour respectively, compared to £5.61 in Teeside.

Not all UK experiences with state aid for inward investment have been so disappointing. Nissan established its Sunderland car plant in 1969, resulting in direct employment of 4,500 people (and many more indirectly) and a major contribution to UK car exports. Nevertheless, a *Financial Times* survey in 2003 found that half the £730 million of grants involved in 50 regional aid projects over the past decade went to 16 companies which have since closed or fallen well short of job creation targets promised in return for this state aid.

Governments have often welcomed foreign producers to the UK in order to stimulate innovation and create employment in the country. State aid has been one method of attracting such firms with these subsidies helping firms locating in the UK to lower both the set-up costs and running costs of their operations in the UK. However, state aid cannot solve all the possible problems facing electronic firms. For example, new technology can change what seems a good investment into a major problem in a very short period of time! In these circumstances state aid can be wasted. Many analysts suggest that if labour costs are significantly lower in other countries, then state aid by the UK government merely delays the inevitable loss of jobs overseas, because it is impossible to give state aid to incoming firms indefinitely to compensate them for high relative costs in the UK. For example, in the late 1990s, the Korean Lucky Goldstar (LG) electronics firm received £40,000 from the UK government *for every job created* in factories set up in South Wales. The problems of such investment and subsidies became clear in 2003 when economic difficulties at home in Korea, coupled with adverse market trends, led LG to announce the closure of its computer screen plant in South Wales with the loss of 900 jobs. In addition, the semiconductor plant which LG had only just built near Newport did not even open for business. It may be that government policy should aim to attract foreign firms producing high value added products into the UK instead of providing state aid in the form of labour subsidies. Government aid to incoming industries has also been criticised on the basis that if that same money had been spent on stimulating small UK firms then more employment would have been created and vital innovation stimulated.

4.6 Technological unemployment

Technological unemployment
Leads to significant changes in labour and capital productivity, resulting in job losses.

This refers to unemployment that is regarded as the result of changes in technology.

(a) *Causes.* Such changes in technology may mean that goods and services which previously used labour as input are now more efficiently produced by using capital equipment, or at least *less labour* in relation to capital equipment than before the new technology was developed. This type of unemployment was considered in Mini Case Study 15.1 earlier in the chapter.

(b) *Remedies*. New technology may create new jobs as well as remove old jobs, so that the *net* effect on unemployment may be difficult to measure. Certainly technical change cannot be avoided and may be an important element in raising productivity in the higher wage developed economies, thereby helping them compete effectively with the lower wage less developed economies.

4.7 Natural rate of unemployment (NRU)

Natural rate of unemployment (NRU)
The rate of unemployment at which there is no excess or deficiency of demand for labour.

This has been described as the (voluntary) unemployment which still exists even if the real wage is at the equilibrium level which 'clears' the labour market. The labour market diagram shown in Figure 15.8 can be used to illustrate the idea of the '**natural rate of unemployment**' (NRU) which was introduced by Milton Friedman. Here labour demand, L^D, reflects the *marginal revenue product* (MRP) of workers, i.e. the extra revenue earned from employing the last worker (*see* Chapter 8). This is downward sloping in line with the assumption of a diminishing *marginal physical product* (MPP) for workers.

- Labour supply, L^S, represents all those workers willing and able (i.e. they have the right skills and are in the right location) to accept jobs at a given real wage.
- The labour force, L^F, shows the total number of workers who consider themselves to be members of the labour force at any given real wage; of course, not all of these are willing or able to accept job offers, perhaps because they are still searching for a better offer or because they have not yet acquired the appropriate skills or are not in an appropriate location.

At the equilibrium real wage (W/P) in Figure 15.8, N_1 workers are willing and able to accept job offers whereas N_2 workers consider themselves to be members of the labour

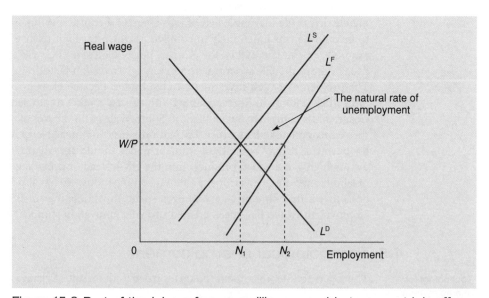

Figure 15.8 Part of the labour force unwilling or unable to accept job offers at the equilibrium real wage. This unemployment ($N_2 - N_1$) is defined as the natural rate of unemployment (NRU).

force. That part of the labour force unwilling or unable to accept job offers at the equilibrium real wage $(N_2 - N_1)$ is defined as being the *natural rate of unemployment* (NRU). In terms of our earlier classification of the unemployed the NRU can be regarded as including both the frictionally and structurally unemployed.

It can be seen that anything that *reduces the labour supply* (the numbers willing and able to accept a job at a given real wage) will, other things being equal, cause the NRU to increase. Possible factors might include an increase in the level or availability of unemployment benefits, thereby encouraging unemployed members of the labour force to engage in more prolonged search activity. An increase in trade union power might also reduce the numbers willing and able to accept a job at a given real wage, especially if the trade union is able to restrict the effective labour supply as part of a strategy for raising wages. A reduced labour supply might also result from increased technological change or increased global competition, both of which change the nature of the labour market skills required for employment. Higher taxes on earned income are also likely to reduce the labour supply at any given real wage.

Similarly, anything that *reduces the labour demand* will, other things equal, cause the NRU to increase. A fall in the marginal revenue product of labour, via a fall in marginal physical productivity or in the product price, might be expected to reduce labour demand. Many economists believe that the two sharp oil price increases in the 1970s had this effect, with the resulting fall in aggregate demand causing firms to cut back on capital spending, reducing the overall capital stock and hence the marginal physical productivity of labour.

4.8 Unemployment and supply-side policies

Supply-side policies
Seek to combat inflation by shifting the aggregate supply curve to the right (increase). Involves focusing on raising the productivity of factor inputs.

Supply-side policies, together with fiscal and monetary policies, will be covered in more detail in Section 9.4 of this chapter, although it is important to mention them here as a remedy for unemployment.

Supply-side policies are based on the belief that output, economic growth and *employment* can be increased by raising aggregate supply. The view is that by allowing competitive market forces to operate, both households and firms will be motivated by financial rewards to increase the supply of their services. Thus, supply-side policies include a reduction in income tax, improvements in government training and retraining schemes, and the reform of both trade unions and the benefit system.

As we noted at the beginning of the chapter, policies aimed at reducing unemployment also have potential impacts on inflation, and it is to this topic that we now turn.

5 INFLATION

Inflation
Average level of prices in the economy rises. Different measures exist (RPI, RPIX, RPIY, etc.).

Inflation is a term often applied to a situation in which there is a persistent tendency for the general level of prices to rise. The 'rate of inflation' over the past twelve months is, in effect, telling us how much extra money we would need now in order to be able to purchase the same 'basket' of goods and services as we did twelve months ago.

In extreme circumstances an economy may suffer *hyperinflation* where there is a rapidly accelerating rise in prices. In a situation of hyperinflation, members of society tend to lose confidence in the ability of their currency to fulfil its functions (*see* Chapter 13, page 301) and there can follow a breakdown in the country's monetary system.

The rate of inflation has varied from a peak of 25% in 1975 to around 2% in more recent years. A number of measures have been used to calculate the rate of inflation in the UK.

5.1 The Retail Price Index (RPI)

Retail Price Index (RPI)
Shows the change from month to month in the cost of a representative 'basket' of goods and services bought by a typical household.

This has been the main official measure in the UK, showing the change from month to month in the cost of a representative 'basket' of goods and services bought by a typical household. The rate of inflation measured using the RPI is often referred to as the *headline* rate of inflation.

In January 2004 the RPI stood at 183.6 which means that average prices have risen by 83.6% between January 1987 and January 2004. As the index is an average, this figure conceals the fact that some prices have increased more rapidly (rent 155%, water 176% and cigarettes 208%), whilst other prices have fallen (audio-visual equipment by around 70%).

Once the RPI has been constructed, the rate of inflation can then be calculated, with the most usual measure being the twelve-monthly change in the RPI. For example, the RPI stood at 183.6 in January 2004. In January 2003 it stood at 179.3 and therefore the annual rate of inflation over the period to January 2004 was:

$$\frac{183.6 - 179.3}{179.3} \times 100\% = 2.4\%$$

Mini Case Study 15.2 looks in more detail at the calculation of the RPI in the UK.

Mini Case Study 15.2

The Retail Price Index (RPI)

The RPI measures the change from month to month in the cost of a representative 'basket' of goods and services of the type bought by a typical household.

A number of stages are involved in the calculation of the RPI. The first stage is to select the items to be included in the index and to weight these items according to their relative importance in the average family budget. Obviously items on which a family spends a large proportion of its income are given heavier weights than those items on which the family spends relatively little. For example, in 2003 the weight given to tea in the index was 1, whereas that for electricity was 14 (out of a total 'all items weight' of 1,000). The weights used are changed annually to reflect the changes in the composition of family expenditure.

The weights used for groups of items are shown in Table 15.4. It can be seen that food has been replaced as the largest item by housing (rent, mortgage interest, rates and council tax, water charges, repairs and dwelling insurance). This is part of a longer-run trend associated with differing income elasticities of demand for the items in the 'basket'.

The second stage in deriving the RPI involves collecting the price data. For most items prices are collected on a specific day each month, usually the Tuesday nearest the middle of the month. Prices are obtained from a sample of retail outlets in some 180 different areas. Care is taken to make sure a representative range of retail outlets, small retailers, supermarkets, department stores, etc., are surveyed. In all, around

Table 15.4 General index of retail prices: group weights

	1987	2003
Food	167	109
Catering	46	51
Alcoholic drink	76	68
Tobacco	38	30
Housing	157	203
Fuel and light	61	29
Household goods	73	72
Household services	44	61
Clothing and footwear	74	51
Personal goods and services	40	41
Motoring expenditure	127	146
Fares and other travel costs	22	20
Leisure goods	47	48
Leisure services	30	71

Source: M. O'Quigley in Griffiths and Wall, *Economics for Business and Management* (FT/Prentice Hall, 2005)

150,000 price quotations are collected each month. An average price is then calculated for each item in the index.

The final stage is to calculate the RPI from all these data. All index numbers must relate to some base period or reference date. In the case of the RPI the base period is January 1987 = 100.

Questions

1 *What can we learn from the data in Table 15.4?*

2 *What changes would you expect for a similar table in ten years' time?*

Answers to questions can be found at the back of the book (page 521).

5.2 RPIX

RPIX
Retail Price Index (RPI) excluding mortgage interest payments.

For policy makers in the UK, however, the RPI has been superseded by the **RPIX** (the RPI excluding mortgage interest payments). The RPIX is referred to as measuring 'underlying' inflation and this was (until 2003 – see below) the subject of the government's 2.5% inflation target. Excluding mortgage interest rates from the RPI eliminates a rather perverse effect, namely that raising the interest rate to moderate inflationary pressure will actually increase the RPI measure of inflation!

5.3 RPIY

RPIY
This is RPIX minus indirect taxes and the council tax.

However, both the RPI and the RPIX are influenced by increases in indirect taxes and in the council tax. If these taxes increase, for example a rise in excise duty on cigarettes to discourage smoking, then the RPIX measure of inflation will increase without any increase in inflationary pressure in the economy. The Bank of England publishes the **RPIY** (RPIX minus VAT, local authority taxes and excise duty) to eliminate this effect.

5.4 Consumer Price Index (CPI)

Consumer Price Index (CPI)
Uses a different 'basket' of goods to the RPI. Now the UK as well as the EU 'official' inflation measure.

This was adopted in December 2003 as the official measure of inflation in the UK and is based on the *Harmonised Index of Consumer Prices* (*HICP*), the official measure in the EU. The European Central Bank aims to keep EU inflation below 2% as measured by the HICP and 2% is now also the target for UK inflation using the CPI.

Note: Inflation and oil prices

Given the surge in oil prices in recent times, the Chancellor of the Exchequer may be regretting his decision in 2003 to change from the RPI to the CPI as the UK's official measure of inflation. This is because the CPI has a higher weighting for energy prices than the RPI or RPIX. In 2005 it has been estimated that high energy prices have caused the CPI measure of inflation to be some 0.5% higher than would have been the case using the RPIX measure.

6 | THE EFFECTS OF INFLATION

The effects of inflation can be identified as arising from either *perfectly anticipated* or *unanticipated inflation*. With perfectly anticipated inflation the rate of inflation has been expected by the various decision-making agents in the economy, such as households and firms, whereas unanticipated inflation is a situation where the economy may under- or over-predict the actual rate of inflation.

6.1 Perfectly anticipated inflation

Perfectly anticipated inflation
Where inflation proceeds at a perfectly foreseen rate so that all possible adjustments for the existence of inflation have been made.

If inflation is perfectly anticipated then everybody knows what the rate of inflation is going to be, say, 5%. As a result the various agents in the economy have been able to adjust their decision making accordingly. In this economy all contracts, interest rates and the tax system would take the correctly foreseen rate of inflation into account. Even the exchange rate would have adjusted to prevent inflation having any adverse effect on the balance of payments. The main costs of perfectly anticipated inflation would then be as follows:

(a) *Shoe-leather costs.* If there is a high, perfectly anticipated rate of inflation then it is likely that the rate of interest offered to savers will increase. Since there is an opportunity cost to holding money, individuals will place their money in interest-bearing assets. Thus, shoe-leather costs will arise since individual members of society, holding more of their wealth in, say, bank accounts, will require frequent visits to the bank to withdraw their money.

Unanticipated inflation
Where inflation has not been foreseen correctly so that any adjustments that have been made are inaccurate.

(b) *Menu costs.* Even though inflation may be perfectly anticipated there is still the cost of frequently changing price labels, vending machine prices and so on. Obviously the faster the rate of change of inflation, then the higher the menu costs will be.

6.2 Unanticipated inflation

In addition to the costs already noted, **unanticipated inflation** brings with it some further costs.

(a) *Redistributional effects.* Different income groups are likely to be affected in different ways. For example, those on fixed incomes will see their purchasing power reduced by inflation, as too will those workers who belong to weak trade unions, unable to obtain wage increases for their members in line with the increase in inflation. Those workers, on the other hand, who belong to powerful trade unions with effective bargaining power are likely to be able to cushion their members against the effects of inflation.

Retired members of society who saved throughout their working lives to provide for their old age will find that their savings are worth less as a result of unanticipated inflation. There is also likely to be a *redistribution* of income away from the income earner to the government. The reason for this is that money incomes normally rise when inflation occurs and income earners, therefore, move into higher tax brackets. This means that the taxpayer will pay a higher proportion of their income in tax, hence a redistribution from the taxpayer to the government. This is called *fiscal drag*. Redistributional effects will also occur, involving movement away from lenders (creditors) to borrowers (debtors). In times of unanticipated inflation, repaid loans will be worth less than they were when the loans were initially obtained, hence the borrower is set to gain while the lender is set to lose.

Example	If the rate of interest is 12% but the rate of inflation is 18% then the *real rate of interest* is in fact negative, at −6%.

(b) *The effect on business.* Unanticipated inflation may make it difficult for businesses to enter into long-term contracts because of the uncertainty of the inflation rate; for example, where inflation is the result of higher than expected costs of production (particularly wages). If the increased costs cannot be matched by price increases then businesses will see their profits reduced, which could eventually lead to bankruptcy. Businesses may also suffer if their unionised workforce take industrial action in support of a wage claim to offset the unanticipated inflation.

(c) *The effect on the balance of payments.* Inflation can cause balance-of-payments problems. For example, if the UK inflation rate is higher than that of its major competitors, the goods and services produced in the UK will be less competitive abroad, whilst goods and services produced abroad will become more competitive in the UK. If the exchange rate fails to adjust accordingly (here depreciate) then, depending on the price elasticity of demand, the cumulative effect could be a deficit on the balance of payments (*see* Chapter 14).

Of course, where extreme inflationary events occur (*hyperinflation*) then the costs are even more severe, as indicated in Mini Case Study 15.3 below for Germany.

Mini Case Study 15.3

German hyperinflation

When people discuss inflation and its problems they often examine inflation in its more 'moderate form's. However, if inflation gets out of hand then it can take on the extreme form sometimes described as 'hyperinflation'. Whilst this word does not have a specific definition it tends to be used for extreme situations where, say, prices are rising in double digit figures on a daily or weekly basis. The example of Germany in the early years of the 1920s is often used as an example.

To illustrate the German experience we can look at changes in the price of a postage stamp in these years.

Table 15.5 **The price of a postage stamp in Germany, 1921–3**

	Deutschmarks
1 April 1921	0.60
1 January 1922	2
1 July	3
1 October	6
15 November	12
15 December	25
15 January 1923	50
1 March	100
1 July	300
1 August	1,000
24 August	20,000
1 September	75,000
20 September	250,000
1 October	2,000,000
10 October	5,000,000
20 October	10,000,000
1 November	100,000,000
5 November	1,000,000,000
12 November	10,000,000,000
20 November	20,000,000,000
26 November	80,000,000,000
1 December	100,000,000,000 or 0.10 new marks

Many stories come from this period in Germany to illustrate the problems of hyperinflation. A famous one tells of a man who filled up his wheelbarrow with deutschmarks to go to the shops, only to be mugged on route to his destination; the robber tipped out the notes and stole the wheelbarrow. Another refers to the Berlin Symphony Orchestra which walked out halfway through an afternoon performance because they had just been paid, knowing that if they waited to the end of the performance their wages would be able to buy so much less. Yet another refers to coffee drinkers in Berlin's cafes who insisted on paying before they drank their cup of coffee, aware that one hour later they might be unable to afford it.

It does not take very much imagination to realise that everyday life would simply break down if faced by such dramatic falls in the value of money.

Historically, annual price increases of less than 5% have not been considered too much of a problem, though lower figures than this have become the stated aim of many advanced industrialised economies. For example, the UK government has for many years instructed the Bank of England to keep inflation (RIPX) below 2.5% per annum and the European Central Bank aims to keep its official measure of inflation (HICP) below 2% per annum.

Source: M. O'Quigley in Griffiths and Wall, *Economics for Business and Management* (FT/Prentice Hall, 2005)

Questions

1 *Why do some suggest that it is useful for us to carefully consider historical cases of hyperinflation, such as that in Germany, even though hyperinflation rarely occurs?*

2 *How might a government seek to bring a situation of hyperinflation under control?*

Answers to questions can be found on the students' side of the Companion Website.

---

7 ECONOMIC THEORY AND INFLATION

A number of approaches have been used in seeking to explain inflationary pressures and suggest policy remedies to control these pressures. Whilst the following discussion may somewhat oversimplify the various approaches, it may be useful in giving an overview of this ongoing debate.

One view of inflation is based on the premise that it is changes in the money supply which bring about changes in the price level. If this view of inflation is to be believed, then in order to control inflation it is necessary to control the growth of the money supply. Central to this (often called the 'monetarist') view of inflation is the *quantity theory of money*.

7.1 The quantity theory of money

Velocity of circulation
The average number of times a unit of money changed hands in a given time period.

Phillips curve
A curve showing the relationship between (price) inflation and unemployment. The original Phillips curve plotted wage inflation against unemployment in the UK over the years 1861–1957.

The simplest form of the quantity theory of money is that based on the work of Irving Fisher, the Fisher equation for exchange being:

$$MV \equiv PT$$

The equation can be analysed in terms of the money supply in circulation determined by the monetary authorities (M) multiplied by the average number of times money changes hands, that is the **velocity of circulation** (V), being identical to the average price level of all transactions (P) multiplied by the total number of transactions (T). The equation for exchange is an identity (denoted by $\equiv$) since both sides of the equation must be equal.

In terms of the Fisher equation, the argument is that in the long run the velocity of circulation (V) and the number of transactions (T) are constant. The velocity of circulation is assumed constant since it depends on institutional factors such as the pattern of payments. The total number of transactions is assumed constant since it is the view of the classical economist that the economy will always return to full employment in the long run. The importance of making these two assumptions is that if both V and T are constant a change in the money supply will cause a proportionate change in the price level.

7.2 The Phillips curve and inflation

Here the emphasis is on excess aggregate demand being the major source of inflationary pressures with the level of unemployment being a proxy (stand-in) variable for the level of aggregate demand. The relationship between unemployment and inflation can be analysed by reference to the *Phillips curve*. The traditional Phillips curve described the inverse relationship between unemployment and the rate of change of money wages (i.e. wage inflation).

The relationship illustrated in Figure 15.9 was presented by A. W. Phillips in 1958 and was based on empirical evidence from the UK over the period 1861 to 1957. What became known as the 'Phillips curve' appeared to indicate a stable relationship between unemployment and inflation, the view being that when the level of demand in the economy increased, unemployment would fall but at the expense of higher inflation. The reason put forward for this is that if there is excess demand in the labour market it will result in a reduction in unemployment. The excess demand for labour will cause an increase in the money wage rate and, since wages are a cost of production, this is likely to lead to an increase in prices, i.e. price inflation.

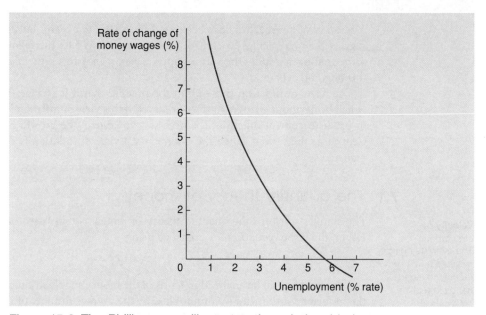

Figure 15.9 The Phillips curve illustrates the relationship between unemployment and inflation. The evidence in the 1950s and most of the 1960s in the UK appeared to support the idea of the Phillips curve, hence policy makers had a clear choice. There was a trade-off between unemployment and inflation, such that a certain level of unemployment could be traded off for a certain rate of inflation.

The Phillips curve relationship between unemployment and inflation behaved throughout the 1950s and most of the 1960s in the way it had for the previous 100 years, and it appeared to offer policy makers a clear choice – a certain level of unemployment could be 'traded off' for a certain rate of inflation (*see* Figure 15.9). Thus, if the policy makers were unhappy with a particular level of unemployment, they could stimulate demand in the economy but the reduction in unemployment would be at the expense of higher inflation. Alternatively, lower inflation would imply higher unemployment.

From the late 1960s, however, the Phillips curve relationship between unemployment and inflation broke down. The rate of inflation associated with a particular level of unemployment was found to be much higher than the traditional Phillips curve predicted and at various times both unemployment and inflation increased. In response to this some analysts began to argue that there was in fact no stable relationship between unemployment and inflation in the long run.

7.3 The expectations-augmented Phillips curve

Proponents of this approach accept that in the short run an inverse relationship between unemployment (aggregate demand) and the rate of inflation might indeed exist, but that in the *long run* there is no relationship. In this view, in the long run the Phillips curve is a vertical line through the NRU – at U_n in Figure 15.10.

The suggestion here is that there will be a whole series of short-run Phillips curves, each representing a *different* expected rate of inflation. This can be seen in Figure 15.10 which shows just two short-run Phillips curves, one with an expected rate of inflation of zero and the other with a 6% expected rate of inflation. We assume that the level of unemployment is initially at the natural rate, i.e. at point A in Figure 15.10, with a zero actual and expected rate of inflation.

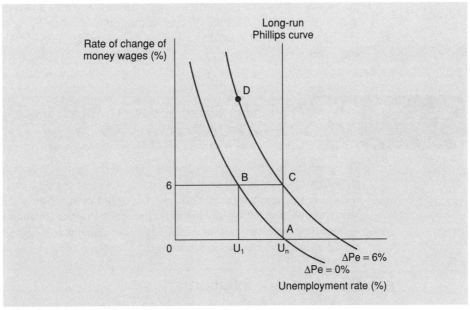

Figure 15.10 The natural rate of unemployment (NRU) is U_n and $\Delta Pe = 0\%$ and $\Delta Pe = 6\%$ represent the short-run Phillips curves with different expectations of inflation. If the government reduces the level of unemployment to U_1 this may cause a 6% rate of inflation. This will have resulted in the economy moving along the short-run Phillips curve from point A to point B. Once the workforce realise that their real income has not increased, since expected inflation equals actual inflation, then newly employed workers will no longer have the incentive to remain in employment. This means that unemployment will rise back to U_n with the economy now being at point C. This means the same level of unemployment but with a higher level of inflation. The long-run Phillips curve thus becomes vertical through the NRU.

The government may, however, be unhappy with a rate of unemployment, U_n, and may take steps to reduce it by stimulating demand in the economy through an expansion of the money supply. As aggregate demand increases, the level of unemployment will fall to U_1 and firms, in attracting extra labour to meet the increase in demand, will have to increase the wage rate, say, by 6%. This increase in the wage rate will soon be followed by an increase in the level of prices. The economy is now at point B in Figure 15.10, moving up the short-run Phillips curve from point A to B. As workers obtain the increase in money wages they will perceive themselves as being better off since they are expecting zero inflation ($\Delta Pe = 0\%$). The workers are, however, suffering from *money illusion* since their real wage has not changed.

This money illusion will not last long and, therefore, point B is only a short-run position. This is because when the workers realise they are no better off, those who have recently obtained employment will no longer have the incentive to remain in employment and so unemployment will increase back to the NRU, U_n. The economy is now at point C in Figure 15.10 with the same level of unemployment as before but with an actual rate of inflation of 6% as opposed to 0% initially. This rate of inflation is now the expected rate of inflation ($\Delta Pe = 6\%$).

If the government now wishes to reduce unemployment again (below U_n) by expanding the money supply, the economy will move along the short-run Phillips curve ($\Delta Pe = 6\%$) to a point such as D and the process will repeat itself. This being the case, the long-run Phillips curve can be viewed as a vertical line through the NRU, U_n joining points A, C and so on.

---

8 AGGREGATE DEMAND, AGGREGATE SUPPLY AND INFLATION

The following discussion makes extensive use of the aggregate demand and aggregate supply analysis presented earlier in this chapter. It will be useful at this point to re-read that analysis before going further. Various types of inflation are often discussed, in particular 'demand-pull' and 'cost-push' inflation, though in practice inflation may involve elements of both types. We can use our earlier aggregate demand and aggregate supply analysis to consider these two types of inflation.

8.1 Demand-pull inflation

Demand-pull inflation
Inflation seen as being caused mainly by an increase in aggregate demand for goods and services.

This is seen as being caused mainly by an increase in the components of aggregate demand (e.g. consumption, investment, public expenditure, exports). A rise in any of these components will shift aggregate demand upwards and to the right from AD_1 to AD_2 in Figure 15.11. This raises the average level of prices from P_1 to P_2 and raises national output from Y_1 to Y_2. The rise in aggregate demand results in many more consumers buying products, but a rise in aggregate output to Y_2 requires a higher price to cover the extra production costs (marginal and average) incurred. With demand-pull inflation we move along the aggregate supply curve to a point where both output and price levels are higher.

The increase in AD could be brought about by an increase in consumer spending, a rise in business confidence leading to an increase in investment, an increase in government expenditure or an increase in the demand for UK goods and services by foreigners. The

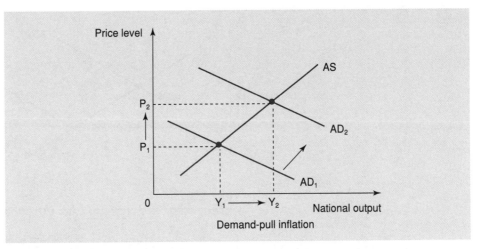

Figure 15.11 Demand-pull inflation can be caused by an increase in aggregate demand (AD). This can be illustrated by a shift in AD from AD_1 to AD_2 and the resulting increase in the price level from P_1 to P_2. The increase in AD may be caused by an increase in consumer expenditure (not associated with an increase in income), government expenditure, investment by firms or foreigners' demand for UK goods and services.

shift in AD from AD_1 to AD_2 can be termed a *demand shock* which causes a single rise in the price level.

In outlining demand-pull inflation it has been assumed that the increase in AD has been the result of an increase in aggregate expenditure, such as government expenditure. This is, in fact, a Keynesian explanation of inflation. However, the increase in AD could have been the result of an increase in the money supply, resulting in a monetary rather than a non-monetary explanation of inflation.

8.2 Cost-push inflation

Cost-push inflation
Inflation seen as being caused mainly by an increase in the costs of production, which firms pass on as higher prices.

This is seen as being caused mainly by an increase in the costs of production, which occurs independently of the level of aggregate demand. Firms then pass on these higher costs to consumers in the form of higher prices. The rise in costs reduces profit margins and results in some firms becoming insolvent so that they exit the market. As a result the aggregate supply curve shifts to the left from AS_1 to AS_2 in Figure 15.12, with less output supplied at any given price. This raises the average level of prices from P_1 to P_2 but reduces national output from Y_1 to Y_2.

With cost-push inflation we move along the aggregate demand curve to a point where output is lower and price levels are higher.

Note
The analysis has assumed throughout that prices adjust more rapidly than input costs so that there is some profit incentive for higher prices to result in extra output. In other words, the AS curves slope upwards from left to right in our diagrams.

An increase in the costs can be represented by a shift in the AS curve to the left. If firms see an increase in their costs they are likely to respond by raising their prices and cutting

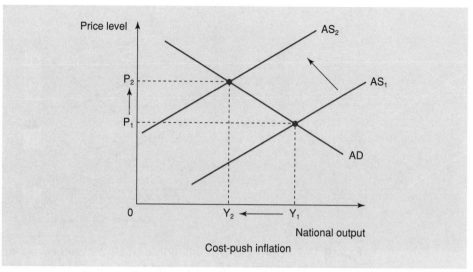

Cost-push inflation

Figure 15.12 Cost-push inflation occurs when there is an increase in the cost of production not associated with AD. If a firm's costs increase they will react by increasing their prices and reducing production. This is represented by a shift to the left in the AS curve and results in an increase in the price level, P_1 to P_2, and a reduction in the real national income from Y_1 to Y_2.

back on production – the result being a reduction in real national income from Y_1 to Y_2 and an increase in the price level from P_1 to P_2. The effect shown in Figure 15.12 can be termed a *supply shock*, bringing about a single rise in the price level. The situation in Figure 15.12 is one of stagflation where there has been an aggregate supply shock such as a rise in oil prices. Firms have passed on their increased costs in higher prices and aggregate demand has fallen, thus leading to an increase in unemployment and, therefore, stagflation.

Cost-push inflation can be the result of an increase in any of the following.

(a) *Wage costs*. Trade unions may push up wages through their bargaining power, with the increase in wages not being matched by an increase in productivity. Wages tend to be the largest cost of production so an increase in wages is likely to have an important effect on a firm's overall costs and, therefore, the prices they charge. This increase in prices is likely to lead to further wage claims and this could result in what is known as the *wage-price spiral*.

(b) *Profits*. This is perhaps less important than an increase in wage costs. There could be a situation where firms use their monopoly power to increase prices in order to increase profit margins. In this situation the increase in the price of the product is not associated with an increase in consumer demand.

(c) *Import prices*. A rise in import prices can be an important contributor to inflation. World commodity prices rose in the early 1970s, as did oil prices, and both led to higher inflation in the UK. Although an increase in import prices can be seen as imported cost-push inflation in the UK, it could have initially been the result of demand-pull inflation in the country in which the product originated.

9 COUNTER-INFLATIONARY POLICIES

The following are possible methods of dealing with inflation and they have all been used in the UK at various times.

9.1 Fiscal policy

Fiscal policy comprises changes in government expenditure and/or taxation and was considered in more detail in Chapter 12. The aim is to affect the level of AD through a policy known as *demand management*. In the case of controlling inflation, this involves reducing government expenditure and/or increasing taxation in what is called a *deflationary fiscal policy*. Such policies are likely to be effective if inflation has been diagnosed as demand-pull since a reduction in government expenditure or an increase in income tax will reduce aggregate demand in the economy. In the 1950s and 1960s fiscal policy was viewed as the main means by which inflation could be controlled.

9.2 Monetary policy

Monetary policy is concerned with influencing the money supply and the interest rate and was considered in more detail in Chapter 13. Until the mid 1970s, monetary policy was viewed as a supplement to fiscal policy; however, it now plays a major role in economic policy in the UK. In terms of controlling inflation, the Bank of England, through the Monetary Policy Committee, can increase the interest rate so as to increase the cost of borrowing. This can be seen as *deflationary monetary policy*. As stated earlier, monetarists view the growth of the money supply as being the main cause of inflation, therefore any control of inflation from a monetarist viewpoint must involve control of the money supply.

9.3 Prices and incomes policy

A prices and incomes policy can be seen as direct intervention in the economy. The aim is to limit and, in certain cases, freeze wage and price increases. In the past they have either been statutory or voluntary. Statutory prices and incomes policies have to be enforced by government legislation, such as that introduced in 1967. With a voluntary prices and incomes policy the government aims to control prices and incomes through voluntary restraint, possibly by obtaining the support of the TUC and the CBI.

If a prices and incomes policy is pursued, the general belief behind it is that inflation is caused by trade unions. Historically, governments have found it difficult to enforce prices and incomes policies since firms have always found ways of circumventing them and unions have often resorted to industrial action against them, particularly if wages have been more strictly controlled than prices.

9.4 Supply-side policies

Some people have suggested that the UK experienced a supply-side 'revolution' during the 1980s and 1990s, which included a wide range of policies that sought to raise the productivity of both labour and capital.

Such 'supply-side' policies have included, amongst others:

- assistance with investment
- trade union reform
- deregulation/privatisation
- making more training grants available
- increasing the number of people at universities
- helping people to set up new firms
- income tax cuts to increase incentives to work
- cuts in welfare payments to encourage people to return to work
- a government commitment to keep inflation low in order to aid investment plans
- cutting government expenditure in order to release resources to the private sector
- abolishing exchange controls in order to allow capital to move freely.

Any increase in labour or capital productivity resulting from these supply-side policies would then shift outwards the production possibility frontier of Chapter 1. Successful supply-side policies would also increase the aggregate supply curve in Figure 15.13, shifting it downwards and to the right from AS_1 to AS_2. The result is shown as raising the equilibrium level of national output (e.g. GDP) from Y_1 to Y_2 and reducing the average price level from P_1 to P_2.

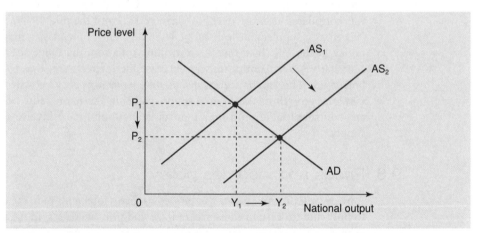

Figure 15.13 The effect of supply-side policies in shifting the aggregate supply curve downwards and to the right, raising equilibrium national income and reducing the average price level.

KEY POINTS

- The ILO (survey) method of measuring the unemployed differs from the claimant (administrative record) methods used in the UK.

- Unemployment in the UK can be disaggregated into regional, occupational, gender, age, ethnically based and qualification-related unemployment.

- The major types of unemployment include frictional (temporary), structural (changing patterns of demand), technological (changing technology), classical ('excessive' real wages) and demand deficient (inadequate demand) categories.

- The natural rate of unemployment (NRU) is the unemployment (labour force minus labour supply) existing at the real wage level which 'clears' the markets.

- The RPI measures movements in the prices of a 'basket' of goods and services bought by a representative UK household. Items with higher income elasticities of demand (e.g. housing, leisure services, catering) are being given increasing weights in the calculation of the RPI.

- RPIX is RPI excluding mortgage interest payments.

- RPIY is RPI excluding mortgage interest payments and indirect taxes.

- The GDP deflator seeks to measure changes in the prices of the entire basket of goods and services produced in the UK. It is found by dividing GDP at current factor cost by GDP at constant factor cost.

- The modern view of the Phillips curve is that there is a short-run trade-off between unemployment and inflation, but no long-run trade-off.

- The natural rate of unemployment is sometimes known as the non-accelerating inflation rate of unemployment (NAIRU).

- Attempts to push unemployment below the natural rate will result in increasing inflation.

- The government sets the inflation target and the Monetary Policy Committee (MPC) then changes interest rates with its primary objective being to meet that inflation target.

- There is evidence that setting an inflation target may itself help to reduce inflation without inhibiting growth.

Further reading

Griffiths, A. and Wall, S. (2006) *Applied Economics*, 11th edition, FT/Prentice Hall, Chapters 22–3.

Griffiths, A. and Wall, S. (2005) *Economics for Business and Management*, FT/Prentice Hall, Chapter 10.

Heather, K. (2004) *Economics Theory in Action*, 4th edition, FT/Prentice Hall, Chapter 15.

Parkin, M., Powell, M. and Matthews, K. (2005) *Economics*, 6th edition, FT/Prentice Hall, Chapters 21 and 28.

Sloman, J. (2006) *Economics*, 6th edition, FT/Prentice Hall, Chapter 14.

Web references

The data sources below offer a range of useful data and information on unemployment and inflation.

Central Office of Information: **http://www.coi.gov.uk/**

Office for National Statistics: **http://www.statistics.gov.uk/**

Treasury: **http://www.hm-treasury.gov.uk/**

Institute of Fiscal Studies: **http://www.ifs.org.uk/**

DfEE: **http://www.dfes.gov.uk/index.shtml**

Low Pay Unit: **http://www.lowpay.gov.uk/**

Equal Opportunities Commission: **http://www.eoc.org.uk/**

Trades Union Congress (TUC) (see Biz/ed link): **http://www.tuc.org.uk/**

Royal Institute of International Affairs: **http://www.riia.org/**

Institute of Fiscal Studies: **http://www.ifs.org.uk/**
Eurostat: **http://www.europa.eu.int/index_en.htm**

Economic models and simulation

Economic modelling is an important aspect of economic analysis. There are a number of sites that offer access to a model for you to use, which can be a useful way of finding out how economic theory works within an environment that claims to reflect reality. In this case variations in variables such as the money supply, rate of interest, exchange rate, rate of inflation, rate of unemployment can be assessed as to how they influence the economy.

Virtual economy: **http://bized.ac.uk/virtual/economy**
WinEcon: **http://www.webecon.bris.ac.uk/winecon/**
National Institute of Economic and Social Research: **http://www.niesr.ac.uk/**

PROGRESS AND REVIEW QUESTIONS

Answers to most questions can be found at the back of the book (pages 522–3). Answers to asterisked questions can be found on the students' side of the Companion Website.

Multiple-choice questions

1 Which *two* of the following are reasons for a government increasing its spending in particular regions of the UK?

   a) Real national income per head is similar in all regions
   b) Real national income per head varies substantially between regions
   c) Unemployment rates are similar in all regions
   d) Unemployment rates vary substantially between regions
   e) Indices of deprivation are similar in all regions

2 Which *three* of the following are often referred to as part of the 'regional problem'?

   a) Inadequate levels of infrastructure
   b) Net migration into the region
   c) Net migration out of the region
   d) Heavy dependence upon a narrow industrial base
   e) Rapid expansion of manufacturing

3 An inflationary gap means that equilibrium GDP:

   a) may be less than, more than, or the same as full-employment GDP
   b) no longer exists in modern economies
   c) equals full-employment GDP
   d) is more than full-employment GDP
   e) is less than full-employment GDP.

4 If the economy experiences inflation, aggregate:

   a) demand increases more slowly than aggregate supply
   b) supply increases faster than aggregate demand
   c) demand and supply increase at about the same rate
   d) demand increases faster than aggregate supply
   e) there is insufficient information to answer the question.

5 Inflation that is higher than expected transfers resources from:

   a) employers to workers and borrowers to lenders
   b) workers to employers and lenders to borrowers
   c) workers to employers and borrowers to lenders
   d) the unemployed to those in work
   e) employers to workers and lenders to borrowers.

6 The government increases the number of job centres and uses more advanced computers to improve the information database. This is an example of a measure to reduce:

   a) demand deficient unemployment
   b) structural unemployment
   c) regional unemployment
   d) frictional unemployment
   e) real wage unemployment
   f) technological unemployment.

7 A new skills training initiative is aimed at increasing the ability of those out of work to take the jobs on offer in a rapidly changing environment. This is an example of a measure to reduce:

   a) demand deficient unemployment
   b) structural unemployment
   c) regional unemployment
   d) frictional unemployment
   e) real wage unemployment
   f) technological unemployment.

8 To offset the downswing in the business cycle, the government announces a major increase in public expenditure. This is an example of a measure to reduce:

   a) demand deficient unemployment
   b) structural unemployment
   c) regional unemployment
   d) frictional unemployment
   e) real wage unemployment
   f) technological unemployment.

9 A programme to support small business start-ups is launched on Tyneside after the recent announcement of further closures in the shipbuilding industry. This is an example of a measure to reduce:

   a) demand deficient unemployment
   b) structural unemployment
   c) regional unemployment
   d) frictional unemployment
   e) real wage unemployment
   f) technological unemployment.

10 The government puts pressure on trade unions to make pay claims which are below the increase in productivity over the past year. This is an example of a measure to reduce:

   a) demand deficient unemployment
   b) structural unemployment
   c) regional unemployment
   d) frictional unemployment
   e) real wage unemployment
   f) technological unemployment.

 ## True/false questions

1 A fall in the rate of inflation means that the average price level is now lower.

2 A rise in the rate of inflation means that the percentage rise in average prices is higher than previously.

3 One of the costs of inflation is that those on variable incomes do better than those on fixed incomes.

4 If a rise in raw material costs feeds through to higher prices we use the term 'cost-push' inflation.

5 The Phillips curve suggests that higher levels of unemployment lead to higher levels of inflation.

6 The Phillips curve suggests that a fall in unemployment is likely to lead to lower rates of wage and price inflation.

7 If injections exceed withdrawals at the 'full capacity' level of national income, then we have a 'deflationary gap'.

8 If withdrawals fall short of injections at the 'full capacity' level of national income, then we have an 'inflationary gap'.

9 A substantial fall in the sterling exchange rate might lead to cost-push inflation in the UK by raising the sterling price of imports.

10 Technological unemployment is involved when new publishing software reduces the number of people needed to produce books.

 ## Data response question

This chapter has dealt mainly with unemployment and inflation. However, as noted in other chapters, balance of payments equilibrium and a high growth rate are two other objectives of policy. The data in the following table represents the outcome of attempts by successive government to achieve these four key objectives, namely low unemployment, low inflation, high growth and balance of payments equilibrium.

1 *Consider any possible conclusions you might draw as regards government policy from the data in the table.*

2 *How might the data achieved in the UK for these four objectives in recent years affect business confidence?*

Table 15.6 Achieved values in the UK for a number of policy objectives

Year	Unemployment as a % of working population	Annual change in RPI (%)	Annual change in GDP (at market prices) (%)	Balance of payments (current account) (£m)
1984	10.7	4.6	2.3	–1,294
1985	10.9	5.7	3.8	–570
1986	11.2	4.0	3.8	–3,614
1987	10.3	4.2	4.5	–7,538
1988	8.3	4.9	5.1	–19,850
1989	6.4	7.8	2.1	–26,321
1990	5.8	9.4	0.0	–22,321
1991	8.1	5.9	–1.5	–10,659
1992	9.8	3.7	0.0	–12,974
1993	10.3	1.6	2.3	–11,919
1994	9.4	2.4	4.3	–6,768
1995	8.1	3.5	2.7	–9,015
1996	7.4	2.4	2.6	–8,709
1997	5.4	3.1	3.5	–1,720
1998	4.6	3.4	2.2	–4,814
1999	4.2	1.5	2.0	–19,729
2000	3.7	3.0	3.0	–19,208
2001	3.3	1.8	2.0	–27,620
2002	3.2	1.7	1.7	–31,289
2003	3.1	2.0	2.2	–32,673
2004	3.1	2.1	2.3	–33,423

Source: Adapted from ONS (2005) *Economic Trends: Annual Supplement*; ONS (2005) *UK Balance of Payments;* ONS (2005) *Data Releases* (various)

 Essay questions

Answers to asterisked questions can be found on the students' side of the Companion Website. All other answers can be found at the back of the book (page 523).

1* Why is unemployment regarded as a problem? What policy measures might be used to tackle this problem?

2 Do you agree that we can only have less unemployment if we are willing to accept higher inflation? Explain your answer.

CHAPTER 16

International trade, international institutions and globalisation

Learning objectives

By the end of this chapter you should be able to:

- Outline the arguments used to support free trade between nations.
- Identify the sources of comparative and competitive advantages between nations.
- Review the contribution of international institutions such as the World Trade Organisation (WTO) to the growth of world trade.
- Assess the arguments and practices used to support protectionism, including the use of regional trading blocs and bilateral arrangements.
- Identify the key characteristics of globalisation and review the impacts of globalisation on international economic and business activity.
- Assess the contribution of relative unit labour costs (RULCs) to international competitiveness and the geographical location of various elements in the value chain.

1 INTRODUCTION

This chapter begins by reviewing the theoretical basis for suggesting that international trade yields patterns of consumption that could not be attained via self-sufficiency. This view as to the benefits of trade is further supported by an analysis which suggests that free trade raises economic welfare (consumer surplus + producer surplus) as compared to protectionism. There follows a review of the arguments for and against protectionism and the methods that can be used to protect domestic markets. The contribution of international institutions such as the World Trade Organisation (WTO) to international trading relationships is reviewed, as is the impact of regional trading blocs, bilateral trading agreements and other inter-governmental developments. The chapter concludes by reviewing the concept of globalisation and its impacts on international economic and business activity. Issues such as the value chain and its reconfiguration via offshoring and outsourcing are considered. The idea of relative unit labour cost (RULC) is introduced and its relevance for international competitiveness reviewed.

2   THE GAINS FROM TRADE

2.1 Why trade internationally?

International trade takes place for a number of reasons. Countries have different factor endowments whether it be plentiful supplies of raw materials, such as copper and zinc, or climatic conditions which allow them to produce items such as bananas, coffee and cotton that many other countries would find too costly to produce. It is easy to see why trade in these products takes place across international boundaries, but there is also a large amount of world trade in products which could be produced in the importing countries. What then is the basis for companies and countries trading products which they have the factor endowments to produce themselves?

David Ricardo in the early nineteenth century developed the *theory of comparative advantage*, which showed the possible gains to be made from specialisation and trade. However, before outlining this theory of comparative advantage it is necessary to consider an earlier theory of *absolute advantage* attributed to Adam Smith and his followers in the later eighteenth century.

Example   Growth of world trade

Whatever the theoretical basis, in practical terms world trade has been growing at an astonishing rate of over 5% per annum in real terms over the past quarter century. For example, between 1980 and 2005 world exports of goods and services more than doubled in real terms, reaching over $8,000 billion in 2005 and accounting for over 23% of world gross domestic product.

2.2 Absolute advantage

Absolute advantage Where, in a 2-country 2-product model, one country can produce one or both product(s) more efficiently than the other.

A country is said to have an *absolute advantage* over another country if it can produce more of a particular product than other countries, with the same amount of resources. If two countries have an absolute advantage in different products it is possible for specialisation to lead to an increase in world output and, therefore, via world trade, to an increase in the welfare of the countries involved. This can be outlined by reference to Table 16.1 which presents hypothetical data for countries A and B.

With one unit of resource, country A can produce 20 units of textiles or 40 units of steel. With the same amount of resource, country B can produce 80 units of textiles or 20 units of steel.

Table 16.1 Absolute advantage

	Output from one unit of resource	
	Textiles	Steel
Country A	20	40
Country B	80	20

In terms of steel production, one unit of resource in country A can produce twice as much output as one unit of resource in country B. However, in terms of textile production, one unit of resource in country B can produce an output which is four times greater than that in country A. In this situation country A is said to have an *absolute advantage* in the production of steel and country B an *absolute advantage* in the production of textiles.

It can be shown that both countries can then gain by specialising in the production of the product in which they have an absolute advantage. This can be seen in Table 16.2, where, by reallocating one unit of resource from textiles to steel in country A and one unit of resource from steel to textiles in country B, world output of *both* products can be increased. This additional world output of both textiles and steel is then traded to the benefit of both countries. There are gains to be made, therefore, from specialisation and trade according to absolute advantage.

Table 16.2 **The gains made from the movement of one unit of resource**

	Textiles	Steel	Movement of one unit of resource from
Country A	−20	+40	textiles to steel
Country B	+80	−20	steel to textiles
World output	+60	+20	

2.3 Comparative advantage

Comparative advantage
Where, in a 2-country 2-product model, one country has a lower opportunity cost ratio than the other.

It is obvious that given the situation of absolute advantage outlined above there are gains to be made from trade. It is not so obvious that there are gains to be made when a country has an absolute advantage in *both* products. In 1817, David Ricardo developed his theory of *comparative advantage* to show that specialisation and trade would still be beneficial to both countries. In this approach, even where a country has an absolute advantage (less resource cost) over the other country in both products, it can still gain by specialisation and trade in that product in which its *absolute advantage is greatest*, i.e. in which it has a comparative advantage. Similarly, the other country which has an absolute disadvantage (higher resource cost) in both products can still gain by specialisation and trade in that product in which its *absolute disadvantage is least*, i.e. in which it also has a comparative advantage.

This example is illustrated in Table 16.3 where country A is more efficient in the production of both textiles and steel. The difference between Tables 16.3 and 16.1 is that country A has improved its output of textiles per unit of resource, possibly through technological change in the textile industry. Although country A is better at producing (has an absolute advantage in) both products, there are still gains to be made through specialisation

Table 16.3 **Comparative advantage**

	Output from one unit of resource	
	Textiles	Steel
Country A	320	40
Country B	80	20

and trade since country A is *relatively* more efficient in the production of textiles. This can be seen by referring to Table 16.3 which shows country A is four times better at producing textiles than country B but only twice as good at producing steel. In this situation country A is said to have a *comparative advantage* in the production of textiles. Country B is one quarter as good as A at producing textiles but half as good as A at producing steel. Whilst B has, therefore, an absolute disadvantage in both products, it is *relatively* least inefficient in the production of steel. In this situation country B is said to have a *comparative advantage* in the production of steel.

The result of specialisation in the two countries according to comparative advantages means there are gains to be made through trade which can benefit both countries, as illustrated in Table 16.4.

Table 16.4 Gains made from the reallocation of resources in a comparative advantage situation

	Textiles	Steel	Movement of resources
Country A	+320	−40	1 unit of resource from steel to textiles
Country B	−240	+60	3 units of resource from textiles to steel
World output	+80	+20	

By reallocating resources within the two countries so that each produces more of the product in which it has a comparative advantage (A in textiles, B in steel) it is possible to increase world output, and so there are gains to be made from specialisation and trade. For example, by reallocating one unit of resource from steel to textiles in country A and three units of resource from textiles to steel in country B, it is possible to increase world output by 80 units of textiles and 20 units of steel.

2.4 Comparative advantage and opportunity cost

In developing the theory of comparative advantage it is possible to use the concept of *opportunity cost*, first introduced in Chapter 1. Referring back to Table 16.3, if it is assumed that all resources are fully employed then it is only possible to produce one more unit of one commodity if resources are reallocated from the production of the other commodity. In country A, the production of one extra unit of textiles requires 1/8 of a unit of steel to be sacrificed. In country B, the production of one extra unit of textiles requires 1/4 of a unit of steel to be sacrificed. In country A, the production of one extra unit of steel requires 8 units of textiles to be sacrificed, whereas in country B the production of 1 extra unit of steel only requires 4 units of textiles to be sacrificed. The opportunity cost ratios are summarised in Table 16.5.

Table 16.5 Opportunity cost ratios

	Opportunity cost of producing one extra unit of textiles	Opportunity cost of producing one extra unit of steel
Country A	$\frac{1}{8}$ unit of steel	8 units of textiles
Country B	$\frac{1}{4}$ unit of steel	4 units of textiles

Ricardo's theory of comparative advantage for a 2-country 2-product model can be re-expressed in terms of opportunity costs:

A country has a comparative advantage in that product for which it has a lower opportunity cost than the other country.

In terms of Table 16.5, country A has a comparative advantage in *textiles* (1/8 steel sacrificed is lower than 1/4 steel sacrificed) whereas country B has a comparative advantage in steel (4 units of textiles sacrificed is lower than 8 units of textiles sacrificed).

Let us now check whether specialisation and trade according to the comparative advantage we have identified really does provide potential benefits for both countries. Suppose country A produces one extra unit of textiles and country B one less unit of textiles (specialises in steel). We have the outcome shown in Table 16.6.

Table 16.6 Specialisation according to comparative advantages (lower opportunity costs)

	Textiles	Steel
Country A	+1	−1/8
Country B	−1	+4
	0	+3⅞

In producing one *extra* unit of textiles, A *sacrifices* 1/8 unit of steel. However, in producing one *less* unit of textiles, B *gains* 4 units of steel. By this marginal reallocation of resources according to our revised definition of comparative advantages (lower opportunity costs), total output of textiles is unchanged but total output of steel has risen. There is clearly potential for this extra output of steel to be traded to the benefit of *both* countries, provided the terms of trade are appropriate.

2.5 Limitations of the theory of comparative advantage

Limitations of the theory can be seen as:

(a) *Returns to scale.* The theory assumes constant opportunity costs, i.e. constant returns to scale, thus ignoring the possibility that economies or diseconomies of scale can be obtained as output increases.

(b) *Full employment.* The assumption is made that there is full employment of the factors of production. Thus, as specialisation takes place, those resources freed by one sector are automatically transferred to the sector in which the country is specialising. This assumption means that it is possible to calculate the opportunity costs.

(c) *Reciprocal demand.* The theory assumes what is known as *double coincidence of wants.* This means that in the example we have used, following specialisation, country A should demand steel from country B, and country B textiles from country A.

(d) *Transport costs.* Transport costs are not included in the theory of comparative advantage. Transport costs, however, increase production costs and therefore offset some of the potential gains made through specialisation.

(e) *Factor mobility.* The theory assumes that resources can be reallocated from the production of one product to another. In the real world, however, resources are likely to be immobile. In the example used above (page 395), it is unlikely that resources can be freely moved from steel to textile production or from textile to steel production.

(**f**) *Free trade*. Free trade is an obvious assumption of the theory of comparative advantage. There are no trade barriers such as tariffs and quotas, for these would limit the scope for specialisation in the two countries. This is unlikely to be the case in the real world. (For a discussion of tariffs and quotas *see* pages 400–402.)

Note: 'Localisation' and trade

Critics point to these various assumptions being so out of line with the real world that the benefits claimed for free trade are unsupportable. For example, adherents of a doctrine opposed to unbridled free trade, namely 'localisation' which proposes that everything that can be produced locally should be produced locally, and to that end nations should protect their economies using trade taxes and legal barriers, though some international trade is still envisaged. The author of the 'localisation' manifesto, Colin Hines, suggests that 'some long-distance trade will still occur for those sectors providing goods and services to other regions of the world that can't provide such items from within their own borders, e.g. certain minerals or cash crops.' However, this is clearly a minimalist view as to the need for a world trading environment.

2.6 National competitive advantage

Michael Porter is well known for his contribution to explaining corporate competitive advantages. However, he sees both *product innovation* and *process innovation* as key elements in determining national competitive advantages. In his view these dynamic elements far outweigh the more static elements of 'factor endowments' in determining success in international trading relationships. Still more so when technology is constantly changing the optimal combination of capital/labour/natural resource inputs for a product, when multinationals are so 'footloose' that they can readily relocate across national boundaries and when capital markets provide investment finance on an increasingly global basis.

Porter identifies six key variables as potentially giving a country a competitive advantage over other countries.

1 *Demand conditions*: the extent and characteristics of domestic demand.
2 *Factor conditions*: transport infrastructure, national resources, human capital endowments, etc.
3 *Firm strategies: structures and rivalries*: the organisation and management of companies and the degree of competition in the market structures in which they operate.
4 *Related and supporting industries*: quality and extent of supply industries, supporting business services, etc.
5 *Government policies*: nature of the regulatory environment, extent of state intervention in industry and the regions, state support for education and vocational training, etc.
6 *Chance*.

Porter's diamond
Highlights four interdependent determinants of national competitive advantages, namely demand conditions, factor conditions, related and supporting industries and firm strategies: structures and rivalries.

Porter's diamond

The first four of these variables form a *diamond* shape, as shown in Figure 16.1, when mapped as the most important determinants of national competitive advantage.

In Porter's view, the four determinants are interdependent. For example, favourable 'demand conditions' will only contribute to national competitive advantage when combined with appropriate 'factor conditions', 'related and supporting industries' and 'firm strategies: structures and rivalries' so that companies are *able* and *willing* to take advantage of the favourable demand conditions. To sustain national competitive advantages in modern, high-technology industries and economies, Porter argues that all four determinants in the

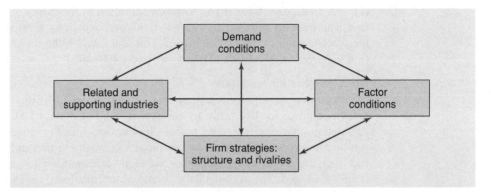

Figure 16.1 Porter's 'diamond', suggesting reasons why one country might have a competitive advantage vis-à-vis other countries.

'diamond' must be favourable. However, in less technology intensive industries and economies, one or two of the four determinants being favourable may be sufficient for a national competitive advantage: e.g. natural resource dependent industries may only need favourable 'factor conditions' (presence of an important natural resource) and appropriate infrastructure to extract and transport that resource.

The last two determinants 'government policies' and 'chance' outlined above can interact with the four key determinants of the diamond to open up new opportunities for national competitive advantage. For example, government policies in the field of education and training may help create R & D and other knowledge-intensive competitive advantage for a nation. Similarly, 'chance' events can play a part, as in the case of Russia supporting a greater US presence in Uzbekistan during the war in Afghanistan in 2001/02, thereby creating new opportunities for US oil companies to exploit the huge oil resources in that country.

Example	National contribution to global exports of goods

The list below (Table 16.7) shows the ranking of different countries in the world export league of goods in 2004. As can be seen China is now the fifth ranked country in terms of the share of world exports of goods.

Table 16.7 Percentage shares of world exports (2004)

Rank	Exporters	Share of world goods exports (%) in 2004
1	US	10.8
2	Germany	9.5
3	Japan	6.5
4	France	5.1
5	China	5.1
6	UK	4.3
7	Canada	3.9
8	Italy	3.9
9	Netherlands	3.8
10	Belgium	3.3

Source: Adapted from WTO data

3 THE TERMS OF TRADE

The preceding sections have outlined how countries specialise in the production of particular products (goods or services) in which they have a comparative advantage. Of course the extent to which any individual country will benefit from specialisation and trade will depend upon the terms under which exports are traded for imports. Referring to the previous analysis, suppose country B exports 60 units of the steel it produces to country A in exchange for 300 units of textiles. The ratio at which steel is externally traded for textiles is 1 unit of steel for 5 units of textiles. The ratio 1:5 can be taken to be the *terms of trade* (*see* also Chapter 14, page 334).

Terms of trade
A ratio of export prices to import prices, usually expressed as an index number with a base year (=100).

At this term of trade of 1:5, steel:textiles, both countries can be seen to benefit. For example, if country A had produced the 60 units of steel *itself* it would have been at the expense of 480 units of textiles, some 180 units of textiles more than it has to give up via trade. The same is true for country B. If country B has itself produced the 300 units of textiles it imports, it would have been at the expense of 75 units of steel, some 15 units of steel more than it has to give up via trade. Specialisation and trade are, therefore, of mutual benefit to both countries, although there is no reason why the benefits are necessarily split equally between the two countries.

However, the terms of trade may take values which do not permit both countries to benefit from specialisation and trade according to comparative advantages.

Pause for thought 1

Would both countries benefit from specialisation and trade if the terms of trade are 1:2, steel:textiles?

4 FREE TRADE AND ECONOMIC WELFARE

We now consider an alternative approach to demonstrate the gains from trade. This approach makes use of the ideas previously considered involving consumer surplus (Chapter 5, page 138) and producer surplus (Chapter 9, page 189).

Box 16.1 Gains from trade

Consumer surplus
The amount consumers are willing to pay for a product over and above the amount they have to pay (market price).

Figure 16.2 shows that free trade could, in theory, bring welfare benefits to an economy previously protected. Suppose the industry is initially completely protected. The domestic price PD will then be determined solely by the intersection of the domestic supply (S_DS_D) and domestic demand (D_DD_D) curves. Suppose that the government now decides to remove these trade barriers and to allow foreign competition. For simplicity, we assume a perfectly elastic 'world' supply curve $P_W - C$, giving a total supply curve (domestic and world) of S_DAC. Domestic price will then be forced down to the world level P_W with domestic demand being $0Q_3$ at this price. To meet this domestic demand, $0Q_2$ will be supplied from domestic sources, with Q_2Q_3 supplied from the rest of the world (i.e. imported). The *consumer surplus*, which is the difference between what consumers

$\rightarrow$

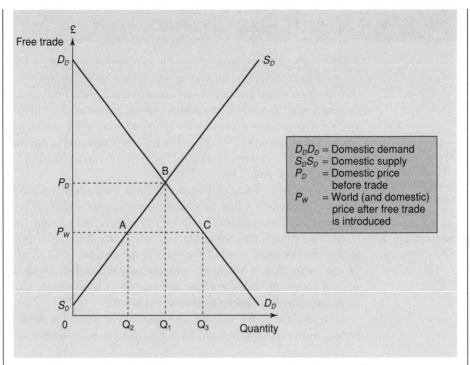

Figure 16.2 Gains from free trade versus no trade.

Producer surplus
The amount producers receive (market price) over and above the amount needed for them to supply the product.

Economic welfare
The sum of consumer and producer surplus.

are prepared to pay and what they have to pay, has risen from D_DBP_D to D_DCP_W. The *producer surplus*, which is the difference between the price the producer receives and the minimum necessary to induce production, has fallen from P_DBS_D to P_WAS_D. The gain in consumer surplus outweighs the loss in producer surplus by the area ABC, which could then be regarded as the *net gain* in **economic welfare** as a result of free trade replacing protectionism.

Pause for thought 2

In the analysis above, what has happened to the area P_WP_DBA?

5 PROTECTIONISM

Government intervention or *protectionism* in international trade can occur for a number of reasons (*see* below), can take a variety of forms and can have both positive and negative effects. Some of the types of protectionist policy are discussed below.

5.1 Tariffs

A tariff is a tax placed on imported commodities with the aim of raising their price and, therefore, discouraging their purchase. A tariff can take the form of a *specific tax*, i.e. a *lump sum tax*, where the tariff is a fixed amount on an imported item. Alternatively, it can be *ad valorem*, in which case it is based on a percentage of the price of the product. As well as raising the price of imports relative to domestic products, tariffs can also act as a source of revenue for the government.

With the aid of Figure 16.3 it is possible to examine the effect of a tariff on a particular imported product. The assumption is made that the world supply, S_w, is *perfectly elastic* at a price of P_w, and that D_d and S_d are domestic demand and domestic supply of the product. Before the imposition of a tariff the domestic price would be set at the world price P_w. At this price domestic demand would be q_4 and domestic producers would be willing to supply q_1, with the excess demand of $q_4 - q_1$ satisfied by importing the product.

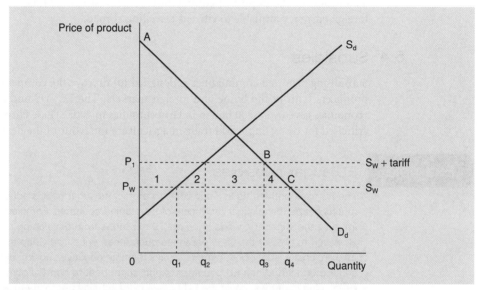

Figure 16.3 The imposition of a tariff causes the domestic price of the product to increase from the world price of P_w to P_1. The introduction of the tariff will reduce consumer surplus by the area $1 + 2 + 3 + 4$. Area 1 is now the benefit to the producer, area 3 now represents tariff revenue to the government and areas 2 and 4 do not benefit anyone. They represent net welfare losses.

If the government then imposes a tariff equal to $P_1 - P_w$, it has the effect of shifting the world supply curve to S_w + tariff. The domestic price will now be P_1 and this will have the dual effect of reducing domestic demand to q_3 and expanding the amount domestic firms are willing to supply to q_2. The desired outcome of the tariff will have been achieved since imports of the product are now only $q_3 - q_2$.

As well as reducing imports, the imposition of the tariff will have other implications. Before the tariff, consumer surplus was ACP_w, while after the tariff the consumer surplus was reduced to ABP_1. Part of this reduction in consumer surplus will go to the government in the form of tariff revenue and this can be represented by area 3 in Figure 16.3, being the amount of the tariff $P_1 - P_w$ multiplied by the imported quantity $q_3 - q_2$. The domestic producers of the product will obtain an increase in their producer surplus of area 1. This then leaves areas 2 and 4 which no party benefits from; they are a *cost to society* and are called *net welfare losses*.

5.2 Quotas

A quota is a physical limit placed on the amount of a product that can be imported over a certain period of time. This works on the basis that once a specified quantity has been imported no more of that product will be allowed into the country. The EU has placed quotas on the imports of textile products from China for the years 2005–07.

5.3 Exchange controls

The use of exchange controls places limits on the amount of foreign currency domestic residents can obtain. Such controls were in operation in the UK until 1979 and acted as a control over the import of commodities, on investment abroad and on the amount of foreign currency available to citizens travelling abroad.

5.4 Subsidies

Subsidising exported commodities is designed to improve the competitiveness of domestic producers both in the home and foreign markets. The EU, US and other 'high income' economies gave over $300 billion in farm subsidies in 2005. These farm subsidies have been criticised for distorting world trade in agriculture in favour of the developed economies.

> **Example**   **EU sugar subsidies**
>
> The EU uses both tariffs and subsidies to protect its sugar beet producers from the much cheaper cane sugar producers of developing countries. For example, the EU could import cane sugar at a world price of £70 per tonne from developing countries in 2005. However, to protect the £360 per tonne quaranteed price (see Chapter 17, page 433) to its own, costly, sugar beet farmers it pays them an effective subsidy of £290 per tonne of sugar produced. When EU countries export sugar beet to non-EU countries (including developing countries) again the EU pays a £290 subsidy per tonne to ensure that the EU farmer receives £360 per tonne, even when the sugar is sold overseas at the world price of £70 per tonne.

5.5 Administrative barriers

These can take a number of different forms, ranging from time-consuming formalities such as official form filling on commodities imported into a particular country to strict health and safety standards such as those regarding the ingredients of imported food.

5.6 Voluntary export restraints

These represent agreements between two countries to limit the export of a particular commodity from one country to the other. *Voluntary export restraints* act as do quotas and have become increasingly popular in recent years.

5.7 Arguments for protection

There are several arguments put forward in favour of protection and these can be outlined in general terms, ignoring the distinction between tariffs and quotas.

(a) *To protect an infant industry.* This is possibly the best known argument for protection. A newly established or *infant industry* is likely to have relatively high costs and, without protection, it might find it difficult to compete with established producers in other countries who are possibly benefiting from economies of scale.

It may be difficult, however, for a government to identify the potential infant industries which are likely to be successful. Also, if the infant industry will ultimately be profitable, obtaining a comparative advantage, the question needs to be asked: why is private business not willing to invest, relying instead on government assistance? An added problem is that it is often difficult for the government to remove the protection once in place, since the infant industry may have grown accustomed to it. The infant industry may never become efficient because of such protection and this means that resources are not being used most efficiently in the economy.

Dumping
Setting a price
below the costs of
production.

(b) *To prevent dumping.* Protectionist measures may be used to counter the threat of *dumping.* Dumping is a term usually used to refer to situations in which a company sells its product in an overseas market at a price lower than its average costs of production, often with the aim of driving an overseas competitor out of business. This is sometimes called *predatory* dumping. Simply charging different prices for a product in home and overseas markets is not necessarily 'dumping'. It may be that the firm in question is practising price discrimination (*see* Chapter 6, page 139), selling at one price in its domestic market and at a lower price in an overseas market where the price elasticity of demand may be highest.

(c) *To protect a strategic industry.* Particular industries may be regarded as strategic in times of war or as essential to the running of the economy. It may, therefore, be viewed as necessary to maintain these industries through protection rather than rely on foreign suppliers. Aerospace, shipbuilding, agriculture and armaments could be classed as strategic industries, and the decision about whether or not to protect them is essentially political.

(d) *To reduce structural unemployment.* A particular industry could have lost its comparative advantage and may be finding it hard to compete with foreign companies. Since the result of this may be structural unemployment (*see* Chapter 15, page 367) and the human costs which go with it, the government may offer temporary protection.

(e) *To aid economic recovery.* This concerns the wider macroeconomic objective of stimulating the economy, with the suggestion that general import controls would lead to a switch in demand from imported to domestically produced products, and with it an increase in domestic output and employment.

5.8 Arguments against protection

There are a number of arguments put forward against protectionism.

(a) *Retaliation.* If the UK imposes import controls, for example on Japanese electrical goods, then Japan may impose import controls on UK products. If this is the case, any gain to UK companies competing with Japanese companies would be offset by the losses made by UK exporters to Japan. The overall result could be a trade war.

(b) *A cost on society.* Protectionist measures impose a cost on society and may result in a misallocation of resources which imposes a cost on society in terms of 'welfare loss'. This has already been discussed with Figure 16.3 suggesting that, following the introduction of a tariff, there would be an increase in the price of the imported product paid by the domestic consumer, a fall in consumer surplus and a resulting loss of welfare.

(c) *Companies may remain inefficient.* Since import controls protect particular industries from foreign competition, it means that they have less incentive to reduce their costs and increase their efficiency.

Mini Case Study 16.1

Trade and food giants

A report in January 2005 by Action Aid charged large global food companies with aggravating poverty in developing countries by dominating markets, buying up seed firms and forcing down prices for staple goods including tea, coffee, milk, bananas and wheat. Some 30 companies now account for a third of the world's processed food, five companies control 75% of the international grain trade and six companies manage 75% of the global pesticide market.

The report finds that two companies dominate sales of half the world's bananas, three trade 85% of the world's tea and one, Wal Mart, now controls 49% of Mexico's retail food sector. It also found that Monsanto controls 91% of the global GM seed market.

Household names including Nestle, Monsanto, Unilever, Tesco, Wal Mart, Bayer and Cargill are all said to have expanded hugely in size, power and influence in the past decade directly because of the trade liberalisation policies being advanced in the US, Britain and other G8 countries.

The report accuses the companies of shutting local companies out of the market, driving down prices, setting international and domestic trade rules to suit themselves, imposing tough standards that poor farmers cannot meet and charging consumers more.

Many food giants are wealthier than the countries in which they do their business. Nestle recorded profits greater than Ghana's GDP in 2002, Unilever profits were a third larger than the national income of Mozambique and Wal Mart profits are bigger than the economies of both countries combined.

Retailers such as Tesco, Ahold, Carrefour and Metro are buying increasing volumes of fruit, vegetables, meat and dairy products in developing countries, but their exacting food safety and environmental standards are driving small farmers out of business, says Action Aid.

Question

How might this case be used in the free trade versus protectionism argument?

Answer to question can be found on the students' side of the Companion Website.

6 INTERNATIONAL FRAMEWORK FOR TRADE

6.1 General Agreement on Tariffs and Trade (GATT)

In 1947 the *General Agreement on Tariffs and Trade* (GATT) was established, with the primary aim of liberalising trade worldwide. With this in mind the member countries, 132 in total, have met periodically in order to negotiate reductions in tariffs and other barriers to trade. A number of 'rounds' of negotiations have taken place since 1947, the most notable being the Kennedy Round (1964–7), the Tokyo Round (1973–9) and the Uruguay Round (1986–93). The Kennedy Round led to a reduction in tariffs of approximately one third as did the Tokyo Round in the 1970s. With the Uruguay Round, negotiations were slow due to the conflicting interests of the member countries of GATT.

GATT has been concerned with the provision of the *most favoured nation* clause which requires that where a tariff reduction is made available by one country to another then this has to be made available to all the other members. A main problem with GATT was that it relied on a voluntary code of compliance. In January 1995 this problem was addressed when GATT came under the umbrella of a new organisation called the World Trade Organisation (WTO).

6.2 World Trade Organisation (WTO)

The World Trade Organisation replaced GATT in 1995 and now has 147 members, with the People's Republic of China, Chinese Taipei and Cambodia being the latest to join. The WTO's members in total account for more than 90% of the value of world trade. The objectives of the WTO are essentially the same as GATT's, namely to reduce tariffs and other barriers to trade and to eliminate discrimination in trade, and by doing so contribute to rising living standards and a fuller use of world resources.

(a) *WTO authority* Trade disputes between member states now come under the auspices of the WTO, which has been given more powers than GATT to enforce compliance, using streamlined disputes procedure with provision for appeals and binding arbitration. Whereas under GATT any single member (including the one violating GATT rules) could block a ruling of unfair trade, the findings of the WTO's disputes panel cannot be blocked by a veto of a member state.

Countries found to be in violation of a WTO principle must remove the cause of that violation or pay compensation to the injured parties. If the offending party fails to comply with a WTO ruling, the WTO can sanction certain types of retaliation by the aggrieved party.

Since its creation in January 1995, more than 240 cases have been brought before the WTO against only 200 cases brought before GATT in the 47 years of its existence. More than half of these have involved the USA and the EU while around one quarter have involved developing countries. The WTO also seeks to provide a forum for further multilateral trade negotiations.

(b) *WTO principles* Both the GATT and its successor the WTO have sought to implement a number of principles:

- *non-discrimination*: the benefits of any trading advantage agreed between two nations (i.e. in bilateral negotiations) must be extended to all nations (i.e. become multilateral). This is sometimes referred to as the 'most-favoured nation' clause;
- *progressive reduction in tariff and non-tariff barriers*: certain exceptions, however, are permitted in specific circumstances. For example, Article 18 allows for the protection of 'infant industries' by the newly industrialising countries, whereas Article 19 permits any country to abstain from a general tariff cut in situations where rising imports might seriously damage domestic production. Similarly, Articles 21–5 allow protection to continue where 'strategic interests' are involved, such as national security;

● *solving trade disputes through consultation rather than retaliation*: again, certain exceptions are permitted. For example, Article 6 permits retaliatory sanctions to be applied if 'dumping' can be proven, i.e. the sale of products at artificially low prices (e.g. below cost). Countries in dispute are expected to negotiate bilaterally, but if these negotiations break down a WTO appointed working-party or panel can investigate the issue and make recommendations. Should any one of the parties refuse to accept this outcome, the WTO can impose fines and/or sanction certain types of retaliation by the aggrieved party.

The WTO has inherited 28 separate accords agreed under the final round of GATT negotiations (the Uruguay Round). These accords sought to extend fair trade rules from industrial products to agricultural products, services, textiles, intellectual property rights and investment.

Mini Case Study 16.2

World trade deal agreed

Ministers from the world's richest and poorest countries struck an eleventh hour deal in August 2004 to boost trade by cutting farm subsidies and import tariffs worldwide. After five days of intense negotiation, the World Trade Organisation agreed to an interim text and set a deadline of December 2005 to hammer out a new global deal. The deal was hailed as 'historic' by the WTO and the main wealthy nations but fiercely attacked by activist groups who condemned it as a 'catastrophe for the poor'.

The deal strikes a compromise between cuts in subsidies for farmers in rich nations and an agreement by poorer countries to open up their markets by cutting tariffs. Under the agreement, key WTO members, including the United States, the EU, Brazil and Japan, have agreed to the eventual elimination of export subsidies. Wealthy nations currently spend about $370 billion (£203 billion) a year on all forms of farm support.

African and Latin American countries say this enables wealthy farmers to 'dump' cheap produce on their markets, annihilating their domestic farming industries. The deal includes a 'down payment' that would see an immediate 20% cut in the maximum permitted payments of subsidies by rich nations.

West African nations dropped a demand that the US's $3 billion (£1.65 billion) a year subsidies to its cotton farmers be treated as a separate issue. Rich countries also agreed to cut tariffs on farm imports that make it tough for poorer countries to compete. The highest agricultural import tariffs will face the biggest cuts, although no figures have yet been agreed.

Nations will have the right to keep higher tariffs on some of the products they consider most important. The deal on farming cleared the way for accords on access to markets for industrial goods and services, such as banking, water and telecommunications. The hard won deal put back on track the negotiations that were launched at Doha, Qatar, in November 2001, but collapsed at a summit in Cancun, Mexico in 2003.

Question

Assess the benefits and costs of the world trade agreement.

Answer to question can be found at the back of the book (page 523).

7 REGIONAL TRADING ARRANGEMENTS (RTAs)

Although the WTO supports multilateral trade, with all nations provided with a level playing field, this movement towards free trade has been accompanied by a parallel movement towards the formation of *regional trading blocs* centred on the EU, North and South America and East Asia, suggesting a movement away from multilateral trading relationships. There is evidence to suggest that the nations of a given region have begun to create more formal and comprehensive trading and economic links with each other and with selected countries/regions outside than was previously the case.

Example | Bilateral trade deals

Free trade areas
Where member countries reduce or abolish restrictions on trade between each other while maintaining their individual protectionist measures against non-members.

The growth in *bilateral* (two-country/two-region) trade deals involving the EU and US in recent years has been criticised by many observers as being unfair on 'weaker' nations and against the *multilateral* principles of the WTO. For example, the EU has created a large number of *Economic Partnership Agreement* (EPAs) with various developing countries, which allow these countries free access to EU markets but only if EU members themselves have free access to the developing country's markets. Many observers fear that this will allow heavily subsidised EU exports to flood the local producers from developing their own businesses.

Customs unions
Where, as well as liberalising trade among members, a common external tariff is established to protect the group from imports from any non-members.

7.1 Types of regional trading arrangements

There are four broad types of regional trading arrangements (RTAs).

1 *Free trade areas*, where member countries reduce or abolish restrictions on trade between each other while maintaining their individual protectionist measures against non-members.

2 *Customs unions*, where, as well as liberalising trade among members, a common external tariff is established to protect the group from imports from any non-members.

Economic unions
Where national economic policies are also harmonised within the common market.

3 *Common markets*, where the customs union is extended to include the free movement of factors of production as well as products within the designated area.

4 *Economic unions*, where national economic policies are also harmonised within the common market.

Example | European Union, NAFTA and ASEAN

Common markets
Where the customs union is extended to include the free movement of factors of production as well as products within the designated area.

The European Union (EU) was founded in January 1958 as a *common market* with six member nations. By 2003 the EU included 15 nations with a combined population of over 370 million and accounted for some 42% of world trade, expanding to 25 nations in 2004 with a population of around 490 million. Some 62% of EU exports go to other member countries. This group originated as a *common* market, the majority of members effectively progressing into a type of *economic union* with the Maastricht Treaty of 1992 and the advent of the euro and its related financial arrangements on 1 January 1999.

In August 1993 the North American Free Trade Agreement (NAFTA) was signed between the US, Canada and Mexico, having grown out of an earlier Canadian–US Free

Trade Agreement (CUFTA). NAFTA, as the name implies, is a *free trade area* with around 56% of NAFTA exports going to member countries, covering a population of 372 million and accounting for 31% of world output and 17% of world trade.

In Asia and the Pacific, the rather 'loose' Association of South-East Asian Nations (ASEAN) with a population of 300 million was formed in August 1967. In 1991 they agreed to form an ASEAN Free Trade Area (AFTA) by the year 2003. A Common External Preference Tariff (CEPT) came into force in 1994 as a formal tariff-cutting mechanism for achieving *free trade* in all goods except agricultural products, natural resources and services.

Mini Case Study 16.3

Regional trading arrangements

The OECD (2005) noted some 70 regional trade arrangements were completed between 2000 and 2004, compared to less than 25 completed in a similar five-year period between 1990 and 1994 a decade earlier. Table 16.8 indicates the importance of the EU, NAFTA and ASEAN regional trading arrangements to trade within the respective regions.

Table 16.8 Regional trading arrangements (RTAs): intra-regional export shares (%)

	1990	1995	2001
EU	64.9	64.0	61.9
NAFTA	42.6	46.1	55.5
ASEAN	67.5	73.1	71.8

Question

What does the data suggest? Can you explain what is happening?

Answer to question can be found on the students' side of the Companion Website.

8   GLOBALISATION

It is widely accepted that the world has become increasingly interconnected in recent decades as the result of economic, technological, political, sociological and cultural forces. To take but one example, in 2005 Troika, the financial services company, estimated that a further 100,000 financial jobs will be 'offshored' from the UK to low cost countries by 2010. The report by Troika noted that there is a growing shift towards offshoring more complex and high paid roles – finance, research, human resources, marketing, actuarial work and underwriting – to countries such as India with its well educated English speaking population. This is on top of the lower skilled service and manufacturing work, such as call-centre operations and assembly workers in factories. As we noted below (page 415) such offshoring was attracted by labour costs some 70% lower in India than in Britain. However, there is considerable debate as to whether such projections merely reflects the continuation of a long established internationalisation process or a deep-seated shift in the structure and operations of the world economy. 'Globalisation' is a much used but often loosely defined term, which many believe should be restricted to situations characterised by this latter perspective.

8.1 Characteristics of globalisation

Of course globalisation is by no means the preserve of economists alone. Indeed it has been approached from the perspective of at least four academic disciplines, within each of which it tends to take on different characteristics.

- *Economists* focus on the growth of international trade and the increase in international capital flows.
- *Political scientists* view globalisation as a process that leads to the undermining of the nation state and the emergence of new forms of governance.
- *Sociologists* view globalisation in terms of the rise of a global culture and the domination of the media by global companies.
- *International relations experts* tend to focus on the emergence of global conflicts and global institutions.

Some argue that globalisation is a long-standing phenomenon and not really anything new, pointing out that world trade and investment as a proportion of world GDP is little different today from what it was a century ago and that international borders were as open at that time as they are today with proportionately just as many people migrating abroad. Nor, from this perspective, should we overestimate the power of today's global corporations. In a major study for the Economic and Social Research Council of the top 214 multinationals over the period 1995–8, Alan Rugman concluded that the vast majority were not pursuing a global strategy, were finding it difficult to make decent profits and were tending to 'de-globalise' by concentrating on tried and trusted markets at home (Elliott, 2002).

However, those who believe that globalisation really is a new phenomenon tend to agree that at least three key elements are commonly involved.

- *Shrinking space.* The lives of all individuals are increasingly interconnected by events worldwide. This is not only a matter of fact but one which people increasingly perceive to be the case, recognising that their jobs, income levels, health and living environment depend on factors outside national and local boundaries.
- *Shrinking time.* With the rapid developments in communication and information technologies, events occurring in one place have almost instantaneous (real time) impacts worldwide. A fall in share prices in Wall Street can have almost immediate consequences for share prices in London, Frankfurt or Tokyo.
- *Disappearing borders.* The nation state and its associated borders seem increasingly irrelevant as 'barriers' to international events and influences. Decisions taken by regional trading blocs (e.g. EU, NAFTA) and supra-national bodies (e.g. IMF, World Trade Organisation) increasingly override national policy making in economic and business affairs as well as in other areas such as law enforcement and human rights.

It may be useful at this point to consider some of the conceptual issues as regards 'globalisation' a little further using a broadly economic perspective.

Different perspectives on globalisation

Of course there are different schools of thought among even those who do accept the reality of globalisation.

- *Hyperglobalists* envisage the global economy as being inhabited by powerless nation states at the mercy of 'footloose' multinational enterprises bestowing jobs and wealth creation opportunities on favoured national clients. National cultural differences are largely seen by these progressively powerful multinationals as merely variations in consumer preferences to be reflected in their international marketing mix.
- *Transformationalists* recognise that globalisation is a powerful force impacting economic, social and political environments, but take a much less prescriptive stance as to what the outcomes of those impacts might be. Predictions as to any end-state of a globalised economy can only be tentative and premature. Here globalisation is seen as involving a complex set of intermittent, uneven processes with unpredictable outcomes rather than a linear progression to a predictable end-state.

It is this more pragmatic transformationalist approach that is most commonly encountered in debates on globalisation. While there may be many theories as to the causes of globalisation, most writers would agree that globalisation is a discontinuous historical process. Its dynamic proceeds in fits and starts and its effects are experienced differentially across the globe. Some regions are more deeply affected by globalisation than others. Even within nation states, some sectors may experience the effects of globalisation more sharply than others. Many have argued that globalisation is tending to reinforce inequalities of power both within and across nation states, resulting in global hierarchies of privilege and control for some, but economic and social exclusion for others.

Box 16.2 attempts to capture some of the characteristics which currently underpin the use of the term 'globalisation' as being something different from what has gone before.

Box 16.2 | ## Globalisation characteristics

New markets

- Growing global markets in services – banking, insurance, transport.
- New financial markets – deregulated, globally linked, working around the clock, with action at a distance in real time, with new instruments such as derivatives.
- Deregulation of antitrust laws and growth of mergers and acquisitions.
- Global consumer markets with global brands.

New actors

- Multinational corporations integrating their production and marketing, dominating world production.
- The World Trade Organisation – the first multilateral organisation with authority to force national governments to comply with trade rules.
- A growing international network of non-governmental organisations (NGOs).
- Regional blocs proliferating and gaining importance – European Union, Association of South-East Asian Nations, Mercosur, North American Free Trade Association, Southern African Development Community, among many others.
- More policy coordination groups – G7, G8, OECD, IMF, World Bank.

New rules and norms

- Market economic policies spreading around the world, with greater privatisation and liberalisation than in earlier decades.
- Widespread adoption of democracy as the choice of political regime.
- Human rights conventions and instruments building up in both coverage and number of signatories – and growing awareness among people around the world.
- Consensus goals and action agenda for development.
- Conventions and agreements on the global environment – biodiversity, ozone layer, disposal of hazardous wastes, desertification, climate change.
- Multilateral agreements in trade, taking on such new agendas as environmental and social conditions.
- New multilateral agreements – for services, intellectual property, communications – more binding on national governments than any previous agreements.
- The (proposed) Multilateral Agreement on Investment.

New (faster and cheaper) methods of communication

- Internet and electronic communications linking many people simultaneously.
- Cellular phones.
- Fax machines.
- Faster and cheaper transport by air, rail, sea and road.
- Computer-aided design and manufacture.

Source: Adapted from World Investment Report (1999) UNCTAD

Some would argue that the 'globalisation tendencies' outlined in Box 16.2 can be at work without this resulting in the end-state of a new geo-economy in which 'market forces are rampant and uncontrollable, and the nation state merely passive and supine' (Dickens, 2003, page 5).

8.2 Indicators of globalisation

Bearing in mind the characteristics of globalisation already outlined in Table 16.9, here we review some selected quantitative indicators relevant to the debate.

New markets

Table 16.9 would certainly seem to confirm the growth of new markets within a more liberalised and deregulated global environment. We have already seen the relevance of foreign direct investment (fdi) to cross-border mergers and acquisitions by multinational enterprises (Chapter 9). Table 16.9 uses data from the United Nations Conference on Trade and Development (UNCTAD) to indicate the progressive increase in regulatory changes affecting fdi by national governments, the overwhelming majority of which are 'more favourable' to fdi flows.

New actors

The rapid growth of MNEs themselves has already been documented in Chapter 7, as for example with employment in the overseas affiliates Table 16.10 throws further light on the increasing globalisation of productive activity by showing the progressive growth in

Table 16.9 Increasing liberalisation of markets on a global scale

National regulatory changes in fdi regimes		
Number of regulatory changes	Number more favourable to fdi	Number less favourable to fdi
1991	82	80	2
1993	103	100	3
1995	107	102	5
1997	158	144	14
1999	146	138	8
2001	206	194	12

Source: Adapted from World Investment Report (2002)

the Transnationality Index (TNI) for the world's largest 100 MNEs in their home economies between 1990 and 2000. The TNI has been defined as the average of three ratios, namely foreign assets: total assets; foreign sales: total sales; and foreign employment: total employment. A rise in the TNI index suggests still more international involvement of the top 100 MNEs outside their home country, which is certainly a pattern strongly supported by the data in Table 16.10.

The EU is home to almost half of the world's largest MNEs and we can see from Table 16.10 that the average Transnationality Index (TNI) for the EU has risen from 56.7 to 67.1 over the 1990–2000 period alone. A still more rapid growth in the TNI is indicated for MNEs with North America as their 'home' base, with Japan alone showing only modest growth. For 'all economies' the greater internationalisation of production is indicated via the TNI rising from 51.1 to 57.8 in the 1990–2000 time period. Closer scrutiny of this data reveals that the driving forces behind these observed increases in TNI have been the

Table 16.10 Transnationality Index for the world's largest 100 MNEs in their home economies, 1990 and 2000

Economy	Average TNI (%)		Number of MNEs	
	1990	2000	1990	2000
European Union	56.7	67.1	48	49
France	50.9	63.2	14	13
Germany	44.4	45.9	9	10
UK	68.5	76.9	12	14
North America	41.2	62.9	30	25
US	38.5	43.0	28	23
Canada	79.2	82.9	2	2
Japan	35.5	35.9	12	16
All Economies	51.1	57.8	100	100

Source: Adapted from World Investment Report (2002)

growth in the foreign sales: total sales and in the foreign employment: total employment components of the TNI.

New actors within a globalised economy are also expected to include growing numbers of multilateral organisations (e.g. WTO), non-governmental organisations (NGOs) and policy coordination groups (e.g. G8/G7). These will be progressively required in an attempt to bring some kind of order to a progressively less nationally supervised and deregulated world trading regime. In addition, the growth of regional trading blocs is often predicted as a collective response to the progressive loss of economic power of individual nation states.

New rules and norms

Not only are new international institutions and trading blocs characteristic of a more globalised economy in which nation states have progressively less influence, but so too are the 'rules and norms' by which they seek to operate. Market-oriented policies, democratic political frameworks, consensus goals involving social and environmental responsibility, and growing multilateral applications of agreed rules were all identified as characteristics of globalisation in Table 16.10 above. Again there is considerable empirical evidence of movements in this direction. Here we note the importance of good governance and transparency, an absence of corruption and appropriate property rights to the establishment of a sustainable globalised economic environment.

The World Bank in its *World Development Report* (2002) has pointed out that good governance – including independent agencies, mechanisms for citizens to monitor public behaviour and rules that constrain corruption – is a key ingredient for growth and prosperity. Chapter 18 (page 472) summarises some important studies and surveys which emphasise the importance of good governance to inward foreign direct investment, productivity growth and rising standards of living.

New methods of communication

Management specialist Stephen Kobrin describes globalisation as driven not by foreign trade and investment but by information flows. It is this latter perspective, which sees globalisation as a process inextricably linked with the creation, distribution and use of knowledge and information, which is the focus here. Many contributors to the globalisation debate regard the technological convergence of information, computer and telecommunications technologies in the late twentieth century as having acted as a key catalyst in the rapid growth of these information-based activities, seen here as the hallmark of the globalised economy.

International communications have grown dramatically, as evidenced by indicators such as the time spent on international telephone calls rising from 33 billion minutes in 1990 to over 90 billion minutes in 2005. Such rapid growth has been fuelled by dramatic reductions in cost; for example, the cost of a three minute telephone call from New York to London in 2005 was less than 2% of the cost in 1930 (OECD, 2005). International travellers have more than doubled in 25 years, from some 260 million travellers a year in 1980 to over 650 million travellers a year in 2005.

Contemporary discourse often seeks to express globalisation in terms of the exponential growth in the creation, processing and dissemination of knowledge and information. For example, an 'index of globalisation' recently compiled jointly by the Carnegie Foundation and ATKearney (a global consultant) gives considerable weight to the proportion of national populations online as well as to the number of Internet hosts and secure servers per capita. These indicators of access to information technology and associated information flows are seen here as proxy variables for 'global openness', to be used in association with the more conventional indicators of investment, capital flows, foreign income as a proportion of national income and convergence between domestic and international prices when compiling the overall globalisation index. Singapore has appeared in several recent surveys as the 'most globalised' country, helped by the fact that its recorded outgoing telephone traffic at 390 minutes per head per year was some four times as much as in the US. Sweden (ranked third) recorded some 44% of households online whilst Finland (ranked fifth) had over 70 web-connected servers (Internet hosts) per 1,000 people whilst Swiss citizens (ranked fourth) spent 400% more time on international phone calls than Americans. In 2005 some 60% of the US population was recorded as 'Internet users', compared to 48% in the European Union and a world average of some 15%.

8.3 Globalisation and the value chain

Value chain
The various activities that are involved in providing a good or service, whether creating, selling or distributing the good or service.

We noted earlier that international business is dominated by MNEs which are increasingly transnational in operation, including horizontally and vertically integrated activities more widely dispersed on a geographical basis. This brings into focus the *value chain* which breaks down the full collection of activities which companies perform into 'primary' and 'secondary' activities.

- *Primary activities* are those required to create the product (whether good or service, including inbound raw materials, components and other inputs) to sell the product and to distribute it to the marketplace.
- *Secondary activities* include a variety of functions such as human resource management, technological development, management information systems and finance for procurement. These secondary activities are required to support the primary activities.

It is useful to remember that an effective international business strategy must encompass *all* parts of the value chain configuration, wherever their geographical location. Here we concentrate on international approaches which might help the firm maximise the sum of these individual activities.

The globalisation characteristics we have noted, namely shrinking space, shrinking time and disappearing borders are giving these MNEs increasing opportunities to move parts of their value chain to different geographical locations. This is often called 'offshoring', when an activity previously performed in one country is moved to another. A key determinant of potential benefits from such 'offshoring' is the relative unit labour costs (RULCs) available in the various geographical locations under consideration.

8.4 Relative unit labour costs (RULCs)

Relative unit labour costs (RULCs)
A key measure of international competitiveness involving relative labour costs, relative labour productivity and relative exchange rates.

One of the major reasons for reconfiguring the value chain is the opportunity to reduce costs of production and raise profits. Data such as that in Table 16.11 provides some indication of the possibilities which exist in this respect.

However, we should not simply look at labour cost figures, no matter how superficially attractive they may seem. Rather we should seek to identify the *relative unit labour costs* (*RULCs*) which are a much better indicator of international competitiveness, as is argued in Box 16.3.

Table 16.11 Labour costs and labour productivity, 2002

Country	Total labour costs* ($ per hour)	Total labour costs ($ per hour) (Index UK = 100)	Labour productivity^ (Index UK = 100)
Mexico	2.3	14.3	40.3
Korea	8.1	50.3	43.5
France	15.9	98.8	135.5
UK	16.1	100.0	100.0
Japan	19.6	121.8	92.0
US	20.3	126.1	125.9
Germany	22.9	142.2	127.4

Source: Adapted from US Department of Labour (2002)

Box 16.3	Relative Unit Labour Costs (RULCs)

Labour costs per unit of output (unit labour costs) depend on both the wage and non-wage costs (e.g. employer National Insurance contributions in the UK) of workers and the recorded output per worker (labour productivity). For example, if the total (wage and non-wage) costs per worker double, but productivity more than doubles, then labour costs per unit will actually fall.

However, the exchange rate must be taken into account when considering international competitiveness, and this also is included in the definition of RULC below. For example, for any given value for labour costs per unit, if the exchange rate of that country's currency falls against a competitor, then its exports become more competitive (cheaper) abroad and imports less competitive (dearer) at home.

$$\text{RULC} = \frac{\text{Relative labour costs}}{\text{Relative labour productivity}} \times \text{Relative exchange rate}$$

This formula emphasises that (compared to some other country) a lower RULC for, say, the UK could be achieved by reducing the UK's relative labour costs, or by raising the UK's relative labour productivity, or by lowering the UK's relative exchange rate, or by some combination of all three.

If we apply the reasoning in Box 16.3 to Table 16.11 above, we can note the following: Mexico has total labour costs per hour which are only around 14% of those in the UK, making Mexico a potentially attractive location for labour intensive production activities, despite the hourly productivity of labour being only around 40% of that in the UK. Although Korea has lower labour costs than the UK its labour productivity is even lower relative to the UK, making it appear rather less attractive than Mexico. Other pair-wise comparisons can be made between other countries. Of course, more data may be needed before multinationals make any final decisions, e.g. the rate of exchange between the respective currencies, the transport and distributive infrastructure, quality of output produced, nearness to key markets and so on.

KEY POINTS

- In a competitive, full employment framework, free trade can be shown to yield a net welfare gain vis-à-vis various protectionist alternatives.

- The General Agreement on Tariffs and Trade (GATT) was established in 1947 and its successor, the World Trade Organisation (WTO), seeks to reduce tariffs and other barriers to trade and to eliminate discrimination in trade.

- Various types of regional trading arrangements have been developed. Free trade areas, customs unions (which have an external tariff barrier), common markets (in which factors of production can also freely move) and economic unions (with harmonisation of member policies) have all been used to influence trading relationships, sometimes creating new trading opportunities (trade creation), sometimes removing existing trading relationships (trade diversion). The implications of trade creation and trade diversion are considered further in Chapter 17.

- Various types of protection have been used by countries, including tariffs, quotas, voluntary export restraints, subsidies, exchange controls, and a range of restrictions involving technological standards, safety, etc.

- Arguments often advanced in favour of protectionist policies include the prevention of dumping, the protection of infant industries and the protection of strategically important industries.

- Arguments against protectionist policies include retaliation and a misallocation of resources on both a national and international scale, leading to welfare loss.

- Globalisation involves greater global inter-connectedness via shrinking space, shrinking time and disappearing borders, and is leading to the geographical relocation of elements of the value chain.

- Relative unit labour costs (RULCs) are a key measure of international competitiveness.

Further reading

Griffiths, A. and Wall, S. (2006) *Applied Economics*, 11th edition, FT/Prentice Hall, Chapters 26–8.

Griffiths, A. and Wall, S. (2005) *Economics for Business and Management*, FT/Prentice Hall, Chapter 10.

Heather, K. (2004) *Economics Theory in Action*, 4th edition, FT/Prentice Hall, Chapters 19 and 20.

Parkin, M., Powell, M. and Matthews, K. (2005) *Economics*, 6th edition, FT/Prentice Hall, Chapters 33 and 34.

Sloman, J. (2006) *Economics*, 6th edition, FT/Prentice Hall, Chapters 15, 23–5.

Web references

You can find current data and information on many aspects of issues involving free trade and protection from the following websites.

National Statistics: **http://www.statistics.gov.uk/** The official UK statistics site.

Eurostat: **http://europa.eu.int/comm/eurostat** The main site for EU statistics.

United Nations: **http://www.un.org** A main source of information and statistics, especially the Trade and Development (UNCTAD) site **http://www.unctad.org/**

World Trade Organisation: **http://www.wto.org** The main site for most sources on trade and protectionism.

Centre for Policy Studies: **http://www.freetrade.org/** US site for free trade issues and key trade statistics.

FITA: **http://www.internationalaffairs.com/Analysis/Topic_Areas/Economy/ Foreign_Trade/ foreign_trade.html** A US site containing very good sources on trade and protectionist issues.

NAFTA: **http://lanic.utexas.edu/la/Mexico/nafta/index.html** A US site for all types of information relating to NAFTA.

Overseas investment into the UK: **www.invest.uk.com**

US exports and overseas business: **www.mac.doc.gov**

ASEAN: **www.aseansec.org**

Chinese business: **www.cbbc.org**

References

Dickens, P. (2003) *Global shift: reshaping the global economic map in the 21st century*, Sage Publications.

Elliott, L. (2002) 'Big business isn't really that big', *Guardian* 2 September.

PROGRESS AND REVIEW QUESTIONS

Answers to most questions can be found at the back of the book (pages 523–4). Answers to asterisked questions can be found on the students' side of the Companion Website.

Multiple-choice questions

1 In a 2-product 2-country model, which *one* of the following corresponds to Ricardo's theory of 'comparative advantage'?

   a) Each country specialising in that product in which it is absolutely most efficient.

   b) Each country specialising in that product in which it is absolutely least efficient.

   c) Each country specialising in that product in which it is relatively most efficient (or relatively least inefficient).

   d) Each country specialising in that product in which the terms of trade are most favourable.

   e) Each country specialising in that product in which the terms of trade are least favourable.

2 Which *one* of the following is often said to be a benefit of specialisation and trade?

   a) Reaching a consumption bundle inside the country's production possibility frontier

   b) Reaching a consumption bundle on the country's production possibility frontier

   c) Reaching a consumption bundle inside the country's terms of trade

   d) Reaching a consumption bundle outside the country's terms of trade

   e) Reaching a consumption bundle outside the country's production possibility frontier

3 Which *two* of the following are often used to support a policy of protectionism?

   a) Mature industry argument
   b) Infant industry argument
   c) Harming strategically important industries
   d) Encouraging 'dumping'
   e) Preventing 'dumping'

4 Where member countries reduce or abolish restrictions on trade between each other while maintaining their individual protectionist measures against non-members

   a) Common market
   b) Economic union
   c) Free trade area
   d) Customs union
   e) Common Agricultural Policy (CAP)

5 Which *one* of the following is NOT a characteristic of the World Trade Organisation (WTO)?

   a) Ensuring that any trading advantage agreed between two nations extends to all nations
   b) Seeking a progressive reduction in tariff and non-tariff barriers (e.g. tariffs)
   c) Allowing retaliatory action where another nation can be shown to have breached WTO rules (e.g. 'dumping')
   d) Supporting the use of non-tariff rather than tariff barriers wherever possible
   e) Solving trade disputes through consultation rather than retaliation

6 Which *three* of the following elements are included in the calculation of relative unit labour costs (RULCs)?

   a) Relative capital costs
   b) Relative labour costs
   c) Relative total factor productivity
   d) Relative labour productivity
   e) Relative exchange rate

7 Which *three* of the following ratios are used in constructing the Transnationality Index?

   a) Foreign employment to total employment
   b) Foreign managers to total managers
   c) Foreign sales to total sales
   d) Foreign costs to total costs
   e) Foreign assets to total assets

8 Which *two* of the following are the most likely effects of the imposition of a tariff on an imported good?

   a) The domestic price of the imported good will fall
   b) Overseas production of the good may be stimulated
   c) Overseas employment will rise
   d) The domestic price of the imported good will rise
   e) Gain of tax revenue by the government

9 Which *one* of the following refers to a situation where a customs union is extended to include the free movement of factors of production and the integration of economic policies?

a) Common market
b) Economic union
c) Free trade area
d) Common Fisheries Policy
e) Common Agricultural Policy

10 Which *three* of the following are often associated with globalisation?

a) Expanding borders
b) Disappearing borders
c) Expanding distance
d) Shrinking distance
e) Shrinking time

 ## Matching terms/concepts

In these questions you will be given a description of a certain aspect of trade and protectionism. Try to match the description with the correct term or expression.

1 Where the member countries of a trading bloc may suffer because they have to buy products from within the bloc when cheaper sources are often available from outside the bloc.

a) The non-tariff effect
b) The trade creation effect
c) The inter-bloc effect
d) The trade diversion effect
e) The multilateral trade effect

2 The form of protection most often used to protect the agricultural sector in EU countries.

a) Voluntary export restraints
b) Exchange controls
c) Time consuming formalities
d) Public sector contracts
e) Tariffs on imports

3 A situation where any advantage given by one member of the WTO to another member must be extended to *all* WTO members.

a) The intra-regional principle
b) The comparative advantage principle
c) The most favoured nation principle
d) The trade diversion principle
e) The excessive invoicing principle

4 A situation where countries export a product at a price below the cost of its production.

a) Full cost pricing
b) Price skimming

c) Dumping
d) New protectionism
e) Price discrimination

5 A protectionist measure whereby members of a regional trading bloc agree to impose an identical rate of protection on all goods imported from non-member countries.

a) Non-tariff agreement
b) Common quota arrangements
c) Technological standards control
d) Common external tariff
e) VER agreements

 ## True/false questions

1 A country has a comparative advantage (in a 2-country 2-product model) in that product in which it has a lower opportunity cost than the other country.

2 Shrinking space, shrinking time and disappearing borders are all characteristics of owner-ship specific advantages.

3 Economists tend to view globalisation in terms of the rise of a global culture and the domina-tion of the media by global companies.

4 A multinational engaged in exploration in one country, component production in another and assembly in a third might be called a vertically integrated multinational.

5 A multinational engaged in the assembly function in three separate countries might be called a vertically integrated multinational.

6 Trade creation describes the situation where the removal of tariff barriers between mem-bers of the trading bloc now enables various products to be purchased at lower prices, thereby stimulating intra-regional trade.

 ## Data response and stimulus questions

1 Mutual benefits of outsourcing/offshoring

A report by the consultants McKinsey in 2003 on offshoring concludes that it is a win-win arrangement for both countries involved. The report estimates that for every $1 previously spent in the US and now outsourced to India, there is a 'global impact' of $1.47. Of that the US itself receives back $1.14 – as a result of cheaper services for consumers, redeploying labour to better paid jobs, additional exports of US goods to India, etc. India receives an extra $0.33 via new wages, extra profits and extra taxes.

Consider some of the implications of these findings.

2 The diagram below represents a particular country, county X, and its demand for and supply of wheat. It can be seen that the world's supply of wheat is infinite at a price of OB.

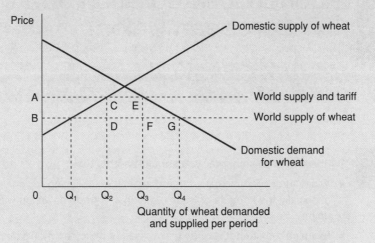

a) Before the introduction of a tariff, what is:
   i)   the domestic production of wheat?
   ii) the domestic demand for wheat?
   iii) the quantity of wheat imported?

b) After the tariff (AB) is introduced, what is:
   i)   the total expenditure on wheat by the residents of country X?
   ii) the loss of consumer surplus suffered by the residents of country X?
   iii) the quantity of wheat now imported?
   iv) the tariff revenue obtained by the government of country X?

 Essay questions

Answers to asterisked questions can be found on the students' side of the Companion Website. All other answers can be found at the back of the book (page 524).

1* Explain the economic basis for supporting free trade.

2 Evaluate the arguments in favour of protectionisms. What measures might be used to provide effective protection?

3* What do you understand by the term 'globalisation'? Consider some of its likely impacts.

Economic integration and the European Union

1   INTRODUCTION

Here we take further the analysis of the regional trading blocs identified in Chapter 16. The protected free trade area known as a 'customs union' invariably creates opportunities for new trade relationships (trade creation) whilst at the same time resulting in the loss of some long established trade relationships (trade diversion). The welfare gains from trade creation are contrasted with the welfare losses from trade diversion which result from developing such trading blocs.

Of course, economic integration may go still further than that of a 'customs union'. If it provides for the free flow of factors of production it becomes a 'common market' and if it goes a stage further, seeking the integration of economic policies, then the term 'economic union' can legitimately be applied. In this chapter we review some of the economic issues which underlie aspects of the workings of such an economic union, using the European Union by way of illustration. The European Union has changed its designation from that of the European Economic Community (1958–86), to European Community (1986–92), to European Union (EU) since 1993. The EU is part of the so-called 'triad' of the global economy, together with North America and South East Asia. It accounts for some 35% of world exports by value and contributes around 28% of world manufacturing output by value. It is clearly an important grouping of nations which creates both market opportunities (and threats) for other nations and for international business generally. This is certainly true for UK based MNEs since around 60% of UK goods are exported to the EU countries and around 54% of UK goods are imported from the EU countries.

Other aspects of harmonised fiscal policies for EU members have already been considered in Chapter 12, harmonised monetary policies in Chapter 13 and the particular issue of the euro as a single currency in Chapter 14.

2   CUSTOMS UNIONS: TRADE CREATION AND TRADE DIVERSION

Customs union
A protected free trade area.

Trade creation
Extra trade resulting from the formation of a trading bloc.

As already noted, a ***customs union*** is a protected free trade area. Those who favour this approach argue that the setting up of such regional trading blocs can enable individual countries within a broad geographical region to purchase products at lower prices because tariff walls between the member countries have been removed; this is the ***trade creation effect***. They also argue that such regional trading arrangements may create opportunities for still deeper integration, such as harmonising tax policies and product standards, while also helping to reduce political conflicts. Supporters also argue that where the world is already organised into trading blocs, then negotiations in favour of free trade are more likely to be successful when individual countries combine to form large and influential trading blocs. A large number of individual countries will, on their own, have little power to bargain successfully with existing trade blocs to secure tariff or subsidy reductions.

Trade diversion
Trade diverted to less efficient producers as a result of the formation of a trading bloc.

On the other hand, the critics of integration warn that regional trading blocs have, historically, tended to be inward looking, as in the 1930s when discriminatory trade blocs were formed to impose tariffs on non-members. Some also argue that member countries may suffer from being inside a regional bloc because they then have to buy products from within the bloc, when cheaper sources are often available from outside; i.e. the ***trade diversion effect***. Critics also argue that such regionalism threatens to erode support for multilateralism in that business groups within a regional bloc will find it easier to obtain protectionist (trade diversionary) deals via preferential pacts than they would in the world of non-discriminatory trade practices favoured by the GATT/WTO.

Figure 17.1 looks in more detail at the trade creation versus trade diversion impacts of establishing a regional trading bloc.

We assume that the domestic country initially has a tariff (t) imposed on imports from two separate countries, A and B, both of which are lower (and constant) cost producers, as indicated by their horizontal supply curves S_A and S_B respectively. We assume the tariff (t) imposed on imports from both A and B rules the less efficient country A out from competing in the domestic market altogether but still allows the relatively more efficient country, B, to compete.

The 'world' supply curve to the domestic market is therefore $S_d + (S_B + t)$ i.e. LNK giving a domestic price of P_d and domestic production of $0q_2$, with imports from country B of q_2q_3, but no trade at all with country A.

Suppose now a regional trading bloc, protected by the common external tariff t, is now formed between the domestic country and country A only. All tariffs between the domestic country and country A are abolished (it is a protected free trade area) so that the 'world' supply curve to the domestic market now becomes LMZ. Price in the domestic market falls to P_d', with imports from country A of q_1q_4 but now no imports from country B.

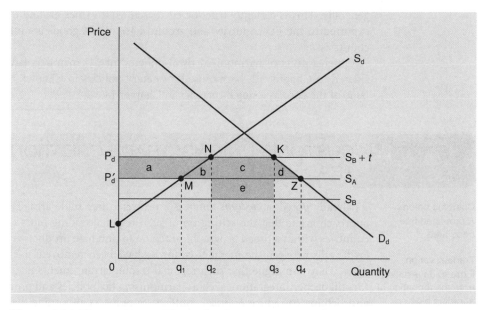

Figure 17.1 The costs and benefits from trade creation and trade diversion. A free trading bloc is established between the domestic country and country A only, with a tariff *t* still levied on country B imports.

We have, in this example, both trade creation and trade diversion.

- *Trade creation:* The result of removing the tariff *t* on trade with country A has created extra trade (with A) of the magnitude $q_1q_2 + q_3q_4$.
- *Trade diversion:* The result of removing the tariff *t only* on country A (i.e. forming a trading bloc with A) has enabled country A to undercut country B (the more efficient producer) in the domestic market. The volume of trade q_2q_3 previously undertaken with B prior to the trading bloc is now undertaken with the less efficient producer A. Trade has been 'diverted' by the formation of the trading bloc.

Using our earlier ideas of consumer and producer surplus, we can seek to measure gains and losses from trade creation and trade diversion. In Figure 17.1, the reduction in price from P_d to P'_d via creating the trading bloc has increased *consumer surplus* by area $(a + b + c + d)$, but reduced *producer surplus* by area a, since domestic production has fallen from q_2 to q_1. The *tariff revenue* $(c + e)$ previously earned on trade with country B is also lost as trade is diverted to tariff free country A.

Box 17.1

Trading blocs, trade creation and trade diversion

As long as the *net* benefits $(b + c + d)$ brought about from trade creation exceed the losses $(c + e)$ brought about from trade diversion, then the formation of the economic trading bloc can be regarded as beneficial overall.

Some general observations can be made from this analysis as to when the above condition is most likely to hold and to support the creation of a trading bloc.

1 *The greater the degree of overlap in the economies of the countries contemplating the formation of an economic bloc*, the greater the likelihood that the bloc will be a trade-creating one. If economies do not overlap, as in the case when a basically agricultural producing country joins a mainly manufacturing country, then there is little scope for trade creation but a great deal of scope for trade diversion.

2 *The greater the differences in production costs between the potential members in their overlapping industries*, the greater the potential for trade creation. Conversely, if the differences in costs are small, so will be the potential gains.

3 *The higher the tariff rates prior to the amalgamation of the economies*, the greater the gains from the associated tariff reductions.

It follows that the greatest gains from the formation of a trading bloc can be achieved if:

● the structure of the economies of potential members overlap;
● the industries that are common to potential members have a wide variation in their costs;
● the level of import tariffs placed by potential members on one another's products is high prior to the formation of the bloc.

3 ORIGINS OF THE EU

Economic union
A common market (*see* above) with attempts to harmonise other economic policies.

Common market
A protected free trade area with free movement of factors of production.

With this economic rationale for trading blocs in mind, we now turn to the more integrated institutional arrangement of the '**economic union**' with its free flow of factors of production and attempted harmonisation of national policies over a wide range of policy areas. We take the European Union as our example, with our particular focus being on the economic principles which underlie selected policy areas. The European Union (EU) has been in existence in various forms for almost 50 years, arguably beginning with the formation of the European Economic Community (EEC) on 1 January 1958 after the signing of the Treaty of Rome, although some would place its origins still earlier – *see* Box 17.2 below. This sought to establish a '**common market**'. By dismantling tariff barriers on industrial trade between members and by imposing a common tariff against non-members, the EEC was to become a protected free trade area or 'customs union' and by eliminating all restrictions on the free movements of goods, capital and persons between member countries it was to become a 'common market'. These were seen by many at the time as the first steps in the creation of an 'economic union' with national economic policies harmonised across the member countries.

The original 'Six' became 'Nine' in 1973, with the accession of the UK, Eire and Denmark, and 'Ten' in 1981 with the entry of Greece. The accession of Spain and Portugal on 1 January 1986 increased the number of member countries to twelve. In January 1995 the 12 became 15, as Austria, Finland and Sweden joined. The population of the EU encompassed over 382 million people in 2004 with a GDP exceeding ECU 9 trillion. The enlargement of the EU to 25 countries in 2004 meant that a further 75 million people were added, together with another 30 million in 2007 when Bulgaria and Romania join.

Box 17.2	European Coal and Steel Community (ECSC)

The historical background to the EU has been covered in some depth elsewhere. Since its foundation the EU has absorbed the two 'communities' which preceded it, i.e. the European Coal and Steel Community (ECSC) and the European Atomic Energy Community (Euratom). The ECSC had been established in 1952 to control the pooled coal and iron and steel resources of the six member countries – France, West Germany, Italy, Belgium, the Netherlands and Luxembourg. By promoting free trade in coal and steel between members and by protecting against non-members, the ECSC revitalised the two war-stricken industries. It was this success which prompted the establishment of the much more ambitious European Economic Community (EEC), subsequently known simply as the European Community (EC). The European Atomic Energy Community (Euratom) had been set up by treaty in 1957 with the same six countries, to promote growth in nuclear industries and the peaceful use of atomic energy.

3.1 Single European Act (SEA)

The *Single European Act* came into force in July 1987. The objective was not simply to create an internal market by removing frontier controls but to remove all barriers to the movement of goods, people and capital. Achieving a single European market has meant, among other things, work on standards, procurement, qualifications, banking, capital movements and exchange regulations, tax 'approximation', communication standards and transport.

3.2 Maastricht Treaty

The Treaty on European Union which was signed at Maastricht on 7 February 1992 represents one of the most fundamental changes to have occurred in the EU since its foundation. Although, legally speaking, merely an extension and amendment to the Treaty of Rome, Maastricht represents a major step for the member states. For the first time many of the political and social imperatives of the Community have been explicitly agreed and delineated. Maastricht takes the EU beyond a 'merely' economic institution and takes it towards the full potential, economic and social union foreseen by many of its founders. Some of its major objectives are as follows:

1 To create economic and social progress through an 'area without internal frontiers' and through economic and monetary union (EMU).
2 To develop a common foreign security and defence policy which 'might lead to common defence'.
3 To introduce a 'citizenship of the Union'.

4 EU LAWS AND REGULATIONS

European Union laws are adopted after passing through various EU bodies, as indicated in Figure 17.2. For example, most laws involving business issues are initiated by proposals from the *European Commission*. These proposals are then passed to the *Council of*

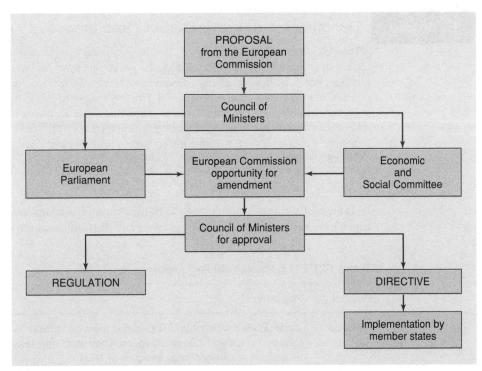

Figure 17.2 An outline of the consultation procedure for law making in the EU.

Ministers for comment, amendment and ultimately approval. However, the *European Parliament* has the power to reject new legislation coming before it (*see* below).

Figure 17.2 summarises the present process which would have been changed if a new EU constitution had been ratified which, following the 'no' vote in the French and Netherlands referendum in 2005 now seems unlikely.

Voting takes place in the Council of Ministers on the basis of a *qualified majority*. Until enlargement of the EU in 2004, 62 out of 87 votes and at least 10 out of 15 countries had to be in favour. Countries have different numbers of votes, with Germany, France, Italy and the UK each having 10 votes. Disagreements on how voting rights should be allocated after enlargement delayed the agreement on a new EU Constitution which in any case failed to be ratified in the French and Netherlands referendums in 2005.

Within this framework European Union law takes four main forms:

Directives
EU objectives are established but the means to achieve them left in hands of individual nations.

Decisions
Binding on all members of the EU.

- *Regulations*: these are applied directly without the need for national measures to implement them.
- *Directives*: these bind members of the EU with respect to objectives but allow individual countries to decide the form and means of implementation; most legislation with respect to banking and finance takes the form of directives.
- *Decisions*: these are binding in all aspects according to whether they are addressed to member states, to institutions or to individuals.
- *Recommendations and opinions*: these are not binding.

EU intervention in legal aspects of business has not always been well received.

Example | **Directives and unintended consequences**

The EU Gender Equality Directive of 2004 was intended to reduce gender discrimination but critics argue that it has had the opposite effect. For example, Direct Line, the insurer, argues that it will have to charge young women drivers £500 more than before to avoid discriminating in their favour. Prior to the Directive the better driving record for young women drivers lower premiums because they made fewer insurance claims for accidents. Young women drivers make 20% fewer claims in total than young men and their claims cost 40% less in value. For female drivers there are 17% fewer claims than for male drivers and these cost 32% less.

Table 17.1 outlines a number of EU horticultural regulations involving fresh produce which have been widely criticised by growers and distributors as too prescriptive.

Table 17.1 EU horticultural regulation

Product	Regulation
Bananas	Under EU regulation 2257/94 bananas must be at least 13.97cm (5.5 inches) long and 2.96cm (1.06 inches) round. They must now have 'abnormal curvature' as defined in an eight-page directive of 1994
Cucumbers	Any that curve more than 10mm per 10cm in length cannot be sold as 'Class 1'
Peaches	Must not be less than 5.6cm in diameter between July and October to be sold as Class 1
Red apples	Cannot be so described if less than 25% of the surface is red
Carrots	Cannot be less than 1.9cm wide at the thick end except in 'baby' varieties

4.1 European Commission (EC)

Since 1995 the *European Commission* has consisted of 20 commissioners appointed by the national governments. On appointment they are expected to act independently of national interests. The five larger member states (France, Germany, UK, Spain and Italy) have two commissioners each and the ten other member states each have one commissioner. The EC is divided into 35 separate director-generals (DGs), each of which deals with specific policy areas. The European Commission is often regarded as the 'pillar' of the EU in the economic policy domain, proposing most business-related legislation.

4.2 European Parliament (EP)

The *European Parliament* consists of members (MEPs) who, since 1979, have been directly elected by member states on a five-year mandate. It has the power to dismiss the European Commission and can therefore exert considerable influence on the EC at times of crisis. For example, in 1999 the EP insisted on the EC appointing a special investigating committee to enquire into alleged irregularities, which it secured under the threat of it dismissing the Commission. Nevertheless, its main influence is on the *legislative process* within which its procedural authority varies depending on the particular policy area.

- *Consultation procedure*: here the EP merely gives an opinion and has no effective sanction over the central decision-making agency, the Council of Ministers (*see* below).
- *Budget treaties*: here the EP has important powers, including that of rejecting the budget in its entirety.
- *Single European Act* (SEA): here the EP must give its assent to the accession of new member states and for Association Agreements with third countries.
- *Co-decision procedure* (*Article 251*): here the power of the EP extends to 37 separate policy areas in each of which the EP can reject legislation coming before it. In effect, the EP is now a co-legislator with the Council of Ministers.

4.3 European Court of Justice (ECJ)

This consists of fifteen judges and nine advocate-generals. The ECJ does not formulate policy but its rulings on matters referred to it involve the interpretation and application of EC law and these play a key part in the implementation and effectiveness of policy proposals over time.

4.4 Council of Ministers

Common Agricultural Policy (CAP)
A system providing support for the production of a range of agricultural products in the EU.

This consists of the ministers of the member states. The actual ministers involved depend on the policy areas in question; for example, the Agricultural Ministers will meet when the policy area is the **Common Agricultural Policy (CAP)**. There are some 100 meetings of the Council of Ministers each year, with the Council of Agricultural Ministers, the Council of Economics and Finance Ministers (Ecofin) and the Council of Foreign Ministers having the most frequent meetings. Meetings are chaired by the minister from the member state which holds the current 'presidency' of the Council for a six-month period. National civil servants support their ministers in these meetings.

Decisions of the Council can use *qualified majority voting* (QMV) in many areas, though *unanimous voting* is required in certain areas (e.g. tax policy). A decision by QMV requires 62 of the 87 votes, distributed according to a weighting system (e.g. France, Germany, Italy and UK have ten votes each, Belgium, Netherlands, Portugal and Greece five votes each and so on).

4.5 European Council

This consists of the heads of state, foreign ministers, EC president and vice president, meeting at least twice yearly. This is responsible for political and strategic decision making.

Pause for thought 1

What did the (aborted) EU constitution have to say on the workings of these institutions?

As we note below, not only is the EU a major destination for UK exports (around 60% of total goods exports) and a major source of UK imports (around 54% of total goods imports), it is also the location in which many subsidiary companies of UK-owned multinationals operate. Indeed, EU laws and regulations often take precedence over UK laws and regulations. For all these reasons the content of EU law is of vital importance to UK individuals and businesses.

Mini Case Study 17.1 looks at the impacts of EU law (in the form of Directives) on perceived 'market failure' in the EU financial sector.

Mini Case Study 17.1

EU directives and regulations

The EU often uses *Directives* in seeking to establish a 'level playing field' to encourage fairer competition within the EU. Although a strict classification of the numerous types of regulation would seem improbable, McKenzie (1998) makes a useful distinction:

- Regulations aimed at *protecting* the consumer from the consequences of market failure.
- Regulations aimed at *preventing* the market failure from happening in the first place.

In terms of the financial sector, the *Deposit Guarantee Directive* of the EU is of the former type. This *protects* customers of accredited EU banks by restoring at least 90% of any losses up to £12,000, which might result from the failure of a particular bank. In part, this is a response to asymmetric information, since customers do not have the information to evaluate the credit-worthiness of a particular bank and might not be able to interpret that information even if it was available.

The *Capital Adequacy Directive* of the EU is of the latter type. This seeks to prevent market failure (such as bank collapse) by directly relating the value of the capital a bank must hold to the riskiness of its business. The idea here is that the greater the value of capital available to a bank, the larger the buffer stock which it can use to absorb any losses. Various elements of the Capital Adequacy Directive force the banks to increase their capital base if the riskiness of their portfolio (indicated by various statistical measures) is deemed to have increased. In part, this is in response to the potential for negative externalities in this sector. One bank failure can invariably lead to a 'domino effect' and risk system collapse with incalculable consequences for the sector as a whole.

In these ways the regulatory system for EU financial markets is seeking to provide a framework within which greater competition between banks can occur while at the same time addressing the fact that greater competition can increase the risks of bank failure. It is seeking both to protect consumers should any mishap occur and at the same time to prevent such a mishap actually occurring.

Overall we can say that those who support any or all of these forms of regulation, on whatever sector of the economy, usually do so in the belief that they improve the allocation of resources in situations characterised by one or more types of market failure.

Questions

1 *Explain what type of 'market failure' is being tackled by the Deposit Guarantee Directive.*

2 *Explain what type of 'market failure' is being tackled by the Capital Adequacy Directive.*

3 *Can you identify any other types of 'market failure' that the EU seeks to tackle by the use of Directives?*

Answers to questions can be found on the students' side of the Companion Website.

5 CHARACTERISTICS OF THE EU

5.1 Country-specific data on the original EU 15

Tables 17.2 and 17.3 present some of the important characteristics of the 25 member countries which now comprise the EU. It shows how diverse they are in terms of population, industrial structure, standard of living, unemployment level and inflation rate. In terms of population the UK is the third largest member, with a smaller proportion engaged in agriculture than in other EU countries and the third largest in services. In overall wealth, however, the UK drops down the rankings. It has the second largest GDP in absolute terms, but comes sixth in terms of GDP per capita, some 15% above the EU average.

Pause for thought 2

How does the data in Table 17.2 help explain the major disagreement between France and the UK on the way forward for the EU?

5.2 EU enlargement

In October 2002, the EU Commission approved the most ambitious expansion plans in its history when ten countries were told that they had met the 'Copenhagen criteria' for membership. The criteria include such aspects as institutional stability, democracy, functioning market economies and adherence to the aims of political, economic and monetary union. These ten countries were deemed to be ready to join in the EU in 2004 while a further two – Bulgaria and Romania – would be due for membership in 2007. Table 17.3 provides some economic data on these countries together with their actual and projected dates of accession.

Establishing the EU 25 will not be easy since even the optimists believe it will take a decade to fully absorb the ten new nations, whose per capita income is less than 40% of the previous EU 15 average. Demands for larger subsidies for farming from the new entrants will become an inevitable problem; e.g. in Poland, 25% of the population gain some income from farming. Others argue that most of the gains will go to countries such as Germany, Austria and Italy which are physically closer to the new entrants.

6 EU COMMON AGRICULTURAL POLICY (CAP)

EAGGF
The European Agricultural Guarantee and Guidance Fund which operates the CAP.

The Common Agricultural Policy (CAP) of the EU provides a useful illustration of an attempt to impose EU-wide policies involving import protection/export support which exert a strong influence on the operations of farms and agri-businesses, both inside and outside the EU. Here we consider the operation of the CAP in some detail.

The formal title for the executive body of the CAP is the European Agricultural Guarantee and Guidance Fund (EAGGF), often known by its French translation of 'Fonds Européen d'Orientation et de Garantie-Agricole' (FEOGA). As its name implies, one of its key roles is in operating the 'guarantee system' for EU farm incomes.

Table 17.2 The EU 15 in the year 2004 prior to enlargement

Member country	Economically active population								Share of EU		
	Population (million)	Agriculture (%)	Industry (%)	Services (%)	GDP € (bn)	GDP per capita € (000s)	GDP (%)	Population (%)	Index of GDP per capita	Unemployment (%)	Inflation (%)
Austria	8.9	7.2	33.2	59.6	233.0	26.4	2.4	2.2	111.2	4.3	2.1
Belgium	10.2	2.5	6.1	71.4	281.8	25.4	2.9	2.7	106.0	7.9	2.3
Denmark	5.5	4.0	27.0	69.0	219.0	34.5	2.0	1.4	145.5	5.6	1.9
Finland	5.3	7.1	27.6	65.3	147.3	26.8	1.5	1.4	112.4	9.0	0.8
France	61.5	4.6	25.9	69.5	1,625.0	24.6	16.5	15.8	103.0	9.4	1.9
Germany	82.2	3.3	37.5	59.2	2,190.0	25.6	23.2	21.8	107.2	9.6	0.9
Greece	11.4	20.4	23.2	56.4	148.7	12.7	1.5	2.8	53.5	9.3	3.0
Ireland	4.1	10.7	27.2	61.1	146.1	32.0	1.4	1.0	133.3	4.6	3.5
Italy	58.9	7.0	32.1	60.9	1,355.9	21.6	13.7	15.3	90.5	8.6	2.8
Luxembourg	0.4	2.8	30.7	66.5	29.5	54.3	0.2	0.1	203.6	3.7	2.2
The Netherlands	16.1	3.9	22.4	73.7	464.8	27.5	4.9	4.2	116.0	3.8	0.8
Portugal	10.7	12.2	31.4	56.4	134.2	12.5	1.4	2.6	52.7	6.2	1.8
Spain	41.1	8.7	29.7	61.6	793.1	17.0	7.6	10.5	71.3	11.3	3.1
Sweden	8.8	2.9	26.1	71.0	285.3	27.7	2.7	2.4	116.0	5.6	1.1
UK	60.9	2.0	26.4	71.0	1,834.0	27.3	18.1	15.8	114.8	5.0	2.1
Total EU	385.2	3.9	28.2	67.9	9,378.3	23.8	100.0	100.0	100.0	8.9	1.9

Notes: 'Total EU' percentages for agriculture, industry and services are weighted averages.
Source: Adapted from European Commission (2005) European Economy

Table 17.3 EU enlargement 2004–07, selected data 2004

	Population (m)	GDP per capita (% of EU average)	General government budget (% of GDP)	Unemployment rate (%)	Inflation (%)
Bulgaria (2007)	7.9	28	1.7	19.9	7.4
Cyprus (2004)	0.8	80	−3.0	4.0	2.0
Czech Republic (2004)	10.2	57	−5.5	8.0	4.5
Estonia (2004)	1.4	42	−0.4	12.4	5.6
Hungary (2004)	10.2	51	−4.1	5.7	9.1
Latvia (2004)	2.4	33	−1.6	13.1	2.5
Lithuania (2004)	3.5	38	−1.9	16.5	1.3
Malta (2004)	0.4	55	−7.0	6.5	2.5
Poland (2004)	38.6	40	−3.9	18.4	5.3
Romania (2007)	22.4	25	−3.4	6.6	34.5
Slovakia (2004)	5.4	48	−5.6	19.4	10.8
Slovenia (2004)	2.0	69	−2.5	5.7	8.6

Source: European Commission (2005) various

Intervention price
The price at which the CAP intervenes to prevent any further fall. Sometimes called the 'guaranteed' price.

Different agricultural products are dealt with in slightly different ways, but the basis of the system is the establishment of a 'target price' for each product (Figure 17.3(a)). The target price is not set with reference to world prices but is based upon the price which producers need to cover costs, including a profit mark-up, in the highest-cost area of production in the EU. The EU then sets an 'intervention' or 'guaranteed' price for the product in that area, about 7–10% below the target price. Should the price be in danger of falling below this level, the Commission intervenes to buy up production to keep the price at or above the 'guaranteed' level. The Commission then sets separate target and **intervention prices** for that product in each area of the Community, related broadly to production costs in that area. As long as the market price in a given area (there are eleven such areas

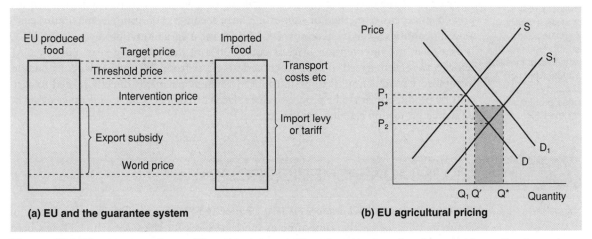

(a) EU and the guarantee system   (b) EU agricultural pricing

Figure 17.3 The system for setting the intervention (guaranteed) price and how the target price P* is maintained in a situation of excess supply.

in the UK) is above the intervention price, the producer will sell his produce at prevailing market prices. In effect the intervention price sets a 'floor' below which market price will not be permitted to fall and is therefore the guaranteed minimum price to producers.

In Figure 17.3(b) an increase in supply of agricultural products to S_1 would, if no action were taken, lower the market price from P_1 to P_2 below the intervention or guaranteed price, P^*. At P^* demand is Q' but supply is Q^*. To keep the price at P^*, the EAGGF will buy up the excess $Q^* - Q'$. In terms of Figure 17.3(b), the demand curve is artificially increased to D_1 by the EAGGF purchase.

If this system of guaranteed minimum prices is to work, EU farmers must be protected from low-priced imports from overseas. To this end, levies or tariffs are imposed on imports of agricultural products. If in Figure 17.3(b) the price of imported food were *higher* than the EU target price then, of course, there would be no need for an import tariff. If, however, the import price is *below* this, say at the 'world price' in Figure 17.3(a), then an appropriate tariff must be calculated. This need not quite cover the difference between 'target' and 'world' price, since the importer still has to pay transport costs within the EU to get the food to market. The tariff must therefore be large enough to raise the import price at the EU frontier to the target price minus transport costs, i.e. 'threshold price'. This calculation takes place in the highest-cost area of production in the EU, so that the import tariff set will more than protect EU producers in areas with lower target prices (i.e. lower-cost areas).

Should an EU producer wish to export an agricultural product, an export subsidy will be paid to bring his receipts up to the intervention price (*see* Figure 17.3(a)), i.e. the minimum price he would receive in the home market. Problems involving this form of subsidy of oil-seed exports have been a major threat to dealings between the EU and the US, with the latter alleging a breach of WTO rules. The system outlined above does not apply to all agricultural products in the EU. About a quarter of these products are covered by different direct subsidy systems, e.g. olive oil and tobacco, and some products such as potatoes, agricultural alcohol and honey are not covered by EU regulation at all.

Note: Cost of CAP to the UK
In a recent book Professor Patrick Minford (2005) puts the cost of the CAP to the UK at around 0.3% to 0.5% of UK national income each year.

Common Fisheries Policy (CFP)
A system which regulates and supports the fishing activities of member states. Common property issues pose problems for the CFP.

Reforms of the CAP over the past decade or so have modified this system which has proved an expensive method of supporting farm incomes. For example, maximum guaranteed quantities (MGQs) have now been set for most agricultural products. If the MGQ is exceeded, the intervention price is cut by 30% in the following year. Further CAP reforms were also agreed in 2003 to come into effect from 2007 onwards. For example, 'compulsory modulation' is to be introduced whereby payments directly related to agricultural production are to be progressively replaced by payments for a wide range of environmental protection activities by EU farmers.

7   COMMON FISHERIES POLICY

The legal basis of the **Common Fisheries Policy (CFP)** was established in the Treaty of Rome in 1958, i.e. at the same time as the legal basis for the CAP. The CFP has been modified over time and, in 1983, a 20-year CFP policy was agreed which would last until 2002. This included the following:

- *Access arrangements* providing for national zones of up to 12 miles (19km) for member states, with limited access for other EC countries, and a 200 mile exclusive EC zone.
- *Quotas or total allowable catches* (TACs) were established for each member state covering around one hundred different fish species.
- *Market support measures* whereby EC support buying would be undertaken in specified circumstances to maintain fish prices and stabilise incomes of fishermen and their fleets.
- *Structural policies* were introduced to help reduce overcapacity, as for example in restricting fishing capacity to specified levels in member countries. Funds were available to help people move out of the fishing sector and to help those remaining become more effective in processing and marketing their fish.

As with the CAP, attempts at a common policy have met with a number of problems, not least the 'common property rights' and public good types of market failure encountered in Chapters 1 and 9. Box 17.3 looks in more detail at these problems for the CFP.

| Box 17.3 | Common property resources and public goods characteristics facing the CFP |

Common property resources (such as the sea) are not, in fact, 'pure public goods' but rather 'quasi-public goods' in that only the first of the two key characteristics (or conditions) for public goods noted in Chapters 1 and 9 apply. The absence of property rights prevents exclusion, thereby fulfilling the 'non-exclusive' condition. However, there is some element of rivalry in that overfishing is technically possible, thereby violating the 'non-rival' condition.

The root problem is associated with that of the free rider. One co-owner of a common property resource may have little or no reason to consider the impacts of his action on other co-owners of the common property resource. Even if conservation of the common property resource (here fish in the sea) is regarded as desirable, he may hope to free ride by using the resource to the full himself while others voluntarily restrict their access. Alternatively, he may regard (given imperfect information) collective agreements to conserve fish stocks as being unrealistic and/or unenforceable, thereby supporting any inclination he might already have to pursue his own self-interest, regardless of its impact on others. Any investment the individual might make in the common property resource (e.g. desisting from overuse; restocking fish supplies) is discouraged by the fact that any returns on that investment cannot be wholly appropriated by that individual because of the absence of property rights.

Take the example of fishing in international waters. Each fisherman (trawler owner) fishes up to the point at which the marginal private benefit = marginal private cost. But since the high seas are a common property resource, the fisherman has no incentive to take into account the impact of his fishing on others. As a result the fisherman's marginal private cost (MPC) understates the true marginal social cost (MSC) of his activity. In the competitive market for fish (horizontal demand curve) shown in Figure 17.4 the outcome is likely to be overfishing. The profit-maximising solution (MPB = MPC) yields F_p fish per time period; the socially optimum solution (MSB = MSC) is only F_s fish per time period.

The main source of this particular market failure involves the institutional environment in which transactions take place. A simple remedy is therefore to change that institutional environment: e.g. let a single owner manage the resource; here the excess of MSC over MPC. A Pigouvian-type charge (*see* Chapter 10) for using the resources (e.g. depleting

→

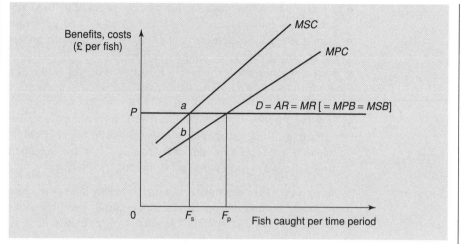

Figure 17.4 Overusing a common property resource.

fish stocks) would shift MPC vertically upwards to MSC, leading to the socially optimum fishing volume of F_s with a charge $a - b$ per fish (Figure 17.4).

Of course, in practice, many common property resources are huge, with single private ownership impractical. In this case public ownership or public regulation of private ownership may be more realistic.

8   EU INDUSTRIAL POLICY

Common External Tariff (CET)
A tariff on all imported products into the EU.

By abolishing industrial tariff and non-tariff barriers at national frontiers, the EU with the 25 current member countries has created a single 'domestic' market of around 460 million people, with opportunities for substantial economies of scale in production. A further 30 million will be added in 2007 when Bulgaria and Romania join. By surrounding this market with a tariff wall, the *Common External Tariff* (CET), member countries are the beneficiaries of these scale economies. The Common External Tariff is common to all members of the EU and is imposed on imports from non-EU countries. Tariff rates differ from one kind of import to another, as can be seen from Table 17.4. The maximum tariff can be higher for some countries than the average (most favoured nation) rate. In addition, non-tariff barriers are often applied, giving even higher overall rates of protectionism.

Raw materials and some types of semi-manufactured goods that are not produced within the EU tend to benefit from low duty rates to stimulate competition within some sectors of the EU. Tariff rates may also be set at a low level for pharmaceutical and IT-related goods.

Figure 17.5 outlines some of the expected effects of the creation of the single market, with reduced tariff and other barriers to trade and the potential economies of scale which result. The diagram represents the arguments in the Cecchini Report of 1988 which predicted that the single market was likely to lead to a staged and progressive reduction in costs and prices for many products. These would then provide opportunities for more

Table 17.4 European Union tariffs

	Average most favoured nation rate	Maximum rate %	Non-tariff barrier %	Overall
Cereals	14.0	15.2	5.0	19.0
Meat	11.2	12.1	64.8	76.0
Dairy	9.7	10.3	100.3	110.0
Other agriculture	8.9	179.7	11.2	20.0
Food products	19.5	236.4	5.0	24.5
Tobacco	47.3	81.9	–	47.3
Clothing	11.6	13.0	10.0	30.6
Footwear	7.4	17.0	–	8.9

Source: EU Commission (various)

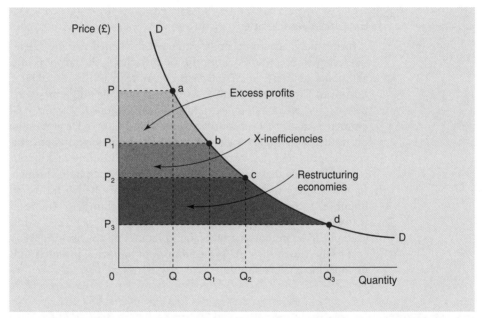

Figure 17.5 The progressively lower costs and associated prices (from P to P_3) resulting from increased competitive pressures via the removal of cost-increasing trade barriers under the single market. Excess profits are eroded ($PabP_1$), X-inefficiencies removed (P_1bcP_2) and restructuring economics attained (P_2cdP_3).

'dynamic effects' to benefit firms, as compared to the more 'static effects' of the conventional trade creation/trade diversion model of Figure 17.1 above.

The removal of tariff barriers would enable firms from other EC (as it then was) countries to sell at lower prices (P_1) in the product market of the member state (say the UK) represented in the diagram. This increased competition would, in the first stage, result in UK firms trimming their profit margins and thereby reducing the *excess profits* ('economic rents') that the UK firms had enjoyed under the previous protectionist regime (area $PabP_1$). In the next stage the UK firms may be forced to further cut their costs and prices (P_2) to compete with the now even lower prices on offer from overseas firms. For example, the overseas firms may, by selling more in the now unprotected UK market, themselves be benefiting from economies of scale. In this second stage the UK firms will be seeking to reduce the excessive costs (often called *X-inefficiencies*) from inefficient practices such as over-manning or high real wages that have resulted from a lack of competitive pressure (area P_1bcP_2). In the third stage the UK firms may be seeking to respond to still further price pressures (P_3) by restructuring their operations to cut their costs further. For example, UK firms may themselves be selling in greater volume at the now lower prices, thereby reaping economies of scale and scope (*see* Chapter 5) via mergers, acquisitions, alliances or new, more productive investments. Put another way there may now be '*economies from restructuring*' (area P_2cdP_3).

X-inefficiencies
Higher costs which are a result of a lack of competitive pressure.

It was argued that these 'dynamic effects' would raise labour and capital productivity in the single market, thereby progressively freeing resources for alternative, more productive uses. In these ways the levels of investment, economic growth and sustainable consumption would increase within the EU.

Empirical evidence

A major macroeconomic study estimated the benefits of the single market to be, over a six-year period, a 6% reduction in the price level, the creation of 5 million jobs and an additional 4.5% rise in GDP over those six years (Nello, S., 2005). Another study by the European Commission (2003) estimated that the single market had, over a ten-year period, created 2.5 million extra jobs and an additional 9% rise in GDP. A less favourable estimate is made by Professor Patrick Minford (2005). He argues that while tariff barriers on industrial imports are small, the EU protects manufacturing through quotas on specific products (e.g. textiles) through anti-dumping measures and other restraints. Minford argues that anti-dumping measures operate both through explicit tariffs being imposed where this is suspected and the threat of such tariffs, which often results in importers raising prices to avoid accusations of dumping. The result, in Minford's view, is to be seen in the high margins by which EU prices exceed world prices – in cars, for example, 69%, in footwear 60% and in radios and televisions 63%. Minford estimates the cost to the UK of such EU protectionism of industrial products to be as high as 2–3% of national income per annum.

9 · EU SOCIAL CHAPTER

By amending and coordinating labour and capital regulations in the member countries, the EU seeks to create a free market in both, leading to a more 'efficient' use of these factors. Here we illustrate some of the economic arguments underpinning the European approach to harmonised policies involving the labour market. What has become known as the European **Social Chapter** is, in fact, a consolidation and extension of long-standing approaches to labour markets by the EU.

Social Chapter
A general term covering various minimum labour market conditions established by directives and regulations in the EU.

● *1956 Treaty of Rome* has a social policy content contained in Articles 117 (promotion of an improved standard of living), 118 (cooperation of states in the social field including employment conditions, training, safety and collective bargaining) and 119 (equal pay). It also set up the European Social Fund to improve employment opportunities and increase mobility.

- *1986 Single European Act* permitted majority voting on 'health and safety' issues which has been the treaty basis for the current directives on maternity rights and working hours.
- *1989 Community Charter on Fundamental Social Rights of Workers* set out an action plan with 47 initiatives in areas such as pay, freedom of association, training, equal treatment, participation, health and safety, and protection of young workers.
- *1992 Treaty on European Union* (Maastricht Treaty) has an annex containing the Agreement on Society Policy. This has come to be known as the Social Chapter. This agreement is additional to the existing Articles 117–19 of the Treaty of Rome as amended by the Single European Act. It agrees to 'continue along the path of the 1989 Community Charter', to permit majority voting in an expanded number of areas (including working conditions, participation and gender equality) and to promote social dialogue between the main employer and union organisations.

9.1 Main directives of the Social Chapter

Approximately 30 directives have so far been adopted, a few of which are summarised below.

- *Pregnant worker protection:* all women, regardless of length of service, are to have 14 weeks' maternity leave during which their jobs will be protected and firms will have to find replacements. (Prior to this directive there was a service requirement of two years for full-timers and five years for part-timers). Women with over 26 weeks' service have the right to maternity pay. The UK has costed the expanded coverage at between £100 and £250 million or between 0.2% and 0.4% of the at-risk female wage bill.
- *Hours restriction:* a maximum of 48 hours is imposed on the working week (with exceptions such as hospital doctors and workers with 'autonomous decision-making powers' such as managers). Other requirements include a four-week paid annual holiday and an eight-hour limitation on shifts.
- *European works councils:* companies employing over 1,000 workers with at least 150 in two or more member states are required to permit a transnational worker council with information and consultation rights over the introduction of new production processes, mergers and plant closures.
- *Young workers:* there is a ban on work for those under 15. For those who are 17 or under and in education, work must be for less than three hours per day: if out of education, the limit is eight hours a day. Five weeks' paid holiday is also required and there is a ban on night work.

The UK had been opposed to many of the regulations and directives associated with the Social Chapter in the Maastricht Treaty of 1992 and secured an opt-out from its provisions. Successive Conservative governments had argued that attempting to impose regulations in such areas as works councils, maternity/paternity rights, equal pay, part-time workers issues, and so on, merely increased labour costs and decreased UK competitiveness.

Example | **UK reluctance to join the social chapter**

German social/labour market policies have been criticised in the UK for making labour too expensive to employ! Although Germany's labour productivity in manufacturing was 20% above that of the UK in the late 1990s, its relative unit labour costs were 64% higher than in the UK. Part of the problem was seen as resulting from the fact that Germany's labour costs have been inflated by non-wage costs (e.g. social benefits) which are 32% of total wage costs in Germany compared to only 18% in the UK.

Nevertheless, the incoming Labour government in the UK adopted many parts of the Social Chapter in 1997 in order to provide basic minimum standards across Europe even if this did result in some increase in labour costs.

9.2 Economic analysis of the Social Chapter

Again we can use the ideas of economic welfare to analyse the economic principles underlying the Social Chapter, which we have seen to be a set of mandated (legally enforceable) regulations establishing *minimum conditions* over a range of labour market areas.

In a competitive world, working conditions are determined by a process of experimentation that tends to make both employees and employers as well off as possible. This can be illustrated with labour demand and supply diagrams. First consider Figure 17.6(a) which uses workplace safety as an example. Suppose a firm provides *no safety*, so that risk of injury is at a maximum (r = max). Demand for labour is illustrated in the diagram as $D[r = max]$ and supply $S[r = max]$. The equilibrium wage will be W_1. Now suppose that the firm provides a *completely safe workplace* so that risk of injury is at a minimum (r = min). This will cause the demand curve for labour to shift downwards to $D[r = 0]$. We saw in Chapter 8 that the marginal revenue product of labour (MRP_L) could, under certain conditions, be regarded as the demand curve for labour. The expenditure by employers on safety measures will now mean that the 'net' MRP_L for any given quantity of labour is the original (gross) value when r = max minus 'safety expenditures' incurred when r = 0. This gives the $D[r = 0]$ curve in Figure 17.6(a). Of course, the supply curve will also shift downwards to $S[r = 0]$ because workers like safety and more workers will now be willing to supply themselves at any given wage. The new equilibrium wage when r = 0 will be W_3.

In practice, some medium risk (r = med) position is likely to be preferable. This equilibrium can be shown in Figure 17.6(b) by adding some 'medium risk' demand and supply curves to those already shown in Figure 17.6(a). Here, B represents a possible equilibrium position for medium risk, which can be seen to be preferable to both employers and employees. For example, point B gives employers higher profits (triangle ABW_2) and

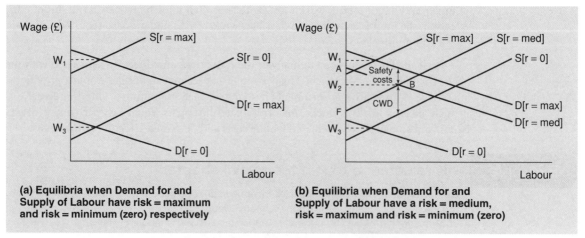

(a) Equilibria when Demand for and Supply of Labour have risk = maximum and risk = minimum (zero) respectively

(b) Equilibria when Demand for and Supply of Labour have a risk = medium, risk = maximum and risk = minimum (zero)

Figure 17.6 In Figure 17.6(a) the labour market equilibrium positions for risk = maximum (W_1) and risk = zero (W_3) are shown. In Figure 17.6(b) the labour market equilibrium for risk = medium is shown with a new equilibrium at W_2 at point B.

workers higher economic rent or surplus payments (triangle W_2BF) than either the $r = max$ or $r = 0$ alternatives as drawn; it also increases employment.

Compensating Wage Differential (CWD)
Extra wages needed to compensate workers for accepting some risk.

Notice from Figure 17.6(b) how B implies a certain '**compensating wage differential**' (CWD) when $r = med$, whereby any given number of workers must now be paid extra, as compared to $r = 0$, for them to supply themselves. Notice also from Figure 17.6(b) how expenditures on safety measures is shown by the vertical downward shift of the demand for labour curve.

Figure 17.7 helps us explore the equilibrium position with medium risk at point B in more detail.

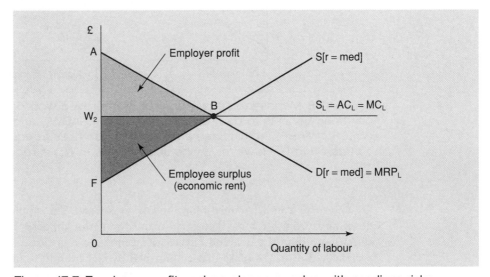

Figure 17.7 Employer profit and employee surplus with medium risks.

- *Employer profits* If we assume a competitive labour market, then the supply of labour is perfectly elastic at the going wage rate W_2 so that wage $= AC_L = MC_L$ (*see* Chapter 8, page 168) so a worker with a MRP_L above W_2 will earn that amount of profit for his/her employer. Summing all these profits on each worker gives total profit ABW_2.
- *Employee surplus ('economic rent')* Where the employee receives a wage (W_2) higher than that needed to induce his/her supply, then this corresponds to an employee surplus or 'economic rent' payment. In Figure 17.7 at the medium risk equilibrium, the total of such employee surplus payments is area W_2BF.

Total welfare at medium risk is the sum of the two areas, i.e. ABF, which is greater than the equivalent total welfares for $r = max$ or $r = 0$, as drawn in Figure 17.6(b) above. In other words, the vertical downward shift of the demand curve reflects the costs to the firm of safety measures, as compared to $r = max$, and the vertical upward shift at the supply curve represents the CWD as compared to $r = 0$.

An important question is: could mandating (i.e. legally prescribing) more safety as in the Directives of the Social Chapter improve on B? One possibility is shown in Figure 17.8. *Mandating* (i.e. legally prescribing) more safety expenditures will shift the

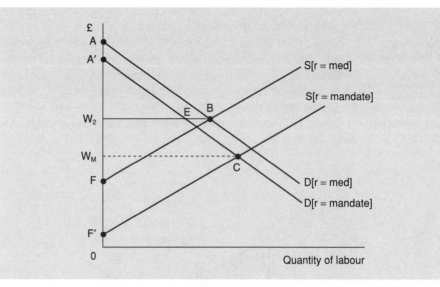

Figure 17.8 Mandating (legally enforcing) improved working conditions can bring benefits to both employers ($A'CW_M > ABW_2$) and employees ($W_MCF' > W_2BF$). In this case employment also rises at equilibrium C compared to B. However, wage flexibility ($W_M < W_2$) is required.

demand curve from $D[r = med]$ down to $D[r = mandate]$. The supply curve will also shift downwards from $S[r = med]$ to $S[r = mandate]$. Let us suppose that the supply curve shifts more than the demand curve, so we move to a position such as C, which is preferable to B in the sense that employment is higher and the sum of employer and employee surpluses is higher. Point C is a Pareto improvement on B: society is better off at C than at B. In other words, the Social Chapter Directive raises economic welfare. However, we could also draw a diagram illustrating the case where the workers do not value the mandate as much as it costs the firms and total economic welfare falls. Note that, whatever happens, the money wage must fall when the mandate is imposed. If wages do not fall (perhaps because of labour-market rigidities) we move to a position such as E with lower employment than B.

Figure 17.8 illustrates the conditions that must be fulfilled if a mandate is to increase employment and make both sides better off. At the same time it raises the question of why, if a position such as C exists which is better than B, the parties have not independently discovered it in the first place. Why do they need government help? Let us now turn to this problem.

Example | Mandated hours

In 2004 the UK implemented the restriction on doctors' hours to a maximum of 58 hours per week, as specified in the EU *Working Time Directive*. Since most junior doctors in the UK hospitals work an average of around 70 hours per week, the NHS has lost some 270,000 hours of their time over a year, the equivalent of 3,700 junior doctors.

9.3 Failures of the competitive labour-market process

The efficiency or surplus-maximising case for mandates (such as the EU Directives for the labour market) is that they overcome obstacles preventing employees and employers from negotiating their own efficient contracts. There are three main types of obstacle that might be involved here: monopsony, externalities and imperfect information.

- *Monopsony* This refers to the case where a firm has buyer power in the market for labour. Such power can be used to block efficient contracts. Thus, suppose that a contract would bring a fall in employer profits, but a larger increase in employee surplus. This contract would represent a 'potential Pareto improvement', in the sense that the gains of the employees would outweigh the losses of the employers the joint surplus would be increased by this contract. Yet the firm would have an incentive to prevent such a contract if it had the power. The firm is interested in its own surplus, not the joint surplus.

- *Externalities* In the labour market externalities are often said to arise in the case of training, as when a firm poaches trained workers from other firms which thereby make a loss on their training activities. The outcome may be too little training from society's point of view, so mandating a minimum level of training or a means by which all companies in an industry pay for training may be needed.

- *Imperfect information* Under this heading we can consider both the question of workers' lack of information about firms and firms' lack of information about workers. If workers are unaware of the hazards they face in the workplace, then they may be unable to accurately assess their preferences for supplying labour to alternative occupations. Firms' ignorance about the quality of their workers might be very real in some circumstances. For this reason, firms might be reluctant to offer company health insurance, or maternity insurance, even though their workers would value such insurance and the company could provide it more cheaply than the workers could buy it themselves. The difficulty from the firm's point of view is that if it alone offers insurance it will tend to attract the bad risks. A form of negative externality – adverse selection – will operate. In terms of Figure 17.8 fear of adverse selection prevents point C being reached. However, if *all* firms are forced to offer insurance, as for example by an EU Directive, then such adverse selection is ruled out. This argument can be used as a basis for mandated company health or maternity benefits.

What our analysis has shown is that certain types of 'market failure' in labour markets may make it beneficial (in terms of raising economic welfare) to insist (mandate) that all parties enforce a particular labour market regulation, i.e. that a Directive of the Social Chapter be adopted.

10 EU COMPETITION POLICY

By seeking to intervene in various monopoly and restrictive practice situations, competition has been encouraged both within and across frontiers. Many European countries have long histories of state intervention in markets so it is hardly surprising that the European Commission accepts the case for intervention by member governments. Apart from agriculture, competition is the only area in which the EU has been able to implement effectively a common policy across member countries. The Commission can intervene to control the behaviour of monopolists, and to increase the degree of competition, through authority derived directly from the Treaty of Rome:

a) *Article 81* prohibits agreements between enterprises which result in the restriction of competition (notably relating to price-fixing, market-sharing, production limitations and other restrictive practices). This article refers to any agreement affecting trade between member states and therefore applies to a large number of British industries.

b) *Article 82* prohibits a dominant firm, or group of firms, from using their market power to exploit consumers.

c) *Articles 87 and 88* prohibit government subsidies to industries or individual firms which will distort, or threaten to distort, competition.

Example	Coca Cola must keep its promises

Coca Cola has over 50% of the EU carbonated drinks market. In 2004 it promised the European Commission that it would allow more competition in this market, to avoid a full investigation. Coca Cola, based in Atlanta, has agreed to give up all its exclusivity arrangements with retailers, who will now be free to buy and sell fizzy drinks from any supplier of their choice. The European Commission was given new legal powers in 2004 to enforce such commitments; for example, it can fine Coca Cola up to 10% of its global revenues if it breaches the commitments it has made over allowing more competition in the carbonated drinks market.

10.1 Cross-border mergers policy

European competition policy has been criticised for its lack of comprehensiveness, but in December 1989 the Council of Ministers agreed for the first time on specific cross-border merger regulations. The criteria for judging whether a merger should be referred to the European Commission covered three aspects.

- First, the companies concerned must have a combined world turnover of more than €5 billion (though for insurance companies the figure was based on total assets rather than turnover).
- Secondly, at least two of the companies concerned in the merger must have an EU-wide turnover of at least €250 million each.
- Thirdly, if both parties to the merger have two-thirds of their business in one and the same member state, the merger was to be subject to national and not EU controls.

The European Commission must be notified of merger proposals which meet the criteria noted above within one week of the announcement of the bid and it will vet each proposed merger against a concept of '*a dominant position*'. Any creation or strengthening of a dominant position will be seen as incompatible with the aims of the EU if it significantly impedes '*effective competition*'.

The European Commission has one month after notification to decide whether to start proceedings and then four months to make a final decision. If a case is being investigated by the European Commission it will *not* also be investigated by national bodies such as the UK Competition Commission, for example. Member states may prevent a merger which has already been permitted by the EU only if it involves public security or some aspects of the media or if competition in the local markets is threatened.

A number of reservations were expressed about this EU legislation on cross-border mergers and acquisitions.

- First, a main aim of the legislation was to introduce a 'one-stop-shop' which meant that merging companies would be liable to *either* European *or* national merger control, but not both. However, as can be seen above, in some situations national merger control could override EU control creating a 'two-stop-shop'!
- Secondly, it was not clear how the rules would apply to non-EU companies. For example, it was quite possible that two US or Japanese companies each with the required amount of sales in the EU, but with no actual EU presence, could merge. While such a case would certainly fall within the EU merger rules, it was not clear how seriously the EU could exercise its powers in such cases.
- Thirdly, guidelines were needed on joint ventures.

10.2 New EU cross-border merger regulations

In March 1998 a number of amendments were made to the scope of EU cross-border merger regulations. The result of these amendments was that the three original criteria for exclusive reference to the European Commission remain, but other criteria were added to give the EU jurisdiction over smaller-sized mergers which would not be large enough to qualify under the €5 billion and €250 million rules described earlier.

As regards joint ventures, the new regulations also make a distinction between 'concentrative' joint ventures and 'cooperative' joint ventures, with the new European Commission rules applying to the first type (which was seen to concentrate power) but not to the second type (which was merely seen as a method to coordinate competitive behaviour).

In 2000, a review of the merger approval system was instigated by the EU. By November 2002 it was announced that a package of reforms would be introduced that would take effect from May 2004. One aspect of the reforms includes the retention of the rule that a merger is unlawful if it 'creates or strengthens a dominant position' but also adds an amendment to the merger regulation to include situations where a merger may be deemed unlawful if it creates 'collective dominance' in a market. This situation might occur when a merger results in the formation or strengthening of an oligopolistic market structure within which a few large firms can coordinate their activities to the detriment of consumers. To date the European Commission has handled around 80 merger cases per year over the past decade.

10.3 Restrictive practices and EU legislation

As in the UK, the EU competition policy seeks to deal with much more than merger activity. The reasoning behind European competition policy is exactly that which created the original European Economic Community (EEC) almost 50 years ago. Competition is viewed as bringing consumers greater choice, lower prices and higher quality goods and services.

The European Commission has a set of *directives* in this area which are designed to underpin 'fair and free' competition. They cover cartels (price-fixing, market-sharing, etc.), government subsidies (direct or indirect subsidies for inefficient enterprises – state and private), the abuse of dominant market position (differential pricing in different markets, exclusive contracts, predatory pricing, etc.), selective distribution (preventing consumers in one market from buying in another in order to maintain high margins in the first market), and mergers and takeovers.

Avoiding excessive use of state aid

One of the most active areas of competition policy has involved *state aid*. The Commission has attempted to restrict the aid paid by member states to their own nationals through Articles 87 and 88 which cover various aspects of the distorting effect that subsidies can have on competition between member states. However, it is likely that the progressive implementation of single market arrangements will result in domestic firms increasing their attempts to obtain state aid from their own governments as a means of helping them meet greater Europe-wide competition. Overall, the amount of aid given by member states to their domestic industry has been running at around 2% of their respective GNPs during the 1990s and early years of the millennium.

Pause for thought 3

Why has the European Commission started to pay more attention to the use of state aid by member countries?

Mini Case Study 17.2 examines this issue of state aid further.

Mini Case Study 17.2

Boeing versus Airbus

Boeing (US) and Airbus (EU) are close rivals in the aircraft industry and each is alleging unfair competition.

AIRBUS	BOEING
Infrastructure aid for A380: $1.7 billion Launch aid (since 1969): $15 billion Launch aid for A350: $1.3 billion	Tax exemptions. Infrastructure and personnel subsidies from Washington State: $7 billion Tax subsidy through US Foreign Sales Corporation: $200 million pa Research and Development grants through Nasa and Pentagon since 1992: $20 billion Infrastructure aid from Japanese government: $1.6 billion

Questions

1 *What does the data suggest?*

2 *What implications might follow from this dispute between these two huge companies?*

Answers to questions can be found at the back of the book (page 524).

10.4 EU competition policy and economic efficiency

In the discussion above for the EU it is clear that there is no presumption that mergers and takeovers are against the public interest, though in specific cases it is recognised that they might be. Here we review the theoretical underpinnings for judging individual mergers and takeovers on a case-by-case basis.

The idea of economic efficiency may usefully be broken down into two separate elements.

Productive efficiency
Where the average total cost of production is at the minimum technically feasible.

Allocative efficiency
Where price is set equal to the marginal cost of producing the last unit.

- *Productive efficiency* This involves using the most efficient combination of resources to produce a given level of output. Only when the firm is producing a given level of output with the least-cost methods of production available do we regard it as having achieved 'productive efficiency'.
- *Allocative efficiency* This is often taken to mean setting a price which corresponds to the marginal cost of production. The idea here is that consumers pay firms exactly what it costs them to produce the last (marginal) unit of output; such a pricing strategy can be shown to be a key condition in achieving a so-called 'Pareto optimum' resource allocation, where it is no longer possible to make someone better off without making someone else worse off. Any deviation of price away from marginal cost is then seen as resulting in 'allocative inefficiency'.

What may pose problems for policy makers is that the impacts of proposed mergers may move these two aspects of economic efficiency in *opposite directions*. For example, economies of scale may result from the merger having increased firm size, with a lower cost of producing any given output thereby improving productive efficiency. However, the greater market power associated with increased size may give the enlarged firm new opportunities to raise price above (or still further above) its costs of production, including marginal costs, thereby reducing allocative efficiency.

We may need to balance the gain in productive efficiency against the loss in allocative efficiency to get a better idea of the *net* overall impact of the merger on the 'public interest'. We noted in earlier chapters that this can often be regarded as the sum of consumer surplus (Chapter 4) and producer surplus (Chapter 5).

Figure 17.9 is useful in illustrating the fact that a proposed merger might move productive and allocative efficiencies in opposite directions. For simplicity we assume the curves displayed to be linear and the firm to be at an initial price/quantity equilibrium of P/Q with marginal cost MC (for a profit-maximising firm MR would have intersected MC at point i). Now suppose that the merger/takeover results in the (enlarged) firm using its market power to raise price from P to P_1, cutting output from Q to Q_1, *but* that at the same time the newly available scale economies cut costs so that MC shifts downwards to MC_1.

Clearly we have to balance a loss of allocative efficiency against a gain in productive efficiency in order to assess the overall impact on the 'public interest'. To do this we can usefully return to the idea of economic welfare and the associated consumer and producer surpluses.

If we regard the total welfare resulting from a resource allocation as being the sum of the consumer surplus and the producer surplus, we have:

Pre-merger	*afd + dfig*
Post-merger	*abc + bckj*

In terms of total welfare (consumer surplus + producer surplus) we can note the following impacts of the merger:

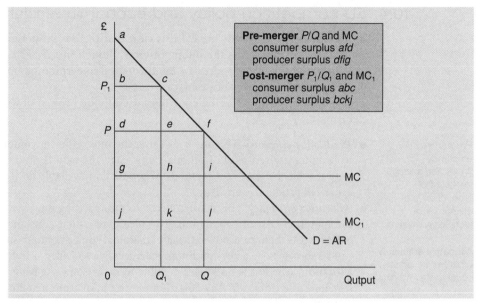

Figure 17.9 The pre-merger and post-merger situations in terms of economic welfare, with the gain shown as area *ghkj* and the loss as area *cflk*.

Gains of welfare	*ghkj*
Loss of welfare	*cflk*

The 'gain of welfare' (*ghkj*) represents the improvement in productive efficiency from the merger, as the Q_1 units still produced require fewer resources than before now that the scale economies have reduced costs (shifting MC down to MC_1).

The 'loss of welfare' (*cflk*) represents the deterioration in allocative efficiency from the merger: price has risen (P to P_1) and marginal costs have fallen (MC to MC_1), further increasing the gap between price and marginal cost. As a result of the price rise from P to P_1, output has fallen from Q to Q_1. This loss of output has reduced economic welfare since society's willingness to pay for these lost $Q - Q_1$ units (the area under the demand curve from $Q - Q_1$, i.e. *cfQQ₁*) exceeds the cost of producing them (the sum of all the marginal costs from $Q - Q_1$) by *cflk*.

Clearly the overall welfare effect ('public interest') could be positive or negative, depending on whether the welfare gains exceed the welfare losses, or vice versa (in Figure 17.9 the losses outweigh the gains). No pre-judgement can therefore be made that a merger will, or will not, be in the public interest. Everything depends on the extent of any price rise and on the demand and cost curve configurations for any proposed merger. It is in this context that an EU Competition Commission investigation and other methods of enquiry into particular proposals might be regarded as important in deciding whether any merger should proceed or be abandoned.

KEY POINTS

● A customs union is a protected free trade area and results in both trade creation with members but trade diversion away from non-members.

- The welfare benefits of a customs union are likely to be larger: a) the more similar the economic structure of potential members, b) the greater the cost variations between the industries of potential members, and c) the greater the tariffs placed on the products of potential members prior to the formation of the customs union.

- The Maastricht Treaty in 1992 sought to widen the scope of the EU beyond a common market to that of an economic and monetary union (EMU).

- There are now 25 member states within the EU, with Austria, Sweden and Finland joining in 1995 and Cyprus, Czech Republic, Estonia, Hungary, Latvia, Lithuania, Malta, Poland, Slovakia and Slovenia joining in 2004. Bulgaria and Romania are to join in 2007.

- The 25 member EU is essentially a regional trading bloc with around 460 million people within a protected free trade area, with a high per capita income of almost £24,000 per annum.

- The EU is the largest trading bloc in the world. It accounts for 20% of world GDP and around 40% of world trade.

- Agriculture is the most regulated sector within the EU. Around 41% of the entire EU budget is spent on various price support and intervention policies involving agricultural products.

- There is a Common Fisheries Policy which faces problems associated with 'common property resources' and which often lead to overfishing.

- The average EU tariff imposed on imported industrial products varies considerably between different products and different countries supplying the imports.

- 'Dynamic effects' of the single European market include curbing excess profits, reducing X-inefficiencies and stimulating economic restructuring.

- The Social Chapter is a term used to cover a wide variety of mandated (i.e. legislated) minimum labour market conditions contained in EU directives and regulations.

- The welfare gains of using mandated directives, rather than voluntary agreements, can be substantial when labour market 'failures' such as monopsony, externalities and imperfect information are present.

Further reading

Griffiths, A. and Wall, S. (2006) *Applied Economics*, 11th edition, FT/Prentice Hall, Chapter 29.

Griffiths, A. and Wall, S. (2005) *Economics for Business and Management*, FT/Prentice Hall, Chapter 14.

Minford, P., Mahambare, V. and Nowell, E. (2005) *Should Britain leave the EU? An economic analysis of a troubled relationship*, Edward Elgar and IEA.

Parkin, M., Powell, M. and Matthews, K. (2003) *Economics*, 5th edition, FT/Prentice Hall, Chapter 6.

Sloman, J. (2006) *Economics*, 6th edition, FT/Prentice Hall, Chapters 3, 12 and 23.

Web references

You can find current data and information on many aspects of the EU from the following sites.

EU: **http://www.europa.eu.int/** This is the official EU website.
Eurostat: **http://europa.eu.int/comm/eurostat/** Main site for EU data.

European Central Bank: **http://www.ecb.int/** The ECB site containing financial statistics and other relevant material on EU finance.

European Investment Bank: **http://eib.eu.int/** The organisation which provides medium term loans to help facilitate European integration.

Some European directorates for statistics and other information:

Agriculture: **http://europa.eu.int/comm/dgs/agriculture/index_en.htm**

Budget: **http://europa.eu.int/comm/dgs/budget/index_en.htm**

Competition: **http://europa.eu.int/comm/dgs/competition/index_en.htm**

Economy/Finance: **http://europa.eu.int/comm/dgs/economy_finance/index_en.htm**

Internal Market: **http://europa.eu.int/comm/dgs/internal_market/index_en.htm**

EU Commission representation in the UK: **http://www.cec.org.uk/** Details on publications/statistics related to the UK.

EU information network for the UK: **http://europe/org/uk/info/** Information and other details on UK regions.

IMF: **http://www.imf.org/** A major source of comparative data for EU/other countries.

OECD: **http://www.oecd.org/** A main source of comparative data for EU/other countries.

PROGRESS AND REVIEW QUESTIONS

Answers to most questions can be found at the back of the book (pages 525–6). Answers to asterisked questions can be found on the students' side of the Companion Website.

 ## Multiple-choice questions

1   Which *two* of the following were key objectives of the European Union's Maastricht Treaty?

   a) To increase the resources available for economic growth
   b) To prevent trade dumping by competitors
   c) To create an area without internal frontiers
   d) To develop a common political entity
   e) To develop a common foreign, security and defence policy

2   Which *two* of the following are key elements of the Common Agricultural Policy (CAP) of the EU?

   a) Subsidies on imported agricultural products
   b) Tariffs on imported agricultural products
   c) Quotas on imported agricultural products
   d) Subsidies to EU exporters of agricultural products
   e) Tariffs on EU exporters of agricultural products

3   Which *one* of the following is where a protected free trade area also involves free movement of factors of production and the harmonisation of economic policies?

   a) Common market
   b) Economic union
   c) Free trade area

d) Customs union

e) Common Agricultural Policy (CAP)

4 Which *one* of the following is a policy designed to reduce spending on the CAP by helping farmers move into other economic activities?

a) The Maximum Guaranteed Quantities policy

b) The European Regional Development Fund initiative

c) The Guidance Fund within the European Agricultural Guarantee and Guidance Fund (EAGGF)

d) The Rural Development policy

e) The Deficiency Payments policy

5 Which *one* of the following represents a situation where the common external tariff imposed by the EU on non-members results in some production being transferred from low-cost producers outside the Union to high-cost producers inside the Union.

a) Dynamic trade gains

b) Trade creation

c) Trade diversion

d) Trade restriction

e) Cost inversion

Data response question

Look carefully at the figure below.

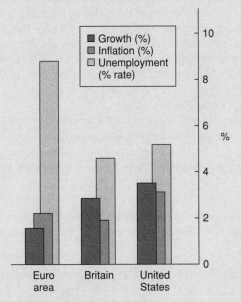

Source: Adapted from OECD data

How does the data shown in the figure contribute to the ongoing debate as to the future direction of the EU?

Case study question

Tyre Directive

Scrap tyres have become a major headache for the UK and other EU governments. A European Directive banned landfills on whole tyres in 2003 and shredded tyres by 2006. The option of dumping tyres in major landfill sites will be closed and new ways will have to be found to dispose of the 13 million tyres that are stockpiled or put in landfills every year in the UK. The problem is huge. The number of tyres is forecast to increase by up to 60% by 2021 as the number of vehicles rises. Every day, 100,000 tyres are taken off cars, vans, trucks, buses and bicycles in the UK. It is widely estimated that there are now more than 200 million tyres lying around. By their very nature, tyres are difficult to dispose of since they are designed not to fall apart while you are driving along the motorway.

Although tyres remain substantially intact for decades, some of their components can break down and enter the environment. Environmental concern centres on the highly toxic additives used in their manufacture, such as zinc, chromium, lead, copper, cadmium and sulphur. The Environment Agency launched a campaign in 2002 in the UK to alert the public and industry to the need to prolong the life of existing tyres and to find new recycling methods. 'You can find landfill sites that cover an entire valley, with black as far as the eye can see,' said an Environment Agency spokesman. 'We have always viewed tyres as a resource, rather than something to be dumped.'

The best use of tyres is probably to retread them, but this is now expensive, and fewer than ever are recycled in this way. According to the Used Tyre Working Group, a joint industry and government initiative sponsored by the main tyre industry associations, just 18% of Britain's tyres are retreaded. A further 48,500 tonnes are converted into 'crumb rubber' used in carpet underlay and to make surfaces such as those on children's playgrounds.

More controversially, 18% are burnt as a 'replacement fuel' in the manufacture of cement. This is fast becoming the most popular way of disposing of them, but it is of increasing concern to environmentalists and scientists. 'Tyre burning emits ultra-fine particles that have a toxicity all of their own,' says Vyvyan Howard, senior lecturer in toxicopathology at Liverpool University. 'The toxicity is even stronger if this contains metals such as nickel and tin, which you get when you throw the whole tyre into the furnace. If the metal content of the particles goes up, then there is going to be an increasing impact on health.' The cement companies deny that they are affecting people's health.

Meanwhile, the UK sends 26% of its tyres to landfill, far less than some other EU countries. France sends almost 50%, Spain 58%, but Holland sends none. The UK is now racking its brains as to how to dispose of the 13 million tyres that accumulate each year. Many believe the onus is on the manufacturers to produce tyres that lend themselves to greater recycling.

Question

What does this Case Study suggest about the relevance of EU legal decisions to UK businesses and individuals? Give examples of possible impacts of this Directive involving tyres on both.

 ## True/false questions

1 Trade creation describes the situation where the removal of tariff barriers between members of the trading bloc now enables various products to be purchased at lower prices, thereby stimulating intra-regional trade.

2 The Maastricht Treaty in 1992 sought to widen the scope of the EU beyond a common market to that of economic and monetary union.

3 Directives of the EU specify the ways in which member countries must achieve an objective.

4 The Guarantee section of the European Agricultural Guarantee and Guidance Fund (EAGGF) seeks to direct smaller, less efficient farmers out of agriculture.

5 X-inefficiencies are those which result from a lack of competitive pressure.

6 The so-called 'dynamic' effects of increased competition from the single market include the removal of excess profits and X-inefficiencies and various economies from restructuring business activity.

7 The Social Chapter involves directives which set mandated objectives but allow countries to choose how to meet those objectives.

8 Monopsony in a labour market refers to a situation where the seller of labour has market power.

 ## Essay questions

Answers can be found at the back of the book (page 526).

1 Under what circumstances would you support the creation of a protected free trade area?

2 Evaluate the arguments for and against the Common Agricultural Policy (CAP).

3 How effective do you believe the single market to be? Justify your reasoning.

4 Why do many believe we need a Social Chapter within the EU?

CHAPTER 18

Growth, sustainable development and the less developed countries

Learning objectives

By the end of this chapter you should be able to:

- Evaluate the contribution of the classical, neo-classical and modern theories of growth to the issue of economic development.

- Identify the key characteristics of 'sustainable development' and examine the conditions required to achieve sustainable growth paths.

- Assess the relative importance of GNP and other 'quality of life' indicators in estimating standards of living.

- Understand the key characteristics of developing economies and their implications for policy initiatives seeking to promote economic development.

- Evaluate the role of the IMF, World Bank and other international institutions and initiatives seeking to promote debt relief and economic development.

1   INTRODUCTION

This chapter first reviews the theoretical basis for economic growth and development in *all* countries, including classical, neo-classical and modern (endogenous) theories of growth. These principles are then applied to the issue of sustainability and to the particular circumstances of the so-called less developed countries (LDCs). It is now acknowledged that political, social, historical and cultural factors work alongside the economic factors when LDCs go through a process of growth and structural change. Although this chapter will focus on the economic issues, reference will be made on occasions to these broader issues. The nature and causes of poverty amongst the nations are very complex, and the remedies are neither easy nor quick. An analysis of the major features of LDCs will shed some light on the peculiar economic and social conditions of production, consumption and distribution of income and wealth which exist in LDCs. This will help us to understand some development approaches and their policy implications. The 'debt crisis' facing many LDCs is considered and the policy responses of the IMF and other international institutions are reviewed.

2 THEORIES OF ECONOMIC GROWTH

We noted in Chapter 11 that the percentage change in real national income is the usual method for measuring the rate of economic growth. Here we consider the classical, neo-classical and modern theories of growth.

2.1 Classical growth theory

Subsistence real wage
Just sufficient to keep one alive.

Classical growth theory
No long-term growth and real wage falls to the subsistence level over this time period.

The *subsistence real wage rate* plays a key role in **classical growth theory**, i.e. the minimum real wage rate required to maintain life. Whenever the actual real wage *exceeds* the subsistence real wage, then population grows and this, combined with diminishing returns to labour, ensures that the actual real wage rate falls back to the subsistence level. On the other hand, when the actual real wage *falls below* the subsistence real wage, then lives are lost and the population declines until the actual real wage rises to the subsistence level. The discouraging prediction of the classical growth theory (Figure 18.1) is that whatever the increase in levels of investment or the improvements in technology, the *long run growth rate* is effectively zero, since equilibrium will only occur with living standards at the subsistence real wage.

This rather dismal prospect was emphasised by analysts of the time such as Thomas Malthus (*see* Box 18.1).

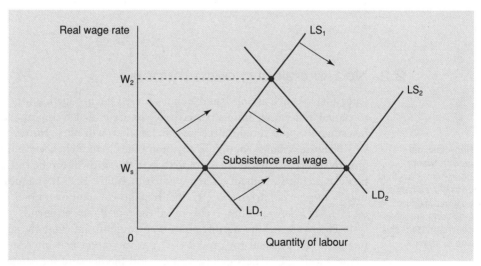

Figure 18.1 An increase in capital equipment and/or technical change increases the marginal revenue product of labour (*see* Chapter 8) and therefore the demand for labour increases from LD$_1$ to LD$_2$. The real wage rises from W$_s$ to W$_2$ in the short run, but the increase in population and labour supply to LS$_2$ in the long run reduces the real wage rate, which then falls back to the original subsistence level W$_s$.

Box 18.1	Population and natural resources

Thomas Malthus (1766–1834) claimed that the human population would, left unchecked, grow exponentially (in a geometric progression). However, food production would grow only linearly (in an arithmetic progression), restricted by the need to bring new, less productive land into cultivation (an earlier forerunner of the theory of diminishing returns). Population would therefore double every 25 years and food production would be unable to keep pace. Periodic famines and high infant mortality, together with occasional wars, were seen by Malthus as the most likely 'checks' to population explosion. Malthus noted that even in nineteenth-century Britain, food production was already falling short of population growth, as evidenced by the high price of bread and increasing public expenditure on relief of the poor.

Malthus failed, however, to perceive that population growth has turned out to have an internal check: as people grow richer and healthier, they have smaller families. Indeed, the growth rate of the human population reached its peak of more than 2% a year in the early 1960s. The rate of increase has been declining ever since. It is now 1.26% and is expected to fall to 0.46% in 2050. The United Nations has estimated that most of the world's population growth will be over by 2100, with the population stabilising at just below 11 billion.

Malthus also failed to take account of developments in agricultural technology. These have squeezed more and more food out of each hectare of land. It is this application of technology and human ingenuity that has boosted food production, not merely in line with, but ahead of, population growth.

2.2 Neo-classical growth theory

Neo-classical growth theory
Short-term growth is possible via capital accumulation but long-term growth is only haphazard and due to chance.

Later analysts such as Solow and Dennison used the production function (relating output to capital and labour inputs respectively) to argue that technical change and additional investment capital could indeed raise national growth rates. However, there is no reason why technical change should be anything other than a chance event under **neo-classical growth theory**, so that there is no prediction that growth can be sustained over time. The neo-classical growth theory is represented in Figure 18.2. It assumes that savers have in mind a *target real interest rate* (R_T) that remains constant over time. This target real interest rate, say 5% per annum, is also called the *rate of time preference*.

In Figure 18.2(a) the starting point is an equilibrium where the supply of capital (KS_1) intersects the demand for capital (KD_1) at the target real interest rate R_T and capital/labour ratio K_1/L_1. The supply of capital and the demand for capital are determined by saving and investment decisions. For example, as real interest rates rise, savings rise and the supply of capital expands. However, as real interest rates rise, less investment projects are now profitable (*see* Box 18.2, page 457) and the demand for capital contracts. We now suppose that technical change occurs which raises the output per unit of capital, so that at any given interest rate there is an increased demand for capital investment, raising the amount of capital per person in production. In the short run this increase in the demand for capital from KD_1 to KD_2 raises the real interest rate to R_2, which is now above the target rate R_T. In Figure 18.2(b) this above-target return to savers shifts sentiments in favour of still more saving at any given real interest rate, increasing (shifting to the right)

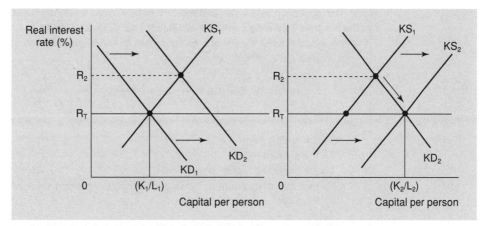

Figure 18.2 In Figure 18.2(a) unexpected technical change raises the marginal productivity of capital and with it the demand for capital from KD_1 to KD_2. This raises the real interest rate *above* the target level for savers R_T. Sentiment shifts in favour of saving in Figure 18.2(b), resulting in an increase in supply of capital from KS_1 to KS_2. Diminishing marginal productivity of capital along KD_2 occurs until the real return on capital falls back to the original real interest rate R_T, and equilibrium is restored with no further shift of sentiment in favour of savings.

the supply of capital from KS_1 to KS_2. As progressively more capital is used per person, the marginal productivity of capital diminishes along the new KD_2 curve. The extra savings and supply of capital will continue until KS_1 has shifted as far as KS_2 in Figure 18.2(b) and the marginal return on capital has fallen to the target real interest rate R_T and no further savings and therefore capital is supplied at any given real interest rate. We now have the new equilibrium situation with a higher capital/labour ratio (K_2/L_2) but with the original real target interest rate of R_T.

Whilst real GDP per person will have grown during the transition period from one equilibrium to another, it will now cease to grow once the real rate of interest has returned to its target level R_T. The marginal productivity of (a now higher volume of) capital will have fallen back to its original level and real GDP per person, whilst higher, will cease to grow. In the absence of continuous technical change, there can only be short-term and transient growth periods under the neo-classical theory.

| Box 18.2 | Demand for capital investment |

Here we consider why the demand for capital schedule (KD in Figure 18.2) is shown as varying inversely with the real rate of interest.

The earliest theories of investment placed considerable emphasis on the importance of the rate of interest, seen here as the compensation required for forgoing current consumption. Irving Fisher used the rate of interest to derive the present value (PV) of an expected future stream of income. By calculating the PV of various alternative investment projects they could then be ranked against each other.

This approach was taken a stage further by Keynes who introduced the concept of the *marginal efficiency of investment* (MEI). The MEI was defined as that rate of discount which would equate the PV of a given stream of future income from a project, with the initial capital outlay (the supply price):

$$S = PV = \frac{R_1}{(1 + i)} + \frac{R_2}{(1 + i)^2} + \frac{R_3}{(1 + i)^3} + \frac{R_n}{(1 + i)^n}$$

where:

    S = the supply price

    PV = the present value

    R = the expected yearly return

    i = that rate of discount necessary to equate the present value of future income with the initial cost of the project

The curve relating the marginal efficiency of investment (i) to the level of investment in Figure 18.3 is negatively sloped for two main reasons. First, the earliest investment projects undertaken are likely to be the most profitable, i.e. offering the highest expected yearly returns (R), and therefore having the highest marginal efficiencies of investment (i). Secondly, as more projects are initiated, they are likely to be less and less profitable, with lower expected yearly returns, and therefore lower MEIs.

The decision on whether to proceed with an investment project will depend on the relationship between the rate of interest (r) and the marginal efficiency of investment (i). If r is less than i, then the annual cost of borrowing funds for an additional project will be less than the expected annual return on the initial capital outlay so that the project will be profitable to undertake. In Figure 18.3, with interest rate r_1, it will be profitable to invest in all projects up to I_1, with I_1 itself breaking even. The MEI schedule is therefore the investment demand schedule, telling us the level of investment that will be undertaken at any given rate of interest.

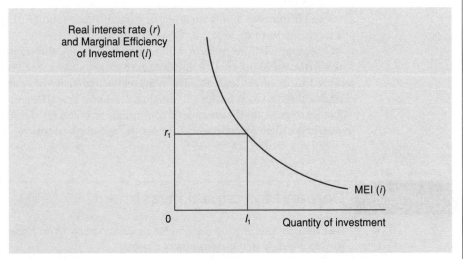

Figure 18.3 The demand for capital (MEI schedule) expands as the real interest rate (r) falls. Extra capital investment results in progressively less productive investment projects with lower marginal efficiencies of investment (i).

2.3 Modern growth theories

Endogenous growth theory Views long-term growth as sustainable and responsive to government policies.

The modern approach to growth is sometimes called *endogenous growth theory* (EGT) and is often associated with the pioneering work of Joseph Schumpeter. The emphasis here is on education and training, research and development and other knowledge-accumulating activities helping to build the potential for continuous technical change, progressively increasing the marginal productivities of both capital and labour, and resulting in prolonged and sustainable periods of economic growth. Unlike neo-classical growth theory, technical change is no longer haphazard and down to chance, but can be fostered and promoted by appropriate policies. Moreover, as the foundations for innovation and entrepreneurship are secured, the probabilities of further technical change and associated economic growth occurring rise significantly. Technical change is no longer regarded as 'unexplainable' and due to chance as in neo-classical theory; instead in the endogenous growth theories technical change becomes itself a variable which can be influenced by policy decisions and should now be included within production functions, alongside the conventional inputs of labour and capital.

Pause for thought 1

What specific policy measures might a government propose in the light of endogenous growth theory?

3   SUSTAINABLE DEVELOPMENT

The term 'sustainable development' is now widely used and its origins can be traced back to the early 1970s when fears were already growing about globally unsustainable social and economic development. An influential academic report entitled *The Limits to Growth* published in 1972 (Meadows *et al.*, 1972) captured this growing unease at attempts by nations to push for ever faster growth, irrespective of impacts on the environment and the general quality of life. The report explored alternative futures as to what might happen as a result of a rapidly growing global human population, including impacts on food production, natural resources and environmental degradation in a finite world. *Limits to Growth* was widely received as a message of impending doom and concluded that sooner or later one or more of these interrelated systems would collapse. The report had a significant impact, partly because it reinforced the growing economic and political uncertainty and fuelled the general pessimism of the time. *Limits to Growth* was followed soon after by the onset of the first oil crisis in late 1973, which compounded fears about finite oil and other energy resources.

3.1 Characteristics of sustainable development

The modern understanding of the concept of 'sustainable development' was perhaps most clearly articulated in 1987 through the publication of a United Nations report entitled *Our Common Future*. This was the final report of a process called the United National World Commission on Environment and Development (WCED). The report is also sometimes known as the Brundtland Report after the Norwegian Prime Minister Gro Harlem Brundtland, the then chair of the WCED. *Our Common Future* is famous for providing the following most widely cited definition of sustainable development. Sustainable development is 'development which meets the needs of the present without compromising the ability of future generations to meet their own needs' (WCED, 1987).

Two years on from the WCED report, preparations began in 1989 for a major international meeting on environment and development. The 'Earth Summit' or to give it its legal title, the UN Conference on Environment and Development (UNCED), was held in June 1992 in Rio De Janeiro in Brazil. Attended by around 30,000 governmental and non-governmental organisations from over 170 countries, the Earth Summit laid down key principles for governments to follow to promote sustainability (Box 18.3). The Johannesburg 'sustainability conference' of 2002 revisited and reinforced many of these principles.

Box 18.3 | ## The Rio Declaration on Environment and Development

The *Rio Declaration on Environment and Development* aims to establish 'a new and equitable global partnership through the creation of new levels of cooperation among states, key sectors of societies and people' by 'working towards international agreements which respect the interests of all and protect the integrity of the global environmental and developmental system' (preamble to the Rio Declaration). The main themes of the Rio Declaration are outlined below. The first ten of twenty seven principles agreed in the declaration give a good idea of the issues covered.

- *Principle 1* Humans are centre of concern for sustainable development
- *Principle 2* Countries must not cause damage to the environment of other states
- *Principle 3* Development must equitably meet developmental and environmental needs of present and future generations
- *Principle 4* Environmental protection is an integral part of the development process
- *Principle 5* Eradicating poverty is an indispensable requirement for sustainable development
- *Principle 6* The special situation and needs of (least) developing countries must be given special priority
- *Principle 7* States have common but differentiated responsibilities to conserve, protect and restore the health and integrity of the Earth's ecosystem
- *Principle 8* States should reduce and eliminate unsustainable patterns of production and consumption and promote appropriate demographic policies
- *Principle 9* States should cooperate to strengthen endogenous capacity-building for sustainable development
- *Principle 10* Need to improve access to environmental information, public awareness and participation

Source: Adapted from *The Rio Declaration* (1992)

The Rio Declaration contains many sensible principles and proclamations. However, a major weakness as an international treaty is its lack of any enforcement or compliance system. In legal terms, the Rio Declaration is what is called 'soft law'. Nevertheless, some of these principles are starting to play important roles in the development of future detailed legal frameworks around trade and the environment.

The *World Summit on Sustainable Development* (WSSD) or, as it was commonly known, the 'Rio + 10' conference, was held in Johannesburg in 2002. The communiqué from this conference acknowledged shortcomings in attempts by developed economies to implement the Rio principles over the past ten years. It placed still greater emphasis than Rio on interdependencies, acknowledging that economic, developmental, environmental and social dimensions must be addressed simultaneously if sustainability is to be achieved.

3.2 Key conditions for sustainable development

It has already been noted that the Brundtland Commission defined 'sustainable development' (SD) as development that meets the needs of the present generation without compromising the ability of future generations to meet their own needs. This would seem to imply at least two key aspects be present if social and economic development is to be regarded as 'sustainable'.

Intergenerational equity
The development process must seek fairness between generations.

- *Intergenerational equity*: namely that the development process seeks to minimise any adverse impacts on future generations. These clearly include avoiding adverse environmental impacts such as excessive resource depletion today reducing the stock available for future use, or excessive levels of pollution emissions and waste disposal today which are beyond the ability of the environment to absorb them, thereby imposing long-term damage.

Intragenerational equity
The development process must seek fairness within the current generation.

- *Intragenerational equity*: namely that the development process seeks to minimise tendencies towards excessive income and wealth inequalities *within and between* nations and groups of nations at any point of time.

Attempts have been made to operationalise these aspects of sustainable development still further. For example, various 'rules' have been devised to reflect views as to what might constitute 'weak' and 'strong' sustainability practices.

Weak sustainability (WS)

Weak sustainability 'rules'
This allows substitution between physical and environmental capital.

Under **WS** 'rules' practical efforts will be made to fully compensate those adversely affected by development:

Constant capital rule
Each generation should pass on to the next generation an aggregate capital stock no smaller in value than the one it inherited.

- *Future generations*: e.g. depletion of scarce resources 'compensated' by income transfers to future generations or by technological developments increasing the efficiency of future resource use (e.g. less resource requirements per unit of output). Significant attempts will be made under WS to 'decouple' adverse environmental effects from economic growth. Support will also be given to the '**constant capital rule**', namely that this generation must pass on to future generations an *aggregate capital stock* no smaller in value than the one it inherited. Less 'environmental capital' (e.g. fewer natural resources) can be passed on so long as it is replaced by an equivalent value of physical capital (e.g. buildings and infrastructure) since physical capital is seen under this 'rule' as a credible substitute for environmental capital. Attempts will be made to capture environmental impacts within the macroeconomic accounts so that the 'constant capital' rule can be monitored.
- *Current generations*: e.g. the poor and those disadvantaged by development must be compensated by various support programmes and other policy measures. Higher priority must be given under WS to attempts to tackle poverty both at home and abroad (e.g. debt relief for developing countries).

Strong sustainability (SS)

Under SS 'rules' attempts will also be made to compensate those adversely affected by development. However, under SS that compensation must be explicitly 'environmental':

- *Future generations:* e.g. the 'constant capital rule' no longer applies. Any loss of environmental capital in this generation must be offset by the addition of an equivalent 'value' of environmental capital to future generations (e.g. deforestation must be fully offset by an equivalent 'value' of tree planting). Physical capital is seen under SS as a highly imperfect substitute for environmental capital. The focus is on the conservation and preservation of ecosystems, landscapes and other 'natural' features.

- *Current generations:* e.g. although there is still concern under SS for support for individuals disadvantaged by development, the focus shifts from individual valuations and concerns to the *collective* value ascribed to ecosystems and other environmental assets.

Box 18.4 looks at the more technical issues underlying the issue of sustainable development.

Box 18.4 | ## Sustainable development: a technical approach

Following Pearce (1998), Figure 18.4 uses *well-being per capita* on the vertical axis and *time* on the horizontal axis, where time is split into three generations of people. Pearce suggests that an economy that develops along a path like A is pursuing *sustainable development*, securing increases in well-being that last over future generations. Even an economy developing along path B is 'sustainable' because later generations are no worse off than the first one: well-being is 'non-declining'. However, the economy on path C is not sustainable because per capita well-being grows then declines for succeeding generations.

Note that sustainable development is not necessarily 'optimal' in that path $C(C_1 + C_2 + C_3)$ yields a total well-being in excess of path $A(A_1 + A_2 + A_3)$.

Sustainability 'rules'

Whatever the concept of 'well-being' applied (GDP or 'quality of life' indices) the condition for sustainable development is that each generation should leave the next

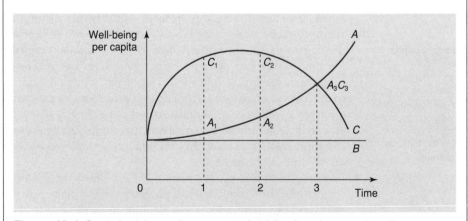

Figure 18.4 Sustainable and non-sustainable development paths.

generation a stock of capital assets no less than the stock it 'inherits'. The next generation will then have the capacity to generate the same (or more) 'well-being' as the previous generation.

At least four types of capital asset are often identified.

1 *Man-made capital* (K_M) – factories, machines, roads, computers, etc.
2 *Human capital* (K_H) – knowledge, skills embodied in people
3 *Natural capital* (K_N) – the stock of environmental assets that provide natural resources to sustain life, to use in production, to help in the assimilation of wastes and provide amenity attractions
4 *Social capital* (K_S) – values and relationships which give a particular society its sense of identify

Weak sustainability rule

● *The total stock of capital ($K_M + K_H + K_N + K_S$) should not fall, though individual elements within it can vary.*

Strong sustainability rule

● *Each element within the total stock of capital should not fall.*

Sustainable development is a key issue for both developed and developing countries. However, it is clearly the developing countries which will have the greatest problems in conforming to either of these sustainability rules. This is especially true if these capital rules are expressed per capita, given the current and projected rapid population growth for the developing countries. Of course, the 'weak sustainability rule' gives more scope for the developing economies. For example, a fall in K_N (per capita) via, say, deforestation in Amazonia can, at least in principle, be offset by investing the monies received in education and training, giving an offsetting rise in K_H (per capita).

The extent to which such offsets are feasible depends on how easily one form of capital can be substituted for another form in terms of its contribution to 'well-being'. If K_M, K_H or K_S (per capita) can more than offset a decline in K_N (per capita) then achieving 'weak sustainability' for both developed and developing countries will at least be more plausible. It is in this context that many are placing their hopes for sustainable development on further advances in technological capabilities, thereby raising output per unit input of these various types of capital asset.

3.3 Measuring sustainable development

General savings rule
For development to
be sustainable (in its
'weak' form), total
savings must at least
cover depreciation
of the four types of
capital (man-made,
human, natural and
social).

It has often been pointed out that an implication for fulfilling the 'weak sustainability rule' is that the total savings of a nation must be greater than the total depreciation of its capital assets ($K_M + K_H + K_N + K_S$). Only then can the nation replenish its capital assets so that they are at least as extensive at the end of the time period as they were at the beginning.

● *The general savings rule: for development to be sustainable (in its weak form) total savings must at least cover depreciation of the four types of capital.*

Estimates (if imperfect) of savings by nations are available from the national accounts as are also estimates of man-made capital depreciation (K_M). Environmental economists have also made progress in developing indicators which seek to capture environmental factors within the national accounts (*see* Box 18.5).

Progress has also been made in developing indicators of human capital depreciation (K_H), which tends of course to be substantial and positive in sign in the poorer developing economies, but via increased education, training and improvements in the quality of life to be negative in sign in the developed economies, implying appreciation of K_H. Indicators for social capital depreciation (K_S) remain somewhat elusive.

A dilemma facing the developing economies, and particularly the poorer LDC grouping, is that savings, expressed as a percentage of GNP, are often insufficient to more than offset any (net) depreciation estimated for the other four capital assets combined. The richer countries would certainly seem to be sustainable in terms of the 'general savings

LDCs
Less developed countries, the precise definition varying across bodies such as the World Bank, UN, OECD.

Box 18.5	Environment and national income account

In recent times attempts have been made to capture environmental costs within a national accounting framework. An *Index of Sustainable Economic Welfare* (ISEW) has been calculated for the US and UK. Essentially, any increase in the GNP figure is adjusted to reflect the following environmental impacts which are often associated with rising GNP:

1 Monies spent correcting environmental damage (i.e. 'defensive' expenditures)
2 Decline in the stock of natural resources (i.e. environmental depreciation)
3 Pollution damage (i.e. monetary value of any environmental damage not corrected).

By failing to take these environmental impacts into account, the conventional GNP figure arguably does not give an accurate indication of *sustainable economic welfare*, i.e. the flow of goods and services that an economy can generate without reducing its future production capacity. Suppose we consider the expenditure method of calculating GNP (*see* Chapter 11). It could be argued that some of the growth in GNP is due to expenditure undertaken to mitigate (offset) the impact of environmental damage. For example, some double-glazing may be undertaken to reduce noise levels from increased traffic flow and does not therefore reflect an increase in economic well-being, merely an attempt to retain the status quo. Such 'defensive expenditures' should be subtracted from the GNP figure (item 1 above). So too should be expenditures associated with a decline in the stock of natural resources. For example, the monetary value of minerals extracted from rock is included in GNP but nothing is subtracted to reflect the loss of unique mineral deposits. 'Environmental depreciation' of this kind should arguably be subtracted from the conventional GNP figure (item 2 above). Finally, some expenditures are incurred to overcome pollution damage which has not been corrected; for example, extra cost of bottled water when purchased because tap water is of poor quality. Additional expenitures of this kind should also be subtracted from the GNP figure, as should the monetary valuation of any environmental damage which has not been corrected (item 3 above).

We are then left with an Index of Sustainable Economic Welfare (ISEW) which subtracts rather more from GNP than the usual depreciation of physical capital:

ISEW = GNP minus depreciation of physical capital
           minus defensive expenditures
           minus depreciation of environmental capital
           minus monetary value of residual pollution.

rule' and in a context of 'weak sustainability'. Problems clearly exist elsewhere, as in much of Africa and in the Middle East, where assets appear to be depreciating faster than they are being replaced and savings are extremely limited.

3.4 Technical change and sustainability

Technical change is not usually included in national savings ratios, although many would argue that it is a factor to be added to general savings. Pearce (1998) suggests a rich economy such as the US would gain an extra three percentage points on its 'genuine savings' measure by adding on technological change. The number is likely to be far less, perhaps zero in many developing economies. However, a major debate is currently under way on the extent to which technological change might become a major factor in supporting sustainable development in the low-income, developing economies.

Figure 18.5 indicates how technological change can play a key role in development in terms of our earlier analysis enhancing human capital (K_H), man-made capital (K_M), social capital (K_S) and arguably even natural capital (K_N). The *Human Development Report* of the United Nations (2001) emphasises the benefits of technology for developing economies, producing drought-tolerant plant varieties for farming in uncertain climates, more efficient industrial processing vaccines for infectious diseases, clean energy sources for domestic and industrial uses. In these ways new technologies support economic growth through productivity gains in agriculture, industry and service activities and by supporting a healthier, more highly educated and skilled workforce.

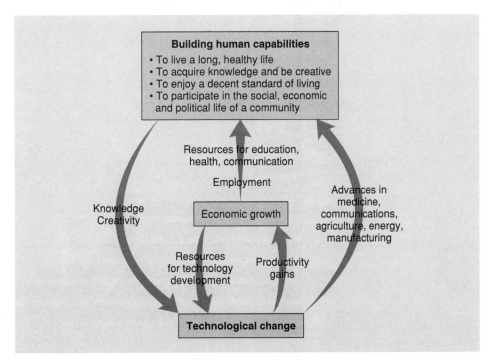

Figure 18.5 How technological change can influence economic growth through a variety of variables, including the development of human capital, physical capital and various types of innovation.

4 GNP DATA, DEVELOPED AND DEVELOPING COUNTRIES

The use of GNP per head as a basis for classifying countries as developed or developing has been much criticised in recent years. Nevertheless, it does give some indication of the huge disparities in standard of living between countries, as can be seen from Figure 18.6.

Before moving to alternative indicators of 'economic well-being' let us briefly review the usefulness of the GNP per head figures represented in Figure 18.6, paying particular attention to the situation of the developing economies. Students of macroeconomics will know that GNP can be measured in the local currency using output, income and expenditure methods. By dividing the figure for GNP (converted into US dollars at the official $/country exchange rate) by the country population, we obtain an average figure for output or income per head. Interesting as this figure undoubtedly is, it has a number of flaws as a measure of comparative living standards in the respective countries.

(a) *Inappropriate exchange rates* Converting the value of GNP expressed in the local currency into a $ equivalent using the *official* exchange rate may misrepresent the actual purchasing power in the local economy. This is because the official exchange rate is

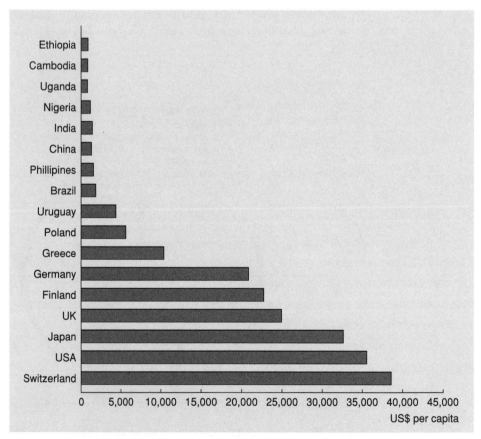

Figure 18.6 Gross national product per head (in 2002) in US $.
Source: World Development Report (2004), World Bank

influenced by a range of complex forces in the foreign exchange markets and may not accurately reflect the purchasing power of one country's currency in another country. A more accurate picture is given if we use *purchasing power parities* (PPPs) rather than official exchange rates when making this conversion (*see* Table 18.1). Purchasing power parities measure how many units of one country's currency are needed to buy *exactly the same basket of goods* as can be bought with a given amount of another country's currency. On this basis Ethiopia's figure rises from $100 to $720 per capita and the Switzerland figure falls from $37,930 to around $31,250 per capita, using 2002 purchasing power parities.

(b) *Differing degrees of non-market economic activity* GNP per capita only includes the money value of recorded (market) transactions involving goods and services. Non-market transactions are excluded. For example, the output of subsistence agriculture, whereby farmers grow food for their own consumption, are excluded from GNP figures. In many less developed economies where there is often a greater degree of non-market economic activity this fact may lead to GNP figures to underestimate the true living standards.

(c) *Varying degrees of inequality* GNP per capita gives an indication of the 'average' standard of living in a country. However, this may reflect the experience of only a small number of people in that country because its *income distribution* may be highly unequal, being skewed in the direction of the wealthier sections of society. For example, instead of using the *arithmetic mean* for GNP per capita, the *median* might be a more useful measure of the 'average', i.e. that figure for which 50% of the population has a higher GNP per capita and 50% has a lower GNP per capita.

(d) *Incidence of externalities* Externalities occur where actions by an individual or group impose costs (or benefits) on others which are not fully 'priced'. Increased pollution is a by-product of many industrial processes, reducing the quality of life for those affected. However, this negative externality may not be reflected in the GNP calculations. Similarly, the GNP figure makes no allowance for the depletion and degradation of natural resources and for the social costs these may impose, e.g. deforestation as a factor in global warming, etc.

For these and other reasons (differing accounting conventions, economic and social practices, etc.) there has been a move towards the use of indicators other than the GNP per capita figure to reflect the 'true' standard of living in various countries, using various 'quality of life' indicators such as life expectancy, medical provision, educational opportunities, etc.

Pause for thought 2

What indicators other than real GNP per head might be used to capture the idea of quality of life?

The United Nations has moved on to publish a Human Development Report since 1990 in which new methods of classification are presented, including a *Human Development Index* which we consider below.

4.1 Human Development Index (HDI) classification

An interesting issue is whether the conventional GNP per capita figure can be merged with 'quality of life' indicators to give an overall index of economic well-being. A first step in this direction has in fact been made with the publication of the United Nations'

Table 18.1 Selected country indicators and rankings (out of 177 countries), 2002

	1 GNP per head ($)	2 Real GNP per head (PPP$)	3 Life expectancy at birth (years)	4 Adult literacy rate (%)	5 Enrolment ratio* (%)	6 Human Development Index (HDI)	7 Rank by real GNP per head (PPP$)	8 Rank by HDI
Ethiopia	100	720	46	42	35	0.359	169	170
Cambodia	280	1,590	57	70	59	0.568	131	130
Uganda	250	1,320	46	69	71	0.493	150	146
Nigeria	290	780	52	67	46	0.466	166	151
India	502	2,570	64	58	55	0.595	117	127
China	940	4,390	71	91	68	0.745	99	94
Philippines	1,020	4,280	70	93	82	0.753	105	83
Brazil	2,850	7,770	68	86	92	0.775	63	72
Uruguay	4,370	7,830	75	98	86	0.883	62	46
Poland	4,570	10,130	74	99	90	0.850	50	37
Greece	11,660	18,240	78	97	86	0.902	29	24
Germany	22,670	26,220	78	99	89	0.925	14	19
Finland	23,510	25,440	78	99	100	0.935	20	13
UK	25,250	25,870	78	99	100	0.936	19	12
Japan	33,550	26,070	82	99	84	0.938	15	9
US	35,020	35,020	77	99	93	0.939	4	8
Switzerland	37,930	31,250	79	99	88	0.936	7	11

* Percentage of population at Levels 1, 2 and 3 (combined) of OECD Literacy Survey.
Source: Adapted from *Human Development Report* (2004), UN; *World Development Report* (2004)

Human Development Index (HDI)
An attempt to broaden the measures of 'quality of life' beyond the GNP per head figure, bringing additional indicators such as education, life expectancy and literacy into focus.

Human Development Index (HDI). In Table 18.1 we present more comprehensive data for 17 countries shown in our earlier Figure 18.6. We also show the rank of these countries (out of 177 countries) in terms of real GNP per head using purchasing power parities and in terms of the Human Development Index. Before commenting further on these rankings it will help if we explore the background to the HDI a little further.

The Human Development Index (HDI) is based on three indicators.

- *Standard of living*, as measured by real GNP per capita (PPS$). Column 2 in Table 18.1.
- *Life expectancy at birth*, in years. Column 3 in Table 18.1.
- *Educational attainment*, as measured by a weighted average of adult literacy (two-thirds weight) and enrolment ratio (one-third weight). Columns 4 and 5 respectively in Table 18.1.

Each of these three indicators is then expressed in *index form*, with a scale set between a minimum value (index = 0) and a maximum value (index = 1) for each indicator.

- *Standard of living*: $100 real GNP per capita (PPP$) is the minimum value (index = 0) and $40,000 is the maximum value (index = 1).
- *Life expectancy at birth*: 25 years is the minimum value (index = 0) and 85 years is the maximum value (index = 1).
- *Educational attainment*: 0% for both adult literacy and enrolment ratios are the minimum values used for calculating the weighted average (index = 0) and 100% for both adult literacy and enrolment ratios and the maximum values used for calculating the weighted average (index = 1).

An index is then calculated for each of these three indicators and the average of these three index numbers is then calculated, as shown for each country in column 6 of Table

18.1. This average of the three separate index numbers is the Human Development Index (HDI). The closer to 1 is the value of the HDI, the closer the country is to achieving the maximum values defined for each of the three indicators.

From columns 7 and 8 of Table 18.1 we can see that the rankings of the countries (in order from 1 to 177) do vary with the type of indicator used. In other words, using a GNP per head indicator, even adjusted for purchasing power parities, gives a different ranking for countries than using the HDI index which brings quality of life aspects into the equation.

The HDI, by bringing together both economic and quality of life indicators, suggests a smaller degree of underdevelopment for some countries than is indicated by economic data alone. For example, the Philippines is 105th out of 177 countries when the GNP per head data is used for ranking (column 7) but rises 22 places to 83rd when the HDI is used for ranking (column 8). For the Philippines it would seem that the relatively high life expectancy at birth and relatively high enrolment ratios into education have helped raise these indicators and thereby the overall HDI. On the other hand, the HDI suggests a greater degree of underdevelopment for some countries than is indicated by economic data alone. For example, India is 117th out of 177 countries when the GNP per head data is used for ranking (column 7) but falls by 10 places to 127th when the HDI is used for ranking (column 8). For India it would seem that the relatively low adult literacy and enrolment ratios have helped reduce the 'education' index which has lowered the overall HDI.

Although only in its infancy, it may be that classification of countries based on indices such as the HDI which bring together both economic and quality of life data may give a more accurate picture of the level of development.

5 MAJOR FEATURES OF LDCS

Clearly the exact definition of which countries are regarded as the less developed countries (LDCs) may depend on the types of classification system adopted. Nevertheless, whatever the precise definition of an LDC, a number of features or characteristics are regarded as fairly typical of any country placed within this category.

1 *Low real income per capita* This is a major indicator of underdevelopment. A comparison with the economically developed countries is striking. For instance, in 2004, an average employed adult in the 49 'least developed countries' earned less than 3% of the average employed adult in the US. Most LDCs exhibit very low ratios of total income (however defined) to total population, resulting in a low value for real income per capita. This is usually the result of low productivity, low savings, low investment, few resources and backward technology, often allied to high levels of population, the latter being determined by complex socio-economic factors.

2 *High population growth rate* Many LDCs have experienced a high population growth rate, although some LDCs in Africa and elsewhere are now experiencing population decline due mainly to a rapidly rising death rate from HIV/AIDS. Despite HIV/AIDS the 49 'least developed countries' have grown at a compound rate of 2.5% per annum over the period 1975–2002, as compared to only 0.6% per annum for the 'high income developed countries'. A major implication of population growth in LDCs has been the growth in the proportion of people who live on the subsistence or 'poverty' line, defined as the minimum calorie intake necessary to stay alive. Even where the population growth rate is not very high (e.g. China) or falling (e.g. India), the absolute size of the population may be very high.

3 *Large-scale unemployment and underemployment* This has been a common feature of many LDCs. Contributory factors often include a low level of economic activity, particularly in the industrial sector. Since labour in LDCs tends to be both more abundant than capital and poorly educated, labour productivity is often quite low. Currently some 1.3 billion people, around one-quarter of the world's population, live on $1 a day or less, with the majority of these people to be found in East and South Asia, Sub-Saharan Africa, Latin America and the Caribbean. Even with low wages an even lower labour productivity can mean high 'relative unit labour costs' in LDCs, which in turn can mean unemployment.

4 *Inequalities in the distribution of income* The pattern of income distribution tends to be less equal in most LDCs in comparison with the developed countries. For example, the *ratio* of shares of income between the richest 10% and poorest 10% is over 87 to 1 in Sierra Leone, compared to a *ratio* of only 6 to 1 in Norway. This reflects the fact that in Sierra Leone the richest 10% have 43.6% of all income, whereas the poorest 10% have only 0.5% (i.e. half of 1%) of all income. In Norway, by way of contrast, the richest 10% have 23.4% of all income, whereas the poorest 10% have 3.9% of all income. A significant disparity in this ratio is evident between developed and developing countries.

5 *Large but neglected agricultural sector* In most LDCs agricultural accounts for 40–85% of the real national income and about 60–90% of total employment. Nevertheless, policy makers in many LDCs have opted for industrialisation, often at the expense of agricultural development, in order to promote rapid economic growth. Such neglect of agriculture has often led to food shortages, poverty and famines.

6 *Volatile export earnings* Foreign trade has tended to contribute relatively little to the national income of many LDCs. The pattern of foreign trade for most LDCs has often been determined by former colonial trade relationships, with today's LDCs remaining net exporters of primary goods and net importers of finished industrial goods. The export income of LDCs from primary goods (such as food and raw materials) sometimes fluctuates quite sharply, in part because of *low price elasticities of demand* for primary goods. For example, fluctuations in export earnings of LDCs have, on occasions, been the result of a substantial increase in supply of primary products allied to a relatively price inelastic demand curve, resulting in a fall in price and a fall in revenue for the exporter of primary goods. The tendency for such products to have relatively *low income elasticity of demand* has also meant that rising prosperity in the developed countries has resulted in only modest increases in demand for primary products from developing countries. In addition, the LDCs have historically often depended on a few key markets, with such a narrow market base increasing the risk factor as regards the prospects for a sustained growth of export earnings.

7 *Market imperfections* In many LDCs markets are imperfect; sometimes they do not even exist. The money markets are just such an example of market failure. These money markets are often divided into two broad categories: a) organised and b) unorganised. The organised sector generally consists of a central bank, commercial banks, cooperative credit banks and development banks. Division of labour and specialisation does not always exist in such money markets, as with the absence of insurance companies. The unorganised sector mainly consists of moneylenders, indigenous banks, pawnbrokers, traders, merchants, landlords and friends. While the organised sector is amenable to financial control, the unorganised sector is not. In many LDCs the unorganised sector still controls a significant section of the money market, chiefly because of its hold over the rural areas. Clearly the existence of such financial dualism has restricted the use of bank cheques and other means of payment. By reducing the volume of monetary transactions this has led to the (less efficient) growth of transactions supported by barter or goods exchange. Further, this lack of an organised money market has deprived the society of an array of financial assets through which savings could have been more effectively mobilised and converted into investment for promoting economic growth. Evidently, a major policy objective in LDCs should be for the organised sector of the money markets to bring the unorganised sector more closely under its control.

8 *Environmental degradation* There is considerable evidence to point to greater environmental degradation in the developing economies. As Robert Dorfman, a well known environmental economist, noted, 'the poorer countries of the world confront tragic choices. They cannot afford drinking water standards as high as those of the industrial countries are accustomed to. They cannot afford to close their pristine areas to polluting industries that would introduce technical know-how and productive capital and that would earn urgently needed foreign exchange. They cannot afford to bar mining companies from their exploited regions. Nor can they afford to impose anti-pollution requirements on these companies that are as strict and expensive as those in richer industrial countries. They should always realise that environmental protection measures are financed out of the stomachs of their own people; the multinationals cannot be made to pay for them.'

Example | **Pollution haven hypotheses**

The suggestion here is that an increasingly important factor in the decisions by multinational firms to locate production facilities in the developing economies is the absence of the strict environmental controls applied in the developed economies. In this sense the developing economies are acting as 'pollution havens', proving particularly attractive to firms in the more toxic-intensive industries which release relatively large amounts of toxic chemicals per unit output. With many variables involved in locational decisions by multinationals, testing this hypothesis by establishing the significance of the single explanatory variable (environmental standard avoidance) is clearly difficult. Some studies do, however, claim to have found evidence that the more toxic-intensive industries have grown most rapidly in the developing economies.

9 *Poor governance* Developing countries feature prominently in international studies citing poor governance and widespread corruption.

Example | **TI Corruption Perception Index**

Transparency International (TI) is a non-governmental organisation founded in 1993 and based in Berlin. It has developed one of the more comprehensive databases on corruption which it defines as an abuse of public office for private gain. The 'TI Corruption Perception Index' correlates a number of surveys, polls and country studies involving the number of bribe requests which those conducting business in some 102 separate countries perceive to have been made to them. A score of 10 indicates a perception that bribe requests are never made in that country, while a score of 0 indicates a perception that bribe requests are always made. A score of 5.0 indicates a perception that there is an equal chance of a bribe being made as not being made. Of the 102 countries included in the 2002 index, 69 scored 5.0 or below; in other words, businessmen perceive that in two-thirds of these countries it is more likely than not that a bribe request will be made in any given transaction. In 2002 Finland scored 10, UK 8.6, US 7.8, China 3.9, India 2.7, Pakistan 2.2 and Indonesia 1.9.

Mini Case Study 18.1 looks more carefully at the linkage between good governance and economic development.

Mini Case Study 18.1

Benefits of good governance

The World Bank (World Development Report, 2002) has pointed out that *good governance* – including independent agencies, mechanisms for citizens to monitor public behaviour, and rules that constrain corruption – is a key ingredient for growth and prosperity. In an early study Barro (1991) had found a positive correlation between economic growth and measures of political stability for 98 countries surveyed between 1960 and 1985. More recent empirical research points in a similar direction, for example confirming that fdi inflows are *inversely* related to measures of corruption, as with Lipsey (1999) observing a strong negative correlation between corruption and the locational choice of US subsidiaries across Asian countries. Similarly, Claugue *et al.* (1999) and Zak (2001) found that productivity and economic growth will improve when governments impartially protect and define property rights. Underpinning these findings is the perception by firms that a non-transparent business environment increases the prevalence of information asymmetries, raises the cost of securing additional information, increases transaction costs (e.g. risk premiums) and creates an uncertain business environment which deters trade and investment. For example, Wallsten (2001) found a strong inverse relationship between investment intentions and the threat of asset expropriation, as well as a propensity for firms to charge higher prices to help pay back their initial capital outlays more rapidly when they felt less secure about the intentions of host governments, the higher prices often inhibiting the penetration and growth phase of product life cycles.

Question
What does the text suggest are the impacts of good governance?

Answer to question can be found on the students' side of the Companion Website.

10 *HIV/AIDS* The low levels of education, income and healthcare services in many developing countries has contributed to the spread of HIV/AIDS, with devastating effects on the countries affected, as indicated by the example below.

Example · HIV/AIDS in Botswana

Botswana has almost 40% of its adult population infected by HIV/AIDS and the average life expectancy will soon be less than 27 years for newborn children, having been as high as 75 years in Botswana only a decade ago. In fact, 11 African countries will soon have life expectancies below 30 years. The dying will outnumber those being born in five African countries, resulting in falling populations. Those dying are the breadwinners as well as the young, and the missing middle generation will not be there to look after either the young or the old in future years.

6   INTERNATIONAL DEVELOPMENT TARGETS

Millennium Development Goals (MDGs) Specific targets set by the UN in 2000 for developing economies – to be achieved by 2015.

Today's political orientations towards development are firmly centred on the use of International Development Targets (IDTs). This approach is usefully illustrated by the *UN Millennium Declaration* which included a commitment to a set of Millennium Development Goals (MDGs), broken down into targets (*see* Table 18.2).

Despite growing recognition for these targets, international development targets are not new. Many previous summits have included targets. What does seem to be new, however, is the seriousness of tackling the issue of development on a broad front, bringing into play economic, social, political, environmental and technological elements in a comprehensive and integrative approach. Effectively monitoring and implementing these targets on a global scale will ultimately determine whether a more coherent approach in principle can result in more effective development in practice. Optimists should note, however, that despite the 'make poverty history' campaign for Africa, some six years into the new millennium, many of the targets in Table 18.2 are already well behind schedule if they are to be met by 2015.

Pause for thought 3

How would you propose implementing a programme that is more than just a 'wish list'?

Table 18.2 The UN Millennium Development Goals (MDGs)

Goals	Targets
Goal 1 Eradicate extreme poverty and hunger	*Target 1* Halve, between 1990 and 2015, the proportion of people whose income is less than one dollar a day
	Target 2 Halve, between 1990 and 2015, the proportion of people who suffer from hunger
Goal 2 Achieve universal primary education	*Target 3* Ensure that, by 2015, children everywhere, boys and girls alike, will be able to complete a full course of primary schooling
Goal 3 Promote gender equality and empower women	*Target 4* Eliminate gender disparity in primary and secondary education, preferably by 2005, and to all levels of education no later than 2015
Goal 4 Reduce child mortality	*Target 5* Reduce by two-thirds, between 1990 and 2015, the under-five mortality rate
Goal 5 Improve maternal health	*Target 6* Reduce by three-quarters, between 1990 and 2015, the maternal mortality ratio
Goal 6 Combat HIV/AIDS, malaria and other diseases	*Target 7* Have halted, by 2015, and begun to reverse the spread of HIV/AIDS
	Target 8 Have halted, by 2015, and begun to reverse the incidence of malaria and other major diseases
Goal 7 Ensure environmental sustainability	*Target 9* Integrate the principles of sustainable development into country policies and programmes and reverse the loss of environmental resources
	Target 10 Halve, by 2015, the proportion of people without sustainable access to safe drinking water

Table 18.2 (*cont'd*)

Goals	Targets
	Target 11 By 2020 to have achieved a significant improvement in the lives of at least 100 million slum dwellers
Goal 8 Develop a global partnership for development	*Target 12* Develop further an open, rule-based, predictable, non-discriminatory trading and financial system (Includes a commitment to good governance, development and poverty reduction – both nationally and internationally)
	Target 13 Address the special needs of the least developed countries
	Target 14 Address the special needs of landlocked countries and small island developing states
	Target 15 Deal comprehensively with the debt problems of developing countries through national and international measures in order to make debt sustainable in the long term
	Target 16 In cooperation with developing countries, develop and implement strategies for decent and productive work for youth
	Target 17 In cooperation with pharmaceutical companies, provide access to affordable essential drugs in developing countries
	Target 18 In cooperation with the private sector, make available the benefits of new technologies, especially information and communications

Source: Adapted from UN sources

7   URBANISATION AND DEVELOPING ECONOMIES

Urbanisation
The tendency of populations in LDCs to concentrate in urban areas during the development process which often involves industrialisation.

'Urban areas' are usually defined in terms of concentrations of non-agricultural workers and non-agricultural production sectors. Although individual country definitions differ, most countries regard settlements involving 2,500–25,000 people as urban areas. Larger urban areas are often termed 'metropolitan areas' as they involve networks of geographically adjacent urban areas, including towns and cities (the latter defined in terms of legal status within countries rather than pure size).

7.1   Impacts of urbanisation

Increased urbanisation is clearly associated with the transfer of workers from agricultural and rural activities to new industrial and service sector employment in towns and cities. Around 50% of the world's population currently lives in areas classified as urban, a rapid increase on the 34% recorded in 1975. By 2020 over 4 billion people (around 60%) of the world's population will live in towns and cities, with the developing countries being the major contributor to this continued growth in urbanisation. The rate of urbanisation has passed its peak in the middle to high income industrial countries, but is far from its peak in much of Asia and Africa. The more rapid pace and less regulated nature of the urban growth in the developing economies has created a number of environmental problems.

Urban living conditions such as crowding, sewage connections, waste collections and water access tend to be far inferior in cities with lower levels of average household incomes. The Mini Case Study below pays particular attention to the issue of sanitation in the context of urbanisation within developing economies.

Mini Case Study 18.2

Sanitation and urbanisation

As the low income developing countries industrialise over the next 25 years, progressively larger discharges of wastewater and solid wastes can be expected in total and per capita. Inadequate investments in waste collection and disposal mean that large quantities of waste enter both groundwater and surface water. Groundwater contamination is less visible but often more serious because it can take decades for polluted aquifers to cleanse themselves and because large numbers of people drink untreated groundwater.

More environmental damage occurs when people try to compensate for inadequate provision. The lack or unreliability of piped water causes households to sink their own wells, which often leads to overpumping and depletion. In cities such as Jakarta, where almost two-thirds of the population relies on groundwater, the water table has declined dramatically since the 1970s. In coastal areas this can cause saline intrusion, sometimes rendering the water permanently unfit for consumption. In, for example, Bangkok excessive pumping has also led to subsidence, cracked pavements, broken water and sewerage pipes, intrusion of seawater and flooding.

Inadequate water supply also prompts people to boil water, thus using energy. The practice is especially common in Asia. In Jakarta more than $50 million is spent each year by households for this purpose – an amount equal to 1% of the city's GDP. Investments in water supply can therefore reduce fuelwood consumption and air pollution.

The health benefits from better water and sanitation are substantial: diarrhoeal death rates are typically about 60% lower among children in households with adequate facilities than among those in households without such facilities. Improved environmental sanitation has economic benefits. Consider the case of sewage collection in Santiago, Chile. The principal justification for investments was the need to reduce the extraordinarily high incidence of typhoid fever in the city. A secondary motive was to maintain access to the markets of industrial countries for Chile's increasingly important exports of fruit and vegetables. To ensure the sanitary quality of these exports, it was essential to stop using raw wastewater in their production. In just the first ten weeks of the cholera epidemic in Peru in the early 1990s, losses from reduced agricultural exports and tourism were estimated at $1 billion – more than three times the amount that the country had invested in water supply and sanitation services during the 1980s.

Question

Outline the costs and benefits of improved sanitation and access to clean water for developing countries.

Answer to question can be found at the back of the book (page 526).

Despite such problems there are a number of factors which make urbanisation so attractive to firms in both developing and developed economies. These are briefly reviewed below.

7.2 Reasons for urbanisation

Why is it that economic activity is so often concentrated in large, urban areas where land prices are often more than 50 times higher and the cost of living four or five times higher than they are in smaller urban or rural areas less than 50 miles away? From the firm's point of view the answer must involve a belief that the perceived benefits more than outweigh the additional costs. Many of these perceived benefits are often grouped under the heading *agglomeration economies*, which refers to the alleged synergies which benefit firms from increases in urban size.

Agglomeration economies
Benefits to firms from the growth in size of urban areas.

● *Localisation economies* Firms benefit from locating close to other firms in the *same* industry since this expands the pool of specialised workers and inputs. It has been shown that in Brazil and the Republic of Korea, if a plant moves from a location shared by 1,000 workers employed by firms in the same industry to one with 10,000 such workers, output will increase by some 15% on average.
● *Urbanisation economies* Firms also benefit from locating close to firms in *different* industries. The presence of a common pool of labour, materials and services provides benefits for all firms, whatever their sector of economic activity. Geographical proximity to other firms can, for example, help in the more rapid diffusion of knowledge, as in the case of 'information spillovers' via firms observing what others are doing, whatever the activities involved. Evidence using patent citations, that information flows increase with geographical proximity and deteriorate with geographical distance. 'Transaction costs' also fall when there is a higher degree of industrial concentration, e.g. the lower search costs now involved in matching workers with employment opportunities.
● *Diversification economies* Large urban areas are less vulnerable to business cycles because of their more diversified economic base.

> **! Pause for thought 4**
>
> *Why is it that so many people in developing countries head for the cities?*

8 AID, TRADE AND DEVELOPMENT

Here we briefly examine the role of both aid and trade in development.

8.1 Foreign aid and development

In theory, foreign aid should raise both consumption and investment in a developing country, since in the absence of foreign aid an LDC will produce less of both consumption and investment goods given its limited resources. However, if the economy has a very high preference for consumption, then most of the foreign aid might be used for consumption purposes with little addition to its future productive capacity. To counter this the aid programmes often seek to designate aid for particular purposes; for example food aid is intended to increase consumption rather than investment, but project aid is usually intended to raise investment rather than consumption.

In the traditional economic models, an increase in access to savings from abroad should raise the growth rate of the borrowing country by increasing its rate of investment. If we aggregate aid from abroad with access to the savings from foreign capital markets, this gives us the variable 'financial resources' (FR). For some LDCs such as Bangladesh and Nepal in Asia and Mali and Senegal in Africa, foreign aid is a significant proportion of the GDP of these economies and hence the impact of additional aid on FR should help increase their growth rates. However, a rise in the flow of FR may raise consumption at the expense of savings/investment so that the overall growth rate suffers. Further, a rise in domestic consumption due to a rise in FR may increase imports and add to the balance of payment problems of many LDCs. They may then have to deflate aggregate demand to reduce imports, adversely affecting economic growth. In addition, many governments of LDCs have used FR for increasing public expenditure on prestige projects which are relatively unproductive.

On the other hand, foreign aid has the potential to increase domestic economic growth rates by supplementing domestic savings to further increase investment and to allow imports of capital items previously restricted by scarce foreign exchange reserves. In this view foreign aid could have a positive and significant influence on growth rates for LDCs.

This is not to deny that a corrupt government in a developing country seeking to maximise its own 'utility function' may use aid money to expand non-productive expenditures, e.g. on military capability, corrupt bureaucracy and very inefficient investments. In such cases, the impact of aid on economic growth will indeed tend to adversely affect growth. For aid to be effective may then depend on careful targeting of both the countries to support through aid and the specific projects to support within those countries. For instance, it has been widely acknowledged that, despite the absence of a positive aid-growth correlation in India, aid inflows in the agricultural sector significantly helped to usher in the 'Green Revolution' in the late 1960s and early 1970s, thereby helping to overcome India's acute problems of food insecurity and famines. Such aid was generally well targeted, as in its allocation to specific areas in north-west India where irrigation facilities were available to reap the benefits of new seed-fertiliser techniques. The inflow of foreign aid to such specific rural areas has helped India to import considerable amounts of new seeds and chemical fertilisers from abroad and to substantially increase the yields of major food crops.

The impact of foreign aid on the economic growth rates of LDCs is clearly likely to vary across different countries. More specially, such impacts will depend on a number of factors such as the following:

(*i*) The effective targeting of aid by both donor and recipient;

(*ii*) The effective use of aid by the recipient;

(*iii*) The current level of economic development and rate of output growth;

(*iv*) The rates of return on investment in both organised and unorganised financial markets;

(*v*) The public infrastructure and the availability of physical human capital;

(*vi*) The level and types of economic regulation.

Without a careful analysis of such a complex set of dynamic socio-economic factors, it is difficult to draw a definite conclusion about the real impact of foreign aid on LDCs.

8.2 Trade and development

In recent years the focus has moved to a broader recognition of the key role of trade to economic development. The World Bank (Dollar and Kraay, 2000) has argued that increased openness to trade raises average incomes and the incomes of the poor, i.e. that there is no relationship between increased openness to trade and rising inequality, if anything quite the opposite. Sebastian Edwards (2000) of the University of California also concludes in a study of 93 countries that there is a close link between openness to trade and rates of productivity growth.

Some of the ways in which protectionism still pervades much of the trade between developed and developing countries has been considered in Chapter 16. What is clear is that the developing countries have been badly damaged both by export subsidies on agricultural and other products by the EU, US and other advanced industrialised countries. Mini Case Study 18.3 looks at some progress in respect of these issues for developing countries in recent World Trade Organisation negotiations, but the precise details and time frame of the outline agreements make the final outcomes less clear.

Mini Case Study 18.3

World trade deal agreed

Ministers from the world's richest and poorest countries struck an eleventh hour deal in August 2004 to boost trade by cutting farm subsidies and import tariffs worldwide. After five days of intense negotiation, the World Trade Organisation agreed to an interim text and set a deadline of December 2005 to hammer out a new global deal. The deal was hailed as 'historic' by the WTO and the main wealthy nations but fiercely attacked by activist groups who condemned it as a 'catastrophe for the poor'.

The deal strikes a compromise between cuts in subsidies for farmers in rich nations and an agreement by poorer countries to open up their markets by cutting tariffs. Under the agreement, key WTO members, including the US, the EU, Brazil and Japan, have agreed to the eventual elimination of export subsidies. Wealthy nations currently spend about $370 billion (£203 billion) a year on all forms of farm support. African and Latin American countries say this enables wealthy farmers to 'dump' cheap produce on their markets, annihilating their domestic farming industries. The deal includes a 'down payment' that would see an immediate 20% cut in the maximum permitted payments of subsidies by rich nations.

West African nations dropped a demand that the US's $3 billion (£1.65 billion) a year subsidies to its cotton farmers be treated as a separate issue. Rich countries also agreed to cut tariffs on farm imports that make it tough for poorer countries to compete. The highest agricultural import tariffs will face the biggest cuts, although no figures have yet been agreed.

Nations will have the right to keep higher tariffs on some of the products they consider most important. The deal on farming cleared the way for accords on access to markets for industrial goods and services, such as banking, water and telecommunications. The hard-won deal put back on track the negotiations that were launched at Doha, Qatar, in November 2001, but collapsed at a summit in Cancun, Mexico in 2003.

The main points

- All 147 members of the World Trade Organisation have agreed on the basis for talks on a trade deal, but still have months of hard negotiations ahead.
- Rich countries have agreed to eliminate all forms of export farm subsidies but can keep some of their domestic support.
- The deal includes a 'down payment' that would see an immediate 20% cut in the maximum permitted subsidy payments by rich nations.
- Europe's multibillion-pound sugar industry is still outside the negotiations.
- West African states failed in their attempt to open separate negotiations over the US's $3 billion (£1.65 billion) of subsidies for its cotton-growers.
- Poorer countries will have to cut import barriers under which the highest get cut the most.
- Developing countries have to negotiate on rules to make customs procedures easier and less expensive for business.

Question

Why do some see the deal as historic and others as a missed opportunity?

Answer to question can be found on the students' side of the Companion Website.

9   DEBT AND DEVELOPMENT

An important economic issue in recent times has been the analysis of the impact of external debt on the economies of the less developed countries (LDCs). The main focus of attention has been the cost of servicing foreign debt and the potential benefits from default. It has been argued that if the cost of debt service is higher than the cost of default, then debt repayment by an LDC is not 'incentive-compatible'. However, a **highly indebted developing country** may still have an incentive to repay because of the fear of losing access to the international capital market.

Highly indebted countries
Those countries with the highest ratio of debt to GDP.

9.1 Reasons for LDC borrowing

The practice of borrowing from foreign countries as a method of promoting economic growth is not new. Historically, most of today's developed countries, including the US, depended significantly on the imports of foreign capital for achieving a high standard of living. Besides the lessons of history, there are a number of sound reasons to explain the borrowing of LDCs from abroad.

(a) Most LDCs have low per capita income and savings. The required rate of economic growth to attain a better standard of living may need a higher level of investment (I) than can be financed by domestic savings (S). Thus, LDCs may wish to borrow foreign capital to eliminate the 'savings gap', i.e. $(I - S) > 0$.

(b) Most LDCs suffer from serious shortages in their foreign exchange earnings as their imports (M) are generally much greater than their exports (X). Such an imbalance, i.e. $(M - X) > 0$ is defined as a 'trade gap' which could be a serious constraint on achieving a higher rate of economic growth and per capita income. Many LDCs depend substantially on the import of capital and intermediate inputs to increase their production. Sometimes food imports may also play a crucial role in averting the threat of hunger and famine. Imports of foreign technology and skills may help ease the trade gap and accelerate economic growth.

(c) Many LDCs suffer from capital scarcity relative to labour supply which, according to orthodox theory, means that they should enjoy higher returns at the margin on capital flows from the developed countries. In capital-abundant countries, the marginal efficiency of capital (MEC) tends to be lower than in the LDCs. It follows that, as long as capital is fully mobile across nations, capital should flow, on efficiency grounds, from the rich to the poor countries to equalise the global MEC. Of course, such capital movements depend on the funds being invested in sectors where the rate of return is higher than the interest rate charged on the use of foreign capital.

9.2 Resolving the debt problem

It has become increasingly clear that past debts are unsustainable for many developing countries. The *ratio* of total debt to GDP is well over 50% for many developing countries and nearly 100% for the 15 most heavily indebted countries, mainly located in Africa and South America. As a result payment of interest on such debts is often three or four times the annual export earnings of such countries, making it impossible for such countries to invest in the improvements in education, health and infrastructure so important for development.

Many attempts have been made over the years to resolve this debt problem, often involving global institutions such as the World Bank and IMF (see below). The *Jubilee 2000 Campaign* mobilised world opinion and led to an easing of the debt burden for many countries. Most recently, the meeting of the eight most advanced industrialised economies (G8) at Edinburgh, UK in June 2005 announced a package of measures whereby 18 of the world's poorest countries will have their debts to the World Bank and IMF wiped out as part of a £30 billion package. A further nine countries are expected to qualify for similar debt relief by 2007, rising to 37 countries shortly thereafter. Unlike previous deals, the debts of the initial eight countries would be eliminated immediately and with them the heavy burden of interest payments in servicing the debt.

10 THE ROLE OF THE IMF AND WORLD BANK

As has been mentioned, both institutions have provided support for LDCs in various ways, but only under specified conditions.

10.1 IMF 'stabilisation programmes'

IMF stabilisation programmes seek to address adverse balance of payments situations whilst retaining price stability and encouraging the resumption of economic growth. The main components of typical IMF stabilisation policies include some or all of the following:

● *fiscal contraction* – a reduction in the public sector deficit through cuts in public expenditure and/or rises in taxation;
● *monetary contraction* – restrictions on credit to the public sector and increases in interest rates;

- *devaluation of the exchange rate* (this is often a pre-condition for the serious negotiation of a stabilisation programme, rather than part of the programme as such);
- *liberalisation of the economy* via reduction or elimination of controls, and privatisation of public sector assets;
- *incomes policy* – wage restraint and removal of subsidies and reduction of transfer payments.

10.2 World Bank 'structural adjustment lending'

Since 1980 the World Bank has been involved in various types of structural adjustment lending (SAL) which accounts for over 20% of World Bank lending. These SAL programmes are non-project related, rather they involve lending to support specific programmes of policy which may involve elements of institutional change. These SAL programmes are generally directed towards improving the 'supply side' of the borrowing countries, intending to initiate and fund change which will ultimately raise productive efficiency in various sectors of the economies.

Figure 18.7 provides a rather stereotyped but useful overview of the IMF 'stabilisation programmes' and the World Bank 'structural adjustment lending' programmes.

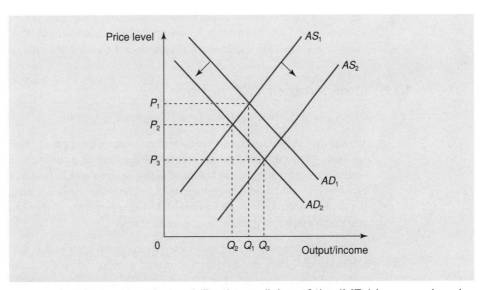

Figure 18.7 Compares the stabilisation policies of the IMF (downward and leftward shift in AD) with the structural adjustment policies of the World Bank (downward and rightward shift in AS).

10.3 Stabilisation

As was noted above, most of the policies involved in the IMF stabilisation programmes have been of a deflationary nature. This results in the downward movement, to the left, of the aggregate demand curve (AD) from AD_1 to AD_2, thus reducing the price level (from P_1 to P_2) but also reducing output (from Q_1 to Q_2). The debtor country may be made more competitive in its exports and import-substitute sectors, benefiting its balance of payments and reducing its debt, but at the cost of lost output and employment.

Various studies of the impact of IMF stabilisation policies from Latin America and elsewhere have suggested that stabilisation causes a fall in labour's share in the distribution of income. A wage freeze has often been involved, reducing the real value of all incomes from labour, especially those employed in the public sector where a wage freeze can be applied most effectively. Stabilisation was often found to be associated with declines in public sector employment.

Cuts in public expenditure have been an important part of many stabilisation programmes, such as health and education, with disproportional effects on the poor and particularly women. Stabilisation has had differing effects on the urban and the rural poor, with the urban poor being hardest hit.

10.4 Structural adjustment

As was noted earlier, most of the World Bank SAL programmes have sought to improve the supply side of the economy. This results in the downward, to the right, movement of the aggregate supply curve (AS) from AS_1 to AS_2 in Figure 18.7, thus reducing the price level (from P_2 to P_3 with AD_2) and increasing output (from Q_2 to Q_3). Clearly the 'medicine' via structural adjustment is rather more palatable in that output and employment rise, but only after possibly difficult changes to labour and capital market practices and institutions to improve supply-side conditions. (Note: for diagrammatic purposes we have assumed that the structural adjustment programme of the World Bank occurs at the same time as the IMF stabilisation programme. Of course they may occur independently.)

10.5 Criticisms of IMF action

Criticisms of the IMF's activities can be grouped as follows:

1 *That IMF programmes are inappropriate* The criticism here is that its approach to policy has been preoccupied with the control of demand and too little concerned with other weaknesses stemming from the productive system of LDCs, e.g. balance of payments problems. By deflating demand the IMF has imposed large adjustment costs on borrowing countries through losses of output and employment, further impoverishing the poor and even destabilising incumbent governments.

2 *That IMF programmes are inflexible* The criticism here is that the IMF has imposed its solutions on LDCs rather than negotiated a more flexible package. This has arguably infringed the sovereignty of states and alienated governments from the measures they are supposed to implement.

3 *That IMF support has been too small, expensive and short term* The programmes have been criticised for having been too small in magnitude and too short term in duration for economies whose underlying problems are rooted in structural weaknesses and who often face secular declines in their terms of trade (fall in export prices relative to import prices).

4 *That the IMF is dominated by a few major industrial countries* The criticism here is that the industrial countries have sometimes used their control of the IMF to promote their own interests, as for example in using the IMF to shift a disproportionate amount of the debt burden onto the debtor countries rather than forcing lenders (e.g. banks) to accept some of the debt burden. It has been alleged that successive American governments have used their influence to favour (or oppose) friendly (or hostile) LDCs.

KEY POINTS

- Of the three main theories of growth, classical, neo-classical and modern (endogenous), only the latter views economic growth as sustainable in the long run and subject to the influence of governmental policies.

- The issue of 'sustainable' development has become more prominent in recent times with its emphasis on both intragenerational and intergenerational equity.

- The 'constant capital rule' states that each generation should pass on to the next generation an aggregate capital stock no smaller in value than the one it inherited.

- There are different ways of classifying countries, including those regarded as the less developed countries (LDCs).

- The conventional measure of real GNP per head has a number of weaknesses as a measure of the standard of living.

- New measures have been devised which also bring quality of life indicators into the equation, an important example being the Human Development Index (HDI) of the UN.

- The LDCs have a number of features which create additional problems for policies aimed at increasing growth.

- In recent times the focus has shifted away from aid and towards trade as a mechanism for supporting economic development.

- The world debt problem bears down heavily on the LDCs and various initiatives involving the IMF and World Bank have sought to resolve some of these problems.

- There has been considerable criticism of the nature of the support mechanisms provided to LDCs, especially those from the IMF.

Further reading

Griffiths, A. and Wall, S. (2006) *Applied Economics*, 11th edition, FT/Prentice Hall, Chapter 30.
Sloman, J. (2006) *Economics*, 6th edition, FT/Prentice Hall, Chapter 26.

Web references

You can find current data and information on many aspects of the developed and less developed countries from the following websites.

Food and Agricultural Organisation: **http://www.fao.org/**
International Monetary Fund (IMF): **http://www.imf.org/**
World Bank: **http://www.worldbank.org/**
World Health Organisation: **http://www.who.int/en/**
United Nations: **http://www.un.org/**
United Nations Industrial Development Organisation: **http://www.unido.org/**
Friends of the Earth: **http://www.foe.co.uk/**
Jubilee 2000: **http://www.jubilee2000uk.org/**
Oxfam: **http://www.oxfam.org.uk/**
European Bank for Reconstruction and Development (EBRD): **http://www.ebrd.org/**
World Trade Organisation (WTO): **http://www.wto.org/**
United Nations Development Program: **http://www.undp.org/**

References

Barro, R. (1991) 'Economic Growth in a Cross-Section of Countries', *Quarterly Journal of Economics*, 106, 20, pages 407–43.

Claugue, C., Keefer, P., Knack, S. and Olson, M. (1999) 'Contract – Intensive Money: Contract Enforcement, Property Rights and Economic Performances', *Journal of Economic Growth*, 4, pages 185–211.

Dollar, D. and Kraay, A. (2000) 'Growth is good for the poor', *World Bank*.

Edwards, S. (2000) 'Trade Development and Poverty Reduction', *World Bank*.

Lipsey, R. E. (1999) 'The Location and Characteristics of US Affiliates in Asia', National Bureau of Economic Research (NBER) Working Paper, Cambridge, Mass.

Meadows, D. H., Meadows, D. L., Randers, J. and Behrens, W. W. (1972) *The Limits to Growth*, Potomac Associates, Washington DC.

Wallsten, S. (2001) 'Ringing in the 20th Century', World Bank Research Working Paper, Washington, DC.

PROGRESS AND REVIEW QUESTIONS

Answers to most questions can be found at the back of the book (page 527). Answers to asterisked questions can be found on the students' side of the Companion Website.

 Multiple-choice questions

1 Which *one* of the following theories of growth predicts that the real wage will remain at the 'subsistence level' and economic growth be zero in the long run?

a) Endogenous growth theory

b) Neo-classical growth theory

c) Classical growth theory

d) Modern growth theory

e) Keynesian growth theory

2 Which *one* of the following theories of growth predicts that long-run growth is possible and that governments can invest in human and physical capital so that future economic growth becomes more likely?

a) Classical growth theory

b) Keynesian growth theory

c) Monetarist growth theory

d) Neo-classical growth theory

e) Endogenous growth theory

3 Which *two* of the following are widely regarded as being important aspects of sustainable development?

   a) Intergenerational inequity
   b) Intragenerational equity
   c) Intragenerational inequity
   d) Intergenerational equity
   e) High levels of consumption expenditure and low levels of saving

4 Which *one* of the following conditions is an important part of the 'strong sustainability rule'?

   a) Total savings need not cover the depreciation value of the stock of capital.
   b) Total stock of capital should not fall over time, though individual elements within that stock can vary.
   c) Each element within the total stock of capital should not fall over time.
   d) Any rise in man-made capital can be regarded as helping offset any fall in natural capital.
   e) Any rise in capital can be regarded as helping offset any fall in natural capital.

5 Which *two* of the following arguments imply that the real GNP per head measure may be a misleading indicator of the standard of living between different countries?

   a) It does not take account of differing rates of inflation.
   b) There are differing degrees of non-market activity between countries.
   c) It does not take account of differing consumer tastes.
   d) It does not take account of exchange rate distortions; the measure should therefore be expressed using 'purchasing power parities'.
   e) The 'income method' of GNP measurement may differ from the 'expenditure method'.

6 Which *three* indicators are currently used in the Human Development Index (HDI)?

   a) Real GNP per capita (PPP$)
   b) Birth rates
   c) Life expectancy at birth
   d) Employment rates
   e) Educational attainment

7 Which *one* of the following is NOT regarded as characteristic of a less developed country (LDC)?

   a) Low real income per capita
   b) Low population growth rate
   c) Large-scale unemployment and under employment
   d) Large but neglected agricultural sector
   e) Substantial inequality in the distribution of income

8 Which *one* of the following measures is NOT usually a part of an IMF stabilisation programme?

   a) Fiscal contraction
   b) Monetary contraction
   c) Liberalisation of the economy (e.g. reduction or elimination of controls)
   d) Incomes policy
   e) Revaluation of the exchange rate

True/false questions

1 The Human Development Index (HDI) pays no attention to economic variables such as real GNP per capita.

2 The World Bank 'structural adjustment lending' (SAL) programmes seek to remedy deficiencies in aggregate demand for the economy.

3 The Millennium Development Goals are aspirations without targets.

4 Good governance is a pre-requisite to effective development.

5 The Corruption Perception Index is a general concept with no measurement indicators.

6 GNP per head is the best indicator of quality of life, especially in developing countries.

Data response question

Look at the data in the table below.

Table 18.3 Exports to GDP ratios (%), 1981–2005

Economy Classification	1981	1984	1987	1990	Date 1993	1996	1999	2002	2005
High-income economies	20	20	21	20	19	21	23	22	21
Developing economies	18	19	19	20	23	24	27	33	36

Source: Adapted from *Global Economic Prospects and the Developing Economies* (2005) World Bank, UNCTAD (various)

What does it suggest in terms of the developed/developing country debate?

Case study question

Offshoring at HSBC

HSBC, one of the world's biggest banks, is creating 500 jobs a month in its service centres in ten locations in Asia and saves $20,000 for every job moved. The bank has already announced 4,500 job cuts in the UK by 2006 as a result of offshoring and half of these have already been achieved. The bank has 13,000 workers in the centres in India, China, Malaysia, the Philippines and Sri Lanka. 'I don't have a precise target but I would be surprised if we had less than 15 global service centres in three years' time, and very surprised if we had less than 25,000 people working in them,' Mr Jebson was quoted as saying.

A HSBC spokesman insisted that his remarks should not be interpreted to mean that further UK jobs were about to be offshored. Mr Jebson revealed that the bank was also considering opening a service centre in Vietnam, where both English and French speakers are available.

Question

What implications does this information on HSBC have for the developed/developing country debate?

Essay questions

Answers to asterisked questions can be found on the students' side of the Companion Website. All other answers can be found at the back of the book (page 527).

1* What are the differences between modern (endogenous) theories of growth and other theories?

2 What features might you identify as characterising a 'lesser developed country' (LDC)?

3* Suggest policy options a government of a developing country might adopt to help it raise the standard of living of its people.

4 Why have the urban centres of developing countries grown so quickly? What are the advantages and disadvantages of such urbanisation?

Chapter 1

Mini Case Study 1.2 Meeting the plan

1 The command economy failed to deliver many benefits to the public for various reasons. First, the production process often involved too many levels of management which made it expensive and difficult to coordinate activity. Secondly, the amount of information needed to plan production of every product and service created an enormous inflexible and costly central bureaucracy. Thirdly, any increased consumer income had to be spent on what was supplied by the authorities rather than on what consumers really wanted. Fourthly, the system did not provide any incentive for workers to work harder and increase productivity because their rewards would not increase in proportion to their extra efforts.

2 There are many clues to indicate the problems of transition from a command to a market economy. For example, in a command economy the skills needed in the nation could be identified from the requirements of specific enterprises meeting their allocated target outputs. However, in a market economy there is no such mechanism and so it is difficult to know how to estimate and then generate the training and skills required in the new, more uncertain, environment where the market, not a central planner, determines the outputs required. In addition, there was no official unemployment in the command economies and therefore no need for social security benefits. In the process of transition, the growth of unemployment and the lack of a social security 'net' to help the poor became a serious problem for transition economies. Finally, in the command economies, officially there was zero inflation, so the transition towards a market economy with often high levels of inflation brought new problems of economic policy.

3 The advantages for the transition countries that are moving from a command to a market economy are many. The firms would be able to benefit from greater flexibility in the sense that entrepreneurs in the transition economies would be given greater freedom to meet market demand and to assess future demand in order to satisfy consumer needs. Workers in these states may also be spurred on to higher productivity by the incentive effect if they can see that more effort brings more reward. An enormous amount of resources may be made available for more productive use during the transition process, as the bureaucracy is dismantled and the price mechanism begins to act as a 'signal' to producers and consumers. All these impacts might, eventually, help to raise output per head (i.e. standard of living in these transition economies as both the quantity and quality of output rises).

However, there are disadvantages for the transition economies during the process of marketisation. For example, there is the danger of an increase in inequality of incomes as those with market power begin to exercise that power. For example, the 'oligarchs', businessmen and politicians with close links to the ruling elite, were often able to buy state assets at knockdown prices. Also since inheritance, skill and knowledge are unequally distributed in nations, the market will reward some more than others, further increasing inequalities. In addition, there is the problem that moving towards the market mechanism will create unemployment – a relatively new experience for such economies. There is also a danger of inflationary pressures as bottlenecks occur in both the labour and goods market, resulting in excess demand and higher prices. There is also a problem, at least in the short run, as transition economies try to build up legal systems to protect property rights. Finally, the transition economies may experience difficulties as they try to establish financial institutions to provide the investment funds that were previously supplied by the state in the form of credits or subsidies.

PROGRESS AND REVIEW QUESTIONS

Multiple-choice questions

1 b)
2 d)
3 d)
4 e)
5 b) and d)
6 c) and d)
7 a) and d)

Case study question

1 Production refers to the transformation of inputs, namely land labour and capital, into outputs, that is goods and services, which are consumed by individuals in order to satisfy wants. The inputs, or resources, are limited in supply hence the problem of scarcity. Labour is one such resource and this is the human input into the production of goods or services. It can be a physical and/or mental input into current production. The production possibility frontier refers to a curve such as that in the figure below which reveals all the possible combinations of two goods (X and Y) that a country can produce within a particular time period when all its resources are fully and efficiently employed.

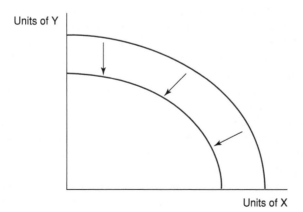

With the introduction of a 35-hour week in France then this represents a reduction in the amount of the labour resource available to the French economy. As a result the production possibility curve will shift inwards and to the left, as shown in the figure.

2 The 'economic problem' refers to the situation in which individuals' wants are unlimited but the resources (land, labour and capital) available to satisfy those wants are limited, i.e. in scarce supply. This situation of scarcity imposes a choice on society as to which wants it wishes to satisfy, hence the economic problem. In the case study it is mentioned that Keynes concluded that economic growth, leading to a shift in the production possibility frontier to the right, would go some way to solving the economic problem of wants which are not satisfied.

True/false questions

1 False
2 True
3 False
4 False
5 True
6 False
7 True
8 True

Essay questions

2 Opportunity cost refers to a situation in which the decision to produce or consume more of one good or service means that the next best alternative is forgone. The concept of opportunity cost often applies at the level of the individual, the firm or the government. Thus if an individual decides to purchase a digital camera, this might mean forgoing the purchase of a DVD recorder. On the other hand, if a firm invests in a new fleet of lorries, it may not be able to extend the size of the factory buildings, and if the government decides to build a new hospital, it may be at the expense of three new schools. In a situation of scarcity and restricted choice, opportunity cost is all important. Every society has to make choices as to *what* goods and services to produce and invariably the production of more of one good or service means less of some other goods and services. In addition to deciding *what* to produce, the decision has also to be made as to *how* to produce. For example, should production be more capital or labour intensive? There is also the decision about *for whom* to produce.

4 There are certain *disadvantages* with planned economies as a means of allocating resources. First, when allocating resources to the production of particular goods and services the planning authority may miscalculate the preferences of the consumer. As a result, there may be an underproduction of certain goods and an overproduction of others. This may lead either to severe shortages of certain goods, with the resultant long queues or rationing, and a glut of others, leading to large stockpiles. This is unlikely to occur with a market economy since resources are automatically allocated to those goods and services the consumer demands. Secondly, since the state owns the productive assets in a planned economy and profits are unavailable, there is arguably a reduced incentive to work harder, whereas in a market economy the reward in the form of profit is a motivational factor. Thirdly, since business is organised as a state monopoly in a planned economy there is a lack of variety in terms of the goods and services produced. Overall, with a market economy there is less bureaucracy and a more efficient allocation of resources than is the case with a planned economy.

Chapter 2

Mini Case Study 2.2 Increase in demand for general air travel

Levels of income are suggested here ('... industry has been hard hit by a sluggish economy'). Air travel has a high income elasticity of demand, so that demand increases more than in proportion to any rise in world income levels, and vice versa for any fall in world income levels. Perceptions as to the safety of air travel and destinations from terrorist attacks are also a significant influence on the demand for world air travel. Fears of health issues (e.g. SARS) involving contracting diseases as a result of air travel are also important here.

Higher oil prices are raising the price of fuel used in air travel and this is a significant part of the total cost of such travel. From the case study we can see that each one dollar increase in price of oil per barrel raises costs to the airline industry by one billion dollars. This extra cost will reduce the possibilities of low-price air fares especially, with higher prices causing a contraction in demand for world air travel. As higher oil prices feed through into higher rates of inflation across the world, real incomes will fall and this will shift the demand for air travel leftwards (i.e. decrease in demand).

PROGRESS AND REVIEW QUESTIONS

Multiple-choice questions

1 a)
2 a)
3 d)
4 e)
5 c)
6 c)

Data response questions

1 a) Quantity demanded refers to the amount of a product consumers are willing and able to purchase at a particular price over a particular period of time. The quantity supplied refers to the amount firms are willing and able to put onto the market at a particular price over a particular period of time.

    b) The equilibrium price is £4 and the equilibrium quantity is 60 units.

    c) *i)* Excess demand of 80 units

       ii) Excess supply of 80 units

    d) New equilibrium price is £3.50 and the new equilibrium quantity is 50 units.

2

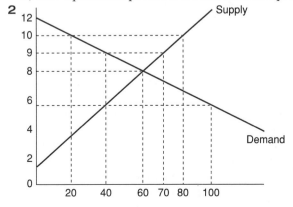

a) As shown in the figure above, the equilibrium price is £8 and the equilibrium quantity is 60,000 units.

b) As can be seen in the figure above, at a price of £9 the quantity demanded is 40,000 *units* whereas the quantity firms want to supply at this price is 70,000. There is excess supply of 30,000 units and, if left to the market, the price will fall to £8, which is the equilibrium price at which the quantity demanded and supplied are exactly equal at 60,000 units.

c) If a maximum price of £6 per unit is introduced by the government then the consequences will be an excess demand of 60,000 units with 100,000 units demanded but only 40,000 units supplied. There will thus be shortages which could lead to the product in question being rationed.

d) If a minimum price of price of £10 is imposed, the quantity demanded and supplied will be 20,000 and 80,000 units respectively. There will therefore be an excess supply of 60,000 units, which could lead to stockpiles of unwanted products.

Case study questions

1 a) The slowing down in house price rises depends on a number of factors. Clearly if there is a slow growth in wages then individuals will be less inclined to enter the housing market or consider a house move. There will be a slowing down in the demand for housing and this will have an effect on the rise in house prices. In addition, if there is a rise in interest rates this will increase the cost of borrowing to finance house purchases and the resulting decrease in demand for houses will slow the rise in house prices. Equally if there are lower expectations in terms of future house price rises, then homeowners are likely to be more cautious when considering a house move.

b)

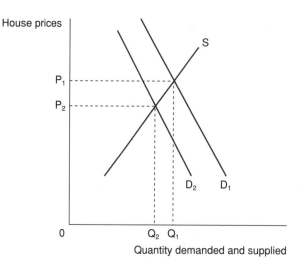

A slowing down in wage growth, a rise in interest rates and lower expectations as to future house price rises by homeowners is likely to lead to a shift in the demand curve for houses to the left, i.e. a decrease in demand from D_1 to D_2.

2 Whilst pub sales are lower following the ban on smoking, they have not fallen as much as many feared. It may even have been the case that non-smokers are now more willing to drink in Irish pubs following the ban.

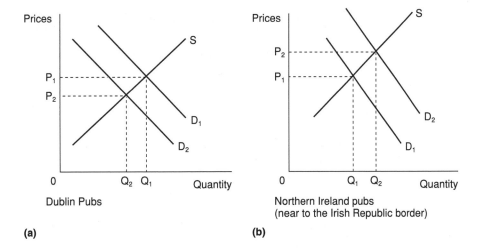

(a) Dublin Pubs

(b) Northern Ireland pubs
(near to the Irish Republic border)

Figure a) above illustrates the possible impact of the Irish smoking ban on pubs in the Republic – the demand for drink having decreased from D_1 to D_2. It may have decreased even further (i.e. to the left of D_2) if non-smokers had not possibly been encouraged into pubs by the smoking ban. The pubs which are likely to have benefited are those in Northern Ireland close to the Irish Republic border, where smoking in pubs is still allowed, hence the increase in demand from D_1 to D_2 in figure b).

True/false questions

1 True
2 True
3 True
4 False
5 True

Essay questions

2 It is possible to use a demand and supply diagram in order to explain the situation. If there is an increase in income, the demand curve for DVD players will shift to the right, assuming DVD players are normal goods. If there is a new technique of production in terms of DVD players, this will reduce the costs of production and the supply curve will shift downwards and to the right, since they are now a more profitable product for the manufacturer to produce. Overall, the demand and supply diagram should be drawn so as to reveal a rise in the equilibrium quantity of DVD players bought and sold. The effect on price depends on the extent to which the respective demand and supply curves shift.

4 Reasons for the sharp increase in the price of oil in recent years might include the following:
- decrease in the supply of oil following the Iraq war;
- faster economic growth worldwide, therefore an increase in the demand for oil from the manufacturing and service sectors;
- restrictions in the supply of oil by the Oil Producing and Exporting Countries (OPEC), a cartel.

Chapter 3

Mini Case Study 3.2 Elasticity of bus and rail travel

1 $PED = \dfrac{\% \text{ change in quantity demanded of X}}{\% \text{ change in price of X}}$

The negative sign is included here (often omitted) and simply tells us that a rise in price will lead to a contraction in demand, and vice versa. The short-run values for bus and rail are both relatively inelastic, with a 1% rise in bus prices resulting in a 0.42 of 1% (i.e. less than 1%) contraction in demand for bus travel. A 1% rise in rail prices resulting in a 0.46 of 1% contraction in demand for rail travel.

2 In the long-run time period, the price elasticity of demand for buses is substantially higher than for rail. Indeed for buses we have (just) a relatively elastic demand, but still a relatively inelastic demand for rail, where a 1% rise in rail prices results in only a 0.65 of 1% contraction in demand for rail travel. Arguably there are more substitutes available for many types of bus travel, with buses more often used for shorter distance travel than trains. Cars, bicycles, walking may be more often available as substitutes for bus journeys than for rail journeys. With more substitutes available we would expect PED to be more elastic, which is the case here.

PROGRESS AND REVIEW QUESTIONS

Multiple-choice questions

1	b)	**6**	b)
2	b)	**7**	a)
3	a)	**8**	d)
4	b)	**9**	c)
5	c)	**10**	e)

Data response questions

1 a) −0.5

b) At a price of £40 the quantity demanded per week is 16 units, which results in total revenue of £640. When the price increases to £60 the quantity demanded per week falls to 12 units giving a total revenue of £720. The effect on total revenue of the price increase is an £80 increase in revenue.

c) 1.5

2 a) DF

b) DE

c) EF

d) ADFC

True/false questions

1 False

2 False

3 True

4 True

5 True

Essay questions

2 Price elasticity of supply is influenced by a number of factors:

- *The existence of spare capacity.* If there is spare capacity then the producer is able to increase supply relatively easily and supply can be seen as being relatively elastic.
- *The availability of stocks.* If stocks of raw materials, partly finished or finished products are readily available then supply will tend to be more elastic.
- *Mobility of the factors of production.* If the factors of production, such as labour and capital are mobile, i.e. able to switch from the production of one good or service to another relatively easily then supply is likely to be relatively elastic.
- The time period. The longer the time period being considered, the more flexible the firm is likely to be in terms of supplying a product. This could involve switching labour from the production of one product to another or ordering new capital equipment.

4 Knowledge of price elasticity of demand is important in determining whether a firm should raise or lower its prices since it will have an effect on total revenue. If the firm is operating in the portion of the demand curve which is relatively elastic, then a reduction in price will result in an increase in total revenue as illustrated in the figure below.

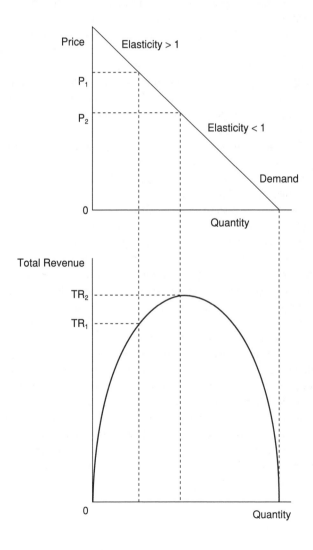

In the figure a reduction in price from P_1 to P_2 will result in an increase in revenue earned from TR_1 to TR_2. If demand is relatively inelastic then an increase in price will lead to an increase in revenue earned by the firm.

Chapter 4

Mini Case Study 4.2 Changing tastes over time

1 There are many reasons for the emergence of new products and the disappearance of others. Products which have been *taken out* of the basket are items which no longer fit the tastes or lifestyle of the country. For example, drinks such as brown ale are not popular with young people who are the main consumers of alcoholic drink and fixed telephones have been superseded by portable phones or mobiles. Shoes are now more of a fashion statement and are being thrown away after a certain time as tastes change rather than repaired. Spaghetti is now available 'fresh' from supermarkets so that the demand for the tinned version is no longer so high. In terms of the products which have been included, these often reflect new patterns of consumption made available by higher real income and reflecting our more hectic 'time scarce' lifestyles. More people are now able to afford to bring home ready-made meals and prepared pet foods and do so as a means of saving time. The growth of incomes in general has also allowed the growth of personal products and services such as designer spectacles, shower gels, golf fees and slimming club fees. Changing tastes are reflected in the inclusion of draught premium lager which is the favourite of young drinkers. What is happening here is that the interaction of changing incomes, tastes, and lifestyles are influencing the types of goods and services consumed.

2 The changes in the products in the shopping basket covering the decades from the 1960s to the 1990s do reflect some of the points covered above. The effects of changes in income levels, lifestyles and technological developments all influenced the content of the basket over time. For example, increasing affluence in the 1960s saw the introduction of meals out in restaurants and this continued into the 1970s in the form of the ability to purchase increased leisure (e.g. visiting stately homes). By the 1980s and 1990s higher real incomes continued to encourage leisure activities (e.g. foreign holidays) and combined with the growth of new technology brought a wide variety of new electronic products into the purchasing range of the typical household.

3 In the next ten years the shopping basket may contain more products and services covering niche markets, e.g. specially packaged holidays to unusual places reflecting the desire for more customised consumption. It is also probable that goods and services suitable to older people will be included in the basket to reflect the rapidly ageing population, e.g. motorised scooters for the infirm. New consumer goods with high technology digital components or products involving sophisticated mobile phone technology may also be included. Products and services which might *disappear* from the basket include basic foodstuffs and personal services such as repairing items which people can now afford to replace. High calorie foodstuffs might disappear as the health issues associated with obesity become higher profile. Greater concern for the environment and health may also put pressure on tobacco and alcohol related products, e.g. bans on smoking in public places and higher taxes on products associated with adverse environmental and health effects.

PROGRESS AND REVIEW QUESTIONS

Multiple-choice questions

1 e)
2 c)
3 a)
4 c)
5 b)

Data response question

Type of product	Substitution effect	Income effect	Total effect
Normal	Positive	Positive	Positive
Inferior (but not Giffen)	Positive	Negative	Positive
Giffen	Positive	Negative	Negative

Case study question

1 In terms of the figure below the consumer is initially in an equilibrium position at point E. Given the introduction of the free flights promotion the consumer could obtain a position such as C. As can be seen, however, E and C lie on the same indifference curve and as such represent the same level of satisfaction. The consumer is therefore indifferent between taking advantage of, and not taking advantage of, the 'free flights' promotion.

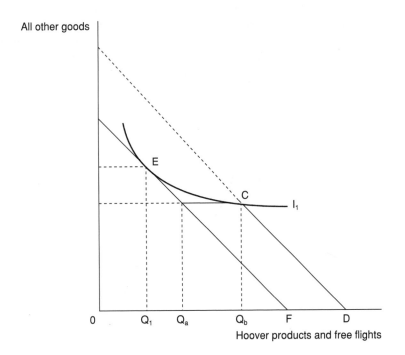

2 The company can learn a number of lessons from the 'free flights' offer, namely:
- It creates uncertainty in the market and could possibly result in a price war.
- It had implications in terms of placing pressure on capacity, with additional labour required plus the factory having to be placed on seven-day working in order to meet the increased demand.
- Consumers were buying the electrical appliances in order to obtain the free flights, hardly a policy to improve brand loyalty.
- The promotion was costly with a high take up of the promotional offer.

True/false questions

1 False
2 True
3 False
4 True
5 False
6 True
7 True

Essay questions

2 An indifference curve is a line which joins all the combinations of two products for which the consumer obtains the same level of satisfaction.

The consumer is in equilibrium, that is at the highest level of satisfaction that his or her income allows, where the budget line is tangential to the highest attainable indifference curve, and this is the point where the slope of the budget line (as given by the relative prices of the two products) is equal to the slope of the indifference curve (the marginal rate of substitution). This can be seen in the figure below at point E which is the position of maximum utility for the consumer, purchasing Y_1 of product Y and X_1 of product X. Any point on the budget line is feasible, but movements to points to the left and right of point E would place the consumer on a lower indifference curve, which represents a lower level of satisfaction.

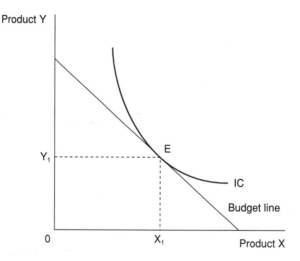

4 In answer to this question see the answer to the data response question above (page 497).

Chapter 5

Mini Case Study 5.2 Morrisons acquires Safeway

Morrisons sees the benefits from purchasing Safeway from both cost and market-based perspectives. On the cost side, some savings from rationalisation will be possible, e.g. head office savings. Other cost benefits from increased size (trebled, from around 5% to over 15% of supermarket turnover) will include various scale economies, e.g. purchasing (discounts), marketing, logistical, etc. Cost savings of £215 million by January 2008 are predicted. On the market-based side, the increased market power from being among the top four UK supermarkets can be exploited in various ways. For example, Wm Morrisons now has a more national geographical coverage (previously a northern-based company) and a much larger market presence. It expects a more focused and uniform market strategy using the successful Morrisons brand (quality and low prices) to boost sales revenue in the previously underperforming Safeway stores. The value discrepancy and valuation ratio hypotheses of merger activity would tend to receive some support from this takeover. The brief materials in the Mini Case Study could be the preliminary to further investigation by students into the pre- and post-merger phases of this deal.

PROGRESS AND REVIEW QUESTIONS

Multiple-choice questions

  1 b)
  2 c)
  3 a)
  4 b)
  5 b)
  6 b)
  7 b)
  8 e)
  9 d)
 10 a)

Case study question

The compensation culture was found by 60% of employers in the study of 500 organisations to be hampering their business. The time and money spent on responding to claims is raising business costs and reducing profits. The study by AON, the insurance broking and risk management group, found that multinationals were even moving business offshore to avoid the growing compensation culture in the UK. Possible remedies might include banning 'no-win-no-fee' adverts and making it more difficult and more expensive for frivolous claims to reach court.

Data response questions

1 a)

Output	TC	TFC	TVC	ATC	AFC	AVC	MC
0	15	15	0			0	
1	30	15	15	30	15	15	15
2	35	15	20	17.5	7.5	10	5
3	39	15	24	13	5	8	4
4	45	15	30	11.25	3.75	7.5	6
5	60	15	45	12	3	9	15

b) Plot the AC and the MC on graph paper. This can be done using the figures given in the above table. Remember to plot the MC at the mid point, i.e. between 1 and 2, etc.

c) Total cost is just that, it is the total cost of producing a particular level of output. Total cost can be divided into total fixed cost (TFC) and total variable cost (TVC), so that TC = TFC + TVC. Average cost (AC) or, as it is often expressed, average total cost (ATC), is the cost per unit and is obtained by dividing total cost by the number of units produced. Average total cost (ATC) comprises average fixed cost and average variable cost so that ATC = AFC + AVC. Average fixed cost is given by AFC = TFC/Q and it declines continuously as out-put increases. This is because the fixed cost is spread over more units of production and is therefore sometimes called 'spreading the overheads'. Average variable cost is given by AVC = TVC/Q. Marginal cost (MC) is the change in the total cost as a result of a change in output of one unit. It can be written as $MC = \dfrac{\Delta TC}{\Delta Q}$. The marginal cost curve cuts the average cost curve at its minimum point.

2 Table 1 suggests that as the plant size increases in terms of car output, then the average production cost of each car reduces. Thus a plant which produces 2 million as opposed to 100,000 cars per annum will see a 44% reduction in average production costs, indicating a benefit of size (economies of scale) in the car industry. Economies of scale clearly vary depending on the type of activity involved. For example, Table 2 suggests that to obtain full economies in terms of advertising then the optimum output per annum is 1 million cars per annum, whereas in terms of *research and development* the optimum output is 5 million. Interestingly, in terms of plant size, then 2 million appears to result in the lowest average production cost and this also represents the optimum output in terms of sales per year.

True/false questions

1 False
2 False
3 True
4 True
5 False
6 True
7 True
8 True
9 False
10 True

Essay questions

2 An *isoquant* can be defined as a curve showing the various combinations of capital and labour required to produce a given quantity of a particular product, in the most efficient way. The slope of the isoquant reveals the marginal rate of technical substitution of labour for capital. This shows how much capital can be replaced by one extra unit of labour, with output remaining constant. An *isocost* line represents the various combinations of captial and labour that the firm can buy for a given expenditure.

By combining the isoquant with the isocost it is possible to determine the *least-cost process of production*. This occurs when the isoquant is tangential to the isocost. At this point it is not possible to produce any more of the product with the resources available to the firm.

4 Economies of scale refer to the fall in long-run average cost as output rises. Economies of scale can be technical, marketing, administrative, etc. Economies of scope refer to lower average costs resulting from a change in the *mix* of production as size increases. In other words, larger firms can be multi-product firms and may choose products which fit together in ways which reduce costs. For example, products which give off heat energy may help reduce energy costs when using this heat to produce other products. Any industry may be chosen, e.g. the car industry.

Chapter 6

Mini Case Study 6.2 Car barriers

1 The 'selective and exclusive distribution' practice (declared illegal in the UK in 2002) meant that dealers could only sell the cars of one company and could not purchase cheaper models of that company's cars from other countries. This monopoly practice has kept new car prices in the UK some 10% to 12% higher than for those same cars in EU countries. In addition, the car companies (suppliers of new cars) seem to be setting the prices of their new cars in line with the prices of similar new cars from their rivals – i.e. they are acting together (collusion) in a monopoly practice.
2 Prices are higher than they otherwise would be in a competitive market, as with the suggestion that car buyers in the UK have been paying on average £1,000 more for new models than elsewhere in the EU. Without this monopoly markets, dealers would have incentives to buy cheaper models of new cars in the EU and sell them at lower prices to UK purchasers, thereby raising their own profits.

PROGRESS AND REVIEW QUESTIONS
Multiple-choice questions

1 a)
2 b)
3 c)
4 b)
5 e)
6 c)
7 c)
8 b)
9 b)

True/false questions

1 True
2 False
3 True
4 True
5 False
6 True
7 True
8 False
9 True
10 True

Essay questions

2 Perfect competition refers to a market structure where firms have no power over the market. This means that they accept the price as set by the market and, therefore, they are known as *price takers*. The lack of market power reveals itself in a number of ways. First, there are many buyers and sellers, none of which is able to influence the market price. Each firm is very small in relation to the whole market and is, therefore, unable to influence total supply and therefore to affect the price charged. Put another way, each firm faces a perfectly elastic demand curve at the price set by the market. Secondly, both the producers and consumers have perfect knowledge; they are aware of the ruling market price. If the producer charges above this price, consumers will purchase their products elsewhere. Thirdly, the product is homogeneous, which means that each unit of the product is identical and of the same quality. Thus, buyers have no preference as to where they purchase the product – they are indifferent – hence the demand curve is perfectly elastic at the going market price. Should any firm seek to charge a higher price than this, there will be no purchasers.

In the short-run equilibrium firms are able to make supernormal profit in perfect competition. The existence of supernormal profit will attract new firms into the industry, since profits act as a 'signal' in a competitive market to enter the industry. The entry of large numbers of new firms into the industry would result in a shift in the industry's supply curve to the right, and the price would be forced down until all the firms in the industry were earning normal profit. In the long-run equilibrium, each firm will be operating at the minimum point on both their short-run and long-run average cost curves, obtaining the full economies of scale.

4 There are a number of assumptions necessary for price discrimination to operate:
- There is a single monopoly supplier of the product.
- The market can be divided into at least two segments.
- There are different demand and marginal revenue curves in the two markets with different price elasticities of demand.
- A single price is charged in each market.
- It is not possible to resell the product between the two markets. The markets are separated, e.g. on the basis of time or geographically.
- The cost of providing the product is the same in the two markets.
- *First degree price discrimination* involves the monopolist in selling each unit of the product separately, charging the highest price each consumer is willing to pay. The producer would thus set a price equal to what each consumer is willing to pay at each point on the demand curve, which in fact becomes the marginal revenue curve. The result is that through perfect price discrimination the monopolist is able to extract the entire consumer surplus.
- *Second degree price discrimination* involves charging a uniform price per unit for a specific quantity (or block) of the product consumed, a lower price per unit for the next block consumed and so on. By this form of price discrimination the monopolist is able to extract some, but not all, of the consumer's surplus.
- *Third degree price discrimination* involves dividing the market into a least two market segments. There are different demand and marginal revenue curves in the two market segments with different elasticities of demand in each segment. The profit maximising condition is that marginal cost for whole output be set equal to marginal revenue in each market segment.

Chapter 7

Mini Case Study 7.2 Cartels and collusion

1 The examples show clearly that cartel activity can take many forms. The cement example provides evidence of *supply fixing* as the three companies refused to supply a certain type of cement. The second example shows a *price fixing* cartel as other companies follow changes in the price of the market leader Vitafoam Ltd. Finally, the 'vitamin cartel' led by the Swiss firm Hoffman La Roche operated both *supply and price fixing* in different markets for vitamins. They were engaged in holding meetings specifically designed to implement their cartel constraints.

2 Cartels are believed to be against the public interest because they use their combined power to control the supply/price of a good or service in order to earn extra profits. Cartel activity is seen as an anti-competitive device by most countries because the practice does not allow the free forces of the market to work. It is an exercise in collective market power which benefits the producer at the expense of the consumer.

3 The conditions necessary for a cartel to be successful are the following. First, that the price elasticity of demand is relatively low; secondly, that the elasticity of supply is also low; thirdly, that there is no tendency for members of the cartel to cheat; and finally, that the barriers to entry in the industry are high. The first two conditions ensure that prices will rise rapidly as the cartel restrains output. The third condition ensures that the supply curve does not become more elastic. The third condition makes sure that it is difficult to enter the industry, i.e. that the supply of the product remains under the control of the cartel.

PROGRESS AND REVIEW QUESTIONS

Multiple-choice questions

1 c)
2 b)
3 c)
4 c)
5 a)
6 c)

Data response question

1 a) A *payoff matrix* is used in order to analyse the behaviour of firms in oligopolistic markets via game theory. Firms in such markets can undertake various strategies which may range from price cutting to promotional campaigns.

b) Firm X will opt for a price cutting strategy since, at best, it will result in profit of 5 if Y opts for advertising, and at worst it could result in profit of 3 if Y opts for price cutting. If firm X had opted for advertising, the best it could receive is a profit of 4 and the worst zero profit. Firm X therefore has a *dominant strategy*, which is to price cut. If the situation is considered from the point of view of firm Y then it will also opt for price cutting for the same reasons. So each firm will end up with profit of 3 each.

c) The payoff matrix reveals that the firms could have done much better if they had colluded and both undertaken an advertising strategy. By doing this they could have each received profit of 4.

True/false questions

1 True
2 False
3 True
4 True
5 False
6 True
7 True
8 False
9 True
10 True

Essay questions

2 Prices often show less variation, i.e. are 'sticky', in oligopolistic markets which involve competition amongst a few major firms which dominate the industry. As a result there is a tendency for firms in this type of market to watch closely the strategies of their competitors because there are only a small number of them in the industry. The kinked demand curve model for oligopoly uses the idea of strategic behaviour to predict relatively stable prices even when costs vary considerably (*see* Figure 7.3). Another feature of oligopoly is that price warfare can break out between the firms – e.g. as one firm decreases price, others have to follow or they will lose customers. This price warfare cannot continue forever because firms will lose all profits, so they will eventually have to stop competing on the basis of price alone. What they then do is to engage in *non-price competition* (e.g. advertising etc.) to secure customers and not change price too often. The 'stickiness' of prices in oligopoly situations is therefore linked to the problems of interdependence between firms in oligopoly markets.

4 There is a level of uncertainty which exists in oligopolistic markets and therefore there is much to be gained from collusion. Collusion is a way of dealing with interdependence since coming to an agreement as to what price should be charged or what level of output should be produced makes it possible for oligopolists to act as a monopoly, thereby achieving maximum profits for the industry.

Collusion can take one of two forms namely *formal* or *informal* (tacit) collusion. Formal collusion is where an agreement is reached between the firms as to what price to charge or what output to produce. This type of formal agreement is sometimes known as a *cartel*. Tacit collusion, on the other hand, is where firms behave in a co-operative way but do not have a formal agreement. The most common form of tacit collusion is *price leadership* where one firm sets the price and the other firms follow. This can occur via *dominant firm price leadership* which is a situation in which the largest or the most efficient firm takes the lead in setting the price which the other firms follow. Alternatively, *barometric firm price leadership* may exist where the price leader may be a small firm but one which has a close knowledge of the market and the prevailing economic conditions.

Chapter 8

Mini Case Study 8.2 Trade unions and labour markets

1 The data suggests a progressive fall in union density since 1991, where union density is the proportion of employees who are members of trade unions. In 1991 some 37.5% of

employees were in trade unions, but only 29% by 2001, although in the next few years this decline stabilised and even rose slightly.

2 The fall in union density is likely to reduce trade union bargaining power. Since less employees are in unions, the costs to management of disagreeing with terms proposed by unions is reduced. For example, any industrial action called by a union because its proposed terms are rejected will have less impact on the employer if few employees are members of the union.

PROGRESS AND REVIEW QUESTIONS

Multiple-choice questions

1 d)
2 c)
3 c)
4 d)
5 b)
6 d)
7 c)
8 a) and c)
9 e)

Data response questions

1 a) With the price of the product at €20 per unit then:

Number of workers	Total product	Marginal physical product (MPP)	Marginal revenue product (MPP × price of the product)
1	10	10	200
2	22	12	240
3	36	14	280
4	44	12	240
5	50	6	120
6	50	0	0

b) If the wage rate is €160 per week then 4 units of labour will be employed.

c) If the wage rate fell to €80, then 5 units of labour will be employed.

2 The table shows that the first three categories of full-time male non-manual workers earn significantly more than the average gross weekly earning for all full-time male workers. However, some non-manual workers in such occupations as sales, personal service and clerical and secretarial work earn less than the average wage. The differences in the earnings between managerial/professionals/technical groups and others may be linked to the differences in productivity – in other words, the high earnings may reflect their higher MRP which in turn may reflect the high level of training and investment in 'human capital' in those occupations. Other reasons include the ability of some occupations – especially professional occupations – to be better able to control the supply of labour to their occupations. Similarly, various groups of labour which do not have strong market power (such as the last three occupations in the non-manual category) have suffered more than proportionately as a result of the observed decline in trade union bargaining positions. Trade union density and power in the manual sector is arguably stronger than in the sales/services and clerical occupations, thus helping to keep the wages of the manual workers relatively high in comparison. Part of the reason for the persistence of these difference in earnings may also be due to 'intergenerational immobility' – i.e. that the children of parents who worked in low income occupations tended to find themselves working in the same type of low paid jobs as their parents. A final reason for some occupations earning less than others might be if a higher proportion of workers in them are employed under monopsony market conditions (*see* Figure 8.6).

True/false questions

1 True
2 False
3 True
4 True
5 True
6 False
7 True
8 True

Essay questions

2 Economic rent is the amount paid to a factor of production, such as labour, over and above that necessary to keep it in its present occupation. The minimum payment necessary to keep the factor of production in its present occupation is called its transfer earnings. The excess of earnings above the *transfer earnings* is called the *economic rent.*

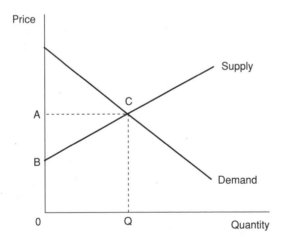

These two concepts can be illustrated by reference to the diagram which refers to a labour market. The equilibrium wage rate in this particular labour market is A and the numbers employed Q. Area ABC represents economic rent and is the amount above the minimum payment necessary to keep labour in the particular industry concerned. The last worker employed may only be willing to work for A, thus he or she obtains zero economic rent. All previous workers would receive economic rent and their transfer earnings are represented by the area 0BCQ.

The elasticity of supply affects economic rent. For example, if the supply curve for labour is perfectly elastic there will be no economic rent. The reason for this is that if the employer reduces the wage rate below that represented by the perfectly elastic supply curve then labour would be unwilling to supply its services. All the return to the factor is then transfer payment. The more inelastic the supply curve, the greater the economic rent.

Chapter 9

Mini Case Study 9.2 Ryanair and Charleroi

1 The regional authorities owning the airports which Ryanair flies to have benefited significantly by subsidising Ryanair. These regional airports were not used effectively before such subsidised arrangements so that regional airports now benefit from using their capacity more efficiently. Since many had already invested in runways which could cope with larger sizes of aircraft, the increase in air traffic meant that the 'fixed' cost of the airport could be spread over more flight arrivals. Tens of thousands of Britons now use Ryanair for weekends in second homes in France. This stimulates employment in and around the airports and in the region as a whole. It has also helped to keep house prices buoyant in some less known areas of Europe, thus helping to make former low growth regions more prosperous.

2 The European Commission's attitude to state aid is enshrined in Articles 87 and 88 of the Treaty of Rome. These indicate that any aid granted by a member state or through state resources which distorts or threatens to distort competition is incompatible with the common market. The only aid permissible is that which is for natural disasters, to promote economic development of low growth areas or which has social or cultural implications. The subsidy to Ryanair was seen as a public subsidy to a private organisation which could distort competition in favour of Ryanair. For example, the Commission ruled that Ryanair had received aid from the Brussels South Charleroi Airport in opening a new air route in the form of cuts in landing and ground handling fees and other subsidies. These had distorted competition to the disadvantage of Brussels National Airport and the airlines flying there. The Commission therefore told Ryanair to repay 4 million euros to the Belgian authorities – about 30% of what the carrier received in subsidies.

3 The implications of the ruling against Ryanair might have repercussions for second tier airports, regional development and consumer choice in the EU. For example, second tier airports may no longer be able to subsidise low cost flights to the same extent as before and the decision may therefore affect the regional development of certain areas of Europe. In addition, the Ryanair ruling might also lead to a decrease of consumer choice if low cost flight companies withdraw from flying to many areas of Europe. There is also the problem that if European states decide to provide money for their state airlines, this itself could be seen as anti-competitive! Of course, the ruling could also have repercussions for UK regions since the ending of flights from those regions to Europe by such low cost airlines discourages UK businessmen and individuals from using regional airports.

PROGRESS AND REVIEW QUESTIONS
Multiple-choice questions

1 b) and d)
2 a) and d)
3 b) and e)
4 a)
5 d)

6 a)

7 b) and c)

8 a) and d)

Case study question

1 The case for state aid to correct market failure can be beneficial from the standpoint of a nation. For example, if a country wants to stimulate the growth of a new industry which is too 'young' to compete, and which needs extra help to become more competitive, then state aid can be used to help such an infant industry. In addition, subsidies might be given to stimulate research and development which is seen as vital for increasing a nation's competitive advantage. Also, if an industrial sector is in the position where its marginal social benefit is greater than the marginal private benefit then the state could subsidise it. In other words, the state could subsidise say, the railways, to relieve road pollution and road congestion. In this way the state is subsidising positive externalities. In some particular instances such as the re-unification of Germany, it was felt that subsidies would help the economy of the old East Germany as it merged with its western counterpart. State aid is also accepted in the EU to help countries when major industries are in structural decline, and retraining and support for a large number of unemployed is needed. Aid is also acceptable when natural disasters occur. Although some of these types of subsidies may be allowed in the EU, it is always difficult to decide on the optimum amount of aid.

2 There are a number of problems with providing state aid. For example, the larger countries of the EU tend to spend more on state aid, which gives clear advantages to those countries at the expense of others, distorting the single market which seeks a 'level playing field'. State aid may prevent firms from becoming efficient so that sectors which arguably should be replaced by other, more competitive sectors, 'stagger on' and wastefully absorb scarce resources. State aid by developed economies is also arguably unfair to developing countries, as the state aid often in effect subsidises exports from developed to developing countries, discouraging domestic firms from growing larger in the developing economies. Such state aid also makes it harder for developing economies to sell their exports to the developed economies, even when they are more efficient in producing these products.

True/false questions

1 False

2 False

3 True

4 False

5 True

6 False

7 False

8 True

Essay questions

2 The arguments put forward for privatisation include the following:
- A view that nationalised industries are inefficient state controlled monopolies and that resources are allocated more efficiently through a competitive market structure. If this view is accepted then a case can be made for privatisation in order to promote competition. Increased competition, as well as leading to a more efficient allocation

of resources, should also make business more responsive to changing patterns of consumer demand.

- Efficiency can be encouraged through less government involvement in the firms' pricing and investment decisions. It could be argued that government officials are not the best individuals to be involved in commercial decision taking.
- The revenue from privatisation has allowed government borrowing to be reduced.
- Privatisation promoted a wider share ownership, at least in the short term.

The arguments against privatisation include the following:

- Privatisation has not necessarily brought about competition. In fact, in a number of instances, privatisation has simply meant the transfer of monopoly ownership from the public sector to the private sector.
- It has been argued that state owned assets were sold off too cheaply.
- Privatisation can be viewed as simply 'selling of the family silver' in order to finance current government expenditure and reduce the size of government borrowing.

4 Most of these reasons are linked to 'market failure'. First, where there are negative externalities (e.g. MSC > MPC) then governments might seek to tax a product to make the price closer to the social cost of production. Secondly, where there are positive externalities (e.g. MSB > MPB) a subsidy may be given, e.g. the government might subsidise rail to get more people to travel by train and therefore reduce car pollution. Thirdly, the government might regulate industries in the public interest, e.g. to assure minimum health and safety standards where it is difficult for consumers to have full information on the provision of a product or service. Fourthly, to provide a 'safety net' of a minimum standard of living for its citizens should they be unfortunate enough to be ill (NHS) or unemployed (employment benefits) etc.

Chapter 10

Mini Case Study 10.2 Alternatives to oil

If biodiesel and similar fuels become widely used in the US and world car markets as a cleaner substitute for petrol, then the demand curve for oil can be expected to decrease substantially over time (shift downwards and to the left). This should mean that both the equilibrium price and quantity of oil will be lower than would otherwise be the case, especially since transport is (together with electricity generation) the main source of demand for oil. A wide range of implications might be discussed such as environmental improvements, climate change, geographical redistribution of income (reallocation from oil to non-oil producers), etc.

PROGRESS AND REVIEW QUESTIONS

Multiple-choice questions

1 c)
2 e)
3 d)
4 c)

Data response questions

1 See Mini Case Study 10.3, Question 1.
2 The following policy options are available for dealing with congestion and traffic related pollution in London. Each has relative merits.

Market based options include:

- *Fuel taxes*, which could include differential taxes between different types of fuel, notably petrol (leaded and unleaded) and diesel. Fuel duty is seen as having a number of advantages: the amount of tax paid varies with the environmental costs, it is simple to administer, road users have discretion about how to respond, it is possible to vary the rate of fuel duty in order to provide an incentive to use environmentally less damaging forms of fuel, and the fuel duty already exists.

- *Graduated vehicle excise duty*, which depends on engine size. The problem with vehicle excise duty is that it is a *fixed cost* and as such bears no relation to vehicle use. There is therefore the risk that a high fixed charge will lead to higher vehicle use by those who have paid the vehicle excise duty. A graduated excise duty, however, could encourage the shift to smaller cars, with a reduction in fuel use and an equivalent reduction in carbon monoxide over the longer term.

- *Parking charges*, the aim of which is to deter motorists from undertaking journeys. There are, however, difficulties with this in that it may encourage through-traffic and driving around in search of uncharged spaces. Parking charges are, however, relatively straightforward to collect and where on-street parking is concerned they represent revenue gains to the authority.

- *Road user charging* is a means of rationing a scarce resource (road space) via the price mechanism. By increasing the cost of travel, the aim of road user charging is to reduce vehicle usage and therefore congestion. First impressions would lead one to think that reduced congestion would have environmental benefits, but some motorists may take longer journeys in order to avoid the charge. If overall traffic flows are reduced, this is likely to lower carbon monoxide and VOC emissions, traffic noise, visual intrusion and community disturbance.

- *Public transport subsidies* in order to reduce public transport fares. The case for a public transport subsidy rests heavily on the argument that the cross elasticity of demand (*see* Chapter 3 Section 4) between private and public transport is non-zero and preferably a high positive value. Evidence would suggest, however, that the cross elasticity of demand is low.

Regulatory or command-and-control options include:

- *Traffic calming*, which is a term used for a range of measures introduced in order to reduce traffic speeds and divert traffic away from areas which are perceived as environmentally sensitive. Traffic calming includes measures such as pedestrianisation, speed humps and narrower lane widths. It could be argued, however, that such physical control measures may result in longer journeys and therefore additional vehicle emissions. Traffic calming schemes require public expenditure and do not provide a monetary return.

- *Stricter enforcement of emission standards* such as requiring all new petrol driven cars to be fitted with catalytic converters. Stricter enforcement of standards requires the addition of monitoring mechanisms such as regular vehicle and/or roadside checks. Catalytic converters have been required on all new cars with petrol engines since 1992 in order to meet EU regulations. This has resulted in a reduction in various emissions, but converters will only act as a temporary check since the benefits of the converter will eventually be outweighed by the growth in traffic.

- *Land-use and transport planning* involving careful decisions in terms of the location of office, leisure and educational facilities, shopping centres and residential areas, taking account of their consequences in terms of transport. Land-use and transport planning can be seen as a long-term policy aimed at addressing the fact that geographically dispersed populations result in increased travel demand and car use, and therefore manipulating the market for land as a means of influencing the transport sector. Since transport is essentially a *derived* demand, a reversal of the trend could result in a reduction in vehicle kilometres travelled by car and an increase in vehicle kilometres travelled by public transport. There are a number of issues raised by this type of measure. First, it is a long-term policy and the benefits are likely to vary depending on how planning policy is implemented; secondly, many cities offer limited scope for manipulation of land use given their historical make-up, and thirdly, there is complexity in terms of the relationship between land use and transport.

True/false questions

1 True
2 False
3 True
4 True
5 False
6 True
7 True
8 True
9 True
10 True

Essay questions

1 The bargaining solution is based on the argument that if *property rights* are assigned (that is the legal rights to a resource) then *bargains* may be undertaken, such that the optimum level of pollution is achieved. If property rights are assigned to the *polluter*, then those who suffer may be prepared to pay the polluter to reduce its scale of activity and therefore the level of pollution. Since what the sufferer is prepared to pay is likely to be greater than the lost revenue to the polluter for reducing its output level, then there is scope for bargaining to take place between the two parties. The amount paid by the sufferers will depend on the relative bargaining strengths of the two parties. If the property rights are assigned to the *sufferers*, then a similar outcome will result. Here the polluter will find it advantageous to compensate the sufferers of pollution and retain an amount of profit. As with the previous example there is scope for bargaining to take place. Whether the polluter compensates the sufferers or the sufferers pay the polluter the outcome is the same, although the income distribution differs.

Some issues raised by the bargaining solution include the following:

- Those affected by pollution often find it difficult to organise themselves since they are likely to be large in number.
- Sufferers may have insufficient funds in order to compensate polluters for the cost of reducing pollution.
- Individual sufferers may not want to take the lead in terms of negotiations with the polluter, preferring to let someone else take the responsibility (free rider problem). They would, however, take advantage of the benefits which relates to a situation.
- If polluters are aware of the fact that they would have to pay compensation to the sufferers for their emissions then they may be encouraged to undertake research and development into more environmentally friendly technology.

- If the sufferers have to compensate polluters for reducing their emission levels then it may encourage other polluting firms to relocate to the area in order to take advantage of the compensation.

2 The potential issues which need to be resolved in terms of ETS being extended to aviation include the following:
   - How the permits are allocated.
   - The basis of trading.
   - How the scheme is monitored.
   - How the scheme is enforced.
   - The administrative costs.
   - Whether it will have an impact on emission levels.
   - The impact on new entrants.
   - The fact that it may act as a potential barrier to entry to the sector.
   - The fact that it is EU specific, therefore creating a potential unfair advantage to world operators.
   - The likely impact on air fares.

3 - Road user charging is a charge for the use of road space and as such by increasing the cost of travel the aim is to reduce vehicle usage.
   - Given the introduction of a road user charge motorists may make longer journeys in order to avoid the charge, with environmental implications.
   - The cross elasticity of demand is likely to be low for public transport use. Lower fares are only one aspect encouraging public transport use. Other factors include, frequency, reliability, safety and quality of the public transport service offered.
   - If there is latent demand for the use of the road space then a switch of travellers from the car to public transport as a result of the subsidy will free up the road space for those who previously did not undertake journeys. As such, traffic will be generated as a result of the subsidy.
   - There are resource implications in terms of financing the public transport subsidy.
   - In terms of acceptance, public transport subsidies are likely to be more acceptable than the introduction of a road user charge.

4 See the answer to Mini Case Study 10.3, question 1, and the Data response question 2.

Chapter 11

Mini Case Study 11.2 National income and consumer behaviour

1 At any given level of national income (Y) there would be less consumer spending (C) since higher mortgage payments and other payments on borrowing would reduce the available (disposable) income for household consumer expenditure. The consumption function (C) would shift downwards.

2 A fall in consumption (C) would reduce aggregate expenditure (E) at any given level of national income/output (Y) in Figure 11.7. This fall in E would reduce the equilibrium value of national income/output in the circular flow.

3 The government might seek to stimulate other aspects of aggregate expenditure (E) to offset the predicted fall in consumer spending (C). For example, it might increase government spending (G). It might also consider reducing various forms of taxation, thereby raising the level of income available to spend after tax. Longer-term strategies might involve reducing the importance of *variable* interest rate mortgages for UK households, e.g. encouraging more mortgage borrowing at *fixed* rates of interest.

PROGRESS AND REVIEW QUESTIONS

Multiple-choice questions

1 a)
2 e)
3 a)
4 b)
5 c)
6 d)
7 e)
8 e)
9 c)
10 c)
11 e)
12 b)

Matching pairs

1 a) iv);   b) i);   c) vii);   d) ii);   e) v);   f) iii)
2 a) vii);   b) viii);   c) i);   d) vi);   e) ii);   f) iii)
3 a) iii);   b) ii);   c) iv);   d) v);   e) i);

Data response and stimulus questions

1 a) GDP and GNP figures at market prices are identical whichever method of measuring national income is chosen.

b) GDP at market prices involves measuring the value of output produced (and income received) which has been inflated in value terms by indirect taxes levied on the goods and services produced but deflated in value terms by subsidies received on those goods and services. These indirect taxes inflate the recorded value of incomes from producing goods and services by £260.4 billion more than subsidies from government deflate the recorded values of incomes from producing goods and services.

c) GDP refers to incomes derived from activities by households and firms using resources located in the UK, whereas GNP measures incomes derived from the ownership of resources by UK residents (and firms) wherever these resources happen to be located. We must therefore add to GDP the incomes earned by UK residents on resources located overseas and subtract incomes earned by overseas residents on resources located in the UK. This *net* value is recorded in the accounts as 'net property income from abroad', which is +£6 billion in Table (i). So GNP at market prices is £6 billion *more* than GDP at market prices.

d) Various types of pensions and state benefits. These are called 'transfer payments' and are excluded from the national income accounts since they are payments received out of tax revenue and do not correspond to production having taken place.

e) Aggregate expenditure is $C + I + G + (X - M)$ and corresponds to the first four values shown in Table (ii).

f) Exports correspond to expenditure on output produced by *domestic* residents and are therefore included in GDP whereas imports correspond to expenditure on output produced by *overseas* residents and are therefore excluded. We must therefore *add* to any expenditure by UK households the expenditure by overseas households on UK exports, and *subtract* from any expenditure by UK households that part which is spent on UK imports. Both exports and imports are valued at current prices, which include indirect taxes and subsidies, and are therefore valued at 'market prices'. In our example, exports fall short of imports by £32.4 billion, hence the negative sign.

g) Expenditure on intermediate outputs or on second-hand products is excluded. Only expenditure on *final* output is included, otherwise there is a danger of double counting.

2 a)

National income (Y)	Tendency to change in national income
0	0
2,000	Increase
4,000	Increase
6,000	Increase
8,000	Increase
10,000	Increase
12,000	No change
14,000	Decrease
16,000	Decrease

b)

National income (Y)	Withdrawals (W)	Injections (J)
0	−2,000	4,000
2,000	−1,000	4,000
4,000	0	4,000
6,000	1,000	4,000
8,000	2,000	4,000
10,000	3,000	4,000
12,000	4,000	4,000
14,000	5,000	4,000
16,000	6,000	4,000

c) Your diagram should look like that in Figure 11.3 (page 242) but with W intersecting J at a value of Y of 12,000. J will be a horizontal line at 4,000 and W will intersect the vertical axis at −2,000 and will intersect the horizontal axis when Y = 4,000.

d) Savings (S) $= -2,000 + 0.2Y$
Taxes (T) $= 0.2Y$
Imports (M) $= 0.1Y$
Withdrawals $= -2,000 + 0.5Y$

e)

National income (Y)	Consumption (C)	Injections (J)	Aggregate expenditure (E)
0	2,000	4,000	6,000
2,000	3,000	4,000	7,000
4,000	4,000	4,000	8,000
6,000	5,000	4,000	9,000
8,000	6,000	4,000	10,000
10,000	7,000	4,000	11,000
12,000	8,000	4,000	12,000
14,000	9,000	4,000	13,000
16,000	10,000	4,000	14,000

f) Your diagram should look like that in Figure 11.6 (page 247). The $E = C + J$ schedule should intersect the 45° line at $Y = 12,000$. The E schedule intersects the vertical axis at a value of 6,000.

g) The equilibrium level of national income is where the 45° line intersects the aggregate expenditure line, i.e. at the 12,000 level of national income. It can be seen from the various tables created in this exercise that the equilibrium level of national income is 12,000 whether the $W = J$ approach or the $Y = E$ approach to equilibrium is taken. This confirms the nature of the relationships between the variables discussed in the chapter.

3 You should draw an initial diagram similar to that shown in Figure 11.3 with equilibrium national income at Y_1. A rise in savings (S) will, other things equal, shift the withdrawals schedule (W) vertically upwards to a new and higher schedule W_1. This new schedule will intersect the unchanged injection schedule (J) at a *lower* level of national income than Y_1. This attempt to save more by everyone (or a significant number of people) may therefore result in less output and employment, hardly a 'virtuous' outcome! Further, with less income available there may be an *actual fall* in aggregate savings as a result of the attempt to save more. For example, in Figure 11.4(a), a reduction in national income (Y) will clearly reduce aggregate savings (S).

4 a) People who receive income from the initial £2.4 billion of government spending will in turn spend some of this on a wide range of goods and services in and around London. Those who receive income from producing these 'secondary' goods and services will in turn spend some of this on yet more goods and services, and so on. The size of the *total* increase in spending is likely to considerably outstrip the original £2.4 billion in initial ('primary') spending. This 'multiplier' effect will be greater the higher the proportion of any extra income that is spent, i.e. the higher the marginal propensity to consume.

b) Much of the multiplier effect will benefit Londoners but it is likely that many outside London will also benefit. For example, the airlines, train and bus companies transporting spectators and contestants to London from around the world and those who work on them or supply them will benefit. Also building and other contracts involving Olympic facilities and services will result in income being earned by companies (and workers) which are based outside London. As these extra incomes are spent outside London, they will create still further incomes and expenditures, and so on.

c) As mentioned in Question a), the higher the proportion of any extra income received which is passed on in the circular flow as extra consumer spending, the larger the final multiplier effect. In other words, the higher the marginal propensity to consume, the larger the final multiplier effect and vice versa. On the other hand, the higher the proportion of any extra income received which is withdrawn from the circular flow as savings, taxes or imports, the smaller the final multiplier effect. In other words, the higher the marginal propensities to save, tax or import, the smaller the final multiplier effect and vice versa.

Essay questions

2 See the text on 'Comparing living standards of different nations' (page 241) which examines this issue. You can also find more on this issue in Chapter 18.

Chapter 12

Mini Case Study 12.2 International comparisons of public expenditure

1 The UK is not, as often suggested, one of the countries where government spending is an excessively high proportion of GDP. In fact, of the 20 countries in the table, the UK is only the 11th highest, with public spending at 37.4% of GDP well behind Sweden's 53.2%. Nor has public spending grown that rapidly over the period 1981–2001 – with the UK only 8th highest out of the 20 countries.

2 Household consumer expenditure on a whole range of leisure related goods and services will grow significantly from this market segment. The surplus capital of parents is being spent on themselves and helping children afford deposits on houses. Businesses such as retail stores and producers of goods ands services will have an incentive to focus more carefully on the tastes and needs of baby boomers given their growing number and wealth (e.g. M&S placing greater emphasis on women's fashion in the 35–55 year age group). Governments must pay attention to the interests of an ever-growing proportion of the electorate. Extra taxes on the income from savings and from holdings of securities (e.g. bonds, shares etc.) may be highly unpopular with this group which have invested their capital in such items. Governments will also recognise that the elderly have both a rich segment (baby boomers) and a poor segment, making the targeting of higher state pension entitlements to the poorer elderly segment a higher priority, rather than increasing the basic state pension for everyone.

Mini Case Study 12.4 The flat tax

1 The Laffer curve does point to extra taxes eventually reducing, rather than raising, tax revenue because of the disincentives they create. However, total tax revenue only starts to fall when the composite (average of all) tax rate rises over 60%. The flat tax supporters are arguing that disincentive effects of taxes occur at much lower rates of tax.

2 The government might argue that the main beneficiaries will be the rich, since the top 10% of income earners pay 50% of all income tax collected. It might also argue that if current personal allowances are maintained, then a flat tax rate of 23%, which would be needed if current tax revenue was to be maintained, would result in 27 million more who lose rather than gain from the change. If no losers were to occur under a flat tax regime, the flat tax rate would have to be set as low as 18% with unchanged personal allowances, resulting in a loss of £20 billion of tax revenue. The government would challenge the opposition to identify who is going to lose from the sharp cuts in government expenditure which would then be necessary.

PROGRESS AND REVIEW QUESTIONS

Multiple-choice questions

1 b) and d)
2 b) and d)
3 a) and c)
4 a) and c)
5 d) and e)
6 b) and e) (Petroleum revenue tax is a direct tax on the profits of oil companies)
7 a) and d)
8 b) and c)

9 d)

10 c) and e)

Data response questions

1 a) The table suggests that a rise in *gross* income for this household from £125 per week to £250 per week results in only a modest rise in net income. For example, an increase in gross income from £150 to £200 per week gives only an extra £15.81 after various deductions. In other words, for an extra £50 per week gross, £34.19 is lost. This suggests an implicit marginal tax rate (or marginal deduction rate) of around 68% (34.19/50).

   b) Tables such as this are often used in discussing the so-called 'poverty trap' where a person on low income may gain very little, or even lose, from an increase in gross earnings. This is because as gross earnings rise, the amount of benefits received decreases while income tax and other deductions increase. The challenge for government policy is to so structure the benefit/tax system that there is sufficient incentive for families to gain by working harder and increasing their gross incomes (or from moving from unemployment to employment). In other words, government policy must try to make these implicit marginal tax/deduction rates much lower than they even are today. It is certainly true that the poverty and unemployment traps are less of a problem than they were a few years ago when many examples were cited where people were actually worse off when their gross income rose because loss of benefit and increase in tax overwhelmed any extra increase in gross income.

2 A 1% rise in VAT cuts the net (after tax) income of the poorest households by more than the net income of the richest households. For example, a 1% rise in VAT cuts the net income of the poorest 10% by over 1.4%, compared to only some 0.7% for the richest 10%. In other words, VAT is a regressive tax.

Case study question

1 The higher rate of income tax certainly does not fall on individuals receiving average (median) income, but largely on those with over three times the gross income of the median individual.

2 This is still the case for households, with the median income household needing to earn over 50% more if it is to pay higher rate tax. However, those households with more children and other dependants will need much more to achieve the same standard of living as households with fewer children/dependants. Therefore they may perceive themselves to be middle income households even when their gross income is well above the median.

Essay questions

2 Some believe that too high a proportion of national income being spent by governments can have adverse effects on the economy. For example, it might 'crowd out' the private sector, with higher taxes and higher interest rates discouraging savings, investments and incentives to take risks. Higher public spending might also stimulate a growth in money supply, with possible inflationary consequences. Reducing the role of the state might help curb the growth of public expenditure, for example more involvement of the private sector in the provision of public services. Improved monitoring of the growth in public expenditure and restrictions on its further growth may help here (e.g. 'golden rule' etc.).

4 The idea of the business cycle can be introduced (Figure 12.3) together with an explanation of what built-in stabilisation actually means and the public expenditure/taxation policy instruments which serve that function. The contrast between built-in stabilisation and discretionary fiscal policy can be examined and the benefits of the former highlighted using Figure 12.4 and its associated analysis.

Chapter 13

Mini Case Study 13.2 Clearing payments

Benefits include higher returns to customers of banks/financial intermediaries as incoming funds are recorded as being received (and therefore earning interest) more quickly. Also, withdrawals of such funds can occur more quickly – increasing liquidity. Higher real incomes and liquidity of households will tend to raise spending and therefore demand for producers. Of course, the profits of bank and financial intermediaries are likely to be reduced and the income of shareholders in these businesses, etc.

PROGRESS AND REVIEW QUESTIONS
Multiple-choice questions

1 d)	**6** e)
2 d)	**7** a)
3 c)	**8** c)
4 e)	**9** a)
5 a) and e)	**10** e)

True/false questions

1 True
2 True
3 True
4 False ('narrow' money)
5 True
6 False (inversely)
7 True
8 False (it is now more important as it impacts exchange rates more strongly)

Case study question

There is clearly a higher risk of default by credit card users in lower income and less credit-worthy segments of the population. This may cause personal and social problems if these users run into credit card debt that they cannot pay, having been attracted by the marketing of credit cards to this large market segment (8 million in the UK). The credit card companies themselves may be charging higher interest rates to cover this default risk both to non-prime and prime users of credit cards, etc.

Essay questions

2 See the discussion on pages 306–13. An efficient financial system underpins the growth of savings, consumption and investment expenditure and arguably (via financing public sector borrowing) government expenditure. We noted in Chapter 11 the importance of these elements to the circular flow of income.

4 Figure 13.6 might be used to show how a decrease in money supply (shift to left) and/or an increase in money demand (shift to right) would result in a higher rate of interest. Factors causing either of these shifts could be discussed.

Chapter 14

Mini Case Study 14.2 Oiling the wheels

1 a) From the case study we can observe at least five main factors which might increase the world demand for oil (i.e. shift it upwards and to the right). First, the increase in real incomes resulting from the economic growth of nations will increase the demand for oil as transport and energy requirements rise. Secondly, if the price of substitute energy sources such as gas rises, the demand for oil would increase as consumers substitute oil for more expensive gas wherever possible. Thirdly, should the renewable substitute sources (wind, sun, wave) prove more expensive or more difficult to provide, then the demand for oil might increase. Fourthly, should climate change reduce average temperatures in some countries then this will increase the demand for oil as a means of supplying heat for domestic and business purposes. Finally, the possible occurrence of a war or other emergency can lead to an increase in demand for oil as nations stockpile oil.

   b) A decrease in the demand for oil could be due to a number of factors such as a slowing down in the global rate of economic growth, a fall in the price and increase in availability of substitute fuels such as gas and renewable energy sources which can be used instead of oil, a tendency for climate change to raise average temperatures, a more stable situation in the oil producing regions, etc.

2 a) If OPEC tried to raise price from $25 to around $45 a barrel, it could do this by limiting the quotas of its members so that the total supply of oil from the OPEC members becomes fixed at a given level. For example, if OPEC wants to raise price from P_E ($25) to P_C ($45) per barrel, it might operate as shown in the diagram below. The supply would be limited to Q_F so that the supply curve becomes SAS_1 instead of SAS, with the price of oil rising to a higher price P_C of say $45 per barrel.

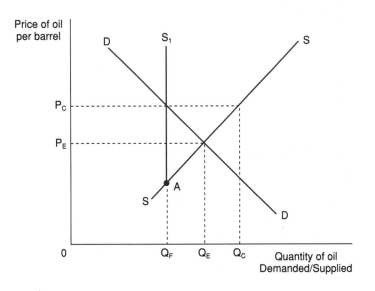

b) OPEC may not always be successful in achieving price P_C for many reasons. For example, there might be a tendency for some of the members of the OPEC cartel to cheat by producing more than their quotas, thus making the supply curve flatter (i.e. change shape from SAS_1 towards SAS). Also, if prices began to rise perhaps other, non-OPEC, oil sources in the world would now become profitable to exploit, thus increasing total (OPEC + non-OPEC) supply of oil and keeping down price.

PROGRESS AND REVIEW QUESTIONS

Multiple-choice questions

  1 b) and d)
  2 b) and d)
  3 a) and d)
  4 b) and c)
  5 a) and d)
  6 c) and e)
  7 a), d) and e)
  8 b) and c)
  9 a) and d)
10 a) and d)
11 b) and c)
12 a) and c)
13 a)

Matching terms/concepts

1 c)
2 b)
3 d)
4 a)
5 e)

True/false questions

1 False (they are separate balances)
2 False (imports become dearer in sterling)
3 True
4 True
5 False (exports dearer abroad and imports cheaper at home)
6 True
7 False (European Central Bank controls these)
8 True

Data response and stimulus questions

1 Anything which increases the relative demand to hold euros rather than sterling will strengthen the euro vis-à-vis sterling, i.e. will cause sterling to depreciate against the euro. Faster growth in eurozone countries relative to the UK might have this effect. So too might increased prospects for UK entry into the single currency – markets are aware that this could only occur at a lower exchange rate for sterling against the euro, so that sterling is likely to fall as markets anticipate UK entry. With a high price elasticity of demand for CD players, the appreciation of sterling against the euro has made imported CD players from rivals cheaper in the UK, so that the sales of these rival CD players can be expected to increase at Sony's expense. The now higher price of Sony exports of CD players to Europe will also result in a significant contraction of eurozone demand for Sony's exports.

2 $July = \dfrac{89.8}{88.0} \times 100 = 102.05$

$August = \dfrac{89.5}{88.0} \times 100 = 101.70$

$September = \dfrac{89.1}{87.6} \times 100 = 101.71$

$October = \dfrac{89.1}{86.4} \times 100 = 103.1$

$November = \dfrac{89.3}{86.3} \times 100 = 103.48$

3 a) £10 billion
  b) £50 billion
  c) £20 billion
  d) −£70 billion

Essay questions

2 When the terms of trade improve on the export side via a rise in prices because of an increase in demand for the products exported rather than an increase in the costs of the products exported. Or, on the import side, when the terms of trade improve because of a fall in price due to a decrease in demand for the products imported rather than those imports being cheaper because of cost reductions by the overseas producers.

4 Potential impacts of higher oil prices on the balance of payments, inflationary pressures and global economic growth are considered in Sections 9 and 10 of the chapter. Whilst the balance of payments of oil exporting countries will improve, the higher oil prices create inflationary pressures and reduce the aggregate demand available for spending on non-oil goods and services. Both these impacts could result in global economic slowdown, with detrimental effects on all economies. However, there is a possibility that technological change and the development of oil substitutes might help restrict the rise in oil prices in the longer run.

Chapter 15

Mini Case Study 15.2 The Retail Price Index (RPI)

1 The 'weights' reflect the relative importance at each date of the product group in a typical household's 'basket' of purchases. With rising real incomes, expenditure on food has become relatively less important since 1987, as has expenditure on alcoholic drink, tobacco, fuel, clothing and footwear, etc. This may be due to these products having low income elasticities of demand and/or consumer tastes shifting against them. The opposite is true for expenditure on housing, motoring, leisure and other types of services.

2 If the 'knowledge' economy continues to grow then a wide range of electronic/IT products used in homes and businesses will play a still more prominent part in tables such as that in the case study. If transport congestion and global warming are tackled by

heavier taxes on road transport then motoring expenditure, fares and other travel costs will certainly have higher group weights, etc.

PROGRESS AND REVIEW QUESTIONS

Multiple-choice questions

1 b) and d)
2 a), c and d)
3 d)
4 d)
5 b)
6 d)
7 b)
8 a)
9 c)
10 e)

True/false questions

1 False (the rate of increase in average prices is now lower)
2 True
3 True
4 True
5 False (lower levels of unemployment lead to higher levels of inflation)
6 False (higher rates of wage and price inflation)
7 False (inflationary gap)
8 True
9 True
10 True

Data response question

1 The period 1984–92 was particularly disappointing, with unemployment averaging almost 10%, inflation almost reaching 10% in 1990, uneven economic growth and a growing balance of payments deficit, at least up to 1990. However, since 1993 unemployment has progressively fallen, inflation has rarely exceeded 3% and economic growth has been steady. However, the balance of payments on current account has moved alarmingly into deficit since 1999.

Conclusions might include a broadly more successful macroeconomic policy over the past ten or so years, perhaps aided by factors such as independence to the Bank of England in setting interest rates helping control inflation, the 'golden rule' and other aspects of monetary and fiscal policy helping generate non-inflationary economic growth. However, one of the four objectives, namely balance of payments equilibrium, still appears difficult to achieve even under such favourable outcomes for the other three objectives.

2 Business confidence is generally raised by low unemployment, steady economic growth and low inflation rates achieved in recent years. These data suggest a business environment characterised by economic stability, in which businesses can have more confidence in the future direction of the economy. This is likely to encourage businesses to invest more and to employ more people, confident that aggregate demand is sufficient to purchase the extra goods and services produced. They can also be reasonably

confident that inflation is unlikely to surge ahead, raising costs and making it difficult to compete with businesses in less inflationary countries.

Essay questions

2 This is the suggestion behind the so-called Phillips curve. However, there are other models which suggest that lower unemployment can be achieved without having to accept higher inflation, for example the expectations-augmented Phillips curve of Section 7.3 (page 381). Supply-side policies of Section 9.4 (page 385) can also help in this respect.

Chapter 16

Mini Case Study 16.2 World trade deal agreed

The WTO rules are such that all 147 member countries must agree. To get an agreement acceptable to so many countries is therefore regarded as a major challenge. Failure to reach this agreement would have undermined the WTO and its multilateral approach to trade, led to a failure of three years of international negotiations for further freeing trade (started at Doha in 2001) and probably resulted in a fresh round of trade wars and bilateral treaties. However, critics point to the limited detail in the draft treaty and the few immediate actions required of member nations, especially the richer ones. They also point to the ability of powerful nations to continue some of their damaging activities (e.g. US cotton subsidies, EU sugar subsidies).

PROGRESS AND REVIEW QUESTIONS

Multiple-choice questions

1 c)
2 e)
3 b) and e)
4 c)
5 d)
6 b), d) and e)
7 a), c) and e)
8 d) and e)
9 b)
10 b), d) and e)

Matching terms/concepts

1 d)
2 e)
3 c)
4 c)
5 d)

True/false questions

1 True
2 False (globalisation)
3 False (sociologists)
4 True

5 False (horizontal integration)

6 True

Data response and stimulus questions

1 The findings suggest that outsourcing parts of the value chain to other countries (off-shoring) can bring benefits to the different countries concerned. The companies from the country doing the offshoring (here the US) can now provide goods and services at lower prices to domestic consumers, raising real living standards. Workers in the US will, it is suggested, tend to be redeployed to higher value added jobs in which the US has a comparative advantage, raising labour productivity and with it wages. As India benefits from extra employment and income (with the multiplier reinforcing these gains) it can afford to import those goods and services from the US (raising US exports). India also gains profits and tax revenue from the offshoring, which can be used to benefit its economy and people further.

2 a) i) OQ_1

ii) OQ_4

iii) O_1Q_4

b) i) $OAE \, Q_3$

ii) AEGB

iii) Q_2Q_3

iv) $Q_2C \, EQ_3$

Essay questions

2 Section 5.7 outlines the case for protectionism. The word 'evaluate' gives you an opportunity to explore both the case for and against protectionism, with Section 5.8 useful in reviewing the arguments against protectionism. The various measures that that can be used to provide effective protection are reviewed in Sections 5.1 to 5.8.

Chapter 17

Mini Case Study 17.2 Boeing versus Airbus

1 The data suggests that both companies receive substantial direct and indirect subsidies from their respective governmental bodies – EU for Airbus and US for Boeing.

2 If the WTO becomes involved in a disputes claim it may rule in favour of one company against the other – giving that company a huge competitive advantage and awarding it huge damages. Of course, the WTO may rule against both companies – making it more difficult for both companies to compete against other competitors on world markets, given the loss of their respective state aid packages. Prices of aircraft on the world markets are likely to increase generally if all such state aid supports are removed from all companies. Some companies are likely to fail or be forced to merge with larger companies who benefit more from scale economies. Many possible implications can be discussed here.

PROGRESS AND REVIEW QUESTIONS

Multiple-choice questions

1 c) and e)
2 b) and d)
3 b)
4 c)
5 c)

Data response question

The data shows lower growth in the euro area being much slower than in Britain or the US but unemployment much higher. This reflects the perception of many that the EU must adapt its policies to become a more dynamic, higher growth, lower unemployment economy than at present. The suggestion of 'reformers' is that the EU has too much regulation and protectionism, and needs to liberalise its markets and reduce bureaucracy and 'red tape'. Included here is the suggestion that too much of the EU expenditure is in supporting agriculture and too little in supporting research, development and innovation.

Case study question

Legal decisions by supra-national bodies such as the EU can have major environmental and commercial impacts. Finding an environmentally acceptable way of disposing of the 13 million tyres that were previously placed annually in landfill sites or stockpiled, will be a major undertaking for UK government and business. The total for landfill represents the disposal of some 26% of UK used tyres each year and since 2003 this has been illegal for whole tyres and will be illegal for shredded tyres by 2006. Businesses in the UK will have to find legal ways for disposing of tyres from company vehicles to replace landfill disposal. These may turn out to be more expensive alternatives given the restricted capacity for many alternatives and the sudden surge in demand for these methods of disposal. Indeed, there are risks that new plans for alternatives such as incineration may be rejected by planners aware of local opposition on health grounds, may face 'green' taxes or even themselves be banned. Some businesses involved in R & D on new, environmentally appropriate methods of disposal are likely to benefit from government grants and high revenues should technological advancements occur. Similarly, businesses involved in alternative disposal methods such as re-treading, carpet underlay, etc., may benefit. Individuals in the UK will face similar problems, with the danger of an increase in 'fly tipping', i.e. individuals dumping unwanted tyres on other people's land if new methods of disposal are more expensive than at present (e.g. garages might now impose a charge for the disposal of damaged tyres) or are unavailable to households.

True/false questions

1 True
2 True
3 False
4 False (Guidance section)
5 True
6 True
7 True
8 False (buyer of labour)

Essay questions

1 ● Where the structure of the economies of potential members overlap
   ● Where the industries that are common to potential members have a wide variation in their costs
   ● Where the level of import tariffs placed by potential members on each others' products is high prior to the formation of the protected free trade area

2 *For CAP*: encourages production of agricultural products to support the needs of the EU population; reduces EU (and member nations) import bill and improves balance of payments; supports small and medium sized farms; encourages maintenance of rural lifestyle/culture, etc.
   Against CAP: very expensive for EU budget; raises EU agricultural prices higher than they need be, increasing inflation rate; stimulates inefficient EU agricultural production; distorts world trade patterns to the disadvantage of developing countries, etc.

3 Single market provides a protected free trade area of some 460 million people with current 25 member countries and major opportunities for economies of scale for EU producers. The resulting lower costs were expected to result in lower prices and therefore lower inflation and higher real living standards for EU citizens. Increased competition was predicted throughout the EU, again helping keep prices low and raising living standards. X-inefficiencies would be eliminated as inefficient practices such as over-manning would no longer be possible. These various 'dynamic effects' would raise labour and capital productivity in the Single Market, thereby freeing resources for alternative, more productive uses. In these ways the levels of investment, economic growth and sustainable consumption would rise.

   Critics argue that various types of market failure, for example, development of monopoly and oligopoly producers have prevented many of these 'dynamic effects' and raised profits of producers rather than the economic welfare of consumers.

4 The Social Chapter refers to the establishment of minimum legal (mandated) conditions in the EU labour market. The suggestion is that without such legal minimum conditions the labour market outcomes would be less favourable in terms of wages and levels of employment as employers with monopsony power would benefit rather than their employees. In addition there would not be a 'level playing field' so that those countries offering less protection to their labour forces would benefit at the expense of countries which provided more responsible conditions of employment.

Chapter 18

Mini Case Study 18.2 Sanitation and urbanisation

The benefits include a healthier population, with much reduced death rates among adults and especially infants, e.g. less typhoid, diarrhoea and other water borne infections. Better water supplies and improved sanitation also help reduce air pollution, since less use of fires is needed to boil water. In addition, businesses can maintain better quality standards for agricultural and other products requiring clean water. Failure to meet these standards can result in loss of markets and business failures in the developing countries.

   Costs include the use of scarce resources in improving sanitation and water quality.

PROGRESS AND REVIEW QUESTIONS
Multiple-choice questions

1 c)
2 e)
3 b) and d)
4 c)
5 b) and d)
6 a), c) and e)
7 b)
8 e)

True/false questions

1 False (this is an important element)
2 False (supply-side policies)
3 False (targets are set)
4 True
5 False (has a scale from 0–10)
6 False (measures such as Human Development Index are more representative)

Data response question

The data suggests that export activity is becoming a progressively more important aspect of total economic activity (GDP) in the developing economies. Indeed, it is now a much higher *proportion* in developing than developed economies. If trade barriers can be reduced in the developed economies then trade (rather than aid) may become a still more important mechanism for economic development in the lower income economies.

Case study question

Whilst service sector (banking) jobs might be lost in the developed economies, they are creating new employment opportunities in the developing economies. The multiplier impact of these new, relatively high paid jobs overseas, will further raise output and employment in the developing countries.

Although jobs are being lost in high income developed economies, large multinational firms are reducing their costs, arguably helping them remain globally competitive and helping to secure many other jobs they provide in the higher income economies.

Essay questions

2 The features that are characteristics of a 'lesser developed country' are considered in some detail in Section 5 (pages 469–72) earlier in the chapter.
4 Section 7 (pages 474–6) reviews some of the reasons why urban centres have grown so quickly (e.g. agglomeration economies) in developing countries. It also considers some of the advantages and disadvantages of urbanisation.

Index

330